Real-Time Data Analysis Exercises

Up-to-date macro data is a great way to engage in and understand the usefulness of macro variables and their impact on the economy. Real-Time Data Analysis exercises communicate directly with the Federal Reserve Bank of St. Louis's FRED site, so every time FRED posts new data, students see new data.

End-of-chapter exercises accompanied by the Real-Time Data Analysis icon 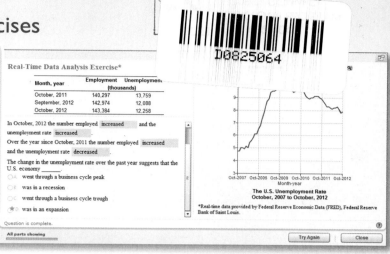 include Real-Time Data versions in **MyEconLab**.

Current News Exercises

Posted regularly, we find the latest microeconomic and macroeconomic news stories, post them, and write auto-graded multi-part exercises that illustrate the economic way of thinking about the news.

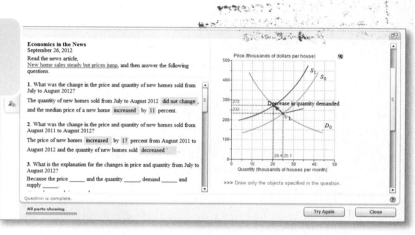

Interactive Homework Exercises

Participate in a fun and engaging activity that helps promote active learning and mastery of important economic concepts.

Pearson's experiments program is flexible and easy for instructors and students to use. For a complete list of available experiments, visit *www.myeconlab.com*.

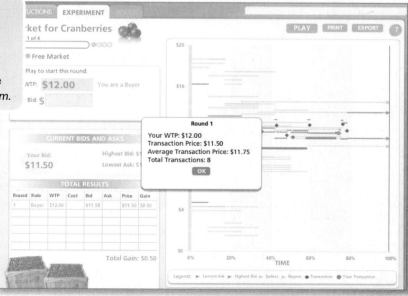

MICROECONOMICS

ELEVENTH EDITION

Global Edition

MICHAEL PARKIN
University of Western Ontario

Boston   Columbus   Indianapolis   New York   San Francisco   Upper Saddle River   Amsterdam
Cape Town   Dubai   London   Madrid   Milan   Munich   Paris   Montréal   Toronto
Delhi   Mexico City   São Paulo   Sydney   Hong Kong   Seoul   Singapore   Taipei   Tokyo

Editor in Chief	Donna Battista	**International Senior Manufacturing Controller**	Trudy Kimber
Executive Acquisitions Editor	Adrienne D'Ambrosio	**Cover Designer**	Jodi Notowitz
International Publisher	Laura Dent	**Cover Images**	Robin Smith/Getty
International Programme Editor	Leandra Paoli	**Director of Media**	Susan Schoenberg
Editorial Project Manager	Sarah Dumouchelle	**MyEconLab Content Project Manager**	Noel Lotz
Executive Marketing Manager	Lori DeShazo	**Executive Media Producer**	Melissa Honig
International Marketing Manager	Dean Erasmus	**Digital Publisher, Economics**	Denise Clinton
Managing Editor	Jeff Holcomb	**Text Design and Project Management**	Integra Software Services, Inc.
Senior Production Project Manager	Nancy Freihofer	**Copyeditor**	Catherine Baum
Operations Specialist	Carol Melville	**Technical Illustrator**	Richard Parkin

Pearson Education Limited
Edinburgh Gate
Harlow
Essex CM20 2JE
England

and Associated Companies throughout the world

Visit us on the World Wide Web at:
www.pearsoned.co.uk

© Pearson Education Limited 2014

ISBN 10: 0-273-79003-X
ISBN 13: 978-0-273-79003-7

British Library Cataloguing-in-Publication Data
A catalogue record for this book is available from the British Library

10 9 8 7 6 5 4 3 2 1
17 16 15 14 13

Typeset in Adobe Garamond Pro by Integra Software Services Inc.
Printed and bound by Courier/Kendallville in the United States of America

The publisher's policy is to use paper manufactured from sustainable forests.

TO ROBIN

Michael Parkin is Professor Emeritus in the Department of Economics at the University of Western Ontario, Canada. Professor Parkin has held faculty appointments at Brown University, the University of Manchester, the University of Essex, and Bond University. He is a past president of the Canadian Economics Association and has served on the editorial boards of the *American Economic Review* and the *Journal of Monetary Economics* and as managing editor of the *Canadian Journal of Economics*. Professor Parkin's research on macroeconomics, monetary economics, and international economics has resulted in over 160 publications in journals and edited volumes, including the *American Economic Review, the Journal of Political Economy,* the *Review of Economic Studies,* the *Journal of Monetary Economics,* and the *Journal of Money, Credit and Banking.* He became most visible to the public with his work on inflation that discredited the use of wage and price controls. Michael Parkin also spearheaded the movement toward European monetary union. Professor Parkin is an experienced and dedicated teacher of introductory economics.

Micro Flexibility

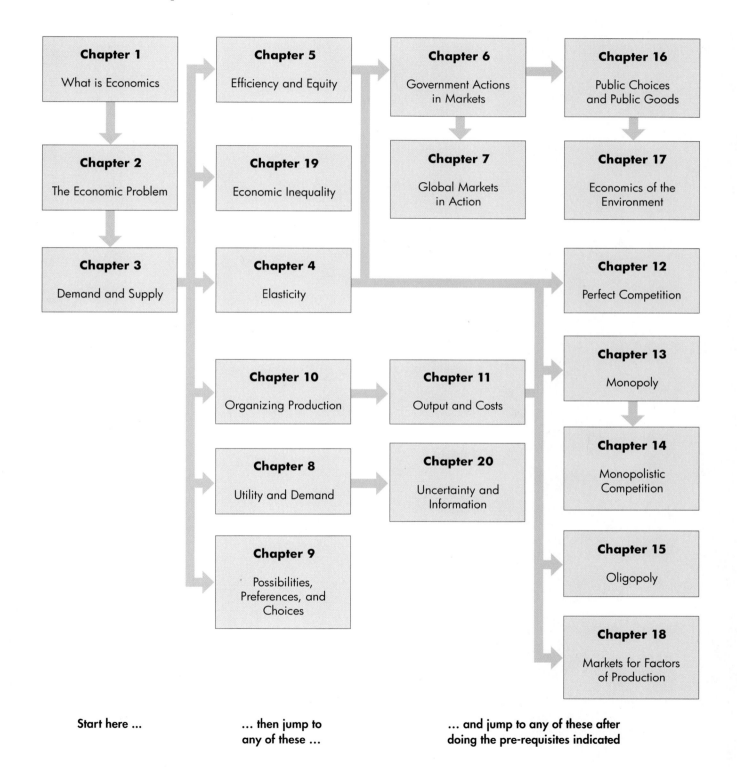

PART TWO
HOW MARKETS WORK   55

The future is always uncertain. But at some times, and now is one such time, the range of possible near-future events is enormous. The major source of this great uncertainty is economic policy. There is uncertainty about the way in which international trade policy will evolve as protectionism is returning to the political agenda. There is uncertainty about exchange rate policy as competitive devaluation rears its head. There is extraordinary uncertainty about monetary policy with the Fed having tripled the quantity of bank reserves and continuing to create more money in an attempt to stimulate a flagging economy but providing no guidance about its eventual exit strategy from stimulus. And there is uncertainty about fiscal policy as a one trillion dollar deficit approaches a fiscal cliff and interacts with an aging population and rising health-care costs to create a national debt time bomb.

In the five years since the subprime mortgage crisis of August 2007 moved economics from the business report to the front page, justified fear has gripped producers, consumers, financial institutions, and governments.

Even the *idea* that the market is an efficient mechanism for allocating scarce resources came into question. Many thoughtful people worried about rising income inequality and some political leaders called for the end of capitalism and the dawn of a new economic order in which tighter regulation reigned in unfettered greed.

Rarely do teachers of economics have such a rich feast on which to draw. And rarely are the principles of economics more surely needed to provide the solid foundation on which to think about economic events and navigate the turbulence of economic life.

Although thinking like an economist can bring a clearer perspective to and deeper understanding of today's events, students don't find the economic way of thinking easy or natural. *Microeconomics* seeks to put clarity and understanding in the grasp of the student through its careful and vivid exploration of the tension between self-interest and the social interest, the role and power of incentives—of opportunity cost and marginal benefit—and demonstrating the possibility that markets supplemented by other mechanisms might allocate resources efficiently.

Parkin students begin to think about issues the way real economists do and learn how to explore difficult policy problems and make more informed decisions in their own economic lives.

The Eleventh Edition Revision

Thoroughly updated, stripped of technical detail where possible, extensively illustrated with well-chosen photographs, enlivened with new applications features that focus on issues at play in today's world, responsive to the suggestions of reviewers and users, and seamlessly integrated with MyEconLab: These are the hallmarks of this eleventh edition of *Microeconomics*.

This comprehensive revision builds on the solid foundation of the previous edition and retains its thorough and careful presentation of the principles of economics, its emphasis on real-world examples and applications, its development of critical thinking skills, its diagrams renowned for pedagogy and clarity, and its path-breaking technology.

Most chapters have been thoroughly reworked to achieve even greater clarity and to place greater emphasis on applications to current issues. Some sections of chapters have been removed and other sections added to cover new issues, particularly those that involve current policy problems.

Current issues organize each chapter. News stories about today's major economic events and debates tie each chapter together, from new abbreviated chapter-opening vignettes to *Reading Between the Lines* and end-of-chapter problems and applications and online practice.

A new feature, Economics in the News, is aimed at better motivating students and showing them how to use the economic toolkit to understand the events and issues they are confronted with in the media. It also helps them to work the related *Economics in the News* end-of-chapter problems and applications.

A second new feature, At Issue, shows two sides of a controversial issue and helps students to apply the economic way of thinking to clarify and debate the issues.

Among the many issues covered in one or more of the two new features described above are:

- Capitalism and its critics in Chapter 1
- Energy independence in Chapter 2
- The relentlessly rising cost of college in Chapter 3
- Price gouging in Chapter 5
- Offshore outsourcing in Chapter 7
- Obamacare in Chapter 16
- Taxing carbon to counter climate change in Chapter 17
- The monopoly power of the NCAA in Chapter 18

Highpoints of the Revision

Most topics are well explained in the previous edition and are hard to improve on. So the highpoints of the current revision are the new *Economics in the News* and *At Issue* features. Nonetheless, three topics have been substantially revised. They are:

- Price discrimination
- Carbon emissions and climate change externalities
- Education and health care

Price Discrimination The key idea we want our students to understand about price discrimination is that it converts consumer surplus into producer surplus and economic profit. To strengthen this insight, I now begin with a brief explanation of the relationship between producer surplus and economic profit. I then use a carefully constructed model of two separated markets to show how discrimination between them can increase producer surplus. I build on this model to show how perfect price discrimination, if it were possible, would grab the entire consumer surplus and convert it to producer surplus. I illustrate the attempt to move toward perfect price discrimination with applications to Microsoft's pricing of Windows and Disney's pricing of tickets to its theme parks.

Carbon Emissions and Climate Change Externalities What Nicholas Stern has called the greatest market failure and what some climate-change skeptics see as a problem that markets will eventually solve gets a thoroughly new treatment. I begin by contrasting the success story of local air quality in the major U.S. cities with the unrelenting rise in atomospheric carbon concentration. I then explain the three methods of coping with environmental externalities: property rights, mandating the use of clean technologies, and taxing or pricing emissions. I explore the ability of each method to achieve an effcient outcome. I also explore the special challenge that arises from the global rather than national scope of carbon emission.

Education and Health Care These two large items of public expenditure are not *public goods* but are examples of goods that have large *positive externalities*. I have expanded and revised my explanation of the problem of delivering an efficient quantity of these goods with an emphasis on the potential role for vouchers in both markets. I also have a new discussion of charter schools and the role they can play. U.S. health-care service and expenditures are placed in a global perspective.

Economics in the News

Complementing *Economics in the News* questions, which have appeared daily in MyEconLab and in end-of-chapter problems in previous editions, a series of new *Economics in the News* boxes help students to answer news-based questions (see an example below). The topics covered by these boxes are:

- The invisible hand and entrepreneurship at work
- The fragile global economy in 2013
- Rising global food costs
- Energy independence cost and inefficiency
- The market for college education
- The market for gasoline
- Elasticities of demand for peanut butter
- The changing market for coat hangers
- The principal–agent problem at JPMorgan Chase
- Cost curves at the checkout line
- Record stores exit
- The falling cost of sequencing DNA
- Microsoft monopoly
- Boeing versus Airbus
- The choice of college major and job prospects

College Major and Job Prospects

The Most Valuable College Major

Which college major is most likely to land you a well-paying job right out of school? Katie Bardaro, an economist at PayScale, a compensation research firm, says biomedical engineering is your best bet. The median salary starts at $53,800 and by mid-career reaches $84,700 and keeps rising. The median salary for all biomedical engineers in 2012 was $88,000.

Some other science and engineering jobs pay more but don't have as good an outlook for jobs growth. The Bureau of Labor Statistics projects that the number of jobs for biomedical engineers will increase from today's 20,000 to 32,000 in 2020—an increase of more than 60 percent. In contrast, the working-age population will increase by only 8 percent by 2020.

Sources: The Bureau of Labor Statistics and *Forbes*, May 15, 2012

THE QUESTIONS

- Why is the number of jobs for biomedical engineering graduates increasing?
- What determines the demand for biomedical engineers and why might it be increasing?
- What determines the supply of biomedical engineers and why might it be increasing?
- What determines whether the wage rate of biomedical engineers will rise?
- Provide a graphical illustration of the market for biomedical engineers in 2012 and 2020.

THE ANSWERS

- The number of jobs for biomedical engineers is growing because *both* demand for and supply of biomedical engineers are increasing.
- The demand for biomedical engineers is *derived* from the demand for biomedical products. The demand for replacement parts for the human body is increasing because technological advances are creating new and improved products.
- The supply of biomedical engineers is determined by the working-age population and the number of people who decide to major in the subject. The supply is increasing because the working-age population is increasing and attracting a larger percentage of people to study biomedical engineering.
- The wage rate of biomedical engineers will rise if the demand for their services increases faster than supply.
- The figure illustrates the market for biomedical engineers in 2012 and in 2020.
- Demand is expected to increase from D_{12} to D_{20}.
- Supply is expected to increase from S_{12} to S_{20}.
- The increase in demand is much greater than the increase in supply.
- The equilibrium quantity (the number of jobs) increases from 20,000 in 2012 to 32,000 in 2020.
- Because demand increases by more than supply, the equilibrium wage rate rises. (The 2020 wage rate is an assumption.)

Biomedical engineers design and build replacement parts for the human body.

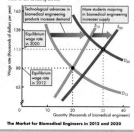

The Market for Biomedical Engineers in 2012 and 2020

At Issue

Seven new *At Issue* boxes engage the student in debate and controversy. An *At Issue* box (see below) introduces an issue and then presents two opposing views. It leaves the matter unsettled so that the student and instructor can continue the argument in class and reach their own conclusions.

The goal of *At Issue* is to motivate the student to think about the opposing arguments and to take a stand on the issues.

The seven issues covered by this feature are:

- The protest against capitalism and the Occupy Wall Street movement
- Do we need a law against price gouging?
- Should Hong Kong increase its minimum wage?
- Is offshore outsourcing good or bad for America?
- Is Obamacare the solution to U.S. health-care problems?
- Should we be doing more to limit carbon emissions?
- Monopoly power at NCAA: Is it good or bad?

 ## Features to Enhance Teaching and Learning

The new features that I have just described are additions to an already powerful teaching and learning package. Here, I briefly review the features retained from the previous edition.

Reading Between the Lines

This Parkin hallmark helps students think like economists by connecting chapter tools and concepts to the world around them. In *Reading Between the Lines*, which appears at the end of each chapter, students apply the tools they have just learned by analyzing an article from a newspaper or news Web site. Each article sheds additional light on the questions first raised in the Chapter Opener. Questions about the article also appear with the end-of-chapter problems and applications.

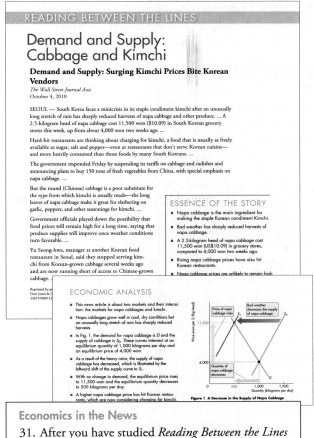

AT **ISSUE**

Should We Be Doing More to Reduce Carbon Emissions?

Economists agree that tackling the global warming problem requires changes in the incentives that people face. The cost of carbon-emitting activities must rise and the cost of clean-energy technologies must fall.

Disagreement centers on *how* to change incentives. Should more countries set targets for cutting carbon emissions at a faster rate and introduce a carbon tax or emissions charges or cap-and-trade to cut emissions? Should clean energy research and development be subsidized?

Yes: *The Stern Review*

- Confronting emitters with a tax or price on carbon imposes low present costs for high future benefits.
- The cost of reducing greenhouse gas emissions to safe levels can be kept to 1 percent of global income each year.
- The future benefits are incomes at least 5 percent and possibly 20 percent higher than they will be with inaction every year forever.
- Climate change is a global problem that requires an international coordinated response.
- Unlike most taxes, which bring deadweight loss, a carbon tax eliminates (or reduces) deadweight loss.
- Strong, deliberate policy action is required to change the incentives that emitters face.
- Policy actions should include:
  1. Emissions limits and emissions trading
  2. Increased subsidies for energy research and development, including the development of low-cost clean technology for generating electricity
  3. Reduced deforestation and research into new drought and flood-resilient crop varieties

Economist Nicholas Stern, principal author of *The Stern Review on the Economics of Climate Change*. Greenhouse gas emission is "the greatest market failure the world has ever seen." To avoid the risk of catastrophic climate change, the upward CO_2 trend must be stopped.

No: The Copenhagen Consensus

- Confronting emitters with a tax or price on carbon imposes high present costs and low future benefits.
- Unless the entire world signs onto an emissions reduction program, free riders will increase their emissions and carbon leakage will occur.
- A global emissions reduction program and carbon tax would lower living standards in the rich countries and slow the growth rate of living standards in developing countries.
- Technology is already advancing and the cost of cleaner energy is falling.
- Fracking technology has vastly expanded the natural gas deposits that can be profitably exploited and replacing coal with gas halves the carbon emissions from electricity generation.
- Free-market price signals will allocate resources to the development of new technologies that stop and eventually reverse the upward trend in greenhouse gasses.

Bjørn Lomborg, President of the Copenhagen Consensus and author of *The Skeptical Environmentalist*. "For little environmental benefit, we could end up sacrificing growth, jobs, and opportunities for the big majority, especially in the developing world."

READING BETWEEN THE LINES

Demand and Supply: Cabbage and Kimchi

Demand and Supply: Surging Kimchi Prices Bite Korean Vendors

The Wall Street Journal Asia
October 4, 2010

SEOUL — South Korea faces a minicrisis in its staple condiment kimchi after an unusually long stretch of rain has sharply reduced harvests of napa cabbage and other produce. ... A 2.5-kilogram head of napa cabbage cost 11,500 won ($10.09) in South Korean grocery stores this week, up from about 4,000 won two weeks ago. ...

Hard-hit restaurants are thinking about charging for kimchi, a food that is usually as freely available as sugar, salt and pepper—even at restaurants that don't serve Korean cuisine—and more heavily consumed than those foods by many South Koreans. ...

The government responded Friday by suspending its tariffs on cabbage and radishes and announcing plans to buy 150 tons of fresh vegetables from China, with special emphasis on napa cabbage. ...

But the round (Chinese) cabbage is a poor substitute for the type from which kimchi is usually made—the long leaves of napa cabbage make it great for slathering on garlic, peppers, and other seasonings for kimchi. ...

Government officials played down the possibility that food prices will remain high for a long time, saying that produce supplies will improve once weather conditions turn favorable. ...

Yu Seong-hwa, manager at another Korean food restaurant in Seoul, said they stopped serving kimchi from Korean-grown cabbage several weeks ago and are now running short of access to Chinese-grown cabbage. ...

Reprinted by p[...]
Dow Jones & [...]
2567570087[...]

ESSENCE OF THE STORY

- Napa cabbage is the main ingredient for making the staple Korean condiment Kimchi.
- Bad weather has sharply reduced harvests of napa cabbage.
- A 2.5-kilogram head of napa cabbage cost 11,500 won (US$10.09) in grocery stores, compared to 4,000 won two weeks ago.
- Rising napa cabbage prices have also hit Korean restaurants.
- Napa cabbage prices are unlikely to remain high [...]

ECONOMIC ANALYSIS

- This news article is about two markets and their interaction: the markets for napa cabbages and kimchi.
- Napa cabbages grow well in cool, dry conditions but an unusually long stretch of rain has sharply reduced harvests.
- In Fig. 1, the demand for napa cabbage is D and the supply of cabbage is S_0. These curves intersect at an equilibrium quantity of 1,000 kilograms per day and an equilibrium price of 4,000 won.
- As a result of the heavy rains, the supply of napa cabbage has decreased, which is illustrated by the leftward shift of the supply curve to S_1.
- With no change in demand, the equilibrium price rises to 11,500 won and the equilibrium quantity decreases to 500 kilograms per day.
- A higher napa cabbage price has hit Korean restaurants, which are now considering charging for kimchi.

Figure 1 A Decrease in the Supply of Napa Cabbage

Economics in the News

31. After you have studied *Reading Between the Lines* on pp. 74–75, answer the following questions.
    a. What happened to the prices of napa cabbage and kimchi in 2011?
    b. What substitutions do you expect might have been made to decrease the quantity of kimchi demanded?

Diagrams That Show the Action

Through the past ten editions, this book has set new standards of clarity in its diagrams; the eleventh edition continues to uphold this tradition. My goal has always been to show "where the economic action is." The diagrams in this book continue to generate an enormously positive response, which confirms my view that graphical analysis is the most powerful tool available for teaching and learning economics.

Because many students find graphs hard to work with, I have developed the entire art program with the study and review needs of the student in mind.

The diagrams feature:

■ Original curves consistently shown in blue

■ Shifted curves, equilibrium points, and other important features highlighted in red

■ Color-blended arrows to suggest movement

■ Graphs paired with data tables

■ Diagrams labeled with boxed notes

■ Extended captions that make each diagram and its caption a self-contained object for study and review.

Economics in Action Boxes

This feature uses boxes within the chapter to address current events and economic occurrences that highlight and amplify the topics covered in the chapter. Instead of simply reporting the current events, the material in the boxes applies the event to an economics lesson, enabling students to see how economics plays a part in the world around them as they read through the chapter.

Some of the many issues covered in these boxes include the best affordable choice of recorded music, movies and DVDs, the cost of selling a pair of shoes, how Apple doesn't make the iPhone, opposing trends in air pollution and carbon concentration, information-age monopolies, is the American dream still alive, and how is income redistributed. A complete list can be found on the inside back cover.

Chapter Openers

Each chapter opens with a student-friendly vignette that raises questions to motivate the student and focus the chapter. This chapter-opening story is woven into the main body of the chapter and is explored in the *Reading Between the Lines* feature that ends each chapter.

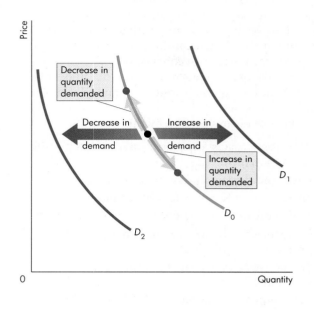

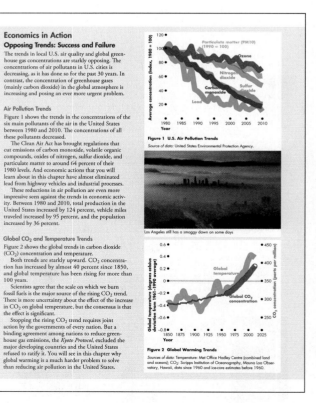

Key Terms

Highlighted terms simplify the student's task of learning the vocabulary of economics. Each highlighted term appears in an end-of-chapter list with its page number, in an end-of-book glossary with its page number, boldfaced in the index and in MyEconLab in the interactive glossary and the Flash Cards.

In-Text Review Quizzes

A review quiz at the end of each major section enables students to determine whether a topic needs further study before moving on. This feature includes a reference to the appropriate MyEconLab study plan to help students further test their understanding.

REVIEW QUIZ

1 What is the distinction between a money price and a relative price?
2 Explain why a relative price is an opportunity cost.
3 Think of examples of goods whose relative price has risen or fallen by a large amount.

You can work these questions in Study Plan 3.1 and get instant feedback.   MyEconLab

End-of-Chapter Study Material

Each chapter closes with a concise summary organized by major topics, a list of key terms with page references, and problems and applications. These learning tools provide students with a summary for review and exam preparation.

Interviews with Economists

Each part closes with an overview of the chapters and a teaser of an interview with a leading economist whose work correlates to what the student is learning. These interviews explore the education and research of these prominent economists and their advice for those who want to continue the study of economics. All past and present interviews I have conducted are available in full in MyEconLab.

 For the Instructor

This book enables you to focus on the economic way of thinking and choose your own course structure in your principles course:

Focus on the Economic Way of Thinking

As an instructor, you know how hard it is to encourage a student to think like an economist. But that is your goal. Consistent with this goal, the text focuses on and repeatedly uses the central ideas: choice; tradeoff; opportunity cost; the margin; incentives; the gains from voluntary exchange; the forces of demand, supply, and equilibrium; the pursuit of economic rent; the tension between self-interest and the social interest; and the scope and limitations of government actions.

Flexible Structure

You have preferences for how you want to teach your course. I have organized this book to enable you to do so. The flexibility chart on p. xi illustrates the book's flexibility. By following the arrows through the chart you can select the path that best fits your preference for course structure. Whether you want to teach a traditional course that blends theory and policy, or one that takes a fast-track through either theory or policy issues, *Microeconomics* gives you the choice.

Instructor's Supplemental Resources

The supplements for instructors are:

- Instructor's Manual
- Solutions Manual
- Test Item Files
- PowerPoint Resources

Instructor's Manual The Instructor's Manual for *Microeconomics* integrates the teaching and learning resources and serves as a guide to all the supplements. Written by Laura A. Wolff of Southern Illinois University Edwardsville, the Instructor's Manual is available electronically from www.pearsonglobaleditions.com/parkin.

Each chapter contains an overview, a list of what's new in the eleventh edition, and ready-to-use lecture notes, which enable a new user of Parkin to walk into a classroom and deliver a polished lecture.

Solutions Manual The comprehensive solutions manual for *Microeconomics* provides instructors with solutions to the Review Quizzes and the end-of-chapter Problems and Applications as well as additional problems and the solutions to these problems. Written by Mark Rush of the University of Florida and reviewed for accuracy by Jeannie Gillmore of the University of Western Ontario, the Solutions Manual is available electronically from www.pearsonglobaleditions.com/parkin.

Test Item Files Three separate Test Item Files with nearly 6,500 questions, provide multiple-choice, true/false, numerical, fill-in-the-blank, short-answer, and essay questions. Mark Rush reviewed and edited all the questions to ensure their clarity and consistency.

New questions were written by Rebecca Stein of the University of Pennsylvania, Svitlana Maksymenko of the University of Pittsburgh, and James K. Self of the University of Indiana, Bloomington.

Questions follow the style and format of the end-of-chapter text problems. End-of-part tests contain integrative questions that cover all the chapters in the part. New to the eleventh edition are news based application questions for each chapter of the text.

Fully networkable and available for Windows® and Macintosh®, TestGen's graphical interface enables instructors to view the Test Item Files, edit and add questions; transfer questions to tests; and print different forms of tests. Tests can be formatted as in any word-processing document with varying fonts, styles, margins, headers, and footers. Search and sort features let the instructor quickly locate questions and arrange them in a preferred order. QuizMaster, working with your school's computer network, automatically grades exams, stores the results, and allows the instructor to view or print a variety of reports.

PowerPoint Resources A set of full-color Microsoft® PowerPoint Presentations for each chapter.

Each chapter contains:

- Lecture notes with all the textbook figures animated, tables from the textbook, and speaking notes from the Instructor's Manuals
- Large-scale versions of all the figures and tables in the textbook, animated for instructors to incorporate into their own slide shows
- Clicker-ready multiple-choice quizzes that test important concepts

The presentations can be used electronically in the classroom or can be printed to create hard copy transparency masters.

In addition, a separate set of PowerPoint lecture notes is available for students in MyEconLab.

Study Guide

The eleventh edition Study Guide by Mark Rush is coordinated with the text, MyEconLab, and the Test Item Files. Each chapter contains key concepts, helpful hints, true/false/uncertain questions, multiple-choice questions, and short-answer questions. Each part allows students to test their cumulative understanding with questions that go across chapters and to work a sample midterm examination. The student is encouraged to explain some common misconceptions as if he or she were the teacher.

MYECONLAB MyEconLab

MyEconLab works hand-in-hand with *Microeconomics*. Robin Bade and I, assisted by Jeannie Gillmore, Laurel Davies, and Sharmistha Nag, have authored and overseen all of the MyEconLab content for *Microeconomics*. Our team has worked hard to ensure that the Parkin MyEconLab is tightly integrated with the book's content and vision.

With comprehensive homework, quiz, test, and tutorial options, instructors can manage all assessment needs in one program.

- All of the Review Quiz questions and end-of-chapter Problems and Applications are assignable and automatically graded in MyEconLab.
- All the Review Quiz questions and end-of-chapter Study Plan Problems and Applications are available for students to work in Study Plan.
- All the end-of-chapter Additional Problems and Applications are not available to students in MyEconLab unless assigned by the instructor.
- Many of the problems and applications are algorithmic, draw-graph, and numerical exercises.
- Test Item File questions are available for assignment as MyEconLab quizzes, tests, or homework.
- The Custom Exercise Builder enables instructors to create their own problems for assignment as test or homework questions.
- The powerful Gradebook records each student's performance and time spent on tests, the study plan, and homework and generates reports by student or by chapter.
- The Pearson eText provides a direct link to the relevant page of the text so that students can view the appropriate section to help them complete an exercise when working through the Study Plan or completing homework assignments.

Economics in the News *Economics in the News* is a turn-key solution to bringing daily news into the classroom. Updated daily during the school year, I upload a microeconomic article and provide links for further information and questions that may be assigned for homework or for classroom discussion.

Auto-Graded *Economics in the News* New to the eleventh edition are auto-graded *Economics in the News* exercises updated regularly throughout the school year. I upload a multi-part microeconomic exercise with links to the relevant article.

Experiments in MyEconLab Experiments are a fun and engaging way to promote active learning and mastery of important economic concepts. Pearson's experiments program is flexible and easy for instructors and students to use.

- Single-player experiments allow your students to play against virtual players from anywhere at any time with an Internet connection.
- Multiplayer experiments allow you to assign and manage a real-time experiment with your class.

Pre- and post-questions for each experiment are available for assignment in MyEconLab.

For a complete list of available experiments, visit www.myeconlab.com.

AACSB and Learning Outcomes All end-of-chapter and Test Item File questions are tagged in two ways: to AACSB standards and to discipline-specific Learning Outcomes. These two separate tagging systems allow instructors to build assessments around desired departmental and course outcomes and track results in MyEconLab's gradebook.

A more detailed walk-through of the student benefits and features of MyEconLab can be found on the inside front cover. Visit www.myeconlab.com for more information and an online demonstration of instructor and student features.

►► Acknowledgments

I thank my current and former colleagues and friends who have taught me so much. They are Jim Davies, Jeremy Greenwood, Ig Horstmann, Peter Howitt, Greg Huffman, David Laidler, Phil Reny, Chris Robinson, John Whalley, Ron Wonnacott, Doug McTaggart, Christopher Findlay, Melanie Powell, Kent Matthews, Rebecca Stein, and Yoram Bauman.

It is a special joy to thank the many outstanding editors, media specialists, and others at Pearson who contributed to the concerted publishing effort that brought this edition to completion. Denise Clinton, Publisher of MyEconLab has played a major role in the evolution of this text since its third edition, and her insights and ideas can still be found in this new edition. Donna Battista, Editor-in-Chief for Economics and Finance, is hugely inspiring and has provided overall direction to the project. As ever, Adrienne D'Ambrosio, Executive Acquisitions Editor for Economics and my sponsoring editor, played a major role in shaping this revision and the many outstanding supplements that accompany it. Adrienne brings intelligence and insight to her work and is the unchallengeable pre-eminent economics editor. Sarah Dumouchelle, Editorial Project Manager, provided a steady hand throughout the revision process, managing our immense supplements program, keeping the supplements authors' contributions on track, and working with rights and permissions advisors. Nancy Freihofer, Senior Production Project Manager, oversaw the production and design process and coordinated the photo research program. Susan Schoenberg, Director of Media, directed the development of MyEconLab; Noel Lotz, Content Lead for MyEconLab, managed a complex and thorough reviewing process for the content of MyEconLab; and Melissa Honig, Senior Media Producer ensured that all our media assets were correctly assembled. Lori Deshazo, Executive Marketing Manager, provided inspired marketing strategy and direction. Catherine Baum provided a careful, consistent, and intelligent copy edit and accuracy check. Jonathan Boylan designed the cover and package and yet again surpassed the challenge of ensuring that we meet the highest design standards. Joe Vetere provided endless technical help with the text and art files. And Heather Johnson with the other members of an outstanding editorial and production team at Integra-Chicago kept the project on track on an impossibly tight schedule.

In preparing this Global edition, I have had the great pleasure of working with economists in the regions in which it will be used. Special Reading Between the Lines and At Issue features have been researched by Monal Abdel-Baki of the American University in Cairo, Egypt; Eddie Cheung Chi Leung of the Open University, Hong Kong; Samer Kherfi of the American University of Sharjah, United Arab Emirates; and Lily Wong of the Temasek Polytechnic, Singapore. I thank these fine and creative economists and teachers for their most helpful contributions. ˙

I thank all of these wonderful people. It has been inspiring to work with them and to share in creating what I believe is a truly outstanding educational tool.

I thank our talented eleventh edition supplements authors and contributors—Laurel Davies, Jeannie Gillmore, Svitlana Maksymenko, Sharmistha Nag, Jim Self, Rebecca Stein, and Laurie Wolff.

I especially thank Mark Rush, who yet again played a crucial role in creating another edition of this text and package. Mark has been a constant source of good advice and good humor.

I thank the many exceptional reviewers who have shared their insights through the various editions of this book. Their contribution has been invaluable.

I thank the people who work directly with me. Jeannie Gillmore provided outstanding research assistance on many topics, including the *Reading Between the Lines* news articles. Richard Parkin created the electronic art files and offered many ideas that improved the figures in this book. Laurel Davies managed an ever-growing and ever more complex MyEconLab database. And Sharmistha Nag has helped me to create *Economics in the News* questions for MyEconLab.

As with the previous editions, this one owes an enormous debt to Robin Bade. I dedicate this book to her and again thank her for her work. I could not have written this book without the tireless and unselfish help she has given me. My thanks to her are unbounded.

Classroom experience will test the value of this book. I would appreciate hearing from instructors and students about how I can continue to improve it in future editions.

Michael Parkin
London, Ontario, Canada
michael.parkin@uwo.ca

Contributors and Supplement Authors

Contributors to Global Edition

Monal Abdel-Baki, The American University in Cairo, Egypt
Eddie Cheung Chi Leung, The Open University of Hong Kong, Hong Kong
Samer Kherfi, American University of Sharjah, United Arab Emirates
Lily Wong, Temasek Polytechnic, Singapore

Supplements Authors

Luke Armstrong, Lee College
Sue Bartlett, University of South Florida
Kelly Blanchard, Purdue University
James Cobbe, Florida State University
Carol Dole, Jacksonville University
Karen Gebhardt, Colorado State University
John Graham, Rutgers University
Jill Herndon, University of Florida
Gary Hoover, University of Alabama
Patricia Kuzyk, Washington State University
Sang Lee, Southeastern Louisiana University
Svitlana Maksymenko, University of Pittsburgh
Robert Martel, University of Connecticut
Katherine McClain, University of Georgia
Russ McCullough, Iowa State University
Barbara Moore, University of Central Florida
James Morley, Washington University in St. Louis
William Mosher, Clark University
Constantin Ogloblin, Georgia Southern University
Edward Price, Oklahoma State University
Mark Rush, University of Florida
James K. Self, University of Indiana, Bloomington
Rebecca Stein, University of Pennsylvania
Michael Stroup, Stephen F. Austin State University
Della Lee Sue, Marist College
Nora Underwood, University of Central Florida
Laura A. Wolff, Southern Illinois University, Edwardsville

Reviewers

Eric Abrams, Hawaii Pacific University
Christopher Adams, Federal Trade Commission
Tajudeen Adenekan, Bronx Community College
John T. Addison, University of South Carolina
Syed Ahmed, Cameron University
Frank Albritton, Seminole Community College
Milton Alderfer, Miami-Dade Community College
William Aldridge, Shelton State Community College
Donald L. Alexander, Western Michigan University
Terence Alexander, Iowa State University

Stuart Allen, University of North Carolina, Greensboro
Sam Allgood, University of Nebraska, Lincoln
Neil Alper, Northeastern University
Alan Anderson, Fordham University
Lisa R. Anderson, College of William and Mary
Jeff Ankrom, Wittenberg University
Fatma Antar, Manchester Community Technical College
Kofi Apraku, University of North Carolina, Asheville
John Atkins, University of West Florida
Moshen Bahmani-Oskooee, University of Wisconsin, Milwaukee
Donald Balch, University of South Carolina
Mehmet Balcilar, Wayne State University
Paul Ballantyne, University of Colorado
Sue Bartlett, University of South Florida
Jose Juan Bautista, Xavier University of Louisiana
Klaus Becker, Texas Tech University
Valerie R. Bencivenga, University of Texas, Austin
Ben Bernanke, Chairman of Federal Reserve
Radha Bhattacharya, California State University, Fullerton
Margot Biery, Tarrant County College, South
John Bittorowitz, Ball State University
David Black, University of Toledo
Kelly Blanchard, Purdue University
S. Brock Blomberg, Claremont McKenna College
William T. Bogart, Case Western Reserve University
Giacomo Bonanno, University of California, Davis
Tan Khay Boon, Nanyard Technological University
Sunne Brandmeyer, University of South Florida
Audie Brewton, Northeastern Illinois University
Baird Brock, Central Missouri State University
Byron Brown, Michigan State University
Jeffrey Buser, Columbus State Community College
Alison Butler, Florida International University
Colleen Callahan, American University
Tania Carbiener, Southern Methodist University
Kevin Carey, American University
Scott Carrell, University of California at Davis
Kathleen A. Carroll, University of Maryland, Baltimore County
Michael Carter, University of Massachusetts, Lowell
Edward Castronova, California State University, Fullerton
Francis Chan, Fullerton College
Ming Chang, Dartmouth College
Subir Chakrabarti, Indiana University-Purdue University
Joni Charles, Texas State University
Adhip Chaudhuri, Georgetown University
Gopal Chengalath, Texas Tech University
Daniel Christiansen, Albion College
Kenneth Christianson, Binghamton University
John J. Clark, Community College of Allegheny County, Allegheny Campus
Cindy Clement, University of Maryland
Meredith Clement, Dartmouth College
Michael B. Cohn, U. S. Merchant Marine Academy

Robert Collinge, University of Texas, San Antonio

Carol Condon, Kean University

Doug Conway, Mesa Community College

Larry Cook, University of Toledo

Bobby Corcoran, retired, Middle Tennessee State University

Kevin Cotter, Wayne State University

James Peery Cover, University of Alabama, Tuscaloosa

Erik Craft, University of Richmond

Eleanor D. Craig, University of Delaware

Jim Craven, Clark College

Jeremy Cripps, American University of Kuwait

Elizabeth Crowell, University of Michigan, Dearborn

Stephen Cullenberg, University of California, Riverside

David Culp, Slippery Rock University

Norman V. Cure, Macomb Community College

James D'Angelo, University of Cincinnati

Dan Dabney, University of Texas, Austin

Andrew Dane, Angelo State University

Joseph Daniels, Marquette University

Gregory DeFreitas, Hofstra University

David Denslow, University of Florida

Shatakshee Dhongde, Rochester Institute of Technology

Mark Dickie, University of Central Florida

James Dietz, California State University, Fullerton

Carol Dole, State University of West Georgia

Ronald Dorf, Inver Hills Community College

John Dorsey, University of Maryland, College Park

Eric Drabkin, Hawaii Pacific University

Amrik Singh Dua, Mt. San Antonio College

Thomas Duchesneau, University of Maine, Orono

Lucia Dunn, Ohio State University

Donald Dutkowsky, Syracuse University

John Edgren, Eastern Michigan University

David J. Eger, Alpena Community College

Harold W. Elder, University of Alabama

Harry Ellis, Jr., University of North Texas

Ibrahim Elsaify, Goldey-Beacom College

Kenneth G. Elzinga, University of Virginia

Patrick Emerson, Oregon State University

Tisha Emerson, Baylor University

Monica Escaleras, Florida Atlantic University

Antonina Espiritu, Hawaii Pacific University

Gwen Eudey, University of Pennsylvania

Barry Falk, Iowa State University

M. Fazeli, Hofstra University

Philip Fincher, Louisiana Tech University

F. Firoozi, University of Texas, San Antonio

Nancy Folbre, University of Massachusetts, Amherst

Kenneth Fong, Temasek Polytechnic (Singapore)

Steven Francis, Holy Cross College

David Franck, University of North Carolina, Charlotte

Mark Frank, Sam Houston State University

Roger Frantz, San Diego State University

Mark Frascatore, Clarkson University

Alwyn Fraser, Atlantic Union College

Marc Fusaro, East Carolina University

James Gale, Michigan Technological University

Susan Gale, New York University

Roy Gardner, Indiana University

Eugene Gentzel, Pensacola Junior College

Kirk Gifford, Brigham Young University-Idaho

Scott Gilbert, Southern Illinois University, Carbondale

Andrew Gill, California State University, Fullerton

Robert Giller, Virginia Polytechnic Institute and State University

Robert Gillette, University of Kentucky

James N. Giordano, Villanova University

Maria Giuili, Diablo College

Susan Glanz, St. John's University

Robert Gordon, San Diego State University

Richard Gosselin, Houston Community College

John Graham, Rutgers University

John Griffen, Worcester Polytechnic Institute

Wayne Grove, Syracuse University

Robert Guell, Indiana State University

William Gunther, University of Southern Mississippi

Jamie Haag, Pacific University, Oregon

Gail Heyne Hafer, Lindenwood University

Rik W. Hafer, Southern Illinois University, Edwardsville

Daniel Hagen, Western Washington University

David R. Hakes, University of Northern Iowa

Craig Hakkio, Federal Reserve Bank, Kansas City

Bridget Gleeson Hanna, Rochester Institute of Technology

Ann Hansen, Westminster College

Seid Hassan, Murray State University

Jonathan Haughton, Suffolk University

Randall Haydon, Wichita State University

Denise Hazlett, Whitman College

Julia Heath, University of Memphis

Jac Heckelman, Wake Forest University

Jolien A. Helsel, Kent State University

James Henderson, Baylor University

Doug Herman, Georgetown University

Jill Boylston Herndon, University of Florida

Gus Herring, Brookhaven College

John Herrmann, Rutgers University

John M. Hill, Delgado Community College

Jonathan Hill, Florida International University

Lewis Hill, Texas Tech University

Steve Hoagland, University of Akron

Tom Hoerger, Fellow, Research Triangle Institute

Calvin Hoerneman, Delta College

George Hoffer, Virginia Commonwealth University

Dennis L. Hoffman, Arizona State University

Paul Hohenberg, Rensselaer Polytechnic Institute

Jim H. Holcomb, University of Texas, El Paso

Robert Holland, Purdue University

Harry Holzer, Georgetown University

Gary Hoover, University of Alabama

Linda Hooks, Washington and Lee University

Jim Horner, Cameron University

Djehane Hosni, University of Central Florida

Harold Hotelling, Jr., Lawrence Technical University

Calvin Hoy, County College of Morris

Ing-Wei Huang, Assumption University, Thailand

Julie Hunsaker, Wayne State University

Beth Ingram, University of Iowa

Jayvanth Ishwaran, Stephen F. Austin State University

Michael Jacobs, Lehman College

S. Hussain Ali Jafri, Tarleton State University

Dennis Jansen, Texas A&M University

Andrea Jao, University of Pennsylvania

Barbara John, University of Dayton

Barry Jones, Binghamton University

Garrett Jones, Southern Florida University

Frederick Jungman, Northwestern Oklahoma State University

Paul Junk, University of Minnesota, Duluth

Leo Kahane, California State University, Hayward

Veronica Kalich, Baldwin-Wallace College

John Kane, State University of New York, Oswego

Eungmin Kang, St. Cloud State University

Arthur Kartman, San Diego State University

Gurmit Kaur, Universiti Teknologi (Malaysia)

Louise Keely, University of Wisconsin, Madison

Manfred W. Keil, Claremont McKenna College

Elizabeth Sawyer Kelly, University of Wisconsin, Madison

Rose Kilburn, Modesto Junior College

Amanda King, Georgia Southern University

John King, Georgia Southern University

Robert Kirk, Indiana University-Purdue University, Indianapolis

Norman Kleinberg, City University of New York, Baruch College

Robert Kleinhenz, California State University, Fullerton

John Krantz, University of Utah

Joseph Kreitzer, University of St. Thomas

Patricia Kuzyk, Washington State University

David Lages, Southwest Missouri State University

W. J. Lane, University of New Orleans

Leonard Lardaro, University of Rhode Island

Kathryn Larson, Elon College

Luther D. Lawson, University of North Carolina, Wilmington

Elroy M. Leach, Chicago State University

Jim Lee, Texas A & M, Corpus Christi

Sang Lee, Southeastern Louisiana University

Robert Lemke, Florida International University

Mary Lesser, Iona College

Philip K. Letting, Harrisburg Area Community College

Jay Levin, Wayne State University

Arik Levinson, University of Wisconsin, Madison

Tony Lima, California State University, Hayward

William Lord, University of Maryland, Baltimore County

Nancy Lutz, Virginia Polytechnic Institute and State University

Brian Lynch, Lakeland Community College

Murugappa Madhavan, San Diego State University

K. T. Magnusson, Salt Lake Community College

Svitlana Maksymenko, University of Pittsburgh

Mark Maier, Glendale Community College

Jean Mangan, Staffordshire University Business School

Denton Marks, University of Wisconsin, Whitewater

Michael Marlow, California Polytechnic State University

Akbar Marvasti, University of Houston

Wolfgang Mayer, University of Cincinnati

John McArthur, Wofford College

Katherine McClain, University of Georgia

Amy McCormick, Mary Baldwin College

Russ McCullough, Iowa State University

Catherine McDevitt, Central Michigan University

Gerald McDougall, Wichita State University

Stephen McGary, Brigham Young University-Idaho

Richard D. McGrath, Armstrong Atlantic State University

Richard McIntyre, University of Rhode Island

John McLeod, Georgia Institute of Technology

Mark McLeod, Virginia Polytechnic Institute and State University

B. Starr McMullen, Oregon State University

Sandra McPherson, Millersville University

Mary Ruth McRae, Appalachian State University

Kimberly Merritt, Cameron University

Charles Meyer, Iowa State University

Peter Mieszkowski, Rice University

John Mijares, University of North Carolina, Asheville

Richard A. Miller, Wesleyan University

Judith W. Mills, Southern Connecticut State University

Glen Mitchell, Nassau Community College

Jeannette C. Mitchell, Rochester Institute of Technology

Khan Mohabbat, Northern Illinois University

Bagher Modjtahedi, University of California, Davis

Michael A. Mogavero, University of Notre Dame

Shahruz Mohtadi, Suffolk University

Barbara Moore, University of Central Florida

W. Douglas Morgan, University of California, Santa Barbara

William Morgan, University of Wyoming

James Morley, Washington University in St. Louis

William Mosher, Clark University

Joanne Moss, San Francisco State University

Nivedita Mukherji, Oakland University

Francis Mummery, Fullerton College

Edward Murphy, Southwest Texas State University

Kevin J. Murphy, Oakland University

Kathryn Nantz, Fairfield University

William S. Neilson, Texas A&M University

Bart C. Nemmers, University of Nebraska, Lincoln

Melinda Nish, Orange Coast College

Anthony O'Brien, Lehigh University

Norman Obst, Michigan State University

Constantin Ogloblin, Georgia Southern University

Neal Olitsky, University of Massachusetts, Dartmouth

Mary Olson, Tulane University

Terry Olson, Truman State University

James B. O'Neill, University of Delaware

Farley Ordovensky, University of the Pacific

Z. Edward O'Relley, North Dakota State University

Donald Oswald, California State University, Bakersfield

Jan Palmer, Ohio University

Michael Palumbo, Chief, Federal Reserve Board

Chris Papageorgiou, Louisiana State University

G. Hossein Parandvash, Western Oregon State College

Randall Parker, East Carolina University

Robert Parks, Washington University

David Pate, St. John Fisher College

James E. Payne, Illinois State University

Donald Pearson, Eastern Michigan University

Steven Peterson, University of Idaho

Mary Anne Pettit, Southern Illinois University, Edwardsville

William A. Phillips, University of Southern Maine

Dennis Placone, Clemson University

Charles Plot, California Institute of Technology, Pasadena

Mannie Poen, Houston Community College

Kathleen Possai, Wayne State University

Ulrika Praski-Stahlgren, University College in Gavle-Sandviken, Sweden

Edward Price, Oklahoma State University

Rula Qalyoubi, University of Wisconsin, Eau Claire

K. A. Quartey, Talladega College

Herman Quirmbach, Iowa State University

Jeffrey R. Racine, University of South Florida

Ramkishen Rajan, George Mason University

Peter Rangazas, Indiana University-Purdue University, Indianapolis

Vaman Rao, Western Illinois University

Laura Razzolini, University of Mississippi

Rob Rebelein, University of Cincinnati

J. David Reed, Bowling Green State University

Robert H. Renshaw, Northern Illinois University

Javier Reyes, University of Arkansas

Jeff Reynolds, Northern Illinois University

Rupert Rhodd, Florida Atlantic University

W. Gregory Rhodus, Bentley College

Jennifer Rice, Indiana University, Bloomington

John Robertson, Paducah Community College

Malcolm Robinson, University of North Carolina, Greensboro

Richard Roehl, University of Michigan, Dearborn

Carol Rogers, Georgetown University

William Rogers, University of Northern Colorado

Thomas Romans, State University of New York, Buffalo

David R. Ross, Bryn Mawr College

Thomas Ross, Baldwin Wallace College

Robert J. Rossana, Wayne State University

Jeffrey Rous, University of North Texas

Rochelle Ruffer, Youngstown State University

Mark Rush, University of Florida

Allen R. Sanderson, University of Chicago

Gary Santoni, Ball State University

Jeffrey Sarbaum, University of North Carolina at Chapel Hill

John Saussy, Harrisburg Area Community College

Don Schlagenhauf, Florida State University

David Schlow, Pennsylvania State University

Paul Schmitt, St. Clair County Community College

Jeremy Schwartz, Hampden-Sydney College

Martin Sefton, University of Nottingham

James K. Self, Indiana University

Esther-Mirjam Sent, University of Notre Dame

Rod Shadbegian, University of Massachusetts, Dartmouth

Neil Sheflin, Rutgers University

Gerald Shilling, Eastfield College

Dorothy R. Siden, Salem State College

Mark Siegler, California State University at Sacramento

Scott Simkins, North Carolina Agricultural and Technical State University

Jacek Siry, University of Georgia

Chuck Skoro, Boise State University

Phil Smith, DeKalb College

William Doyle Smith, University of Texas, El Paso

Sarah Stafford, College of William and Mary

Rebecca Stein, University of Pennsylvania

Frank Steindl, Oklahoma State University

Jeffrey Stewart, New York University

Allan Stone, Southwest Missouri State University

Courtenay Stone, Ball State University

Paul Storer, Western Washington University

Richard W. Stratton, University of Akron

Mark Strazicich, Ohio State University, Newark

Michael Stroup, Stephen F. Austin State University

Robert Stuart, Rutgers University

Della Lee Sue, Marist College

Abdulhamid Sukar, Cameron University

Terry Sutton, Southeast Missouri State University

Gilbert Suzawa, University of Rhode Island

David Swaine, Andrews University

Jason Taylor, Central Michigan University

Mark Thoma, University of Oregon

Janet Thomas, Bentley College

Kiril Tochkov, SUNY at Binghamton

Kay Unger, University of Montana
Anthony Uremovic, Joliet Junior College
David Vaughn, City University, Washington
Don Waldman, Colgate University
Francis Wambalaba, Portland State University
Sasiwimon Warunsiri, University of Colorado at Boulder
Rob Wassmer, California State University, Sacramento
Paul A. Weinstein, University of Maryland, College Park
Lee Weissert, St. Vincent College
Robert Whaples, Wake Forest University
David Wharton, Washington College
Mark Wheeler, Western Michigan University
Charles H. Whiteman, University of Iowa
Sandra Williamson, University of Pittsburgh

Brenda Wilson, Brookhaven Community College
Larry Wimmer, Brigham Young University
Mark Witte, Northwestern University
Willard E. Witte, Indiana University
Mark Wohar, University of Nebraska, Omaha
Laura Wolff, Southern Illinois University, Edwardsville
Cheonsik Woo, Vice President, Korea Development Institute
Douglas Wooley, Radford University
Arthur G. Woolf, University of Vermont
John T. Young, Riverside Community College
Michael Youngblood, Rock Valley College
Peter Zaleski, Villanova University
Jason Zimmerman, South Dakota State University
David Zucker, Martha Stewart Living Omnimedia

1

WHAT IS ECONOMICS?

After studying this chapter, you will be able to:

◆ Define economics and distinguish between microeconomics and macroeconomics

◆ Explain the two big questions of economics

◆ Explain the key ideas that define the economic way of thinking

◆ Explain how economists go about their work as social scientists and policy advisers

Is economics about money: How people make it and spend it? Is it about business, government, and jobs? Is it about why some people and some nations are rich and others poor? Economics is about all these things. But its core is the study of *choices* and their *consequences*.

Your life will be shaped by the choices that you make and the challenges that you face. To face those challenges and seize the opportunities they present, you must understand the powerful forces at play. The economics that you're about to learn will become your most reliable guide. This chapter gets you started by describing the questions that economists try to answer and looking at how economists think as they search for the answers.

Definition of Economics

A fundamental fact dominates our lives: We want more than we can get. Our inability to get everything we want is called **scarcity**. Scarcity is universal. It confronts all living things. Even parrots face scarcity!

Not only do I want a cracker—we all want a cracker!

© The New Yorker Collection 1985
Frank Modell from cartoonbank.com. All Rights Reserved.

Think about the things that *you* want and the scarcity that *you* face. You want to go to a good school, college, or university. You want to live in a well-equipped, spacious, and comfortable home. You want the latest smart phone and the fastest Internet connection for your laptop or iPad. You want some sports and recreational gear—perhaps some new running shoes, or a new bike. You want much more time than is available to go to class, do your homework, play sports and games, read novels, go to the movies, listen to music, travel, and hang out with your friends. And you want to live a long and healthy life.

What you can afford to buy is limited by your income and by the prices you must pay. And your time is limited by the fact that your day has 24 hours.

You want some other things that only governments provide. You want to live in a safe neighborhood in a peaceful and secure world, and enjoy the benefits of clean air, lakes, rivers, and oceans.

What governments can afford is limited by the taxes they collect. Taxes lower people's incomes and compete with the other things they want to buy.

What *everyone* can get—what *society* can get—is limited by the productive resources available. These resources are the gifts of nature, human labor and ingenuity, and all the previously produced tools and equipment.

Because we can't get everything we want, we must make *choices*. You can't afford *both* a laptop *and* an iPhone, so you must *choose* which one to buy. You can't spend tonight *both* studying for your next test *and* going to the movies, so again, you must *choose* which one to do. Governments can't spend a tax dollar on *both* national defense *and* environmental protection, so they must *choose* how to spend that dollar.

Your choices must somehow be made consistent with the choices of *others*. If you choose to buy a laptop, someone else must choose to sell it. Incentives reconcile choices. An **incentive** is a reward that encourages an action or a penalty that discourages one. Prices act as incentives. If the price of a laptop is too high, more will be offered for sale than people want to buy. And if the price is too low, fewer will be offered for sale than people want to buy. But there is a price at which choices to buy and sell are consistent.

> **Economics** is the social science that studies the *choices* that individuals, businesses, governments, and entire societies make as they cope with *scarcity* and the *incentives* that influence and reconcile those choices.

The subject has two parts:

- Microeconomics
- Macroeconomics

Microeconomics is the study of the choices that individuals and businesses make, the way these choices interact in markets, and the influence of governments. Some examples of microeconomic questions are: Why are people downloading more movies? How would a tax on e-commerce affect eBay?

Macroeconomics is the study of the performance of the national economy and the global economy. Some examples of macroeconomic questions are: Why is the U.S. unemployment rate so high? Can the Federal Reserve make our economy expand by cutting interest rates?

◆ REVIEW QUIZ

1 List some examples of the scarcity that you face.
2 Find examples of scarcity in today's headlines.
3 Find an example of the distinction between microeconomics and macroeconomics in today's headlines.

You can work these questions in Study Plan 1.1 and get instant feedback.   MyEconLab

◆ Two Big Economic Questions

Two big questions summarize the scope of economics:

- How do choices end up determining *what, how,* and *for whom* goods and services are produced?
- Do the choices that people make in the pursuit of their own *self-interest* unintentionally promote the broader *social interest*?

What, How, and For Whom?

Goods and services are the objects that people value and produce to satisfy wants. *Goods* are physical objects such as cell phones and automobiles. *Services* are tasks performed for people such as cell-phone service and auto-repair service.

What? *What* we produce varies across countries and changes over time. In the United States today, agriculture accounts for 1 percent of total production, manufactured goods for 22 percent, and services (retail and wholesale trade, health care, and education are the biggest ones) for 77 percent. In contrast, in China today, agriculture accounts for 10 percent of total production, manufactured goods for 47 percent, and services for 43 percent. Figure 1.1 shows these numbers and also the percentages for Brazil, which fall between those for the United States and China.

What determines these patterns of production? How do choices end up determining the quantities of cell phones, automobiles, cell-phone service, auto-repair service, and the millions of other items that are produced in the United States and around the world?

How? *How* we produce is described by the technologies and resources that we use. The resources used to produce goods and services are called **factors of production**, which are grouped into four categories:

- Land
- Labor
- Capital
- Entrepreneurship

Land The "gifts of nature" that we use to produce goods and services are called **land**. In economics, *land* is what in everyday language we call *natural resources*. It includes land in the everyday sense

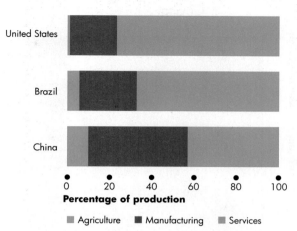

FIGURE 1.1   What Three Countries Produce

Percentage of production

■ Agriculture   ■ Manufacturing   ■ Services

Agriculture and manufacturing are small percentages of production in rich countries such as the United States and large percentages of production in poorer countries such as China. Most of what is produced in the United States is services.

Source of data: CIA Factbook 2012, Central Intelligence Agency.

————— MyEconLab animation —————

together with minerals, oil, gas, coal, water, air, forests, and fish.

Our land surface and water resources are renewable and some of our mineral resources can be recycled. But the resources that we use to create energy are nonrenewable—they can be used only once.

Labor The work time and work effort that people devote to producing goods and services is called **labor**. Labor includes the physical and mental efforts of all the people who work on farms and construction sites and in factories, shops, and offices.

The *quality* of labor depends on **human capital**, which is the knowledge and skill that people obtain from education, on-the-job training, and work experience. You are building your own human capital right now as you work on your economics course, and your human capital will continue to grow as you gain work experience.

Human capital expands over time. Today, 88 percent of the adult population of the United States have completed high school and 30 percent have a college or university degree. Figure 1.2 shows these measures of human capital in the United States and its growth over the past 110 years.

FIGURE 1.2   A Measure of Human
Capital

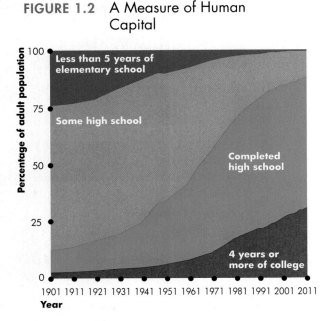

In 2011, 30 percent of the population had 4 years or more
of college, up from 2 percent in 1901. A further 58 percent
had completed high school, up from 10 percent in 1901.

Source of data: U.S. Census Bureau, *Statistical Abstract of the
United States*, 2012.

——————— MyEconLab animation ———————

Capital The tools, instruments, machines, buildings,
and other constructions that businesses use to produce goods and services are called **capital**.

In everyday language, we talk about money,
stocks, and bonds as being "capital." These items are
financial capital. Financial capital plays an important
role in enabling businesses to borrow the funds that
they use to buy physical capital. But financial capital
is not used to produce goods and services and it is
not a factor of production.

Entrepreneurship The human resource that organizes
labor, land, and capital is called **entrepreneurship**.
Entrepreneurs are the drivers of economic progress.
They develop new ideas about what and how to produce, make business decisions, and bear the risks that
arise from these decisions.

What determines how the factors of production
are used to produce each good and service?

For Whom? *Who* consumes the goods and services
that are produced depends on the incomes that people earn. People with large incomes can buy a wide
range of goods and services. People with small
incomes have fewer options and can afford a smaller
range of goods and services.

People earn their incomes by selling the services of
the factors of production they own:

■ Land earns **rent**.
■ Labor earns **wages**.
■ Capital earns **interest**.
■ Entrepreneurship earns **profit**.

Which factor of production earns the most
income? The answer is labor. In 2011, wages were 68
percent of total income and the incomes from land,
capital, and entrepreneurship 32 percent. These
shares have been remarkably constant over time.

Knowing how income is shared among the factors of production doesn't tell us how it is shared
among individuals. And the distribution of income
among individuals is extremely unequal. You know
of some people who earn very large incomes:
Angelina Jolie earns $10 million per movie; and the
New York Yankees pays Alex Rodriguez $27.5 mil-
lion a year.

You know of even more people who earn very
small incomes. Servers at McDonald's average around
$7.25 an hour; checkout clerks, cleaners, and textile
and leather workers all earn less than $10 an hour.

You probably know about other persistent differences in incomes. Men, on average, earn more than
women; whites earn more than minorities; college
graduates earn more than high-school graduates.

We can get a good sense of who consumes the
goods and services produced by looking at the percentages of total income earned by different groups
of people. The 20 percent of people with the lowest
incomes earn about 5 percent of total income, while
the richest 20 percent earn close to 50 percent of
total income. So on average, people in the richest 20
percent earn more than 10 times the incomes of
those in the poorest 20 percent. There is even huge
inequality within the richest 20 percent and the top 1
percent earns almost 15 percent of total income.

Why is the distribution of income so unequal?

Economics provides some answers to all these
questions about *what, how*, and *for whom* goods and
services are produced and much of the rest of this
book will help you to understand those answers.

We're now going to look at the second big question of economics: Does the pursuit of self-interest
unintentionally promote the social interest?

Does the Pursuit of Self-Interest Unintentionally Promote the Social Interest?

Every day, you and 314 million other Americans, along with 6.7 billion people in the rest of the world, make economic choices that result in *what, how*, and *for whom* goods and services are produced. These choices are made by people who are pursuing their self-interest.

Self-Interest You make a choice in your **self-interest** if you think that choice is the best one available for you. All the choices that people make about how to use their time and other resources are made in the pursuit of self-interest. When you allocate your time or your budget, you do what makes the most sense to you. You might think about how your choices affect other people and take into account how you feel about that, but it is how *you* feel that influences your choice. You order a home delivery pizza because you're hungry, not because the delivery person needs a job. And when the pizza delivery person shows up at your door, he's not doing you a favor. He's pursuing *his* self-interest and hoping for a tip and another call next week.

The big question is: Is it possible that all the choices that each one of us makes in the pursuit of self-interest could end up achieving an outcome that is best for everyone?

Social Interest An outcome is in the **social interest** if it is best for society as a whole. It is easy to see how you decide what is in *your* self-interest. But how do you decide if something is in the social interest? To help you answer this question, imagine a scene like that in *Economics in the News* on the next page.

Ted, an entrepreneur, creates a new business. He hires a thousand workers and pays them $20 an hour, $1 an hour more than they earned in their old jobs. Ted's business is extremely profitable and his own earnings increase by $1 million per week.

You can see that Ted's decision to create the business is in his self-interest—he gains $1 million a week. You can also see that the decisions to work for Ted are in the self-interest of the workers—they gain $1 an hour (say $40 a week). And the decisions of Ted's customers must be in their self-interest otherwise they wouldn't buy from him. But is this outcome in the social interest?

The economist's answer is "Yes." It is in the social interest because it makes everyone better off. There are no losers.

Efficiency and the Social Interest Economists use the everyday word "efficient" to describe a situation that can't be improved upon. Resource use is **efficient** if it is *not* possible to make someone better off without making someone else worse off. If it *is* possible to make someone better off without making anyone worse off, society can be made better off and the situation is not efficient.

In the Ted story everyone is better off, so it improves efficiency and the outcome is in the social interest. But notice that it would also have been efficient if the workers and customers had gained nothing and Ted had gained even more than $1 million a week. But would that efficient outcome be in the social interest?

Many people have trouble seeing the outcome in which Ted is the only winner as being in the social interest. They say that the social interest requires Ted to share some of his gain either with his workers in higher wages or with his customers in lower prices, or with both groups.

Fair Shares and the Social Interest The idea that the social interest requires "fair shares" is a deeply held one. Think about what you regard as a fair share. To help you, imagine the following game.

I put $100 on the table and tell someone you don't know and who doesn't know you to *propose* a share of the money between the two of you. If you *accept* the proposed share, you each get the agreed upon shares. If you don't accept the proposed share, you both get nothing.

It would be efficient—you would both be better off—if the proposer offered to take $99 and leave you with $1 and you accepted that offer.

But would you accept the $1? If you are like most people, the idea that the other person gets 99 times as much as you is just too much to stomach. "No way" you say and the $100 disappears. That outcome is inefficient. You have both given up something.

When the game I've just described is played in a classroom experiment, about a half of the players reject offers of below $30.

So fair shares matters. But what is *fair*? There isn't a crisp definition of fairness to match that of efficiency. Reasonable people have a variety of views about it. Almost everyone agrees that too much inequality is unfair. But how much is too much? And inequality of what: income, wealth, or the *opportunity* to work, earn an income, and accumulate wealth?

You will examine efficiency again in Chapter 2 and efficiency and fairness in Chapter 5.

Questions about the social interest are hard ones to answer and they generate discussion, debate, and disagreement. Four issues in today's world put some flesh on these questions. The issues are:

- Globalization
- Information-age monopolies
- Climate change
- Economic instability

Globalization The term *globalization* means the expansion of international trade, borrowing and lending, and investment.

When Nike produces sports shoes, people in Malaysia get work; and when China Airlines buys new airplanes, Americans who work at Boeing in Seattle build them. While globalization brings expanded production and job opportunities for some workers, it destroys many American jobs. Workers across the manufacturing industries must learn new skills, take service jobs, which are often lower-paid, or retire earlier than previously planned.

Globalization is in the self-interest of those consumers who buy low-cost goods and services produced in other countries; and it is in the self-interest of the multinational firms that produce in low-cost regions and sell in high-price regions. But is globalization in the self-interest of the low-wage worker in Malaysia who sews your new running shoes and the displaced shoemaker in Atlanta? Is it in the social interest?

◆ ECONOMICS IN THE NEWS

The Invisible Hand

From Brewer to Bio-Tech Entrepreneur

Kiran Mazumdar-Shaw trained to become a master brewer and learned about enzymes, the stuff from which bio-pharmaceuticals are made. Discovering it was impossible for a woman in India to become a master brewer, the 25-year-old Kiran decided to create a bio-pharmaceutical business.

Kiran's firm, Biocom, employed uneducated workers who loved their jobs and the living conditions made possible by their high wages. But when a labor union entered the scene and unionized the workers, a furious Kiran fired the workers, automated their jobs, and hired a smaller number of educated workers. Biocom continued to grow and today, Kiran's wealth exceeds $1 billion.

Kiran has become wealthy by developing and producing bio-pharmaceuticals that improve people's lives. But Kiran is sharing her wealth in creative ways. She has opened a cancer treatment center to help thousands of patients who are too poor to pay and created a health insurance scheme.

Source of information: Ariel Levy, "Drug Test"
The New Yorker, January 2, 2012

THE QUESTIONS

- Whose decisions in the story were taken in self-interest?
- Whose decisions turned out to be in the social interest?
- Did any of the decisions harm the social interest?

THE ANSWERS

- All the decisions—Kiran's, the workers', the union's, and the firm's customers'—are taken in the pursuit of self-interest.
- Kiran's decisions serve the social interest: She creates jobs that benefit her workers and products that benefit her customers. And her charitable work brings yet further social benefits.
- The labor union's decision might have harmed the social interest because it destroyed the jobs of uneducated workers.

Kiran Mazumdar-Shaw, founder and CEO of Biocom

Information-Age Monopolies The technological change of the past forty years has been called the *Information Revolution.*

Gordon Moore, who founded the chip-maker Intel, and Bill Gates, a co-founder of Microsoft, held privileged positions in this revolution. For many years, Intel chips were the only available chips and Windows was the only available operating system for the original IBM PC and its clones. The PC and Mac competed, but the PC had a huge market share.

An absence of competition gave Intel and Microsoft the power and ability to sell their products at prices far above the cost of production. If the prices of chips and Windows had been lower, many more people would have been able to afford a computer and would have chosen to buy one.

The information revolution has clearly served your self-interest: It has provided your cell phone, laptop, loads of handy applications, and the Internet. It has also served the self-interest of Bill Gates of Microsoft and Gordon Moore of Intel, both of whom have seen their wealth soar.

But did the information revolution best serve the social interest? Did Microsoft produce the best possible Windows operating system and sell it at a price that was in the social interest? Did Intel make the right quality of chips and sell them in the right quantities for the right prices? Or was the quality too low and the price too high? Would the social interest have been better served if Microsoft and Intel had faced competition from other firms?

Climate Change Climate change is a huge political issue today. Every serious political leader is acutely aware of the problem and of the popularity of having proposals that might lower carbon emissions.

Burning fossil fuels to generate electricity and to power airplanes, automobiles, and trucks pours a staggering 28 billion tons—4 tons per person—of carbon dioxide into the atmosphere each year.

Two thirds of the world's carbon emissions comes from the United States, China, the European Union, Russia, and India. The fastest growing emissions are coming from India and China.

The amount of global warming caused by economic activity and its effects are uncertain, but the emissions continue to grow and pose huge risks.

Every day, when you make self-interested choices to use electricity and gasoline, you contribute to carbon emissions; you leave your carbon footprint. You can lessen your carbon footprint by walking, riding a bike, taking a cold shower, or planting a tree.

But can each one of us be relied upon to make decisions that affect the Earth's carbon-dioxide concentration in the social interest? Must governments change the incentives we face so that our self-interested choices are also in the social interest? How can governments change incentives? How can we encourage the use of wind and solar power to replace the burning of fossil fuels that brings climate change?

Economic Instability The years between 1993 and 2007 brought remarkable economic stability, so much so that they've been called the *Great Moderation.* During those years, the U.S. and global economies were on a roll. Incomes in the United States increased by 30 percent and incomes in China tripled. Even the economic shockwaves of 9/11 brought only a small dip in the strong pace of U.S. and global economic expansion.

Flush with funds and offering record low interest rates, banks went on a lending spree to home buyers. Rapidly rising home prices made home owners feel well off and they were happy to borrow and spend. Home loans were bundled into securities that were sold and resold to banks around the world.

◆ AT **ISSUE**

The Protest against Market Capitalism

Market capitalism is an economic system in which individuals own all the land and capital and are free to buy and sell land, capital, and goods and services in markets. Billions of self-interested choices and their coordination in markets determine what, how, and for whom goods and services are produced. There is no supreme planner guiding the use of scarce resources and the outcome is unintended and unforeseeable.

Centrally planned socialism is an economic system in which the government owns all the land and capital, directs workers to jobs, and decides what, how, and for whom to produce. The Soviet Union, several Eastern European countries, and China have used this system in the past but have now abandoned it.

Our economy today is a **mixed economy**, which is market capitalism with government regulation.

The **Protest**

The protest against market capitalism takes many forms. Historically, **Karl Marx** and other communist and socialist thinkers wanted to replace it with *socialism* and *central planning*. Today, thousands of people who feel let down by the economic system want less market capitalism and more government regulation. The **Occupy Wall Street** movement is a visible example of today's protest. Protesters say:

- Big corporations (especially big banks) have too much power and influence on governments.
- Democratically elected governments can do a better job of allocating resources and distributing income than uncoordinated markets. More regulation in the social interest is needed—to serve "human need, not corporate greed."
- In a market, for every winner, there is a loser. Big corporations are the winners. Workers and unemployed people are the losers.

An Occupy Wall Street protester

The **Economist's Response**

Economists agree that market capitalism isn't perfect. But they argue that it is the best system available and while some government intervention and regulation can help, it is equally likely to harm the social interest. **Adam Smith** (see p. 53) gave the first systematic account of how market capitalism works. He says:

- The self-interest of big corporations is *maximum profit*. But an *invisible hand* leads decisions made in pursuit of self-interest to *unintentionally* promote the social interest.
- Politicians are ill-equipped to regulate corporations or to intervene in markets and those who think they can improve on the market outcome are most likely wrong.
- In a market, buyers get what they want for less than they would be willing to pay and sellers earn a profit. Both buyers and sellers gain. A market transaction is a "win-win" event.

"It is not from the benevolence of the butcher, the brewer, or the baker that we expect our dinner, but from their regard to their own interest."
The Wealth of Nations,
1776

Adam Smith

In 2006, as interest rates began to rise and the rate at which home prices were rising slowed, borrowers defaulted on their loans. What started as a trickle became a flood. As more people defaulted, banks took losses that totaled billions of dollars by the summer of 2007. Financial markets are global and a bank in France was the first to feel the pain that soon gripped the entire global financial system.

Banks take in deposits from people and businesses and get more funds by borrowing from each other and from other firms. Banks use these funds to make loans. All the banks' choices to borrow and lend and the choices of people and businesses to lend to and borrow from banks are made in self-interest. But does this lending and borrowing serve the social interest? Is there too much borrowing and lending or too little?

◆ ECONOMICS IN THE NEWS

A Fragile Global Economy

Global Economy Recovering, but Major Risks Remain
In mid-2007, the U.S. mortgage market crashed and triggered a global financial and economic crisis. In mid-2012, the global economy, still recovering from that crisis, remained in a fragile state with more than 1 in 10 people unemployed in Europe. Another global crisis, this time starting in Europe, was feared.

Source: *OECD Press Release,* May 22, 2012

THE DATA

Unemployment Rates
(percentage of labor force)

	United States	Euro Area	OECD
2012	8.1	10.8	8.0
2013	7.9	11.1	7.9

THE QUESTIONS

- With the information provided in the news clip and the data table, what caused the financial and economic crisis of 2007?
- Has the world fully recovered from that crisis?
- Where is the greatest unemployment? Where is unemployment falling and where is it rising?
- Why does the existence of persistent high unemployment present a puzzle for economists?

THE ANSWERS

- Problems in the U.S. mortgage market brought the global economy crashing in 2007.
- Even 5 years later in 2012, the recovery was incomplete and a second crisis was feared.
- Europe has the greatest unemployment. Unemployment is falling a bit in the United States and the OECD as a whole but is rising in Europe.
- Unemployment is a puzzle because it is in no one's self-interest. It seems to be a waste of resources and doesn't seem to contribute to overcoming scarcity.

In Spain, 1 in 4 people who want a job can't find one.

When the banks got into trouble, the Federal Reserve (the Fed) bailed them out with big loans backed by taxpayer dollars. Did the Fed's bailout of troubled banks serve the social interest? Or might the Fed's rescue action encourage banks to repeat their dangerous lending in the future?

Banks weren't the only recipients of public funds. General Motors was saved by a government bailout. GM makes its decisions in its self-interest. The government bailout of GM also served the firm's self-interest. Did the bailout also serve the social interest?

We've looked at four topics and asked many questions that illustrate the big question: Can choices made in the pursuit of self-interest also promote the social interest? We've asked questions but not answered them because we've not yet explained the economic principles needed to do so.

◆ REVIEW QUIZ

1. Describe the broad facts about *what, how,* and *for whom* goods and services are produced.
2. Use headlines from the recent news to illustrate the potential for conflict between self-interest and the social interest.

You can work these questions in Study Plan 1.2 and get instant feedback.   MyEconLab

By working through this book, you will discover the economic principles that help economists figure out when the social interest is being served, when it is not, and what might be done when it is not being served. We will return to each of the unanswered questions in future chapters.

The Economic Way of Thinking

The questions that economics tries to answer tell us about the *scope of economics,* but they don't tell us how economists *think* and go about seeking answers to these questions. You're now going to see how economists go about their work.

We're going to look at six key ideas that define the *economic way of thinking.* These ideas are

- A choice is a *tradeoff.*
- People make *rational choices* by comparing *benefits* and *costs.*
- *Benefit* is what you gain from something.
- *Cost* is what you *must give up* to get something.
- Most choices are "*how-much*" choices made at the *margin.*
- Choices respond to *incentives.*

A Choice Is a Tradeoff

Because we face scarcity, we must make choices. And when we make a choice, we select from the available alternatives. For example, you can spend Saturday night studying for your next economics test or having fun with your friends, but you can't do both of these activities at the same time. You must choose how much time to devote to each. Whatever choice you make, you could have chosen something else.

You can think about your choices as tradeoffs. A **tradeoff** is an exchange—giving up one thing to get something else. When you choose how to spend your Saturday night, you face a tradeoff between studying and hanging out with your friends.

Making a Rational Choice

Economists view the choices that people make as rational. A **rational choice** is one that compares costs and benefits and achieves the greatest benefit over cost for the person making the choice.

Only the wants of the person making a choice are relevant to determine its rationality. For example, you might like your coffee black and strong but your friend prefers his milky and sweet. So it is rational for you to choose espresso and for your friend to choose cappuccino.

The idea of rational choice provides an answer to the first question: *What* goods and services will be produced and in what quantities? The answer is those that people rationally choose to buy!

But how do people choose rationally? Why do more people choose an iPod rather than a Zune? Why has the U.S. government chosen to build an interstate highway system and not an interstate high-speed railroad system? The answers turn on comparing benefits and costs.

Benefit: What You Gain

The **benefit** of something is the gain or pleasure that it brings and is determined by **preferences**—by what a person likes and dislikes and the intensity of those feelings. If you get a huge kick out of "Guitar Hero," that video game brings you a large benefit. And if you have little interest in listening to Yo Yo Ma playing a Vivaldi cello concerto, that activity brings you a small benefit.

Some benefits are large and easy to identify, such as the benefit that you get from being in school. A big piece of that benefit is the goods and services that you will be able to enjoy with the boost to your earning power when you graduate. Some benefits are small, such as the benefit you get from a slice of pizza.

Economists measure benefit as the most that a person is *willing to give up* to get something. You are willing to give up a lot to be in school. But you would give up only an iTunes download for a slice of pizza.

Cost: What You *Must* Give Up

The **opportunity cost** of something is the highest-valued alternative that must be given up to get it.

To make the idea of opportunity cost concrete, think about *your* opportunity cost of being in school. It has two components: the things you can't afford to buy and the things you can't do with your time.

Start with the things you can't afford to buy. You've spent all your income on tuition, residence fees, books, and a laptop. If you weren't in school, you would have spent this money on tickets to ball games and movies and all the other things that you enjoy. But that's only the start of your opportunity cost. You've also given up the opportunity to get a job. Suppose that the best job you could get if you weren't in school is working at Citibank as a teller earning $25,000 a year. Another part of your opportunity cost of being in school is all the things that you could buy with the extra $25,000 you would have.

As you well know, being a student eats up many hours in class time, doing homework assignments, preparing for tests, and so on. To do all these school activities, you must give up many hours of what would otherwise be leisure time spent with your friends.

So the opportunity cost of being in school is all the good things that you can't afford and don't have the spare time to enjoy. You might want to put a dollar value on that cost or you might just list all the items that make up the opportunity cost.

The examples of opportunity cost that we've just considered are all-or-nothing costs—you're either in school or not in school. Most situations are not like this one. They involve choosing *how much* of an activity to do.

How Much? Choosing at the Margin

You can allocate the next hour between studying and chatting online with your friends, but the choice is not all or nothing. You must decide how many minutes to allocate to each activity. To make this decision, you compare the benefit of a little bit more study time with its cost—you make your choice at the **margin**.

The benefit that arises from an increase in an activity is called **marginal benefit**. For example, your marginal benefit from one more night of study before a test is the boost it gives to your grade. Your marginal benefit doesn't include the grade you're already achieving without that extra night of work.

The *opportunity cost* of an *increase* in an activity is called **marginal cost**. For you, the marginal cost of studying one more night is the cost of not spending that night on your favorite leisure activity.

To make your decisions, you compare marginal benefit and marginal cost. If the marginal benefit from an extra night of study exceeds its marginal cost, you study the extra night. If the marginal cost exceeds the marginal benefit, you don't study the extra night.

Choices Respond to Incentives

Economists take human nature as given and view people as acting in their self-interest. All people— you, other consumers, producers, politicians, and public servants—pursue their self-interest.

Self-interested actions are not necessarily *selfish* actions. You might decide to use your resources in ways that bring pleasure to others as well as to yourself. But a self-interested act gets the most benefit for *you* based on *your* view about benefit.

The central idea of economics is that we can predict the self-interested choices that people make by looking at the *incentives* they face. People undertake those activities for which marginal benefit exceeds marginal cost; and they reject options for which marginal cost exceeds marginal benefit.

For example, your economics instructor gives you a problem set and tells you these problems will be on the next test. Your marginal benefit from working these problems is large, so you diligently work them. In contrast, your math instructor gives you a problem set on a topic that she says will never be on a test. You get little marginal benefit from working these problems, so you decide to skip most of them.

Economists see incentives as the key to reconciling self-interest and social interest. When our choices are *not* in the social interest, it is because of the incentives we face. One of the challenges for economists is to figure out the incentives that result in self-interested choices being in the social interest.

Economists emphasize the crucial role that institutions play in influencing the incentives that people face as they pursue their self-interest. Laws that protect private property and markets that enable voluntary exchange are the fundamental institutions. You will learn as you progress with your study of economics that where these institutions exist, self-interest can indeed promote the social interest.

REVIEW QUIZ

1　Explain the idea of a tradeoff and think of three tradeoffs that you have made today.
2　Explain what economists mean by rational choice and think of three choices that you've made today that are rational.
3　Explain why opportunity cost is the best forgone alternative and provide examples of some opportunity costs that you have faced today.
4　Explain what it means to choose at the margin and illustrate with three choices at the margin that you have made today.
5　Explain why choices respond to incentives and think of three incentives to which you have responded today.

You can work these questions in Study Plan 1.3 and get instant feedback.   MyEconLab

Economics as Social Science and Policy Tool

Economics is both a social science and a toolkit for advising on policy decisions.

Economist as Social Scientist

As social scientists, economists seek to discover how the economic world works. In pursuit of this goal, like all scientists, economists distinguish between positive and normative statements.

Positive Statements A *positive* statement is about what *is*. It says what is currently believed about the way the world operates. A positive statement might be right or wrong, but we can test it by checking it against the facts. "Our planet is warming because of the amount of coal that we're burning" is a positive statement. We can test whether it is right or wrong.

A central task of economists is to test positive statements about how the economic world works and to weed out those that are wrong. Economics first got off the ground in the late 1700s, so it is a young science compared with, for example, physics, and much remains to be discovered.

Normative Statements A *normative* statement is about what *ought to be*. It depends on values and cannot be tested. Policy goals are normative statements. For example, "We ought to cut our use of coal by 50 percent" is a normative policy statement. You may agree or disagree with it, but you can't test it. It doesn't assert a fact that can be checked.

Unscrambling Cause and Effect Economists are particularly interested in positive statements about cause and effect. Are computers getting cheaper because people are buying them in greater quantities? Or are people buying computers in greater quantities because they are getting cheaper? Or is some third factor causing both the price of a computer to fall and the quantity of computers bought to increase?

To answer such questions, economists create and test economic models. An **economic model** is a description of some aspect of the economic world that includes only those features that are needed for the purpose at hand. For example, an economic model of a cell-phone network might include features such as the prices of calls, the number of cell-phone users, and the volume of calls. But the model would ignore cell-phone colors and ringtones.

A model is tested by comparing its predictions with the facts. But testing an economic model is difficult because we observe the outcomes of the simultaneous change of many factors. To cope with this problem, economists look for natural experiments (situations in the ordinary course of economic life in which the one factor of interest is different and other things are equal or similar); conduct statistical investigations to find correlations; and perform economic experiments by putting people in decision-making situations and varying the influence of one factor at a time to discover how they respond.

Economist as Policy Adviser

Economics is useful. It is a toolkit for advising governments and businesses and for making personal decisions. Some of the most famous economists work partly as policy advisers.

For example, Jagdish Bhagwati of Columbia University, whom you will meet on p. 54, has advised governments and international organizations on trade and economic development issues.

Alan B. Krueger of Princeton University is on leave and serving as the chief economic adviser to President Barack Obama and head of the President's Council of Economic Advisers.

All the policy questions on which economists provide advice involve a blend of the positive and the normative. Economics can't help with the normative part—the policy goal. But for a given goal, economics provides a method of evaluating alternative solutions—comparing marginal benefits and marginal costs and finding the solution that makes the best use of the available resources.

REVIEW QUIZ

1 Distinguish between a positive statement and a normative statement and provide examples.
2 What is a model? Can you think of a model that you might use in your everyday life?
3 How do economists try to disentangle cause and effect?
4 How is economics used as a policy tool?

You can work these questions in Study Plan 1.4 and get instant feedback.   MyEconLab

SUMMARY

Key Points

Definition of Economics (p. 2)

- All economic questions arise from scarcity—from the fact that wants exceed the resources available to satisfy them.
- Economics is the social science that studies the choices that people make as they cope with scarcity.
- The subject divides into microeconomics and macroeconomics.

Working Problem 1 will give you a better understanding of the definition of economics.

Two Big Economic Questions (pp. 3–9)

- Two big questions summarize the scope of economics:

  1. How do choices end up determining *what*, *how*, and *for whom* goods and services are produced?
  2. When do choices made in the pursuit of *self-interest* also promote the *social interest*?

Working Problems 2 and 3 will give you a better understanding of the two big questions of economics.

The Economic Way of Thinking (pp. 10–11)

- Every choice is a tradeoff—exchanging more of something for less of something else.
- People make rational choices by comparing benefit and cost.
- Cost—*opportunity cost*—is what you must give up to get something.
- Most choices are "how much" choices made at the *margin* by comparing marginal benefit and marginal cost.
- Choices respond to incentives.

Working Problems 4 and 5 will give you a better understanding of the economic way of thinking.

Economics as Social Science and Policy Tool (p. 12)

- Economists distinguish between positive statements—what is—and normative statements—what ought to be.
- To explain the economic world, economists create and test economic models.
- Economics is a toolkit used to provide advice on government, business, and personal economic decisions.

Working Problem 6 will give you a better understanding of economics as social science and policy tool.

Key Terms

Benefit, 10
Capital, 4
Economic model, 12
Economics, 2
Efficient, 5
Entrepreneurship, 4
Factors of production, 3
Goods and services, 3
Human capital, 3
Incentive, 2

Interest, 4
Labor, 3
Land, 3
Macroeconomics, 2
Margin, 11
Marginal benefit, 11
Marginal cost, 11
Microeconomics, 2
Opportunity cost, 10
Preferences, 10

Profit, 4
Rational choice, 10
Rent, 4
Scarcity, 2
Self-interest, 5
Social interest, 5
Tradeoff, 10
Wages, 4

STUDY PLAN PROBLEMS AND APPLICATIONS

MyEconLab   You can work Problems 1 to 6 in MyEconLab Chapter 1 Study Plan and get instant feedback.

Definition of Economics (Study Plan 1.1)

1. Apple Inc. decides to make iTunes freely available in unlimited quantities.
   a. Does Apple's decision change the incentives that people face?
   b. Is Apple's decision an example of a microeconomic or a macroeconomic issue?

Two Big Economic Questions (Study Plan 1.2)

2. Which of the following pairs does not match?
   a. Labor and wages
   b. Land and rent
   c. Entrepreneurship and profit
   d. Capital and profit

3. Explain how the following news headlines concern self-interest and the social interest.
   a. Starbucks Expands in China
   b. McDonald's Moves into Gourmet Coffee
   c. Food Must Be Labeled with Nutrition Data

The Economic Way of Thinking (Study Plan 1.3)

4. The night before an economics test, you decide to go to the movies instead of staying home and working your MyEconLab Study Plan. You get 50 percent on your test compared with the 70 percent that you normally score.
   a. Did you face a tradeoff?
   b. What was the opportunity cost of your evening at the movies?

5. **Costs Soar for London Olympics**
   The regeneration of East London, the site of the 2012 Olympic Games, is set to add extra £1.5 billion to taxpayers' bill.
   > Source: *The Times*, London, July 6, 2006

   Is the cost of regenerating East London an opportunity cost of hosting the 2012 Olympic Games? Explain why or why not.

Economics as Social Science and Policy Tool

(Study Plan 1.4)

6. Which of the following statements is positive, which is normative, and which can be tested?
   a. The United States should cut its imports.
   b. China is the largest trading partner of the United States.
   c. If the price of antiretroviral drugs increases, HIV/AIDS sufferers will decrease their consumption of the drugs.

ADDITIONAL PROBLEMS AND APPLICATIONS

MyEconLab   You can work these problems in MyEconLab if assigned by your instructor.

Definition of Economics

7. **Hundreds Line up for 5 p.m. Ticket Giveaway**
   By noon, hundreds of Eminem fans had lined up for a chance to score free tickets to the concert.
   > Source: *Detroit Free Press*, May 18, 2009

   When Eminem gave away tickets, what was free and what was scarce? Explain your answer.

Two Big Economic Questions

8. How does the creation of a successful movie influence *what, how*, and *for whom* goods and services are produced?

9. How does a successful movie illustrate self-interested choices that are also in the social interest?

The Economic Way of Thinking

10. Before starring in *Iron Man*, Robert Downey Jr. had appeared in 45 movies that grossed an average of $5 million on the opening weekend. In contrast, *Iron Man* grossed $102 million.
    a. How do you expect the success of *Iron Man* to influence the opportunity cost of hiring Robert Downey Jr.?
    b. How have the incentives for a movie producer to hire Robert Downey Jr. changed?

11. What might be an incentive for you to take a class in summer school? List some of the benefits and costs involved in your decision. Would your choice be rational?

Economics as Social Science and Policy Tool

12. Look at today's *Wall Street Journal*. What is the leading economic news story? With which of the big economic questions does it deal and what tradeoffs does it discuss or imply?

13. Provide two microeconomic statements and two macroeconomic statements. Classify your statements as positive or normative. Explain why.

APPENDIX

Graphs in Economics

After studying this appendix, you will be able to:

◆ Make and interpret a scatter diagram

◆ Identify linear and nonlinear relationships and relationships that have a maximum and a minimum

◆ Define and calculate the slope of a line

◆ Graph relationships among more than two variables

Graphing Data

A graph represents a quantity as a distance on a line. In Fig. A1.1, a distance on the horizontal line represents temperature, measured in degrees Fahrenheit. A movement from left to right shows an increase in temperature. The point 0 represents zero degrees Fahrenheit. To the right of 0, the temperature is positive. To the left of 0, the temperature is negative (as indicated by the minus sign). A distance on the vertical line represents height, measured in thousands of feet. The point 0 represents sea level. Points above 0 represent feet above sea level. Points below 0 represent feet below sea level (indicated by a minus sign).

In Fig. A1.1, the two scale lines are perpendicular to each other and are called *axes*. The vertical line is the y-axis, and the horizontal line is the x-axis. Each axis has a zero point, which is shared by the two axes and called the *origin*.

To make a two-variable graph, we need two pieces of information: the value of the variable x and the value of the variable y. For example, off the coast of Alaska, the temperature is 32 degrees—the value of x. A fishing boat is located at 0 feet above sea level—the value of y. These two bits of information appear as point A in Fig. A1.1. A climber at the top of Mount McKinley on a cold day is 20,320 feet above sea level in a zero-degree gale. These two pieces of information appear as point B. On a warmer day, a climber might be at the peak of Mt. McKinley when the temperature is 32 degrees, at point C.

We can draw two lines, called *coordinates*, from point C. One, called the x-coordinate, runs from C to the vertical axis. This line is called "the x-coordinate"

FIGURE A1.1   Making a Graph

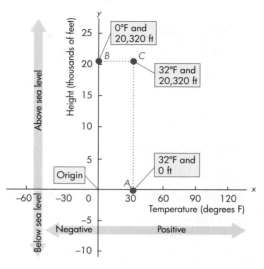

Graphs have axes that measure quantities as distances. Here, the horizontal axis (x-axis) measures temperature, and the vertical axis (y-axis) measures height. Point A represents a fishing boat at sea level (0 on the y-axis) on a day when the temperature is 32°F. Point B represents a climber at the top of Mt. McKinley, 20,320 feet above sea level at a temperature of 0°F. Point C represents a climber at the top of Mt. McKinley, 20,320 feet above sea level at a temperature of 32°F.

— **MyEconLab** animation —

because its length is the same as the value marked off on the x-axis. The other, called the y-coordinate, runs from C to the horizontal axis. This line is called "the y-coordinate" because its length is the same as the value marked off on the y-axis.

We describe a point on a graph by the values of its x-coordinate and its y-coordinate. For example, at point C, x is 32 degrees and y is 20,320 feet.

A graph like that in Fig. A1.1 can be made using any quantitative data on two variables. The graph can show just a few points, like Fig. A1.1, or many points. Before we look at graphs with many points, let's reinforce what you've just learned by looking at two graphs made with economic data.

Economists measure variables that describe *what*, *how*, and *for whom* goods and services are produced. These variables are quantities produced and prices. Figure A1.2 shows two examples of economic graphs.

FIGURE A1.2   Two Graphs of Economic Data

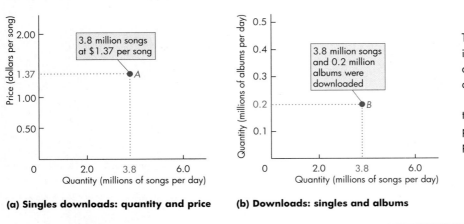

(a) Singles downloads: quantity and price

(b) Downloads: singles and albums

The graph in part (a) tells us that in 2010, 3.8 million songs per day were downloaded at an average price of $1.37 per song.

The graph in part (b) tells us that in 2010, 3.8 million songs per day and 0.2 million albums per day were downloaded.

MyEconLab animation

Figure A1.2(a) is a graph about song downloads in 2010. The *x*-axis measures the quantity of songs downloaded per day and the *y*-axis measures the price of a song. Point *A* tells us what the quantity and price were. You can "read" this graph as telling you that in 2010, 3.8 million songs a day were downloaded at an average price of $1.37 per song.

Figure A1.2(b) is a graph about song and album downloads in 2010. The *x*-axis measures the quantity of songs downloaded per day and the *y*-axis measures the quantity of albums downloaded per day. Point *B* tells us what these quantities were. You can "read" this graph as telling you that in 2010, 3.8 million songs a day and 0.2 million albums were downloaded.

The three graphs that you've just seen tell you how to make a graph and how to read a data point on a graph, but they don't improve on the raw data. Graphs become interesting and revealing when they contain a number of data points because then you can visualize the data.

Economists create graphs based on the principles in Figs. A1.1 and A1.2 to reveal, describe, and visualize the relationships among variables. We're now going to look at some examples. These graphs are called scatter diagrams.

Scatter Diagrams

A **scatter diagram** is a graph that plots the value of one variable against the value of another variable for a number of different values of each variable. Such a graph reveals whether a relationship exists between

two variables and describes their relationship.

The table in Fig. A1.3 shows some data on two variables: the number of tickets sold at the box office and the number of DVDs sold for nine of the most popular movies in 2011.

What is the relationship between these two variables? Does a big box office success generate a large volume of DVD sales? Or does a box office success mean that fewer DVDs are sold?

We can answer these questions by making a scatter diagram. We do so by graphing the data in the table. In the graph in Fig. A1.3, each point shows the number of box office tickets sold (the *x* variable) and the number of DVDs sold (the *y* variable) of one of the movies. There are nine movies, so there are nine points "scattered" within the graph.

The point labeled *A* tells us that *Fast Five* sold 27 million tickets at the box office and 2 million DVDs. The points in the graph form a pattern, which reveals that larger box office sales are associated with larger DVD sales. But the points also tell us that this association is weak. You can't predict DVD sales with any confidence by knowing only the number of tickets sold at the box office.

Figure A1.4 shows two scatter diagrams of economic variables. Part (a) shows the relationship between income and expenditure, on average, during a ten-year period. Each point represents income and expenditure in a given year. For example, point *A* shows that in 2006, income was $33,000 and expenditure was $31,000. This graph shows that as income increases, so does expenditure, and the relationship is a close one.

FIGURE A1.3   A Scatter Diagram

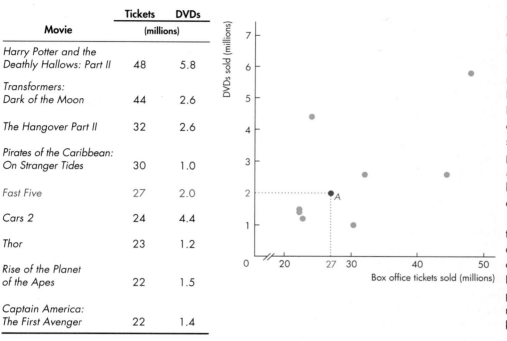

Movie	Tickets	DVDs
	(millions)	
Harry Potter and the Deathly Hallows: Part II	48	5.8
Transformers: Dark of the Moon	44	2.6
The Hangover Part II	32	2.6
Pirates of the Caribbean: On Stranger Tides	30	1.0
Fast Five	27	2.0
Cars 2	24	4.4
Thor	23	1.2
Rise of the Planet of the Apes	22	1.5
Captain America: The First Avenger	22	1.4

The table lists the number of tickets sold at the box office and the number of DVDs sold for nine popular movies.

The scatter diagram reveals the relationship between these two variables. Each point shows the values of the two variables for a specific movie. For example, point A shows the point for *Fast Five*, which sold 27 million tickets at the box office and 2 million DVDs.

The pattern formed by the points shows that there is a tendency for large box office sales to bring greater DVD sales. But you couldn't predict how many DVDs a movie would sell just by knowing its box office sales.

MyEconLab animation

Figure A1.4(b) shows a scatter diagram of U.S. inflation and unemployment from 2001 through 2011. Here, the points show no relationship between the two variables, but 2010 had a high unemployment rate and low inflation rate.

You can see that a scatter diagram conveys a wealth of information, and it does so in much less space than we have used to describe only some of its features. But you do have to "read" the graph to obtain all this information.

FIGURE A1.4   Two Economic Scatter Diagrams

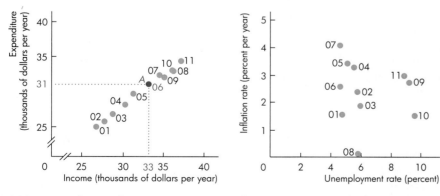

(a) Income and expenditure

(b) Unemployment and inflation

The scatter diagram in part (a) shows the relationship between income and expenditure from 2001 to 2011. Point A shows that in 2006, income was $33 (thousand) on the x-axis and expenditure was $31 (thousand) on the y-axis. This graph shows that as income rises, so does expenditure and the relationship is a close one.

The scatter diagram in part (b) shows a weak relationship between unemployment and inflation in the United States during most of the years.

MyEconLab animation

Breaks in the Axes The graph in Fig. A1.4(a) has breaks in its axes, as shown by the small gaps. The breaks indicate that there are jumps from the origin, 0, to the first values recorded.

The breaks are used because the lowest values of income and expenditure exceed $25,000. If we made this graph with no breaks in its axes, there would be a lot of empty space, all the points would be crowded into the top right corner, and it would be difficult to see whether a relationship exists between these two variables. By breaking the axes, we are able to bring the relationship into view.

Putting a break in one or both axes is like using a zoom lens to bring the relationship into the center of the graph and magnify it so that the relationship fills the graph.

Misleading Graphs Breaks can be used to highlight a relationship, but they can also be used to mislead—to make a graph that lies. The most common way of making a graph lie is to put a break in the axis and either to stretch or compress the scale. For example, suppose that in Fig. A1.4(a), the *y*-axis that measures expenditure ran from zero to $35,000 while the *x*-axis was the same as the one shown. The graph would now create the impression that despite a huge increase in income, expenditure had barely changed.

To avoid being misled, it is a good idea to get into the habit of always looking closely at the values and the labels on the axes of a graph before you start to interpret it.

Correlation and Causation A scatter diagram that shows a clear relationship between two variables, such as Fig. A1.4(a), tells us that the two variables have a high correlation. When a high correlation is present, we can predict the value of one variable from the value of the other variable. But correlation does not imply causation.

Sometimes a high correlation is a coincidence, but sometimes it does arise from a causal relationship. It is likely, for example, that rising income causes rising expenditure (Fig. A1.4a) and that high unemployment makes for a slack economy in which prices don't rise quickly, so the inflation rate is low (Fig. A1.4b).

You've now seen how we can use graphs in economics to show economic data and to reveal relationships. Next, we'll learn how economists use graphs to construct and display economic models.

 ## Graphs Used in Economic Models

The graphs used in economics are not always designed to show real-world data. Often they are used to show general relationships among the variables in an economic model.

An *economic model* is a stripped-down, simplified description of an economy or of a component of an economy such as a business or a household. It consists of statements about economic behavior that can be expressed as equations or as curves in a graph. Economists use models to explore the effects of different policies or other influences on the economy in ways that are similar to the use of model airplanes in wind tunnels and models of the climate.

You will encounter many different kinds of graphs in economic models, but there are some repeating patterns. Once you've learned to recognize these patterns, you will instantly understand the meaning of a graph. Here, we'll look at the different types of curves that are used in economic models, and we'll see some everyday examples of each type of curve. The patterns to look for in graphs are the four cases in which

- Variables move in the same direction.
- Variables move in opposite directions.
- Variables have a maximum or a minimum.
- Variables are unrelated.

Let's look at these four cases.

Variables That Move in the Same Direction

Figure A1.5 shows graphs of the relationships between two variables that move up and down together. A relationship between two variables that move in the same direction is called a **positive relationship** or a **direct relationship**. A line that slopes upward shows such a relationship.

Figure A1.5 shows three types of relationships: one that has a straight line and two that have curved lines. All the lines in these three graphs are called curves. Any line on a graph—no matter whether it is straight or curved—is called a *curve*.

A relationship shown by a straight line is called a **linear relationship**. Figure A1.5(a) shows a linear relationship between the number of miles traveled in

FIGURE A1.5   Positive (Direct) Relationships

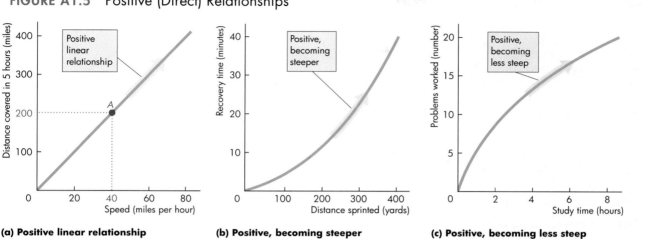

(a) Positive linear relationship   **(b) Positive, becoming steeper**   **(c) Positive, becoming less steep**

Each part shows a positive (direct) relationship between two variables. That is, as the value of the variable measured on the x-axis increases, so does the value of the variable measured on the y-axis. Part (a) shows a linear positive relationship—as the two variables increase together, we move along a straight line.

Part (b) shows a positive relationship such that as the two variables increase together, we move along a curve that becomes steeper.

Part (c) shows a positive relationship such that as the two variables increase together, we move along a curve that becomes flatter.

MyEconLab animation

5 hours and speed. For example, point *A* shows that you will travel 200 miles in 5 hours if your speed is 40 miles an hour. If you double your speed to 80 miles an hour, you will travel 400 miles in 5 hours.

Figure A1.5(b) shows the relationship between distance sprinted and recovery time (the time it takes the heart rate to return to its normal resting rate). This relationship is an upward-sloping one that starts out quite flat but then becomes steeper as we move along the curve away from the origin. The reason this curve becomes steeper is that the additional recovery time needed from sprinting an additional 100 yards increases. It takes less than 5 minutes to recover from sprinting 100 yards but more than 10 minutes to recover from 200 yards.

Figure A1.5(c) shows the relationship between the number of problems worked by a student and the amount of study time. This relationship is an upward-sloping one that starts out quite steep and becomes flatter as we move along the curve away from the origin. Study time becomes less productive as the student spends more hours studying and becomes more tired.

Variables That Move in Opposite Directions

Figure A1.6 shows relationships between things that move in opposite directions. A relationship between variables that move in opposite directions is called a **negative relationship** or an **inverse relationship**.

Figure A1.6(a) shows the relationship between the hours spent playing squash and the hours spent playing tennis when the total time available is 5 hours. One extra hour spent playing tennis means one hour less spent playing squash and vice versa. This relationship is negative and linear.

Figure A1.6(b) shows the relationship between the cost per mile traveled and the length of a journey. The longer the journey, the lower is the cost per mile. But as the journey length increases, even though the cost per mile decreases, the fall in the cost per mile is smaller the longer the journey. This feature of the relationship is shown by the fact that the curve slopes downward, starting out steep at a short journey length and then becoming flatter as the journey length increases. This relationship arises because some of the costs are fixed, such as auto insurance, and the fixed costs are spread over a longer journey.

FIGURE A1.6   Negative (Inverse) Relationships

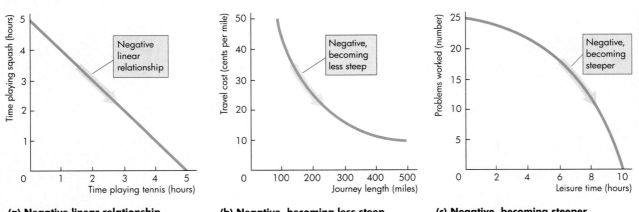

(a) **Negative linear relationship**   (b) **Negative, becoming less steep**   (c) **Negative, becoming steeper**

Each part shows a negative (inverse) relationship between two variables. Part (a) shows a linear negative relationship. The total time spent playing tennis and squash is 5 hours. As the time spent playing tennis increases, the time spent playing squash decreases, and we move along a straight line.

Part (b) shows a negative relationship such that as the journey length increases, the travel cost decreases as we move along a curve that becomes less steep.

Part (c) shows a negative relationship such that as leisure time increases, the number of problems worked decreases as we move along a curve that becomes steeper.

 MyEconLab animation

Figure A1.6(c) shows the relationship between the amount of leisure time and the number of problems worked by a student. Increasing leisure time produces an increasingly large reduction in the number of problems worked. This relationship is a negative one that starts out with a gentle slope at a small number of leisure hours and becomes steeper as the number of leisure hours increases. This relationship is a different view of the idea shown in Fig. A1.5(c).

Variables That Have a Maximum or a Minimum

Many relationships in economic models have a maximum or a minimum. For example, firms try to make the maximum possible profit and to produce at the lowest possible cost. Figure A1.7 shows relationships that have a maximum or a minimum.

Figure A1.7(a) shows the relationship between rainfall and wheat yield. When there is no rainfall, wheat will not grow, so the yield is zero. As the rainfall increases up to 10 days a month, the wheat yield increases. With 10 rainy days each month, the wheat yield reaches its maximum at 40 bushels an acre (point A). Rain in excess of 10 days a month starts to lower the yield of wheat. If every day is rainy, the wheat suffers from a lack of sunshine and the yield decreases to zero. This relationship is one that starts out sloping upward, reaches a maximum, and then slopes downward.

Figure A1.7(b) shows the reverse case—a relationship that begins sloping downward, falls to a minimum, and then slopes upward. Most economic costs are like this relationship. An example is the relationship between the cost per mile and the speed of the car. At low speeds, the car is creeping in a traffic snarl-up. The number of miles per gallon is low, so the cost per mile is high. At high speeds, the car is traveling faster than its efficient speed, using a large quantity of gasoline, and again the number of miles per gallon is low and the cost per mile is high. At a speed of 55 miles an hour, the cost per mile is at its minimum (point B). This relationship is one that starts out sloping downward, reaches a minimum, and then slopes upward.

FIGURE A1.7   Maximum and Minimum Points

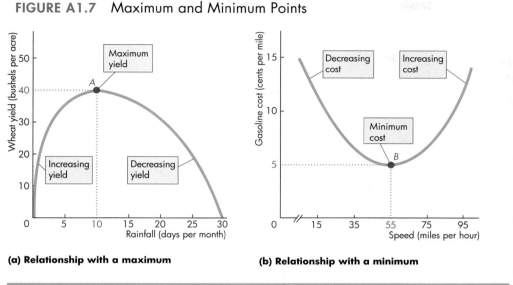

(a) Relationship with a maximum

(b) Relationship with a minimum

Part (a) shows a relationship that has a maximum point, *A*. The curve slopes upward as it rises to its maximum point, is flat at its maximum, and then slopes downward.

Part (b) shows a relationship with a minimum point, *B*. The curve slopes downward as it falls to its minimum, is flat at its minimum, and then slopes upward.

MyEconLab animation

Variables That Are Unrelated

There are many situations in which no matter what happens to the value of one variable, the other variable remains constant. Sometimes we want to show the independence between two variables in a graph, and Fig. A1.8 shows two ways of achieving this.

In describing the graphs in Fig. A1.5 through Fig. A1.7, we have talked about curves that slope upward or slope downward, and curves that become less steep or steeper. Let's spend a little time discussing exactly what we mean by *slope* and how we measure the slope of a curve.

FIGURE A1.8   Variables That Are Unrelated

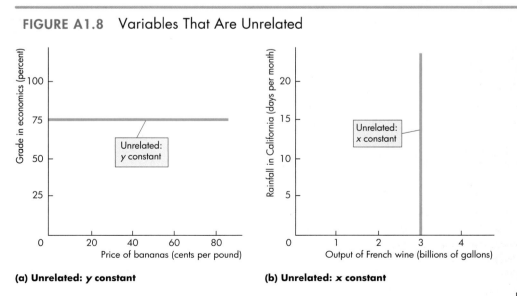

(a) Unrelated: *y* constant

(b) Unrelated: *x* constant

This figure shows how we can graph two variables that are unrelated. In part (a), a student's grade in economics is plotted at 75 percent on the *y*-axis regardless of the price of bananas on the *x*-axis. The curve is horizontal.

In part (b), the output of the vineyards of France on the *x*-axis does not vary with the rainfall in California on the *y*-axis. The curve is vertical.

MyEconLab animation

◆ The Slope of a Relationship

We can measure the influence of one variable on another by the slope of the relationship. The **slope** of a relationship is the change in the value of the variable measured on the *y*-axis divided by the change in the value of the variable measured on the *x*-axis. We use the Greek letter Δ (*delta*) to represent "change in." Thus Δ*y* means the change in the value of the variable measured on the *y*-axis, and Δ*x* means the change in the value of the variable measured on the *x*-axis. Therefore the slope of the relationship is

$$\text{Slope} = \frac{\Delta y}{\Delta x}.$$

If a large change in the variable measured on the *y*-axis (Δ*y*) is associated with a small change in the variable measured on the *x*-axis (Δ*x*), the slope is large and the curve is steep. If a small change in the variable measured on the *y*-axis (Δ*y*) is associated with a large change in the variable measured on the *x*-axis (Δ*x*), the slope is small and the curve is flat.

We can make the idea of slope clearer by doing some calculations.

The Slope of a Straight Line

The slope of a straight line is the same regardless of where on the line you calculate it. The slope of a straight line is constant. Let's calculate the slope of the positive relationship in Fig. A1.9. In part (a),

---

FIGURE A1.9   The Slope of a Straight Line

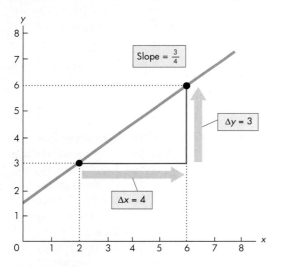

(a) Positive slope

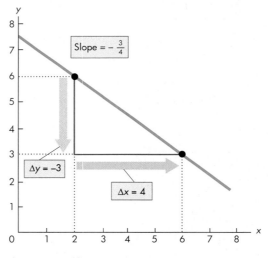

(b) Negative slope

To calculate the slope of a straight line, we divide the change in the value of the variable measured on the *y*-axis (Δ*y*) by the change in the value of the variable measured on the *x*-axis (Δ*x*) as we move along the line.

Part (a) shows the calculation of a positive slope. When *x* increases from 2 to 6, Δ*x* equals 4. That change in *x*

brings about an increase in *y* from 3 to 6, so Δ*y* equals 3. The slope (Δ*y*/Δ*x*) equals 3/4.

Part (b) shows the calculation of a negative slope. When *x* increases from 2 to 6, Δ*x* equals 4. That increase in *x* brings about a decrease in *y* from 6 to 3, so Δ*y* equals −3. The slope (Δ*y*/Δ*x*) equals −3/4.

 MyEconLab animation

when x increases from 2 to 6, y increases from 3 to 6. The change in x is +4—that is, Δx is 4. The change in y is +3—that is, Δy is 3. The slope of that line is

$$\frac{\Delta y}{\Delta x} = \frac{3}{4}.$$

In part (b), when x increases from 2 to 6, y decreases from 6 to 3. The change in y is *minus* 3—that is, Δy is -3. The change in x is *plus* 4—that is, Δx is 4. The slope of the curve is

$$\frac{\Delta y}{\Delta x} = \frac{-3}{4}.$$

Notice that the two slopes have the same magnitude (3/4), but the slope of the line in part (a) is positive ($+3/+4 = 3/4$) while that in part (b) is negative ($-3/+4 = -3/4$). The slope of a positive relationship is positive; the slope of a negative relationship is negative.

The Slope of a Curved Line

The slope of a curved line is trickier. The slope of a curved line is not constant, so the slope depends on where on the curved line we calculate it. There are two ways to calculate the slope of a curved line: You can calculate the slope at a point, or you can calculate the slope across an arc of the curve. Let's look at the two alternatives.

Slope at a Point To calculate the slope at a point on a curve, you need to construct a straight line that has the same slope as the curve at the point in question. Figure A1.10 shows how this is done. Suppose you want to calculate the slope of the curve at point A. Place a ruler on the graph so that the ruler touches point A and no other point on the curve, then draw a straight line along the edge of the ruler. The straight red line is this line, and it is the tangent to the curve at point A. If the ruler touches the curve only at point A, then the slope of the curve at point A must be the same as the slope of the edge of the ruler. If the curve and the ruler do not have the same slope, the line along the edge of the ruler will cut the curve instead of just touching it.

Now that you have found a straight line with the same slope as the curve at point A, you can calculate the slope of the curve at point A by calculating the slope of the straight line. Along the straight line, as x

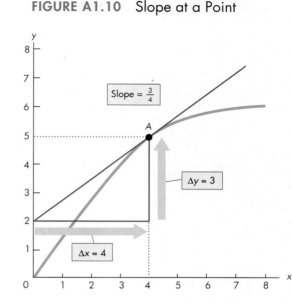

FIGURE A1.10   Slope at a Point

To calculate the slope of the curve at point A, draw the red line that just touches the curve at A—the tangent. The slope of this straight line is calculated by dividing the change in y by the change in x along the red line. When x increases from 0 to 4, Δx equals 4. That change in x is associated with an increase in y from 2 to 5, so Δy equals 3. The slope of the red line is 3/4, so the slope of the curve at point A is 3/4.

━━━━━━━━━ MyEconLab animation ━━━━━

increases from 0 to 4 (Δx is 4) y increases from 2 to 5 (Δy is 3). Therefore the slope of the straight line is

$$\frac{\Delta y}{\Delta x} = \frac{3}{4}.$$

So the slope of the curve at point A is 3/4.

Slope Across an Arc An arc of a curve is a piece of a curve. Fig. A1.11 shows the same curve as in Fig. A1.10, but instead of calculating the slope at point A, we are now going to calculate the slope across the arc from point B to point C. You can see that the slope of the curve at point B is greater than at point C. When we calculate the slope across an arc, we are calculating the average slope between two points. As we move along the arc from B to C, x increases from 3 to 5 and y increases from 4.0 to 5.5. The change in x is 2 (Δx is 2), and the change in y is 1.5 (Δy is 1.5).

FIGURE A1.11   Slope Across an Arc

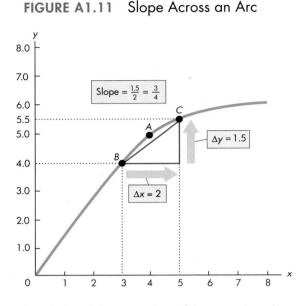

To calculate the average slope of the curve along the arc BC, draw a straight line from point B to point C. The slope of the line BC is calculated by dividing the change in y by the change in x. In moving from B to C, the increase in x is 2 (Δx equals 2) and the change in y is 1.5 (Δy equals 1.5). The slope of the line BC is 1.5 divided by 2, or 3/4. So the slope of the curve across the arc BC is 3/4.

MyEconLab animation

Therefore the slope is

$$\frac{\Delta y}{\Delta x} = \frac{1.5}{2} = \frac{3}{4}.$$

So the slope of the curve across the arc BC is 3/4.

This calculation gives us the slope of the curve between points B and C. The actual slope calculated is the slope of the straight line from B to C. This slope approximates the average slope of the curve along the arc BC. In this particular example, the slope across the arc BC is identical to the slope of the curve at point A, but the calculation of the slope of a curve does not always work out so neatly. You might have fun constructing some more examples and a few counter examples.

You now know how to make and interpret a graph. So far, we've limited our attention to graphs of two variables. We're now going to learn how to graph more than two variables.

Graphing Relationships Among More Than Two Variables

We have seen that we can graph the relationship between two variables as a point formed by the x- and y-coordinates in a two-dimensional graph. You might be thinking that although a two-dimensional graph is informative, most of the things in which you are likely to be interested involve relationships among many variables, not just two. For example, the amount of ice cream consumed depends on the price of ice cream and the temperature. If ice cream is expensive and the temperature is low, people eat much less ice cream than when ice cream is inexpensive and the temperature is high. For any given price of ice cream, the quantity consumed varies with the temperature; and for any given temperature, the quantity of ice cream consumed varies with its price.

Figure A1.12 shows a relationship among three variables. The table shows the number of gallons of ice cream consumed each day at two different temperatures and at a number of different prices of ice cream. How can we graph these numbers?

To graph a relationship that involves more than two variables, we use the *ceteris paribus* assumption.

Ceteris Paribus

Ceteris paribus (often shortened to *cet par*) means "if all other relevant things remain the same." To isolate the relationship of interest in a laboratory experiment, a scientist holds everything constant except for the variable whose effect is being studied. Economists use the same method to graph a relationship that has more than two variables.

Figure A1.12 shows an example. There, you can see what happens to the quantity of ice cream consumed when the price of ice cream varies but the temperature is held constant.

The curve labeled 70°F shows the relationship between ice cream consumption and the price of ice cream if the temperature remains at 70°F. The numbers used to plot that curve are those in the first two columns of the table. For example, if the temperature is 70°F, 10 gallons are consumed when the price is $2.75 a scoop and 18 gallons are consumed when the price is $2.25 a scoop.

The curve labeled 90°F shows the relationship between ice cream consumption and the price of ice cream if the temperature remains at 90°F. The

FIGURE A1.12   Graphing a Relationship Among Three Variables

Price (dollars per scoop)	Ice cream consumption (gallons per day)	
	70°F	90°F
2.00	25	50
2.25	18	36
2.50	13	26
2.75	**10**	**20**
3.00	7	14
3.25	5	10
3.50	3	6

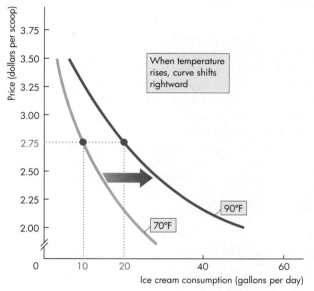

Ice cream consumption depends on its price and the temperature. The table tells us how many gallons of ice cream are consumed each day at different prices and two different temperatures. For example, if the price is $2.75 a scoop and the temperature is 70°F, 10 gallons of ice cream are consumed.

To graph a relationship among three variables, the value of one variable is held constant. The graph shows the relationship between price and consumption when temperature is held constant. One curve holds temperature at 70°F and the other holds it at 90°F.

A change in the price of ice cream brings a movement along one of the curves—along the blue curve at 70°F and along the red curve at 90°F.

When the temperature *rises* from 70°F to 90°F, the curve that shows the relationship between consumption and price *shifts* rightward from the blue curve to the red curve.

MyEconLab animation

numbers used to plot that curve are those in the first and third columns of the table. For example, if the temperature is 90°F, 20 gallons are consumed when the price is $2.75 a scoop and 36 gallons are consumed when the price is $2.25 a scoop.

When the price of ice cream changes but the temperature is constant, you can think of what happens in the graph as a movement along one of the curves. At 70°F there is a movement along the blue curve and at 90°F there is a movement along the red curve.

When Other Things Change

The temperature is held constant along each of the curves in Fig. A1.12, but in reality the temperature changes. When that event occurs, you can think of what happens in the graph as a shift of the curve. When the temperature rises from 70°F to 90°F, the curve that shows the relationship between ice cream consumption and the price of ice cream shifts rightward from the blue curve to the red curve.

You will encounter these ideas of movements along and shifts of curves at many points in your study of economics. Think carefully about what you've just learned and make up some examples (with assumed numbers) about other relationships.

With what you have learned about graphs, you can move forward with your study of economics. There are no graphs in this book that are more complicated than those that have been explained in this appendix.

MATHEMATICAL NOTE
Equations of Straight Lines

If a straight line in a graph describes the relationship between two variables, we call it a linear relationship. Figure 1 shows the *linear relationship* between a person's expenditure and income. This person spends $100 a week (by borrowing or spending previous savings) when income is zero. Out of each dollar earned, this person spends 50 cents (and saves 50 cents).

All linear relationships are described by the same general equation. We call the quantity that is measured on the horizontal axis (or x-axis) $x,$ and we call the quantity that is measured on the vertical axis (or y-axis) y. In the case of Fig. 1, x is income and y is expenditure.

A Linear Equation

The equation that describes a straight-line relationship between x and y is

$$y = a + bx.$$

In this equation, a and b are fixed numbers and they are called *constants*. The values of x and y vary, so these numbers are called *variables*. Because the equation describes a straight line, the equation is called a *linear equation*.

The equation tells us that when the value of x is zero, the value of y is a. We call the constant a the y-axis intercept. The reason is that on the graph the straight line hits the y-axis at a value equal to a. Figure 1 illustrates the y-axis intercept.

For positive values of x, the value of y exceeds a. The constant b tells us by how much y increases above a as x increases. The constant b is the slope of the line.

Slope of Line

As we explain in the chapter, the *slope* of a relationship is the change in the value of y divided by the change in the value of x. We use the Greek letter Δ (delta) to represent "change in." So Δy means the change in the value of the variable measured on the y-axis, and Δx means the change in the value of the variable measured on the x-axis. Therefore the slope of the relationship is

$$\text{Slope} = \frac{\Delta y}{\Delta x}.$$

To see why the slope is b, suppose that initially the value of x is x_1, or $200 in Fig. 2. The corresponding value of y is y_1, also $200 in Fig. 2. The equation of the line tells us that

$$y_1 = a + bx_1. \tag{1}$$

Now the value of x increases by Δx to $x_1 + \Delta x$ (or $400 in Fig. 2). And the value of y increases by Δy to $y_1 + \Delta y$ (or $300 in Fig. 2).

The equation of the line now tells us that

$$y_1 + \Delta y = a + b(x_1 + \Delta x). \tag{2}$$

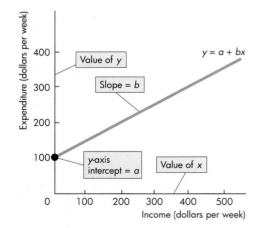

Figure 1 Linear Relationship

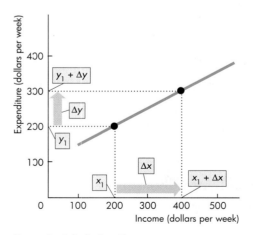

Figure 2 Calculating Slope

To calculate the slope of the line, subtract equation (1) from equation (2) to obtain

$$\Delta y = b \Delta x \qquad (3)$$

and now divide equation (3) by Δx to obtain

$$\Delta y / \Delta x = b.$$

So the slope of the line is b.

Position of Line

The y-axis intercept determines the position of the line on the graph. Figure 3 illustrates the relationship between the y-axis intercept and the position of the line. In this graph, the y-axis measures saving and the x-axis measures income.

When the y-axis intercept, a, is positive, the line hits the y-axis at a positive value of y—as the blue line does. Its y-axis intercept is 100. When the y-axis intercept, a, is zero, the line hits the y-axis at the origin—as the purple line does. Its y-axis intercept is 0. When the y-axis intercept, a, is negative, the line hits the y-axis at a negative value of y—as the red line does. Its y-axis intercept is -100.

As the equations of the three lines show, the value of the y-axis intercept does not influence the slope of the line. All three lines have a slope equal to 0.5.

Positive Relationships

Figure 1 shows a positive relationship—the two variables x and y move in the same direction. All positive relationships have a slope that is positive. In the equation of the line, the constant b is positive. In this example, the y-axis intercept, a, is 100. The slope b equals $\Delta y / \Delta x$, which in Fig. 2 is 100/200 or 0.5. The equation of the line is

$$y = 100 + 0.5x.$$

Negative Relationships

Figure 4 shows a negative relationship—the two variables x and y move in the opposite direction. All negative relationships have a slope that is negative. In the equation of the line, the constant b is negative. In the example in Fig. 4, the y-axis intercept, a, is 30. The slope, b, equals $\Delta y / \Delta x$, which is $-20/2$ or -10. The equation of the line is

$$y = 30 + (-10)x$$

or

$$y = 30 - 10x.$$

Example

A straight line has a y-axis intercept of 50 and a slope of 2. What is the equation of this line?
The equation of a straight line is

$$y = a + bx$$

where a is the y-axis intercept and b is the slope. So the equation is

$$y = 50 + 2x.$$

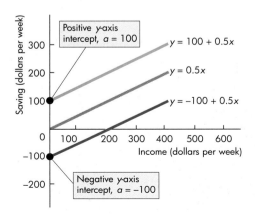

Figure 3 The y-Axis Intercept

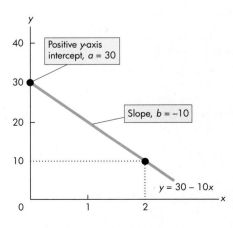

Figure 4 Negative Relationship

REVIEW QUIZ

1 Explain how we "read" the three graphs in Figs. A1.1 and A1.2.

2 Explain what scatter diagrams show and why we use them.

3 Explain how we "read" the three scatter diagrams in Figs. A1.3 and A1.4.

4 Draw a graph to show the relationship between two variables that move in the same direction.

5 Draw a graph to show the relationship between two variables that move in opposite directions.

6 Draw a graph to show the relationship between two variables that has (i) a maximum and (ii) a minimum.

7 Which of the relationships in Questions 4 and 5 is a positive relationship and which is a negative relationship?

8 What are the two ways of calculating the slope of a curved line?

9 How do we graph a relationship among more than two variables?

10 Explain what change will bring a *movement along* a curve.

11 Explain what change will bring a *shift* of a curve.

You can work these questions in Study Plan 1.A and get instant feedback.   MyEconLab

SUMMARY

Key Points

Graphing Data (pp. 15–18)

- A graph is made by plotting the values of two variables x and y at a point that corresponds to their values measured along the x-axis and the y-axis.

- A scatter diagram is a graph that plots the values of two variables for a number of different values of each.

- A scatter diagram shows the relationship between the two variables. It shows whether they are positively related, negatively related, or unrelated.

Graphs Used in Economic Models (pp. 18–21)

- Graphs are used to show relationships among variables in economic models.

- Relationships can be positive (an upward-sloping curve), negative (a downward-sloping curve), positive and then negative (have a maximum point), negative and then positive (have a minimum point), or unrelated (a horizontal or vertical curve).

The Slope of a Relationship (pp. 22–24)

- The slope of a relationship is calculated as the change in the value of the variable measured on the y-axis divided by the change in the value of the variable measured on the x-axis—that is, $\Delta y/\Delta x$.

- A straight line has a constant slope.

- A curved line has a varying slope. To calculate the slope of a curved line, we calculate the slope at a point or across an arc.

Graphing Relationships Among More Than Two Variables (pp. 24–25)

- To graph a relationship among more than two variables, we hold constant the values of all the variables except two.

- We then plot the value of one of the variables against the value of another.

- A *cet par* change in the value of a variable on an axis of a graph brings a movement along the curve.

- A change in the value of a variable held constant along the curve brings a shift of the curve.

Key Terms

Ceteris paribus, 24
Direct relationship, 18
Inverse relationship, 19

Linear relationship, 18
Negative relationship, 19
Positive relationship, 18

Scatter diagram, 16
Slope, 22

STUDY PLAN PROBLEMS AND APPLICATIONS

MyEconLab   You can work Problems 1 to 11 in MyEconLab Chapter 1A Study Plan and get instant feedback.

Use the following spreadsheet to work Problems 1 to 3. The spreadsheet provides data on the U.S. economy: Column A is the year, column B is the inflation rate, column C is the interest rate, column D is the growth rate, and column E is the unemployment rate.

	A	B	C	D	E
1	2001	1.6	3.4	1.1	4.7
2	2002	2.4	1.6	1.8	5.8
3	2003	1.9	1.0	2.5	6.0
4	2004	3.3	1.4	3.5	5.5
5	2005	3.4	3.2	3.1	5.1
6	2006	2.5	4.7	2.7	4.6
7	2007	4.1	4.4	1.9	4.6
8	2008	0.1	1.5	−0.3	5.8
9	2009	2.7	0.2	−3.5	9.3
10	2010	1.5	0.1	3.0	9.6
11	2011	3.0	0.1	1.7	9.0

1. Draw a scatter diagram of the inflation rate and the interest rate. Describe the relationship.
2. Draw a scatter diagram of the growth rate and the unemployment rate. Describe the relationship.
3. Draw a scatter diagram of the interest rate and the unemployment rate. Describe the relationship.

Use the following news clip to work Problems 4 to 6.
Avengers **Shatters More Records:**

Movie	Theaters (number)	Revenue (dollars per theater)
Marvel's The Avengers	4,349	$23,696
Dark Shadows	3,755	$7,906
Think Like a Man	2,052	$2,834
The Hunger Games	2,531	$1,780

Source: boxofficemojo.com,
Data for weekend of May 11–12, 2012

4. Draw a graph of the relationship between the revenue per theater on the *y*-axis and the number of theaters on the *x*-axis. Describe the relationship.
5. Calculate the slope of the relationship between 3,755 and 2,052 theaters.
6. Calculate the slope of the relationship between 2,052 and 2,531 theaters.

7. Calculate the slope of the following relationship.

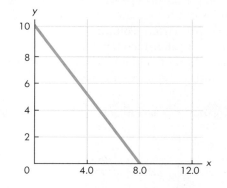

Use the following relationship to work Problems 8 and 9.

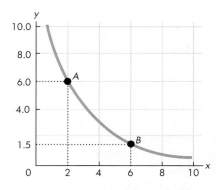

8. Calculate the slope of the relationship at point *A* and at point *B*.
9. Calculate the slope across the arc *AB*.

Use the following table to work Problems 10 and 11. The table gives the price of a balloon ride, the temperature, and the number of rides a day.

Price (dollars per ride)	Balloon rides (number per day)		
	50°F	70°F	90°F
5	32	40	50
10	27	32	40
15	18	27	32

10. Draw a graph to show the relationship between the price and the number of rides, when the temperature is 70°F. Describe this relationship.
11. What happens in the graph in Problem 10 if the temperature rises to 90°F?

ADDITIONAL PROBLEMS AND APPLICATIONS

MyEconLab   You can work these problems in MyEconLab if assigned by your instructor.

Use the following spreadsheet to work Problems 12 to 14. The spreadsheet provides data on oil and gasoline: Column A is the year, column B is the price of oil (dollars per barrel), column C is the price of gasoline (cents per gallon), column D is U.S. oil production, and column E is the U.S. quantity of gasoline refined (both in millions of barrels per day).

	A	B	C	D	E
1	2001	26	146	5.8	8.6
2	2002	26	139	5.7	8.8
3	2003	31	160	5.7	8.9
4	2004	42	190	5.4	9.1
5	2005	57	231	5.2	9.2
6	2006	66	262	5.1	9.3
7	2007	72	284	5.1	9.3
8	2008	100	330	5.0	9.0
9	2009	62	241	5.4	9.0
10	2010	79	284	5.5	9.0
11	2011	95	358	5.7	8.7

12. Draw a scatter diagram of the price of oil and the quantity of U.S. oil produced. Describe the relationship.
13. Draw a scatter diagram of the price of gasoline and the quantity of gasoline refined. Describe the relationship.
14. Draw a scatter diagram of the quantity of U.S. oil produced and the quantity of gasoline refined. Describe the relationship.

Use the following data to work Problems 15 to 17. Draw a graph that shows the relationship between the two variables x and y:

x	0	1	2	3	4	5
y	25	24	22	18	12	0

15. a. Is the relationship positive or negative?
    b. Does the slope of the relationship become steeper or flatter as the value of x increases?
    c. Think of some economic relationships that might be similar to this one.
16. Calculate the slope of the relationship between x and y when x equals 3.
17. Calculate the slope of the relationship across the arc as x increases from 4 to 5.
18. Calculate the slope of the curve in the figure in the next column at point A.

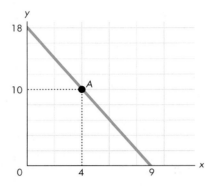

Use the following relationship to work Problems 19 and 20.

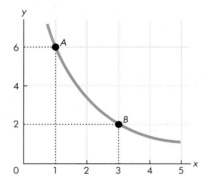

19. Calculate the slope at point A and at point B.
20. Calculate the slope across the arc AB.

Use the following table to work Problems 21 to 23. The table gives information about umbrellas: price, the number purchased, and rainfall in inches.

Price	Umbrellas (number purchased per day)		
(dollars per umbrella)	0 inches	1 inch	2 inches
20	4	7	8
30	2	4	7
40	1	2	4

21. Draw a graph to show the relationship between the price and the number of umbrellas purchased, holding the amount of rainfall constant at 1 inch. Describe this relationship.
22. What happens in the graph in Problem 21 if the price rises and rainfall is constant?
23. What happens in the graph in Problem 21 if the rainfall increases from 1 inch to 2 inches?

2

THE ECONOMIC PROBLEM

After studying this chapter, you will be able to:

- ◆ Define the production possibilities frontier and use it to calculate opportunity cost
- ◆ Distinguish between production possibilities and preferences and describe an efficient allocation of resources
- ◆ Explain how current production choices expand future production possibilities
- ◆ Explain how specialization and trade expand production possibilities
- ◆ Describe the economic institutions that coordinate decisions

How can we lower the cost of food production in the desert regions of the world? How do we know when we are using our resources efficiently? How can we become more productive? Is it really true that both buyers and sellers gain from trade?

In this chapter, you study an economic model that answers these questions.

At the end of the chapter, in *Reading Between the Lines*, we'll apply what you've learned to understanding why the Gulf states gain from trading oil for food and how hydroponic farming is lowering the cost of their domestic food production.

◆▶ Production Possibilities and Opportunity Cost

Every working day, in mines, factories, shops, and offices and on farms and construction sites across the United States, 142 million people produce a vast variety of goods and services valued at $60 billion. But the quantities of goods and services that we can produce are limited by our available resources and by technology. And if we want to increase our production of one good, we must decrease our production of something else—we face a tradeoff. You are now going to study the limits to production.

The **production possibilities frontier** (*PPF*) is the boundary between those combinations of goods and services that can be produced and those that cannot. To illustrate the *PPF*, we look at a *model economy* in which the quantities produced of only two goods change, while the quantities produced of all the other goods and services remains the same.

Let's look at the production possibilities frontier for cola and pizza, which represent *any* pair of goods or services.

Production Possibilities Frontier

The *production possibilities frontier* for cola and pizza shows the limits to the production of these two goods, given the total resources and technology available to produce them. Figure 2.1 shows this production possibilities frontier. The table lists combinations of the quantities of pizza and cola that can be produced in a month and the figure graphs these combinations. The *x*-axis shows the quantity of pizzas produced, and the *y*-axis shows the quantity of cola produced.

The *PPF* illustrates *scarcity* because the points outside the frontier are *unattainable*. These points describe wants that can't be satisfied.

We can produce at any point *inside* the *PPF* or *on* the *PPF*. These points are *attainable*. For example, we can produce 4 million pizzas and 5 million cans of cola. Figure 2.1 shows this combination as point *E* and as possibility *E* in the table.

Moving along the *PPF* from point *E* to point *D* (possibility *D* in the table) we produce more cola and less pizza: 9 million cans of cola and 3 million pizzas. Or moving in the opposite direction from point *E* to point *F* (possibility *F* in the table), we produce more pizza and less cola: 5 million pizzas and no cola.

FIGURE 2.1   Production Possibilities Frontier

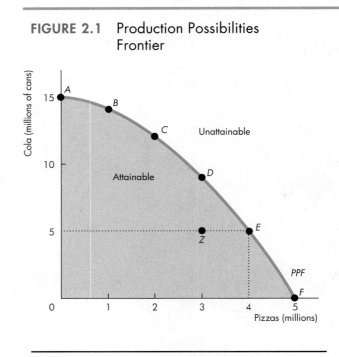

Possibility	Pizzas (millions)		Cola (millions of cans)
A	0	and	15
B	1	and	14
C	2	and	12
D	3	and	9
E	4	and	5
F	5	and	0

The table lists six production possibilities for cola and pizzas. Row *A* tells us that if we produce no pizzas, the maximum quantity of cola we can produce is 15 million cans. Points *A*, *B*, *C*, *D*, *E*, and *F* in the figure represent the rows of the table. The curve passing through these points is the production possibilities frontier (*PPF*).

The *PPF* separates the attainable from the unattainable. Production is possible at any point *inside* the orange area or *on* the frontier. Points outside the frontier are unattainable. Points inside the frontier, such as point *Z*, are inefficient because resources are wasted or misallocated. At such points, it is possible to use the available resources to produce more of either or both goods.

MyEconLab animation

Production Efficiency

We achieve **production efficiency** if we produce goods and services at the lowest possible cost. This outcome occurs at all the points *on the PPF*. At points *inside* the *PPF*, production is inefficient because we are giving up more than necessary of one good to produce a given quantity of the other good.

For example, at point *Z* in Fig. 2.1, we produce 3 million pizzas and 5 million cans of cola, but we have enough resources to produce 3 million pizzas and 9 million cans of cola. Our pizzas cost more cola than necessary. We can get them for a lower cost. Only when we produce *on the PPF* do we incur the lowest possible cost of production.

Production inside the *PPF* is *inefficient* because resources are either *unused* or *misallocated* or both.

Resources are *unused* when they are idle but could be working. For example, we might leave some of the factories idle or some workers unemployed.

Resources are *misallocated* when they are assigned to tasks for which they are not the best match. For example, we might assign skilled pizza chefs to work in a cola factory and skilled cola workers to cook pizza in a pizzeria. We could get more pizzas *and* more cola if we reassigned these workers to the tasks that more closely match their skills.

Tradeoff Along the *PPF*

A choice *along* the *PPF* involves a *tradeoff*. Tradeoffs like that between cola and pizza arise in every imaginable real-world situation in which a choice must be made. At any given time, we have a fixed amount of labor, land, capital, and entrepreneurship and a given state of technology. We can employ these resources and technology to produce goods and services, but we are limited in what we can produce.

When doctors want to spend more on AIDS and cancer research, they face a tradeoff: more medical research for less of some other things. When Congress wants to spend more on education and health care, it faces a tradeoff: more education and health care for less national defense or homeland security. When an environmental group argues for less logging, it is suggesting a tradeoff: greater conservation of endangered wildlife for less paper. When you want a higher grade on your next test, you face a tradeoff: spend more time studying and less leisure or sleep time.

All the tradeoffs you've just considered involve a cost—an opportunity cost.

Opportunity Cost

The **opportunity cost** of an action is the highest-valued alternative forgone. The *PPF* makes this idea precise and enables us to calculate opportunity cost. Along the *PPF*, there are only two goods, so there is only one alternative forgone: some quantity of the other good. To produce more pizzas we must produce less cola. The opportunity cost of producing an additional pizza is the cola we *must* forgo. Similarly, the opportunity cost of producing an additional can of cola is the quantity of pizza we must forgo.

In Fig. 2.1, if we move from point *C* to point *D*, we produce an additional 1 million pizzas but 3 million fewer cans of cola. The additional 1 million pizzas *cost* 3 million cans of cola. Or 1 pizza costs 3 cans of cola.

Opportunity Cost Is a Ratio

Opportunity cost is a ratio. It is the decrease in the quantity produced of one good divided by the increase in the quantity produced of another good as we move along the production possibilities frontier.

Because opportunity cost is a ratio, the opportunity cost of producing an additional can of cola is equal to the *inverse* of the opportunity cost of producing an additional pizza. Check this proposition by returning to the calculations we've just worked through. When we move along the *PPF* from *C* to *D*, the opportunity cost of a pizza is 3 cans of cola. The inverse of 3 is 1/3. If we decrease the production of pizza and increase the production of cola by moving from *D* to *C*, the opportunity cost of a can of cola must be 1/3 of a pizza. That is exactly the number that we calculated for the move from *D* to *C*.

Increasing Opportunity Cost

The opportunity cost of a pizza increases as the quantity of pizzas produced increases. The outward-bowed shape of the *PPF* reflects increasing opportunity cost. When we produce a large quantity of cola and a small quantity of pizza—between points *A* and *B* in Fig. 2.1—the frontier has a gentle slope. An increase in the quantity of pizzas costs a small decrease in the quantity of cola—the opportunity cost of a pizza is a small quantity of cola.

When we produce a large quantity of pizzas and a small quantity of cola—between points *E* and *F* in Fig. 2.1—the frontier is steep. A given increase in the quantity of pizzas *costs* a large decrease in the quantity of cola, so the opportunity cost of a pizza is a large quantity of cola.

◆ ECONOMICS IN THE NEWS

Cost of Global Food Up Again

The cost of global food has increased by 8 percent since December 2011. All key food items cost more, except for rice. Asia's strong demand for food imports has contributed to this increase, notwithstanding bumper harvests.

Source: *Food Price Watch*, World Bank, April 2012

THE QUESTIONS

- How does the *PPF* illustrate the effect of Asia's strong demand for food imports on the cost of food?
- How does the *PPF* illustrate the effect of a bumper harvest?

THE ANSWERS

- The figure shows the global *PPF* for food and other goods and services.
- Before the bumper harvest, the *PPF* is PPF_0 and before Asia's strong demand for food, the world is producing at point *A*.
- Asia's strong demand for food brings an increase in food production and a decrease in the production of other goods and services, which is illustrated as a movement along the *PPF* from point *A* to point *B*.
- At point *B*, the *PPF* slope is steeper than at point *A*, which means that the opportunity cost of food is higher at point *B* than at point *A*.

- A bumper harvest increases the production of food at each level of production of other goods and services.
- The *PPF* illustrates the effects of a bumper harvest as an outward shift of the *PPF* from PPF_0 to PPF_1 in the figure.
- The bumper harvest lowered the opportunity cost of food, but the news clip says that this effect was not sufficient to offset the rise in opportunity cost resulting from Asia's strong demand.

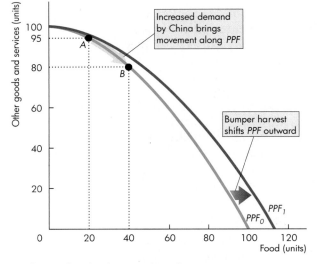

PPF for Food and Other Goods and Services

The *PPF* is bowed outward because resources are not all equally productive in all activities. People with many years of experience working for PepsiCo are good at producing cola but not very good at making pizzas. So if we move some of these people from PepsiCo to Domino's, we get a small increase in the quantity of pizzas but a large decrease in the quantity of cola.

Similarly, people who have spent years working at Domino's are good at producing pizzas, but they have no idea how to produce cola. So if we move some of these people from Domino's to PepsiCo, we get a small increase in the quantity of cola but a large decrease in the quantity of pizzas. The more of either good we try to produce, the less productive are the additional resources we use to produce that good and the larger is the opportunity cost of a unit of that good.

How do we choose among the points on the *PPF*? How do we know which point is the best?

◆ REVIEW QUIZ

1 How does the production possibilities frontier illustrate scarcity?
2 How does the production possibilities frontier illustrate production efficiency?
3 How does the production possibilities frontier show that every choice involves a tradeoff?
4 How does the production possibilities frontier illustrate opportunity cost?
5 Why is opportunity cost a ratio?
6 Why does the *PPF* bow outward and what does that imply about the relationship between opportunity cost and the quantity produced?

You can work these questions in Study Plan 2.1 and get instant feedback.   MyEconLab

◆ Using Resources Efficiently

We achieve *production efficiency* at every point on the *PPF*, but which point is best? The answer is the point on the *PPF* at which goods and services are produced in the quantities that provide the greatest possible benefit. When goods and services are produced at the lowest possible cost and in the quantities that provide the greatest possible benefit, we have achieved **allocative efficiency**.

The questions that we raised when we reviewed the four big issues in Chapter 1 are questions about allocative efficiency. To answer such questions, we must measure and compare costs and benefits.

The *PPF* and Marginal Cost

The **marginal cost** of a good is the opportunity cost of producing one more unit of it. We calculate marginal cost from the slope of the *PPF*. As the quantity of pizzas produced increases, the *PPF* gets steeper and the marginal cost of a pizza increases. Figure 2.2 illustrates the calculation of the marginal cost of a pizza.

Begin by finding the opportunity cost of pizza in blocks of 1 million pizzas. The cost of the first million pizzas is 1 million cans of cola; the cost of the second million pizzas is 2 million cans of cola; the cost of the third million pizzas is 3 million cans of cola, and so on. The bars in part (a) illustrate these calculations.

The bars in part (b) show the cost of an average pizza in each of the 1 million pizza blocks. Focus on the third million pizzas—the move from *C* to *D* in part (a). Over this range, because 1 million pizzas cost 3 million cans of cola, one of these pizzas, on average, costs 3 cans of cola—the height of the bar in part (b).

Next, find the opportunity cost of each additional pizza—the marginal cost of a pizza. The marginal cost of a pizza increases as the quantity of pizzas produced increases. The marginal cost at point *C* is less than it is at point *D*. On average over the range from *C* to *D*, the marginal cost of a pizza is 3 cans of cola. But it exactly equals 3 cans of cola only in the middle of the range between *C* and *D*.

The red dot in part (b) indicates that the marginal cost of a pizza is 3 cans of cola when 2.5 million pizzas are produced. Each black dot in part (b) is interpreted in the same way. The red curve that passes through these dots, labeled *MC*, is the marginal cost curve. It shows the marginal cost of a pizza at each quantity of pizzas as we move along the *PPF*.

FIGURE 2.2   The *PPF* and Marginal Cost

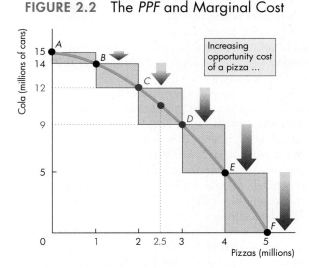

(a) *PPF* and opportunity cost

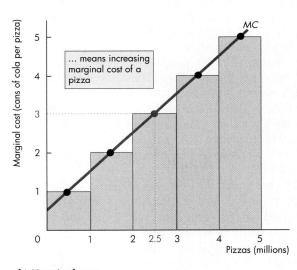

(b) Marginal cost

Marginal cost is calculated from the slope of the *PPF*. As the quantity of pizzas produced increases, the *PPF* gets steeper and the marginal cost of a pizza increases. The bars in part (a) show the opportunity cost of pizza in blocks of 1 million pizzas. The bars in part (b) show the cost of an average pizza in each of these 1 million blocks. The red curve, *MC*, shows the marginal cost of a pizza at each point along the *PPF*. This curve passes through the center of each of the bars in part (b).

———— MyEconLab animation ————

Preferences and Marginal Benefit

The **marginal benefit** from a good or service is the benefit received from consuming one more unit of it. This benefit is subjective. It depends on people's **preferences**—people's likes and dislikes and the intensity of those feelings.

Marginal benefit and *preferences* stand in sharp contrast to *marginal cost* and *production possibilities*. Preferences describe what people like and want and the production possibilities describe the limits or constraints on what is feasible.

We need a concrete way of illustrating preferences that parallels the way we illustrate the limits to production using the *PPF*.

The device that we use to illustrate preferences is the **marginal benefit curve**, which is a curve that shows the relationship between the marginal benefit from a good and the quantity consumed of that good. Note that the *marginal benefit curve* is *unrelated* to the *PPF* and cannot be derived from it.

We measure the marginal benefit from a good or service by the most that people are *willing to pay* for an additional unit of it. The idea is that you are willing to pay less for a good than it is worth to you but you are not willing to pay more: The most you are willing to pay for something is its marginal benefit.

It is a general principle that the more we have of any good or service, the smaller is its marginal benefit and the less we are willing to pay for an additional unit of it. This tendency is so widespread and strong that we call it a principle—the *principle of decreasing marginal benefit*.

The basic reason why marginal benefit decreases is that we like variety. The more we consume of any one good or service, the more we tire of it and would prefer to switch to something else.

Think about your willingness to pay for a pizza. If pizza is hard to come by and you can buy only a few slices a year, you might be willing to pay a high price to get an additional slice. But if pizza is all you've eaten for the past few days, you are willing to pay almost nothing for another slice.

You've learned to think about cost as opportunity cost, not as a dollar cost. You can think about marginal benefit and willingness to pay in the same way. The marginal benefit, measured by what you are willing to pay for something, is the quantity of other goods and services that you are willing to forgo. Let's continue with the example of cola and pizza and illustrate preferences this way.

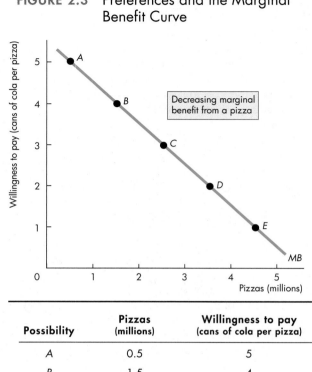

FIGURE 2.3   Preferences and the Marginal Benefit Curve

Possibility	Pizzas (millions)	Willingness to pay (cans of cola per pizza)
A	0.5	5
B	1.5	4
C	2.5	3
D	3.5	2
E	4.5	1

The smaller the quantity of pizzas available, the more cola people are willing to give up for an additional pizza. With 0.5 million pizzas available, people are willing to pay 5 cans of cola per pizza. But with 4.5 million pizzas, people are willing to pay only 1 can of cola per pizza. Willingness to pay measures marginal benefit. A universal feature of people's preferences is that marginal benefit decreases.

———— MyEconLab animation ————

Figure 2.3 illustrates preferences as the willingness to pay for pizza in terms of cola. In row *A*, with 0.5 million pizzas available, people are willing to pay 5 cans of cola per pizza. As the quantity of pizzas increases, the amount that people are willing to pay for a pizza falls. With 4.5 million pizzas available, people are willing to pay only 1 can of cola per pizza.

Let's now use the concepts of marginal cost and marginal benefit to describe allocative efficiency.

FIGURE 2.4   Efficient Use of Resources

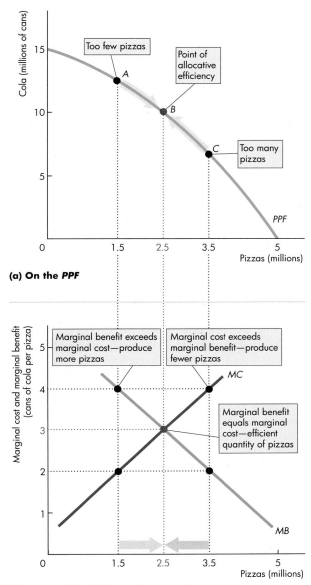

(a) On the PPF

(b) Marginal benefit equals marginal cost

The greater the quantity of pizzas produced, the smaller is the marginal benefit (*MB*) from pizza—the less cola people are willing to give up to get an additional pizza. But the greater the quantity of pizzas produced, the greater is the marginal cost (*MC*) of a pizza—the more cola people must give up to get an additional pizza. When marginal benefit equals marginal cost, resources are being used efficiently.

MyEconLab animation

Allocative Efficiency

At *any* point on the *PPF*, we cannot produce more of one good without giving up some other good. At the *best* point on the *PPF*, we cannot produce more of one good without giving up some other good that provides greater benefit. We are producing at the point of allocative efficiency—the point on the *PPF* that we prefer above all other points.

Suppose in Fig. 2.4, we produce 1.5 million pizzas. The marginal cost of a pizza is 2 cans of cola, and the marginal benefit from a pizza is 4 cans of cola. Because someone values an additional pizza more highly than it costs to produce, we can get more value from our resources by moving some of them out of producing cola and into producing pizza.

Now suppose we produce 3.5 million pizzas. The marginal cost of a pizza is now 4 cans of cola, but the marginal benefit from a pizza is only 2 cans of cola. Because the additional pizza costs more to produce than anyone thinks it is worth, we can get more value from our resources by moving some of them away from producing pizza and into producing cola.

Suppose we produce 2.5 million pizzas. Marginal cost and marginal benefit are now equal at 3 cans of cola. This allocation of resources between pizzas and cola is efficient. If more pizzas are produced, the forgone cola is worth more than the additional pizzas. If fewer pizzas are produced, the forgone pizzas are worth more than the additional cola.

REVIEW QUIZ

1 What is marginal cost? How is it measured?
2 What is marginal benefit? How is it measured?
3 How does the marginal benefit from a good change as the quantity produced of that good increases?
4 What is allocative efficiency and how does it relate to the production possibilities frontier?
5 What conditions must be satisfied if resources are used efficiently?

You can work these questions in Study Plan 2.2 and get instant feedback.   MyEconLab

You now understand the limits to production and the conditions under which resources are used efficiently. Your next task is to study the expansion of production possibilities.

Economic Growth

During the past 30 years, production per person in the United States has doubled. The expansion of production possibilities is called **economic growth**. Economic growth increases our *standard of living,* but it doesn't overcome scarcity and avoid opportunity cost. To make our economy grow, we face a trade-off—the faster we make production grow, the greater is the opportunity cost of economic growth.

The Cost of Economic Growth

Economic growth comes from technological change and capital accumulation. **Technological change** is the development of new goods and of better ways of producing goods and services. **Capital accumulation** is the growth of capital resources, including *human capital.*

Technological change and capital accumulation have vastly expanded our production possibilities. We can produce automobiles that provide us with more transportation than was available when we had only horses and carriages. We can produce satellites that provide global communications on a much larger scale than that available with the earlier cable technology. But if we use our resources to develop new technologies and produce capital, we must decrease our production of consumption goods and services. New technologies and new capital have an opportunity cost. Let's look at this opportunity cost.

Instead of studying the *PPF* of pizzas and cola, we'll hold the quantity of cola produced constant and examine the *PPF* for pizzas and pizza ovens. Figure 2.5 shows this *PPF* as the blue curve PPF_0. If we devote no resources to producing pizza ovens, we produce at point *A.* If we produce 3 million pizzas, we can produce 6 pizza ovens at point *B.* If we produce no pizza, we can produce 10 ovens at point *C.*

The amount by which our production possibilities expand depends on the resources we devote to technological change and capital accumulation. If we devote no resources to this activity (point *A*), our *PPF* remains the blue curve PPF_0 in Fig. 2.5. If we cut the current pizza production and produce 6 ovens (point *B*), then in the future, we'll have more capital and our *PPF* will rotate outward to the position shown by the red curve PPF_1. The fewer resources we use for producing pizza and the more resources we use for producing ovens, the greater is the expansion of our future production possibilities.

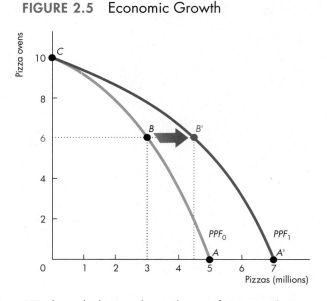

FIGURE 2.5   Economic Growth

PPF_0 shows the limits to the production of pizzas and pizza ovens, with the production of all other goods and services remaining the same. If we devote no resources to producing pizza ovens and produce 5 million pizzas, our production possibilities will remain the same at PPF_0. But if we decrease pizza production to 3 million and produce 6 ovens, at point *B,* our production possibilities expand. After one period, the *PPF* rotates outward to PPF_1 and we can produce at point *B'*, a point outside the original PPF_0. We can rotate the *PPF* outward, but we cannot avoid opportunity cost. The opportunity cost of producing more pizzas in the future is fewer pizzas today.

MyEconLab animation

Economic growth brings enormous benefits in the form of increased consumption in the future, but it is not free and it doesn't abolish scarcity.

In Fig. 2.5, to make economic growth happen we must use some resources to produce new ovens, which leaves fewer resources to produce pizzas. To move to *B'* in the future, we must move from *A* to *B* today. The opportunity cost of more pizzas in the future is fewer pizzas today. Also, on the new *PPF,* we still face a tradeoff and opportunity cost.

The ideas about economic growth that we have explored in the setting of the pizza industry also apply to nations. Hong Kong and the United States provide a striking case study.

Economics in Action

Hong Kong Catching Up to the United States

In 1969, the production possibilities per person in the United States were more than four times those in Hong Kong (see the figure). The United States devotes one fifth of its resources to accumulating capital and in 1969 was at point *A* on its *PPF*. Hong Kong devotes one third of its resources to accumulating capital and in 1969, Hong Kong was at point *A* on its *PPF*.

Since 1969, both countries have experienced economic growth, but because Hong Kong devotes a bigger fraction of its resources to accumulating capital, its production possibilities have expanded more quickly.

By 2011, production possibilities per person in Hong Kong had reached 94 percent of those in the United States. If Hong Kong continues to devote more resources to accumulating capital than the United States does (at point *B* on its 2011 *PPF*), it will continue to grow more rapidly. But if Hong Kong decreases its capital accumulation (moving to point *D* on its 2011 *PPF*), then its rate of economic growth will slow.

Hong Kong is typical of the fast-growing Asian economies, which include Taiwan, Thailand, South Korea, China, and India. Production possibilities

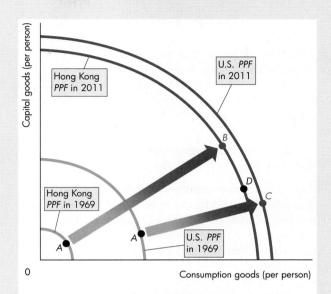

Economic Growth in the United States and Hong Kong

expand in these countries by between 5 percent and almost 10 percent a year.

If such high economic growth rates are maintained, these other Asian countries will continue to close the gap between themselves and the United States, as Hong Kong is doing.

A Nation's Economic Growth

The experiences of the United States and Hong Kong make a striking example of the effects of our choices about consumption and capital accumulation on the rate of economic growth.

If a nation devotes all its factors of production to producing consumption goods and services and none to advancing technology and accumulating capital, its production possibilities in the future will be the same as they are today.

To expand production possibilities in the future, a nation must devote fewer resources to producing current consumption goods and services and some resources to accumulating capital and developing new technologies. As production possibilities expand, consumption in the future can increase. The decrease in today's consumption is the opportunity cost of tomorrow's increase in consumption.

REVIEW QUIZ

1 What generates economic growth?
2 How does economic growth influence the production possibilities frontier?
3 What is the opportunity cost of economic growth?
4 Why has Hong Kong experienced faster economic growth than the United States?
5 Does economic growth overcome scarcity?

You can work these questions in Study Plan 2.3 and get instant feedback.   MyEconLab

Next, we're going to study another way in which we expand our production possibilities—the amazing fact that *both* buyers and sellers gain from specialization and trade.

Gains from Trade

People can produce for themselves all the goods and services that they consume, or they can produce one good or a few goods and trade with others. Producing only one good or a few goods is called *specialization*. We are going to learn how people gain by specializing in the production of the good in which they have a *comparative advantage* and trading with others.

Comparative Advantage and Absolute Advantage

A person has a **comparative advantage** in an activity if that person can perform the activity at a lower opportunity cost than anyone else. Differences in opportunity costs arise from differences in individual abilities and from differences in the characteristics of other resources.

No one excels at everything. One person is an outstanding pitcher but a poor catcher; another person is a brilliant lawyer but a poor teacher. In almost all human endeavors, what one person does easily, someone else finds difficult. The same applies to land and capital. One plot of land is fertile but has no mineral deposits; another plot of land has outstanding views but is infertile. One machine has great precision but is difficult to operate; another is fast but often breaks down.

Although no one excels at everything, some people excel and can outperform others in a large number of activities—perhaps even in all activities. A person who is more productive than others has an **absolute advantage**.

Absolute advantage involves comparing productivities—production per hour—whereas comparative advantage involves comparing opportunity costs.

A person who has an absolute advantage does not have a *comparative* advantage in every activity. John Grisham is a better lawyer and a better author of fast-paced thrillers than most people. He has an absolute advantage in these two activities. But compared to others, he is a better writer than lawyer, so his *comparative* advantage is in writing.

Because ability and resources vary from one person to another, people have different opportunity costs of producing various goods. These differences in opportunity cost are the source of comparative advantage.

Let's explore the idea of comparative advantage by looking at two smoothie bars: one operated by Liz and the other operated by Joe.

Liz's Smoothie Bar Liz produces smoothies and salads. In Liz's high-tech bar, she can turn out either a smoothie or a salad every 2 minutes—see Table 2.1. If Liz spends all her time making smoothies, she can produce 30 an hour. And if she spends all her time making salads, she can also produce 30 an hour. If she splits her time equally between the two, she can produce 15 smoothies and 15 salads an hour. For each additional smoothie Liz produces, she must decrease her production of salads by one, and for each additional salad she produces, she must decrease her production of smoothies by one. So

Liz's opportunity cost of producing 1 smoothie is 1 salad,

and

Liz's opportunity cost of producing 1 salad is 1 smoothie.

Liz's customers buy smoothies and salads in equal quantities, so she splits her time equally between the two items and produces 15 smoothies and 15 salads an hour.

Joe's Smoothie Bar Joe also produces smoothies and salads, but his bar is smaller than Liz's. Also, Joe has only one blender, and it's a slow, old machine. Even if Joe uses all his resources to produce smoothies, he can produce only 6 an hour—see Table 2.2. But Joe is good at making salads. If he uses all his resources to make salads, he can produce 30 an hour.

Joe's ability to make smoothies and salads is the same regardless of how he splits an hour between the two tasks. He can make a salad in 2 minutes or a smoothie in 10 minutes. For each additional smoothie

TABLE 2.1   Liz's Production Possibilities

Item	Minutes to produce 1	Quantity per hour
Smoothies	2	30
Salads	2	30

TABLE 2.2 Joe's Production Possibilities

Item	Minutes to produce 1	Quantity per hour
Smoothies	10	6
Salads	2	30

Joe produces, he must decrease his production of salads by 5. And for each additional salad he produces, he must decrease his production of smoothies by 1/5 of a smoothie. So

> Joe's opportunity cost of producing 1 smoothie is 5 salads,

and

> Joe's opportunity cost of producing 1 salad is 1/5 of a smoothie.

Joe's customers, like Liz's, buy smoothies and salads in equal quantities. So Joe spends 50 minutes of each hour making smoothies and 10 minutes of each hour making salads. With this division of his time, Joe produces 5 smoothies and 5 salads an hour.

Liz's Comparative Advantage In which of the two activities does Liz have a comparative advantage? Recall that comparative advantage is a situation in which one person's opportunity cost of producing a good is lower than another person's opportunity cost of producing that same good. Liz has a comparative advantage in producing smoothies. Her opportunity cost of a smoothie is 1 salad, whereas Joe's opportunity cost of a smoothie is 5 salads.

Joe's Comparative Advantage If Liz has a comparative advantage in producing smoothies, Joe must have a comparative advantage in producing salads. Joe's opportunity cost of a salad is 1/5 of a smoothie, whereas Liz's opportunity cost of a salad is 1 smoothie.

Achieving the Gains from Trade

Liz and Joe run into each other one evening in a singles bar. After a few minutes of getting acquainted, Liz tells Joe about her amazing smoothie business. Her only problem, she tells Joe, is that she would like to produce more because potential customers leave when her lines get too long.

Joe is hesitant to risk spoiling his chances by telling Liz about his own struggling business, but he takes the risk. Joe explains to Liz that he spends 50 minutes of every hour making 5 smoothies and 10 minutes making 5 salads. Liz's eyes pop. "Have I got a deal for you!" she exclaims.

Here's the deal that Liz sketches on a paper napkin. Joe stops making smoothies and allocates all his time to producing salads; Liz stops making salads and allocates all her time to producing smoothies. That is, they both specialize in producing the good in which they have a comparative advantage. Together they produce 30 smoothies and 30 salads—see Table 2.3(b).

They then trade. Liz sells Joe 10 smoothies and Joe sells Liz 20 salads—the price of a smoothie is 2 salads—see Table 2.3(c).

After the trade, Joe has 10 salads—the 30 he produces minus the 20 he sells to Liz. He also has the 10 smoothies that he buys from Liz. So Joe now has increased the quantities of smoothies and salads that he can sell to his customers—see Table 2.3(d).

TABLE 2.3 Liz and Joe Gain from Trade

(a) Before trade	Liz	Joe
Smoothies	15	5
Salads	15	5

(b) Specialization	Liz	Joe
Smoothies	30	0
Salads	0	30

(c) Trade	Liz	Joe
Smoothies	sell 10	buy 10
Salads	buy 20	sell 20

(d) After trade	Liz	Joe
Smoothies	20	10
Salads	20	10

(e) Gains from trade	Liz	Joe
Smoothies	+5	+5
Salads	+5	+5

Liz has 20 smoothies—the 30 she produces minus the 10 she sells to Joe. She also has the 20 salads that she buys from Joe. Liz has increased the quantities of smoothies and salads that she can sell to her customers—see Table 2.3(d). Liz and Joe both gain 5 smoothies and 5 salads an hour—see Table 2.3(e).

To illustrate her idea, Liz grabs a fresh napkin and draws the graphs in Fig. 2.6. The blue *PPF* in part (a) shows Joe's production possibilities. Before trade, he is producing 5 smoothies and 5 salads an hour at point *A*. The blue *PPF* in part (b) shows Liz's production possibilities. Before trade, she is producing 15 smoothies and 15 salads an hour at point *A*.

Liz's proposal is that they each specialize in producing the good in which they have a comparative advantage. Joe produces 30 salads and no smoothies at point *B* on his *PPF*. Liz produces 30 smoothies and no salads at point *B* on her *PPF*.

Liz and Joe then trade smoothies and salads at a price of 2 salads per smoothie or 1/2 a smoothie per salad. Joe gets smoothies for 2 salads each, which is less than the 5 salads it costs him to produce a smoothie. Liz gets salads for 1/2 a smoothie each, which is less than the 1 smoothie that it costs her to produce a salad.

With trade, Joe has 10 smoothies and 10 salads at point *C*—a gain of 5 smoothies and 5 salads. Joe moves to a point *outside* his *PPF*.

With trade, Liz has 20 smoothies and 20 salads at point *C*—a gain of 5 smoothies and 5 salads. Liz moves to a point *outside* her *PPF*.

Despite Liz being more productive than Joe, both of them gain from specializing—producing the good in which they have a comparative advantage—and trading.

FIGURE 2.6   The Gains from Trade

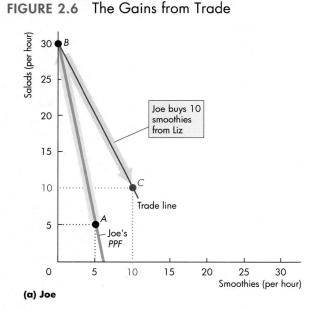

(a) Joe

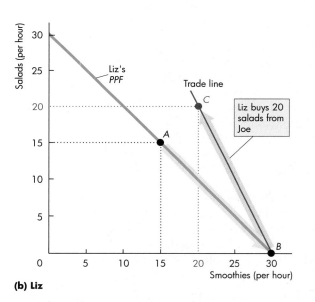

(b) Liz

Initially, Joe produces at point *A* on his *PPF* in part (a), and Liz produces at point *A* on her *PPF* in part (b). Joe's opportunity cost of producing a salad is less than Liz's, so Joe has a comparative advantage in producing salads. Liz's opportunity cost of producing a smoothie is less than Joe's, so Liz has a comparative advantage in producing smoothies.

If Joe specializes in making salads, he produces 30 salads and no smoothies at point *B* on his *PPF*. If Liz specializes

in making smoothies, she produces 30 smoothies and no salads at point *B* on her *PPF*. They exchange salads for smoothies along the red "Trade line." Liz buys salads from Joe for less than her opportunity cost of producing them. Joe buys smoothies from Liz for less than his opportunity cost of producing them. Each goes to point *C*—a point outside his or her *PPF*. With specialization and trade, Joe and Liz gain 5 smoothies and 5 salads each with no extra resources.

◆ ECONOMICS IN THE NEWS

Energy Independence

Is U.S. Energy Independence Finally Within Reach?
"Energy self-sufficiency is now in sight," says energy economist Phil Verleger.... Small energy companies using such controversial techniques as hydraulic fracturing, along with horizontal drilling, are unlocking vast oil and natural gas deposits trapped in shale in places like Pennsylvania, North Dakota, and Texas.

Source *NPR*, March 7, 2012

THE DATA

Energy Production and Consumption
(quadrillion Btu)

	Production	Imports	Consumption
Coal	22	−1	21
Natural gas	25	0	25
Oil	12	24	36
Nuclear	8	0	8
Renewables	8	0	8
Total	75	23	98

THE QUESTIONS

- What energy sources does the United States buy from other countries?
- Why is the United States *not* energy independent? Use a *PPF* graph to explain your answer.
- How can it become efficient for the United States to be energy independent?

THE ANSWERS

- The data table shows that the United States imports oil—buys oil from other countries. Oil imports are double U.S. oil production and two thirds of oil consumed.
- The United States is not energy independent because other countries have a comparative advantage in energy production. It costs less to buy some of our energy from other countries than to produce it all ourselves.
- The figure shows the U.S. *PPF* for energy and all other goods and services. We produce on the *PPF* at point *A*.
- To produce 60 quadrillion Btu, the production of other goods and services falls from 100 units to 90 units. The opportunity cost of 60 quadrillion Btu of energy is 10 units of other goods and services.
- The figure also shows a red "Trade line." The United States can buy (or sell) energy along that line. (It is like the trade line in Fig. 2.6). We can move along the trade line and consume at point *B*,

by buying (importing) 20 quadrillion Btu of energy at a cost of 10 units of other good and services.

- To be energy independent, we would forgo 30 units of other goods and services and produce and consume at point *C*.
- At point *C*, the United States consumes the same amount of energy as at point *B*, but the opportunity cost of the energy is higher than the opportunity cost of imported energy.
- For it to become efficient for the United States to be energy independent, the *PPF* must shift outward and the opportunity cost of energy must fall.
- Technological advances in hydraulic fracturing (fracking) and horizontal drilling and opening more gas wells will shift the *PPF* outward and lower the opportunity cost of energy.

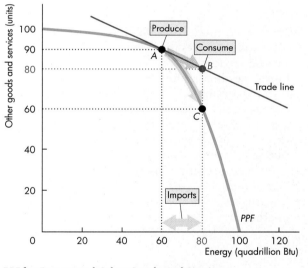

PPF for Energy and Other Goods and Services

◆ REVIEW QUIZ

1 What gives a person a comparative advantage?
2 Distinguish between comparative advantage and absolute advantage.
3 Why do people specialize and trade?
4 What are the gains from specialization and trade?
5 What is the source of the gains from trade?

You can work these questions in Study Plan 2.4 and get instant feedback.   MyEconLab

◆ Economic Coordination

For 7 billion people to specialize and produce millions of different goods and services, individual choices must somehow be coordinated. Two competing coordination systems have been used: central economic planning and markets (see *At Issue*, p. 8).

Central economic planning works badly because economic planners don't know people's production possibilities and preferences, so production ends up *inside* the *PPF* and the wrong things are produced.

Decentralized coordination works best but to do so it needs four complementary social institutions. They are

- Firms
- Markets
- Property rights
- Money

Firms

A **firm** is an economic unit that hires factors of production and organizes them to produce and sell goods and services.

Firms coordinate a huge amount of economic activity. For example, Wal-Mart buys or rents large buildings, equips them with storage shelves and checkout lanes, and hires labor. Wal-Mart directs the labor and decides what goods to buy and sell.

But Sam Walton would not have become one of the wealthiest people in the world if Wal-Mart produced everything that it sells. He became rich by specializing in providing retail services and buying from other firms that specialize in producing goods (just as Liz and Joe did). This trade needs markets.

Markets

In ordinary speech, the word *market* means a place where people buy and sell goods such as fish, meat, fruits, and vegetables.

In economics, a **market** is any arrangement that enables buyers and sellers to get information and to do business with each other. An example is the world oil market, which is not a place but a network of producers, consumers, wholesalers, and brokers who buy and sell oil. In the world oil market, decision makers make deals by using the Internet. Enterprising individuals and firms, each pursuing their own self-interest, have profited by making markets—by standing ready to buy or sell items in which they specialize. But markets can work only when property rights exist.

Property Rights

The social arrangements that govern the ownership, use, and disposal of anything that people value are called **property rights**. *Real property* includes land and buildings—the things we call property in ordinary speech—and durable goods such as plant and equipment. *Financial property* includes stocks and bonds and money in the bank. *Intellectual property* is the intangible product of creative effort. This type of property includes books, music, computer programs, and inventions of all kinds and is protected by copyrights and patents.

Where property rights are enforced, people have the incentive to specialize and produce the goods and services in which they have a comparative advantage. Where people can steal the production of others, resources are devoted not to production but to protecting possessions.

Money

Money is any commodity or token that is generally acceptable as a means of payment. Liz and Joe don't need money. They can exchange salads and smoothies. In principle, trade in markets can exchange any item for any other item. But you can perhaps imagine how complicated life would be if we exchanged goods for other goods. The "invention" of money makes trading in markets much more efficient.

Circular Flows Through Markets

Trading in markets for goods and services and factors of production creates a circular flow of expenditures and incomes. Figure 2.7 shows the circular flows. Households specialize and choose the quantities of labor, land, capital, and entrepreneurial services to sell or rent to firms. Firms choose the quantities of factors of production to hire. These (red) flows go through the *factor markets*. Households choose the quantities of goods and services to buy, and firms choose the quantities to produce. These (red) flows go through the *goods markets*. Households receive incomes and make expenditures on goods and services (the green flows).

How do markets coordinate all these decisions?

FIGURE 2.7   Circular Flows in the Market Economy

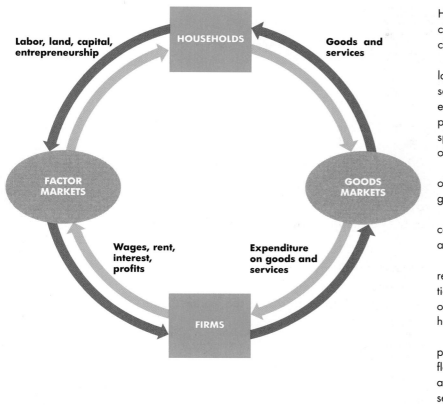

Households and firms make economic choices and markets coordinate these choices.

Households choose the quantities of labor, land, capital, and entrepreneurial services to sell or rent to firms in exchange for wages, rent, interest, and profits. Households also choose how to spend their incomes on the various types of goods and services available.

Firms choose the quantities of factors of production to hire and the quantities of goods and services to produce.

Goods markets and factor markets coordinate these choices of households and firms.

The counterclockwise red flows are real flows—the flow of factors of production from households to firms and the flow of goods and services from firms to households.

The clockwise green flows are the payments for the red flows. They are the flow of incomes from firms to households and the flow of expenditure on goods and services from households to firms.

— MyEconLab animation —

Coordinating Decisions

Markets coordinate decisions through price adjustments. Suppose that some people who want to buy hamburgers are not able to do so. To make buying and selling plans the same, either more hamburgers must be offered for sale or buyers must scale down their appetites (or both). A rise in the price of a hamburger produces this outcome. It encourages producers to offer more hamburgers for sale and encourages some people to change their lunch plans. When the price is right, buying plans and selling plans match.

Alternatively, suppose that more hamburgers are available than people want to buy. In this case, more hamburgers must be bought or fewer hamburgers must be offered for sale (or both). A fall in the price of a hamburger achieves this outcome. It encourages people to buy more hamburgers and it encourages firms to produce a smaller quantity of hamburgers.

REVIEW QUIZ

1 Why are social institutions such as firms, markets, property rights, and money necessary?
2 What are the main functions of markets?
3 What are the flows in the market economy that go from firms to households and the flows from households to firms?

You can work these questions in Study Plan 2.5 and get instant feedback.   MyEconLab

◆ You have now begun to see how economists approach economic questions. *Reading Between the Lines* on pp. 46–47 provides an opportunity to apply what you've learned about the *PPF* and opportunity cost to see why some nations import almost all of their food and how technological advances can lower food production costs.

Food: Import and Expand Production Possibilities

Technology, Growth, and Food Security

Financial Times
April 3, 2012

Private farming companies are turning to the latest techniques to help fill the domestic production gap. One area of focus is hydroponics, where nutrient solutions are used to feed plants in greenhouses, to overcome both the shortage of water and the extreme heat. Using hydroponics can reduce the use of water by 40–60 percent, farmers say.

But with domestic production still providing just a fraction of overall needs, most Gulf governments have looked overseas to secure food supplies, investing tens of billions of dollars buying farming property.

It is not just in Qatar where the private sector is taking the first steps to domestic production. In the United Arab Emirates, a number of hydroponics farms have been set up in recent years and are now starting to play a more important role in the market. Saudi Arabia has also seen new agricultural companies emerge. …

Last year, Abu Dhabi announced it was set to launch Baniyas, the largest aquaponics center in the world, a project that started with lettuces but was set to expand to other vegetables. Aquaponics uses water that fish live in, beneath the plants, offering extra nutrients to the lettuces. …

The Gulf's finite and declining reserves of naturally occurring underground water are the central challenge to the sustainability of desert agriculture operations. Groundwater supplies used for farming are replenished with desalinated water, which lacks the same nutrients. Water is also being consumed much faster than it is being replenished. …

Although the food supply balance will remain heavily weighted toward imports, increasing what small-scale production there is can only contribute to overall food security.

ESSENCE OF THE STORY

- The Arab Gulf nations import most of their food.

- To ensure a secure food supply, Gulf countries have invested heavily and bought farming property overseas.

- Domestic food production is being increased by using desalinated water.

- Hydroponic farms are producing more food and use 40 to 60 percent less water than conventional farms.

ECONOMIC ANALYSIS

- The Arab Gulf nations are rich in oil and poor in water. They have a low opportunity cost of producing oil and a high opportunity cost of producing food, so they have a comparative advantage in producing oil.

- Figure 1 shows the Gulf nations' production possibilities frontier, *PPF*.

- These nations can trade oil for food along the red trade line. This line shows the terms on which the Gulf states can exchange oil for food. Its slope is the opportunity cost of food on the world market.

- The Gulf nations produce at point *A*, where the opportunity cost of food production equals the opportunity cost of food on the world market.

- They consume at point *B* by exporting oil and importing food.

- Because most of their food is imported, the Gulf states want to have some control over production in the nations that produce the food. For this reason, the Gulf states buy farmland in other countries. By this means, they improve the security of their food sources.

- But buying foreign farms doesn't change production possibilities in the Gulf states. It just makes the sources of imports more secure. The farmland is a resource in a foreign economy and influences that economy's production possibilities.

- Another way of improving food security is to increase domestic production. But as Fig. 1 shows, increasing production beyond point *A* incurs a much higher opportunity cost than it is necessary to incur.

- But food production can be increased with no decrease in oil production if the Gulf states can increase their production possibilities.

- That is what advances in agricultural technology can achieve.

- By using hydroponic technology, the Gulf nations can produce more food from a given amount of scarce water and land resources.

- Figure 2 illustrates the effects on hydroponic technology and the Gulf states' production possibilities frontier. When this technological advance occurs, the *PPF* shifts outward from PPF_0 to PPF_1.

- Notice that on PPF_1, the opportunity cost of food is lower than on PPF_0. As a result, the Gulf nations increase the quantity of food they produce and decrease the quantity of food they import.

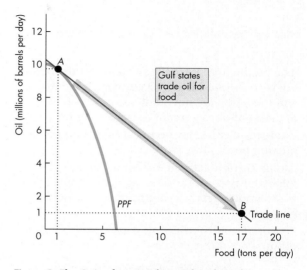

Figure 1 The Gains from Trade in Oil and Food

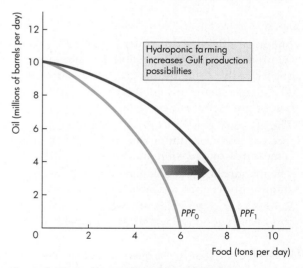

Figure 2 Expanding Food Production Possibilities

SUMMARY

Key Points

Production Possibilities and Opportunity Cost

(pp. 32–34)

- The production possibilities frontier is the boundary between production levels that are attainable and those that are not attainable when all the available resources are used to their limit.
- Production efficiency occurs at points on the production possibilities frontier.
- Along the production possibilities frontier, the opportunity cost of producing more of one good is the amount of the other good that must be given up.
- The opportunity cost of all goods increases as the production of the good increases.

Working Problems 1 to 3 will give you a better understanding of production possibilities and opportunity cost.

Using Resources Efficiently (pp. 35–37)

- Allocative efficiency occurs when goods and services are produced at the least possible cost and in the quantities that bring the greatest possible benefit.
- The marginal cost of a good is the opportunity cost of producing one more unit of it.
- The marginal benefit from a good is the benefit received from consuming one more unit of it and is measured by the willingness to pay for it.
- The marginal benefit of a good decreases as the amount of the good available increases.
- Resources are used efficiently when the marginal cost of each good is equal to its marginal benefit.

Working Problems 4 to 10 will give you a better understanding of the efficient use of resources.

Economic Growth (pp. 38–39)

- Economic growth, which is the expansion of production possibilities, results from capital accumulation and technological change.
- The opportunity cost of economic growth is forgone current consumption.
- The benefit of economic growth is increased future consumption.

Working Problem 11 will give you a better understanding of economic growth.

Gains from Trade (pp. 40–43)

- A person has a comparative advantage in producing a good if that person can produce the good at a lower opportunity cost than everyone else.
- People gain by specializing in the activity in which they have a comparative advantage and trading with others.

Working Problems 12 and 13 will give you a better understanding of the gains from trade.

Economic Coordination (pp. 44–45)

- Firms coordinate a large amount of economic activity, but there is a limit to the efficient size of a firm.
- Markets coordinate the economic choices of people and firms.
- Markets can work efficiently only when property rights exist.
- Money makes trading in markets more efficient.

Working Problem 14 will give you a better understanding of economic coordination.

Key Terms

Absolute advantage, 40	Marginal benefit, 36	Preferences, 36
Allocative efficiency, 35	Marginal benefit curve, 36	Production efficiency, 33
Capital accumulation, 38	Marginal cost, 35	Production possibilities frontier, 32
Comparative advantage, 40	Market, 44	Property rights, 44
Economic growth, 38	Money, 44	Technological change, 38
Firm, 44	Opportunity cost, 33	

STUDY PLAN PROBLEMS AND APPLICATIONS

MyEconLab   You can work Problems 1 to 20 in MyEconLab Chapter 2 Study Plan and get instant feedback.

Production Possibilities and Opportunity Cost

(Study Plan 2.1)

Use the following information to work Problems 1 to 3. Brazil produces ethanol from sugar, and the land used to grow sugar can be used to grow food crops. Suppose that Brazil's production possibilities for ethanol and food crops are as follows

Ethanol (barrels per day)		Food crops (tons per day)
70	and	0
64	and	1
54	and	2
40	and	3
22	and	4
0	and	5

1. a. Draw a graph of Brazil's *PPF* and explain how your graph illustrates scarcity.
    b. If Brazil produces 40 barrels of ethanol a day, how much food must it produce to achieve production efficiency?
    c. Why does Brazil face a tradeoff on its *PPF*?

2. a. If Brazil increases its production of ethanol from 40 barrels per day to 54 barrels per day, what is the opportunity cost of the additional ethanol?
    b. If Brazil increases its production of food crops from 2 tons per day to 3 tons per day, what is the opportunity cost of the additional food?
    c. What is the relationship between your answers to parts (a) and (b)?

3. Does Brazil face an increasing opportunity cost of ethanol? What feature of Brazil's *PPF* illustrates increasing opportunity cost?

Using Resources Efficiently (Study Plan 2.2)

Use the above table to work Problems 4 and 5.

4. Define marginal cost and calculate Brazil's marginal cost of producing a ton of food when the quantity produced is 2.5 tons per day.

5. Define marginal benefit, explain how it is measured, and explain why the data in the table does not enable you to calculate Brazil's marginal benefit from food.

6. Distinguish between *production efficiency* and *allocative efficiency*. Explain why many production possibilities achieve production efficiency but only one achieves allocative efficiency.

Use the following graphs to work Problems 7 to 10. Harry enjoys tennis but wants a high grade in his economics course. The graphs show his *PPF* for these two "goods" and his *MB* curve from tennis.

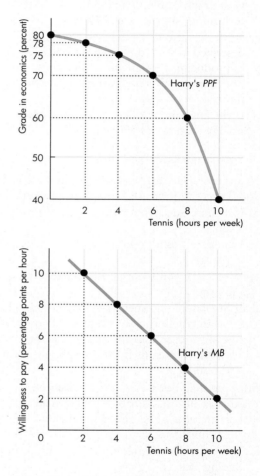

7. What is Harry's marginal cost of tennis if he plays for (i) 3 hours a week; (ii) 5 hours a week; and (iii) 7 hours a week?

8. a. If Harry uses his time to achieve allocative efficiency, what is his economics grade and how many hours of tennis does he play?
    b. Explain why Harry would be worse off getting a grade higher than your answer to part (a).

9. If Harry becomes a tennis superstar with big earnings from tennis, what happens to his *PPF*, *MB* curve, and his efficient time allocation?

10. If Harry suddenly finds high grades in economics easier to attain, what happens to his *PPF*, his *MB* curve, and his efficient time allocation?

Economic Growth (Study Plan 2.3)

11. A farm grows wheat and produces pork. The marginal cost of producing each of these products increases as more of it is produced.
    a. Make a graph that illustrates the farm's *PPF*.
    b. The farm adopts a new technology that allows it to use fewer resources to fatten pigs. Use your graph to illustrate the impact of the new technology on the farm's *PPF*.
    c. With the farm using the new technology described in part (b), has the opportunity cost of producing a ton of wheat increased, decreased, or remained the same? Explain and illustrate your answer.
    d. Is the farm more efficient with the new technology than it was with the old one? Why?

Gains from Trade (Study Plan 2.4)

12. In an hour, Sue can produce 40 caps or 4 jackets and Tessa can produce 80 caps or 4 jackets.
    a. Calculate Sue's opportunity cost of producing a cap.
    b. Calculate Tessa's opportunity cost of producing a cap.
    c. Who has a comparative advantage in producing caps?
    d. If Sue and Tessa specialize in producing the good in which each of them has a comparative advantage, and they trade 1 jacket for 15 caps, who gains from the specialization and trade?

13. Suppose that Tessa buys a new machine for making jackets that enables her to make 20 jackets an hour. (She can still make only 80 caps per hour.)
    a. Who now has a comparative advantage in producing jackets?
    b. Can Sue and Tessa still gain from trade?
    c. Would Sue and Tessa still be willing to trade 1 jacket for 15 caps? Explain your answer.

Economic Coordination (Study Plan 2.5)

14. For 50 years, Cuba has had a centrally planned economy in which the government makes the big decisions on how resources will be allocated.
    a. Why would you expect Cuba's production possibilities (per person) to be smaller than those of the United States?
    b. What are the social institutions that Cuba might lack that help the United States to achieve allocative efficiency?

Economics in the News (Study Plan 2.N)

Use the following data to work Problems 15 to 17. Brazil produces ethanol from sugar at a cost of 83 cents per gallon. The United States produces ethanol from corn at a cost of $1.14 per gallon. Sugar grown on one acre of land produces twice the quantity of ethanol as the corn grown on an acre. The United States imports 5 percent of the ethanol it uses and produces the rest itself. Since 2003, U.S. ethanol production has more than doubled and U.S. corn production has increased by 45 percent.

15. a. Does Brazil or the United States have a comparative advantage in producing ethanol?
    b. Sketch the *PPF* for ethanol and other goods and services for the United States.
    c. Sketch the *PPF* for ethanol and other goods and services for Brazil.

16. a. Do you expect the opportunity cost of producing ethanol in the United States to have increased since 2003? Explain why.
    b. Do you think the United States has achieved production efficiency in its manufacture of ethanol? Explain why or why not.
    c. Do you think the United States has achieved allocative efficiency in its manufacture of ethanol? Explain why or why not.

17. Sketch a figure similar to Fig. 2.6 on p. 42 to show how both the United States and Brazil can gain from specialization and trade.

Use this news clip to work Problems 18 to 20.
Time for Tea
Americans are switching to loose-leaf tea for its health benefits. Tea could be grown in the United States, but picking tea leaves would be costly because it can only be done by workers and not by machine.

Source: *The Economist*, July 8, 2005

18. a. Sketch *PPF*s for the production of tea and other goods and services in India and in the United States.
    b. Sketch marginal cost curves for the production of tea in India and in the United States.

19. a. Sketch the marginal benefit curves for tea in the United States before and after Americans began to appreciate the health benefits of loose tea.
    b. Explain how the quantity of loose tea that achieves allocative efficiency has changed.
    c. Does the change in preferences toward tea affect the opportunity cost of producing tea?

20. Explain why the United States does not produce tea and instead imports it from India.

ADDITIONAL PROBLEMS AND APPLICATIONS

MyEconLab   You can work these problems in MyEconLab if assigned by your instructor.

Production Possibilities and Opportunity Cost

Use the following table to work Problems 21 and 22. Suppose that Yucatan's production possibilities are

Food (pounds per month)		Sunscreen (gallons per month)
300	and	0
200	and	50
100	and	100
0	and	150

21. a. Draw a graph of Yucatan's *PPF* and explain how your graph illustrates a tradeoff.
    b. If Yucatan produces 150 pounds of food per month, how much sunscreen must it produce if it achieves production efficiency?
    c. What is Yucatan's opportunity cost of producing 1 pound of food?
    d. What is Yucatan's opportunity cost of producing 1 gallon of sunscreen?
    e. What is the relationship between your answers to parts (c) and (d)?

22. What feature of a *PPF* illustrates increasing opportunity cost? Explain why Yucatan's opportunity cost does or does not increase.

Using Resources Efficiently

23. In problem 21, what is the marginal cost of a pound of food in Yucatan when the quantity produced is 150 pounds per day? What is special about the marginal cost of food in Yucatan?

24. The table describes the preferences in Yucatan.

Sunscreen (gallons per month)	Willingness to pay (pounds of food per gallon)
25	3
75	2
125	1

    a. What is the marginal benefit from sunscreen and how is it measured?
    b. Draw a graph of Yucatan's marginal benefit from sunscreen.

Use the following news clip to work Problems 25 and 26.

Malaria Eradication Back on the Table

In response to the Gates Malaria Forum in October 2007, countries are debating the pros and cons of eradication. Dr. Arata Kochi of the World Health Organization believes that with enough money malaria cases could be cut by 90 percent, but he believes that it would be very expensive to eliminate the remaining 10 percent of cases. He concluded that countries should not strive to eradicate malaria.

Source: *The New York Times*, March 4, 2008

25. Is Dr. Kochi talking about *production efficiency* or *allocative efficiency* or both?

26. Make a graph with the percentage of malaria cases eliminated on the *x*-axis and the marginal cost and marginal benefit of driving down malaria cases on the *y*-axis. On your graph:
    (i) Draw a marginal cost curve that is consistent with Dr. Kochi's opinion.
    (ii) Draw a marginal benefit curve that is consistent with Dr. Kochi's opinion.
    (iii) Identify the quantity of malaria eradicated that achieves allocative efficiency.

Economic Growth

27. Capital accumulation and technological change bring economic growth, which means that the *PPF* keeps shifting outward: Production that was unattainable yesterday becomes attainable today; production that is unattainable today will become attainable tomorrow. Why doesn't this process of economic growth mean that scarcity is being defeated and will one day be gone?

Gains from Trade

Use the following data to work Problems 28 and 29. Kim can produce 40 pies or 400 cakes an hour. Liam can produce 100 pies or 200 cakes an hour.

28. a. Calculate Kim's opportunity cost of a pie and Liam's opportunity cost of a pie.
    b. If each spends 30 minutes of each hour producing pies and 30 minutes producing cakes, how many pies and cakes does each produce?
    c. Who has a comparative advantage in producing pies? Who has a comparative advantage in producing cakes?

29. a. Draw a graph of Kim's *PPF* and Liam's *PPF*.
    b. On your graph, show the point at which each produces when they spend 30 minutes of each hour producing pies and 30 minutes producing cakes.
    c. On your graph, show what Kim produces and what Liam produces when they specialize.

d. When they specialize and trade, what are the total gains from trade?

e. If Kim and Liam share the total gains equally, what trade takes place between them?

Use the following information to work Problems 30 and 31.

Before the Civil War, the South traded with the North and with England. The South sold cotton and bought manufactured goods and food. During the war, one of President Lincoln's first actions was to blockade the ports and prevent this trade. The South increased its production of munitions and food.

30. In what did the South have a comparative advantage?

31. a. Draw a graph to illustrate production, consumption, and trade in the South before the Civil War.

b. Was the South consuming inside, on, or outside its *PPF*? Explain your answer.

c. Draw a graph to show the effects of the Civil War on consumption and production in the South.

d. Did the Civil War change any opportunity costs in the South? If so, did the opportunity cost of everything increase? Did the opportunity cost of any items decrease? Illustrate your answer with appropriate graphs.

Use the following information to work Problems 32 and 33.

He Shoots! He Scores! He Makes Movies!
NBA All-star Baron Davis and his school friend, Cash Warren, premiered their first movie *Made in America* at the Sundance Festival in January 2008. The movie, based on gang activity in South Central Los Angeles, received good reviews.

Source: *The New York Times,* February 24, 2008

32. a. Does Baron Davis have an absolute advantage in basketball and movie directing and is this the reason for his success in both activities?

b. Does Baron Davis have a comparative advantage in basketball or movie directing or both and is this the reason for his success in both activities?

33. a. Sketch a *PPF* between playing basketball and producing other goods and services for Baron Davis and for yourself.

b. How do you (and people like you) and Baron Davis (and people like him) gain from specialization and trade?

Economic Coordination

34. Indicate on a graph of the circular flows in the market economy, the real and money flows in which the following items belong:

a. You buy an iPad from the Apple Store.

b. Apple Inc. pays the designers of the iPad.

c. Apple Inc. decides to expand and rents an adjacent building.

d. You buy a new e-book from Amazon.

e. Apple Inc. hires a student as an intern during the summer.

Economics in the News

35. After you have studied *Reading Between the Lines* on pp. 46–47, answer the following questions.

a. How does the rich endowment of oil and the poor endowment of water influence opportunity cost and comparative advantage in the Gulf states?

b. Why do the Gulf states import most of their food?

c. Why do the Gulf states buy foreign farmland and how do these purchases influence production possibilities in the foreign economy and the Gulf states?

d. On Fig. 2 on p. 47, show how hydroponic farming increases domestic food production and decreases food imports.

36. **Lots of Little Screens**
Inexpensive broadband access has created a generation of television producers for whom the Internet is their native medium. As they redirect the focus from TV to computers, cell phones, and iPods, the video market is developing into an open digital network.

Source: *The New York Times,* December 2, 2007

a. How has inexpensive broadband changed the production possibilities of video entertainment and other goods and services?

b. Sketch a *PPF* for video entertainment and other goods and services before broadband.

c. Show how the arrival of inexpensive broadband has changed the *PPF*.

d. Sketch a marginal benefit curve for video entertainment.

e. Show how the new generation of TV producers for whom the Internet is their native medium might have changed the marginal benefit from video entertainment.

f. Explain how the efficient quantity of video entertainment has changed.

Your Economic Revolution

Three periods in human history stand out as ones of economic revolution. The first, the *Agricultural Revolution,* occurred 10,000 years ago. In what is today Iraq, people learned to domesticate animals and plant crops. People stopped roaming in search of food and settled in villages, towns, and cities where they specialized in the activities in which they had a comparative advantage and developed markets in which to exchange their products. Wealth increased enormously.

Economics was born during the *Industrial Revolution,* which began in England during the 1760s. For the first time, people began to apply science and create new technologies for the manufacture of textiles and iron, to create steam engines, and to boost the output of farms.

You are studying economics at a time that future historians will call the *Information Revolution.* Over the entire world, people are embracing new information technologies and prospering on an unprecedented scale.

During all three economic revolutions, many have prospered but many have been left behind. It is the range of human progress that poses the greatest question for economics and the one that Adam Smith addressed in the first work of economic science: What causes the differences in wealth among nations?

Many people had written about economics before **Adam Smith***, but he made economics a science. Born in 1723 in Kirkcaldy, a small fishing town near Edinburgh, Scotland, Smith was the only child of the town's customs officer. Lured from his professorship (he was a full professor at 28) by a wealthy Scottish duke who gave him a pension of £300 a year—ten times the average income at that time—Smith devoted ten years to writing his masterpiece:* An Inquiry into the Nature and Causes of the **Wealth of Nations***, published in 1776.*

Why, Adam Smith asked , are some nations wealthy while others are poor? He was pondering these questions at the height of the Industrial Revolution, and he answered by emphasizing the power of the division of labor and free markets in raising labor productivity.

To illustrate his argument, Adam Smith described two pin factories. In the first, one person, using the hand tools available in the 1770s, could make 20 pins a day. In the other, by using those same hand tools but breaking the process into a number of individually small operations in which people specialize—by the division of labor—ten people could make a staggering 48,000 pins a day. One draws

Every individual who intends only his own gain is led by an invisible hand to promote an end (the public good) which was no part of his intention.

ADAM SMITH
The Wealth of Nations

out the wire, another straightens it, a third cuts it, a fourth points it, a fifth grinds it. Three specialists make the head, and a fourth attaches it. Finally, the pin is polished and packaged.

But a large market is needed to support the division of labor: One factory employing ten workers would need to sell more than 15 million pins a year to stay in business!

JAGDISH BHAGWATI is University Professor at Columbia University. Born in India in 1934, he studied at Cambridge University in England, MIT, and Oxford University before returning to India. He returned to teach at MIT in 1968 and moved to Columbia in 1980. A prolific scholar, Professor Bhagwati also writes in leading newspapers and magazines throughout the world. He has been much honored for both his scientific work and his impact on public policy. His greatest contributions are in international trade but extend also to developmental problems and the study of political economy.

Michael Parkin talked with Jagdish Bhagwati about his work and the progress that economists have made in understanding the benefits of economic growth and international trade since the pioneering work of Adam Smith.

Professor Bhagwati, what attracted you to economics?

When you come from India, where poverty hits the eye, it is easy to be attracted to economics, which can be used to bring prosperity and create jobs to pull up the poor into gainful employment.

I learned later that there are two broad types of economist: those who treat the subject as an arid mathematical toy and those who see it as a serious social science.

If Cambridge, where I went as an undergraduate, had been interested in esoteric mathematical economics, I would have opted for something else. But the Cambridge economists from whom I learned—many among the greatest figures in the discipline—saw economics as a social science. I therefore saw the power of economics as a tool to address India's poverty and was immediately hooked.

After Cambridge and MIT, you went to Oxford and then back to India. What did you do in India?

I joined the Planning Commission in New Delhi, where my first big job was to find ways of raising the bottom 30 percent of India's population out of poverty to a "minimum income" level.

And what did you prescribe?

My main prescription was to "grow the pie." My research suggested that the share of the bottom 30 percent of the pie did not seem to vary dramatically with differences in economic and political systems. So growth in the pie seemed to be the principal (but not the only) component of an anti-poverty strategy. To supplement growth's good effects on the poor, the Indian planners were also dedicated to education, health, social reforms, and land reforms. Also, the access of the lowest-income and socially disadvantaged groups to the growth process and its benefits was to be improved in many ways, such as extension of credit without collateral.

Today, this strategy has no rivals. Much empirical work shows that where growth has occurred, poverty has lessened. It is nice to know that one's basic take on an issue of such central importance to humanity's well-being has been borne out by experience!

> My main prescription was to "grow the pie." … Much empirical work shows that where growth has occurred, poverty has lessened.

*Read the full interview with Jagdish Bhagwati in **MyEconLab**.

DEMAND AND SUPPLY

After studying this chapter, you will be able to:

◆ Describe a competitive market and think about a price as an opportunity cost

◆ Explain the influences on demand

◆ Explain the influences on supply

◆ Explain how demand and supply determine prices and quantities bought and sold

◆ Use the demand and supply model to make predictions about changes in prices and quantities

In 2010, the prices of napa cabbage and kimchi in Korea rose rapidly. Why do some prices rise? And why do some prices fall, and some fluctuate?

This chapter answers these questions. The demand and supply model that you're about to study is the main tool of economics. It explains how prices are determined and how they guide the use of resources to influence What, How, and For Whom goods and services are produced.

At the end of the chapter in *Reading Between the Lines*, we'll apply the demand and supply model to the Korean markets for napa cabbage and kimchi and explain why their prices increased in 2010 and why the price rises are expected to be temporary.

55

◆▶ Markets and Prices

When you need a new pair of running shoes, want a bagel and a latte, plan to upgrade your cell phone, or need to fly home for Thanksgiving, you must find a place where people sell those items or offer those services. The place in which you find them is a *market*. You learned in Chapter 2 (p. 44) that a market is any arrangement that enables buyers and sellers to get information and to do business with each other.

A market has two sides: buyers and sellers. There are markets for *goods* such as apples and hiking boots, for *services* such as haircuts and tennis lessons, for *factors of production* such as computer programmers and earthmovers, and for other manufactured *inputs* such as memory chips and auto parts. There are also markets for money such as Japanese yen and for financial securities such as Yahoo! stock. Only our imagination limits what can be traded in markets.

Some markets are physical places where buyers and sellers meet and where an auctioneer or a broker helps to determine the prices. Examples of this type of market are the New York Stock Exchange and the wholesale fish, meat, and produce markets.

Some markets are groups of people spread around the world who never meet and know little about each other but are connected through the Internet or by telephone and fax. Examples are the e-commerce markets and the currency markets.

But most markets are unorganized collections of buyers and sellers. You do most of your trading in this type of market. An example is the market for basketball shoes. The buyers in this $3 billion-a-year market are the 45 million Americans who play basketball (or who want to make a fashion statement). The sellers are the tens of thousands of retail sports equipment and footwear stores. Each buyer can visit several different stores, and each seller knows that the buyer has a choice of stores.

Markets vary in the intensity of competition that buyers and sellers face. In this chapter, we're going to study a **competitive market**—a market that has many buyers and many sellers, so no single buyer or seller can influence the price.

Producers offer items for sale only if the price is high enough to cover their opportunity cost. And consumers respond to changing opportunity cost by seeking cheaper alternatives to expensive items.

We are going to study how people respond to *prices* and the forces that determine prices. But to pursue these tasks, we need to understand the relationship between a price and an opportunity cost.

In everyday life, the *price* of an object is the number of dollars that must be given up in exchange for it. Economists refer to this price as the **money price**.

The *opportunity cost* of an action is the highest-valued alternative forgone. If, when you buy a cup of coffee, the highest-valued thing you forgo is some gum, then the opportunity cost of the coffee is the *quantity* of gum forgone. We can calculate the quantity of gum forgone from the money prices of the coffee and the gum.

If the money price of coffee is $1 a cup and the money price of gum is 50¢ a pack, then the opportunity cost of one cup of coffee is two packs of gum. To calculate this opportunity cost, we divide the price of a cup of coffee by the price of a pack of gum and find the *ratio* of one price to the other. The ratio of one price to another is called a **relative price**, and a *relative price is an opportunity cost.*

We can express the relative price of coffee in terms of gum or any other good. The normal way of expressing a relative price is in terms of a "basket" of all goods and services. To calculate this relative price, we divide the money price of a good by the money price of a "basket" of all goods (called a *price index*). The resulting relative price tells us the opportunity cost of the good in terms of how much of the "basket" we must give up to buy it.

The demand and supply model that we are about to study determines *relative prices,* and the word "price" means *relative* price. When we predict that a price will fall, we do not mean that its *money* price will fall—although it might. We mean that its *relative* price will fall. That is, its price will fall *relative* to the average price of other goods and services.

◆ REVIEW QUIZ

1 What is the distinction between a money price and a relative price?
2 Explain why a relative price is an opportunity cost.
3 Think of examples of goods whose relative price has risen or fallen by a large amount.

You can work these questions in Study Plan 3.1 and get instant feedback.   MyEconLab

Let's begin our study of demand and supply, starting with demand.

◗ Demand

If you demand something, then you

1. Want it.
2. Can afford it.
3. Plan to buy it.

Wants are the unlimited desires or wishes that people have for goods and services. How many times have you thought that you would like something "if only you could afford it" or "if it weren't so expensive"? Scarcity guarantees that many—perhaps most—of our wants will never be satisfied. Demand reflects a decision about which wants to satisfy.

The **quantity demanded** of a good or service is the amount that consumers plan to buy during a given time period at a particular price. The quantity demanded is not necessarily the same as the quantity actually bought. Sometimes the quantity demanded exceeds the amount of goods available, so the quantity bought is less than the quantity demanded.

The quantity demanded is measured as an amount per unit of time. For example, suppose that you buy one cup of coffee a day. The quantity of coffee that you demand can be expressed as 1 cup per day, 7 cups per week, or 365 cups per year.

Many factors influence buying plans, and one of them is the price. We look first at the relationship between the quantity demanded of a good and its price. To study this relationship, we keep all other influences on buying plans the same and we ask: How, other things remaining the same, does the quantity demanded of a good change as its price changes?

The law of demand provides the answer.

The Law of Demand

The **law of demand** states:

> Other things remaining the same, the higher the price of a good, the smaller is the quantity demanded; and the lower the price of a good, the greater is the quantity demanded.

Why does a higher price reduce the quantity demanded? For two reasons:

■ Substitution effect
■ Income effect

Substitution Effect When the price of a good rises, other things remaining the same, its *relative* price—its opportunity cost—rises. Although each good is unique, it has *substitutes*—other goods that can be used in its place. As the opportunity cost of a good rises, the incentive to economize on its use and switch to a substitute becomes stronger.

Income Effect When a price rises, other things remaining the same, the price rises *relative* to income. Faced with a higher price and an unchanged income, people cannot afford to buy all the things they previously bought. They must decrease the quantities demanded of at least some goods and services. Normally, the good whose price has increased will be one of the goods that people buy less of.

To see the substitution effect and the income effect at work, think about the effects of a change in the price of an energy bar. Several different goods are substitutes for an energy bar. For example, an energy drink could be consumed instead of an energy bar.

Suppose that an energy bar initially sells for $3 and then its price falls to $1.50. People now substitute energy bars for energy drinks—the substitution effect. And with a budget that now has some slack from the lower price of an energy bar, people buy even more energy bars—the income effect. The quantity of energy bars demanded increases for these two reasons.

Now suppose that an energy bar initially sells for $3 and then the price doubles to $6. People now buy fewer energy bars and more energy drinks—the substitution effect. And faced with a tighter budget, people buy even fewer energy bars—the income effect. The quantity of energy bars demanded decreases for these two reasons.

Demand Curve and Demand Schedule

You are now about to study one of the two most used curves in economics: the demand curve. You are also going to encounter one of the most critical distinctions: the distinction between *demand* and *quantity demanded*.

The term **demand** refers to the entire relationship between the price of a good and the quantity demanded of that good. Demand is illustrated by the demand curve and the demand schedule. The term *quantity demanded* refers to a point on a demand curve—the quantity demanded at a particular price.

Figure 3.1 shows the demand curve for energy bars. A **demand curve** shows the relationship between the quantity demanded of a good and its price when all other influences on consumers' planned purchases remain the same.

The table in Fig. 3.1 is the demand schedule for energy bars. A *demand schedule* lists the quantities demanded at each price when all the other influences on consumers' planned purchases remain the same. For example, if the price of a bar is 50¢, the quantity demanded is 22 million a week. If the price is $2.50, the quantity demanded is 5 million a week. The other rows of the table show the quantities demanded at prices of $1.00, $1.50, and $2.00.

We graph the demand schedule as a demand curve with the quantity demanded on the *x*-axis and the price on the *y*-axis. The points on the demand curve labeled *A* through *E* correspond to the rows of the demand schedule. For example, point *A* on the graph shows a quantity demanded of 22 million energy bars a week at a price of 50¢ a bar.

Willingness and Ability to Pay Another way of looking at the demand curve is as a willingness-and-ability-to-pay curve. The willingness and ability to pay is a measure of *marginal benefit.*

If a small quantity is available, the highest price that someone is willing and able to pay for one more unit is high. But as the quantity available increases, the marginal benefit of each additional unit falls and the highest price that someone is willing and able to pay also falls along the demand curve.

In Fig. 3.1, if only 5 million energy bars are available each week, the highest price that someone is willing to pay for the 5 millionth bar is $2.50. But if 22 million energy bars are available each week, someone is willing to pay 50¢ for the last bar bought.

A Change in Demand

When any factor that influences buying plans changes, other than the price of the good, there is a **change in demand**. Figure 3.2 illustrates an increase in demand. When demand increases, the demand curve shifts rightward and the quantity demanded at each price is greater. For example, at $2.50 a bar, the quantity demanded on the original (blue) demand curve is 5 million energy bars a week. On the new (red) demand curve, at $2.50 a bar, the quantity demanded is 15 million bars a week. Look closely at the numbers in the table and check that the quantity demanded at each price is greater.

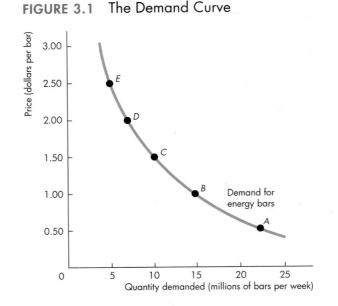

FIGURE 3.1   The Demand Curve

	Price (dollars per bar)	Quantity demanded (millions of bars per week)
A	0.50	22
B	1.00	15
C	1.50	10
D	2.00	7
E	2.50	5

The table shows a demand schedule for energy bars. At a price of 50¢ a bar, 22 million bars a week are demanded; at a price of $1.50 a bar, 10 million bars a week are demanded. The demand curve shows the relationship between quantity demanded and price, other things remaining the same. The demand curve slopes downward: As the price falls, the quantity demanded increases.

The demand curve can be read in two ways. For a given price, the demand curve tells us the quantity that people plan to buy. For example, at a price of $1.50 a bar, people plan to buy 10 million bars a week. For a given quantity, the demand curve tells us the maximum price that consumers are willing and able to pay for the last bar available. For example, the maximum price that consumers will pay for the 15 millionth bar is $1.00.

————MyEconLab animation——

FIGURE 3.2   An Increase in Demand

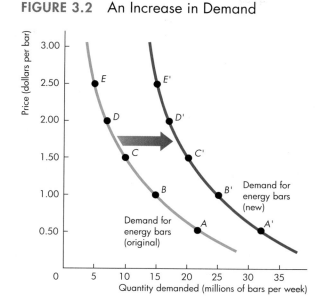

A change in any influence on buying plans other than the price of the good itself results in a new demand schedule and a shift of the demand curve. A change in income changes the demand for energy bars. At a price of $1.50 a bar, 10 million bars a week are demanded at the original income (row C of the table) and 20 million bars a week are demanded at the new higher income (row C'). A rise in income increases the demand for energy bars. The demand curve shifts *rightward*, as shown by the shift arrow and the resulting red curve.

Original demand schedule Original income		New demand schedule New higher income		
	Price (dollars per bar)	Quantity demanded (millions of bars per week)	Price (dollars per bar)	Quantity demanded (millions of bars per week)
A	0.50	22	A' 0.50	32
B	1.00	15	B' 1.00	25
C	1.50	10	C' 1.50	20
D	2.00	7	D' 2.00	17
E	2.50	5	E' 2.50	15

————— MyEconLab animation —————

Six main factors bring changes in demand. They are changes in

- The prices of related goods
- Expected future prices
- Income
- Expected future income and credit
- Population
- Preferences

Prices of Related Goods The quantity of energy bars that consumers plan to buy depends in part on the prices of substitutes for energy bars. A **substitute** is a good that can be used in place of another good. For example, a bus ride is a substitute for a train ride; a hamburger is a substitute for a hot dog; and an energy drink is a substitute for an energy bar. If the price of a substitute for an energy bar rises, people buy less of the substitute and more energy bars. For example, if the price of an energy drink rises, people buy fewer energy drinks and more energy bars. The demand for energy bars increases.

The quantity of energy bars that people plan to buy also depends on the prices of complements with energy bars. A **complement** is a good that is used in conjunction with another good. Hamburgers and fries are complements, and so are energy bars and exercise. If the price of an hour at the gym falls, people buy more gym time *and more* energy bars.

Expected Future Prices If the expected future price of a good rises and if the good can be stored, the opportunity cost of obtaining the good for future use is lower today than it will be in the future when people expect the price to be higher. So people retime their purchases—they substitute over time. They buy more of the good now before its price is expected to rise (and less afterward), so the demand for the good today increases.

For example, suppose that a Florida frost damages the season's orange crop. You expect the price of orange juice to rise, so you fill your freezer with enough frozen juice to get you through the next six months. Your current demand for frozen orange juice has increased, and your future demand has decreased.

Similarly, if the expected future price of a good falls, the opportunity cost of buying the good today is high relative to what it is expected to be in the future. So again, people retime their purchases. They buy less of the good now before its price is expected to fall, so the demand for the good decreases today and increases in the future.

Computer prices are constantly falling, and this fact poses a dilemma. Will you buy a new computer now, in time for the start of the school year, or will you wait until the price has fallen some more? Because people expect computer prices to keep falling, the current demand for computers is less (and the future demand is greater) than it otherwise would be.

Income Consumers' income influences demand. When income increases, consumers buy more of most goods; and when income decreases, consumers buy less of most goods. Although an increase in income leads to an increase in the demand for *most* goods, it does not lead to an increase in the demand for *all* goods. A **normal good** is one for which demand increases as income increases. An **inferior good** is one for which demand decreases as income increases. As incomes increase, the demand for air travel (a normal good) increases and the demand for long-distance bus trips (an inferior good) decreases.

Expected Future Income and Credit When expected future income increases or credit becomes easier to get, demand for a good might increase now. For example, a salesperson gets the news that she will receive a big bonus at the end of the year, so she goes into debt and buys a new car right now, rather than waiting until she receives the bonus.

Population Demand also depends on the size and the age structure of the population. The larger the population, the greater is the demand for all goods and services; the smaller the population, the smaller is the demand for all goods and services.

For example, the demand for parking spaces or movies or just about anything that you can imagine is much greater in New York City (population 7.5 million) than it is in Boise, Idaho (population 150,000).

Also, the larger the proportion of the population in a given age group, the greater is the demand for the goods and services used by that age group.

For example, during the 1990s, a decrease in the college-age population decreased the demand for college places. During those same years, the number of Americans aged 85 years and over increased by more than 1 million. As a result, the demand for nursing home services increased.

TABLE 3.1   The Demand for Energy Bars

The Law of Demand

The quantity of energy bars demanded

Decreases if:	Increases if:
■ The price of an energy bar rises	■ The price of an energy bar falls

Changes in Demand

The demand for energy bars

Decreases if:	Increases if:
■ The price of a substitute falls	■ The price of a substitute rises
■ The price of a complement rises	■ The price of a complement falls
■ The expected future price of an energy bar falls	■ The expected future price of an energy bar rises
■ Income falls*	■ Income rises*
■ Expected future income falls or credit becomes harder to get*	■ Expected future income rises or credit becomes easier to get*
■ The population decreases	■ The population increases

*An energy bar is a normal good.

Preferences Demand depends on preferences. *Preferences* determine the value that people place on each good and service. Preferences depend on such things as the weather, information, and fashion. For example, greater health and fitness awareness has shifted preferences in favor of energy bars, so the demand for energy bars has increased.

Table 3.1 summarizes the influences on demand and the direction of those influences.

A Change in the Quantity Demanded Versus a Change in Demand

Changes in the influences on buying plans bring either a change in the quantity demanded or a change in demand. Equivalently, they bring either a movement along the demand curve or a shift of the demand curve. The distinction between a change in the quantity demanded and a change in demand is the same as that between a movement along the demand curve and a shift of the demand curve.

A point on the demand curve shows the quantity demanded at a given price, so a movement along the demand curve shows a **change in the quantity demanded**. The entire demand curve shows demand, so a shift of the demand curve shows a *change in demand*. Figure 3.3 illustrates these distinctions.

Movement Along the Demand Curve If the price of the good changes but no other influence on buying plans changes, we illustrate the effect as a movement along the demand curve.

A fall in the price of a good increases the quantity demanded of it. In Fig. 3.3, we illustrate the effect of a fall in price as a movement down along the demand curve D_0.

A rise in the price of a good decreases the quantity demanded of it. In Fig. 3.3, we illustrate the effect of a rise in price as a movement up along the demand curve D_0.

A Shift of the Demand Curve If the price of a good remains constant but some other influence on buying plans changes, there is a change in demand for that good. We illustrate a change in demand as a shift of the demand curve. For example, if more people work out at the gym, consumers buy more energy bars regardless of the price of a bar. That is what a rightward shift of the demand curve shows—more energy bars are demanded at each price.

In Fig. 3.3, there is a *change in demand* and the demand curve shifts when any influence on buying plans changes, other than the price of the good. Demand *increases* and the demand curve *shifts rightward* (to the red demand curve D_1) if the price of a substitute rises, the price of a complement falls, the expected future price of the good rises, income increases (for a normal good), expected future income or credit increases, or the population increases. Demand *decreases* and the demand curve *shifts leftward* (to the red demand curve D_2) if the price of a substitute falls, the price of a complement rises, the expected future price of the good falls, income decreases (for a normal good), expected future income or credit decreases, or the population decreases. (For an inferior good, the effects of changes in income are in the opposite direction to those described above.)

FIGURE 3.3 A Change in the Quantity Demanded Versus a Change in Demand

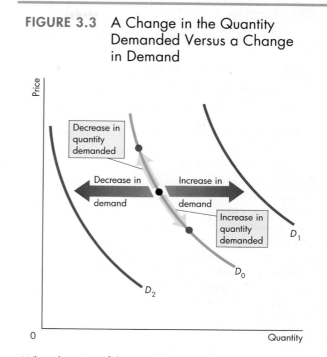

When the price of the good changes, there is a movement along the demand curve and *a change in the quantity demanded*, shown by the blue arrows on demand curve D_0. When any other influence on buying plans changes, there is a shift of the demand curve and a *change in demand*. An increase in demand shifts the demand curve rightward (from D_0 to D_1). A decrease in demand shifts the demand curve leftward (from D_0 to D_2).

MyEconLab animation

REVIEW QUIZ

1 Define the quantity demanded of a good or service.
2 What is the law of demand and how do we illustrate it?
3 What does the demand curve tell us about the price that consumers are willing to pay?
4 List all the influences on buying plans that change demand, and for each influence, say whether it increases or decreases demand.
5 Why does demand not change when the price of a good changes with no change in the other influences on buying plans?

You can work these questions in Study Plan 3.2 and get instant feedback.   MyEconLab

► Supply

If a firm supplies a good or service, the firm

1. Has the resources and technology to produce it.
2. Can profit from producing it.
3. Plans to produce it and sell it.

A supply is more than just having the *resources* and the *technology* to produce something. *Resources and technology* are the constraints that limit what is possible.

Many useful things can be produced, but they are not produced unless it is profitable to do so. Supply reflects a decision about which technologically feasible items to produce.

The **quantity supplied** of a good or service is the amount that producers plan to sell during a given time period at a particular price. The quantity supplied is not necessarily the same amount as the quantity actually sold. Sometimes the quantity supplied is greater than the quantity demanded, so the quantity sold is less than the quantity supplied.

Like the quantity demanded, the quantity supplied is measured as an amount per unit of time. For example, suppose that GM produces 1,000 cars a day. The quantity of cars supplied by GM can be expressed as 1,000 a day, 7,000 a week, or 365,000 a year. Without the time dimension, we cannot tell whether a particular quantity is large or small.

Many factors influence selling plans, and again one of them is the price of the good. We look first at the relationship between the quantity supplied of a good and its price. Just as we did when we studied demand, to isolate the relationship between the quantity supplied of a good and its price, we keep all other influences on selling plans the same and ask: How does the quantity supplied of a good change as its price changes when other things remain the same?

The law of supply provides the answer.

The Law of Supply

The **law of supply** states:

Other things remaining the same, the higher the price of a good, the greater is the quantity supplied; and the lower the price of a good, the smaller is the quantity supplied.

Why does a higher price increase the quantity supplied? It is because *marginal cost increases.* As the quantity produced of any good increases, the marginal cost of producing the good increases. (See Chapter 2, p. 35 to review marginal cost.)

It is never worth producing a good if the price received for the good does not at least cover the marginal cost of producing it. When the price of a good rises, other things remaining the same, producers are willing to incur a higher marginal cost, so they increase production. The higher price brings forth an increase in the quantity supplied.

Let's now illustrate the law of supply with a supply curve and a supply schedule.

Supply Curve and Supply Schedule

You are now going to study the second of the two most used curves in economics: the supply curve. You're also going to learn about the critical distinction between *supply* and *quantity supplied*.

The term **supply** refers to the entire relationship between the price of a good and the quantity supplied of it. Supply is illustrated by the supply curve and the supply schedule. The term *quantity supplied* refers to a point on a supply curve—the quantity supplied at a particular price.

Figure 3.4 shows the supply curve of energy bars. A **supply curve** shows the relationship between the quantity supplied of a good and its price when all other influences on producers' planned sales remain the same. The supply curve is a graph of a supply schedule.

The table in Fig. 3.4 sets out the supply schedule for energy bars. A *supply schedule* lists the quantities supplied at each price when all the other influences on producers' planned sales remain the same. For example, if the price of an energy bar is 50¢, the quantity supplied is zero—in row *A* of the table. If the price of an energy bar is $1.00, the quantity supplied is 6 million energy bars a week—in row *B*. The other rows of the table show the quantities supplied at prices of $1.50, $2.00, and $2.50.

To make a supply curve, we graph the quantity supplied on the *x*-axis and the price on the *y*-axis. The points on the supply curve labeled *A* through *E* correspond to the rows of the supply schedule. For example, point *A* on the graph shows a quantity supplied of zero at a price of 50¢ an energy bar. Point *E* shows a quantity supplied of 15 million bars at $2.50 an energy bar.

FIGURE 3.4   The Supply Curve

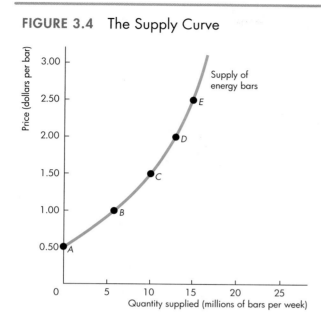

	Price (dollars per bar)	Quantity supplied (millions of bars per week)
A	0.50	0
B	1.00	6
C	1.50	10
D	2.00	13
E	2.50	15

The table shows the supply schedule of energy bars. For example, at a price of $1.00, 6 million bars a week are supplied; at a price of $2.50, 15 million bars a week are supplied. The supply curve shows the relationship between the quantity supplied and the price, other things remaining the same. The supply curve slopes upward: As the price of a good increases, the quantity supplied increases.

A supply curve can be read in two ways. For a given price, the supply curve tells us the quantity that producers plan to sell at that price. For example, at a price of $1.50 a bar, producers are planning to sell 10 million bars a week. For a given quantity, the supply curve tells us the minimum price at which producers are willing to sell one more bar. For example, if 15 million bars are produced each week, the lowest price at which a producer is willing to sell the 15 millionth bar is $2.50.

MyEconLab animation

Minimum Supply Price The supply curve can be interpreted as a minimum-supply-price curve—a curve that shows the lowest price at which someone is willing to sell. This lowest price is the *marginal cost*.

If a small quantity is produced, the lowest price at which someone is willing to sell one more unit is low. But as the quantity produced increases, the marginal cost of each additional unit rises, so the lowest price at which someone is willing to sell an additional unit rises along the supply curve.

In Fig. 3.4, if 15 million bars are produced each week, the lowest price at which someone is willing to sell the 15 millionth bar is $2.50. But if 10 million bars are produced each week, someone is willing to accept $1.50 for the last bar produced.

A Change in Supply

When any factor that influences selling plans other than the price of the good changes, there is a **change in supply**. Six main factors bring changes in supply. They are changes in

- The prices of factors of production
- The prices of related goods produced
- Expected future prices
- The number of suppliers
- Technology
- The state of nature

Prices of Factors of Production The prices of the factors of production used to produce a good influence its supply. To see this influence, think about the supply curve as a minimum-supply-price curve. If the price of a factor of production rises, the lowest price that a producer is willing to accept for that good rises, so supply decreases. For example, during 2008, as the price of jet fuel increased, the supply of air travel decreased. Similarly, a rise in the minimum wage decreases the supply of hamburgers.

Prices of Related Goods Produced The prices of related goods that firms produce influence supply. For example, if the price of energy gel rises, firms switch production from bars to gel. The supply of energy bars decreases. Energy bars and energy gel are *substitutes in production*—goods that can be produced by using the same resources. If the price of beef rises, the supply of cowhide increases. Beef and cowhide are *complements in production*—goods that must be produced together.

Expected Future Prices If the expected future price of a good rises, the return from selling the good in the future increases and is higher than it is today. So supply decreases today and increases in the future.

The Number of Suppliers The larger the number of firms that produce a good, the greater is the supply of the good. As new firms enter an industry, the supply in that industry increases. As firms leave an industry, the supply in that industry decreases.

Technology The term "technology" is used broadly to mean the way that factors of production are used to produce a good. A technology change occurs when a new method is discovered that lowers the cost of producing a good. For example, new methods used in the factories that produce computer chips have lowered the cost and increased the supply of chips.

The State of Nature The state of nature includes all the natural forces that influence production. It includes the state of the weather and, more broadly, the natural environment. Good weather can increase the supply of many agricultural products and bad weather can decrease their supply. Extreme natural events such as earthquakes, tornadoes, and hurricanes can also influence supply.

Figure 3.5 illustrates an increase in supply. When supply increases, the supply curve shifts rightward and the quantity supplied at each price is larger. For example, at $1.00 per bar, on the original (blue) supply curve, the quantity supplied is 6 million bars a week. On the new (red) supply curve, the quantity supplied is 15 million bars a week. Look closely at the numbers in the table in Fig. 3.5 and check that the quantity supplied is larger at each price.

Table 3.2 summarizes the influences on supply and the directions of those influences.

A Change in the Quantity Supplied Versus a Change in Supply

Changes in the influences on selling plans bring either a change in the quantity supplied or a change in supply. Equivalently, they bring either a movement along the supply curve or a shift of the supply curve.

A point on the supply curve shows the quantity supplied at a given price. A movement along the supply curve shows a **change in the quantity supplied**. The entire supply curve shows supply. A shift of the supply curve shows a *change in supply*.

FIGURE 3.5   An Increase in Supply

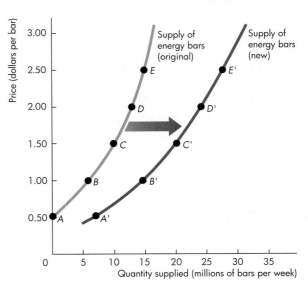

Original supply schedule Old technology			New supply schedule New technology		
	Price (dollars per bar)	Quantity supplied (millions of bars per week)		Price (dollars per bar)	Quantity supplied (millions of bars per week)
A	0.50	0	A'	0.50	7
B	1.00	6	B'	1.00	15
C	1.50	10	C'	1.50	20
D	2.00	13	D'	2.00	25
E	2.50	15	E'	2.50	27

A change in any influence on selling plans other than the price of the good itself results in a new supply schedule and a shift of the supply curve. For example, a new, cost-saving technology for producing energy bars changes the supply of energy bars. At a price of $1.50 a bar, 10 million bars a week are supplied when producers use the old technology (row C of the table) and 20 million energy bars a week are supplied when producers use the new technology (row C'). An advance in technology *increases* the supply of energy bars. The supply curve shifts *rightward*, as shown by the shift arrow and the resulting red curve.

MyEconLab animation

Figure 3.6 illustrates and summarizes these distinctions. If the price of the good changes and other things remain the same, there is a *change in the quantity supplied* of that good. If the price of the good falls, the quantity supplied decreases and there is a movement down along the supply curve S_0. If the price of the good rises, the quantity supplied increases and there is a movement up along the supply curve S_0. When any other influence on selling plans changes, the supply curve shifts and there is a *change in supply*. If supply increases, the supply curve shifts rightward to S_1. If supply decreases, the supply curve shifts leftward to S_2.

TABLE 3.2   The Supply of Energy Bars

The Law of Supply

The quantity of energy bars supplied

Decreases if:	*Increases if:*
■ The price of an energy bar falls	■ The price of an energy bar rises

---

Changes in Supply

The supply of energy bars

Decreases if:	*Increases if:*
■ The price of a factor of production used to produce energy bars rises	■ The price of a factor of production used to produce energy bars falls
■ The price of a substitute in production rises	■ The price of a substitute in production falls
■ The price of a complement in production falls	■ The price of a complement in production rises
■ The expected future price of an energy bar rises	■ The expected future price of an energy bar falls
■ The number of suppliers of bars decreases	■ The number of suppliers of bars increases
■ A technology change decreases energy bar production	■ A technology change increases energy bar production
■ A natural event decreases energy bar production	■ A natural event increases energy bar production

---

FIGURE 3.6   A Change in the Quantity Supplied Versus a Change in Supply

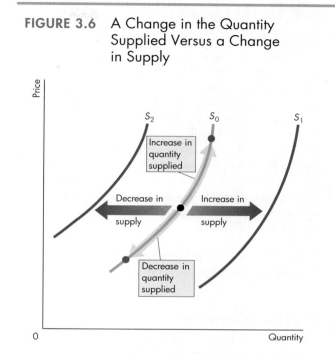

When the price of the good changes, there is a movement along the supply curve and a *change in the quantity supplied*, shown by the blue arrows on supply curve S_0. When any other influence on selling plans changes, there is a shift of the supply curve and a *change in supply*. An increase in supply shifts the supply curve rightward (from S_0 to S_1), and a decrease in supply shifts the supply curve leftward (from S_0 to S_2).

—— MyEconLab animation ——

REVIEW QUIZ

1 Define the quantity supplied of a good or service.
2 What is the law of supply and how do we illustrate it?
3 What does the supply curve tell us about the producer's minimum supply price?
4 List all the influences on selling plans, and for each influence, say whether it changes supply.
5 What happens to the quantity of cell phones supplied and the supply of cell phones if the price of a cell phone falls?

You can work these questions in Study Plan 3.3 and get instant feedback.   MyEconLab

Now we're going to combine demand and supply and see how prices and quantities are determined.

Market Equilibrium

We have seen that when the price of a good rises, the quantity demanded *decreases* and the quantity supplied *increases*. We are now going to see how the price adjusts to coordinate buying plans and selling plans and achieve an equilibrium in the market.

An *equilibrium* is a situation in which opposing forces balance each other. Equilibrium in a market occurs when the price balances buying plans and selling plans. The **equilibrium price** is the price at which the quantity demanded equals the quantity supplied. The **equilibrium quantity** is the quantity bought and sold at the equilibrium price. A market moves toward its equilibrium because

- Price regulates buying and selling plans.
- Price adjusts when plans don't match.

Price as a Regulator

The price of a good regulates the quantities demanded and supplied. If the price is too high, the quantity supplied exceeds the quantity demanded. If the price is too low, the quantity demanded exceeds the quantity supplied. There is one price at which the quantity demanded equals the quantity supplied. Let's work out what that price is.

Figure 3.7 shows the market for energy bars. The table shows the demand schedule (from Fig. 3.1) and the supply schedule (from Fig. 3.4). If the price is 50¢ a bar, the quantity demanded is 22 million bars a week but no bars are supplied. There is a shortage of 22 million bars a week. The final column of the table shows this shortage. At a price of $1.00 a bar, there is still a shortage but only of 9 million bars a week.

If the price is $2.50 a bar, the quantity supplied is 15 million bars a week but the quantity demanded is only 5 million. There is a surplus of 10 million bars a week.

The one price at which there is neither a shortage nor a surplus is $1.50 a bar. At that price, the quantity demanded equals the quantity supplied: 10 million bars a week. The equilibrium price is $1.50 a bar, and the equilibrium quantity is 10 million bars a week.

Figure 3.7 shows that the demand curve and the supply curve intersect at the equilibrium price of $1.50 a bar. At each price *above* $1.50 a bar, there is a surplus of bars. For example, at $2.00 a bar, the surplus is 6

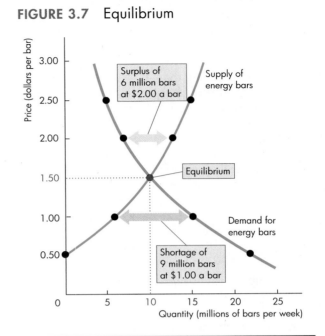

FIGURE 3.7   Equilibrium

Price (dollars per bar)	Quantity demanded	Quantity supplied	Shortage (–) or surplus (+)
	(millions of bars per week)		
0.50	22	0	–22
1.00	15	6	–9
1.50	**10**	**10**	**0**
2.00	7	13	+6
2.50	5	15	+10

The table lists the quantity demanded and the quantity supplied as well as the shortage or surplus of bars at each price. If the price is $1.00 a bar, 15 million bars a week are demanded and 6 million bars are supplied. There is a shortage of 9 million bars a week, and the price rises.

If the price is $2.00 a bar, 7 million bars a week are demanded and 13 million bars are supplied. There is a surplus of 6 million bars a week, and the price falls.

If the price is $1.50 a bar, 10 million bars a week are demanded and 10 million bars are supplied. There is neither a shortage nor a surplus, and the price does not change. The price at which the quantity demanded equals the quantity supplied is the equilibrium price, and 10 million bars a week is the equilibrium quantity.

———MyEconLab animation———

million bars a week, as shown by the blue arrow. At each price *below* $1.50 a bar, there is a shortage of bars. For example, at $1.00 a bar, the shortage is 9 million bars a week, as shown by the red arrow.

Price Adjustments

You've seen that if the price is below equilibrium, there is a shortage and that if the price is above equilibrium, there is a surplus. But can we count on the price to change and eliminate a shortage or a surplus? We can, because such price changes are beneficial to both buyers and sellers. Let's see why the price changes when there is a shortage or a surplus.

A Shortage Forces the Price Up Suppose the price of an energy bar is $1. Consumers plan to buy 15 million bars a week, and producers plan to sell 6 million bars a week. Consumers can't force producers to sell more than they plan, so the quantity that is actually offered for sale is 6 million bars a week. In this situation, powerful forces operate to increase the price and move it toward the equilibrium price. Some producers, noticing lines of unsatisfied consumers, raise the price. Some producers increase their output. As producers push the price up, the price rises toward its equilibrium. The rising price reduces the shortage because it decreases the quantity demanded and increases the quantity supplied. When the price has increased to the point at which there is no longer a shortage, the forces moving the price stop operating and the price comes to rest at its equilibrium.

A Surplus Forces the Price Down Suppose the price of a bar is $2. Producers plan to sell 13 million bars a week, and consumers plan to buy 7 million bars a week. Producers cannot force consumers to buy more than they plan, so the quantity that is actually bought is 7 million bars a week. In this situation, powerful forces operate to lower the price and move it toward the equilibrium price. Some producers, unable to sell the quantities of energy bars they planned to sell, cut their prices. In addition, some producers scale back production. As producers cut the price, the price falls toward its equilibrium. The falling price decreases the surplus because it increases the quantity demanded and decreases the quantity supplied. When the price has fallen to the point at which there is no longer a surplus, the forces moving the price stop operating and the price comes to rest at its equilibrium.

The Best Deal Available for Buyers and Sellers
When the price is below equilibrium, it is forced upward. Why don't buyers resist the increase and refuse to buy at the higher price? The answer is because they value the good more highly than its current price and they can't satisfy their demand at the current price. In some markets—for example, the markets that operate on eBay—the buyers might even be the ones who force the price up by offering to pay a higher price.

When the price is above equilibrium, it is bid downward. Why don't sellers resist this decrease and refuse to sell at the lower price? The answer is because their minimum supply price is below the current price and they cannot sell all they would like to at the current price. Sellers willingly lower the price to gain market share.

At the price at which the quantity demanded and the quantity supplied are equal, neither buyers nor sellers can do business at a better price. Buyers pay the highest price they are willing to pay for the last unit bought, and sellers receive the lowest price at which they are willing to supply the last unit sold.

When people freely make offers to buy and sell and when demanders try to buy at the lowest possible price and suppliers try to sell at the highest possible price, the price at which trade takes place is the equilibrium price—the price at which the quantity demanded equals the quantity supplied. The price coordinates the plans of buyers and sellers, and no one has an incentive to change it.

REVIEW QUIZ

1 What is the equilibrium price of a good or service?
2 Over what range of prices does a shortage arise? What happens to the price when there is a shortage?
3 Over what range of prices does a surplus arise? What happens to the price when there is a surplus?
4 Why is the price at which the quantity demanded equals the quantity supplied the equilibrium price?
5 Why is the equilibrium price the best deal available for both buyers and sellers?

You can work these questions in Study Plan 3.4 and get instant feedback.   MyEconLab

▶ Predicting Changes in Price and Quantity

The demand and supply model that we have just studied provides us with a powerful way of analyzing influences on prices and the quantities bought and sold. According to the model, a change in price stems from a change in demand, a change in supply, or a change in both demand and supply. Let's look first at the effects of a change in demand.

An Increase in Demand

If more people join health clubs, the demand for energy bars increases. The table in Fig. 3.8 shows the original and new demand schedules for energy bars as well as the supply schedule of energy bars.

The increase in demand creates a shortage at the original price and to eliminate the shortage, the price must rise.

Figure 3.8 shows what happens. The figure shows the original demand for and supply of energy bars. The original equilibrium price is $1.50 an energy bar, and the equilibrium quantity is 10 million energy bars a week. When demand increases, the demand curve shifts rightward. The equilibrium price rises to $2.50 an energy bar, and the quantity supplied increases to 15 million energy bars a week, as highlighted in the figure. There is an *increase in the quantity supplied* but *no change in supply*—a movement along, but no shift of, the supply curve.

A Decrease in Demand

We can reverse this change in demand. Start at a price of $2.50 a bar with 15 million energy bars a week being bought and sold, and then work out what happens if demand decreases to its original level. Such a decrease in demand might arise if people switch to energy gel (a substitute for energy bars). The decrease in demand shifts the demand curve leftward. The equilibrium price falls to $1.50 a bar, the quantity supplied decreases, and the equilibrium quantity decreases to 10 million bars a week.

We can now make our first two predictions:

1. When demand increases, the price rises and the quantity increases.
2. When demand decreases, the price falls and the quantity decreases.

FIGURE 3.8   The Effects of a Change in Demand

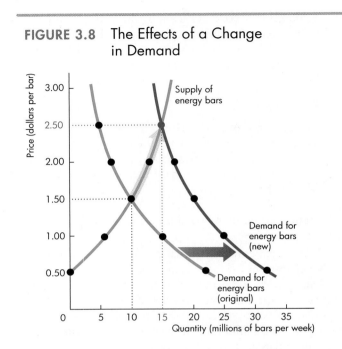

Price (dollars per bar)	Quantity demanded (millions of bars per week)		Quantity supplied (millions of bars per week)
	Original	New	
0.50	22	32	0
1.00	15	25	6
1.50	**10**	20	**10**
2.00	7	17	13
2.50	5	**15**	**15**

Initially, the demand for energy bars is the blue demand curve. The equilibrium price is $1.50 a bar, and the equilibrium quantity is 10 million bars a week. When more health-conscious people do more exercise, the demand for energy bars increases and the demand curve shifts rightward to become the red curve.

At $1.50 a bar, there is now a shortage of 10 million bars a week. The price of a bar rises to a new equilibrium of $2.50. As the price rises to $2.50, the quantity supplied increases—shown by the blue arrow on the supply curve—to the new equilibrium quantity of 15 million bars a week. Following an increase in demand, the quantity supplied increases but supply does not change—the supply curve does not shift.

MyEconLab animation

ECONOMICS IN THE NEWS

The Market for College Education

Obama Decries Rising Cost of College Education
President Obama told colleges, "You can't assume that you'll just jack up tuition every single year. ... In the coming decade, 60 percent of new jobs will require more than a high school diploma... Higher education is not a luxury. It's an economic imperative that every family in America should be able to afford."

Source: *The Associated Press*, January 27, 2012

THE DATA

The scatter diagram provides data on college enrollments and tuition from 1981 through 2010.

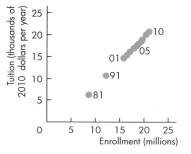

THE QUESTIONS

- What does the scatter diagram tell us?
- Why has college tuition increased? Is it because demand increased or supply increased?

THE ANSWERS

- The scatter diagram tells us that both tuition and enrollments have increased every year.
- An increase in demand brings a rise in the price (tuition) and an increase in the quantity (enrollments).
- An increase in supply brings a fall in the price and an increase in the quantity.
- Because both the price (tuition) and quantity (enrollments) have increased, the demand for college education has increased.
- The figure shows the market for college education.
- The supply curve of college education, S, slopes upward because the principle of increasing opportunity cost applies to college education just as it does to other goods and services.

- In 2001, the demand for college education was D_{2001}. The equilibrium tuition was \$15,000 and 16 million students were enrolled in college.
- Between 2001 and 2010:
  1) Income per person increased
  2) Population increased, and
  3) More new jobs required higher education.
- These (and possibly other) factors increased the demand for a college education. The demand curve shifted rightward to D_{2010}. Equilibrium tuition increased to \$21,000 and the quantity supplied increased to 21 million students.

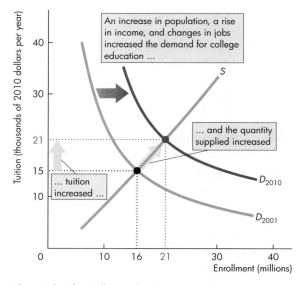

The Market for College Education

An Increase in Supply

When Nestlé (the producer of PowerBar) and other energy bar producers switch to a new cost-saving technology, the supply of energy bars increases. Figure 3.9 shows the new supply schedule (the same one that was shown in Fig. 3.5). What are the new equilibrium price and quantity? The price falls to $1.00 a bar, and the quantity increases to 15 million bars a week. You can see why by looking at the quantities demanded and supplied at the old price of $1.50 a bar. The new quantity supplied at that price is 20 million bars a week, and there is a surplus. The price falls. Only when the price is $1.00 a bar does the quantity supplied equal the quantity demanded.

Figure 3.9 illustrates the effect of an increase in supply. It shows the demand curve for energy bars and the original and new supply curves. The initial equilibrium price is $1.50 a bar, and the equilibrium quantity is 10 million bars a week. When supply increases, the supply curve shifts rightward. The equilibrium price falls to $1.00 a bar, and the quantity demanded increases to 15 million bars a week, highlighted in the figure. There is an *increase in the quantity demanded* but *no change in demand*—a movement along, but no shift of, the demand curve.

A Decrease in Supply

Start out at a price of $1.00 a bar with 15 million bars a week being bought and sold. Then suppose that the cost of labor or raw materials rises and the supply of energy bars decreases. The decrease in supply shifts the supply curve leftward. The equilibrium price rises to $1.50 a bar, the quantity demanded decreases, and the equilibrium quantity decreases to 10 million bars a week.

We can now make two more predictions:

1. When supply increases, the price falls and the quantity increases.
2. When supply decreases, the price rises and the quantity decreases.

You've now seen what happens to the price and the quantity when either demand or supply changes while the other one remains unchanged. In real markets, both demand and supply can change together. When this happens, to predict the changes in price and quantity, we must combine the effects that you've just seen. That is your final task in this chapter.

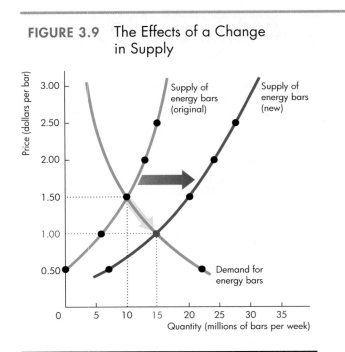

FIGURE 3.9   The Effects of a Change in Supply

Price (dollars per bar)	Quantity demanded (millions of bars per week)	Quantity supplied (millions of bars per week)	
		Original	New
0.50	22	0	7
1.00	15	6	15
1.50	10	10	20
2.00	7	13	25
2.50	5	15	27

Initially, the supply of energy bars is shown by the blue supply curve. The equilibrium price is $1.50 a bar, and the equilibrium quantity is 10 million bars a week. When the new cost-saving technology is adopted, the supply of energy bars increases and the supply curve shifts rightward to become the red curve.

At $1.50 a bar, there is now a surplus of 10 million bars a week. The price of an energy bar falls to a new equilibrium of $1.00 a bar. As the price falls to $1.00, the quantity demanded increases—shown by the blue arrow on the demand curve—to the new equilibrium quantity of 15 million bars a week. Following an increase in supply, the quantity demanded increases but demand does not change—the demand curve does not shift.

MyEconLab animation

◆ ECONOMICS IN THE NEWS

The Market for Gasoline

Gas Prices: Down and Headed Lower

The price of gasoline has been falling for more than a month. With oil prices also falling, more falls at the pump are expected.

Source: CNN Money, May 4, 2012

THE DATA

	Quantity (millions of gallons per week)	Price (dollars per gallon)
April 6, 2012	365	4.00
May 4, 2012	372	3.85

THE QUESTIONS

- What does the data table tell us?
- Why did the price of gasoline decrease? Is it because demand changed or because supply changed, and in which direction?

THE ANSWERS

- The data table tells us that between April and May 2012, the quantity of gasoline used increased and the price of gasoline fell.
- An increase in demand brings an increase in the quantity and a rise in the price.
- An increase in supply brings an increase in the quantity and a fall in the price.
- Because the quantity of gasoline used increased and the price of gasoline fell, there must have been in increase in the supply of gasoline.
- The supply of gasoline increases if the price of a factor of production used to produce gasoline falls. The news clip says the price of oil, which is used to produce gasoline, is falling. So the fall in the price of oil is the source of the increase in the supply.
- The figure illustrates the market for gasoline in 2012.
- The demand curve D_{April} shows the demand. In early April, the supply curve was S_0, the price was $4.00 per gallon, and the quantity used was 365 million gallons per day.
- By the end of April and early May, the lower price of oil had increased the supply of gasoline to S_1. The price fell to $3.85 per gallon and the quantity used increased to 372 million gallons per day.

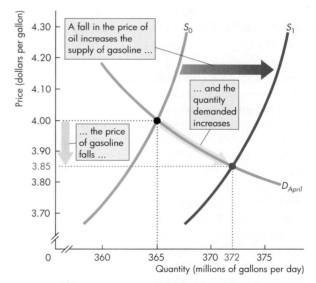

The Market for Gasoline in April 2012

- The lower price brought an increase in the quantity of gasoline demanded, which is shown by the movement along the demand curve.

All the Possible Changes in Demand and Supply

Figure 3.10 brings together and summarizes the effects of all the possible changes in demand and supply. With what you've learned about the effects of a change in *either* demand or supply, you can predict what happens if *both* demand and supply change together. Let's begin by reviewing what you already know.

Change in Demand with No Change in Supply The first row of Fig. 3.10, parts (a), (b), and (c), summarizes the effects of a change in demand with no change in supply. In part (a), with no change in either demand or supply, neither the price nor the quantity changes. With an *increase* in demand and no change in supply in part (b), both the price and quantity increase. And with a *decrease* in demand and no change in supply in part (c), both the price and the quantity decrease.

Change in Supply with No Change in Demand The first column of Fig. 3.10, parts (a), (d), and (g), summarizes the effects of a change in supply with no change in demand. With an *increase* in supply and no change in demand in part (d), the price falls and quantity increases. And with a *decrease* in supply and no change in demand in part (g), the price rises and the quantity decreases.

Increase in Both Demand and Supply You've seen that an increase in demand raises the price and increases the quantity. And you've seen that an increase in supply lowers the price and increases the quantity. Fig. 3.10(e) combines these two changes. Because either an increase in demand or an increase in supply increases the quantity, the quantity also increases when both demand and supply increase. But the effect on the price is uncertain. An increase in demand raises the price and an increase in supply lowers the price, so we can't say whether the price will rise or fall when both demand and supply increase. We need to know the magnitudes of the changes in demand and supply to predict the effects on price. In the example in Fig. 3.10(e), the price does not change. But notice that if demand increases by slightly more than the amount shown in the figure, the price will rise. And if supply increases by slightly more than the amount shown in the figure, the price will fall.

Decrease in Both Demand and Supply Figure 3.10(i) shows the case in which demand and supply *both decrease*. For the same reasons as those we've just reviewed, when both demand and supply decrease, the quantity decreases, and again the direction of the price change is uncertain.

Decrease in Demand and Increase in Supply You've seen that a decrease in demand lowers the price and decreases the quantity. And you've seen that an increase in supply lowers the price and increases the quantity. Fig. 3.10(f) combines these two changes. Both the decrease in demand and the increase in supply lower the price, so the price falls. But a decrease in demand decreases the quantity and an increase in supply increases the quantity, so we can't predict the direction in which the quantity will change unless we know the magnitudes of the changes in demand and supply. In the example in Fig. 3.10(f), the quantity does not change. But notice that if demand decreases by slightly more than the amount shown in the figure, the quantity will decrease; if supply increases by slightly more than the amount shown in the figure, the quantity will increase.

Increase in Demand and Decrease in Supply Figure 3.10(h) shows the case in which demand increases and supply decreases. Now, the price rises, and again the direction of the quantity change is uncertain.

REVIEW QUIZ

What is the effect on the price and quantity of MP3 players (such as the iPod) if

1 The price of a PC falls or the price of an MP3 download rises? (Draw the diagrams!)
2 More firms produce MP3 players or electronics workers' wages rise? (Draw the diagrams!)
3 Any two of the events in questions 1 and 2 occur together? (Draw the diagrams!)

You can work these questions in Study Plan 3.5 and get instant feedback.   MyEconLab

◆ To complete your study of demand and supply, take a look at *Reading Between the Lines* on pp. 74–75, which explains why the prices of napa cabbage and kimchi increased in 2010. Try to get into the habit of using the demand and supply model to understand price changes in your everyday life.

FIGURE 3.10   The Effects of All the Possible Changes in Demand and Supply

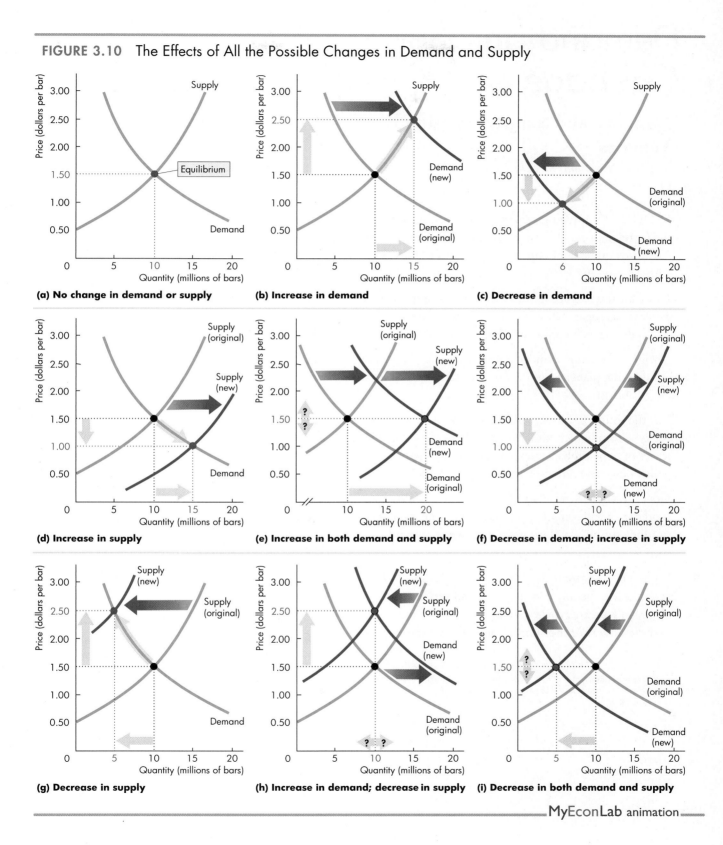

(a) **No change in demand or supply**

(b) **Increase in demand**

(c) **Decrease in demand**

(d) **Increase in supply**

(e) **Increase in both demand and supply**

(f) **Decrease in demand; increase in supply**

(g) **Decrease in supply**

(h) **Increase in demand; decrease in supply**

(i) **Decrease in both demand and supply**

MyEconLab animation

Demand and Supply: Cabbage and Kimchi

Demand and Supply: Surging Kimchi Prices Bite Korean Vendors

The Wall Street Journal Asia
October 4, 2010

SEOUL — South Korea faces a minicrisis in its staple condiment kimchi after an unusually long stretch of rain has sharply reduced harvests of napa cabbage and other produce. ... A 2.5-kilogram head of napa cabbage cost 11,500 won ($10.09) in South Korean grocery stores this week, up from about 4,000 won two weeks ago. ...

Hard-hit restaurants are thinking about charging for kimchi, a food that is usually as freely available as sugar, salt and pepper—even at restaurants that don't serve Korean cuisine—and more heavily consumed than those foods by many South Koreans. ...

The government responded Friday by suspending its tariffs on cabbage and radishes and announcing plans to buy 150 tons of fresh vegetables from China, with special emphasis on napa cabbage. ...

But the round (Chinese) cabbage is a poor substitute for the type from which kimchi is usually made—the long leaves of napa cabbage make it great for slathering on garlic, peppers, and other seasonings for kimchi. ...

Government officials played down the possibility that food prices will remain high for a long time, saying that produce supplies will improve once weather conditions turn favorable. ...

Yu Seong-hwa, manager at another Korean food restaurant in Seoul, said they stopped serving kimchi from Korean-grown cabbage several weeks ago and are now running short of access to Chinese-grown cabbage. ...

ESSENCE OF THE STORY

- Napa cabbage is the main ingredient for making the staple Korean condiment Kimchi.

- Bad weather has sharply reduced harvests of napa cabbage.

- A 2.5-kilogram head of napa cabbage cost 11,500 won (US$10.09) in grocery stores, compared to 4,000 won two weeks ago.

- Rising napa cabbage prices have also hit Korean restaurants.

- Napa cabbage prices are unlikely to remain high for a long time—supplies of the cabbage will improve once weather conditions turn favorable.

ECONOMIC ANALYSIS

- This news article is about two markets and their interaction: the markets for napa cabbages and kimchi.

- Napa cabbages grow well in cool, dry conditions but an unusually long stretch of rain has sharply reduced harvests.

- In Fig. 1, the demand for napa cabbage is D and the supply of cabbage is S_0. These curves intersect at an equilibrium quantity of 1,000 kilograms per day and an equilibrium price of 4,000 won.

- As a result of the heavy rains, the supply of napa cabbage has decreased, which is illustrated by the leftward shift of the supply curve to S_1.

- With no change in demand, the equilibrium price rises to 11,500 won and the equilibrium quantity decreases to 500 kilograms per day.

- A higher napa cabbage price has hit Korean restaurants, which are now considering charging for kimchi.

- Figure 2 shows the demand curve D and the supply curve S_0 of kimchi. These curves determine an equilibrium price of 2,500 won per plate and an equilibrium quantity of 5,000 plates per day.

- Napa cabbage is a factor of production used to make kimchi. A rise in the price of napa cabbage brings a decrease in the supply of kimchi, which is shown by a leftward shift of the supply curve to S_1.

- The equilibrium price rises to 4,000 won per plate and the equilibrium quantity decreases to 3,000 plates per day.

- When favorable weather returns, the supply of napa cabbage will return to its normal level and the supply curve in Fig. 1 will return to S_0. The price of napa cabbage will return to its normal level of 4,000 won per 2.5-kilogram head.

- When the price of napa cabbage returns to its normal level, the supply of kimchi will also return to its normal level and the supply curve in Fig. 2 will return to S_0. The price of kimchi will return to its normal level of 2,500 won per plate.

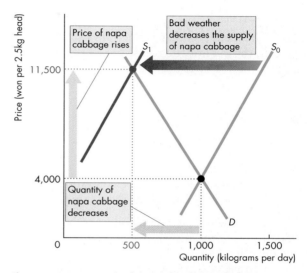

Figure 1 A Decrease in the Supply of Napa Cabbage

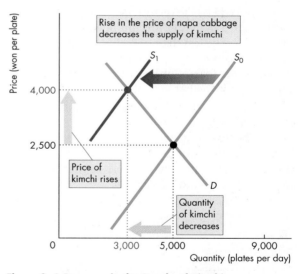

Figure 2 A Decrease in the Supply of Kimchi

MATHEMATICAL NOTE

Demand, Supply, and Equilibrium

Demand Curve

The law of demand says that as the price of a good or service falls, the quantity demanded of that good or service increases. We can illustrate the law of demand by drawing a graph of the demand curve or writing down an equation. When the demand curve is a straight line, the following equation describes it:

$$P = a - bQ_D,$$

where P is the price and Q_D is the quantity demanded. The a and b are positive constants.

The demand equation tells us three things:

1. The price at which no one is willing to buy the good (Q_D is zero). That is, if the price is a, then the quantity demanded is zero. You can see the price a in Fig. 1. It is the price at which the demand curve hits the y-axis—what we call the demand curve's "y-intercept."

2. As the price falls, the quantity demanded increases. If Q_D is a positive number, then the price P must be less than a. As Q_D gets larger, the price P becomes smaller. That is, as the quantity increases, the maximum price that buyers are willing to pay for the last unit of the good falls.

3. The constant b tells us how fast the maximum price that someone is willing to pay for the good falls as the quantity increases. That is, the constant b tells us about the steepness of the demand curve. The equation tells us that the slope of the demand curve is $-b$.

Supply Curve

The law of supply says that as the price of a good or service rises, the quantity supplied of that good or service increases. We can illustrate the law of supply by drawing a graph of the supply curve or writing down an equation. When the supply curve is a straight line, the following equation describes it:

$$P = c + dQ_S,$$

where P is the price and Q_S is the quantity supplied. The c and d are positive constants.

The supply equation tells us three things:

1. The price at which sellers are not willing to supply the good (Q_S is zero). That is, if the price is c, then no one is willing to sell the good. You can see the price c in Fig. 2. It is the price at which the supply curve hits the y-axis—what we call the supply curve's "y-intercept."

2. As the price rises, the quantity supplied increases. If Q_S is a positive number, then the price P must be greater than c. As Q_S increases, the price P becomes larger. That is, as the quantity increases, the minimum price that sellers are willing to accept for the last unit rises.

3. The constant d tells us how fast the minimum price at which someone is willing to sell the good rises as the quantity increases. That is, the constant d tells us about the steepness of the supply curve. The equation tells us that the slope of the supply curve is d.

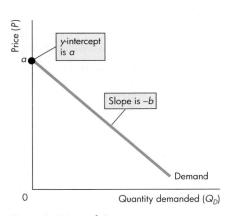

Figure 1 Demand Curve

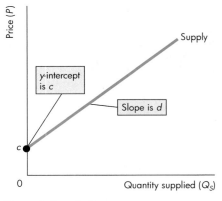

Figure 2 Supply Curve

Market Equilibrium

Demand and supply determine market equilibrium. Figure 3 shows the equilibrium price (P^*) and equilibrium quantity (Q^*) at the intersection of the demand curve and the supply curve.

We can use the equations to find the equilibrium price and equilibrium quantity. The price of a good adjusts until the quantity demanded Q_D equals the quantity supplied Q_S. So at the equilibrium price (P^*) and equilibrium quantity (Q^*),

$$Q_D = Q_S = Q^*.$$

To find the equilibrium price and equilibrium quantity, substitute Q^* for Q_D in the demand equation and Q^* for Q_S in the supply equation. Then the price is the equilibrium price (P^*), which gives

$$P^* = a - bQ^*$$
$$P^* = c + dQ^*.$$

Notice that

$$a - bQ^* = c + dQ^*.$$

Now solve for Q^*:

$$a - c = bQ^* + dQ^*$$
$$a - c = (b + d)Q^*$$
$$Q^* = \frac{a - c}{b + d}.$$

To find the equilibrium price, (P^*), substitute for Q^* in either the demand equation or the supply equation.

Using the demand equation, we have

$$P^* = a - b\left(\frac{a - c}{b + d}\right)$$
$$P^* = \frac{a(b + d) - b(a - c)}{b + d}$$
$$P^* = \frac{ad + bc}{b + d}.$$

Alternatively, using the supply equation, we have

$$P^* = c + d\left(\frac{a - c}{b + d}\right)$$
$$P^* = \frac{c(b + d) + d(a - c)}{b + d}$$
$$P^* = \frac{ad + bc}{b + d}.$$

An Example

The demand for ice-cream cones is

$$P = 800 - 2Q_D.$$

The supply of ice-cream cones is

$$P = 200 + 1Q_S.$$

The price of a cone is expressed in cents, and the quantities are expressed in cones per day.

To find the equilibrium price (P^*) and equilibrium quantity (Q^*), substitute Q^* for Q_D and Q_S and P^* for P. That is,

$$P^* = 800 - 2Q^*$$
$$P^* = 200 + 1Q^*$$

Now solve for Q^*:

$$800 - 2Q^* = 200 + 1Q^*$$
$$600 = 3Q^*$$
$$Q^* = 200.$$

And

$$P^* = 800 - 2(200)$$
$$= 400.$$

The equilibrium price is \$4 a cone, and the equilibrium quantity is 200 cones per day.

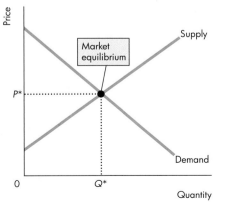

Figure 3 Market Equilibrium

SUMMARY

Key Points

Markets and Prices (p. 56)

- A competitive market is one that has so many buyers and sellers that no single buyer or seller can influence the price.
- Opportunity cost is a relative price.
- Demand and supply determine relative prices.

Working Problem 1 will give you a better understanding of markets and prices.

Demand (pp. 57–61)

- Demand is the relationship between the quantity demanded of a good and its price when all other influences on buying plans remain the same.
- The higher the price of a good, other things remaining the same, the smaller is the quantity demanded—the law of demand.
- Demand depends on the prices of related goods (substitutes and complements), expected future prices, income, expected future income and credit, the population, and preferences.

Working Problems 2 to 5 will give you a better understanding of demand.

Supply (pp. 62–65)

- Supply is the relationship between the quantity supplied of a good and its price when all other influences on selling plans remain the same.
- The higher the price of a good, other things remaining the same, the greater is the quantity supplied—the law of supply.

- Supply depends on the prices of factors of production used to produce a good, the prices of related goods produced, expected future prices, the number of suppliers, technology, and the state of nature.

Working Problems 6 to 9 will give you a better understanding of supply.

Market Equilibrium (pp. 66–67)

- At the equilibrium price, the quantity demanded equals the quantity supplied.
- At any price above the equilibrium price, there is a surplus and the price falls.
- At any price below the equilibrium price, there is a shortage and the price rises.

Working Problems 10 and 11 will give you a better understanding of market equilibrium.

Predicting Changes in Price and Quantity (pp. 68–73)

- An increase in demand brings a rise in the price and an increase in the quantity supplied. A decrease in demand brings a fall in the price and a decrease in the quantity supplied.
- An increase in supply brings a fall in the price and an increase in the quantity demanded. A decrease in supply brings a rise in the price and a decrease in the quantity demanded.
- An increase in demand and an increase in supply bring an increased quantity but an uncertain price change. An increase in demand and a decrease in supply bring a higher price but an uncertain change in quantity.

Working Problems 12 and 13 will give you a better understanding of predicting changes in price and quantity.

Key Terms

Change in demand, 58
Change in supply, 63
Change in the quantity
     demanded, 61
Change in the quantity supplied, 64
Competitive market, 56
Complement, 59
Demand, 57

Demand curve, 58
Equilibrium price, 66
Equilibrium quantity, 66
Inferior good, 60
Law of demand, 57
Law of supply, 62
Money price, 56
Normal good, 60

Quantity demanded, 57
Quantity supplied, 62
Relative price, 56
Substitute, 59
Supply, 62
Supply curve, 62

STUDY PLAN PROBLEMS AND APPLICATIONS

MyEconLab   You can work Problems 1 to 17 in MyEconLab Chapter 3 Study Plan and get instant feedback.

Markets and Prices (Study Plan 3.1)

1. William Gregg owned a mill in South Carolina. In December 1862, he placed a notice in the *Edgehill Advertiser* announcing his willingness to exchange cloth for food and other items. Here is an extract:

   1 yard of cloth for 1 pound of bacon
   2 yards of cloth for 1 pound of butter
   4 yards of cloth for 1 pound of wool
   8 yards of cloth for 1 bushel of salt

   a. What is the relative price of butter in terms of wool?
   b. If the money price of bacon was 20¢ a pound, what do you predict was the money price of butter?
   c. If the money price of bacon was 20¢ a pound and the money price of salt was $2.00 a bushel, do you think anyone would accept Mr. Gregg's offer of cloth for salt?

Demand (Study Plan 3.2)

2. The price of food increased during the past year.
   a. Explain why the law of demand applies to food just as it does to all other goods and services.
   b. Explain how the substitution effect influences food purchases and provide some examples of substitutions that people might make when the price of food rises and other things remain the same.
   c. Explain how the income effect influences food purchases and provide some examples of the income effect that might occur when the price of food rises and other things remain the same.

3. Place the following goods and services into pairs of likely substitutes and pairs of likely complements. (You may use an item in more than one pair.) The goods and services are

   coal, oil, natural gas, wheat, corn, rye, pasta, pizza, sausage, skateboard, roller blades, video game, laptop, iPod, cell phone, text message, email, phone call, voice mail

4. During 2010, the average income in China increased by 10 percent. Compared to 2009,

how do you expect the following would change:
   a. The demand for beef. Explain your answer.
   b. The demand for rice. Explain your answer.

5. In January 2010, the price of gasoline was $2.70 a gallon. By spring 2010, the price had increased to $3.00 a gallon. Assume that there were no changes in average income, population, or any other influence on buying plans. Explain how the rise in the price of gasoline would affect
   a. The demand for gasoline.
   b. The quantity of gasoline demanded.

Supply (Study Plan 3.3)

6. In 2008, the price of corn increased by 35 percent and some cotton farmers in Texas stopped growing cotton and started to grow corn.
   a. Does this fact illustrate the law of demand or the law of supply? Explain your answer.
   b. Why would a cotton farmer grow corn?

Use the following information to work Problems 7 to 9.

Dairies make low-fat milk from full-cream milk. In the process of making low-fat milk, the dairies produce cream, which is made into ice cream. In the market for low-fat milk, the following events occur one at a time:

   (i)   The wage rate of dairy workers rises.
   (ii)   The price of cream rises.
   (iii) The price of low-fat milk rises.
   (iv)   With the period of low rainfall extending, dairies raise their expected price of low-fat milk next year.
   (v)   With advice from health-care experts, dairy farmers decide to switch from producing full-cream milk to growing vegetables.
   (vi)   A new technology lowers the cost of producing ice cream.

7. Explain the effect of each event on the supply of low-fat milk.
8. Use a graph to illustrate the effect of each event.
9. Does any event (or events) illustrate the law of supply?

Market Equilibrium (Study Plan 3.4)

10. "As more people buy computers, the demand for Internet service increases and the price of Internet service decreases. The fall in the price of Internet service decreases the supply of Internet service." Explain what is wrong with this statement.

11. The demand and supply schedules for gum are

Price (cents per pack)	Quantity demanded	Quantity supplied
	(millions of packs a week)	
20	180	60
40	140	100
60	100	140
80	60	180
100	20	220

   a. Draw a graph of the market for gum and mark in the equilibrium price and quantity.

   b. Suppose that the price of gum is 70¢ a pack. Describe the situation in the gum market and explain how the price adjusts.

   c. Suppose that the price of gum is 30¢ a pack. Describe the situation in the gum market and explain how the price adjusts.

Predicting Changes in Price and Quantity

(Study Plan 3.5)

12. The following events occur one at a time:
    (i)   The price of crude oil rises.
    (ii) The price of a car rises.
    (iii) All speed limits on highways are abolished.
    (iv) Robots cut car production costs.
    Which of these events will increase or decrease (state which occurs)
    a. The demand for gasoline?
    b. The supply of gasoline?
    c. The quantity of gasoline demanded?
    d. The quantity of gasoline supplied?

13. In Problem 11, a fire destroys some factories that produce gum and the quantity of gum supplied decreases by 40 million packs a week at each price.
    a. Explain what happens in the market for gum and draw a graph to illustrate the changes.
    b. If at the time the fire occurs there is an increase in the teenage population, which increases the quantity of gum demanded by 40 million packs a week at each price, what are the new equilibrium price and quantity of gum? Illustrate these changes on your graph.

14. **Indian Weddings Boost Gold Price Hopes**
    Indian weddings traditionally take place between late September and December. The predilection for jewelery at this time usually gives a big boost to gold sales, and the record shows the price of gold has generally risen during this period.
    Source: *Financial News*, September 9, 2011
    a. Describe the changes in demand and supply in the market for gold in India during the wedding season.
    b. Given that the wedding season is a predictable event, how might expectations influence the market for gold in India?

15. **Pump Prices on Pace to Top 2009 High by Weekend**
    The cost of filling up the car is rising as the crude oil price soars and pump prices may exceed the peak price of 2009.
    Source: *USA Today*, January 7, 2010
    a. Does demand for or the supply of gasoline or both change when the price of oil soars?
    b. Use a demand-supply graph to illustrate what happens to the equilibrium price of gasoline and the equilibrium quantity of gasoline bought when the price of oil soars.

Economics in the News (Study Plan 3.N)

16. **American to Cut Flights, Charge for Luggage**
    American Airlines announced that it will charge passengers $15 for their first piece of checked luggage and cut domestic flights as it grapples with record-high fuel prices.
    Source: *Boston Herald*, May 22, 2008
    a. According to the news clip, what is the influence on the supply of American Airlines flights?
    b. Explain how supply changes.

17. **Frigid Florida Winter is Bad News for Tomato Lovers**
    An unusually cold January in Florida destroyed entire fields of tomatoes. Florida's growers are shipping only a quarter of their usual 5 million pounds a week. The price has risen from $6.50 for a 25-pound box a year ago to $30 now.
    Source: *USA Today*, March 3, 2010
    a. Make a graph to illustrate the market for tomatoes in January 2009 and January 2010.
    b. On the graph, show how the events in the news clip influence the market for tomatoes.
    c. Why is the news "bad for tomato lovers"?

ADDITIONAL PROBLEMS AND APPLICATIONS

MyEconLab   You can work these problems in MyEconLab if assigned by your instructor.

Markets and Prices

18. What features of the world market for crude oil make it a competitive market?

19. The money price of a textbook is $90 and the money price of the Wii game *Super Mario Galaxy* is $45.

    a. What is the opportunity cost of a textbook in terms of the Wii game?

    b. What is the relative price of the Wii game in terms of textbooks?

Demand

20. The price of gasoline has increased during the past year.

    a. Explain why the law of demand applies to gasoline just as it does to all other goods and services.

    b. Explain how the substitution effect influences gasoline purchases and provide some examples of substitutions that people might make when the price of gasoline rises and other things remain the same.

    c. Explain how the income effect influences gasoline purchases and provide some examples of the income effects that might occur when the price of gasoline rises and other things remain the same.

21. Think about the demand for the three game consoles: Xbox, PS3, and Wii. Explain the effect of the following events on the demand for Xbox games and the quantity of Xbox games demanded, other things remaining the same.

    a. The price of an Xbox falls.

    b. The prices of a PS3 and a Wii fall.

    c. The number of people writing and producing Xbox games increases.

    d. Consumers' incomes increase.

    e. Programmers who write code for Xbox games become more costly to hire.

    f. The expected future price of an Xbox game falls.

    g. A new game console that is a close substitute for Xbox comes onto the market.

Supply

22. Classify the following pairs of goods and services as substitutes in production, complements in production, or neither.

    a. Bottled water and health club memberships

    b. French fries and baked potatoes

    c. Leather purses and leather shoes

    d. Hybrids and SUVs

    e. Diet coke and regular coke

23. As the prices of homes fell across the United States in 2008, the number of homes offered for sale decreased.

    a. Does this fact illustrate the law of demand or the law of supply? Explain your answer.

    b. Why would home owners decide not to sell?

24. **G.M. Cuts Production for Quarter**

    General Motors cut its fourth-quarter production schedule by 10 percent because Ford Motor, Chrysler, and Toyota sales declined in August.

    Source: *The New York Times*, September 5, 2007

    Explain whether this news clip illustrates a change in the supply of cars or a change in the quantity supplied of cars.

Market Equilibrium

Use the following figure to work Problems 25 and 26.

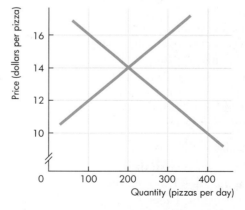

25. a. Label the curves. Which curve shows the willingness to pay for a pizza?

    b. If the price of a pizza is $16, is there a shortage or a surplus and does the price rise or fall?

c. Sellers want to receive the highest possible price, so why would they be willing to accept less than $16 a pizza?

26. a. If the price of a pizza is $12, is there a shortage or a surplus and does the price rise or fall?

b. Buyers want to pay the lowest possible price, so why would they be willing to pay more than $12 for a pizza?

27. The demand and supply schedules for potato chips are

Price (cents per bag)	Quantity demanded	Quantity supplied
	(millions of bags per week)	
50	160	130
60	150	140
70	140	150
80	130	160
90	120	170
100	110	180

a. Draw a graph of the potato chip market and mark in the equilibrium price and quantity.

b. If the price is 60¢ a bag, is there a shortage or a surplus, and how does the price adjust?

Predicting Changes in Price and Quantity

28. In Problem 27, a new dip increases the quantity of potato chips that people want to buy by 30 million bags per week at each price.

a. Does the demand for chips change? Does the supply of chips change? Describe the change.

b. How do the equilibrium price and equilibrium quantity of chips change?

29. In Problem 27, if a virus destroys potato crops and the quantity of potato chips produced decreases by 40 million bags a week at each price, how does the supply of chips change?

30. If the virus in Problem 29 hits just as the new dip in Problem 28 comes onto the market, how do the equilibrium price and equilibrium quantity of chips change?

Economics in the News

31. After you have studied *Reading Between the Lines* on pp. 74–75, answer the following questions.

a. What happened to the prices of napa cabbage and kimchi in 2011?

b. What substitutions do you expect might have been made to decrease the quantity of kimchi demanded?

c. What influenced the demand for kimchi in 2010 and what influenced the quantity of kimchi demanded?

d. What influenced the supply of kimchi during 2010 and how did supply change?

e. How did the combination of the factors you have noted in parts (d) and (e) influence the price and quantity of kimchi?

f. Was the change in quantity of kimchi a change in the quantity demanded or a change in the quantity supplied?

32. **Strawberry Prices Drop as Late Harvest Hits Market**

Shoppers bought strawberries in March for $1.25 a pound rather than the $3.49 a pound they paid last year. With the price so low, some growers plowed over their strawberry plants to make way for spring melons; others froze their harvests and sold them to juice and jam makers.

Source: *USA Today*, April 5, 2010

a. Explain how the market for strawberries would have changed if growers had not plowed in their plants but offered locals "you pick for free."

b. Describe the changes in demand and supply in the market for strawberry jam.

33. **"Popcorn Movie" Experience Gets Pricier**

Cinemas are raising the price of popcorn. Demand for field corn, which is used for animal feed, corn syrup, and ethanol, has increased and its price has exploded. That's caused some farmers to shift from growing popcorn to easier-to-grow field corn.

Source: *USA Today*, May 24, 2008

Explain and illustrate graphically the events described in the news clip in the market for

a. Popcorn

b. Movie tickets

34. **Watch Out for Rising Dry-Cleaning Bills**

In the past year, the price of dry-cleaning solvent doubled. More than 4,000 dry cleaners across the United States disappeared as budget-conscious consumers cut back. This year the price of hangers used by dry cleaners is expected to double.

Source: *CNN Money*, June 4, 2012

a. Explain the effect of rising solvent prices on the market for dry cleaning.

b. Explain the effect of consumers becoming more budget conscious along with the rising price of solvent on the price of dry cleaning.

c. If the price of hangers does rise this year, do you expect additional dry cleaners to disappear? Explain why or why not.

4

ELASTICITY

After studying this chapter, you will be able to:

◆ Define, calculate, and explain the factors that influence the price elasticity of demand

◆ Define, calculate, and explain the factors that influence the income elasticity of demand and the cross elasticity of demand

◆ Define, calculate, and explain the factors that influence the elasticity of supply

In December 2011, taxi fares in Singapore rose by 20 percent and customer numbers fell by 30 percent. But by April 2012, customers returned and cabbies' earnings were up.

To explain these responses to a price hike, we use the neat tool that you study in this chapter: elasticity.

At the end of the chapter, in *Reading Between the Lines*, we use the concept of elasticity to explain what was happening in Singapore's taxi market in 2011 and 2012. But we begin by explaining elasticity in a familiar setting: the market for pizza.

▶ Price Elasticity of Demand

You know that when supply decreases, the equilibrium price rises and the equilibrium quantity decreases. But does the price rise by a large amount and the quantity decrease by a little? Or does the price barely rise and the quantity decrease by a large amount?

The answer depends on the responsiveness of the quantity demanded of a good to a change in its price. If the quantity demanded is not very responsive to a change in the price, the price rises a lot and the equilibrium quantity doesn't change much. If the quantity demanded *is* very responsive to a change in the price, the price barely rises and the equilibrium quantity changes a lot.

You might think about the responsiveness of the quantity demanded of a good to a change in its price in terms of the slope of the demand curve. If the demand curve is steep, the quantity demanded of the good isn't very responsive to a change in the price. If the demand curve is almost flat, the quantity demanded *is* very responsive to a change in the price.

But the slope of a demand curve depends on the units in which we measure the price and the quantity—we can make the curve steep or almost flat just by changing the units in which we measure the price and the quantity. Also we often want to compare the demand for different goods and services and quantities of these goods are measured in unrelated units. For example, a pizza producer might want to compare the demand for pizza with the demand for soft drinks. Which quantity demanded is more responsive to a price change? This question can't be answered by comparing the slopes of two demand curves. The units of measurement of pizza and soft drinks are unrelated. But the question *can* be answered with a measure of responsiveness that is *independent* of units of measurement. Elasticity is such a measure.

The **price elasticity of demand** is a units-free measure of the responsiveness of the quantity demanded of a good to a change in its price when all other influences on buying plans remain the same.

Calculating Price Elasticity of Demand

We calculate the *price elasticity of demand* by using the formula:

$$\text{Price elasticity of demand} = \frac{\text{Percentage change in quantity damanded}}{\text{Percentage change in price}}.$$

To calculate the price elasticity of demand for pizza, we need to know the quantity demanded of pizza at two different prices, when all other influences on buying plans remain the same.

Figure 4.1 zooms in on a section of the demand curve for pizza and shows how the quantity demanded responds to a small change in price. Initially, the price is $20.50 a pizza and 9 pizzas an hour are demanded—the original point. The price then falls to $19.50 a pizza, and the quantity demanded increases to 11 pizzas an hour—the new point. When the price falls by $1 a pizza, the quantity demanded increases by 2 pizzas an hour.

To calculate the price elasticity of demand, we express the change in price as a percentage of the *average price* and the change in the quantity demanded as a percentage of the *average quantity*. By using the average price and average quantity, we calculate the elasticity at a point on the demand curve midway between the original point and the new point.

The original price is $20.50 and the new price is $19.50, so the price change is $1 and the average price is $20 a pizza. Call the percentage change in the price $\%\Delta P$, then

$$\%\Delta P = \Delta P/P_{ave} \times 100 = (\$1/\$20) \times 100 = 5\%.$$

The original quantity demanded is 9 pizzas and the new quantity demanded is 11 pizzas, so the quantity change is 2 pizzas and the average quantity demanded is 10 pizzas. Call the percentage change in the quantity demanded $\%\Delta Q$, then

$$\%\Delta Q = \Delta Q/Q_{ave} \times 100 = (2/10) \times 100 = 20\%.$$

The price elasticity of demand equals the percentage change in the quantity demanded (20 percent) divided by the percentage change in price (5 percent) and is 4. That is,

$$\text{Price elasticity of demand} = \frac{\%\Delta Q}{\%\Delta P}$$

$$= \frac{20\%}{5\%} = 4.$$

Average Price and Quantity Notice that we use the *average* price and *average* quantity. We do this because it gives the most precise measurement of elasticity—at the *midpoint* between the original price and the new price. If the price falls from $20.50 to $19.50, the $1 price change is 4.9 percent of $20.50. The 2 pizza change in quantity is 22.2 percent of 9 pizzas, the original quantity. So if we use

FIGURE 4.1   Calculating the Elasticity of Demand

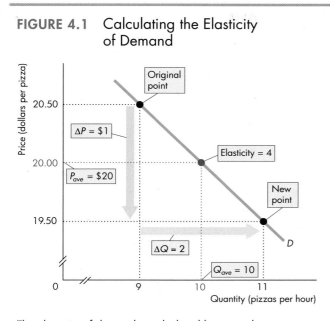

The elasticity of demand is calculated by using the formula:*

$$\text{Price elasticity of demand} = \frac{\text{Percentage change in quantity demanded}}{\text{Percentage change in price}}$$

$$= \frac{\%\Delta Q}{\%\Delta P}$$

$$= \frac{\Delta Q/Q_{ave}}{\Delta P/P_{ave}}$$

$$= \frac{2/10}{1/20} = 4.$$

This calculation measures the elasticity at an average price of $20 a pizza and an average quantity of 10 pizzas an hour.

* In the formula, the Greek letter delta (Δ) stands for "change in" and %Δ stands for "percentage change in."

——————— MyEconLab animation ———————

these numbers, the price elasticity of demand is 22.2 divided by 4.9, which equals 4.5. But if the price rises from $19.50 to $20.50, the $1 price change is 5.1 percent of $19.50. The 2 pizza change in quantity is 18.2 percent of 11 pizzas, the original quantity. So if we use these numbers, the price elasticity of demand is 18.2 divided by 5.1, which equals 3.6.

By using percentages of the *average* price and *average* quantity, we get the *same value* for the elasticity regardless of whether the price falls from $20.50 to $19.50 or rises from $19.50 to $20.50.

Percentages and Proportions Elasticity is the ratio of two percentage changes, so when we divide one percentage change by another, the 100s cancel. A percentage change is a *proportionate* change multiplied by 100. The proportionate change in price is $\Delta P/P_{ave}$, and the proportionate change in quantity demanded is $\Delta Q/Q_{ave}$. So if we divide $\Delta Q/Q_{ave}$ by $\Delta P/P_{ave}$ we get the same answer as we get by using percentage changes.

A Units-Free Measure Now that you've calculated a price elasticity of demand, you can see why it is a *units-free measure*. Elasticity is a units-free measure because the percentage change in each variable is independent of the units in which the variable is measured. The ratio of the two percentages is a number without units.

Minus Sign and Elasticity When the price of a good *rises*, the quantity demanded *decreases*. Because a *positive* change in price brings a *negative* change in the quantity demanded, the price elasticity of demand is a negative number. But it is the magnitude, or *absolute value*, of the price elasticity of demand that tells us how responsive the quantity demanded is. So to compare price elasticities of demand, we use the *magnitude* of the elasticity and ignore the minus sign.

Inelastic and Elastic Demand

If the quantity demanded remains constant when the price changes, then the price elasticity of demand is zero and the good is said to have a **perfectly inelastic demand**. One good that has a very low price elasticity of demand (perhaps zero over some price range) is insulin. Insulin is of such importance to some diabetics that if the price rises or falls, they do not change the quantity they buy.

If the percentage change in the quantity demanded equals the percentage change in the price, then the price elasticity equals 1 and the good is said to have a **unit elastic demand**.

Between perfectly inelastic demand and unit elastic demand is a general case in which *the percentage change in the quantity demanded is less than the percentage change in the price*. In this case, the price elasticity of demand is between zero and 1 and the good is said to have an **inelastic demand**. Food and shelter are examples of goods with inelastic demand.

If the quantity demanded changes by an infinitely large percentage in response to a tiny price change, then the price elasticity of demand is infinity and the good is said to have a **perfectly elastic demand**. An example of a good that has a very high elasticity of demand (almost infinite) is a soft drink from two campus machines located side by side. If the two machines offer the same soft drinks for the same price, some people buy from one machine and some from the other. But if one machine's price is higher than the other's, by even a small amount, no one buys from the machine with the higher price. Drinks from the two machines are perfect substitutes. The demand for a good that has a perfect substitute is perfectly elastic.

Between unit elastic demand and perfectly elastic demand is another general case in which *the percentage change in the quantity demanded exceeds the percentage change in price*. In this case, the price elasticity of demand is greater than 1 and the good is said to have an **elastic demand**. Automobiles and furniture are examples of goods that have elastic demand.

Figure 4.2 shows three demand curves that cover the entire range of possible elasticities of demand that you've just reviewed. In Fig. 4.2(a), the quantity demanded is constant regardless of the price, so this demand is perfectly inelastic. In Fig. 4.2(b), the percentage change in the quantity demanded equals the percentage change in price, so this demand is unit elastic. In Fig. 4.2(c), the price is constant regardless of the quantity demanded, so this figure illustrates a perfectly elastic demand.

You now know the distinction between elastic and inelastic demand. But what determines whether the demand for a good is elastic or inelastic?

The Factors that Influence the Elasticity of Demand

The elasticity of demand for a good depends on

- The closeness of substitutes
- The proportion of income spent on the good
- The time elapsed since the price change

Closeness of Substitutes The closer the substitutes for a good, the more elastic is the demand for it. Oil as fuel or raw material for chemicals has no close substitutes so the demand for oil is inelastic. Plastics are close substitutes for metals, so the demand for metals is elastic.

The degree of substitutability depends on how narrowly (or broadly) we define a good. For example, a personal computer has no close substitutes, but a Dell PC is a close substitute for a Hewlett-Packard PC. So the elasticity of demand for personal computers is lower than the elasticity of demand for a Dell or a Hewlett-Packard.

In everyday language we call goods such as food and shelter *necessities* and goods such as exotic vacations *luxuries*. A necessity has poor substitutes, so it generally has an inelastic demand. A luxury usually has many substitutes, one of which is not buying it. So a luxury generally has an elastic demand.

Proportion of Income Spent on the Good Other things remaining the same, the greater the proportion of income spent on a good, the more elastic (or less inelastic) is the demand for it.

FIGURE 4.2 Inelastic and Elastic Demand

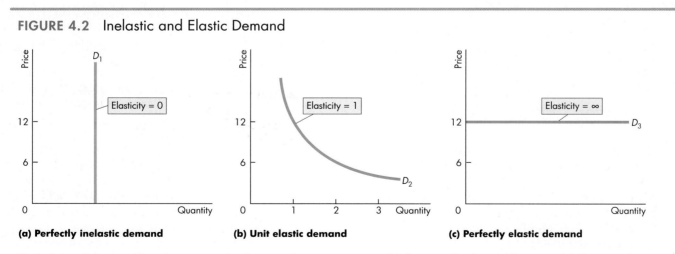

(a) Perfectly inelastic demand   **(b) Unit elastic demand**   **(c) Perfectly elastic demand**

Each demand illustrated here has a constant elasticity. The demand curve in part (a) illustrates the demand for a good that has a zero elasticity of demand. The demand curve in part (b) illustrates the demand for a good with a unit elasticity of demand. And the demand curve in part (c) illustrates the demand for a good with an infinite elasticity of demand.

Think about your own elasticity of demand for chewing gum and housing. If the price of gum rises, you consume almost as much as before. Your demand for gum is inelastic. If apartment rents rise, you look for someone to share with. Your demand for housing is not as inelastic as your demand for gum. Why the difference? Housing takes a big chunk of your budget, and gum takes little. You barely notice the higher price of gum, while the higher rent puts your budget under severe strain.

Time Elapsed Since Price Change The longer the time that has elapsed since a price change, the more elastic is demand. When the price of oil increased by 400 percent during the 1970s, people barely changed the quantity of oil and gasoline they bought. But gradually, as more efficient auto and airplane engines were developed, the quantity bought decreased. The demand for oil became more elastic as more time elapsed following the huge price hike.

Elasticity Along a Linear Demand Curve

Elasticity of demand is not the same as slope. And a good way to see this fact is by studying a demand curve that has a constant slope but a varying elasticity.

The demand curve in Fig. 4.3 is linear, which means that it has a constant slope. Along this demand curve, a $5 rise in the price brings a decrease of 10 pizzas an hour.

But the price elasticity of demand is not constant along this demand curve. To see why, let's calculate some elasticities.

At the midpoint of the demand curve, the price is $12.50 and the quantity is 25 pizzas per hour. If the price rises from $10 to $15 a pizza the quantity demanded decreases from 30 to 20 pizzas an hour and the average price and average quantity are at the midpoint of the demand curve. So

$$\text{Price elasticity of demand} = \frac{10/25}{5/12.50}$$
$$= 1.$$

That is, at the midpoint of a linear demand curve, the price elasticity of demand is 1.

At prices *above* the midpoint, the price elasticity of demand is greater than 1: Demand is elastic. To see that demand is elastic, let's calculate the elasticity when the price rises from $15 to $25 a pizza. You can see that quantity demanded decreases from 20 to zero pizzas an hour. The average price is $20 a pizza, and

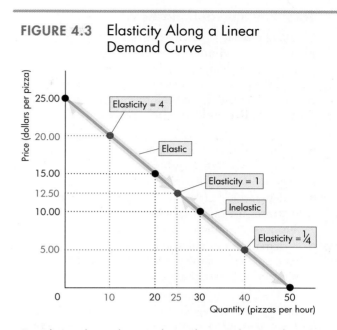

FIGURE 4.3   Elasticity Along a Linear Demand Curve

On a linear demand curve, demand is unit elastic at the midpoint (elasticity is 1), elastic above the midpoint, and inelastic below the midpoint.

───────── MyEconLab animation ─────────

the average quantity is 10 pizzas. Putting these numbers into the elasticity formula,

$$\text{Price elasticity of demand} = \frac{\Delta Q/Q_{ave}}{\Delta P/P_{ave}}$$
$$= \frac{20/10}{10/20}$$
$$= 4.$$

That is, the price elasticity of demand at an average price of $20 a pizza is 4.

At prices *below* the midpoint, the price elasticity of demand is less than 1: Demand is inelastic. For example, if the price rises from zero to $10 a pizza, the quantity demanded decreases from 50 to 30 pizzas an hour. The average price is now $5 and the average quantity is 40 pizzas an hour. So

$$\text{Price elasticity of demand} = \frac{20/40}{10/5}$$
$$= 1/4.$$

That is, the price elasticity of demand at an average price of $5 a pizza is 1/4.

Total Revenue and Elasticity

The **total revenue** from the sale of a good equals the price of the good multiplied by the quantity sold. When a price changes, total revenue also changes. But a cut in the price does not always decrease total revenue. The change in total revenue depends on the elasticity of demand in the following way:

- If demand is elastic, a 1 percent price cut increases the quantity sold by more than 1 percent and total revenue increases.
- If demand is inelastic, a 1 percent price cut increases the quantity sold by less than 1 percent and total revenue decreases.
- If demand is unit elastic, a 1 percent price cut increases the quantity sold by 1 percent and total revenue does not change.

In Fig. 4.4(a), over the price range from $25 to $12.50, demand is elastic. Over the price range from $12.50 to zero, demand is inelastic. At a price of $12.50, demand is unit elastic.

Figure 4.4(b) shows total revenue. At a price of $25, the quantity sold is zero, so total revenue is zero. At a price of zero, the quantity demanded is 50 pizzas an hour and total revenue is again zero. A price cut in the elastic range brings an increase in total revenue—the percentage increase in the quantity demanded is greater than the percentage decrease in price. A price cut in the inelastic range brings a decrease in total revenue—the percentage increase in the quantity demanded is less than the percentage decrease in price. At unit elasticity, total revenue is at a maximum.

Figure 4.4 shows how we can use this relationship between elasticity and total revenue to estimate elasticity using the total revenue test. The **total revenue test** is a method of estimating the price elasticity of demand by observing the change in total revenue that results from a change in the price, when all other influences on the quantity sold remain the same.

- If a price cut increases total revenue, demand is elastic.
- If a price cut decreases total revenue, demand is inelastic.
- If a price cut leaves total revenue unchanged, demand is unit elastic.

FIGURE 4.4 Elasticity and Total Revenue

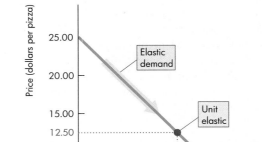

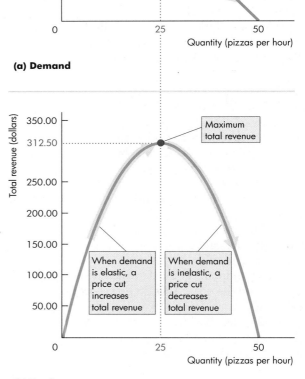

(a) Demand

(b) Total revenue

When demand is elastic, in the price range from $25 to $12.50, a decrease in price (part a) brings an increase in total revenue (part b). When demand is inelastic, in the price range from $12.50 to zero, a decrease in price (part a) brings a decrease in total revenue (part b). When demand is unit elastic, at a price of $12.50 (part a), total revenue is at a maximum (part b).

MyEconLab animation

Economics in Action
Elastic and Inelastic Demand

The real-world price elasticities of demand in the table range from 1.52 for metals, the item with the most elastic demand in the table, to 0.05 for oil, the item with the most inelastic demand in the table. The demand for food is also inelastic.

Oil and food, which have poor substitutes and inelastic demand, might be classified as necessities. Furniture and motor vehicles, which have good substitutes and elastic demand, might be classified as luxuries.

Price Elasticities of Demand

Good or Service	Elasticity
Elastic Demand	
Metals	1.52
Electrical engineering products	1.39
Mechanical engineering products	1.30
Furniture	1.26
Motor vehicles	1.14
Instrument engineering products	1.10
Transportation services	1.03
Inelastic Demand	
Gas, electricity, and water	0.92
Chemicals	0.89
Clothing	0.64
Banking and insurance services	0.56
Housing services	0.55
Agricultural and fish products	0.42
Books, magazines, and newspapers	0.34
Food	0.12
Cigarettes	0.11
Soft drinks	0.05
Oil	0.05

Sources of data: Ahsan Mansur and John Whalley, "Numerical Specification of Applied General Equilibrium Models: Estimation, Calibration, and Data," in *Applied General Equilibrium Analysis,* eds. Herbert E. Scarf and John B. Shoven (New York: Cambridge University Press, 1984), 109, and Henri Theil, Ching-Fan Chung, and James L. Seale, Jr., *Advances in Econometrics, Supplement I,* 1989, *International Evidence on Consumption Patterns* (Greenwich, Conn.: JAI Press Inc., 1989), Emilio Pagoulatos and Robert Sorensen, "What Determines the Elasticity of Industry Demand," *International Journal of Industrial Organization,* 1986, and Geoffrey Heal, Columbia University, Web site.

Price Elasticities of Demand for Food

The price elasticity of demand for food in the United States is estimated to be 0.12. This elasticity is an average over all types of food. The demand for most food items is inelastic, but there is a wide range of elasticities as the figure below shows for a range of fruits, vegetables, and meats.

The demand for grapes and beef is elastic. The demand for oranges is unit elastic. These food items, especially grapes and beef, have many good substitutes. Florida winter tomatoes have closer substitutes than tomatoes in general, so the demand for the Florida winter variety is more elastic (less inelastic) than the demand for tomatoes.

Carrots and cabbage, on which we spend a very small proportion of income, have an almost zero elastic demand.

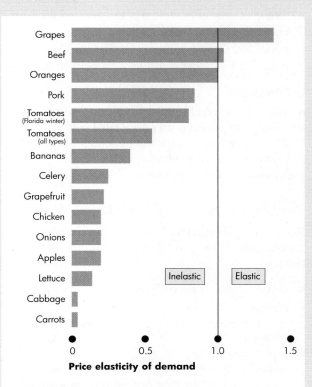

Price Elasticities of Demand for Food

Sources of data: Kuo S. Huang, *U.S. demand for food: A complete system of price and income effects* U.S. Dept. of Agriculture, Economic Research Service, Washington, DC, 1985, J. Scott Shonkwiler and Robert D. Emerson, "Imports and the Supply of Winter Tomatoes: An Application of Rational Expectations", *American Journal of Agricultural Economics,* Vol. 64, No. 4 (Nov., 1982), pp. 634–641 and Kuo S. Huang, "A Further Look at Flexibilities and Elasticities", *American Journal of Agricultural Economics,* Vol. 76, No. 2 (May, 1994), pp. 313–317.

◆ ECONOMICS IN THE NEWS

The Elasticity of Demand for Peanut Butter

Peanut Butter Prices to Rise 30 to 40 Percent
Scott Karns, president and CEO of Karns Foods, said "People are still going to need it for their family. It's still an extremely economical item." Patty Nolan, who is on a fixed income, said "I love peanut butter so I'm using a little less so I don't go through it."

Source: *The Patriot-News*, November 2, 2011

THE DATA

	Quantity (millions of tons per year)	Price (dollars per pound)
2011	350	2.00
2012	300	2.80

THE QUESTIONS

■ Does the news clip imply that the demand for peanut butter is elastic or inelastic?

■ If the data are two points on the demand curve for peanut butter, what is the price elasticity of demand?

THE ANSWERS

■ The two remarks in the news clip suggest that the quantity of peanut butter demanded will decrease when the price rises, but not by much. The demand for peanut butter is inelastic.

■ The data table says the price of peanut butter increased by $0.80 with an average price of $2.40, so the price increased by 33.3 percent. The quantity demanded decreased by 50 million tons with an average quantity of 325 million tons, so the quantity demanded decreased by 15.4 percent. The price elasticity of demand is 15.4 percent divided by 33.3 percent, which equals 0.46.

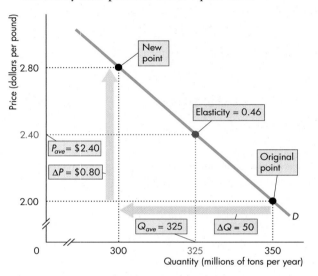

Calculating the Price Elasticity of Demand for Peanut Butter

Your Expenditure and Your Elasticity

When the price of a good changes, the change in your expenditure on the good depends on *your* elasticity of demand.

■ If your demand for the good is elastic, a 1 percent price cut increases the quantity you buy by more than 1 percent and your expenditure on the item increases.

■ If your demand for the good is inelastic, a 1 percent price cut increases the quantity you buy by less than 1 percent and your expenditure on the item decreases.

■ If your demand for the good is unit elastic, a 1 percent price cut increases the quantity you buy by 1 percent and your expenditure on the item does not change.

So if you spend more on an item when its price falls, your demand for that item is elastic; if you spend the same amount, your demand is unit elastic; and if you spend less, your demand is inelastic.

◆ REVIEW QUIZ

1 Why do we need a units-free measure of the responsiveness of the quantity demanded of a good or service to a change in its price?
2 Define the price elasticity of demand and show how it is calculated.
3 What makes the demand for some goods elastic and the demand for other goods inelastic?
4 Why is the demand for a luxury generally more elastic (or less inelastic) than the demand for a necessity?
5 What is the total revenue test?

You can work these questions in Study Plan 4.1 and get instant feedback.   MyEconLab

You've now completed your study of the *price* elasticity of demand. Two other elasticity concepts tell us about the effects of other influences on demand. Let's look at these other elasticities of demand.

More Elasticities of Demand

Suppose the economy is expanding and people are enjoying rising incomes. You know that a change in income changes demand. So this increased prosperity brings an increase in the demand for most types of goods and services. By how much will a rise in income increase the demand for pizza? This question is answered by the income elasticity of demand.

Income Elasticity of Demand

The **income elasticity of demand** is a measure of the responsiveness of the demand for a good or service to a change in income, other things remaining the same. It tells us by how much a demand curve shifts at a given price.

The income elasticity of demand is calculated by using the formula:

$$\text{Income elasticity of demand} = \frac{\text{Percentage change in quantity demanded}}{\text{Percentage change in income}}.$$

Income elasticities of demand can be positive or negative and they fall into three interesting ranges:

- Positive and greater than 1 (*normal* good, income elastic)
- Positive and less than 1 (*normal* good, income inelastic)
- Negative (*inferior* good)

Income Elastic Demand Suppose that the price of pizza is constant and 9 pizzas an hour are bought. Then incomes rise from $975 to $1,025 a week. No other influence on buying plans changes and the quantity of pizzas sold increases to 11 an hour.

The change in the quantity demanded is +2 pizzas. The average quantity is 10 pizzas, so the quantity demanded increases by 20 percent. The change in income is +$50 and the average income is $1,000, so incomes increase by 5 percent. The income elasticity of demand for pizza is

$$\frac{20\%}{5\%} = 4.$$

The demand for pizza is income elastic. The percentage increase in the quantity of pizza demanded exceeds the percentage increase in income.

Economics in Action
Necessities and Luxuries

The table shows estimates of some real-world income elasticities of demand. The demand for a necessity such as food or clothing is income inelastic, while the demand for a luxury such as transportation, which includes airline and foreign travel, is income elastic.

But what is a necessity and what is a luxury depends on the level of income. For people with a low income, food and clothing can be luxuries. So the level of income has a big effect on income elasticities of demand. The figure shows this effect on the income elasticity of demand for food in 10 countries. In countries with low incomes, such as Tanzania and India, the income elasticity of demand for food is high. In countries with high incomes, such as the United States, the income elasticity of

Some Real-World Income Elasticities of Demand

Income Elastic Demand

Airline travel	5.82
Movies	3.41
Foreign travel	3.08
Electricity	1.94
Restaurant meals	1.61
Local buses and trains	1.38
Haircuts	1.36
Automobiles	1.07

Income Inelastic Demand

Tobacco	0.86
Alcoholic drinks	0.62
Furniture	0.53
Clothing	0.51
Newspapers and magazines	0.38
Telephone	0.32
Food	0.14

Sources of data: H.S. Houthakker and Lester D. Taylor, *Consumer Demand in the United States* (Cambridge, Mass.: Harvard University Press, 1970), and Henri Theil, Ching-Fan Chung, and James L. Seale, Jr., *Advances in Econometrics, Supplement 1, 1989, International Evidence on Consumption Patterns* (Greenwich, Conn.: JAI Press, Inc., 1989).

demand for food is low. That is, as income increases, the income elasticity of demand for food decreases. Low-income consumers spend a larger percentage of any increase in income on food than do high-income consumers.

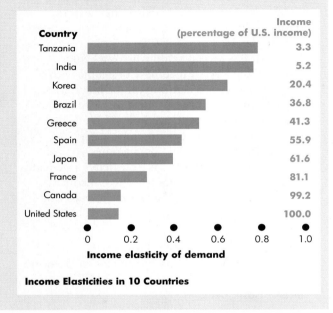

Income Elasticities in 10 Countries

Income Inelastic Demand If the income elasticity of demand is positive but less than 1, demand is income inelastic. The percentage increase in the quantity demanded is positive but less than the percentage increase in income.

Whether demand is income elastic or income inelastic has an important implication for the percentage of income spent on a good. If the demand for a good is *income elastic,* the percentage of income spent on that good *increases* as income increases. And if the demand for a good is *income inelastic,* the percentage of income spent on that good *decreases* as income increases.

Inferior Goods If the income elasticity of demand is negative, the good is an *inferior* good. The quantity demanded of an inferior good and the amount spent on it *decrease* when income increases. Goods in this category include small motorcycles, potatoes, and rice. Low-income consumers buy these goods and spend a large percentage of their incomes on them.

Cross Elasticity of Demand

The burger shop next to your pizzeria has just raised the prices of its burgers. You know that pizzas and burgers are substitutes. You also know that when the price of a substitute for pizza *rises,* the demand for pizza *increases.* But how big is the influence of the price of burgers on the demand for pizza?

You know, too, that pizza and soft drinks are complements. And you know that if the price of a complement of pizza *rises,* the demand for pizza *decreases.* So you wonder, by how much will a rise in the price of a soft drink decrease the demand for your pizza?

To answer this question, you need to know about the cross elasticity of demand for pizza. Let's examine this elasticity measure.

We measure the influence of a change in the price of a substitute or complement by using the concept of the cross elasticity of demand. The **cross elasticity of demand** is a measure of the responsiveness of the demand for a good to a change in the price of a substitute or complement, other things remaining the same.

We calculate the *cross elasticity of demand* by using the formula:

$$\text{Cross elasticity of demand} = \frac{\text{Percentage change in quantity demanded}}{\text{Percentage change in price of a substitute or complement}}.$$

The cross elasticity of demand can be positive or negative. If the cross elasticity of demand is *positive,* demand and the price of the other good change in the *same* direction, so the two goods are *substitutes.* If the cross elasticity of demand is *negative,* demand and the price of the other good change in *opposite* directions, so the two goods are *complements.*

Substitutes Suppose that the price of pizza is constant and people buy 9 pizzas an hour. Then the price of a burger rises from $1.50 to $2.50. No other influence on buying plans changes and the quantity of pizzas bought increases to 11 an hour.

The change in the quantity demanded at the current price is +2 pizzas—the new quantity, 11 pizzas, minus the original quantity, 9 pizzas. The average quantity is 10 pizzas. So the quantity of pizzas demanded increases by 20 percent. That is,

$$\Delta Q/Q_{ave} \times 100 = (+2/10) \times 100 = +20\%.$$

The change in the price of a burger, a substitute for pizza, is +$1—the new price, $2.50, minus the original price, $1.50. The average price is $2 a burger. So the price of a burger rises by 50 percent. That is,

$$\Delta P / P_{ave} \times 100 = (+\$1/\$2) \times 100 = +50\%.$$

So the cross elasticity of demand for pizza with respect to the price of a burger is

$$\frac{+20\%}{+50\%} = 0.4.$$

Figure 4.5 illustrates the cross elasticity of demand. Because pizza and burgers are substitutes, when the price of a burger rises, the demand for pizza increases. The demand curve for pizza shifts rightward from D_0 to D_1. Because a *rise* in the price of a burger brings an *increase* in the demand for pizza, the cross elasticity of demand for pizza with respect to the price of a burger is *positive*. Both the price and the quantity change in the same direction.

Complements Now suppose that the price of pizza is constant and 11 pizzas an hour are bought. Then the price of a soft drink rises from $1.50 to $2.50. No other influence on buying plans changes and the quantity of pizzas bought falls to 9 an hour.

FIGURE 4.5 Cross Elasticity of Demand

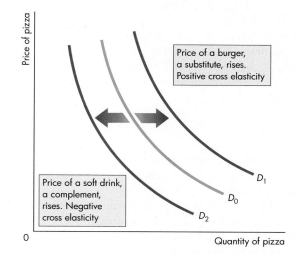

A burger is a *substitute* for pizza. When the price of a burger rises, the demand for pizza increases and the demand curve for pizza shifts rightward from D_0 to D_1. The cross elasticity of demand is *positive*.

A soft drink is a *complement* of pizza. When the price of a soft drink rises, the demand for pizza decreases and the demand curve for pizza shifts leftward from D_0 to D_2. The cross elasticity of demand is *negative*.

MyEconLab animation

◆ ECONOMICS IN THE NEWS

More Peanut Butter Demand Elasticities

Peanut Butter Related Markets
Professor Timothy Mathews teaches economics at Kennesaw State University, Georgia, the nation's number one peanut producing state. The data table below shows his guesses about some demand elasticities for peanut butter.

Source: Timothy Mathews

THE DATA

Income elasticity	−0.31
Cross elasticity peanut butter and grape jelly	−0.27
Cross elasticity peanut butter and American cheese	+0.18

THE QUESTIONS

■ What do the data provided tell us about the demand for peanut butter? Is it a normal good?

■ Is grape jelly a substitute for or a complement of peanut butter? Is American cheese a substitute for or a complement of peanut butter?

THE ANSWERS

■ The income elasticity of demand for peanut butter is *negative*, which means that peanut butter is an *inferior good*. People buy less peanut butter as income rises.

■ The cross elasticity of demand of peanut butter with respect to the price of grape jelly is *negative*, which means that peanut butter and grape jelly are *complements*.

■ The cross elasticity of demand of peanut butter with respect to the price of American cheese is *positive*, which means that peanut butter and American cheese are *substitutes*.

The change in the quantity demanded is the opposite of what we've just calculated: The quantity of pizzas demanded decreases by 20 percent (−20%).

The change in the price of a soft drink, a rise of $1 from $1.50 to $2.50, is the same as the change in the price of a burger that we've just calculated. That is, the price rises by 50 percent (+50%).

So the cross elasticity of demand for pizza with respect to the price of a soft drink is

$$\frac{-20\%}{+50\%} = -0.4.$$

Because pizza and soft drinks are complements, when the price of a soft drink rises, the demand for pizza decreases.

In Fig. 4.5, when the price of soft drinks rises the demand curve for pizza shifts leftward from D_0 to D_2. Because a *rise* in the price of a soft drink brings a *decrease* in the demand for pizza, the cross elasticity of demand for pizza with respect to the price of a soft drink is *negative*. The price and quantity change in *opposite* directions.

The magnitude of the cross elasticity of demand determines how far the demand curve shifts. The larger the cross elasticity (absolute value), the greater is the change in demand and the larger is the shift in the demand curve.

If two items are close substitutes, such as two brands of spring water, the cross elasticity is large. If two items are close complements, such as movies and popcorn, the cross elasticity is large.

If two items are somewhat unrelated to each other, such as newspapers and orange juice, the cross elasticity is small—perhaps even zero.

REVIEW QUIZ

1 What does the income elasticity of demand measure?
2 What does the sign (positive/negative) of the income elasticity tell us about a good?
3 What does the cross elasticity of demand measure?
4 What does the sign (positive/negative) of the cross elasticity of demand tell us about the relationship between two goods?

You can work these questions in Study Plan 4.2 and get instant feedback.   MyEconLab

◆ Elasticity of Supply

You know that when demand increases, the equilibrium price rises and the equilibrium quantity increases. But does the price rise by a large amount and the quantity increase by a little? Or does the price barely rise and the quantity increase by a large amount?

The answer depends on the responsiveness of the quantity supplied to a change in the price. If the quantity supplied is not very responsive to price, then an increase in demand brings a large rise in the price and a small increase in the equilibrium quantity. If the quantity supplied is highly responsive to price, then an increase in demand brings a small rise in the price and a large increase in the equilibrium quantity.

The problems that arise from using the slope of the supply curve to indicate responsiveness are the same as those we considered when discussing the responsiveness of the quantity demanded, so we use a units-free measure—the elasticity of supply.

Calculating the Elasticity of Supply

The **elasticity of supply** measures the responsiveness of the quantity supplied to a change in the price of a good when all other influences on selling plans remain the same. It is calculated by using the formula:

$$\text{Elasticity of supply} = \frac{\text{Percentage change in quantity supplied}}{\text{Percentage change in price}}.$$

We use the same method that you learned when you studied the elasticity of demand. (Refer back to p. 85 to check this method.)

Elastic and Inelastic Supply If the elasticity of supply is greater than 1, we say that supply is elastic and if the elasticity of supply is less than 1, we say that supply is inelastic.

Suppose that when the price rises from $20 to $21, the quantity supplied increases from 10 to 20 pizzas per hour. The price rise is $1 and the average price is $20.50, so the price rises by 4.9 percent of the average price. The quantity increases from 10 to 20 pizzas an hour, so the increase is 10 pizzas, the average quantity is 15 pizzas, and the quantity increases by 67 percent. The elasticity of supply is equal to 67 percent divided by 4.9 percent, which equals 13.67. Because the elasticity of supply exceeds 1 (in this case by a lot), supply is elastic.

In contrast, suppose that when the price rises from $20 to $30, the quantity of pizza supplied increases from 10 to 13 per hour. The price rise is $10 and the average price is $25, so the price rises by 40 percent of the average price. The quantity increases from 10 to 13 pizzas an hour, so the increase is 3 pizzas, the average quantity is 11.5 pizzas an hour, and the quantity increases by 26 percent. The elasticity of supply is equal to 26 percent divided by 40 percent, which equals 0.65. Now, because the elasticity of supply is less than 1, supply is inelastic.

Figure 4.6 shows the range of elasticities of supply. If the quantity supplied is fixed regardless of the price, the supply curve is vertical and the elasticity of supply is zero. Supply is perfectly inelastic. This case is shown in Fig. 4.6(a). A special intermediate case occurs when the percentage change in price equals the percentage change in quantity. Supply is then unit elastic. This case is shown in Fig. 4.6(b). No matter how steep the supply curve is, if it is linear and passes through the origin, supply is unit elastic. If there is a price at which sellers are willing to offer any quantity for sale, the supply curve is horizontal and the elasticity of supply is infinite. Supply is perfectly elastic. This case is shown in Fig. 4.6(c).

The Factors That Influence the Elasticity of Supply

The elasticity of supply of a good depends on

- Resource substitution possibilities
- Time frame for the supply decision

Resource Substitution Possibilities Some goods and services can be produced only by using unique or rare productive resources. These items have a low, perhaps even a zero, elasticity of supply. Other goods and services can be produced by using commonly available resources that could be allocated to a wide variety of alternative tasks. Such items have a high elasticity of supply.

A Van Gogh painting is an example of a good with a vertical supply curve and a zero elasticity of supply. At the other extreme, wheat can be grown on land that is almost equally good for growing corn, so it is just as easy to grow wheat as corn. The opportunity cost of wheat in terms of forgone corn is almost constant. As a result, the supply curve of wheat is almost horizontal and its elasticity of supply is very large. Similarly, when a good is produced in many different countries (for example, sugar and beef), the supply of the good is highly elastic.

The supply of most goods and services lies between these two extremes. The quantity produced

FIGURE 4.6   Inelastic and Elastic Supply

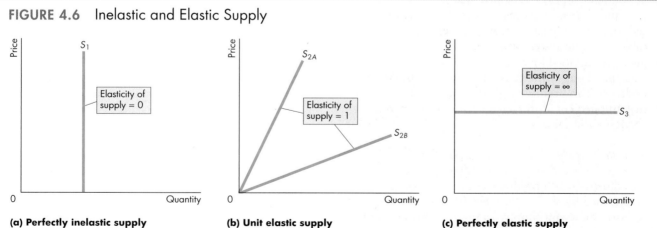

(a) Perfectly inelastic supply   **(b) Unit elastic supply**   **(c) Perfectly elastic supply**

Each supply illustrated here has a constant elasticity. The supply curve in part (a) illustrates the supply of a good that has a zero elasticity of supply. Each supply curve in part (b) illustrates the supply of a good with a unit elasticity of supply. All linear supply curves that pass through the origin illustrate supplies that are unit elastic. The supply curve in part (c) illustrates the supply of a good with an infinite elasticity of supply.

can be increased but only by incurring a higher cost. If a higher price is offered, the quantity supplied increases. Such goods and services have an elasticity of supply between zero and infinity.

Time Frame for the Supply Decision To study the influence of the amount of time elapsed since a price change, we distinguish three time frames of supply:

■ Momentary supply
■ Short-run supply
■ Long-run supply

Momentary Supply When the price of a good changes, the immediate response of the quantity supplied is determined by the *momentary supply* of that good.

Some goods, such as fruits and vegetables, have a perfectly inelastic momentary supply—a vertical supply curve. The quantities supplied depend on crop-planting decisions made earlier. In the case of oranges, for example, planting decisions have to be made many years in advance of the crop being available. Momentary supply is perfectly inelastic because, on a given day, no matter what the price of oranges, producers cannot change their output. They have picked, packed, and shipped their crop to market, and the quantity available for that day is fixed.

In contrast, some goods have a perfectly elastic momentary supply. Long-distance phone calls are an example. When many people simultaneously make a call, there is a big surge in the demand for telephone cables, computer switching, and satellite time. The quantity supplied increases, but the price remains constant. Long-distance carriers monitor fluctuations in demand and reroute calls to ensure that the quantity supplied equals the quantity demanded without changing the price.

Short-Run Supply The response of the quantity supplied to a price change when only *some* of the possible adjustments to production can be made is determined by *short-run supply*. Most goods have an inelastic short-run supply. To increase output in the short run, firms must work their labor force overtime and perhaps hire additional workers. To decrease their output in the short run, firms either lay off workers or reduce their hours of work. With the passage of time, firms can make more adjustments, perhaps training additional workers or buying additional tools and other equipment.

For the orange grower, if the price of oranges falls, some pickers can be laid off and oranges left on the trees to rot. Or if the price of oranges rises, the grower can use more fertilizer and improved irrigation to increase the yields of their existing trees.

But an orange grower can't change the number of trees producing oranges in the short run.

Long-Run Supply The response of the quantity supplied to a price change after *all* the technologically possible ways of adjusting supply have been exploited is determined by *long-run supply*. For most goods and services, long-run supply is elastic and perhaps perfectly elastic.

For the orange grower, the long run is the time it takes new tree plantings to grow to full maturity—about 15 years. In some cases, the long-run adjustment occurs only after a completely new production plant has been built and workers have been trained to operate it—typically a process that might take several years.

REVIEW QUIZ

1 Why do we need a units-free measure of the responsiveness of the quantity supplied of a good or service to a change in its price?
2 Define the elasticity of supply and show how it is calculated.
3 What are the main influences on the elasticity of supply that make the supply of some goods elastic and the supply of other goods inelastic?
4 Provide examples of goods or services whose elasticities of supply are (a) zero, (b) greater than zero but less than infinity, and (c) infinity.
5 How does the time frame over which a supply decision is made influence the elasticity of supply? Explain your answer.

You can work these questions in Study Plan 4.3 and get instant feedback.   MyEconLab

◆ You have now learned about the elasticities of demand and supply. Table 4.1 summarizes all the elasticities that you've met in this chapter. In the next chapter, we study the efficiency of competitive markets. But first study *Reading Between the Lines* on pp. 98–99, which puts the elasticity of demand to work and looks at the market for taxi rides in Singapore.

TABLE 4.1   A Compact Glossary of Elasticities

Price Elasticities of Demand

A relationship is described as	When its magnitude is	Which means that
Perfectly elastic	Infinity	The smallest possible increase in price causes an infinitely large decrease in the quantity demanded*
Elastic	Less than infinity	The percentage decrease in the quantity demanded exceeds the percentage increase in price
Unit elastic	1	The percentage decrease in the quantity demanded equals the percentage increase in price
Inelastic	Less than 1 but greater than zero	The percentage decrease in the quantity demanded is less than the percentage increase in price
Perfectly inelastic	Zero	The quantity demanded is the same at all prices

Cross Elasticities of Demand

A relationship is described as	When its value is	Which means that
Close substitutes	Large	The smallest possible increase in the price of one good causes an infinitely large increase in the quantity* demanded of the other good
Substitutes	Positive	If the price of one good increases, the quantity demanded of the other good also increases
Unrelated goods	Zero	If the price of one good increases, the quantity demanded of the other good remains the same
Complements	Negative	If the price of one good increases, the quantity demanded of the other good decreases

Income Elasticities of Demand

A relationship is described as	When its value is	Which means that
Income elastic (normal good)	Greater than 1	The percentage increase in the quantity demanded is greater than the percentage increase in income*
Income inelastic (normal good)	Less than 1 but greater than zero	The percentage increase in the quantity demanded is greater than zero but less than the percentage increase in income
Negative (inferior good)	Less than zero	When income increases, quantity demanded decreases

Elasticities of Supply

A relationship is described as	When its magnitude is	Which means that
Perfectly elastic	Infinity	The smallest possible increase in price causes an infinitely large increase in the quantity supplied*
Elastic	Less than infinity but greater than 1	The percentage increase in the quantity supplied exceeds the percentage increase in the price
Unit elastic	1	The percentage increase in the quantity supplied equals the percentage increase in the price
Inelastic	Greater than zero but less than 1	The percentage increase in the quantity supplied is less than the percentage increase in the price
Perfectly inelastic	Zero	The quantity supplied is the same at all prices

*In each description, the directions of change may be reversed. For example, in this case, the smallest possible *decrease* in price causes an infinitely large *increase* in the quantity demanded.

The Elasticity of Demand for Taxi Rides

Cabbies Earning More After Fare Hike

The Straits Times, Singapore
April 10, 2012

CABBIES' earnings have risen by up to 30 percent since a fare revision last December, which had initially dampened passenger numbers.

ComfortDelGro, the biggest operator here with about 15,600 taxis, said average net income per cab per day has risen by 12 percent to $210.93. It translates to a monthly income of $5,906 (based on 28 days because of days off), or about $2,953 per driver per shift.

Trans-Cab, the second biggest operator with about 4,400 taxis, said its drivers have seen a 20 to 30 percent rise in earnings.

Taxi fares underwent a slew of changes in December, including a 20-cent rise in flagdown fare. On average, the cost of a typical cab ride during the peak period rose by about 20 percent.

Within the first couple of weeks, cabbies were lamenting that business had dropped—by as much as 30 percent. Cabby Joseph Ho, 52, said demand has stabilized since and "people have accepted the fare increase." He added that "it is easier to get customers now, even during the peak hours."

But even as earnings have improved, industry observers said the gains would be eroded if operating costs continue to rise.

Source: The Straits Times. © Singapore Press Holdings Limited. Reproduced with permission.

ESSENCE OF THE STORY

- In Singapore, the price of a cab ride rose by about 20 percent in December 2011.

- Immediately following the price rise, the number of passengers decreased by around 30 percent.

- After a few weeks, cabbies' earnings began to increase.

- By April 2012, cab drivers' earnings had increased by between 20 and 30 percent.

- The cost of operating a taxi is rising.

ECONOMIC ANALYSIS

- Using information in this news article, we can estimate the price elasticity of demand for taxi rides.

- The news report says that when the price of a cab ride rose by 20 percent, passenger numbers dropped by 30 percent.

- These percentages are the ones that people ordinarily use, so they are percentages of the initial price and quantity.

- Figure 1 illustrates this information. The price is initially $10.00 per ride and the quantity demanded is 100 rides per day. (The numbers are examples and chosen to make our calculations as clear as possible).

- To calculate the price elasticity of demand, we use the mid-point formula.

- The change in price was $2.00 per ride and the average price was $11.00, so the percentage change in price was

  $2.00 × 100 ÷ $11.00 = 18.18 percent.

- The change in quantity was 30 rides and the average quantity was 85, so the percentage change in quantity was

  30 × 100 ÷ 85 = 35.29 percent.

- Dividing the percentage change in quantity demanded by the percentage change in price, we get the estimate of the price elasticity of demand, which is:

  35.29 percent ÷ 18.18 percent = 1.94.

- The demand for taxi rides is elastic—the price elasticity of demand is greater than 1. This makes sense because cab rides have close substitutes such as taking a bus or driving one's own car.

- Because demand is elastic, when the price increased, the total revenue of taxi operators (what the news article calls "earnings") *decreased*. In the numerical example in Fig.1, it decreased from $1,000 per day to $840 per day ($840 = $12.00 × 70).

- By April 2012, taxi operators were earning 20 to 30 percent more than before the price rise. The news article says that "demand stabilized."

- Demand didn't "stabilize": It increased. We know that demand increased because total revenue increased by a greater percentage than the price increased. So the quantity of cab rides must have increased.

- Figure 2 shows what happened assuming that the estimated price elasticity of demand is correct.

- Total revenue (earnings) of cabbies increased as a combined consequence of the higher fares and the increase in demand.

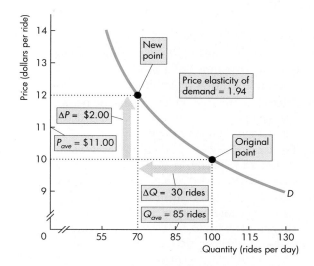

Figure 1 The Price Elasticity of Demand for Taxi Rides

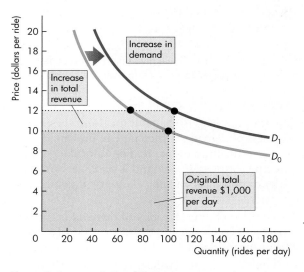

Figure 2 Increase in Total Revenue

- Why did the demand for cab rides increase? The news article provides the clue. The cost of operating taxis increased. But the biggest component of that cost is the cost of fuel.

- But a higher cost of fuel increases the price of public transport and of driving one's own car. Because the prices of these substitutes for cab rides increased, the demand for cab rides increased.

- It seemed to the cab drivers as if their customers had "accepted" the fare increase, but they were merely responding to price signals.

99

SUMMARY

Key Points

Price Elasticity of Demand (pp. 84–90)

- Elasticity is a measure of the responsiveness of the quantity demanded of a good to a change in its price, other things remaining the same.
- Price elasticity of demand equals the percentage change in the quantity demanded divided by the percentage change in the price.
- The larger the magnitude of the price elasticity of demand, the greater is the responsiveness of the quantity demanded to a given price change.
- If demand is elastic, a cut in price leads to an increase in total revenue. If demand is unit elastic, a cut in price leaves total revenue unchanged. And if demand is inelastic, a cut in price leads to a decrease in total revenue.
- Price elasticity of demand depends on how easily one good serves as a substitute for another, the proportion of income spent on the good, and the length of time elapsed since the price change.

Working Problems 1 to 8 will give you a better understanding of the price elasticity of demand.

More Elasticities of Demand (pp. 91–94)

- Income elasticity of demand measures the responsiveness of demand to a change in income, other things remaining the same. For a normal good, the income elasticity of demand is positive. For an inferior good, the income elasticity of demand is negative.
- When the income elasticity of demand is greater than 1 (income elastic), the percentage of income spent on the good increases as income increases.
- When the income elasticity of demand is less than 1 (income inelastic and inferior), the percentage of income spent on the good decreases as income increases.
- Cross elasticity of demand measures the responsiveness of the demand for one good to a change in the price of a substitute or a complement, other things remaining the same.
- The cross elasticity of demand with respect to the price of a substitute is positive. The cross elasticity of demand with respect to the price of a complement is negative.

Working Problems 9 to 16 will give you a better understanding of cross and income elasticities of demand.

Elasticity of Supply (pp. 94–96)

- Elasticity of supply measures the responsiveness of the quantity supplied of a good to a change in its price, other things remaining the same.
- The elasticity of supply is usually positive and ranges between zero (vertical supply curve) and infinity (horizontal supply curve).
- Supply decisions have three time frames: momentary, short run, and long run.
- Momentary supply refers to the response of the quantity supplied to a price change at the instant that the price changes.
- Short-run supply refers to the response of the quantity supplied to a price change after some of the technologically feasible adjustments in production have been made.
- Long-run supply refers to the response of the quantity supplied to a price change when all the technologically feasible adjustments in production have been made.

Working Problems 17 and 18 will give you a better understanding of the elasticity of supply.

Key Terms

Cross elasticity of demand, 92	Inelastic demand, 85	Total revenue, 88
Elastic demand, 86	Perfectly elastic demand, 85	Total revenue test, 88
Elasticity of supply, 94	Perfectly inelastic demand, 85	Unit elastic demand, 85
Income elasticity of demand, 91	Price elasticity of demand, 84	

STUDY PLAN PROBLEMS AND APPLICATIONS

MyEconLab   You can work Problems 1 to 18 in MyEconLab Chapter 4 Study Plan and get instant feedback.

Price Elasticity of Demand (Study Plan 4.1)

1. Rain spoils the strawberry crop, the price rises from $4 to $6 a box, and the quantity demanded decreases from 1,000 to 600 boxes a week.
   a. Calculate the price elasticity of demand over this price range.
   b. Describe the demand for strawberries.

2. If the quantity of dental services demanded increases by 10 percent when the price of dental services falls by 10 percent, is the demand for dental services inelastic, elastic, or unit elastic?

3. The demand schedule for hotel rooms is

Price (dollars per night)	Quantity demanded (millions of rooms per night)
200	100
250	80
400	50
500	40
800	25

   a. What happens to total revenue when the price falls from $400 to $250 a night and from $250 to $200 a night?
   b. Is the demand for hotel rooms elastic, inelastic, or unit elastic?

4. The figure shows the demand for pens.

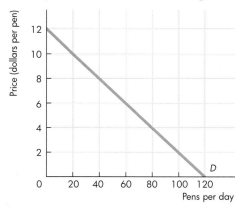

   Calculate the elasticity of demand when the price rises from $4 to $6 a pen. Over what price range is the demand for pens elastic?

5. In 2003, when music downloading first took off, Universal Music slashed the average price of a CD from $21 to $15. The company expected the price cut to boost the quantity of CDs sold by 30 percent, other things remaining the same.

   a. What was Universal Music's estimate of the price elasticity of demand for CDs?
   b. If you were making the pricing decision at Universal Music, what would be your pricing decision? Explain your decision.

6. The demand for illegal drugs is inelastic. Much of the expenditure on illegal drugs comes from crime. Assuming these statements to be correct,
   a. How will a successful campaign that decreases the supply of drugs influence the price of illegal drugs and the amount spent on them?
   b. What will happen to the amount of crime?
   c. What is the most effective way of decreasing the quantity of illegal drugs bought and decreasing the amount of drug-related crime?

7. **The Grip of Gas**
   U.S. drivers are ranked as the least sensitive to changes in the price of gasoline. For example, if the price rose from $3 to $4 per gallon and stayed there for a year U.S. purchases of gasoline would fall only about 5 percent.
   Source: *Slate*, September 27, 2005
   a. Calculate the price elasticity of demand for gasoline. Is the demand for gasoline elastic, unit elastic, or inelastic?
   b. Explain how the price rise from $3 to $4 a gallon changes the total revenue from gasoline sales.

8. **Spam Sales Rise as Food Costs Soar**
   Sales of Spam are rising as consumers realize that Spam and other lower-cost foods can be substituted for costlier cuts of meat as a way of controlling their already stretched food budgets.
   Source: *AOL Money & Finance*, May 28, 2008
   a. Is Spam a normal good or an inferior good? Explain.
   b. Would the income elasticity of demand for Spam be negative or positive? Explain.

More Elasticities of Demand (Study Plan 4.2)

9. When Judy's income increased from $130 to $170 a week, she increased her demand for concert tickets by 15 percent and decreased her demand for bus rides by 10 percent. Calculate Judy's income elasticity of demand for (a) concert tickets and (b) bus rides.

10. If a 12 percent rise in the price of orange juice decreases the quantity of orange juice demanded by 22 percent and increases the quantity of apple juice demanded by 14 percent, calculate the
   a. Price elasticity of demand for orange juice.
   b. Cross elasticity of demand for apple juice with respect to the price of orange juice.

11. If a 5 percent rise in the price of sushi increases the quantity of soy sauce demanded by 2 percent and decreases the quantity of sushi demanded by 1 percent, calculate the
   a. Price elasticity of demand for sushi.
   b. Cross elasticity of demand for soy sauce with respect to the price of sushi.

12. **Swelling Textbook Costs Have College Students Saying "Pass"**
   Textbook prices have doubled and risen faster than average prices for the past two decades. Sixty percent of students do not buy textbooks. Some students hunt for used copies and sell them back at the end of the semester; some buy online, which is often cheaper than the campus store; some use the library copy and wait till it's free; some share the book with a classmate.
   Source: *Washington Post*, January 23, 2006

   Explain what this news clip implies about
   a. The price elasticity of demand for college textbooks.
   b. The income elasticity of demand for college textbooks.
   c. The cross elasticity of demand for college textbooks from the campus bookstore with respect to the online price of a textbook.

Use the following information to work Problems 13 to 15.

As Gas Costs Soar, Buyers Flock to Small Cars
Faced with high gas prices, Americans are substituting smaller cars for SUVs. In April 2008, Toyota Yaris sales increased 46 percent and Ford Focus sales increased 32 percent from a year earlier. SUV sales decreased 25 percent in 2008 and Chevrolet Tahoe sales fell 35 percent. Full-size pickup sales decreased 15 percent in 2008 and Ford F-Series pickup sales decreased by 27 percent in April 2008. The effect of a downsized vehicle fleet on fuel consumption is unknown. In California in January 2008, gasoline consumption was 4 percent lower and the price of gasoline 30 percent higher than in January 2007.
   Source: *The New York Times*, May 2, 2009

13. Calculate the price elasticity of demand for gasoline in California.
14. Calculate the cross elasticity of demand for
   a. Toyota Yaris with respect to the price of gasoline.
   b. Ford Focus with respect to the price of gasoline.
15. Calculate the cross elasticity of demand for
   a. Chevrolet Tahoe with respect to the price of gasoline.
   b. A full-size pickup with respect to the price of gasoline.

16. **Home Depot Earnings Hammered**
   As gas and food prices increased and home prices slumped, people had less extra income to spend on home improvements. And the improvements that they made were on small inexpensive types of repairs and not major big-ticket items.
   Source: CNN, May 20, 2008

   a. What does this news clip imply about the income elasticity of demand for big-ticket home-improvement items?
   b. Would the income elasticity of demand be greater or less than 1? Explain.

Elasticity of Supply (Study Plan 4.3)

17. The table sets out the supply schedule of jeans.

Price (dollars per pair)	Quantity supplied (millions of pairs per year)
120	24
125	28
130	32
135	36

   Calculate the elasticity of supply when
   a. The price rises from $125 to $135 a pair.
   b. The average price is $125 a pair.

18. **Study Ranks Honolulu Third Highest for "Unaffordable Housing"**
   A study ranks Honolulu number 3 in the world for the most unaffordable housing market in urban locations, behind Los Angeles and San Diego and is deemed "severely unaffordable." With significant constraints on the supply of land for residential development, housing inflation has resulted.
   Source: *Hawaii Reporter*, September 11, 2007

   a. Would the supply of housing in Honolulu be elastic or inelastic?
   b. Explain how the elasticity of supply plays an important role in influencing how rapidly housing prices in Honolulu rise.

ADDITIONAL PROBLEMS AND APPLICATIONS

MyEconLab   You can work these problems in MyEconLab if assigned by your instructor.

Price Elasticity of Demand

19. With higher fuel costs, airlines raised their average fare from 75¢ to $1.25 per passenger mile and the number of passenger miles decreased from 2.5 million a day to 1.5 million a day.

    a. What is the price elasticity of demand for air travel over this price range?

    b. Describe the demand for air travel.

20. The figure shows the demand for DVD rentals.

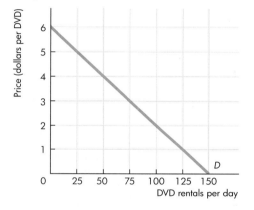

    a. Calculate the elasticity of demand when the price of a DVD rental rises from $3 to $5.

    b. At what price is the elasticity of demand for DVD rentals equal to 1?

Use the following table to work Problems 21 to 23.
The demand schedule for computer chips is

Price (dollars per chip)	Quantity demanded (millions of chips per year)
200	50
250	45
300	40
350	35
400	30

21. a. What happens to total revenue if the price falls from $400 to $350 a chip and from $350 to $300 a chip?

    b. At what price is total revenue at a maximum?

22. At an average price of $350, is the demand for chips elastic, inelastic, or unit elastic? Use the total revenue test to answer this question.

23. At $250 a chip, is the demand for chips elastic or inelastic? Use the total revenue test to answer this question.

24. Your price elasticity of demand for bananas is 4. If the price of bananas rises by 5 percent, what is

    a. The percentage change in the quantity of bananas you buy?

    b. The change in your expenditure on bananas?

25. **As Gasoline Prices Soar, Americans Slowly Adapt**

    As gas prices rose in March 2008, Americans drove 11 billion fewer miles than in March 2007. Realizing that prices are not going down, Americans are adapting to higher energy costs. Americans spend 3.7 percent of their disposable income on transportation fuels. How much we spend on gasoline depends on the choices we make: what car we drive, where we live, how much time we spend driving, and where we choose to go. For many people, higher energy costs mean fewer restaurant meals, deferred weekend outings with the kids, less air travel, and more time closer to home.

    Source: *International Herald Tribune*, May 23, 2008

    a. List and explain the elasticities of demand that are implicitly referred to in the news clip.

    b. Why, according to the news clip, is the demand for gasoline inelastic?

More Elasticities of Demand

Use this information to work Problems 26 and 27.

Economy Forces Many to Shorten Summer Vacation Plans

This year Americans are taking fewer exotic holidays by air and instead are visiting local scenic places by car. The global financial crisis has encouraged many Americans to cut their holiday budgets.

Source: *USA Today*, May 22, 2009

26. Given the prices of the two holidays, is the income elasticity of demand for exotic holidays positive or negative? Are exotic holidays a normal good or an inferior good? Are local holidays a normal good or an inferior good?

27. Are exotic holidays and local holidays substitutes? Explain your answer.

28. When Alex's income was $3,000, he bought 4 bagels and 12 donuts a month. Now his income is $5,000 and he buys 8 bagels and 6 donuts a month.

Calculate Alex's income elasticity of demand for

a. Bagels.

b. Donuts.

29. **Wal-Mart's Recession-Time Pet Project**

During the recession, Wal-Mart moved its pet food and supplies to in front of its other fast-growing business, baby products. Retail experts point out that kids and pets tend to be fairly recession-resistant businesses—even in a recession, dogs will be fed and kids will get their toys.

Source: *CNN*, May 13, 2008

a. What does this news clip imply about the income elasticity of demand for pet food and baby products?

b. Would the income elasticity of demand be greater or less than 1? Explain.

30. If a 5 percent fall in the price of chocolate sauce increases the quantity of chocolate sauce demanded by 10 percent and increases the quantity of ice cream demanded by 15 percent, calculate the

a. Price elasticity of demand for chocolate sauce.

b. Cross elasticity of demand for ice cream with respect to the price of chocolate sauce.

31. **Netflix to Offer Online Movie Viewing**

Online movie rental service Netflix has introduced a new feature to allow customers to watch movies and television series on their personal computers. Netflix competes with video rental retailer Blockbuster, which added an online rental service to the in-store rental service.

Source: *CNN*, January 16, 2007

a. How will online movie viewing influence the price elasticity of demand for in-store movie rentals?

b. Would the cross elasticity of demand for online movies and in-store movie rentals be negative or positive? Explain.

c. Would the cross elasticity of demand for online movies with respect to high-speed Internet service be negative or positive? Explain.

32. **To Love, Honor, and Save Money**

In a survey of caterers and event planners, nearly half of them said that they were seeing declines in wedding spending in response to the economic slowdown; 12% even reported wedding cancellations because of financial concerns.

Source: *Time*, June 2, 2008

a. Based upon this news clip, are wedding events a normal good or inferior good? Explain.

b. Are wedding events more a necessity or a luxury? Would the income elasticity of demand be greater than 1, less than 1, or equal to 1? Explain.

Elasticity of Supply

33. The supply schedule of long-distance phone calls is

Price (cents per minute)	Quantity supplied (millions of minutes per day)
10	200
20	400
30	600
40	800

Calculate the elasticity of supply when

a. The price falls from 40¢ to 30¢ a minute.

b. The average price is 20¢ a minute.

34. **Weak Coal Prices Hit China's Third-Largest Coal Miner**

The chairman of Yanzhou Coal Mining reported that the recession had decreased the demand for coal, with its sales falling by 11.9 percent to 7.92 million tons from 8.99 million tons a year earlier, despite a 10.6 percent cut in the price.

Source: *Dow Jones*, April 27, 2009

Calculate the price elasticity of supply of coal. Is the supply of coal elastic or inelastic?

Economics in the News

35. After you have studied *Reading Between the Lines* on pp. 98–99, answer the following questions.

a. Why is it likely that the elasticity of demand for taxi rides is greater than 1? List all the factors that make this fact seem reasonable.

b. Using the price elasticity value calculated in the analysis on p. 99, find the change in the quantity of cab trips demanded if the price rises by 30 percent.

c. Using your answer to part (b), what happens to total revenue? Will it increase, decrease, or remain constant?

d. What influences on spending might have contributed to the increase in demand for taxi trips other than the ones discussed in the analysis on p. 99?

e. What is the relationship between taxi rides, bus rides, and driving one's own car? What is the sign of the cross elasticities of demand among these three modes of transport?

5

EFFICIENCY
AND EQUITY

After studying this chapter, you will be able to:

◆ Describe the alternative methods of allocating scarce resources

◆ Explain the connection between demand and marginal benefit and define consumer surplus; and explain the connection between supply and marginal cost and define producer surplus

◆ Explain the conditions under which markets are efficient and inefficient

◆ Explain the main ideas about fairness and evaluate claims that markets result in unfair outcomes

When you order a pizza, your *self-interested* choice influences how resources are used. A market coordinates your choice with the self-interested choices of a pizza cook and a delivery person to fill your order. Do markets allocate resources between pizza and everything else efficiently?

Markets generate huge income inequality: *You* can afford to buy a pizza but it might be an unaffordable luxury for a very poor person. Is this situation fair?

You're now going to learn how economists approach these questions. At the end of the chapter, in *Reading Between the Lines*, you will apply what you've learned to see how congestion pricing could end the rush-hour crawl and make our road use efficient.

◢ Resource Allocation Methods

Resources are scarce, so they must be allocated somehow. The goal of this chapter is to evaluate the ability of markets to allocate resources efficiently and fairly. But to see whether the market does a good job, we must compare it with its alternatives. What are the alternative methods of allocating scarce resources?

Eight alternative methods might be used. They are

- Market price
- Command
- Majority rule
- Contest
- First-come, first-served
- Lottery
- Personal characteristics
- Force

Let's briefly examine each method.

Market Price

When a market price allocates a scarce resource, the people who are willing and able to pay that price get the resource. Two kinds of people decide not to pay the market price: those who can afford to pay but choose not to buy and those who are too poor and simply can't afford to buy.

For many goods and services, distinguishing between those who choose not to buy and those who can't afford to buy doesn't matter. But for a few items, it does matter. For example, poor people can't afford to pay school fees and doctors' fees. Because poor people can't afford items that most people consider to be essential, these items are usually allocated by one of the other methods.

Command

A **command system** allocates resources by the order (command) of someone in authority. In the U.S. economy, the command system is used extensively inside firms and government departments. For example, if you have a job, most likely someone tells you what to do. Your labor is allocated to specific tasks by a command.

A command system works well in organizations in which the lines of authority and responsibility are clear and it is easy to monitor the activities being per-

formed. But a command system works badly when the range of activities to be monitored is large and when it is easy for people to fool those in authority. North Korea uses a command system and it works so badly that it even fails to deliver an adequate supply of food.

Majority Rule

Majority rule allocates resources in the way that a majority of voters choose. Societies use majority rule to elect representative governments that make some of the biggest decisions. For example, majority rule decides the tax rates that end up allocating scarce resources between private use and public use. And majority rule decides how tax dollars are allocated among competing uses such as education and health care.

Majority rule works well when the decisions being made affect large numbers of people and self-interest must be suppressed to use resources most effectively.

Contest

A contest allocates resources to a winner (or a group of winners). Sporting events use this method. Andy Roddick competes with other tennis professionals, and the winner gets the biggest payoff. But contests are more general than those in a sports arena, though we don't normally call them contests. For example, Bill Gates won a contest to provide the world's personal computer operating system.

Contests do a good job when the efforts of the "players" are hard to monitor and reward directly. When a manager offers everyone in the company the opportunity to win a big prize, people are motivated to work hard and try to become the winner. Only a few people end up with a big prize, but many people work harder in the process of trying to win. The total output produced by the workers is much greater than it would be without the contest.

First-Come, First-Served

A first-come, first-served method allocates resources to those who are first in line. Many casual restaurants won't accept reservations. They use first-come, first-served to allocate their scarce tables. Highway space is allocated in this way too: The first to arrive at the on-ramp gets the road space. If too many vehicles enter the highway, the speed slows and people wait in line for some space to become available.

First-come, first-served works best when, as in the above examples, a scarce resource can serve just one user at a time in a sequence. By serving the user who arrives first, this method minimizes the time spent waiting for the resource to become free.

Lottery

Lotteries allocate resources to those who pick the winning number, draw the lucky cards, or come up lucky on some other gaming system. State lotteries and casinos reallocate millions of dollars worth of goods and services every year.

But lotteries are more widespread than jackpots and roulette wheels in casinos. They are used to allocate landing slots to airlines at some airports, places in the New York and Boston marathons, and have been used to allocate fishing rights and the electromagnetic spectrum used by cell phones.

Lotteries work best when there is no effective way to distinguish among potential users of a scarce resource.

Personal Characteristics

When resources are allocated on the basis of personal characteristics, people with the "right" characteristics get the resources. Some of the resources that matter most to you are allocated in this way. For example, you will choose a marriage partner on the basis of personal characteristics. But this method can also be used in unacceptable ways. Allocating the best jobs to white, Anglo-Saxon males and discriminating against visible minorities and women is an example.

Force

Force plays a crucial role, for both good and ill, in allocating scarce resources. Let's start with the ill.

War, the use of military force by one nation against another, has played an enormous role historically in allocating resources. The economic supremacy of European settlers in the Americas and Australia owes much to the use of this method.

Theft, the taking of the property of others without their consent, also plays a large role. Both large-scale organized crime and small-scale petty crime collectively allocate billions of dollars worth of resources annually.

But force plays a crucial positive role in allocating resources. It provides the state with an effective method of transferring wealth from the rich to the poor, and it provides the legal framework in which voluntary exchange in markets takes place.

A legal system is the foundation on which our market economy functions. Without courts to enforce contracts, it would not be possible to do business. But the courts could not enforce contracts without the ability to apply force if necessary. The state provides the ultimate force that enables the courts to do their work.

More broadly, the force of the state is essential to uphold the principle of the rule of law. This principle is the bedrock of civilized economic (and social and political) life. With the rule of law upheld, people can go about their daily economic lives with the assurance that their property will be protected—that they can sue for violations against their property (and be sued if they violate the property of others).

Free from the burden of protecting their property and confident in the knowledge that those with whom they trade will honor their agreements, people can get on with focusing on the activity in which they have a comparative advantage and trading for mutual gain.

REVIEW QUIZ

1 Why do we need methods of allocating scarce resources?
2 Describe the alternative methods of allocating scarce resources.
3 Provide an example of each allocation method that illustrates when it works well.
4 Provide an example of each allocation method that illustrates when it works badly.

You can work these questions in Study Plan 5.1 and get instant feedback.   MyEconLab

In the next sections, we're going to see how a market can achieve an efficient use of resources, examine the obstacles to efficiency, and see how sometimes an alternative method might improve on the market. After looking at efficiency, we'll turn our attention to the more difficult issue of fairness.

Benefit, Cost, and Surplus

Resources are allocated efficiently and in the *social interest* when they are used in the ways that people value most highly. You saw in Chapter 2 that this outcome occurs when the quantities produced are at the point on the *PPF* at which marginal benefit equals marginal cost (see pp. 35–37). We're now going to see whether competitive markets produce the efficient quantities.

We begin on the demand side of a market.

Demand, Willingness to Pay, and Value

In everyday life, we talk about "getting value for money." When we use this expression, we are distinguishing between *value* and *price*. Value is what we get, and price is what we pay.

The value of one more unit of a good or service is its marginal benefit. We measure marginal benefit by the maximum price that is willingly paid for another unit of the good or service. But willingness to pay determines demand. *A demand curve is a marginal benefit curve.*

In Fig. 5.1(a), Lisa is willing to pay $1 for the 30th slice of pizza and $1 is her marginal benefit from that slice. In Fig. 5.1(b), Nick is willing to pay $1 for the 10th slice of pizza and $1 is his marginal benefit from that slice. But at what quantity is the market willing to pay $1 for the marginal slice? The answer is provided by the *market demand curve*.

Individual Demand and Market Demand

The relationship between the price of a good and the quantity demanded by one person is called *individual demand*. And the relationship between the price of a good and the quantity demanded by all buyers is called *market demand*.

> The market demand curve is the horizontal sum of the individual demand curves and is formed by adding the quantities demanded by all the individuals at each price.

Figure 5.1(c) illustrates the market demand for pizza if Lisa and Nick are the only people in the market. Lisa's demand curve in part (a) and Nick's demand curve in part (b) sum horizontally to the market demand curve in part (c).

FIGURE 5.1   Individual Demand, Market Demand, and Marginal Social Benefit

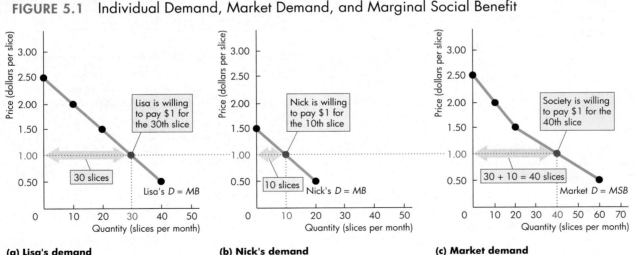

(a) Lisa's demand   **(b) Nick's demand**   **(c) Market demand**

At a price of $1 a slice, the quantity demanded by Lisa is 30 slices and the quantity demanded by Nick is 10 slices, so the quantity demanded by the market is 40 slices. Lisa's demand curve in part (a) and Nick's demand curve in part (b) sum horizontally to the market demand curve in part (c). The market demand curve is the marginal social benefit (*MSB*) curve.

MyEconLab animation

At a price of $1 a slice, Lisa demands 30 slices and Nick demands 10 slices, so the market quantity demanded at $1 a slice is 40 slices.

For Lisa and Nick, their demand curves are their marginal benefit curves. For society, the market demand curve is the marginal benefit curve. We call the marginal benefit to the entire society *marginal social benefit*. So the market demand curve is also the *marginal social benefit (MSB) curve.*

Consumer Surplus

We don't always have to pay as much as we are willing to pay. We get a bargain. When people buy something for less than it is worth to them, they receive a consumer surplus. **Consumer surplus** is the excess of the benefit received from a good over the amount paid for it. We can calculate consumer surplus as the marginal benefit (or value) of a good minus its price, summed over the quantity bought.

Figure 5.2(a) shows Lisa's consumer surplus from pizza when the price is $1 a slice. At this price, she buys 30 slices a month because the 30th slice is worth exactly $1 to her. But Lisa is willing to pay $2 for the 10th slice, so her marginal benefit from this slice is

$1 more than she pays for it—she receives a surplus of $1 on the 10th slice.

Lisa's consumer surplus is the sum of the surpluses on *all of the slices she buys*. This sum is the area of the green triangle—the area below the demand curve and above the market price line. The area of this triangle is equal to its base (30 slices) multiplied by its height ($1.50) divided by 2, which is $22.50. The area of the blue rectangle in Fig. 5.2(a) shows what Lisa pays for 30 slices of pizza.

Figure 5.2(b) shows Nick's consumer surplus, and part (c) shows the consumer surplus for the market. The consumer surplus for the market is the sum of the consumer surpluses of Lisa and Nick.

All goods and services have decreasing marginal benefit, so people receive more benefit from their consumption than the amount they pay.

Supply and Marginal Cost

Your next task is to see how market supply reflects marginal cost. The connection between supply and cost closely parallels the related ideas about demand and benefit that you've just studied. Firms are in business to make a profit. To do so, they must sell

FIGURE 5.2   Demand and Consumer Surplus

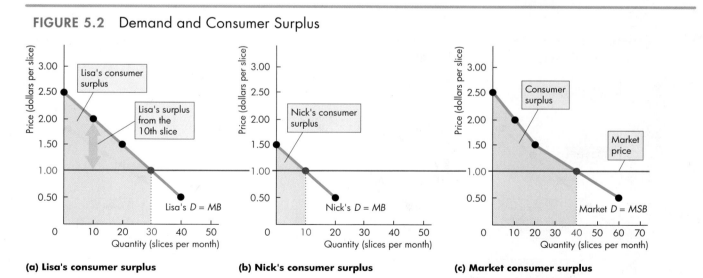

(a) Lisa's consumer surplus   **(b) Nick's consumer surplus**   **(c) Market consumer surplus**

Lisa is willing to pay $2 for her 10th slice of pizza in part (a). At a market price of $1 a slice, Lisa receives a surplus of $1 on the 10th slice. The green triangle shows her consumer surplus on the 30 slices she buys at $1 a slice. The

green triangle in part (b) shows Nick's consumer surplus on the 10 slices that he buys at $1 a slice. The green area in part (c) shows the consumer surplus for the market. The blue rectangles show the amounts spent on pizza.

their output for a price that exceeds the cost of production. Let's investigate the relationship between cost and price.

Supply, Cost, and Minimum Supply-Price

Firms make a profit when they receive more from the sale of a good or service than the cost of producing it. Just as consumers distinguish between value and price, so producers distinguish between *cost* and *price*. Cost is what a firm gives up when it produces a good or service and price is what a firm receives when it sells the good or service.

The cost of producing one more unit of a good or service is its marginal cost. Marginal cost is the minimum price that producers must receive to induce them to offer one more unit of a good or service for sale. But the minimum supply-price determines supply. *A supply curve is a marginal cost curve.*

In Fig. 5.3(a), Maria is willing to produce the 100th pizza for $15, her marginal cost of that pizza. In Fig. 5.3(b), Max is willing to produce the 50th pizza for $15, his marginal cost.

What quantity is this market willing to produce for $15 a pizza? The answer is provided by the *market supply curve*.

Individual Supply and Market Supply

The relationship between the price of a good and the quantity supplied by one producer is called *individual supply*. And the relationship between the price of a good and the quantity supplied by all producers is called *market supply*.

> The market supply curve is the horizontal sum of the individual supply curves and is formed by adding the quantities supplied by all the producers at each price.

Figure 5.3(c) illustrates the market supply of pizzas if Maria and Max are the only producers. Maria's supply curve in part (a) and Max's supply curve in part (b) sum horizontally to the market supply curve in part (c).

At a price of $15 a pizza, Maria supplies 100 pizzas and Max supplies 50 pizzas, so the quantity supplied by the market at $15 a pizza is 150 pizzas.

For Maria and Max, their supply curves are their marginal cost curves. For society, the market supply curve is its marginal cost curve. We call the society's marginal cost *marginal social cost*. So the market supply curve is also the *marginal social cost (MSC) curve*.

FIGURE 5.3 Individual Supply, Market Supply, and Marginal Social Cost

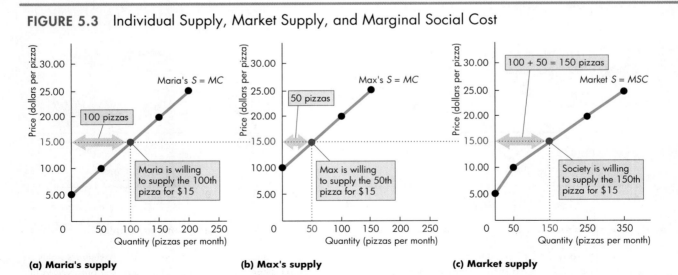

(a) Maria's supply

(b) Max's supply

(c) Market supply

At a price of $15 a pizza, the quantity supplied by Maria is 100 pizzas and the quantity supplied by Max is 50 pizzas, so the quantity supplied by the market is 150 pizzas. Maria's

supply curve in part (a) and Max's supply curve in part (b) sum horizontally to the market supply curve in part (c). The market supply curve is the marginal social cost (MSC) curve.

MyEconLab animation

Producer Surplus

When price exceeds marginal cost, the firm receives a producer surplus. **Producer surplus** is the excess of the amount received from the sale of a good or service over the cost of producing it. We calculate producer surplus as the price received minus the marginal cost (or minimum supply-price), summed over the quantity sold.

Figure 5.4(a) shows Maria's producer surplus from pizza when the price is $15 a pizza. At this price, she sells 100 pizzas a month because the 100th pizza costs her $15 to produce. But Maria is willing to produce the 50th pizza for her marginal cost, which is $10, so she receives a surplus of $5 on this pizza.

Maria's producer surplus is the sum of the surpluses on the pizzas she sells. This sum is the area of the blue triangle—the area below the market price and above the supply curve. The area of this triangle is equal to its base (100) multiplied by its height ($10) divided by 2, which is $500.

The red area below the supply curve in Fig. 5.4(a) shows what it costs Maria to produce 100 pizzas.

The area of the blue triangle in Fig. 5.4(b) shows Max's producer surplus and the blue area in Fig. 5.4(c) shows the producer surplus for the market.

The producer surplus for the market is the sum of the producer surpluses of Maria and Max.

Consumer surplus and producer surplus can be used to measure the efficiency of a market. Let's see how we can use these concepts to study the efficiency of a competitive market.

REVIEW QUIZ

1 What is the relationship between the marginal benefit, value, and demand?
2 What is the relationship between individual demand and market demand?
3 What is consumer surplus? How is it measured?
4 What is the relationship between the marginal cost, minimum supply-price, and supply?
5 What is the relationship between individual supply and market supply?
6 What is producer surplus? How is it measured?

You can work these questions in Study Plan 5.2 and get instant feedback.   MyEconLab

---

FIGURE 5.4   Supply and Producer Surplus

(a) Maria's producer surplus   **(b) Max's producer surplus**   **(c) Market producer surplus**

Maria is willing to produce the 50th pizza for $10 in part (a). At a market price of $15 a pizza, Maria gets a surplus of $5 on the 50th pizza. The blue triangle shows her producer surplus on the 100 pizzas she sells at $15 each.

The blue triangle in part (b) shows Max's producer surplus on the 50 pizzas that he sells at $15 each. The blue area in part (c) shows producer surplus for the market. The red areas show the cost of producing the pizzas sold.

MyEconLab animation

Is the Competitive Market Efficient?

Figure 5.5(a) shows the market for pizza. The market forces that you studied in Chapter 3 (pp. 66–67) pull the pizza market to its equilibrium price of $15 a pizza and equilibrium quantity of 10,000 pizzas a day. Buyers enjoy a consumer surplus (green area) and sellers enjoy a producer surplus (blue area), but is this competitive equilibrium efficient?

Efficiency of Competitive Equilibrium

You've seen that the market demand curve for a good or service tells us the marginal social benefit from it. You've also seen that the market supply curve of a good or service tells us the marginal social cost of producing it.

Equilibrium in a competitive market occurs when the quantity demanded equals the quantity supplied at the intersection of the demand curve and the supply curve. At this intersection point, marginal social benefit on the demand curve equals marginal social cost on the supply curve. This equality is the condition for allocative efficiency. So in equilibrium, a competitive market achieves allocative efficiency.

Figure 5.5 illustrates the efficiency of competitive equilibrium. The demand curve and the supply curve intersect in part (a) and marginal social benefit equals marginal social cost in part (b).

If production is less than 10,000 pizzas a day, the marginal pizza is valued more highly than it costs to produce. If production exceeds 10,000 pizzas a day, the marginal pizza costs more to produce than the value that consumers place on it. Only when 10,000 pizzas a day are produced is the marginal pizza worth exactly what it costs.

The competitive market pushes the quantity of pizzas produced to its efficient level of 10,000 a day. If production is less than 10,000 pizzas a day, a shortage raises the price, which increases production. If production exceeds 10,000 pizzas a day, a surplus of pizzas lowers the price, which decreases production. So a competitive pizza market is efficient.

Figure 5.5(a) also shows the consumer surplus and producer surplus. The sum of consumer surplus and producer surplus is called **total surplus**. When the efficient quantity is produced, total surplus is maximized. Buyers and sellers acting in their self-interest end up promoting the social interest.

FIGURE 5.5   An Efficient Market for Pizza

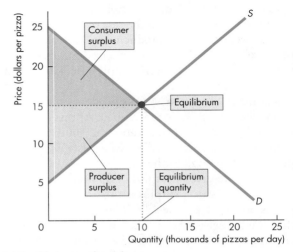

(a) Equilibrium and surpluses

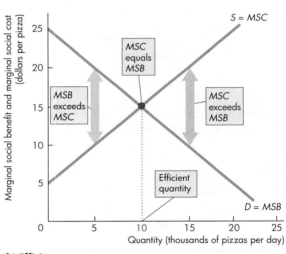

(b) Efficiency

Competitive equilibrium in part (a) occurs when the quantity demanded equals the quantity supplied. Resources are used efficiently in part (b) when marginal social benefit, *MSB*, equals marginal social cost, *MSC*. Total surplus, which is the sum of consumer surplus (the green triangle) and producer surplus (the blue triangle) is maximized.

The efficient quantity in part (b) is the same as the equilibrium quantity in part (a). The competitive pizza market produces the efficient quantity of pizzas.

MyEconLab animation

Economics in Action
Seeing the Invisible Hand

Adam Smith said that each participant in a competitive market is "led by *an invisible hand* to promote an end [the efficient use of resources] which was no part of his intention" (see p. 8). Smith believed that the invisible hand sends resources to the uses in which they have the highest value.

You can't *see* an invisible hand, but you can imagine one, and you can see its consequences in the cartoon and in today's world.

Umbrella for Sale The cold drinks vendor has cold drinks and shade and he has a marginal cost and a minimum supply-price of each. The reader on the park bench has a marginal benefit and willingness to pay for each. The reader's marginal benefit from shade exceeds the vendor's marginal cost; but the vendor's marginal cost of a cold drink exceeds the reader's marginal benefit. They trade the umbrella. The vendor gets a producer surplus from selling the shade for more than its marginal cost, and the reader gets a consumer surplus from buying the shade for less than its marginal benefit. Both are better off and the umbrella has moved to its highest-valued use.

The Invisible Hand at Work Today The market economy relentlessly performs the activity illustrated in the cartoon to achieve an efficient allocation of resources.

Suppose that a Florida frost cuts the supply of tomatoes. With fewer tomatoes available, the marginal social benefit increases. A shortage of tomatoes raises their price, so the market allocates the quantity available to the people who value them most highly.

If a new technology cuts the cost of producing a smart phone, the supply of smart phones increases and the price of a smart phone falls. The lower price

encourages an increase in the quantity demanded of this now less-costly tool. The marginal social benefit from a smart phone is brought to equality with its lower marginal social cost.

Market Failure

Markets do not always achieve an efficient outcome. We call a situation in which a market delivers an inefficient outcome one of **market failure**. Market failure can occur because too little of an item is produced (underproduction) or too much is produced (overproduction). We'll describe these two market failure outcomes and then see why they arise.

Underproduction In Fig. 5.6(a), the quantity of pizzas produced is 5,000 a day. At this quantity, consumers are willing to pay $20 for a pizza that costs only $10 to produce. By producing only 5,000 pizzas a day, total surplus is smaller than its maximum possible level. The quantity produced is inefficient—there is underproduction.

We measure the scale of inefficiency by **deadweight loss**, which is the decrease in total surplus that results

FIGURE 5.6   Underproduction and Overproduction

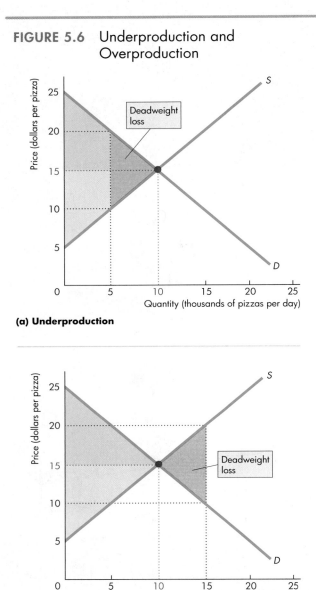

(a) Underproduction

(b) Overproduction

If 5,000 pizzas a day are produced, in part (a), total surplus (the sum of the green and blue areas) is smaller than its maximum by the amount of the deadweight loss (the gray triangle). At all quantities below 10,000 pizzas a day, the benefit from one more pizza exceeds its cost.

If 15,000 pizzas a day are produced, in part (b), total surplus is also smaller than its maximum by the amount of the deadweight loss. At all quantities in excess of 10,000 pizzas a day, the cost of one more pizza exceeds its benefit.

—— MyEconLab animation ——

from an inefficient level of production. The gray triangle in Fig. 5.6(a) shows the deadweight loss.

Overproduction In Fig. 5.6(b), the quantity of pizzas produced is 15,000 a day. At this quantity, consumers are willing to pay only $10 for a pizza that costs $20 to produce. By producing the 15,000th pizza, $10 of resources are wasted. Again, the gray triangle shows the deadweight loss, which reduces the total surplus to less than its maximum.

Inefficient production creates a deadweight loss that is borne by the entire society: It is a social loss.

Sources of Market Failure

Obstacles to efficiency that bring market failure and create deadweight losses are

- Price and quantity regulations
- Taxes and subsidies
- Externalities
- Public goods and common resources
- Monopoly
- High transactions costs

Price and Quantity Regulations *Price regulations* that put a cap on the rent a landlord is permitted to charge and laws that require employers to pay a minimum wage sometimes block the price adjustments that balance the quantity demanded and the quantity supplied and lead to underproduction. *Quantity regulations* that limit the amount that a farm is permitted to produce also lead to underproduction.

Taxes and Subsidies *Taxes* increase the prices paid by buyers and lower the prices received by sellers. So taxes decrease the quantity produced and lead to underproduction. *Subsidies*, which are payments by the government to producers, decrease the prices paid by buyers and increase the prices received by sellers. So subsidies increase the quantity produced and lead to overproduction.

Externalities An *externality* is a cost or a benefit that affects someone other than the seller or the buyer. An *external cost* arises when an electric utility burns coal and emits carbon dioxide. The utility doesn't consider the cost of climate change when it decides how much power to produce. The result is overproduction. An *external benefit* arises when an apartment owner installs a smoke detector and decreases her neighbor's fire risk. She doesn't consider the benefit to her neighbor when she decides how many detectors to install. The result is underproduction.

Public Goods and Common Resources A *public good* is a good or service that is consumed simultaneously by everyone even if they don't pay for it. National defense is an example. Competitive markets would underproduce national defense because it is in each person's interest to free ride on everyone else and avoid paying for her or his share of such a good.

A *common resource* is owned by no one but is available to be used by everyone. Atlantic salmon is an example. It is in everyone's self-interest to ignore the costs they impose on others when they decide how much of a common resource to use. The result is that the resource is overused.

Monopoly A *monopoly* is a firm that is the sole provider of a good or service. Local water supply and cable television are supplied by firms that are monopolies. The monopoly's self-interest is to maximize its profit. Because the monopoly has no competitors, it can set the price to achieve its self-interested goal. To achieve its goal, a monopoly produces too little and charges too high a price. It leads to underproduction.

High Transactions Costs When you go to Starbucks, you pay for more than the coffee. You pay your share of the cost of the barrista's time, the espresso maker, and the decor. When you buy your first apartment, you will pay for more than the apartment. You will buy the services of an agent and a lawyer. Economists call the costs of the services that enable a market to bring buyers and sellers together **transactions costs**.

It is costly to operate *any* market so to use market price to allocate resources, it must be worth bearing the transactions costs. Some markets are too costly to operate. For example, it is too costly to operate a market in time slots on a local tennis court. Instead of a market, the court uses first-come, first-served: You hang around until the court becomes vacant and "pay" with your waiting time. When transactions costs are high, the market might underproduce.

You now know the conditions under which resource allocation is efficient. You've seen how a competitive market can be efficient, and you've seen some obstacles to efficiency. Can alternative allocation methods improve on the market?

Alternatives to the Market

When a market is inefficient, can one of the alternative nonmarket methods that we described at the beginning of this chapter do a better job? Sometimes it can.

Often, majority rule might be used in an attempt to improve the allocation of resources. But majority rule has its own shortcomings. A group that pursues the self-interest of its members can become the majority. For example, a price or quantity regulation that creates inefficiency is almost always the result of a self-interested group becoming the majority and imposing costs on the minority. Also, with majority rule, votes must be translated into actions by bureaucrats who have their own agendas based on their self-interest.

Managers in firms issue commands and avoid the transactions costs that they would incur if they went to a market every time they needed a job done.

First-come, first-served works best in some situations. Think about the scene at a busy ATM. Instead of waiting in line people might trade places at a "market" price. But someone would need to ensure that trades were honored. At a busy ATM, first-come, first-served is the most efficient arrangement.

There is no one efficient mechanism that allocates all resources efficiently. But markets, when supplemented by other mechanisms such as majority rule, command systems, and first-come, first-served, do an amazingly good job.

REVIEW QUIZ

1 Do competitive markets use resources efficiently? Explain why or why not.
2 What is deadweight loss and under what conditions does it occur?
3 What are the obstacles to achieving an efficient allocation of resources in the market economy?

You can work these questions in Study Plan 5.3 and get instant feedback. **MyEconLab**

Is an efficient allocation of resources also a fair allocation? Does the competitive market provide people with fair incomes for their work? Do people always pay a fair price for the things they buy? Don't we need the government to step into some competitive markets to prevent the price from rising too high or falling too low? Let's now study these questions.

Is the Competitive Market Fair?

When a natural disaster strikes, such as a severe winter storm or a hurricane, the prices of many essential items jump. The reason prices jump is that the demand and willingness to pay for these items has increased, but the supply has not changed. So the higher prices achieve an efficient allocation of scarce resources. News reports of these price hikes almost never talk about efficiency. Instead, they talk about equity or fairness. The claim that is often made is that it is unfair for profit-seeking dealers to cheat the victims of natural disaster.

Similarly, when low-skilled people work for a wage that is below what most would regard as a "living wage," the media and politicians talk of employers taking unfair advantage of their workers.

How do we decide whether something is fair or unfair? You know when you *think* something is unfair, but how do you *know?* What are the *principles* of fairness?

Philosophers have tried for centuries to answer this question. Economists have offered their answers too. But before we look at the proposed answers, you should know that there is no universally agreed upon answer.

Economists agree about efficiency. That is, they agree that it makes sense to make the economic pie as large as possible and to produce it at the lowest possible cost. But they do not agree about equity. That is, they do not agree about what are fair shares of the economic pie for all the people who make it. The reason is that ideas about fairness are not exclusively economic ideas. They touch on politics, ethics, and religion. Nevertheless, economists have thought about these issues and have a contribution to make. Let's examine the views of economists on this topic.

To think about fairness, think of economic life as a game—a serious game. All ideas about fairness can be divided into two broad groups. They are

- It's not fair if the *result* isn't fair.
- It's not fair if the *rules* aren't fair.

It's Not Fair If the *Result* Isn't Fair

The earliest efforts to establish a principle of fairness were based on the view that the result is what matters. The general idea was that it is unfair if people's incomes are too unequal. For example, it is unfair

that a bank president earns millions of dollars a year while a bank teller earns only thousands of dollars. It is unfair that a store owner makes a larger profit and her customers pay higher prices in the aftermath of a winter storm.

During the nineteenth century, economists thought they had made an incredible discovery: Efficiency requires equality of incomes. To make the economic pie as large as possible, it must be cut into equal pieces, one for each person. This idea turns out to be wrong. But there is a lesson in the reason that it is wrong, so this idea is worth a closer look.

Utilitarianism The nineteenth-century idea that only equality brings efficiency is called *utilitarianism*. **Utilitarianism** is a principle that states that we should strive to achieve "the greatest happiness for the greatest number." The people who developed this idea were known as utilitarians. They included the most eminent thinkers, such as Jeremy Bentham and John Stuart Mill.

Utilitarians argued that to achieve "the greatest happiness for the greatest number," income must be transferred from the rich to the poor up to the point of complete equality—to the point at which there are no rich and no poor.

They reasoned in the following way: First, everyone has the same basic wants and a similar capacity to enjoy life. Second, the greater a person's income, the smaller is the marginal benefit of a dollar. The millionth dollar spent by a rich person brings a smaller marginal benefit to that person than the marginal benefit that the thousandth dollar spent brings to a poorer person. So by transferring a dollar from the millionaire to the poorer person, more is gained than is lost. The two people added together are better off.

Figure 5.7 illustrates this utilitarian idea. Tom and Jerry have the same marginal benefit curve, *MB*. (Marginal benefit is measured on the same scale of 1 to 3 for both Tom and Jerry.) Tom is at point *A*. He earns \$5,000 a year, and his marginal benefit from a dollar is 3 units. Jerry is at point *B*. He earns \$45,000 a year, and his marginal benefit from a dollar is 1 unit. If a dollar is transferred from Jerry to Tom, Jerry loses 1 unit of marginal benefit and Tom gains 3 units. So together, Tom and Jerry are better off—they are sharing the economic pie more efficiently. If a second dollar is transferred, the same thing happens: Tom gains more than Jerry loses. And the same is true for every dollar transferred until they both reach point *C*. At point *C*, Tom and Jerry have \$25,000

FIGURE 5.7   Utilitarian Fairness

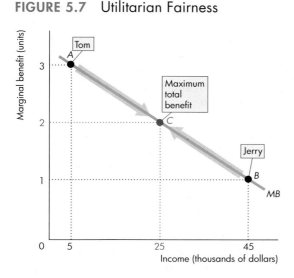

Tom earns $5,000 and has 3 units of marginal benefit at point A. Jerry earns $45,000 and has 1 unit of marginal benefit at point B. If income is transferred from Jerry to Tom, Jerry's loss is less than Tom's gain. Only when each of them has $25,000 and 2 units of marginal benefit (at point C) can the sum of their total benefit increase no further.

───── MyEconLab animation ─────

each and a marginal benefit of 2 units. Now they are sharing the economic pie in the most efficient way. It brings the greatest happiness to Tom and Jerry.

The Big Tradeoff   One big problem with the utilitarian ideal of complete equality is that it ignores the costs of making income transfers. Recognizing the costs of making income transfers leads to what is called the **big tradeoff**, which is a tradeoff between efficiency and fairness.

The big tradeoff is based on the following facts. Income can be transferred from people with high incomes to people with low incomes only by taxing the high incomes. Taxing people's income from employment makes them work less. It results in the quantity of labor being less than the efficient quantity. Taxing people's income from capital makes them save less. It results in the quantity of capital being less than the efficient quantity. With smaller quantities of both labor and capital, the quantity of goods and services produced is less than the efficient quantity. The economic pie shrinks.

The tradeoff is between the size of the economic pie and the degree of equality with which it is shared. The greater the amount of income redistribution through income taxes, the greater is the inefficiency—the smaller is the economic pie.

There is a second source of inefficiency. A dollar taken from a rich person does not end up as a dollar in the hands of a poorer person. Some of the dollar is spent on administration of the tax and transfer system. The cost of tax-collecting agencies, such as the Internal Revenue Service (IRS), and welfare-administering agencies, such as the Centers for Medicare and Medicaid, must be paid with some of the taxes collected. Also, taxpayers hire accountants, auditors, and lawyers to help them ensure that they pay the correct amount of taxes. These activities use skilled labor and capital resources that could otherwise be used to produce goods and services that people value.

When all these costs are taken into account, taking a dollar from a rich person does not give a dollar to a poor person. It is possible that with high taxes, people with low incomes might end up being worse off. Suppose, for example, that highly taxed entrepreneurs decide to work less hard and shut down some of their businesses. Low-income workers get fired and must seek other, perhaps even lower-paid, work.

Today, because of the big tradeoff, no one says that fairness requires complete equality of incomes.

Make the Poorest as Well Off as Possible   A new solution to the big-tradeoff problem was proposed by philosopher John Rawls in a classic book entitled *A Theory of Justice*, published in 1971. Rawls says that, taking all the costs of income transfers into account, the fair distribution of the economic pie is the one that makes the poorest person as well off as possible. The incomes of rich people should be taxed, and after paying the costs of administering the tax and transfer system, what is left should be transferred to the poor. But the taxes must not be so high that they make the economic pie shrink to the point at which the poorest person ends up with a smaller piece. A bigger share of a smaller pie can be less than a smaller share of a bigger pie. The goal is to make the piece enjoyed by the poorest person as big as possible. Most likely, this piece will not be an equal share.

The "fair results" idea requires a change in the results after the game is over. Some economists say that these changes are themselves unfair and propose a different way of thinking about fairness.

It's Not Fair If the *Rules* Aren't Fair

The idea that it's not fair if the rules aren't fair is based on a fundamental principle that seems to be hardwired into the human brain: the symmetry principle. The **symmetry principle** is the requirement that people in similar situations be treated similarly. It is the moral principle that lies at the center of all the big religions and that says, in some form or other, "Behave toward other people in the way you expect them to behave toward you."

In economic life, this principle translates into *equality of opportunity*. But equality of opportunity to do what? This question is answered by the philosopher Robert Nozick in a book entitled *Anarchy, State, and Utopia*, published in 1974.

Nozick argues that the idea of fairness as an outcome or result cannot work and that fairness must be based on the fairness of the rules. He suggests that fairness obeys two rules:

1. The state must enforce laws that establish and protect private property.
2. Private property may be transferred from one person to another only by voluntary exchange.

The first rule says that everything that is valuable must be owned by individuals and that the state must ensure that theft is prevented. The second rule says that the only legitimate way a person can acquire property is to buy it in exchange for something else that the person owns. If these rules, which are the only fair rules, are followed, then the result is fair. It doesn't matter how unequally the economic pie is shared, provided that the pie is made by people, each one of whom voluntarily provides services in exchange for the share of the pie offered in compensation.

These rules satisfy the symmetry principle. If these rules are not followed, the symmetry principle is broken. You can see these facts by imagining a world in which the laws are not followed.

First, suppose that some resources or goods are not owned. They are common property. Then everyone is free to participate in a grab to use them. The strongest will prevail. But when the strongest prevails, the strongest effectively *owns* the resources or goods in question and prevents others from enjoying them.

Second, suppose that we do not insist on voluntary exchange for transferring ownership of resources from one person to another. The alternative is *involuntary* transfer. In simple language, the alternative is theft.

Both of these situations violate the symmetry principle. Only the strong acquire what they want. The weak end up with only the resources and goods that the strong don't want.

In a majority-rule political system, the strong are those in the majority or those with enough resources to influence opinion and achieve a majority.

In contrast, if the two rules of fairness are followed, everyone, strong and weak, is treated in a similar way. All individuals are free to use their resources and human skills to create things that are valued by themselves and others and to exchange the fruits of their efforts with all others. This set of arrangements is the only one that obeys the symmetry principle.

Fair Rules and Efficiency If private property rights are enforced and if voluntary exchange takes place in a competitive market with none of the obstacles described above (p. 115), resources will be allocated efficiently.

According to the Nozick fair rules view, no matter how unequal is the resulting distribution of income and wealth, it will be fair.

It would be better if everyone were as well off as those with the highest incomes, but scarcity prevents that outcome and the best attainable outcome is the efficient one.

Case Study: A Generator Shortage in a Natural Disaster

Hurricane Katrina shut down electricity supplies over a wide area and increased the demand for portable generators. What is the fair way to allocate the available generators?

If the market price is used, the outcome is efficient. Sellers *and buyers* are better off and no one is worse off. But people who own generators make a larger profit and the generators go to those who want them most and can afford them. Is that fair?

On the Nozick rules view, the outcome is fair. On the fair outcome view, the outcome might be considered unfair. But what are the alternatives? They are command, majority rule, contest, first-come-first-served, lottery, personal characteristics, and force. Except by chance, none of these methods delivers an allocation of generators that is either fair or efficient. It is unfair in the rules view because the distribution involves involuntary transfers of resources among citizens. It is unfair in the results view because the poorest don't end up being made as well off as possible.

◆ AT ISSUE

Price Gouging

Price gouging is the practice of offering an essential item for sale following a natural disaster at a price much higher price than its normal price.

In the aftermath of Hurricane Katrina, John Shepperson bought 19 generators and rented a U-Haul truck to transport them from his Kentucky home to a town in Mississippi that had lost its electricity supply. He offered the generators to eager buyers at twice the price he had paid for them. But before Mr. Shepperson had made a sale, the Mississippi police confiscated the generators and put him in jail for four days for price gouging.

In Favor of a Law Against Price Gouging

Supporters of laws against price gouging say:

- It unfairly exploits vulnerable needy buyers.
- It unfairly rewards unscrupulous sellers.
- In situations of extraordinary shortage, prices should be regulated to prevent these abuses and scarce resources should be allocated by one of the non-market mechanisms such as majority vote or equal shares for all.

Should the price that this seller of generators may charge be regulated?

The Economist's Response

Economists say that preventing a voluntary market transaction leads to inefficiency—it makes some people worse off without making anyone better off.

- In the figure below, when the demand for generators increases from D_0 to D_1, the equilibrium price rises from \$200 to \$600.
- Calling the price rise "gouging" and blocking it with a law prevents additional units from being made available and creates a deadweight loss.

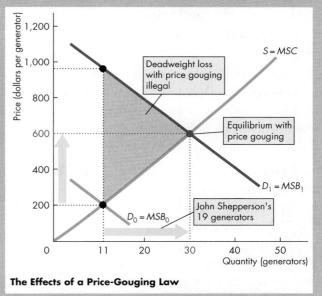

The Effects of a Price-Gouging Law

◆ REVIEW QUIZ

1 What are the two big approaches to thinking about fairness?
2 What is the utilitarian idea of fairness and what is wrong with it?
3 Explain the big tradeoff. What idea of fairness has been developed to deal with it?
4 What is the idea of fairness based on fair rules?

You can work these questions in Study Plan 5.4 and get instant feedback.   MyEconLab

◆ You've now studied efficiency and equity (fairness), the two biggest issues that run through the whole of economics. *Reading Between the Lines* on pp. 120–121 looks at an example of an efficiency in our economy today. At many points throughout this book—and in your life—you will return to and use the ideas you've learned in this chapter. We start to apply these ideas in the next chapter where we study some sources of *in*efficiency and *un*fairness.

Making Traffic Flow Efficiently

Rail No Cure-All for Metro Atlanta's Traffic Congestion

The Atlanta Journal-Constitution
September 6, 2011

… On its face, the problem seems simple. If a person who commutes alone by car takes the train instead, then that's one less car on the road. … Multiple experts told PolitiFact Georgia that even if thousands of drivers take the train rather than a major road, congestion on that road doesn't end.

It might drop initially, but travelers soon notice the better traffic. Commuters who once avoided the road return. Others take additional trips, or start using it during peak traffic times. People who car pooled start commuting alone.

Eventually, congestion returns, said Anthony Downs, a Brookings Institution fellow who has studied traffic congestion for decades. He thinks congestion is extremely hard to avoid, and likely will grow worse. Brookings is a liberal-leaning think tank. …

A 2009 University of Toronto study that analyzed interstate highway and vehicle travel data across the United States found there is little evidence that additional public transit reduces traffic. Other researchers have come to similar conclusions.

But there's another important side to the traffic conundrum … : Decades of research shows that additional highway lanes don't end gridlock, either. As with rail, drivers fill up the new lanes. Once again, they're stuck in traffic.

… In the end, though, the bulk of the experts we interviewed agreed that the one tested way to cut down on gridlock is "congestion pricing." That's when drivers pay a surcharge to use roads during peak traffic hours. Cities such as London and Singapore have used the strategy and eased downtown traffic.

ESSENCE OF THE STORY

- There is little evidence that additional public transit or additional freeway lanes reduces road congestion.

- If one car user takes the train, so there is one less car on the road, traffic flows faster and others are encouraged to switch from train to car, so eventually congestion returns.

- Additional drivers fill up new highway lanes and again, congestion returns.

- The one tested way to reduce congestion is congestion pricing—paying to use roads during peak traffic hours.

- London and Singapore use this method to keep traffic moving.

ECONOMIC ANALYSIS

- The Texas Transportation Institute says that in 2010 on 10 stretches of Atlanta's most congested corridors, 2 million person hours and 6.6 million gallons of gasoline were wasted at a cost of $302 million; and on the nation's 328 most congested corridors, 78 million person hours and 284 million gallons of gasoline were wasted at a cost of $12.6 billion.

- When one additional vehicle enters an uncongested road, it imposes no costs on other road users. But when one additional vehicle enters a congested road, the traffic slows and time and gasoline costs increase for all road users.

- The figures show the marginal social cost curve (MSC) for a road that can carry 15,000 vehicles per hour with no congestion. Up to 15,000 vehicles per hour, $MSC = 0$. Above 15,000 vehicles per hour congestion occurs and MSC increases as more vehicles enter the road.

- During the night and at off-peak parts of the day, the marginal social benefit (MSB) and demand for road space is low and there is no congestion.

- Figure 1 illustrates off-peak road use. The demand and marginal benefit curve is $D_o = MSB_o$; the marginal cost curve is MSC; and the equilibrium and efficient outcome occurs at a zero price for road use.

- Figure 2 illustrates road use at a peak congestion time. The demand and marginal benefit curve is $D_p = MSB_p$ and with a zero price for road use, 40,000 vehicles per

hour enter the road. There is a deadweight loss (of time and gasoline) shown by the gray triangle.

- Imposing a congestion charge of $2 per mile brings an equilibrium at 25,000 vehicles per hour, which is the efficient quantity. In this situation, total surplus, the sum of consumer surplus (green) *plus* producer surplus (blue), is maximized.

- Singapore has the world's most sophisticated congestion pricing with the price displayed on gantries (see photo), and the price rises as congestion increases and falls as congestion eases.

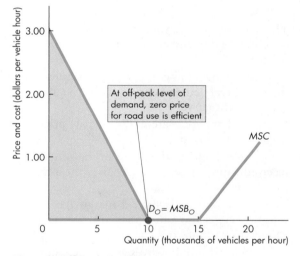

Figure 1 Off-Peak Road Use

Traffic grinds to a halt on a U.S. freeway, but electronic Road Pricing (ERP) keeps vehicles moving in Singapore.

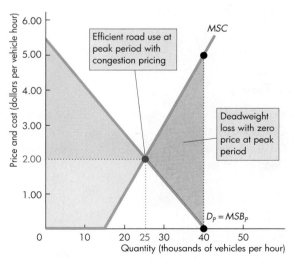

Figure 2 Peak Road Use

SUMMARY

Key Points

Resource Allocation Methods (pp. 106–107)

- Because resources are scarce, some mechanism must allocate them.
- The alternative allocation methods are market price; command; majority rule; contest; first-come, first-served; lottery; personal characteristics; and force.

Working Study Plan Problems 1 and 2 will give you a better understanding of resource allocation methods.

Benefit, Cost, and Surplus (pp. 108–111)

- The maximum price willingly paid is marginal benefit, so a demand curve is also a marginal benefit curve.
- The market demand curve is the horizontal sum of the individual demand curves and is the marginal social benefit curve.
- Value is what people are *willing to* pay; price is what people *must* pay.
- Consumer surplus is the excess of the benefit received from a good or service over the amount paid for it.
- The minimum supply-price is marginal cost, so a supply curve is also a marginal cost curve.
- The market supply curve is the horizontal sum of the individual supply curves and is the marginal social cost curve.
- Cost is what producers pay; price is what producers receive.

- Producer surplus is the excess of the amount received from the sale of a good or service over the cost of producing it.

Working Study Plan Problems 3 to 10 will give you a better understanding of benefit, cost, and surplus.

Is the Competitive Market Efficient? (pp. 112–115)

- In a competitive equilibrium, marginal social benefit equals marginal social cost and resource allocation is efficient.
- Buyers and sellers acting in their self-interest end up promoting the social interest.
- Total surplus, consumer surplus plus producer surplus, is maximized.
- Producing less than or more than the efficient quantity creates deadweight loss.
- Price and quantity regulations; taxes and subsidies; externalities; public goods and common resources; monopoly; and high transactions costs can lead to market failure.

Working Study Plan Problems 11 to 13 will give you a better understanding of the efficiency of competitive markets.

Is the Competitive Market Fair? (pp. 116–119)

- Ideas about fairness can be divided into two groups: fair *results* and fair *rules*.
- Fair-results ideas require income transfers from the rich to the poor.
- Fair-rules ideas require property rights and voluntary exchange.

Working Study Plan Problems 14 and 15 will give you a better understanding of the fairness of competitive markets.

Key Terms

Big tradeoff, 117	Market failure, 113	Transactions costs, 115
Command system, 106	Producer surplus, 111	Utilitarianism, 116
Consumer surplus, 109	Symmetry principle, 118	
Deadweight loss, 113	Total surplus, 112	

MyEconLab   You can work Problems 1 to 17 in MyEconLab Chapter 5 Study Plan and get instant feedback.

Resource Allocation Methods (Study Plan 5.1)

Use the following information to work Problems 1 and 2.

At Chez Panisse, the restaurant in Berkeley that is credited with having created California cuisine, reservations are essential. At Mandarin Dynasty, a restaurant near the University of California San Diego, reservations are recommended. At Eli Cannon's, a restaurant in Middletown, Connecticut, reservations are not accepted.

1. a. Describe the method of allocating scarce table resources at these three restaurants.

    b. Why do you think restaurants have different reservations policies?

2. Why do you think restaurants don't use the market price to allocate their tables?

Benefit, Cost, and Surplus (Study Plan 5.2)

Use the following table to work Problems 3 to 5.
The table gives the demand schedules for train travel for the only buyers in the market, Ann, Beth, and Cy.

Price (dollars per mile)	Quantity demanded (miles)		
	Ann	Beth	Cy
3	30	25	20
4	25	20	15
5	20	15	10
6	15	10	5
7	10	5	0
8	5	0	0
9	0	0	0

3. a. Construct the market demand schedule.

    b. What is the maximum price that each traveler, Ann, Beth, and Cy, is willing to pay to travel 20 miles? Why?

4. a. What is the marginal social benefit when the total distance travelled is 60 miles?

    b. When the three people travel a total of 60 miles, how many miles does each travel and what is the marginal private benefit of each traveler?

5. a. What is each traveler's consumer surplus when the price is $4 a mile?

    b. What is the market consumer surplus when the price is $4 a mile?

Use the following table to work Problems 6 to 8.
The table gives the supply schedules of hot air balloon rides for the only sellers in the market, Xavier, Yasmin, and Zack.

Price (dollars per ride)	Quantity supplied (rides per week)		
	Xavier	Yasmin	Zack
100	30	25	20
90	25	20	15
80	20	15	10
70	15	10	5
60	10	5	0
50	5	0	0
40	0	0	0

6. a. Construct the market supply schedule.

    b. What are the minimum prices that Xavier, Yasmin, and Zack are willing to accept to supply 20 rides? Why?

7. a. What is the marginal social cost when the total number of rides is 30?

    b. What is the marginal cost for each supplier when the total number of rides is 30 and how many rides does each of the firms supply?

8. When the price is $70 a ride, what is each firm's producer surplus? What is the market producer surplus?

Use the following news clip to work Problems 9 and 10.

eBay Saves Billions for Bidders

If you think you would save money by bidding on eBay auctions, you would likely be right. Two Maryland researchers calculated the difference between the actual purchase price paid for auction items and the top price bidders stated they were willing to pay. They found that the difference averaged at least $4 per auction.

Source: *InformationWeek*, January 28, 2008

9. What method is used to allocate goods on eBay? How does the allocation method used by eBay auctions influence consumer surplus?

10. a. Can an eBay auction give the seller a surplus?

    b. On a graph show the consumer surplus and producer surplus from an eBay auction.

Is the Competitive Market Efficient? (Study Plan 5.3)

11. The figure illustrates the competitive market for cell phones.

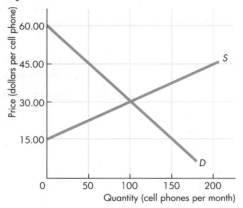

    a. What are the equilibrium price and equilibrium quantity of cell phones?

    b. Shade in and label the consumer surplus at the competitive equilibrium.

    c. Shade in and label the producer surplus at the competitive equilibrium.

    d. Calculate total surplus at the competitive equilibrium.

    e. Is the competitive market for cell phones efficient?

12. The table gives the demand and supply schedules for sunscreen.

Price (dollars per bottle)	Quantity demanded	Quantity supplied
	(bottles per day)	
0	400	0
5	300	100
10	200	200
15	100	300
20	0	400

Sunscreen factories are required to limit production to 100 bottles a day.

    a. What is the maximum price that consumers are willing to pay for the 100th bottle?

    b. What is the minimum price that producers are willing to accept for the 100th bottle?

    c. Describe the situation in this market.

13. Explain why each restaurant in Problem 1 might be using an efficient allocation method.

Is the Competitive Market Fair? (Study Plan 5.4)

14. Explain why the allocation method used by each restaurant in Problem 1 is fair or not fair.

15. In Problem 12, how can the 100 bottles available be allocated to beach-goers? Which possible methods would be fair and which would be unfair?

Economics in the News (Study Plan 5.N)

16. **The World's Largest Tulip and Flower Market**

    Every day 20 million tulips, roses, and other cut flowers are auctioned at the Dutch market called *The Bloemenveiling*. Each day 55,000 Dutch auctions take place, matching buyers and sellers.

    Source: Tulip-Bulbs.com

    A Dutch auction is one in which the auctioneer starts by announcing the highest price. If no one offers to buy the flowers, the auctioneer lowers the price until a buyer is found.

    a. What method is used to allocate flowers at the Bloemenveiling?

    b. How does a Dutch flower auction influence consumer surplus and producer surplus?

    c. Are the flower auctions at the Bloemenveiling efficient?

17. **Wii Sells Out Across Japan**

    After a two-month TV-ad blitz for Wii in Japan, demand was expected to exceed supply. Yodobashi Camera was selling Wii games on a first-come, first-served basis. Eager customers showed up early and those who tried to join the line after 6 or 7 a.m. were turned away—many rushed off to the smaller stores that were holding raffles to decide who got a Wii.

    Source: *Gamespot News*, December 1, 2006

    a. Why was the quantity demanded of Wii expected to exceed the quantity supplied?

    b. Did Nintendo produce the efficient quantity of Wii? Explain.

    c. Can you think of reasons why Nintendo might want to underproduce and leave the market with fewer Wii than people want to buy?

    d. What are the two methods of resource allocation described in the news clip? Is either method of allocating Wii efficient?

    e. What do you think some of the people who managed to buy a Wii did with it?

    f. Explain which is the fairer method of allocating the Wii: the market price or the two methods described in the news clip.

ADDITIONAL PROBLEMS AND APPLICATIONS

MyEconLab   You can work these problems in MyEconLab if assigned by your instructor.

Resource Allocation Methods

18. At McDonald's, no reservations are accepted; at Puck's at St. Louis Art Museum, reservations are accepted; at the Bissell Mansion restaurant, reservations are essential. Describe the method of allocating table resources in these three restaurants. Why do you think restaurants have different reservations policies?

Benefit, Cost, and Surplus

Use the following table to work Problems 19 to 22. The table gives the supply schedules for jet-ski rides by the only suppliers: Rick, Sam, and Tom.

Price (dollars per ride)	Quantity supplied (rides per day)		
	Rick	Sam	Tom
10.00	0	0	0
12.50	5	0	0
15.00	10	5	0
17.50	15	10	5
20.00	20	15	10

19. What is each owner's minimum supply-price of 10 rides a day?

20. Which owner has the largest producer surplus when the price of a ride is $17.50? Explain.

21. What is the marginal social cost of 45 rides a day?

22. Construct the market supply schedule of jet-ski rides.

23. The table gives the demand and supply schedules for sandwiches.

Price (dollars per sandwich)	Quantity demanded	Quantity supplied
	(sandwiches per hour)	
0	300	0
1	250	50
2	200	100
3	150	150
4	100	200
5	50	250
6	0	300

a. What is the maximum price that consumers are willing to pay for the 200th sandwich?

b. What is the minimum price that producers are willing to accept for the 200th sandwich?

c. If 200 sandwiches a day are available, what is the total surplus?

24. **"Two Buck Chuck" Wine Cult**

"Two Buck Chuck" is a cheap, good wine. After a year flooding the West Coast market, it is still being sold by the case to wine lovers. An over-abundance of grapes has made the wine cheap to bottle—about 5 million cases so far.

Source: *CBS*, June 2, 2003

How has "Two Buck Chuck" influenced the consumer surplus from wine, the producer surplus for its producer, and the producer surplus for the producers of other wines?

Is the Competitive Market Efficient?

25. Use the data in the table in Problem 23.

a. If the sandwich market is efficient, what is the consumer surplus, what is the producer surplus, and what is the total surplus?

b. If the demand for sandwiches increases and sandwich makers produce the efficient quantity, what happens to producer surplus and deadweight loss?

Use the following news clip to work Problems 26 to 28.

The Right Price for Digital Music

Apple's $1.29-for-the-latest-songs model isn't perfect and isn't it too much to pay for music that appeals to just a few people? What we need is a system that will be profitable but fair to music lovers. The solution: Price song downloads according to demand. The more people who download a particular song, the higher will be the price of that song; the fewer people who buy a particular song, the lower will be the price of that song. That is a free-market solution—the market would determine the price.

Source: *Slate*, December 5, 2005

Assume that the marginal social cost of downloading a song from the iTunes Store is zero. (This assumption means that the cost of operating the iTunes Store doesn't change if people download more songs.)

26. a. Draw a graph of the market for downloadable music with a price of $1.29 for all the latest songs. On your graph, show consumer surplus and producer surplus.

b. With a price of $1.29 for all the latest songs, is the market efficient or inefficient? If it is inefficient, show the deadweight loss on your graph.

27. If the pricing scheme described in the news clip were adopted, how would consumer surplus, producer surplus, and the deadweight loss change?

28. a. If the pricing scheme described in the news clip were adopted, would the market be efficient or inefficient? Explain.

    b. Is the pricing scheme described in the news clip a "free-market solution"? Explain.

29. Only 1 percent of the world supply of water is fit for human consumption. Some places have more water than they can use; some could use much more than they have. The 1 percent available would be sufficient if only it were in the right place.

    a. What is the major problem in achieving an efficient use of the world's water?

    b. If there were a global market in water, like there is in oil, how do you think the market would be organized?

    c. Would a free world market in water achieve an efficient use of the world's water resources? Explain why or why not.

Is the Competitive Market Fair?

30. Use the information in Problem 28. Would a free world market in water achieve a fair use of the world's water resources? Explain why or why not and be clear about the concept of fairness that you are using.

31. The winner of the men's and women's tennis singles at the U.S. Open is paid twice as much as the runner-up, but it takes two players to have a singles final. Is the compensation arrangement fair?

32. **The Scandal of Phone Call Price Gouging by Prisons**

    In most states, the phone company guarantees the prison a commission of a percentage on every call. The average commission is 42% of the cost of the call, but in some states it is 60%. So 60% of what families pay to receive a collect call from their imprisoned relative has nothing to do with the cost of the phone service. Also, the phone company that offers the highest commission is often the company to get the prison contract.

    Source: *The Guardian*, May 23, 2012

    a. Who is practicing price gouging: the prison, the phone company, or both? Explain.

    b. Evaluate the "fairness" of the prison's commission.

Economics in the News

33. After you have studied *Reading Between the Lines* on pp. 120–121, answer the following questions.

    a. What is the method used to allocate highway space in the United States and what is the method used in Singapore?

    b. Who benefits from the U.S. method of highway resource allocation? Explain your answer using the ideas of marginal social benefit, marginal social cost, consumer surplus, and producer surplus.

    c. Who benefits from the Singaporean method of highway resource allocation? Explain your answer using the ideas of marginal social benefit, marginal social cost, consumer surplus, and producer surplus.

    d. If road use were rationed by limiting drivers with even-date birthdays to drive only on even days (and odd-date birthdays to drive only on odd days), would highway use be more efficietn? Explain your answer.

34. **Fight over Water Rates; Escondido Farmers Say Increase Would Put Them Out of Business**

    Agricultural users of water pay less than residential and business users. Since 1993, water rates have increased by more than 90 percent for residential customers and by only 50 percent for agricultural users.

    Source: *The San Diego Union-Tribune*, June 14, 2006

    a. Do you think that the allocation of water between agricultural and residential users is likely to be efficient? Explain your answer.

    b. If agricultural users paid a higher price, would the allocation of resources be more efficient?

    c. If agricultural users paid a higher price, what would happen to consumer surplus and producer surplus from water?

    d. Is the difference in price paid by agricultural and residential users fair?

6

GOVERNMENT ACTIONS IN MARKETS

After studying this chapter, you will be able to:

◆ Explain how a rent ceiling creates a housing shortage

◆ Explain how a minimum wage law creates unemployment

◆ Explain the effects of a tax

◆ Explain the effects of production quotas and subsidies

◆ Explain how markets for illegal goods work

Can governments raise incomes of low-paid workers with a minimum wage law and cap rents to help low-income renters live in affordable housing? Who *really* pays the sales tax: buyers or sellers? Do subsidies to farmers and production limits help to make markets efficient? How do markets work in the "underground economy" where people trade illegal goods?

These are the questions you study in this chapter. And in *Reading Between the Lines* at the end of the chapter, we apply what you have learned to the labor markets of Hong Kong and Singapore and see how a minimum wage, which brings greater unemployment, isn't the only way to raise wage rates.

◀ A Housing Market with a Rent Ceiling

We spend more of our income on housing than on any other good or service, so it isn't surprising that rents can be a political issue. When rents are high, or when they jump by a large amount, renters might lobby the government for limits on rents.

A government regulation that makes it illegal to charge a price higher than a specified level is called a **price ceiling** or **price cap**.

The effects of a price ceiling on a market depend crucially on whether the ceiling is imposed at a level that is above or below the equilibrium price.

A price ceiling set *above the equilibrium price* has no effect. The reason is that the price ceiling does not constrain the market forces. The force of the law and the market forces are not in conflict. But a price ceiling *below the equilibrium price* has powerful effects on a market. The reason is that the price ceiling attempts to prevent the price from regulating the quantities demanded and supplied. The force of the law and the market forces are in conflict.

When a price ceiling is applied to a housing market, it is called a **rent ceiling**. A rent ceiling set below the equilibrium rent creates

- A housing shortage
- Increased search activity
- A black market

A Housing Shortage

At the equilibrium price, the quantity demanded equals the quantity supplied. In a housing market, when the rent is at the equilibrium level, the quantity of housing supplied equals the quantity of housing demanded and there is neither a shortage nor a surplus of housing.

But at a rent set below the equilibrium rent, the quantity of housing demanded exceeds the quantity of housing supplied—there is a shortage. So if a rent ceiling is set below the equilibrium rent, there will be a shortage of housing.

When there is a shortage, the quantity available is the quantity supplied, and somehow this quantity must be allocated among the frustrated demanders. One way in which this allocation occurs is through increased search activity.

Increased Search Activity

The time spent looking for someone with whom to do business is called **search activity**. We spend some time in search activity almost every time we make a purchase. When you're shopping for the latest hot new cell phone, and you know four stores that stock it, how do you find which store has the best deal? You spend a few minutes on the Internet, checking out the various prices. In some markets, such as the housing market, people spend a lot of time checking the alternatives available before making a choice.

When a price is regulated and there is a shortage, search activity increases. In the case of a rent-controlled housing market, frustrated would-be renters scan the newspapers, not only for housing ads but also for death notices! Any information about newly available housing is useful, and apartment seekers race to be first on the scene when news of a possible supplier breaks.

The *opportunity cost* of a good is equal not only to its price but also to the value of the search time spent finding the good. So the opportunity cost of housing is equal to the rent (a regulated price) plus the time and other resources spent searching for the restricted quantity available. Search activity is costly. It uses time and other resources, such as phone calls, automobiles, and gasoline that could have been used in other productive ways.

A rent ceiling controls only the rent portion of the cost of housing. The cost of increased search activity might end up making the full cost of housing *higher* than it would be without a rent ceiling.

A Black Market

A rent ceiling also encourages illegal trading in a **black market**, an illegal market in which the equilibrium price exceeds the price ceiling. Black markets occur in rent-controlled housing and many other markets. For example, scalpers run black markets in tickets for big sporting events and rock concerts.

When a rent ceiling is in force, frustrated renters and landlords constantly seek ways of increasing rents. One common way is for a new tenant to pay a high price for worthless fittings, such as charging $2,000 for threadbare drapes. Another is for the tenant to pay an exorbitant price for new locks and keys—called "key money."

The level of a black market rent depends on how tightly the rent ceiling is enforced. With loose enforcement, the black market rent is close to the unregulated rent. But with strict enforcement, the black market rent is equal to the maximum price that a renter is willing to pay.

Figure 6.1 illustrates the effects of a rent ceiling. The demand curve for housing is D and the supply curve is S. A rent ceiling is imposed at $800 a month. Rents that exceed $800 a month are in the gray-shaded illegal region in the figure. You can see that the equilibrium rent, where the demand and supply curves intersect, is in the illegal region.

At a rent of $800 a month, the quantity of housing supplied is 60,000 units and the quantity demanded is 100,000 units. So with a rent of $800 a month, there is a shortage of 40,000 units of housing.

To rent the 60,000th unit, someone is willing to pay $1,200 a month. They might pay this amount by incurring search costs that bring the total cost of housing to $1,200 a month, or they might pay a black market price of $1,200 a month. Either way, they end up incurring a cost that exceeds what the equilibrium rent would be in an unregulated market.

Inefficiency of a Rent Ceiling

A rent ceiling set below the equilibrium rent results in an inefficient underproduction of housing services. The *marginal social benefit* of housing exceeds its *marginal social cost* and a deadweight loss shrinks the producer surplus and consumer surplus (Chapter 5, pp. 112–114).

Figure 6.2 shows this inefficiency. The rent ceiling ($800 per month) is below the equilibrium rent ($1,000 per month) and the quantity of housing supplied (60,000 units) is less than the efficient quantity (80,000 units).

Because the quantity of housing supplied (the quantity available) is less than the efficient quantity, there is a deadweight loss, shown by the gray triangle. Producer surplus shrinks to the blue triangle and consumer surplus shrinks to the green triangle. The red rectangle represents the potential loss from increased search activity. This loss is borne by consumers and the full loss from the rent ceiling is the sum of the deadweight loss and the increased cost of search.

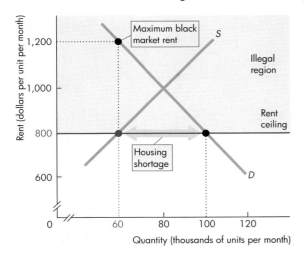

FIGURE 6.1   A Rent Ceiling

A rent above the rent ceiling of $800 a month is illegal (in the gray-shaded illegal region). At a rent of $800 a month, the quantity of housing supplied is 60,000 units. Frustrated renters spend time searching for housing and they make deals with landlords in a black market. Someone is willing to pay $1,200 a month for the 60,000th unit.

MyEconLab animation

FIGURE 6.2   The Inefficiency of a Rent Ceiling

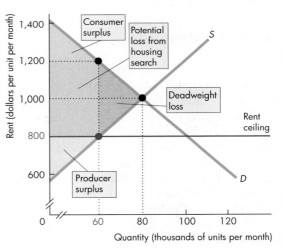

Without a rent ceiling, the market produces an efficient 80,000 units of housing at a rent of $1,000 a month. A rent ceiling of $800 a month decreases the quantity of housing supplied to 60,000 units. Producer surplus and consumer surplus shrink and a deadweight loss arises. The red rectangle represents the cost of resources used in increased search activity. The full loss from the rent ceiling equals the sum of the red rectangle and gray triangle.

MyEconLab animation

Are Rent Ceilings Fair?

Rent ceilings might be inefficient, but don't they achieve a fairer allocation of scarce housing? Let's explore this question.

Chapter 5 (pp. 116–118) reviews two key ideas about fairness. According to the *fair rules* view, anything that blocks voluntary exchange is unfair, so rent ceilings are unfair. But according to the *fair result* view, a fair outcome is one that benefits the less well off. So according to this view, the fairest outcome is the one that allocates scarce housing to the poorest. To see whether rent ceilings help to achieve a fairer outcome in this sense, we need to consider how the market allocates scarce housing resources in the face of a rent ceiling.

Blocking rent adjustments doesn't eliminate scarcity. Rather, because it decreases the quantity of housing available, it creates an even bigger challenge for the housing market. Somehow, the market must ration a smaller quantity of housing and allocate that housing among the people who demand it.

When the rent is not permitted to allocate scarce housing, what other mechanisms are available, and are *they* fair? Some possible mechanisms are

- A lottery
- First-come, first-served
- Discrimination

A lottery allocates housing to those who are lucky, not to those who are poor. First-come, first-served (a method used to allocate housing in England after World War II) allocates housing to those who have the greatest foresight and who get their names on a list first, not to the poorest. Discrimination allocates scarce housing based on the views and self-interest of the owner of the housing. In the case of public housing, what counts is the self-interest of the bureaucracy that administers the allocation.

In principle, self-interested owners and bureaucrats could allocate housing to satisfy some criterion of fairness, but they are not likely to do so. Discrimination based on friendship, family ties, and criteria such as race, ethnicity, or sex is more likely to enter the equation. We might make such discrimination illegal, but we cannot prevent it from occurring.

It is hard, then, to make a case for rent ceilings on the basis of fairness. When rent adjustments are blocked, other methods of allocating scarce housing resources operate that do not produce a fair outcome.

Economics in Action
Rent Control Winners: The Rich and Famous

New York, San Francisco, London, and Paris, four of the world's great cities, have rent ceilings in some part of their housing markets. Boston had rent ceilings for many years but abolished them in 1997. Many other U.S. cities do not have, and have never had, rent ceilings. Among them are Atlanta, Baltimore, Chicago, Dallas, Philadelphia, Phoenix, and Seattle.

To see the effects of rent ceilings in practice we can compare the housing markets in cities with ceilings with those without ceilings. We learn two main lessons from such a comparison.

First, rent ceilings definitely create a housing shortage. Second, they do lower the rents for some but raise them for others.

A survey* conducted in 1997 showed that the rents of housing units *actually available for rent* were 2.5 times the average of all rents in New York but equal to the average rent in Philadelphia. The winners from rent ceilings are the families that have lived in a city for a long time. In New York, these families include some rich and famous ones. The voting power of the winners keeps the rent ceilings in place. Mobile newcomers are the losers in a city with rent ceilings.

The bottom line is that, in principle and in practice, rent ceilings are inefficient and unfair.

---

* William Tucker, "How Rent Control Drives Out Affordable Housing," Cato Policy Analysis No. 274, May 21, 1997, Cato Institute.

REVIEW QUIZ

1 What is a rent ceiling and what are its effects if it is set above the equilibrium rent?
2 What are the effects of a rent ceiling that is set below the equilibrium rent?
3 How are scarce housing resources allocated when a rent ceiling is in place?
4 Why does a rent ceiling create an inefficient and unfair outcome in the housing market?

You can work these questions in Study Plan 6.1 and get instant feedback.   MyEconLab

You now know how a price ceiling (rent ceiling) works. Next, we'll learn about the effects of a price floor by studying a minimum wage in a labor market.

A Labor Market with a Minimum Wage

For each one of us, the labor market is the market that influences the jobs we get and the wages we earn. Firms decide how much labor to demand, and the lower the wage rate, the greater is the quantity of labor demanded. Households decide how much labor to supply, and the higher the wage rate, the greater is the quantity of labor supplied. The wage rate adjusts to make the quantity of labor demanded equal to the quantity supplied.

When wage rates are low, or when they fail to keep up with rising prices, labor unions might turn to governments and lobby for a higher wage rate.

A government regulation that makes it illegal to charge a price lower than a specified level is called a **price floor**.

The effects of a price floor on a market depend crucially on whether the floor is imposed at a level that is above or below the equilibrium price.

A price floor set *below the equilibrium price* has no effect. The reason is that the price floor does not constrain the market forces. The force of the law and the market forces are not in conflict. But a price floor *above the equilibrium price* has powerful effects on a market. The reason is that the price floor attempts to prevent the price from regulating the quantities demanded and supplied. The force of the law and the market forces are in conflict.

When a price floor is applied to a labor market, it is called a **minimum wage**. A minimum wage imposed at a level that is above the equilibrium wage creates unemployment. Let's look at the effects of a minimum wage.

Minimum Wage Brings Unemployment

At the equilibrium price, the quantity demanded equals the quantity supplied. In a labor market, when the wage rate is at the equilibrium level, the quantity of labor supplied equals the quantity of labor demanded: There is neither a shortage of labor nor a surplus of labor.

But at a wage rate above the equilibrium wage, the quantity of labor supplied exceeds the quantity of labor demanded—there is a surplus of labor. So when a minimum wage is set above the equilibrium wage, there is a surplus of labor. The demand for labor determines the level of employment, and the surplus of labor is unemployed.

FIGURE 6.3   Minimum Wage and Unemployment

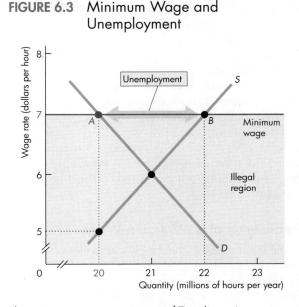

The minimum wage rate is set at $7 an hour. Any wage rate below $7 an hour is illegal (in the gray-shaded illegal region). At the minimum wage of $7 an hour, 20 million hours are hired but 22 million hours are available. Unemployment—*AB*—of 2 million hours a year is created. With only 20 million hours demanded, someone is willing to supply the 20 millionth hour for $5.

MyEconLab animation

Figure 6.3 illustrates the effect of the minimum wage on unemployment. The demand for labor curve is *D* and the supply of labor curve is *S*. The horizontal red line shows the minimum wage set at $7 an hour. A wage rate below this level is illegal, in the gray-shaded illegal region of the figure. At the minimum wage rate, 20 million hours of labor are demanded (point *A*) and 22 million hours of labor are supplied (point *B*), so 2 million hours of available labor are unemployed.

With only 20 million hours demanded, someone is willing to supply that 20 millionth hour for $5. Frustrated unemployed workers spend time and other resources searching for hard-to-find jobs.

Is the Minimum Wage Fair?

The minimum wage is unfair on both views of fairness: It delivers an unfair *result* and imposes an unfair *rule*.

The *result* is unfair because only those people who have jobs and keep them benefit from the minimum wage. The unemployed end up worse off than they would be with no minimum wage. Some of those who search for jobs and find them end up worse off because of the increased cost of job search they incur. Also those who search and find jobs aren't always the least well off. When the wage rate doesn't allocate labor, other mechanisms determine who finds a job. One such mechanism is discrimination, which is yet another source of unfairness.

The minimum wage imposes an unfair *rule* because it blocks voluntary exchange. Firms are willing to hire more labor and people are willing to work more, but they are not permitted by the minimum wage law to do so.

Inefficiency of a Minimum Wage

In the labor market, the supply curve measures the marginal social cost of labor to workers. This cost is leisure forgone. The demand curve measures the marginal social benefit from labor. This benefit is the value of the goods and services produced. An unregu-

lated labor market allocates the economy's scarce labor resources to the jobs in which they are valued most highly. The market is efficient.

The minimum wage frustrates the market mechanism and results in unemployment and increased job search. At the quantity of labor employed, the marginal social benefit of labor exceeds its marginal social cost and a deadweight loss shrinks the firms' surplus and the workers' surplus.

Figure 6.4 shows this inefficiency. The minimum wage ($7 an hour) is above the equilibrium wage ($6 an hour) and the quantity of labor demanded and employed (20 million hours) is less than the efficient quantity (21 million hours).

Because the quantity of labor employed is less than the efficient quantity, there is a deadweight loss, shown by the gray triangle. The firms' surplus shrinks to the blue triangle and the workers' surplus shrinks to the green triangle. The red rectangle shows the potential loss from increased job search, which is borne by workers. The full loss from the minimum wage is the sum of the deadweight loss and the increased cost of job search.

◆ AT ISSUE

Should Hong Kong Increase its Minimum Wage?

Hong Kong's minimum wage was increased to HK$28 per hour in May 2011. At that time, the world economy had just recovered from recession, and there were concerns that the rise in the minimum wage might raise the unemployment rate. In November 2012, a 7.1 percent rise to HK$30 per hour was being debated in the Legislative Council. Should Hong Kong increase its minimum wage?

Yes, It Should

Lee Cheuk-yan, union leader and member of the Legislative Council, says:

- The minimum wage should be raised but to $33 per hour rather than $30 per hour to keep pace with rising prices and to maintain the *real wage*.
- Because the Hong Kong economy is growing, a rise in the minimum wage is unlikely to increase unemployment.
- Official statistics show that after the minimum wage was increased to HK$28 per hour, the unemployment rate didn't increase.
- Many workers have changed industries and moved to higher paid jobs.
- Company bankruptcies have not increased.

No, It Shouldn't

- Miriam Lau, a member of the Legislative Council, says that the current minimum wage of HK$28 threatens to raise the unemployment rate.
- But if the minimum wage rate is increased further to HK$32 per hour, the unemployment rate may double, she says.
- Lau also says low-skilled, older, immigrant, and disabled workers are most affected.
- Simon Wong, president of the Federation of Restaurants, says high labor costs have led to lower employment and a decline in service quality.
- *The Economist* magazine says that minimum wage laws burden firms with bureaucratic red tape that discourages them from hiring.

FIGURE 6.4 The Inefficiency of a Minimum Wage

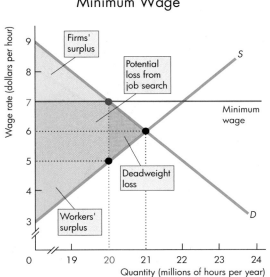

A minimum wage decreases employment. Firms' surplus (blue area) and workers' surplus (green area) shrink and a dead-weight loss (gray area) arises. Job search increases and the red area shows the loss from this activity.

—————— MyEconLab animation ——————

Next we're going to study a more widespread government action in markets: taxes. We'll see how taxes change prices and quantities. You will discover the surprising fact that while the government can impose a tax, it can't decide who will pay the tax! You will also see that a tax creates a deadweight loss.

Taxes

Everything you earn and almost everything you buy is taxed. Income taxes and Social Security taxes are deducted from your earnings and sales taxes are added to the bill when you buy something. Employers also pay a Social Security tax for their workers, and producers of tobacco products, alcoholic drinks, and gasoline pay a tax every time they sell something.

Who *really* pays these taxes? Because the income tax and Social Security tax are deducted from your pay, and the sales tax is added to the prices that you pay, isn't it obvious that *you* pay these taxes? And isn't it equally obvious that your employer pays the employer's contribution to the Social Security tax and that tobacco producers pay the tax on cigarettes?

You're going to discover that it isn't obvious who *really* pays a tax and that lawmakers don't make that decision. We begin with a definition of tax incidence.

Tax Incidence

Tax incidence is the division of the burden of a tax between buyers and sellers. When the government imposes a tax on the sale of a good,* the price paid by buyers might rise by the full amount of the tax, by a lesser amount, or not at all. If the price paid by buyers rises by the full amount of the tax, then the burden of the tax falls entirely on buyers—the buyers pay the tax. If the price paid by buyers rises by a lesser amount than the tax, then the burden of the tax falls partly on buyers and partly on sellers. And if the price paid by buyers doesn't change at all, then the burden of the tax falls entirely on sellers.

Tax incidence does not depend on the tax law. The law might impose a tax on sellers or on buyers, but the outcome is the same in either case. To see why, let's look at the tax on cigarettes in New York City.

A Tax on Sellers

On July 1, 2002, Mayor Bloomberg put a tax of $1.50 a pack on cigarettes sold in New York City. To work out the effects of this tax on the sellers of cigarettes, we begin by examining the effects on demand and supply in the market for cigarettes.

—————————

*These propositions also apply to services and factors of production (land, labor, and capital).

In Fig. 6.5, the demand curve is D, and the supply curve is S. With no tax, the equilibrium price is $3 per pack and 350 million packs a year are bought and sold.

A tax on sellers is like an increase in cost, so it decreases supply. To determine the position of the new supply curve, we add the tax to the minimum price that sellers are willing to accept for each quantity sold. You can see that without the tax, sellers are willing to offer 350 million packs a year for $3 a pack. So with a $1.50 tax, they will offer 350 million packs a year only if the price is $4.50 a pack. The supply curve shifts to the red curve labeled S + *tax on sellers*.

Equilibrium occurs where the new supply curve intersects the demand curve at 325 million packs a year. The price paid by buyers rises by $1 to $4 a pack. And the price received by sellers falls by 50¢ to $2.50 a pack. So buyers pay $1 of the tax and sellers pay the other 50¢.

A Tax on Buyers

Suppose that instead of taxing sellers, New York City taxes cigarette buyers $1.50 a pack.

A tax on buyers lowers the amount they are willing to pay sellers, so it decreases demand and shifts the demand curve leftward. To determine the position of this new demand curve, we subtract the tax from the maximum price that buyers are willing to pay for each quantity bought. You can see, in Fig. 6.6, that without the tax, buyers are willing to buy 350 million packs a year for $3 a pack. So with a $1.50 tax, they are willing to buy 350 million packs a year only if the price including the tax is $3 a pack, which means that they're willing to pay sellers only $1.50 a pack. The demand curve shifts to become the red curve labeled D – *tax on buyers*.

Equilibrium occurs where the new demand curve intersects the supply curve at a quantity of 325 million packs a year. The price received by sellers is $2.50 a pack, and the price paid by buyers is $4.

Equivalence of Tax on Buyers and Sellers

You can see that the tax on buyers in Fig. 6.6 has the same effects as the tax on sellers in Fig. 6.5. In both cases, the equilibrium quantity decreases to 325 million packs a year, the price paid by buyers rises to $4 a pack, and the price received by sellers falls to $2.50 a pack. Buyers pay $1 of the $1.50 tax, and sellers pay the other 50¢ of the tax.

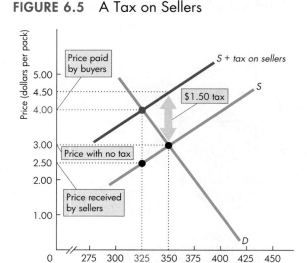

FIGURE 6.5   A Tax on Sellers

With no tax, 350 million packs a year are bought and sold at $3 a pack. A tax on sellers of $1.50 a pack shifts the supply curve from S to S + *tax on sellers*. The equilibrium quantity decreases to 325 million packs a year, the price paid by buyers rises to $4 a pack, and the price received by sellers falls to $2.50 a pack. The tax raises the price paid by buyers by less than the tax and lowers the price received by sellers, so buyers and sellers share the burden of the tax.

MyEconLab animation

Can We Share the Burden Equally? Suppose that Mayor Bloomberg wants the burden of the cigarette tax to fall equally on buyers and sellers and declares that a 75¢ tax be imposed on each. Is the burden of the tax then shared equally?

You can see that it is not. The tax is still $1.50 a pack. You've seen that the tax has the same effect regardless of whether it is imposed on sellers or buyers. So imposing half the tax on sellers and half on buyers is like an average of the two cases you've just examined. (Draw the demand-supply graph and work out what happens in this case. The demand curve shifts downward by 75¢ and the supply curve shifts upward by 75¢. The new equilibrium quantity is still 325 million packs a year. Buyers pay $4 a pack, of which 75¢ is tax. Sellers receive $3.25 from buyers, but pay a 75¢ tax, so sellers net $2.50 a pack.)

When a transaction is taxed, there are two prices: the price paid by buyers, which includes the tax; and the price received by sellers, which excludes the tax.

FIGURE 6.6   A Tax on Buyers

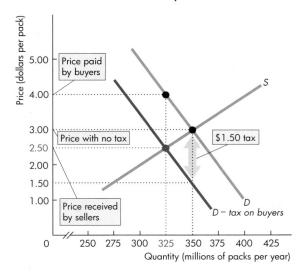

With no tax, 350 million packs a year are bought and sold at $3 a pack. A tax on buyers of $1.50 a pack shifts the demand curve from D to D – tax on buyers. The equilibrium quantity decreases to 325 million packs a year, the price paid by buyers rises to $4 a pack, and the price received by sellers falls to $2.50 a pack. The tax raises the price paid by buyers by less than the tax and lowers the price received by sellers, so buyers and sellers share the burden of the tax.

——————— MyEconLab animation ———

Buyers respond to the price that *includes* the tax and sellers respond to the price that *excludes* the tax.

A tax is like a wedge between the price buyers pay and the price sellers receive. The size of the wedge determines the effects of the tax, not the side of the market on which the government imposes the tax.

The Social Security Tax The Social Security tax is an example of a tax that Congress imposes equally on both buyers and sellers. But the principles you've just learned apply to this tax too. The market for labor, not Congress, decides how the burden of the Social Security tax is divided between firms and workers.

In the New York City cigarette tax example, buyers bear twice the burden of the tax borne by sellers. In special cases, either buyers or sellers bear the entire burden. The division of the burden of a tax between buyers and sellers depends on the elasticities of demand and supply, as you will now see.

Tax Incidence and Elasticity of Demand

The division of the tax between buyers and sellers depends in part on the elasticity of demand. There are two extreme cases:

- Perfectly inelastic demand—buyers pay.
- Perfectly elastic demand—sellers pay.

Perfectly Inelastic Demand Figure 6.7 shows the market for insulin, a vital daily medication for those with diabetes. Demand is perfectly inelastic at 100,000 doses a day, regardless of the price, as shown by the vertical demand curve D. That is, a diabetic would sacrifice all other goods and services rather than not consume the insulin dose that provides good health. The supply curve of insulin is S. With no tax, the price is $2 a dose and the quantity is 100,000 doses a day.

If insulin is taxed at 20¢ a dose, we must add the tax to the minimum price at which drug companies are willing to sell insulin. The result is the new supply curve S + *tax*. The price rises to $2.20 a dose, but the quantity does not change. Buyers pay the entire tax of 20¢ a dose.

FIGURE 6.7   Tax with Perfectly Inelastic Demand

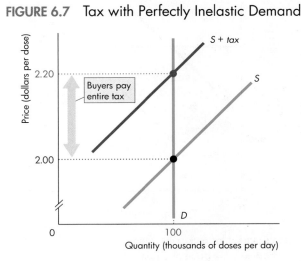

In this market for insulin, demand is perfectly inelastic. With no tax, the price is $2 a dose and the quantity is 100,000 doses a day. A tax of 20¢ a dose shifts the supply curve to S + *tax*. The price rises to $2.20 a dose, but the quantity bought does not change. Buyers pay the entire tax.

——————— MyEconLab animation ———

Perfectly Elastic Demand Figure 6.8 shows the market for pink marker pens. Demand is perfectly elastic at $1 a pen, as shown by the horizontal demand curve *D*. If pink pens are less expensive than the other colors, everyone uses pink. If pink pens are more expensive than other colors, no one uses pink. The supply curve is *S*. With no tax, the price of a pink pen is $1 and the quantity is 4,000 pens a week.

Suppose that the government imposes a tax of 10¢ a pen on pink marker pens but not on other colors. The new supply curve is *S + tax*. The price remains at $1 a pen, and the quantity decreases to 1,000 pink pens a week. The 10¢ tax leaves the price paid by buyers unchanged but lowers the amount received by sellers by the full amount of the tax. Sellers pay the entire tax of 10¢ a pink pen.

We've seen that when demand is perfectly inelastic, buyers pay the entire tax and when demand is perfectly elastic, sellers pay the entire tax. In the usual case, demand is neither perfectly inelastic nor perfectly elastic and the tax is split between buyers and sellers. But the division depends on the elasticity of demand: The more inelastic the demand, the larger is the amount of the tax paid by buyers.

FIGURE 6.8   Tax with Perfectly Elastic Demand

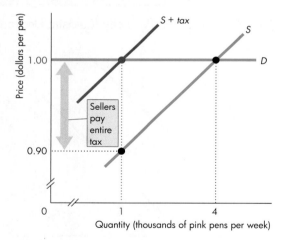

Quantity (thousands of pink pens per week)

In this market for pink pens, demand is perfectly elastic. With no tax, the price of a pen is $1 and the quantity is 4,000 pens a week. A tax of 10¢ a pink pen shifts the supply curve to *S + tax*. The price remains at $1 a pen, and the quantity of pink pens sold decreases to 1,000 a week. Sellers pay the entire tax.

―――― MyEconLab animation ――――

Tax Incidence and Elasticity of Supply

The division of the tax between buyers and sellers also depends, in part, on the elasticity of supply. Again, there are two extreme cases:

- Perfectly inelastic supply—sellers pay.
- Perfectly elastic supply—buyers pay.

Perfectly Inelastic Supply Figure 6.9(a) shows the market for water from a mineral spring that flows at a constant rate that can't be controlled. Supply is perfectly inelastic at 100,000 bottles a week, as shown by the supply curve *S*. The demand curve for the water from this spring is *D*. With no tax, the price is 50¢ a bottle and the quantity is 100,000 bottles.

Suppose this spring water is taxed at 5¢ a bottle. The supply curve does not change because the spring owners still produce 100,000 bottles a week, even though the price they receive falls. But buyers are willing to buy the 100,000 bottles only if the price is 50¢ a bottle, so the price remains at 50¢ a bottle. The tax reduces the price received by sellers to 45¢ a bottle, and sellers pay the entire tax.

Perfectly Elastic Supply Figure 6.9(b) shows the market for sand from which computer-chip makers extract silicon. Supply of this sand is perfectly elastic at a price of 10¢ a pound, as shown by the supply curve *S*. The demand curve for sand is *D*. With no tax, the price is 10¢ a pound and 5,000 pounds a week are bought.

If this sand is taxed at 1¢ a pound, we must add the tax to the minimum supply-price. Sellers are now willing to offer any quantity at 11¢ a pound along the curve *S + tax*. A new equilibrium is determined where the new supply curve intersects the demand curve: at a price of 11¢ a pound and a quantity of 3,000 pounds a week. The tax has increased the price buyers pay by the full amount of the tax—1¢ a pound—and has decreased the quantity sold. Buyers pay the entire tax.

We've seen that when supply is perfectly inelastic, sellers pay the entire tax, and when supply is perfectly elastic, buyers pay the entire tax. In the usual case, supply is neither perfectly inelastic nor perfectly elastic and the tax is split between buyers and sellers. But how the tax is split depends on the elasticity of supply: The more elastic the supply, the larger is the amount of the tax paid by buyers.

FIGURE 6.9   Tax and the Elasticity of Supply

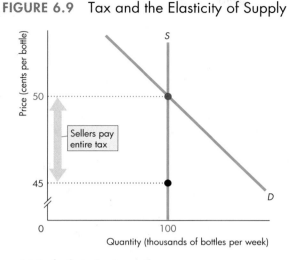

(a) Perfectly inelastic supply

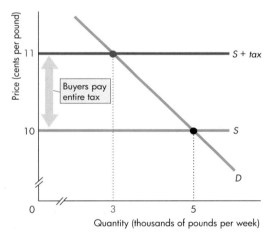

(b) Perfectly elastic supply

Part (a) shows the market for water from a mineral spring. Supply is perfectly inelastic. With no tax, the price is 50¢ a bottle. With a tax of 5¢ a bottle, the price remains at 50¢ a bottle. The number of bottles bought remains the same, but the price received by sellers decreases to 45¢ a bottle. Sellers pay the entire tax.

Part (b) shows the market for sand. Supply is perfectly elastic. With no tax, the price is 10¢ a pound. A tax of 1¢ a pound increases the minimum supply-price to 11¢ a pound. The supply curve shifts to *S + tax*. The price increases to 11¢ a pound. Buyers pay the entire tax.

—— MyEconLab animation ——

Taxes and Efficiency

A tax drives a wedge between the buying price and the selling price and results in inefficient underproduction. The price buyers pay is also the buyers' willingness to pay, which measures *marginal social benefit*. The price sellers receive is also the sellers' minimum supply-price, which equals *marginal social cost*.

A tax makes marginal social benefit exceed marginal social cost, shrinks the producer surplus and consumer surplus, and creates a deadweight loss.

Figure 6.10 shows the inefficiency of a tax on MP3 players. The demand curve, *D*, shows marginal social benefit, and the supply curve, *S*, shows marginal social cost. Without a tax, the market produces the efficient quantity (5,000 players a week).

With a tax, the sellers' minimum supply-price rises by the amount of the tax and the supply curve shifts to *S + tax*. This supply curve does *not* show marginal social cost. The tax component isn't a *social* cost of

FIGURE 6.10   Taxes and Efficiency

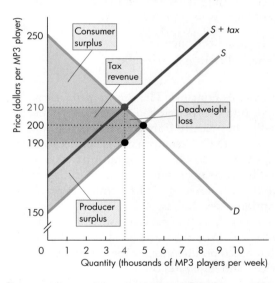

With no tax, 5,000 players a week are produced. With a $20 tax, the buyers' price rises to $210, the sellers' price falls to $190, and the quantity decreases to 4,000 players a week. Consumer surplus shrinks to the green area, and the producer surplus shrinks to the blue area. Part of the loss of consumer surplus and producer surplus goes to the government as tax revenue (the purple area) and part becomes a deadweight loss (the gray area).

—— MyEconLab animation ——

production. It is a transfer of resources to the government. At the new equilibrium quantity (4,000 players a week), both consumer surplus and producer surplus shrink. Part of each surplus goes to the government in tax revenue—the purple area; part becomes a deadweight loss—the gray area.

Only in the extreme cases of perfectly inelastic demand and perfectly inelastic supply does a tax not change the quantity bought and sold so that no deadweight loss arises.

Taxes and Fairness

We've examined the incidence and the efficiency of taxes. But when political leaders debate tax issues, it is fairness, not incidence and efficiency, that gets the most attention. Democrats complain that Republican tax cuts are unfair because they give the benefits of lower taxes to the rich. Republicans counter that it is fair that the rich get most of the tax cuts because they pay most of the taxes. No easy answers are available to the questions about the fairness of taxes.

Economists have proposed two conflicting principles of fairness to apply to a tax system:

- The benefits principle
- The ability-to-pay principle

The Benefits Principle The *benefits principle* is the proposition that people should pay taxes equal to the benefits they receive from the services provided by government. This arrangement is fair because it means that those who benefit most pay the most taxes. It makes tax payments and the consumption of government-provided services similar to private consumption expenditures.

The benefits principle can justify high fuel taxes to pay for freeways, high taxes on alcoholic beverages and tobacco products to pay for public health-care services, and high rates of income tax on high incomes to pay for the benefits from law and order and from living in a secure environment, from which the rich might benefit more than the poor.

The Ability-to-Pay Principle The *ability-to-pay principle* is the proposition that people should pay taxes according to how easily they can bear the burden of the tax. A rich person can more easily bear the burden than a poor person can, so the ability-to-pay principle can reinforce the benefits principle to justify high rates of income tax on high incomes.

Economics in Action
Workers and Consumers Pay the Most Tax

Because the elasticity of the supply of labor is low and the elasticity of demand for labor is high, workers pay most of the personal income taxes and most of the Social Security taxes. Because the elasticities of demand for alcohol, tobacco, and gasoline are low and the elasticities of supply are high, the burden of these taxes (excise taxes) falls more heavily on buyers than on sellers.

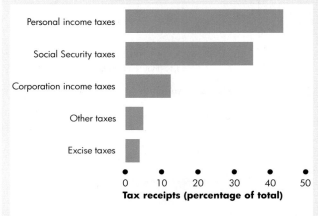

U.S. Taxes

Source of data: Budget of the United States Government, Fiscal Year 2012, Historical Tables, Table 2.2.

REVIEW QUIZ

1   How does the elasticity of demand influence the incidence of a tax, the tax revenue, and the deadweight loss?
2   How does the elasticity of supply influence the incidence of a tax, the quantity bought, the tax revenue, and the deadweight loss?
3   Why is a tax inefficient?
4   When would a tax be efficient?
5   What are the two principles of fairness that are applied to tax systems?

You can work these questions in Study Plan 6.3 and get instant feedback.   MyEconLab

Your next task is to study production quotas and subsidies, tools that are used to influence the markets for farm products.

Production Quotas and Subsidies

An early or late frost, a hot dry summer, and a wet spring present just a few of the challenges that fill the lives of farmers with uncertainty and sometimes with economic hardship. Fluctuations in the weather bring fluctuations in farm output and prices and sometimes leave farmers with low incomes. To help farmers avoid low prices and low incomes, governments intervene in the markets for farm products.

Price floors that work a bit like the minimum wage that you've already studied might be used. But as you've seen, this type of government action creates a surplus and is inefficient. These same conclusions apply to the effects of a price floor for farm products.

Governments often use two other methods of intervention in the markets for farm products:

- Production quotas
- Subsidies

Production Quotas

In the markets for sugarbeets, tobacco leaf, and cotton (among others), governments have, from time to time, imposed production quotas. A **production quota** is an upper limit to the quantity of a good that may be produced in a specified period. To discover the effects of a production quota, let's look at what a quota does to the market for sugarbeets.

Suppose that the growers of sugarbeets want to limit total production to get a higher price. They persuade the government to introduce a production quota on sugarbeets.

The effect of the production quota depends on whether it is set below or above the equilibrium quantity. If the government introduced a production quota above the equilibrium quantity, nothing would change because sugarbeet growers would already be producing less than the quota. But a production quota set *below the equilibrium quantity* has big effects, which are

- A decrease in supply
- A rise in price
- A decrease in marginal cost
- Inefficient underproduction
- An incentive to cheat and overproduce

Figure 6.11 illustrates these effects.

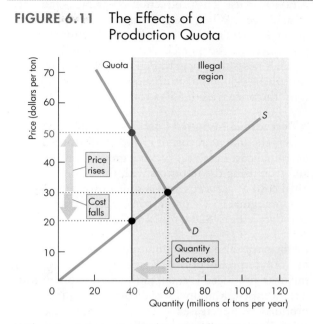

FIGURE 6.11   The Effects of a Production Quota

With no quota, growers produce 60 million tons a year and the price is $30 a ton. A production quota of 40 million tons a year restricts total production to that amount. The quantity produced decreases to 40 million tons a year, the price rises to $50 a ton, and the farmers' marginal cost falls to $20 a ton. Because marginal social cost (on the supply curve) is less than marginal social benefit (on the demand curve), a deadweight loss arises from the underproduction.

MyEconLab animation

A Decrease in Supply A production quota on sugarbeets decreases the supply of sugarbeets. Each grower is assigned a production limit that is less than the amount that would be produced—and supplied—without the quota. The total of the growers' limits equals the quota, and any production in excess of the quota is illegal.

The quantity supplied becomes the amount permitted by the production quota, and this quantity is fixed. The supply of sugarbeets becomes perfectly inelastic at the quantity permitted under the quota.

In Fig. 6.11, with no quota, growers would produce 60 million tons of sugarbeets a year—the market equilibrium quantity. With a production quota set at 40 million tons a year, the gray-shaded area shows the illegal region. As in the case of price ceilings and price floors, market forces and political forces are in conflict in this illegal region.

The vertical red line labeled "Quota" becomes the supply curve of sugarbeets at prices above $20 a ton.

A Rise in Price The production quota raises the price of sugarbeets. When the government sets a production quota, it leaves market forces free to determine the price. Because the quota decreases the supply of sugarbeets, it raises the price. In Fig. 6.11, with no quota, the price is $30 a ton. With a quota of 40 million tons, the price rises to $50 a ton.

A Decrease in Marginal Cost The production quota lowers the marginal cost of growing sugarbeets. Marginal cost decreases because growers produce less and stop using the resources with the highest marginal cost. Sugarbeet growers slide down their supply (and marginal cost) curves. In Fig. 6.11, marginal cost decreases to $20 a ton.

Inefficiency The production quota results in inefficient underproduction. Marginal social benefit at the quantity produced is equal to the market price, which has increased. Marginal social cost at the quantity produced has decreased and is less than the market price. So marginal social benefit exceeds marginal social cost and a deadweight loss arises.

An Incentive to Cheat and Overproduce The production quota creates an incentive for growers to cheat and produce more than their individual production limit. With the quota, the price exceeds marginal cost, so the grower can get a larger profit by producing one more unit. Of course, if all growers produce more than their assigned limit, the production quota becomes ineffective, and the price falls to the equilibrium (no quota) price.

To make the production quota effective, growers must set up a monitoring system to ensure that no one cheats and overproduces. But it is costly to set up and operate a monitoring system and it is difficult to detect and punish producers who violate their quotas.

Because of the difficulty of operating a quota, producers often lobby governments to establish a quota and provide the monitoring and punishment systems that make it work.

Subsidies

In the United States, the producers of peanuts, sugarbeets, milk, wheat, and many other farm products receive subsidies. A **subsidy** is a payment made by the government to a producer. A large and controversial Farm Bill passed by Congress in 2008 renewed and extended a wide range of subsidies.

The effects of a subsidy are similar to the effects of a tax but they go in the opposite directions. These effects are

- An increase in supply
- A fall in price and increase in quantity produced
- An increase in marginal cost
- Payments by government to farmers
- Inefficient overproduction

Figure 6.12 illustrates the effects of a subsidy to peanut farmers.

An Increase in Supply In Fig. 6.12, with no subsidy, the demand curve *D* and the supply curve *S* determine the price of peanuts at $40 a ton and the quantity of peanuts at 40 million tons a year.

Suppose that the government introduces a subsidy of $20 a ton to peanut farmers. A subsidy is like a negative tax. A tax is equivalent to an increase in cost, so a subsidy is equivalent to a decrease in cost. The subsidy brings an increase in supply.

To determine the position of the new supply curve, we subtract the subsidy from the farmers' minimum supply-price. In Fig. 6.12, with no subsidy, farmers are willing to offer 40 million tons a year at a price of $40 a ton. With a subsidy of $20 a ton, they will offer 40 million tons a year if the price is as low as $20 a ton. The supply curve shifts to the red curve labeled *S − subsidy*.

A Fall in Price and Increase in Quantity Produced The subsidy lowers the price of peanuts and increases the quantity produced. In Fig. 6.12, equilibrium occurs where the new supply curve intersects the demand curve at a price of $30 a ton and a quantity of 60 million tons a year.

An Increase in Marginal Cost The subsidy lowers the price paid by consumers but increases the marginal cost of producing peanuts. Marginal cost increases because farmers grow more peanuts, which means that they must begin to use some resources that are less ideal for growing peanuts. Peanut farmers slide up their supply (and marginal cost) curves. In Fig. 6.12, marginal cost increases to $50 a ton.

Payments by Government to Farmers The government pays a subsidy to peanut farmers on each ton of peanuts produced. In this example, farmers increase production to 60 million tons a year and receive a

FIGURE 6.12   The Effects of a Subsidy

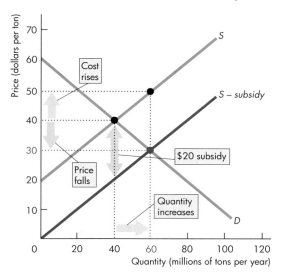

With no subsidy, farmers produce 40 million tons a year at $40 a ton. A subsidy of $20 a ton shifts the supply curve rightward to *S – subsidy*. The equilibrium quantity increases to 60 million tons a year, the price falls to $30 a ton, and the price plus the subsidy received by farmers rises to $50 a ton. In the new equilibrium, marginal social cost (on the supply curve) exceeds marginal social benefit (on the demand curve) and the subsidy results in inefficient overproduction.

MyEconLab animation

subsidy of $20 a ton. So peanut farmers receive payments from the government that total $1,200 million a year.

Inefficient Overproduction The subsidy results in inefficient overproduction. At the quantity produced with the subsidy, marginal social benefit is equal to the market price, which has fallen. Marginal social cost has increased and it exceeds the market price. Because marginal social cost exceeds marginal social benefit, the increased production brings inefficiency.

Subsidies spill over to the rest of the world. Because a subsidy lowers the domestic market price, subsidized farmers will offer some of their output for sale on the world market. The increase in supply on the world market lowers the price in the rest of the world. Faced with lower prices, farmers in other countries decrease production and receive smaller revenues.

Economics in Action
Rich High-Cost Farmers the Winners

Farm subsidies are a major obstacle to achieving an efficient use of resources in the global markets for farm products and are a source of tension between the United States, Europe, and developing nations.

The United States and the European Union are the world's two largest and richest economies. They also pay their farmers the biggest subsidies, which create inefficient overproduction of food in these rich economies.

At the same time, U.S. and European subsidies make it more difficult for farmers in the developing nations of Africa, Asia, and Central and South America to compete in global food markets. Farmers in these countries can often produce at a lower opportunity cost than the U.S. and European farmers.

Two rich countries, Australia and New Zealand, have stopped subsidizing farmers. The result has been an improvement in the efficiency of farming in these countries. New Zealand is so efficient at producing lamb and dairy products that it has been called the Saudi Arabia of milk (an analogy with Saudi Arabia's huge oil reserve and production.)

International opposition to U.S. and European farm subsidies is strong. Opposition to farm subsidies inside the United States and Europe is growing, but it isn't as strong as the pro-farm lobby, so don't expect an early end to these subsidies.

◆ REVIEW QUIZ

1 Summarize the effects of a production quota on the market price and the quantity produced.
2 Explain why a production quota is inefficient.
3 Explain why a voluntary production quota is difficult to operate.
4 Summarize the effects of a subsidy on the market price and the quantity produced.
5 Explain why a subsidy is inefficient.

You can work these questions in Study Plan 6.4 and get instant feedback.   MyEconLab

Governments intervene in some markets by making it illegal to trade in a good. Let's now see how these markets work.

Markets for Illegal Goods

The markets for many goods and services are regulated, and buying and selling some goods is illegal. The best-known examples of such goods are drugs, such as marijuana, cocaine, ecstasy, and heroin.

Despite the fact that these drugs are illegal, trade in them is a multibillion-dollar business. This trade can be understood by using the same economic model and principles that explain trade in legal goods. To study the market for illegal goods, we're first going to examine the prices and quantities that would prevail if these goods were not illegal. Next, we'll see how prohibition works. Then we'll see how a tax might be used to limit the consumption of these goods.

A Free Market for a Drug

Figure 6.13 shows the market for a drug. The demand curve, D, shows that, other things remaining the same, the lower the price of the drug, the larger is the quantity of the drug demanded. The supply curve, S, shows that, other things remaining the same, the lower the price of the drug, the smaller is the quantity supplied. If the drug were not illegal, the quantity bought and sold would be Q_C and the price would be P_C.

A Market for an Illegal Drug

When a good is illegal, the cost of trading in the good increases. By how much the cost increases and who bears the cost depend on the penalties for violating the law and the degree to which the law is enforced. The larger the penalties and the better the policing, the higher are the costs. Penalties might be imposed on sellers, buyers, or both.

Penalties on Sellers Drug dealers in the United States face large penalties if their activities are detected. For example, a marijuana dealer could pay a $200,000 fine and serve a 15-year prison term. A heroin dealer could pay a $500,000 fine and serve a 20-year prison term. These penalties are part of the cost of supplying illegal drugs, and they bring a decrease in supply—a leftward shift in the supply curve. To determine the new supply curve, we add the cost of breaking the law to the minimum price that drug dealers are willing to accept. In Fig. 6.13, the cost of breaking the law by selling drugs (*CBL*) is added to the minimum price that

FIGURE 6.13   A Market for an Illegal Good

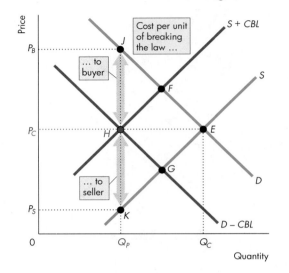

The demand curve for drugs is D, and the supply curve is S. If drugs are not illegal, the quantity bought and sold is Q_C at a price of P_C—point E. If selling drugs is illegal, the cost of breaking the law by selling drugs (*CBL*) is added to the minimum supply-price and supply decreases to $S + CBL$. The market moves to point F. If buying drugs is illegal, the cost of breaking the law is subtracted from the maximum price that buyers are willing to pay, and demand decreases to $D - CBL$. The market moves to point G. With both buying and selling illegal, the supply curve and the demand curve shift and the market moves to point H. The market price remains at P_C, but the market price plus the penalty for buying rises—point J—and the market price minus the penalty for selling falls—point K.

MyEconLab animation

dealers will accept and the supply curve shifts leftward to $S + CBL$. If penalties were imposed only on sellers, the market equilibrium would move from point E to point F.

Penalties on Buyers In the United States, it is illegal to *possess* drugs such as marijuana, cocaine, ecstasy, and heroin. Possession of marijuana can bring a prison term of 1 year, and possession of heroin can bring a prison term of 2 years. Penalties fall on buyers, and the cost of breaking the law must be subtracted from the value of the good to determine the maximum price buyers are willing to pay for the drugs. Demand decreases, and the demand curve shifts leftward. In Fig. 6.13, the demand curve shifts to $D - CBL$. If penalties were imposed only on buyers, the market equilibrium would move from point E to point G.

Penalties on Both Sellers and Buyers

If penalties are imposed on both sellers *and* buyers, both supply and demand decrease and both the supply curve and the demand curve shift. In Fig. 6.13, the costs of breaking the law are the same for both buyers and sellers, so both curves shift leftward by the same amount. The market equilibrium moves to point H. The market price remains at the competitive market price P_C, but the quantity bought decreases to Q_P. Buyers pay P_C plus the cost of breaking the law, which equals P_B. Sellers receive P_C minus the cost of breaking the law, which equals P_S.

The larger the penalties and the greater the degree of law enforcement, the larger is the decrease in demand and/or supply. If the penalties are heavier on sellers, the supply curve shifts farther than the demand curve and the market price rises above P_C. If the penalties are heavier on buyers, the demand curve shifts farther than the supply curve and the market price falls below P_C. In the United States, the penalties on sellers are larger than those on buyers, so the quantity of drugs traded decreases and the market price increases compared with a free market.

With high enough penalties and effective law enforcement, it is possible to decrease demand and/or supply to the point at which the quantity bought is zero. But in reality, such an outcome is unusual. It does not happen in the United States in the case of illegal drugs. The key reason is the high cost of law enforcement and insufficient resources for the police to achieve effective enforcement. Because of this situation, some people suggest that drugs (and other illegal goods) should be legalized and sold openly but also taxed at a high rate in the same way that legal drugs such as alcohol are taxed. How would such an arrangement work?

Legalizing and Taxing Drugs

From your study of the effects of taxes, it is easy to see that the quantity bought of a drug could be decreased if the drug was legalized and taxed. Imposing a sufficiently high tax could decrease the supply, raise the price, and achieve the same decrease in the quantity bought as does a prohibition on drugs. The government would collect a large tax revenue.

Illegal Trading to Evade the Tax It is likely that an extremely high tax rate would be needed to cut the quantity of drugs bought to the level prevailing with a prohibition. It is also likely that many drug dealers and consumers would try to cover up their activities to evade the tax. If they did act in this way, they would face the cost of breaking the law—the tax law. If the penalty for tax law violation is as severe and as effectively policed as drug-dealing laws, the analysis we've already conducted applies also to this case. The quantity of drugs bought would depend on the penalties for law breaking and on the way in which the penalties are assigned to buyers and sellers.

Taxes Versus Prohibition: Some Pros and Cons Which is more effective: prohibition or taxes? In favor of taxes and against prohibition is the fact that the tax revenue can be used to make law enforcement more effective. It can also be used to run a more effective education campaign against illegal drug use. In favor of prohibition and against taxes is the fact that prohibition sends a signal that might influence preferences, decreasing the demand for illegal drugs. Also, some people intensely dislike the idea of the government profiting from trade in harmful substances.

◆ REVIEW QUIZ

1 How does the imposition of a penalty for selling an illegal drug influence demand, supply, price, and the quantity of the drug consumed?
2 How does the imposition of a penalty for possessing an illegal drug influence demand, supply, price, and the quantity of the drug consumed?
3 How does the imposition of a penalty for selling *or* possessing an illegal drug influence demand, supply, price, and the quantity of the drug consumed?
4 Is there any case for legalizing drugs?

You can work these questions in Study Plan 6.5 and get instant feedback.   MyEconLab

◆ You now know how to use the demand and supply model to predict prices, to study government actions in markets, and to study the sources and costs of inefficiency. In *Reading Between the Lines* on pp. 144–145, you will see how to apply what you've learned to the labor markets of Hong Kong and Singapore and contrast two ways of raising the wage rates of the low paid.

Minimum Wage in Hong Kong and Singapore

City's Minimum Wage to be Set at HK$28 an Hour

China Daily - Hong Kong Edition, November 11, 2010

The city's new minimum wage finally has been released. The HK$28 an hour base is roughly the cost of two cartons of milk, a fast food meal, or four premium beers.

Secretary for Labor and Welfare Matthew Cheung Kin-chung said the new wage … represented an average wage increase of 16.9 percent affecting some 314,600 employees. …

Cheung said the impact on employment will be relatively mild, "especially when viewed against the improving economic and labor market conditions." …

Unionist lawmaker Lee Cheuk-yan said he was disappointed with the rate saying it will be based on figures two years old before its implementation, adding HK$28 an hour was not enough to provide for a family. He favored the HK$33 an hour rate supported by employee groups. …

Reprinted by permission of The China Daily, Hong Kong Edition

SNEF on Why Minimum Wage Won't Work

The Straits Times, October 13, 2010

The nasty consequences include raising business costs, driving up joblessness, pushing up costs of living, and eroding Singapore's competitive edge. …

On the point that a minimum wage would give workers a decent wage, the Singapore National Employers Federation (SNEF) said the argument is fallacious.

The reason: If the wage is set too high, employers will hesitate to hire low-skilled workers, who will suffer as the jobs move abroad.

As for the point that a high enough minimum wage can stimulate the economy, the SNEF said it can also cause prices to rise and result in inflation. …

SNEF believe the better way to help low-wage workers is to raise their skills through a "minimum skills" approach.

Source: The Straits Times. © Singapore Press Holdings Limited. Reproduced with permission.

ESSENCE OF THE STORY

- A rise in the minimum wage for Hong Kong to HK$28 per hour is proposed.

- The minimum wage increases by 16.9 percent and affects 314,600 workers.

- The impact on employment is predicted to be mild because labor market conditions are improving.

- Unions wanted the wage to rise to HK$33 per hour.

- The Singapore government does not favor setting a minimum wage.

- If the wage is set too high, employers will not hire low-skilled workers.

- Singapore believes that it is better to help low-wage workers by raising their skills.

ECONOMIC ANALYSIS

- The Legislative Council in Hong Kong has proposed a 16.9 percent rise in the minimum wage from HK$23.95 per hour to HK$28 (US$3.60) per hour.

- The increased wage is expected to affect 314,600 workers.

- An effective minimum wage is imposed above the market equilibrium wage.

- Figure 1 illustrates the market for low-skilled labor in Hong Kong before and after the change in the minimum wage. The supply of labor curve is S and initially, the demand for labor curve is D_0.

- At the old minimum wage of HK$23.95 per hour, 314,600 workers are employed on demand for labor curve D_0.

- The quantity of labor supplied exceeds the quantity demanded and the double-headed arrow shows the amount of unemployment at the old minimum wage.

- When the minimum wage rate rises to HK$28 per hour, the quantity of labor supplied increases in a movement along the supply curve S.

- The news article says that economic and labor market conditions are improving. This can be interpreted to mean that the demand for low-skilled labor is increasing. In Fig. 1, the demand curve shifts rightward to D_1.

- The combination of the rise in the minimum wage and the increase in demand for labor leaves the quantity of labor employed unchanged at 314,600 (an assumption).

- Unemployment increases as shown by the longer double-headed arrow at the minimum wage of HK$28 per hour.

- The Singapore National Employers Federation (SNEF) understands that a minimum wage brings unemployment and wants to help low-wage workers by raising their skills through training and increasing their productivity.

- Figure 2 shows the labor market in Singapore. The supply of labor curve is S and initially, the demand for labor curve is D_0. The wage rate is S$4.50 per hour and 2.8 million workers are employed.

- Raising workers' skills and increasing their productivity makes them more valuable to employers, so the demand for labor increases.

- In Fig. 2, the demand for labor curve shifts D_1. The equilibrium wage rate rises to S$5.50 per hour and employment increases to 3 million workers.

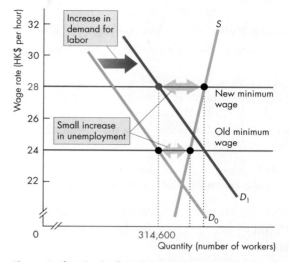

Figure 1 The Rise in the Minimum Wage in Hong Kong

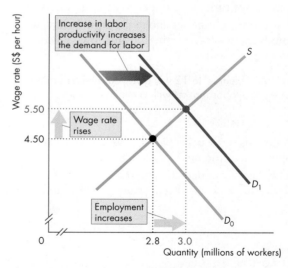

Figure 2 Increase in Productivity in Singapore

- Contrast this outcome with that of a rise in the minimum wage. Both policies increase the wage rate of employed workers, but only the Singapore policy increases employment and avoids unemployment.

- The Singapore policy is efficient and the Hong Kong policy is inefficient.

145

SUMMARY

Key Points

A Housing Market with a Rent Ceiling (pp. 128–130)

- A rent ceiling that is set above the equilibrium rent has no effect.
- A rent ceiling that is set below the equilibrium rent creates a housing shortage, increased search activity, and a black market.
- A rent ceiling that is set below the equilibrium rent is inefficient and unfair.

Working Problems 1 to 6 will give you a better understanding of a housing market with a rent ceiling.

A Labor Market with a Minimum Wage (pp. 131–133)

- A minimum wage set below the equilibrium wage rate has no effect.
- A minimum wage set above the equilibrium wage rate creates unemployment and increases the amount of time people spend searching for a job.
- A minimum wage set above the equilibrium wage rate is inefficient, unfair, and hits low-skilled young people hardest.

Working Problems 7 to 12 will give you a better understanding of a labor market with a minimum wage.

Taxes (pp. 133–138)

- A tax raises the price paid by buyers, but usually by less than the tax.
- The elasticity of demand and the elasticity of supply determine the share of a tax paid by buyers and sellers.

- The less elastic the demand or the more elastic the supply, the larger is the share of the tax paid by buyers.
- If demand is perfectly elastic or supply is perfectly inelastic, sellers pay the entire tax. And if demand is perfectly inelastic or supply is perfectly elastic, buyers pay the entire tax.

Working Problems 13 to 15 will give you a better understanding of taxes.

Production Quotas and Subsidies (pp. 139–141)

- A production quota leads to inefficient underproduction, which raises the price.
- A subsidy is like a negative tax. It lowers the price, increases the cost of production, and leads to inefficient overproduction.

Working Problems 16 and 17 will give you a better understanding of production quotas and subsidies.

Markets for Illegal Goods (pp. 142–143)

- Penalties on sellers increase the cost of selling the good and decrease the supply of the good.
- Penalties on buyers decrease their willingness to pay and decrease the demand for the good.
- Penalties on buyers and sellers decrease the quantity of the good, raise the price buyers pay, and lower the price sellers receive.
- Legalizing and taxing can achieve the same outcome as penalties on buyers and sellers.

Working Problem 18 will give you a better understanding of markets for illegal goods.

Key Terms

Black market, 128
Minimum wage, 131
Price cap, 128
Price ceiling, 128

Price floor, 131
Production quota, 139
Rent ceiling, 128
Search activity, 128

Subsidy, 140
Tax incidence, 133

STUDY PLAN PROBLEMS AND APPLICATIONS

MyEconLab   You can work Problems 1 to 18 in MyEconLab Chapter 6 Study Plan and get instant feedback.

A Housing Market with a Rent Ceiling (Study Plan 6.1)

Use the following graph of the market for rental housing in Townsville to work Problems 1 and 2.

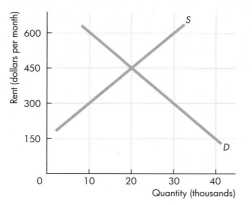

1. a. What are the equilibrium rent and equilibrium quantity of rental housing?
    b. If a rent ceiling is set at $600 a month, what is the quantity of housing rented and what is the shortage of housing?

2. If a rent ceiling is set at $300 a month, what is the quantity of housing rented, the shortage of housing, and the maximum price that someone is willing to pay for the last unit of housing available?

Use the following news clip to work Problems 3 to 6.

Capping Gasoline Prices

As gasoline prices rise, many people are calling for price caps, but price caps generate a distorted reflection of reality, which leads buyers and suppliers to act in ways inconsistent with the price cap. By masking reality, price caps only make matters worse.

Source: *Pittsburgh Tribune-Review*,
September 12, 2005

Suppose that a price ceiling is set below the equilibrium price of gasoline.

3. How does the price cap influence the quantity of gasoline supplied and the quantity demanded?

4. How does the price cap influence
   a. The quantity of gasoline sold and the shortage or surplus of gasoline?
   b. The maximum price that someone is willing to pay for the last gallon of gasoline available on a black market?

5. Draw a graph to illustrate the effects of a price ceiling set below the equilibrium price in the market for gasoline.

6. Explain the various ways in which a price ceiling on gasoline that is set below the equilibrium price would make buyers and sellers of gasoline better off or worse off. What would happen to total surplus and deadweight loss in this market?

A Labor Market with a Minimum Wage

(Study Plan 6.2)

Use the following data to work Problems 7 to 9.

The table gives the demand and supply schedules of teenage labor.

Wage rate (dollars per hour)	Quantity demanded	Quantity supplied
	(hours per month)	
4	3,000	1,000
5	2,500	1,500
6	2,000	2,000
7	1,500	2,500
8	1,000	3,000

7. Calculate the equilibrium wage rate, the number of hours worked, and the quantity of unemployment.

8. If a minimum wage for teenagers is set at $5 an hour, how many hours do they work and how many hours of teenage labor are unemployed?

9. If a minimum wage for teenagers is set at $7 an hour,
   a. How many hours do teenagers work and how many hours are unemployed?
   b. Demand for teenage labor increases by 500 hours a month. What is the wage rate paid to teenagers and how many hours of teenage labor are unemployed?

Use the following news clip to work Problems 10 to 12.

India Steps Up Pressure for Minimum Wage for Its Workers in the Gulf

Oil-rich countries in the [Persian] Gulf, already confronted by strong labor protests, are facing renewed pressure from India to pay minimum wages for unskilled workers. With five million immigrant workers in the region, India is trying to win better conditions for their citizens.

Source: *International Herald Tribune*,
March 27, 2008

Suppose that the Gulf countries paid a minimum wage above the equilibrium wage to Indian workers.

10. How would the market for labor be affected in the Gulf countries? Draw a supply and demand graph to illustrate your answer.

11. How would the market for labor be affected in India? Draw a supply and demand graph to illustrate your answer. [Be careful: the minimum wage is in the Gulf countries, not in India.]

12. Would migrant Indian workers be better off or worse off or unaffected by this minimum wage?

Taxes (Study Plan 6.3)

13. The table gives the demand and supply schedules for chocolate brownies.

Price (cents per brownie)	Quantity demanded	Quantity supplied
	(millions per day)	
50	5	3
60	4	4
70	3	5
80	2	6
90	1	7

a. If brownies are not taxed, what is the price of a brownie and how many are bought?

b. If sellers are taxed 20¢ a brownie, what is the price? How many are sold? Who pays the tax?

c. If buyers are taxed 20¢ a brownie, what is the price? How many are bought? Who pays the tax?

14. **Will Cuts on China's Luxury Goods Tax Prevent Chinese from Buying Abroad?**

Last year Chinese tourists bought almost two-thirds of luxury goods sold in Europe. If you look at China's luxury goods tax, it is easy to see why shopping overseas is so popular. According to the Chinese Ministry of Commerce, prices for luxury goods in China are 45% higher than in Hong Kong, 51% higher than the United States, and 72% higher than France.

Source: PRLog, March 21, 2012

a. Explain why it is "easy to see why shopping overseas is so popular" with wealthy Chinese shoppers.

b. Who pays most of the Chinese luxury tax: sellers or buyers? Explain your answer.

c. Explain how a cut in China's luxury tax rate will change the quantity of luxury goods purchased in China.

15. **How to Take a Gas Holiday**

High fuel prices will probably keep Americans closer to home this summer, despite the gas-tax "holiday" that would shave 18¢ off every gallon.

Source: *Time*, May 19, 2008

Would the price of gasoline that consumers pay fall by 18¢ a gallon? How would consumer surplus change? Explain your answers.

Production Quotas and Subsidies (Study Plan 6.4)

Use the following data to work Problems 16 and 17. The demand and supply schedules for rice are

Price (dollars per box)	Quantity demanded	Quantity supplied
	(boxes per week)	
1.20	3,000	1,500
1.30	2,750	2,000
1.40	2,500	2,500
1.50	2,250	3,000
1.60	2,000	3,500

16. Calculate the price, the marginal cost of rice, and the quantity produced if the government sets a production quota of 2,000 boxes a week.

17. Calculate the price, the marginal cost of rice, and the quantity produced if the government introduces a subsidy of $0.30 a box.

Markets for Illegal Goods (Study Plan 6.5)

18. The figure illustrates the market for a banned substance.

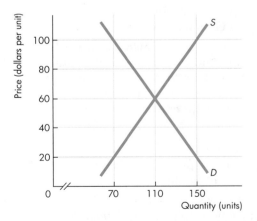

Calculate the market price and the quantity consumed if a penalty of $20 a unit is imposed on

a. Sellers only.

b. Buyers only.

c. Both sellers and buyers.

ADDITIONAL PROBLEMS AND APPLICATIONS

MyEconLab   You can work these problems in MyEconLab if assigned by your instructor.

A Housing Market with a Rent Ceiling

Use this news clip to work Problems 19 and 20.

Despite Protests, Rent Board Sets 7.25% Increase

New York's Rent Guidelines Board voted for a rent increase of up to 7.25 percent over the next two years on rent-stabilized apartments. A survey reported that last year costs for the owners of rent-stabilized buildings rose by 7.8 percent. In addition there is growing concern about the ability of the middle class to afford to live in New York City.

Source: *The New York Times*, June 28, 2006

19. a. If rents for rent-stabilized apartments do not increase, how do you think the market for rental units in New York City will develop?

   b. Are rent ceilings in New York City helpful to the middle class? Why or why not?

20. a. Explain the effect of the increase in the rent ceiling on the quantity of rent-stabilized apartments.

   b. Why is rent stabilization a source of conflict between renters and owners of apartments?

A Labor Market with a Minimum Wage

Use the following news clip to work Problems 21 and 22.

Malaysia Passes Its First Minimum Wage Law

About 3.2 million low-income workers across Malaysia are expected to benefit from the country's first minimum wage, which the government says will transform Malaysia into a high-income nation. Employer groups argue that paying the minimum wage, which is not based on productivity or performance would raise their costs and reduce business profits.

Source: *The New York Times*, May 1, 2012

21. On a graph of the market for low-skilled labor, show the effect of the minimum wage on the quantity of labor employed.

22. Explain the effects of the minimum wage on the workers' surplus, the firms' surplus, and the efficiency of the market for low-skilled workers.

Taxes

23. Use the news clip in Problem 21.

   a. If the Malaysian government cut the tax on business profits, would it offset the effect of the minimum wage on employment? Explain.

   b. Would a cut in the Social Security tax that small businesses pay offset the effect of the higher minimum wage on employment? Explain.

24. The demand and supply schedules for tulips are

Price (dollars per bunch)	Quantity demanded	Quantity supplied
	(bunches per week)	
10	100	40
12	90	60
14	80	80
16	70	100
18	60	120

   a. If tulips are not taxed, what is the price and how many bunches are bought?

   b. If tulips are taxed $6 a bunch, what are the price and quantity bought? Who pays the tax?

25. **Cigarette Taxes, Black Markets, and Crime: Lessons from New York's 50-Year Losing Battle**

   New York City has the highest cigarette taxes in the country. During the four months following the recent tax hike, sales of taxed cigarettes in the city fell by more than 50 percent as consumers turned to the city's bustling black market. The thriving illegal market for cigarettes has diverted billions of dollars from legitimate businesses and governments to criminals.

   Source: Cato Institute, February 6, 2003

   a. How has the market for cigarettes in New York City responded to the high cigarette taxes?

   b. How does the emergence of a black market impact the elasticity of demand in a legal market?

   c. Why might an increase in the tax rate actually cause a decrease in the tax revenue?

Production Quotas and Subsidies

Use the following news clip to work Problems 26 to 28.

Crop Prices Erode Farm Subsidy Program

High corn and soybean prices mean farmers are making the most money in their lives. The reason: Grain prices are far too high to trigger payouts under the U.S. primary farm-subsidy program's "price support" formula. The market has done what Congress couldn't do and that is "slash farm subsidies."

Source: *The Wall Street Journal*, July 25, 2011

26. a. Why are U.S. soybean farmers subsidized?

b. Explain how a subsidy paid to soybean farmers affects the price of soybean and the marginal cost of producing it.

27. Show in a graph how a subsidy paid to soybean farmers affects the consumer surplus and the producer surplus from soybean. Does the subsidy make the soybean market more efficient or less efficient? Explain.

28. In the market for corn with a price support, explain why the corn price has risen and ended up being too high to "trigger payouts."

Markets for Illegal Goods

29. The table gives the demand and supply schedules for an illegal drug.

Price (dollars per unit)	Quantity demanded	Quantity supplied
	(units per day)	
50	500	300
60	400	400
70	300	500
80	200	600
90	100	700

a. If there are no penalties on buying or selling the drug, what is the price and how many units are consumed?

b. If the penalty on sellers is $20 a unit, what are the price and quantity consumed?

c. If the penalty on buyers is $20 a unit, what are the price and quantity consumed?

Economics in the News

30. After you have studied *Reading Between the Lines* on pp. 144–145, answer the following questions.

a. How is Hong Kong trying to raise the wage rate paid to low-skilled workers?

b. How is Singapore trying to raise the wage rate paid to its low-skilled workers?

c. Which of the two policies is efficient and which one is inefficient and why?

d. Draw a graph of the labor market of Hong Kong and show the inefficiency you've described in part (c).

e. Draw a graph of the labor market of Singapore and show the change in the gains from trade that results from increasing labor productivity.

31. **Hollywood: Organized Crime Hits the Movies**
The Mexican army seized 1,180 disc burners and

3.14 million copies of movies and TV shows from 23 warehouses in a move to fight piracy that costs Hollywood about $590 million a year.

Source: Bloomberg *Businessweek*, April 7, 2011

Assume that the marginal cost of producing a DVD (legal or illegal) is a constant $3 and that legal DVDs bear an additional marginal cost of $5 each in royalty payments to film studios.

a. Draw a graph of the market for counterfeit DVDs, assuming that there are no effective penalties on either buyers or sellers for breaking the law.

b. How do the events reported in the news clip change the market outcome? Show the effects in your graph.

c. With no penalty on buyers, if a penalty for breaking the law is imposed on sellers at more than $5 a disc, how does the market work and what is the equilibrium price?

d. With no penalty on sellers, if a penalty for breaking the law is imposed on buyers at more than $5 a disc, how does the market work and what is the equilibrium price?

e. What is the marginal benefit of an illegal DVD in the situations described in parts (c) and (d)?

f. In light of your answer to part (e), why does law enforcement usually focus on sellers rather than buyers?

32. **Drivers Feel the Pinch as Diesel Hits $4 a Gallon**
"The high price of gasoline is hurting our economy," said Mark Kirsch, a trucker, who organized a rally in Washington. "It's hurting middle-class people."

Source: *The Washington Post*, April 29, 2008

Explain to truck drivers why a cap on the price of gasoline would hurt middle-class people more than the high price of gasoline hurts.

33. On December 31, 1776, Rhode Island established wage controls to limit wages to 70¢ a day for carpenters and 42¢ a day for tailors.

a. Are these wage controls a price ceiling or a price floor? Why might they have been introduced?

b. If these wage controls are effective, would you expect to see a surplus or a shortage of carpenters and tailors?

7

GLOBAL MARKETS IN ACTION

After studying this chapter, you will be able to:

◆ Explain how markets work with international trade

◆ Identify the gains from international trade and its winners and losers

◆ Explain the effects of international trade barriers

◆ Explain and evaluate arguments used to justify restricting international trade

iPhones, Wii games, and Nike shoes are just three of the items that you might buy that are not produced in the United States. They are produced abroad in Asia and manufactured by workers who earn a fraction of what an American worker earns.

Isn't globalization of production killing good American jobs? How can we compete with people whose wages are a fraction of our own? Why do we go to such lengths to trade and communicate with others in faraway places?

You will find some answers in this chapter. And in *Reading Between the Lines* at the end of the chapter, you can apply what you've learned and examine the effects of a tariff that the Obama government has put on solar panels imported from China.

How Global Markets Work

Because we trade with people in other countries, the goods and services that we can buy and consume are not limited by what we can produce. The goods and services that we buy from other countries are our **imports**; and the goods and services that we sell to people in other countries are our **exports**.

International Trade Today

Global trade today is enormous. In 2011, global exports and imports were $22 trillion, which is one third of the value of global production. The United States is the world's largest international trader and accounts for 10 percent of world exports and 13 percent of world imports. Germany and China, which rank 2 and 3 behind the United States, lag by a large margin.

In 2011, total U.S. exports were $2.1 trillion, which is about 14 percent of the value of U.S. production. Total U.S. imports were $2.7 trillion, which is about 18 percent of total expenditure in the United States.

We trade both goods and services. In 2011, exports of services were about one third of total exports and imports of services were about one fifth of total imports.

What Drives International Trade?

Comparative advantage is the fundamental force that drives international trade. Comparative advantage (see Chapter 2, p. 40) is a situation in which a person can perform an activity or produce a good or service at a lower opportunity cost than anyone else. This same idea applies to nations. We can define *national comparative advantage* as a situation in which a nation can perform an activity or produce a good or service at a lower opportunity cost than any other nation.

The opportunity cost of producing a T-shirt is lower in China than in the United States, so China has a comparative advantage in producing T-shirts. The opportunity cost of producing an airplane is lower in the United States than in China, so the United States has a comparative advantage in producing airplanes.

You saw in Chapter 2 how Liz and Joe reap gains from trade by specializing in the production of the good at which they have a comparative advantage and then trading with each other. Both are better off.

Economics in Action
We Trade Services for Oil

We import huge amounts of oil—almost $350 billion in 2011. How do we pay for all this oil? The answer is by exporting business, professional, and technical services, airplanes, food and drinks, and chemicals. We also trade a large quantity of automobiles, but we both export and import them (mainly in trade with Canada).

U.S. Exports and Imports in 2011

Source of data: Bureau of Economic Analysis.

This same principle applies to trade among nations. Because China has a comparative advantage at producing T-shirts and the United States has a comparative advantage at producing airplanes, the people of both countries can gain from specialization and trade. China can buy airplanes from the United States at a lower opportunity cost than that at which Chinese firms can produce them. And Americans can buy T-shirts from China for a lower opportunity cost than that at which U.S. firms can produce them. Also, through international trade, Chinese producers can get higher prices for their T-shirts and Boeing can sell airplanes for a higher price. Both countries gain from international trade.

Let's now illustrate the gains from trade that we've just described by studying demand and supply in the global markets for T-shirts and airplanes.

Why the United States Imports T-Shirts

The United States imports T-shirts because the rest of the world has a comparative advantage in producing T-shirts. Figure 7.1 illustrates how this comparative advantage generates international trade and how trade affects the price of a T-shirt and the quantities produced and bought.

The demand curve D_{US} and the supply curve S_{US} show the demand and supply in the U.S. domestic market only. The demand curve tells us the quantity of T-shirts that Americans are willing to buy at various prices. The supply curve tells us the quantity of T-shirts that U.S. garment makers are willing to sell at various prices—that is, the quantity supplied at each price when all T-shirts sold in the United States are produced in the United States.

Figure 7.1(a) shows what the U.S. T-shirt market would be like with no international trade. The price

of a shirt would be $8 and 40 million shirts a year would be produced by U.S. garment makers and bought by U.S. consumers.

Figure 7.1(b) shows the market for T-shirts with international trade. Now the price of a T-shirt is determined in the world market, not the U.S. domestic market. The world price of a T-shirt is less than $8, which means that the rest of the world has a comparative advantage in producing T-shirts. The world price line shows the world price at $5 a shirt.

The U.S. demand curve, D_{US}, tells us that at $5 a shirt, Americans buy 60 million shirts a year. The U.S. supply curve, S_{US}, tells us that at $5 a shirt, U.S. garment makers produce 20 million T-shirts a year. To buy 60 million T-shirts when only 20 million are produced in the United States, we must import T-shirts from the rest of the world. The quantity of T-shirts imported is 40 million a year.

FIGURE 7.1   A Market with Imports

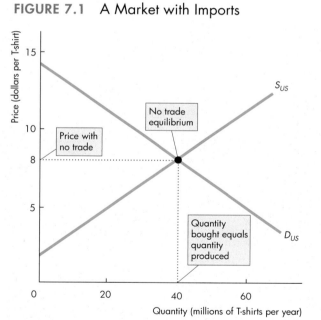

(a) Equilibrium with no international trade

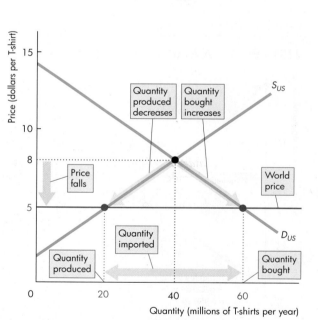

(b) Equilibrium in a market with imports

Part (a) shows the U.S. market for T-shirts with no international trade. The U.S. domestic demand curve D_{US} and U.S. domestic supply curve S_{US} determine the price of a T-shirt at $8 and the quantity of T- shirts produced and bought in the United States at 40 million a year.

Part (b) shows the U.S. market for T-shirts with interna-

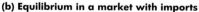

tional trade. World demand for and world supply of T-shirts determine the world price of a T-shirt, which is $5. The price in the U.S. market falls to $5 a shirt. U.S. purchases of T-shirts increase to 60 million a year, and U.S. production of T-shirts decreases to 20 million a year. The United States imports 40 million T-shirts a year.

Why the United States Exports Airplanes

Figure 7.2 illustrates international trade in airplanes. The demand curve D_{US} and the supply curve S_{US} show the demand and supply in the U.S. domestic market only. The demand curve tells us the quantity of airplanes that U.S. airlines are willing to buy at various prices. The supply curve tells us the quantity of airplanes that U.S. aircraft makers are willing to sell at various prices.

Figure 7.2(a) shows what the U.S. airplane market would be like with no international trade. The price of an airplane would be $100 million and 400 airplanes a year would be produced by U.S. aircraft makers and bought by U.S. airlines.

Figure 7.2(b) shows the U.S. airplane market with international trade. Now the price of an airplane is determined in the world market and the world price is higher than $100 million, which means that the United States has a comparative advantage in produc-

ing airplanes. The world price line shows the world price at $150 million.

The U.S. demand curve, D_{US}, tells us that at $150 million an airplane, U.S. airlines buy 200 airplanes a year. The U.S. supply curve, S_{US}, tells us that at $150 million an airplane, U.S. aircraft makers produce 700 airplanes a year. The quantity produced in the United States (700 a year) minus the quantity purchased by U.S. airlines (200 a year) is the quantity of airplanes exported, which is 500 airplanes a year.

REVIEW QUIZ

1 Describe the situation in the market for a good or service that the United States imports.
2 Describe the situation in the market for a good or service that the United States exports.

You can work these questions in Study Plan 7.1 and get instant feedback.   MyEconLab

---

FIGURE 7.2   A Market with Exports

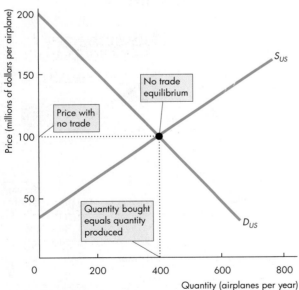

(a) Equilibrium without international trade

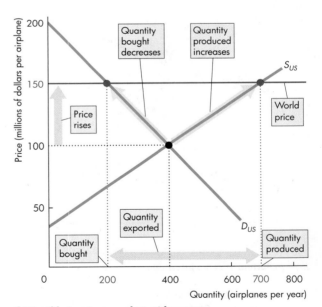

(b) Equilibrium in a market with exports

In part (a), the U.S. market with no international trade, the U.S. domestic demand curve D_{US} and the U.S. domestic supply curve S_{US} determine the price of an airplane at $100 million and 400 airplanes are produced and bought each year.

In part (b), the U.S. market with international trade,

world demand and world supply determine the world price, which is $150 million per airplane. The price in the U.S. market rises. U.S. airplane production increases to 700 a year, and U.S. purchases of airplanes decrease to 200 a year. The United States exports 500 airplanes a year.

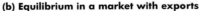 MyEconLab animation

Winners, Losers, and the Net Gain from Trade

In Chapter 1 (see pp. 6–7), we asked whether globalization is in the self-interest of the low-wage worker in Malaysia who sews your new running shoes and the shoemaker in Atlanta—whether it is in the social interest. We're now going to answer these questions. You will learn why producers complain about cheap foreign imports, but consumers of imports never complain.

Gains and Losses from Imports

We measure the gains and losses from imports by examining their effect on consumer surplus, producer surplus, and total surplus. In the importing country the winners are those whose surplus increases and the losers are those whose surplus decreases.

Figure 7.3(a) shows what consumer surplus and producer surplus would be with no international trade in T-shirts. U.S. domestic demand, D_{US}, and U.S. domestic supply, S_{US}, determine the price and quantity. The green area shows consumer surplus and the blue area shows producer surplus. Total surplus is the sum of consumer surplus and producer surplus.

Figure 7.3(b) shows how these surpluses change when the U.S. market opens to imports. The U.S. price falls to the world price. The quantity bought increases to the quantity demanded at the world price and consumer surplus expands from A to the larger green area $A + B + D$. The quantity produced in the United States decreases to the quantity supplied at the world price and producer surplus shrinks to the smaller blue area C.

Part of the gain in consumer surplus, the area B, is a loss of producer surplus—a redistribution of total surplus. But the other part of the increase in consumer surplus, the area D, is a net gain. This increase in total surplus results from the lower price and increased purchases and is the gain from imports.

FIGURE 7.3   Gains and Losses in a Market with Imports

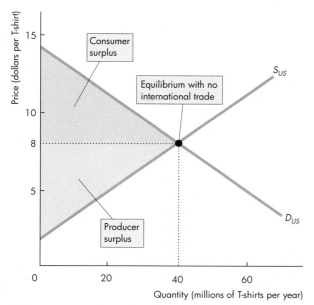

(a) Consumer surplus and producer surplus with no international trade

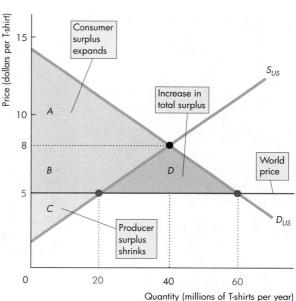

(b) Gains and losses from imports

In part (a), with no international trade, the green area shows the consumer surplus and the blue area shows the producer surplus.

In part (b), with international trade, the price falls to the

world price of $5 a shirt. Consumer surplus expands from area A to the area $A + B + D$. Producer surplus shrinks to area C. Area B is a transfer of surplus from producers to consumers. Area D is an increase in total surplus—the gain from imports.

Gains and Losses from Exports

We measure the gains and losses from exports just like we measured those from imports, by their effect on consumer surplus, producer surplus, and total surplus.

Figure 7.4(a) shows the situation with no international trade. Domestic demand, D_{US}, and domestic supply, S_{US}, determine the price and quantity, the consumer surplus, and the producer surplus.

Figure 7.4(b) shows how the consumer surplus and producer surplus change when the good is exported. The price rises to the world price. The quantity bought decreases to the quantity demanded at the world price and the consumer surplus shrinks to the green area A. The quantity produced increases to the quantity supplied at the world price and the producer surplus expands to the blue area $B + C + D$.

Part of the gain in producer surplus, the area B, is a loss in consumer surplus—a redistribution of the total surplus. But the other part of the increase in producer surplus, the area D, is a net gain. This increase in total

surplus results from the higher price and increased production and is the gain from exports.

Gains for All

You've seen that both imports and exports bring gains. Because one country's exports are other countries' imports, international trade brings gain for all countries. International trade is a win-win game.

REVIEW QUIZ

1 How is the gain from imports distributed between consumers and domestic producers?
2 How is the gain from exports distributed between consumers and domestic producers?
3 Why is the net gain from international trade positive?

You can work these questions in Study Plan 7.2 and get instant feedback.   MyEconLab

---

FIGURE 7.4   Gains and Losses in a Market with Exports

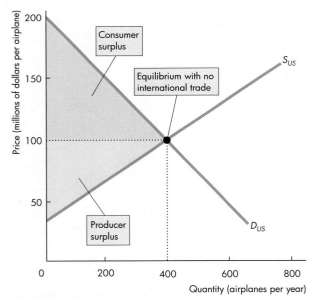

(a) Consumer surplus and producer surplus with no international trade

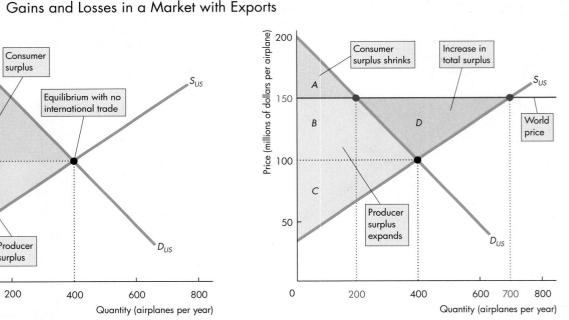

(b) Gains and losses from exports

In part (a), the U.S. market with no international trade, the green area shows the consumer surplus and the blue area shows the producer surplus. In part (b), the U.S. market with international trade, the price rises to the world price.

Consumer surplus shrinks to area A. Producer surplus expands from area C to the area $B + C + D$. Area B is a transfer of surplus from consumers to producers. Area D is an increase in total surplus—the gain from exports.

MyEconLab animation

◆ International Trade Restrictions

Governments use four sets of tools to influence international trade and protect domestic industries from foreign competition. They are

- Tariffs
- Import quotas
- Other import barriers
- Export subsidies

Tariffs

A **tariff** is a tax on a good that is imposed by the importing country when an imported good crosses its international boundary. For example, the government of India imposes a 100 percent tariff on wine imported from California. So when an Indian imports a $10 bottle of Californian wine, he pays the Indian government a $10 import duty.

Tariffs raise revenue for governments and serve the self-interest of people who earn their incomes in import-competing industries. But as you will see, restrictions on free international trade decrease the gains from trade and are not in the social interest.

The Effects of a Tariff To see the effects of a tariff, let's return to the example in which the United States imports T-shirts. With free trade, the T-shirts are imported and sold at the world price. Then, under pressure from U.S. garment makers, the U.S. government imposes a tariff on imported T-shirts. Buyers of T-shirts must now pay the world price plus the tariff. Several consequences follow and Fig. 7.5 illustrates them.

Figure 7.5(a) shows the situation with free international trade. The United States produces 20 million T-shirts a year and imports 40 million a year at the world price of $5 a shirt. Figure 7.5(b) shows what happens with a tariff set at $2 per T-shirt.

FIGURE 7.5 The Effects of a Tariff

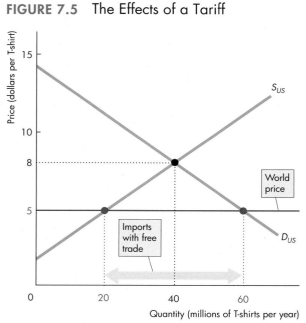

(a) Free trade

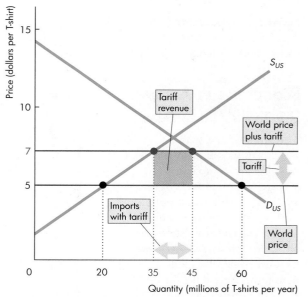

(b) Market with tariff

The world price of a T-shirt is $5. With free trade in part (a), Americans buy 60 million T-shirts a year. U.S. garment makers produce 20 million T-shirts a year and the United States imports 40 million a year.

With a tariff of $2 per T-shirt in part (b), the price in

the U.S. market rises to $7 a T-shirt. U.S. production increases, U.S. purchases decrease, and the quantity imported decreases. The U.S. government collects a tariff revenue of $2 on each T-shirt imported, which is shown by the purple rectangle.

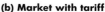

The following changes occur in the market for T-shirts:

- The price of a T-shirt in the United States rises by $2.
- The quantity of T-shirts bought in the United States decreases.
- The quantity of T-shirts produced in the United States increases.
- The quantity of T-shirts imported into the United States decreases.
- The U.S. government collects a tariff revenue.

Rise in Price of a T-Shirt To buy a T-shirt, Americans must pay the world price plus the tariff, so the price of a T-shirt rises by the $2 tariff to $7. Figure 7.5(b) shows the new domestic price line, which lies $2 above the world price line. The price rises by the full amount of the tariff. The buyer pays the entire tariff because supply from the rest of the world is perfectly elastic (see Chapter 6, p. 137).

Decrease in Purchases The higher price of a T-shirt brings a decrease in the quantity demanded along the demand curve. Figure 7.5(b) shows the decrease from 60 million T-shirts a year at $5 a shirt to 45 million a year at $7 a shirt.

Increase in Domestic Production The higher price of a T-shirt stimulates domestic production, and U.S. garment makers increase the quantity supplied along the supply curve. Figure 7.5(b) shows the increase from 20 million T-shirts at $5 a shirt to 35 million a year at $7 a shirt.

Decrease in Imports T-shirt imports decrease by 30 million, from 40 million to 10 million a year. Both the decrease in purchases and the increase in domestic production contribute to this decrease in imports.

Tariff Revenue The government's tariff revenue is $20 million—$2 per shirt on 10 million imported shirts—shown by the purple rectangle.

Winners, Losers, and the Social Loss from a Tariff A tariff on an imported good creates winners and losers and a social loss. When the U.S. government imposes a tariff on an imported good,

- U.S. consumers of the good lose.
- U.S. producers of the good gain.
- U.S. consumers lose more than U.S. producers gain.
- Society loses: a deadweight loss arises.

U.S. Consumers of the Good Lose Because the price of a T-shirt in the United States rises, the quantity of T-shirts demanded decreases. The combination of a higher price and smaller quantity bought decreases consumer surplus—the loss to U.S. consumers that arises from a tariff.

Economics in Action

U.S. Tariffs Almost Gone

The Smoot-Hawley Act, which was passed in 1930, took U.S. tariffs to a peak average rate of 20 percent in 1933. (One third of imports was subject to a 60 percent tariff.) The **General Agreement on Tariffs and Trade (GATT)** was established in 1947. Since then tariffs have fallen in a series of negotiating rounds, the most significant of which are identified in the figure. Tariffs are now as low as they have ever been but import quotas and other trade barriers persist.

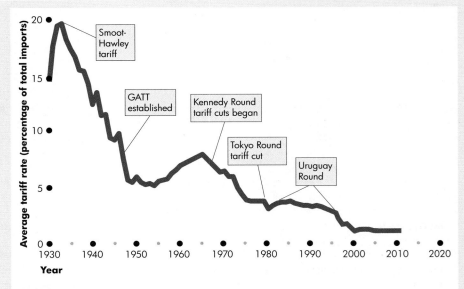

Tariffs: 1930–2011

Sources of data: U.S. Bureau of the Census, *Historical Statistics of the United States, Colonial Times to 1970*, Bicentennial Edition, Part 1 (Washington, D.C., 1975); Series U-212: updated from *Statistical Abstract of the United States:* various editions.

U.S. Producers of the Good Gain Because the price of an imported T-shirt rises by the amount of the tariff, U.S. T-shirt producers are now able to sell their T-shirts for the world price plus the tariff. At the higher price, the quantity of T-shirts supplied by U.S. producers increases. The combination of a higher price and larger quantity produced increases producer surplus—the gain to U.S. producers from the tariff.

U.S. Consumers Lose More Than U.S. Producers Gain
Consumer surplus decreases for four reasons: Some becomes producer surplus, some is lost in a higher cost of production (domestic producers have higher costs than foreign producers), some is lost because imports decrease, and some goes to the government as tariff revenue. Figure 7.6 shows these sources of lost consumer surplus.

Figure 7.6(a) shows the consumer surplus and producer surplus with free international trade in T-shirts. Figure 7.6(b) shows the consumer surplus and producer surplus with a $2 tariff on imported T-shirts. By comparing Fig. 7.6(b) with Fig. 7.6(a), you can see how a tariff changes these surpluses.

Consumer surplus—the green area—shrinks for four reasons. First, the higher price transfers surplus from consumers to producers. The blue area B represents this loss (and gain of producer surplus). Second, domestic production costs more than imports. The supply curve S_{US} shows the higher cost of production and the gray area C shows this loss of consumer surplus. Third, some of the consumer surplus is transferred to the government. The purple area D shows this loss (and gain of government revenue). Fourth, some of the consumer surplus is lost because imports decrease. The gray area E shows this loss.

Society Loses: A Deadweight Loss Arises Some of the loss of consumer surplus is transferred to producers and some is transferred to the government and spent on government programs that people value. But the increase in production cost and the loss from decreased imports is transferred to no one: It is a social loss—a deadweight loss. The gray areas labeled C and E represent this deadweight loss. Total surplus decreases by the area $C + E$.

FIGURE 7.6 The Winners and Losers from a Tariff

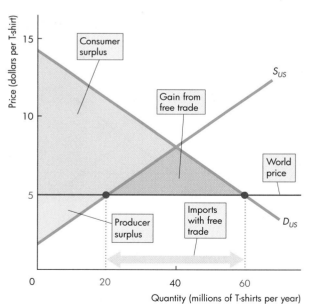

(a) Free trade

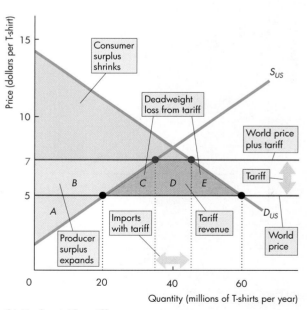

(b) Market with tariff

The world price of a T-shirt is $5. In part (a), with free trade, the United States imports 40 million T-shirts. Consumer surplus, producer surplus, and the gains from free trade are as large as possible.

In part (b), a tariff of $2 per T-shirt raises the U.S. price

of a T-shirt to $7. The quantity imported decreases. Consumer surplus shrinks by the areas B, C, D, and E. Producer surplus expands by area B. The government's tariff revenue is area D, and the tariff creates a deadweight loss equal to the area $C + E$.

MyEconLab animation

Import Quotas

We now look at the second tool for restricting trade: import quotas. An **import quota** is a restriction that limits the maximum quantity of a good that may be imported in a given period.

Most countries impose import quotas on a wide range of items. The United States imposes them on food products such as sugar and bananas and manufactured goods such as textiles and paper.

Import quotas enable the government to satisfy the self-interest of the people who earn their incomes in the import-competing industries. But you will discover that like a tariff, an import quota decreases the gains from trade and is not in the social interest.

The Effects of an Import Quota

The effects of an import quota are similar to those of a tariff. The price rises, the quantity bought decreases, and the quantity produced in the United States increases. Figure 7.7 illustrates the effects.

Figure 7.7(a) shows the situation with free international trade. Figure 7.7(b) shows what happens with an import quota of 10 million T-shirts a year. The U.S. supply curve of T-shirts becomes the domestic supply curve, S_{US}, plus the quantity that the import quota permits. So the supply curve becomes $S_{US} + quota$. The price of a T-shirt rises to $7, the quantity of T-shirts bought in the United States decreases to 45 million a year, the quantity of T-shirts produced in the United States increases to 35 million a year, and the quantity of T-shirts imported into the United States decreases to the quota quantity of 10 million a year. All the effects of this quota are identical to the effects of a $2 per shirt tariff, as you can check in Fig. 7.5(b).

Winners, Losers, and the Social Loss from an Import Quota

An import quota creates winners and losers that are similar to those of a tariff but with an interesting difference.

FIGURE 7.7   The Effects of an Import Quota

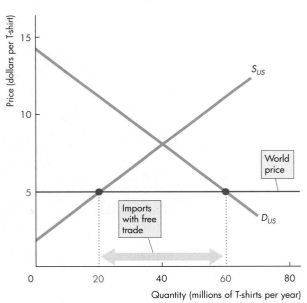

(a) Free trade

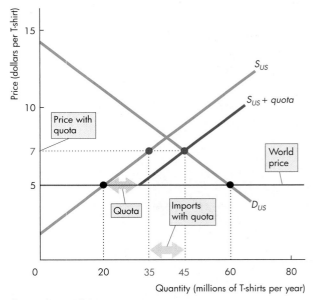

(b) Market with import quota

With free international trade, in part (a), Americans buy 60 million T-shirts at the world price. The United States produces 20 million T-shirts and imports 40 million a year. With an import quota of 10 million T-shirts a year, in part (b),

the supply of T-shirts in the United States is shown by the curve $S_{US} + quota$. The price in the United States rises to $7 a T-shirt. U.S. production increases, U.S. purchases decrease, and the quantity of T-shirts imported decreases.

MyEconLab animation

When the government imposes an import quota,

- U.S. consumers of the good lose.
- U.S. producers of the good gain.
- Importers of the good gain.
- Society loses: a deadweight loss arises.

Figure 7.8 shows these gains and losses from a quota. By comparing Fig. 7.8(b) with a quota and Fig. 7.8(a) with free trade, you can see how an import quota of 10 million T-shirts a year changes the consumer and producer surpluses.

Consumer surplus—the green area—shrinks. This decrease is the loss to consumers from the import quota. The decrease in consumer surplus is made up of four parts. First, some of the consumer surplus is transferred to producers. The blue area *B* represents this loss of consumer surplus (and gain of producer surplus). Second, part of the consumer surplus is lost because the domestic cost of production is higher

than the world price. The gray area *C* represents this loss. Third, part of the consumer surplus is transferred to importers who buy T-shirts for $5 (the world price) and sell them for $7 (the U.S. domestic price). The two blue areas *D* represent this loss of consumer surplus and profit for importers. Fourth, part of the consumer surplus is lost because imports decrease. The gray area *E* represents this loss.

The loss of consumer surplus from the higher cost of production and the decrease in imports is a social loss—a deadweight loss. The gray areas labeled *C* and *E* represent this deadweight loss. Total surplus decreases by the area *C + E*.

You can now see the one difference between a quota and a tariff. A tariff brings in revenue for the government while a quota brings a profit for the importers. All the other effects are the same, provided the quota is set at the same quantity of imports that results from the tariff.

FIGURE 7.8   The Winners and Losers from an Import Quota

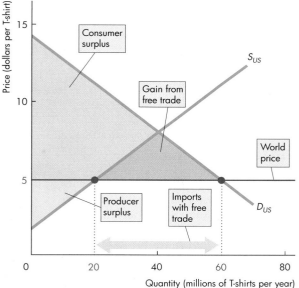

(a) Free trade

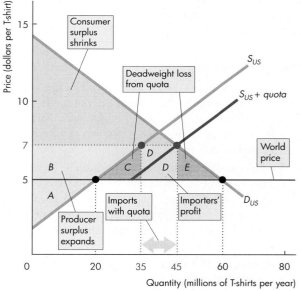

(b) Market with import quota

The world price of a T-shirt is $5. In part (a), with free trade, the United States produces 20 million T-shirts a year and imports 40 million T-shirts. Consumer surplus, producer surplus, and the gain from free international trade (darker green area) are as large as possible.

In part (b), the import quota raises the price of a T-shirt to $7. The quantity imported decreases. Consumer surplus shrinks by the areas *B*, *C*, *D*, and *E*. Producer surplus expands by area *B*. Importers' profit is the two areas *D*, and the quota creates a deadweight loss equal to *C + E*.

◆ ECONOMICS IN THE NEWS

The Changing Market for Coat Hangers

Your Dry Cleaning Bill Is About to Get Worse
The price of wire hangers is a big deal for a dry cleaner, and that price will rise when the Commerce Department puts a 21 percent tariff on hangers made in Vietnam. The tariff is in response to a wire-hanger export subsidy paid to producers in Vietnam.

Source: CNN Money, June 4, 2012

SOME FACTS

Albert J. Parkhouse invented the wire hanger in Jackson, Michigan, in 1903 and for almost 100 years, the United States produced and exported wire hangers. During the past 20 years, China and Vietnam have become the major lowest-cost producers.

THE PROBLEM

Explain why the United States has switched from exporting to importing wire hangers. Also explain the effects of the 21 percent tariff. Does Vietnam's export subsidy make the tariff efficient? Illustrate your explanations with a graph.

THE SOLUTION

- Initially, the opportunity cost of producing a wire hanger was lower in the United States than in the rest of the world. The United States had a comparative advantage in producing wire hangers and exported them.

- Today, the opportunity cost of producing a wire hanger is lower in China and Vietnam than in the United States (and other countries). China and Vietnam have a comparative advantage in producing wire hangers, so the United States imports them.

- By imposing a 21 percent tariff on wire hangers, the price in the United States rises above the world price by this percentage.

- The higher price decreases the quantity of wire hangers demanded in the United States, increases the quantity that U.S. producers supply, and decreases U.S. imports of wire hangers.

- The figure illustrates the U.S. market for wire hangers. The demand curve D_{US} and the supply curve S_{US} are assumed not to change. The U.S. price with no international trade is 10 cents per hanger.

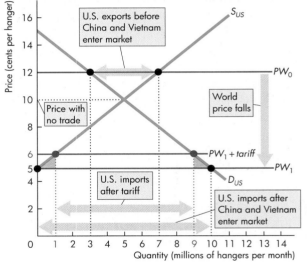

U.S. Market for Wire Hangers

- With a world price PW_0 of 12 cents a hanger, the United States had a comparative advantage in hangers, so it produced 7 million hangers a month, used 3 million, and exported 4 million. The figure shows the quantity of U.S. exports.

- When the world price falls to PW_1 at 5 cents a hanger, the United States stops producing hangers and imports 10 million a month.

- With a 21 percent tariff, the price in the United States rises to $PW_1 + tariff$. U.S. hanger production now becomes 1 million a month, the quantity used decreases to 9 million, and imports decrease to 8 million.

- The fact that the tariff is a response to Vietnam's export subsidy does not make the tariff efficient. It creates a deadweight loss shown by the two gray triangles.

Other Import Barriers

Two sets of policies that influence imports are

- Health, safety, and regulation barriers
- Voluntary export restraints

Health, Safety, and Regulation Barriers Thousands of detailed health, safety, and other regulations restrict international trade. For example, U.S. food imports are examined by the Food and Drug Administration to determine whether the food is "pure, wholesome, safe to eat, and produced under sanitary conditions." The discovery of BSE (mad cow disease) in just one U.S. cow in 2003 was enough to close down international trade in U.S. beef. The European Union bans imports of most genetically modified foods, such as U.S.-produced soybeans. Although regulations of the type we've just described are not designed to limit international trade, they have that effect.

Voluntary Export Restraints A *voluntary export restraint* is like a quota allocated to a foreign exporter of a good. This type of trade barrier isn't common. It was initially used during the 1980s when Japan voluntarily limited its exports of car parts to the United States.

Export Subsidies

A *subsidy* is a payment by the government to a producer. You studied the effects of a subsidy on the quantity produced and the price of a subsidized farm product in Chapter 6, pp. 140–141.

An *export subsidy* is a payment by the government to the producer of an exported good. Export subsidies are illegal under a number of international agreements, including the North American Free Trade Agreement (NAFTA), and the rules of the World Trade Organization (WTO).

Although export subsidies are illegal, the subsidies that the U.S. and European Union governments pay to farmers end up increasing domestic production, some of which gets exported. These exports of subsidized farm products make it harder for producers in other countries, notably in Africa and Central and South America, to compete in global markets. Export subsidies bring gains to domestic producers, but they result in inefficient underproduction in the rest of the world and create a deadweight loss.

Economics in Action
Self-Interest Beats the Social Interest

The **World Trade Organization (WTO)** is an international body established by the world's major trading nations for the purpose of supervising international trade and lowering the barriers to trade.

In 2001, at a meeting of trade ministers from all the WTO member-countries held in Doha, Qatar, an agreement was made to begin negotiations to lower tariff barriers and quotas that restrict international trade in farm products and services. These negotiations are called the **Doha Development Agenda** or the **Doha Round**.

In the period since 2001, thousands of hours of conferences in Cancún in 2003, Geneva in 2004, and Hong Kong in 2005, and ongoing meetings at WTO headquarters in Geneva, costing millions of taxpayers' dollars, have made disappointing progress.

Rich nations, led by the United States, the European Union, and Japan, want greater access to the markets of developing nations in exchange for allowing those nations greater access to the markets of the rich world, especially those for farm products.

Developing nations, led by Brazil, China, India, and South Africa, want access to the markets of farm products of the rich world, but they also want to protect their infant industries.

With two incompatible positions, these negotiations are stalled and show no signs of a breakthrough. The self-interests of rich nations and developing nations are preventing the achievement of the social interest.

REVIEW QUIZ

1 What are the tools that a country can use to restrict international trade?
2 Explain the effects of a tariff on domestic production, the quantity bought, and the price.
3 Explain who gains and who loses from a tariff and why the losses exceed the gains.
4 Explain the effects of an import quota on domestic production, consumption, and price.
5 Explain who gains and who loses from an import quota and why the losses exceed the gains.

You can work these questions in Study Plan 7.3 and get instant feedback. MyEconLab

The Case Against Protection

You've just seen that free trade promotes prosperity and protection is inefficient. Yet trade is restricted with tariffs, quotas, and other barriers. Why? Seven arguments for trade restrictions are that protecting domestic industries from foreign competition

- Helps an infant industry grow
- Counteracts dumping
- Saves domestic jobs
- Allows us to compete with cheap foreign labor
- Penalizes lax environmental standards
- Prevents rich countries from exploiting developing countries
- Reduces offshore outsourcing that sends good U.S. jobs to other countries

Helps an Infant Industry Grow

Comparative advantages change with on-the-job experience—*learning-by-doing*. When a new industry or a new product is born—an *infant industry*—it is not as productive as it will become with experience. It is argued that such an industry should be protected from international competition until it can stand alone and compete.

It is true that learning-by-doing can change comparative advantage, but this fact doesn't justify protecting an infant industry. Firms anticipate and benefit from learning-by-doing without protection from foreign competition.

When Boeing started to build airplanes, productivity was at first low. But after a period of learning-by-doing, huge productivity gains followed. Boeing didn't need a tariff to achieve these productivity gains.

Counteracts Dumping

Dumping occurs when a foreign firm sells its exports at a lower price than its cost of production. Dumping might be used by a firm that wants to gain a global monopoly. In this case, the foreign firm sells its output at a price below its cost to drive domestic firms out of business. When the domestic firms have gone, the foreign firm takes advantage of its monopoly position and charges a higher price for its product. Dumping is illegal under the rules of the World Trade Organization and is usually regarded as a justification for temporary tariffs, which are called *countervailing duties*.

But it is virtually impossible to detect dumping because it is hard to determine a firm's costs. As a result, the test for dumping is whether a firm's export price is below its domestic price. But this test is weak because it is rational for a firm to charge a low price in a market in which the quantity demanded is highly sensitive to price and a higher price in a market in which demand is less price-sensitive.

Saves Domestic Jobs

First, free trade does destroy some jobs, but it also creates other jobs. It brings about a global rationalization of labor and allocates labor resources to their highest-valued activities. International trade in textiles has cost tens of thousands of U.S. jobs as U.S. textile mills and other factories closed. But tens of thousands of jobs have been created in other countries as textile mills opened. And tens of thousands of U.S. workers have better-paying jobs than as textile workers because U.S. export industries have expanded and created new jobs. More jobs have been created than destroyed.

Although protection can save particular jobs, it does so at a high cost. For example, until 2005, U.S. textile jobs were protected by an international agreement called the Multifiber Arrangement. The U.S. International Trade Commission (ITC) has estimated that because of import quotas, 72,000 jobs existed in the textile industry that would otherwise have disappeared and that the annual clothing expenditure in the United States was $15.9 billion ($160 per family) higher than it would have been with free trade. Equivalently, the ITC estimated that each textile job saved cost $221,000 a year.

Imports don't only destroy jobs. They create jobs for retailers that sell imported goods and for firms that service those goods. Imports also create jobs by creating income in the rest of the world, some of which is spent on U.S.-made goods and services.

Allows Us to Compete with Cheap Foreign Labor

With the removal of tariffs on trade between the United States and Mexico, people said we would hear a "giant sucking sound" as jobs rushed to Mexico. That didn't happen. Why?

Because low-wage labor is low-productivity labor. If a U.S. autoworker earns $30 an hour and produces 15 units of output an hour, the average labor cost of a unit of output is $2. If a Mexican auto assembly worker earns $3 an hour and produces 1 unit of output an hour, the average labor cost of a unit of output is $3. Other things remaining the same, the higher a worker's productivity, the higher is the worker's wage rate. High-wage workers have high productivity; low-wage workers have low productivity.

It is *comparative advantage*, not wage differences, that drive international trade and that enable us to compete with Mexico and Mexico to compete with us.

Penalizes Lax Environmental Standards

Another argument for protection is that it provides an incentive to poor countries to raise their environmental standards—free trade with the richer and "greener" countries is a reward for improved environmental standards.

This argument for protection is weak. First, a poor country cannot afford to be as concerned about its environmental standard as a rich country can. Today, some of the worst pollution of air and water is found in China, Mexico, and the former communist countries of Eastern Europe. But only a few decades ago, London and Los Angeles topped the pollution league chart. The best hope for cleaner air in Beijing and Mexico City is rapid income growth, which free trade promotes. As incomes in developing countries grow, they have the *means* to match their desires to improve their environment. Second, a poor country may have a comparative advantage at doing "dirty" work, which helps it to raise its income and at the same time enables the global economy to achieve higher environmental standards than would otherwise be possible.

Prevents Rich Countries from Exploiting Developing Countries

Another argument for protection is that international trade must be restricted to prevent the people of the rich industrial world from exploiting the poorer people of the developing countries and forcing them to work for slave wages.

Child labor and near-slave labor are serious problems. But by trading with poor countries, we increase the demand for the goods that these countries produce and increase the demand for their labor. When the demand for labor in developing countries increases, the wage rate rises. So, rather than exploiting people in developing countries, trade can improve their opportunities and increase their incomes.

Reduces Offshore Outsourcing that Sends Good U.S. Jobs to Other Countries

Offshore outsourcing—buying goods, components, or services from firms in other countries—brings gains from trade identical to those of any other type of trade. We could easily change the names of the items traded from T-shirts and airplanes (the examples in the previous sections of this chapter) to banking services and call center services (or any other pair of services). A U.S. bank might export banking services to Indian firms, and Indians might provide call center services to U.S. firms. This type of trade would benefit both Americans and Indians, provided the United States has a comparative advantage in banking services and India has a comparative advantage in call center services.

Despite the gain from specialization and trade that offshore outsourcing brings, many people believe that it also brings costs that eat up the gains. Why?

A major reason is that it seems to send good U.S. jobs to other countries. It is true that some manufacturing and service jobs are going overseas. But others are expanding at home. The United States imports call center services, but it exports education, health care, legal, financial, and a host of other types of services. The number of jobs in these sectors is expanding and will continue to expand.

The exact number of jobs that have moved to lower-cost offshore locations is not known, and estimates vary. But even the highest estimate is small compared to the normal rate of job creation and labor turnover.

Gains from trade do not bring gains for every single person. Americans, on average, gain from offshore outsourcing, but some people lose. The losers are those who have invested in the human capital to do a specific job that has now gone offshore.

Unemployment benefits provide short-term temporary relief for these displaced workers. But the long-term solution requires retraining and the acquisition of new skills.

Beyond bringing short-term relief through unemployment benefits, government has a larger role to play. By providing education and training, it can enable the labor force of the twenty-first century to engage in the ongoing learning and sometimes rapid retooling that jobs we can't foresee today will demand.

Schools, colleges, and universities will expand and become better at doing their job of producing a more highly educated and flexible labor force.

◆ AT **ISSUE**

Is Offshore Outsourcing Bad or Good for America?

Citibank, Bank of America, Apple, Nike, and Wal-Mart engage in offshore outsourcing when they buy finished goods, components, or services from firms in other countries. Buying goods and components has been going on for centuries, but buying *services* such as customer support call center services, is new and is made possible by the development of low-cost telephone and Internet service.

Should this type of offshore outsourcing be discouraged and penalized with taxes and regulations?

Bad	Good
<ul><li>In his 2012 *State of the Union Address*, President Obama said, "A business that wants to outsource jobs shouldn't get a tax deduction for doing it. ... It is time to stop rewarding businesses that ship jobs overseas, and start rewarding companies that create jobs right here in America."</li><li>A survey conducted in 2004 found that 69 percent of Americans think outsourcing hurts the U.S. economy and only 17 percent think it helps.</li></ul>	<ul><li>Economist N. Gregory Mankiw, when Chair of President George W. Bush's Council of Economic Advisers, said, "I think outsourcing ... is probably a plus for the economy in the long run."</li><li>Mankiw went on to say that it doesn't matter whether "items produced abroad come on planes, ships, or over fiber-optic cables ... the economics is basically the same."</li><li>What Greg Mankiw is saying is that the economic analysis of the gains from international trade—exactly the same as what you have studied on pp. 153–156 above—applies to all types of international trade.</li><li>Offshore outsourcing, like all other forms of international trade, is a source of gains for all.</li></ul>

Have these Indian call center workers destroyed American jobs? Or does their work benefit American workers?

Avoiding Trade Wars

We have reviewed the arguments commonly heard in favor of protection and the counterarguments against it. But one counterargument to protection that is general and quite overwhelming is that protection invites retaliation and can trigger a trade war.

A trade war is a contest in which when one country raises its import tariffs, other countries retaliate wth increases of their own, which trigger yet further increases from the first country.

A trade war occurred during the Great Depression of the 1930s when the United States introduced the Smoot-Hawley tariff. Country after country retaliated with its own tariff, and in a short period, world trade had almost disappeared. The costs to all countries were large and led to a renewed international resolve to avoid such self-defeating moves in the future. The costs also led to attempts to liberalize trade following World War II.

Why Is International Trade Restricted?

Why, despite all the arguments against protection, is trade restricted? There are two key reasons:

- Tariff revenue
- Rent seeking

Tariff Revenue Government revenue is costly to collect. In developed countries such as the United States, a well-organized tax collection system is in place that can generate billions of dollars of income tax and sales tax revenues.

But governments in developing countries have a difficult time collecting taxes from their citizens. Much economic activity takes place in an informal economy with few financial records. The one area in which economic transactions are well recorded is international trade. So tariffs on international trade are a convenient source of revenue in these countries.

Rent Seeking Rent seeking is the major reason why international trade is restricted. **Rent seeking** is lobbying for special treatment by the government to create economic profit or to divert consumer surplus or producer surplus away from others. Free trade increases consumption possibilities *on average*, but not everyone shares in the gain and some people even lose. Free trade brings benefits to some and imposes costs on others, with total benefits exceeding total costs. The uneven distribution of costs and benefits is the principal obstacle to achieving more liberal international trade.

Returning to the example of trade in T-shirts and airplanes, the benefits from free trade accrue to all the producers of airplanes and to those producers of T-shirts that do not bear the costs of adjusting to a smaller garment industry. These costs are transition costs, not permanent costs. The costs of moving to free trade are borne by the garment producers and their employees who must become producers of other goods and services in which the United States has a comparative advantage.

The number of winners from free trade is large, but because the gains are spread thinly over a large number of people, the gain per person is small. The winners could organize and become a political force lobbying for free trade. But political activity is costly. It uses time and other scarce resources and the gains per person are too small to make the cost of political activity worth bearing.

In contrast, the number of losers from free trade is small, but the loss per person is large. Because the loss per person is large, the people who lose *are* willing to incur considerable expense to lobby against free trade.

Both the winners and losers weigh benefits and costs. Those who gain from free trade weigh the benefits it brings against the cost of achieving it. Those who lose from free trade and gain from protection weigh the benefit of protection against the cost of maintaining it. The protectionists undertake a larger quantity of political lobbying than the free traders.

Compensating Losers

If, in total, the gains from free international trade exceed the losses, why don't those who gain compensate those who lose so that everyone is in favor of free trade?

Some compensation does take place. When Congress approved the North American Free Trade Agreement (NAFTA) with Canada and Mexico, it set up a $56 million fund to support and retrain workers who lost their jobs as a result of the new trade agreement. During NAFTA's first six months, only 5,000 workers applied for benefits under this scheme. The losers from international trade are also compensated indirectly through the normal unemployment compensation arrangements. But only limited attempts are made to compensate those who lose.

The main reason why full compensation is not attempted is that the costs of identifying all the losers and estimating the value of their losses would be enormous. Also, it would never be clear whether a person who has fallen on hard times is suffering because of free trade or for other reasons that might be largely under her or his control. Furthermore, some people who look like losers at one point in time might, in fact, end up gaining. The young autoworker who loses his job in Michigan and becomes a computer assembly worker in Minneapolis might resent the loss of work and the need to move. But a year later, looking back on events, he counts himself fortunate.

Because we do not, in general, compensate the losers from free international trade, protectionism is a popular and permanent feature of our national economic and political life.

> ## REVIEW QUIZ
>
> 1 What are the infant industry and dumping arguments for protection? Are they correct?
> 2 Can protection save jobs and the environment and prevent workers in developing countries from being exploited?
> 3 What is offshore outsourcing? Who benefits from it and who loses?
> 4 What are the main reasons for imposing a tariff?
> 5 Why don't the winners from free trade win the political argument?
>
> You can work these questions in Study Plan 7.4 and get instant feedback.   MyEconLab

◆ We end this chapter on global markets in action in *Reading Between the Lines* on pp. 168–169, where we apply what you've learned by looking at the effects of a U.S. tariff on imports of solar panels from China.

A Tariff on Solar Panels

U.S. Proposes Anti-Dumping Duty on Chinese Solar Cell Imports

Financial Times
May 18, 2012

The U.S. department of commerce has proposed antidumping duties on imports of Chinese solar cells, raising the threat of a trade dispute and dividing the American solar industry over the decision.

The proposed tariffs for dumping—selling at less than fair value—are about 31 percent for 61 named Chinese suppliers, and about 250 percent for other imports from China.

The decision follows a collapse in prices for solar components caused by global manufacturing overcapacity after aggressive expansion, particularly in China.

The result has been good news for companies seeking to supply solar power to homes or the grid, making them more competitive against fossil fuels, but has crushed margins for panel manufacturers and made it hard for higher-cost U.S. producers to compete. The U.S. commerce department's decision is subject to confirmation in October and a final determination from the U.S. International Trade Commission.

The department said that as "critical circumstances exist," it would instruct U.S. Customs to start requiring cash deposits or bonds to the value of the duties for all imports of Chinese solar cells starting from 90 days ago.

The action follows an antidumping complaint from SolarWorld, a German company that manufactures in the United States, and six other companies. ...

The pressure on U.S. solar manufacturing has been politically difficult for President Barack Obama's administration, which has repeatedly stressed the opportunities for job creation in renewable energy.

ESSENCE OF THE STORY

- The United States has imposed a tariff of 31 percent on solar panel imports from 61 supliers in China.

- The Commerce Department says Chinese exporters were dumping cut-price panels on the U.S. market.

- Low-price Chinese imports have benefited firms that install solar panels in homes but have lowered the profits of U.S. panel manufacturers.

- The Obama administration has been under political pressure and to create U.S. jobs in the renewable energy sector.

ECONOMIC ANALYSIS

- As the world strives to replace carbon-emitting power stations with renewable energy sources, solar panels have become more popular and the cost of producing a solar panel has fallen.

- Solar panels are produced in the United States, China, and many other countries.

- Today, U.S. producers are struggling to compete with Chinese producers and have persuaded the U.S. government to protect them with a 30 percent tariff.

- Assume that initially, all the solar panels installed in the United States were manufactured here.

- Figure 1 shows this situation. The demand curve is D_{US} and the supply curve is S_{US}. The world price (PW_0) is $200 per panel, which equals the U.S. price with no trade. The quantity of solar panels demanded equals the quantity supplied at 4,000 units a week.

- As Chinese firms enter the market for solar panels, the world price falls to $170 per panel ($PW_1$).

- U.S. producers cannot compete, so they cut production to 1,000 units a week. Units installed increase to 5,000 a week and 4,000 a week are imported.

- Some producer surplus is transferred to consumer surplus and total surplus increases (the dark green area).

- Figure 2 shows the effect of a punitive tariff of 30 percent. A punitive tariff is one that makes it impossible for the foreign producer to compete.

- When the tariff is imposed, the price in the United States rises to $200 per panel.

- At this price, the quantity of solar panels produced in the United States increases by 3,000 units a week, the quantity installed decreases by 1,000 units a week, and imports are completely squeezed out.

- U.S. producers of solar panels are happy because producer surplus increases (the blue area).

- U.S. consumers and installers of solar panels lose and their loss exceeds the gain in producer surplus. The gray triangle shows the deadweight loss created.

- Because the tariff eliminates imports, the U.S. government collects no tariff revenue.

- A situation similar to that shown in Fig. 2 is present in the markets for the other items with a punitive tariff mentioned in the news article.

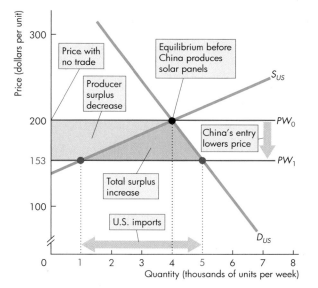

Figure 1   China Enters Solar Panel Market

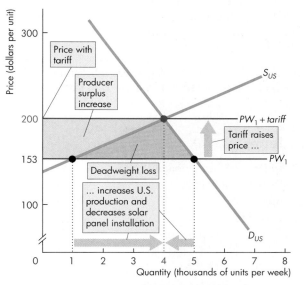

Figure 2   U.S. Puts Tariff on Solar Panel Imports

169

SUMMARY

Key Points

How Global Markets Work (pp. 152–154)

- Comparative advantage drives international trade.
- If the world price of a good is lower than the domestic price, the rest of the world has a comparative advantage in producing that good and the domestic country gains by producing less, consuming more, and importing the good.
- If the world price of a good is higher than the domestic price, the domestic country has a comparative advantage in producing that good and gains by producing more, consuming less, and exporting the good.

Working Problems 1 to 6 will give you a better understanding of how global markets work.

Winners, Losers, and the Net Gain from Trade (pp. 155–156)

- Compared to a no-trade situation, in a market with imports, consumer surplus is larger, producer surplus is smaller, and total surplus is larger with free international trade.
- Compared to a no-trade situation, in a market with exports, consumer surplus is smaller, producer surplus is larger, and total surplus is larger with free international trade.

Working Problems 7 and 8 will give you a better understanding of winners, losers, and the net gains from trade.

International Trade Restrictions (pp. 157–163)

- Countries restrict international trade by imposing tariffs, import quotas, and other import barriers.
- Trade restrictions raise the domestic price of imported goods, lower the quantity imported, decrease consumer surplus, increase producer surplus, and create a deadweight loss.

Working Problems 9 to 20 will give you a better understanding of international trade restrictions.

The Case Against Protection (pp. 164–167)

- Arguments that protection helps infant industry to grow and counteracts dumping are weak.
- Arguments that protection saves jobs, allows us to compete with cheap foreign labor, is needed to penalize lax environmental standards, and prevents exploitation of developing countries are flawed.
- Offshore outsourcing is just a new way of reaping gains from trade and does not justify protection.
- Trade restrictions are popular because protection brings a small loss per person to a large number of people and a large gain per person to a small number of people. Those who gain have a stronger political voice than those who lose and it is too costly to identify and compensate losers.

Working Problem 21 will give you a better understanding of the case against protection.

Key Terms

Doha Development Agenda
     (Doha Round), 163
Dumping, 164
Exports, 152

General Agreement on Tariffs and
     Trade (GATT), 158
Import quota, 160
Imports, 152
Offshore outsourcing, 165

Rent seeking, 167
Tariff, 157
World Trade Organization
     (WTO), 163

STUDY PLAN PROBLEMS AND APPLICATIONS

MyEconLab   You can work Problems 1 to 21 in MyEconLab Chapter 7 Study Plan and get instant feedback.

How Global Markets Work (Study Plan 7.1)

Use the following information to work Problems 1 to 3.

Wholesalers of roses (the firms that supply your local flower shop with roses for Valentine's Day) buy and sell roses in containers that hold 120 stems. The table provides information about the wholesale market for roses in the United States. The demand schedule is the wholesalers' demand and the supply schedule is the U.S. rose growers' supply.

Price (dollars per container)	Quantity demanded	Quantity supplied
	(millions of containers per year)	
100	15	0
125	12	2
150	9	4
175	6	6
200	3	8
225	0	10

Wholesalers can buy roses at auction in Aalsmeer, Holland, for $125 per container.

1. a. Without international trade, what would be the price of a container of roses and how many containers of roses a year would be bought and sold in the United States?

   b. At the price in your answer to part (a), does the United States or the rest of the world have a comparative advantage in producing roses?

2. If U.S. wholesalers buy roses at the lowest possible price, how many do they buy from U.S. growers and how many do they import?

3. Draw a graph to illustrate the U.S. wholesale market for roses. Show the equilibrium in that market with no international trade and the equilibrium with free trade. Mark the quantity of roses produced in the United States, the quantity imported, and the total quantity bought.

Use the following news clip to work Problems 4 and 5.

Underwater Oil Discovery to Transform Brazil into a Major Exporter

A huge underwater oil field discovered late last year has the potential to transform Brazil into a sizable exporter. Fifty years ago, Petrobras was formed as a trading company to import oil to support Brazil's growing economy. Two years ago, Brazil reached its long-sought goal of energy self-sufficiency.

Source: *International Herald Tribune*, January 11, 2008

4. Describe Brazil's comparative advantage in producing oil and explain why its comparative advantage has changed.

5. a. Draw a graph to illustrate the Brazilian market for oil and explain why Brazil was an importer of oil until a few years ago.

   b. Draw a graph to illustrate the Brazilian market for oil and explain why Brazil may become an exporter of oil in the near future.

6. **The End of Cheap Chinese Goods**

   Beginning in the 1990s, as China emerged as a major exporter, the prices of many goods fell. For example, clothing prices fell through 2007 when they bottomed out. But as China's labor costs started to rise, clothing production moved from China to other countries.

   Source: *The New York Times*, October 21, 2011

   a. Explain why China emerged as a major exporter of clothing through 2007.

   b. Explain why cheap Chinese goods are disappearing. Explain why China no longer exports cheap clothing.

Winners, Losers, and the Net Gain from Trade (Study Plan 7.2)

7. In the news clip in Problem 6, who will gain and who will lose from the trade in goods that the news clip predicts?

8. Use the information on the U.S. wholesale market for roses in Problem 1 to

   a. Explain who gains and who loses from free international trade in roses compared to a situation in which Americans buy only roses grown in the United States.

   b. Draw a graph to illustrate the gains and losses from free trade.

   c. Calculate the gain from international trade.

International Trade Restrictions (Study Plan 7.3)

Use the following news clip to work Problems 9 and 10.

Steel Tariffs Appear to Have Backfired on Bush

President Bush set aside his free-trade principles last year and imposed heavy tariffs on imported steel to help out struggling mills in Pennsylvania and West Virginia. Some economists say the tariffs may have cost more jobs than they saved, by driving up costs for automakers and other steel users.

Source: *The Washington Post*, September 19, 2003

9. a. Explain how a high tariff on steel imports can help domestic steel producers.

    b. Explain how a high tariff on steel imports can harm steel users.

10. Draw a graph of the U.S. market for steel to show how a high tariff on steel imports

    i.   Helps U.S. steel producers.

    ii. Harms U.S. steel users.

    iii. Creates a deadweight loss.

Use the information on the U.S. wholesale market for roses in Problem 1 to work Problems 11 to 16.

11. If the United States puts a tariff of $25 per container on imports of roses, explain how the U.S. price of roses, the quantity of roses bought, the quantity produced in the United States, and the quantity imported change.

12. Who gains and who loses from this tariff?

13. Draw a graph of the U.S. market for roses to illustrate the gains and losses from the tariff and on the graph identify the gains and losses, the tariff revenue, and the deadweight loss created.

14. If the United States puts an import quota on roses of 5 million containers, what happens to the U.S. price of roses, the quantity of roses bought, the quantity produced in the United States, and the quantity imported?

15. Who gains and who loses from this quota?

16. Draw a graph to illustrate the gains and losses from the import quota and on the graph identify the gains and losses, the importers' profit, and the deadweight loss.

Use the following news clip to work Problems 17 and 18.

Car Sales Go Up as Prices Tumble

Car affordability in Australia is now at its best in 20 years, fueling a surge in sales as prices tumble. In 2000, Australia cut the tariff to 15 percent and on January 1, 2005, it cut the tariff to 10 percent.

Source: *Courier Mail*, February 26, 2005

17. Explain who gains and who loses from the lower tariff on imported cars.

18. Draw a graph to show how the price of a car, the quantity of cars bought, the quantity of cars produced in Australia, and the quantity of cars imported into Australia changed.

Use the following news clip to work Problems 19 and 20.

A New Food Crisis Is on Our Plates

Over the past year the price of corn has risen 52 percent, wheat 49 percent, and soybeans 28 percent. Alarmed at spiking food prices, a score of countries, including Russia and Ukraine, have banned food exports to make sure they can feed their own people first.

Source: *Sydney Morning Herald*, February 22, 2011

19. a. What are the benefits to a country from importing food?

    b. What costs might arise from relying on imported food?

20. If a country restricts food exports, what effect does this restriction have in that country on the price of food, the quantity of food it produces, the quantity of food it consumes, and the quantity of food it exports?

The Case Against Protection (Study Plan 7.4)

21. **Chinese Tire Maker Rejects U.S. Charge of Defects**

    U.S. regulators ordered the recall of more than 450,000 faulty tires. The Chinese producer of the tires disputed the allegations and hinted that the recall might be an effort by foreign competitors to hamper Chinese exports to the United States. Mounting scrutiny of Chinese-made goods has become a source of new trade frictions between the United States and China and fueled worries among regulators, corporations, and consumers about the risks associated with many products imported from China.

    Source: *International Herald Tribune*, June 26, 2007

    a. What does the information in the news clip imply about the comparative advantage of producing tires in the United States and China?

    b. Could product quality be a valid argument against free trade?

    c. How would the product-quality argument against free trade be open to abuse by domestic producers of the imported good?

ADDITIONAL PROBLEMS AND APPLICATIONS

MyEconLab   You can work these problems in MyEconLab if assigned by your instructor.

How Global Markets Work

22. Suppose that the world price of sugar is 10 cents a pound, the United States does not trade internationally, and the equilibrium price of sugar in the United States is 20 cents a pound. The United States then begins to trade internationally.

    a. How does the price of sugar in the United States change?

    b. Do U.S. consumers buy more or less sugar?

    c. Do U.S. sugar growers produce more or less sugar?

    d. Does the United States export or import sugar and why?

23. Suppose that the world price of steel is $100 a ton, India does not trade internationally, and the equilibrium price of steel in India is $60 a ton. India then begins to trade internationally.

    a. How does the price of steel in India change?

    b. How does the quantity of steel produced in India change?

    c. How does the quantity of steel bought by India change?

    d. Does India export or import steel and why?

24. A semiconductor is a key component in your laptop, cell phone, and iPod. The table provides information about the market for semiconductors in the United States.

Price (dollars per unit)	Quantity demanded	Quantity supplied
	(billions of units per year)	
10	25	0
12	20	20
14	15	40
16	10	60
18	5	80
20	0	100

    Producers of semiconductors can get $18 a unit on the world market.

    a. With no international trade, what would be the price of a semiconductor and how many semiconductors a year would be bought and sold in the United States?

    b. Does the United States have a comparative advantage in producing semiconductors?

25. **Act Now, Eat Later**

    The hunger crisis in poor countries has its roots in U.S. and European policies of subsidizing the diversion of food crops to produce biofuels like corn-based ethanol. That is, doling out subsidies to put the world's dinner into the gas tank.

    Source: *Time*, May 5, 2008

    a. What is the effect on the world price of corn of the increased use of corn to produce ethanol in the United States and Europe?

    b. How does the change in the world price of corn affect the quantity of corn produced in a poor developing country with a comparative advantage in producing corn, the quantity it consumes, and the quantity that it either exports or imports?

Winners, Losers, and the Net Gain from Trade

26. Draw a graph of the market for corn in the poor developing country in Problem 25(b) to show the changes in consumer surplus, producer surplus, and deadweight loss that arise.

Use the following news clip to work Problems 27 and 28.

South Korea to Resume U.S. Beef Imports

South Korea will reopen its market to most U.S. beef. South Korea banned imports of U.S. beef in 2003 amid concerns over a case of mad cow disease in the United States. The ban closed what was then the third-largest market for U.S. beef exporters.

Source: CNN, May 29, 2008

27. a. Explain how South Korea's import ban on U.S. beef affected beef producers and consumers in South Korea.

    b. Draw a graph of the market for beef in South Korea to illustrate your answer to part (a). Identify the changes in consumer surplus, producer surplus, and deadweight loss.

28. a. Assuming that South Korea is the only importer of U.S. beef, explain how South Korea's import ban on U.S. beef affected beef producers and consumers in the United States.

    b. Draw a graph of the market for beef in the United States to illustrate your answer to part (a). Identify the changes in consumer surplus, producer surplus, and deadweight loss.

International Trade Restrictions

Use the following information to work Problems 29 to 31.

Before 1995, trade between the United States and Mexico was subject to tariffs. In 1995, Mexico joined NAFTA and all U.S. and Mexican tariffs have gradually been removed.

29. Explain how the price that U.S. consumers pay for goods from Mexico and the quantity of U.S. imports from Mexico have changed. Who are the winners and who are the losers from this free trade?

30. Explain how the quantity of U.S. exports to Mexico and the U.S. government's tariff revenue from trade with Mexico have changed.

31. Suppose that in 2013, tomato growers in Florida lobby the U.S. government to impose an import quota on Mexican tomatoes. Explain who in the United States would gain and who would lose from such a quota.

Use the following information to work Problems 32 and 33.

Suppose that in response to huge job losses in the U.S. textile industry, Congress imposes a 100 percent tariff on imports of textiles from China.

32. Explain how the tariff on textiles will change the price that U.S. buyers pay for textiles, the quantity of textiles imported, and the quantity of textiles produced in the United States.

33. Explain how the U.S. and Chinese gains from trade will change. Who in the United States will lose and who will gain?

Use the following information to work Problems 34 and 35.

With free trade between Australia and the United States, Australia would export beef to the United States. But the United States imposes an import quota on Australian beef.

34. Explain how this quota influences the price that U.S. consumers pay for beef, the quantity of beef produced in the United States, and the U.S. and the Australian gains from trade.

35. Explain who in the United States gains from the quota on beef imports and who loses.

The Case Against Protection

36. **Trading Up**

The cost of protecting jobs in uncompetitive sectors through tariffs is high: Saving a job in the sugar industry costs American consumers $826,000 in higher prices a year; saving a dairy industry job costs $685,000 per year; and saving a job in the manufacturing of women's handbags costs $263,000.

    Source: *The New York Times*, June 26, 2006

a. What are the arguments for saving the jobs mentioned in this news clip?

b. Explain why these arguments are faulty.

c. Is there any merit to saving these jobs?

Economics in the News

37. After you have studied *Reading Between the Lines* on pp. 168–169, answer the following questions.

a. What events put U.S. solar panel producers under pressure?

b. Explain how a tariff on solar panel imports changes domestic production, consumption, and imports of solar panels.

c. Illustrate your answer to part (b) with an appropriate graphical analysis assuming that imports are not completely eliminated.

d. Explain how a tariff on solar panel imports changes consumer surplus and producer surplus.

e. Explain the four sources of loss of consumer surplus that result from a tariff on solar panel imports.

f. Illustrate your answer to part (e) with an appropriate graphical analysis.

38. **Aid May Grow for Laid-Off Workers**

Expansion of the Trade Adjustment Assistance (TAA) program would improve the social safety net for the 21st century, as advances permit more industries to take advantage of cheap foreign labor—even for skilled, white-collar work. By providing special compensation to more of globalization's losers and retraining them for stable jobs at home, an expanded program could begin to ease the resentment and insecurity arising from the new economy.

    Source: *The Washington Post*, July 23, 2007

a. Why does the United States engage in international trade if it causes U.S. workers to lose their jobs?

b. Explain how an expansion of the TAA program will make it easier for the United States to move toward freer international trade.

The Amazing Market

PART TWO

The five chapters that you've just studied explain how markets work. The market is an amazing instrument. It enables people who have never met and who know nothing about each other to interact and do business. It also enables us to allocate our scarce resources to the uses that we value most highly. Markets can be very simple or highly organized. Markets are ancient and they are modern.

A simple and ancient market is one that the American historian Daniel J. Boorstin describes in *The Discoverers* (p. 161). In the late fourteenth century,

> *The Muslim caravans that went southward from Morocco across the Atlas Mountains arrived after twenty days at the shores of the Senegal River. There the Moroccan traders laid out separate piles of salt, of beads from Ceutan coral, and cheap manufactured goods. Then they retreated out of sight. The local tribesmen, who lived in the strip mines where they dug their gold, came to the shore and put a heap of gold beside each pile of Moroccan goods. Then they, in turn, went out of view, leaving the Moroccan traders either to take the gold offered for a particular pile or to reduce the pile of their merchandise to suit the offered price in gold. Once again the Moroccan traders withdrew, and the process went on. By this system of commercial etiquette, the Moroccans collected their gold.*

Organized and modern markets are auctions on e-Bay and U.S. government auction of the airwaves that cell phone companies use. Susan Athey, whom you will meet on the following page, is a world-renowned expert on the design of auctions.

Everything and anything that can be exchanged is traded in markets to the benefit of both buyers and sellers.

Alfred Marshall *(1842–1924) grew up in an England that was being transformed by the railroad and by the expansion of manufacturing. Mary Paley was one of Marshall's students at Cambridge, and when Alfred and Mary married, in 1877, celibacy rules barred Alfred from continuing to teach at Cambridge. By 1884, with more liberal rules, the Marshalls returned to Cambridge, where Alfred became Professor of Political Economy.*

Many economists had a hand in refining the demand and supply model, but the first thorough and complete statement of the model as we know it today was set out by Alfred Marshall, with the help of Mary Paley Marshall. Published in 1890, this monumental treatise, The Principles of Economics, *became the textbook on economics on both sides of the Atlantic for almost half a century.*

"The forces to be dealt with are . . . so numerous, that it is best to take a few at a time. . . . Thus we begin by isolating the primary relations of supply, demand, and price."

ALFRED MARSHALL
The Principles of Economics

SUSAN ATHEY is Professor of Economics at Harvard University. Born in 1970, she completed high school in three years, wrapped up three majors—in economics, mathematics, and computer science—at Duke University at 20, completed her Ph.D. at Stanford University at 24, and was voted tenure at MIT and Stanford at 29. After teaching at MIT for six years and Stanford for five years, she moved to Harvard in 2006. Among her many honors and awards, the most prestigious is the John Bates Clark Medal given to the best economist under 40. She is the first woman to receive this award.

Professor Athey's research is broad both in scope and style. A government that wants to auction natural resources will turn to her fundamental discoveries (and possibly consult with her) before deciding how to organize the auction. An economist who wants to test a theory using a large data set will use her work on statistics and econometrics.

Michael Parkin talked with Susan Athey about her research, what economists have learned about designing markets, and her advice to students.

Professor Athey, what sparked your interest in economics?

I was studying mathematics and computer science, but I felt that the subjects were not as relevant as I would like. I discovered economics through a research project with a professor who was working on auctions. I had a summer job working for a firm that sold computers to the government through auctions. Eventually my professor, Bob Marshall, wrote two articles on the topic and testified before Congress to help reform the system for government procurement of computers. That really inspired me and showed me the power of economic ideas to change the world and to make things work more efficiently.

What is the connection between an auction and the supply and demand model?

The basic laws of supply and demand can be seen in evidence in an auction market like eBay. The more sellers that are selling similar products, the lower the prices they can expect to achieve. Similarly the more buyers there are demanding those objects, the higher the prices the sellers can achieve.

An important thing for an auction marketplace is to attract a good balance of buyers and sellers so that both the buyers and the sellers find it more profitable to transact in that marketplace rather than using some other mechanism. From a seller's perspective, the more bidders there are on the platform, the greater the demand and the higher the prices. And from the buyer's perspective, the more sellers there are on the platform, the greater the supply and the lower the prices.

> The basic laws of supply and demand can be seen in evidence in an auction market like eBay.

Can we think of an auction as a mechanism for finding the equilibrium price and quantity?

Exactly. We can think of the whole collection of auctions on eBay as being a mechanism to discover a market clearing price, and individual items might sell a little higher or a little lower but over all we believe that the prices on eBay auctions will represent equilibrium prices.

*Read the full interview with Susan Athey in MyEconLab.

8

UTILITY AND DEMAND

After studying this chapter, you will be able to:

- ◆ Explain the limits to consumption and describe preferences using the concept of utility

- ◆ Explain the marginal utility theory of consumer choice

- ◆ Use marginal utility theory to predict the effects of changes in prices and incomes and to explain the paradox of value

- ◆ Describe some new ways of explaining consumer choices

You want Adele's album *21*. Will you buy a CD for $9.99, or will you download it for $10.99? What determines our choices about how we buy recorded music?

You know that diamonds are expensive and water is cheap. Doesn't that seem odd? Why do we place a higher value on useless diamonds than on essential-to-life water?

The theory of consumer choice that you're going to study in this chapter answers questions like the ones we've just posed. *Reading Between the Lines* at the end of the chapter applies what you learn to a debate about whether sugary drinks should be banned or taxed to discourage their consumption.

Consumption Choices

The choices that you make as a buyer of goods and services—your consumption choices—are influenced by many factors. We can summarize them under two broad headings:

- Consumption possibilities
- Preferences

Consumption Possibilities

Your consumption possibilities are all the things that you can afford to buy. You can afford many different combinations of goods and services, but they are all limited by your income and by the prices that you must pay. For example, you might decide to spend a big part of your income on a gym membership and personal trainer and little on movies and music, or you might spend lots on movies and music and use the free gym at school.

The easiest way to describe consumption possibilities is to consider a model consumer who buys only two items. That's what we'll now do. We'll study the consumption possibilities of Lisa, who buys only movies and soda.

A Consumer's Budget Line Consumption possibilities are limited by income and by the prices of movies and soda. When Lisa spends all her income, she reaches the limits to her consumption possibilities. We describe this limit with a **budget line**, which marks the boundary between those combinations of goods and services that a household can afford to buy and those that it cannot afford.

Figure 8.1 illustrates Lisa's consumption possibilities of movies and soda and her budget line. Lisa has an income of $40 a month, the price of a movie is $8, and the price of soda is $4 a case. Rows A through F in the table show six possible ways of allocating $40 to these two goods. For example, in row A Lisa buys 10 cases of soda and sees no movies; in row F she sees 5 movies and buys no soda; and in row C she sees 2 movies and buys 6 cases of soda.

Points A through F in the graph illustrate the possibilities presented in the table, and the line passing through these points is Lisa's budget line.

The budget line constrains choices: It marks the boundary between what is affordable and unaffordable. Lisa can afford all the points on the budget line and inside it. Points outside the line are unaffordable.

FIGURE 8.1   Lisa's Budget Line

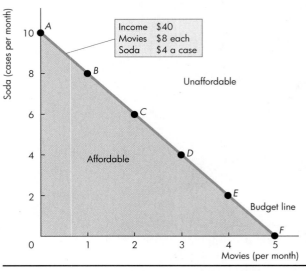

Possibility	Movies		Soda	
	Quantity	Expenditure (dollars)	Cases	Expenditure (dollars)
A	0	0	10	40
B	1	8	8	32
C	**2**	**16**	**6**	**24**
D	3	24	4	16
E	4	32	2	8
F	5	40	0	0

The graph and the table show six possible ways in which Lisa can allocate $40 to movies and soda. In row C and at point C, she sees 2 movies and buys 6 cases of soda. The line AF is Lisa's budget line and is a boundary between what she can afford and what she cannot afford. Her choices must lie along the line AF or inside the orange area.

─────── MyEconLab animation ───────

Changes in Consumption Possibilities Consumption possibilities change when income or prices change. A rise in income shifts the budget line outward but leaves its slope unchanged. A change in a price changes the slope of the line[1]. Our goal is to predict the effects of such changes on consumption choices. To do so, we must determine the choice a consumer makes. The budget line shows what is possible; preferences determine which possibility is chosen. We'll now describe a consumer's preferences.

─────────

[1] Chapter 9 explains an alternative model of consumer choice and pp. 203–204 provides some detail on how changes in income and prices change the budget line.

Preferences

Lisa's income and the prices that she faces limit her consumption choices, but she still has lots of choice. The choice that she makes depends on her **preferences**—a description of her likes and dislikes.

You saw one way that economists use to describe preferences in Chapter 2 (p. 36), the concept of *marginal benefit* and the *marginal benefit curve*. But you also saw in Chapter 5 (p. 108) that a marginal benefit curve is also a demand curve. The goal of a theory of consumer choice is to derive the demand curve from a deeper account of how consumers make their buying plans. That is, we want to *explain what determines demand and marginal benefit*.

To achieve this goal, we need a deeper way of describing preferences. One approach to this problem uses the idea of utility, and defines **utility** as the benefit or satisfaction that a person gets from the consumption of goods and services. We distinguish two utility concepts:

- Total utility
- Marginal utility

Total Utility The total benefit that a person gets from the consumption of all the different goods and services is called **total utility**. Total utility depends on the level of consumption—more consumption generally gives more total utility.

To illustrate the concept of total utility, think about Lisa's choices. We tell Lisa that we want to measure her utility from movies and soda. We can use any scale that we wish to measure her total utility and we give her two starting points: (1) We will call the total utility from no movies and no soda zero utility; and (2) We will call the total utility she gets from seeing 1 movie a month 50 units.

We then ask Lisa to tell us, using the same scale, how much she would like 2 movies, and more, up to 10 movies a month. We also ask her to tell us, on the same scale, how much she would like 1 case of soda a month, 2 cases, and more, up to 10 cases a month.

In Table 8.1, the columns headed "Total utility" show Lisa's answers. Looking at those numbers, you can say a lot about how much Lisa likes soda and movies. She says that 1 case of soda gives her 75 units of utility—50 percent more than the utility that she gets from seeing 1 movie. You can also see that her total utility from soda climbs more slowly than her total utility from movies. This difference turns on the second utility concept: *marginal utility*.

TABLE 8.1   Lisa's Utility from Movies and Soda

Movies			Soda		
Quantity (per month)	Total utility	Marginal utility	Cases (per month)	Total utility	Marginal utility
0	0		0	0	
		 50			 75
1	50		1	75	
		 40			 48
2	90		2	123	
		 32			 36
3	122		3	159	
		 28			 24
4	150		4	183	
		 26			 22
5	176		5	205	
		 24			 20
6	200		6	225	
		 22			 13
7	222		7	238	
		 20			 10
8	242		8	248	
		 17			 7
9	259		9	255	
		 16			 5
10	275		10	260	

Marginal Utility We define **marginal utility** as the *change* in total utility that results from a one-unit increase in the quantity of a good consumed.

In Table 8.1, the columns headed "Marginal utility" show Lisa's marginal utility from movies and soda. You can see that if Lisa increases the soda she buys from 1 to 2 cases a month, her total utility from soda increases from 75 units to 123 units. For Lisa, the marginal utility from the second case each month is 48 units (123 − 75).

The marginal utility numbers appear midway between the quantities of soda because it is the *change* in the quantity she buys from 1 to 2 cases that produces the marginal utility of 48 units.

Marginal utility is *positive*, but it *diminishes* as the quantity of a good consumed increases.

Positive Marginal Utility All the things that people enjoy and want more of have a positive marginal utility. Some objects and activities can generate negative marginal utility—and lower total utility. Two examples are hard labor and polluted air. But all the goods and services that people value and that we are thinking about here have positive marginal utility: Total utility increases as the quantity consumed increases.

Diminishing Marginal Utility As Lisa sees more movies, her total utility from movies increases but her marginal utility from movies decreases. Similarly, as she

FIGURE 8.2   Total Utility and Marginal Utility

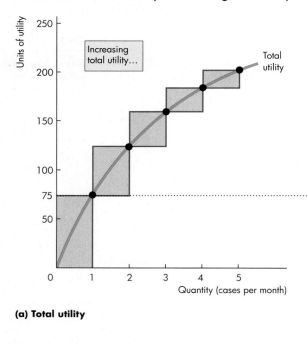

(a) Total utility

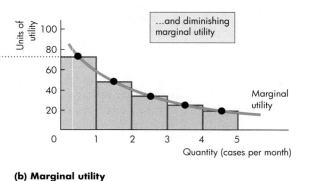

(b) Marginal utility

The figure graphs Lisa's total utility and marginal utility from soda based on the numbers for the first 5 cases of soda a month in Table 8.1. Part (a) shows her total utility—increasing total utility. The bars along the total utility curve show the extra total utility from each additional case of soda—marginal utility. Part (b) shows Lisa's diminishing marginal utility from soda.

MyEconLab animation

consumes more soda, her total utility from soda increases but her marginal utility from soda decreases.

The tendency for marginal utility to decrease as the consumption of a good increases is so general and universal that we give it the status of a *principle*—the principle of **diminishing marginal utility**.

You can see Lisa's diminishing marginal utility by calculating a few numbers. Her marginal utility from soda decreases from 75 units from the first case to 48 units from the second case and to 36 units from the third. Her marginal utility from movies decreases from 50 units for the first movie to 40 units for the second and 32 units for the third. Lisa's marginal utility diminishes as she buys more of each good.

Your Diminishing Marginal Utility You've been studying all day and into the evening, and you've been too busy finishing an assignment to shop for soda. A friend drops by with a can of soda. The utility you get from that soda is the marginal utility from your first soda of the day—from *one* can. On another day you've been on a soda binge. You've been working on an assignment, but you've guzzled 10 cans of soda while doing so, and are now totally wired. You are happy enough to have one more can, but the thrill that you get from it is not very large. It is the marginal utility from the *eleventh* can in a day.

Graphing Lisa's Utility Schedules Figure 8.2(a) illustrates Lisa's total utility from soda. The more soda Lisa consumes in a month, the more total utility she gets. Her total utility curve slopes upward.

Figure 8.2(b) illustrates Lisa's marginal utility from soda. It is a graph of the marginal utility numbers in Table 8.1. This graph shows Lisa's diminishing marginal utility from soda. Her marginal utility curve slopes downward as she consumes more soda.

We've described Lisa's consumption possibilities and preferences. Your next task is to see how Lisa chooses what to consume.

REVIEW QUIZ

1 Explain how a consumer's income and the prices of goods limit consumption possibilities.
2 What is utility and how do we use the concept of utility to describe a consumer's preferences?
3 What is the distinction between total utility and marginal utility?
4 What is the key assumption about marginal utility?

You can work these questions in Study Plan 8.1 and get instant feedback.   MyEconLab

Utility-Maximizing Choice

Consumers want to get the most utility possible from their limited resources. They make the choice that maximizes utility. To discover this choice, we combine the constraint imposed by the budget and the consumer's preferences and find the point on the budget line that gives the consumer the maximum attainable utility. Let's find Lisa's utility-maximizing choice.

A Spreadsheet Solution

Lisa's most direct way of finding the quantities of movies and soda that maximize her utility is to make a table in a spreadsheet with the information and calculations shown in Table 8.2. Let's see what that table tells us.

Find the Just-Affordable Combinations Table 8.2 shows the combinations of movies and soda that Lisa can afford and that exhaust her $40 income. For example, in row *A*, Lisa buys only soda and at $4 a case she can buy 10 cases. In row *B*, Lisa sees 1 movie and buys 8 cases of soda. She spends $8 on the movie. At $4 a case, she spends $32 on soda and can buy 8 cases. The combination in row *B* just exhausts her $40. The combinations shown in the table are the same as those plotted on her budget line in Fig. 8.1.

We noted that the budget line shows that Lisa can also afford any combination *inside* the budget line. The quantities in those combinations would be smaller than the ones shown in Table 8.2 and they do not exhaust her $40. But smaller quantities don't maximize her utility. Why? The marginal utilities of movies and soda are positive, so the more of each that Lisa buys, the more total utility she gets.

Find the Total Utility for Each Just-Affordable Combination Table 8.2 shows the total utility that Lisa gets from the just-affordable quantities of movies and soda. The second and third columns show the numbers for movies and fourth and fifth columns show those for soda. The center column adds the total utility from movies to the total utility from soda. This number, the total utility from movies *and* soda, is what Lisa wants to maximize.

In row *A* of the table, Lisa sees no movies and buys 10 cases of soda. She gets no utility from movies and 260 units of utility from soda. Her total utility from movies and soda (the center column) is 260 units.

TABLE 8.2 Lisa's Utility-Maximizing Choice

	Movies $8		Total utility from movies and soda	Soda $4	
	Quantity (per month)	Total utility		Total utility	Cases (per month)
A	0	0	260	260	10
B	1	50	298	248	8
C	2	90	315	225	6
D	3	122	305	183	4
E	4	150	273	123	2
F	5	176	176	0	0

In row *C* of the table, Lisa sees 2 movies and buys 6 cases of soda. She gets 90 units of utility from movies and 225 units of utility from soda. Her total utility from movies and soda is 315 units. This combination of movies and soda maximizes Lisa's total utility. That is, given the prices of movies and soda, Lisa's best choice when she has $40 to spend is to see 2 movies and buy 6 cases of soda.

If Lisa sees 1 movie, she can buy 8 cases of soda, but she gets only 298 units of total utility—17 units less than the maximum attainable. If she sees 3 movies, she can buy only 4 cases of soda. She gets 305 units of total utility—10 units less than the maximum attainable.

Consumer Equilibrium We've just described Lisa's consumer equilibrium. A **consumer equilibrium** is a situation in which a consumer has allocated all of his or her available income in the way that maximizes his or her total utility, given the prices of goods and services. Lisa's consumer equilibrium is 2 movies and 6 cases of soda.

To find Lisa's consumer equilibrium, we did something that an economist might do but that a consumer is not likely to do: We measured her total utility from all the affordable combinations of movies and soda and then, by inspection of the numbers, selected the combination that gives the highest total utility. There is a more natural way of finding a consumer's equilibrium—a way that uses the idea that choices are made at the margin, as you first met in Chapter 1. Let's look at this approach.

Choosing at the Margin

When you go shopping you don't do utility calculations. But you do decide how to allocate your budget, and you do so in a way that you think is best for you. If you could make yourself better off by spending a few more dollars on an extra unit of one item and the same number of dollars less on something else, you would make that change. So, when you've allocated your budget in the best possible way, you can't make yourself better off by spending more on one item and less on others.

Marginal Utility per Dollar Economists interpret your best possible choice by using the idea of marginal utility per dollar. *Marginal utility* is the increase in total utility that results from consuming *one more unit* of a good. **Marginal utility per dollar** is the *marginal utility* from a good that results from spending *one more dollar* on it.

The distinction between these two marginal concepts is clearest for a good that is infinitely divisible, such as gasoline. You can buy gasoline by the smallest fraction of a gallon and literally choose to spend one more or one less dollar at the pump. The increase in total utility that results from spending one more dollar at the pump is the marginal utility per dollar from gasoline. When you buy a movie ticket or a case of soda, you must spend your dollars in bigger lumps. To buy our marginal movie ticket or case of soda, you must spend the price of one unit and your total utility increases by the marginal utility from that item. So to calculate the marginal utility per dollar for movies (or soda), we must divide marginal utility from the good by its price.

Call the marginal utility from movies MU_M and the price of a movie P_M. Then the *marginal utility per dollar from movies* is

$$MU_M/P_M.$$

Call the marginal utility from soda MU_S and the price of a case of soda P_S. Then the *marginal utility per dollar from soda* is

$$MU_S/P_S.$$

By comparing the marginal utility per dollar from all the goods that a person buys, we can determine whether the budget has been allocated in the way that maximizes total utility.

Let's see how we use the marginal utility per dollar to define a utility-maximizing rule.

Utility-Maximizing Rule A consumer's total utility is maximized by following the rule:

- Spend all the available income
- Equalize the marginal utility per dollar for all goods

Spend All the Available Income Because more consumption brings more utility, only those choices that exhaust income can maximize utility. For Lisa, combinations of movies and soda that leave her with money to spend don't give her as much total utility as those that exhaust her $40 per month income.

Equalize the Marginal Utility per Dollar The basic idea behind this rule is to move dollars from good A to good B if doing so increases the utility from good A by more than it decreases the utility from good B. Such a utility-increasing move is possible if the marginal utility per dollar from good A *exceeds* that from good B.

But buying more of good A decreases its marginal utility. And buying less of good B increases its marginal utility. So by moving dollars from good A to good B, total utility rises, but the gap between the marginal utilities per dollar gets smaller.

As long as the gap exists—as long as the marginal utility per dollar from good A exceeds that from good B—total utility can be increased by spending more on A and less on B. But when enough dollars have been moved from B to A to make the two marginal utilities per dollar equal, total utility cannot be increased further. Total utility is maximized.

Lisa's Marginal Calculation Let's apply the basic idea to Lisa. To calculate Lisa's marginal utility per dollar, we divide her marginal utility numbers for each quantity of each good by the price of the good. The table in Fig. 8.3 shows these calculations for Lisa, and the graph illustrates the situation on Lisa's budget line. The rows of the table are three of her affordable combinations of movies and soda.

Too Much Soda and Too Few Movies In row B, Lisa sees 1 movie a month and consumes 8 cases of soda a month. Her marginal utility from seeing 1 movie a month is 50 units. Because the price of a movie is $8, Lisa's marginal utility per dollar from movies is 50 units divided by $8, or 6.25 units of utility per dollar.

Lisa's marginal utility from soda when she consumes 8 cases of soda a month is 10 units. Because the price of soda is $4 a case, Lisa's marginal utility per dollar from soda is 10 units divided by $4, or 2.50 units of utility per dollar.

When Lisa sees 1 movie and consumes 8 cases of soda a month, her marginal utility per dollar from soda is *less than* her marginal utility per dollar from movies. That is,

$$MU_S/P_S < MU_M/P_M.$$

If Lisa spent an extra dollar on movies and a dollar less on soda, her total utility would increase. She would get 6.25 units from the extra dollar spent on movies and lose 2.50 units from the dollar less spent on soda. Her total utility would increase by 3.75 units (6.25 − 2.50).

Too Little Soda and Too Many Movies In row *D*, Lisa sees 3 movies a month and consumes 4 cases of soda. Her marginal utility from seeing the third movie a month is 32 units. At a price of $8 a movie, Lisa's marginal utility per dollar from movies is 32 units divided by $8, or 4 units of utility per dollar.

Lisa's marginal utility from soda when she buys 4 cases a month is 24 units. At a price of $4 a case, Lisa's marginal utility per dollar from soda is 24 units divided by $4, or 6 units of utility per dollar.

When Lisa sees 3 movies and consumes 4 cases of soda a month, her marginal utility from soda *exceeds* her marginal utility from movies. That is,

$$MU_S/P_S > MU_M/P_M.$$

If Lisa spent an extra dollar on soda and a dollar less on movies, her total utility would increase. She would get 6 units from the extra dollar spent on soda and she would lose 4 units from the dollar less spent on movies. Her total utility would increase by 2 units (6 − 4).

Utility-Maximizing Movies and Soda In Fig. 8.3, if Lisa moves from row *B* to row *C*, she increases the movies she sees from 1 to 2 a month and decreases the soda she consumes from 8 to 6 cases a month. Her marginal utility per dollar from movies falls to 5 and her marginal utility per dollar from soda rises to 5.

Similarly, if Lisa moves from row *D* to row *C*, she decreases the movies she sees from 3 to 2 a month and increases the soda she consumes from 4 to 6 cases a month. Her marginal utility per dollar from movies rises to 5 and her marginal utility per dollar from soda falls to 5.

When Lisa sees 2 movies and consumes 6 cases of soda a month, her marginal utility per dollar from soda *equals* her marginal utility per dollar from

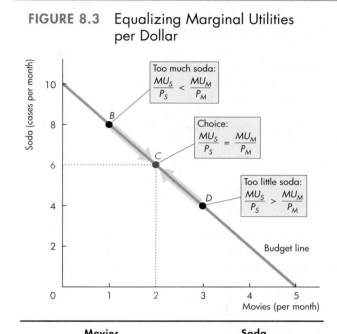

FIGURE 8.3 Equalizing Marginal Utilities per Dollar

	Movies ($8 each)			Soda ($4 per case)		
	Quantity	Marginal utility	Marginal utility per dollar	Cases	Marginal utility	Marginal utility per dollar
B	1	50	6.25	8	10	2.50
C	2	40	5.00	6	20	5.00
D	3	32	4.00	4	24	6.00

The graph shows Lisa's budget line and identifies three points on it. The rows of the table describe these points.

At point *B* (row *B*), with 1 movie and 8 cases of soda, Lisa's marginal utility per dollar from soda is less than that from movies: Buy less soda and see more movies.

At point *D* (row *D*), with 3 movies and 4 cases of soda, Lisa's marginal utility per dollar from soda is greater than that from movies: Buy more soda and see fewer movies.

At point *C* (row *C*), with 2 movies and 6 cases of soda, Lisa's marginal utility per dollar from soda is equal to that from movies: Lisa's utility is maximized.

—— MyEconLab animation ——

movies. That is,

$$MU_S/P_S = MU_M/P_M.$$

Lisa can't move from this allocation of her budget without making herself worse off.

The Power of Marginal Analysis

The method we've just used to find Lisa's utility-maximizing choice of movies and soda is an example of the power of marginal analysis. Lisa doesn't need a computer and a spreadsheet program to maximize utility. She can achieve this goal by comparing the marginal gain from having more of one good with the marginal loss from having less of another good.

The rule that she follows is simple: If the marginal utility per dollar from movies exceeds the marginal utility per dollar from soda, see more movies and buy less soda; if the marginal utility per dollar from soda exceeds the marginal utility per dollar from movies, buy more soda and see fewer movies.

More generally, if the marginal gain from an action exceeds the marginal loss, take the action. You will meet this principle time and again in your study of economics, and you will find yourself using it when you make your own economic choices, especially when you must make big decisions.

Revealing Preferences

When we introduced the idea of utility, we arbitrarily chose 50 units as Lisa's total utility from 1 movie, and we pretended that we asked Lisa to tell us how many units of utility she got from different quantities of soda and movies.

You're now about to discover that we don't need to ask Lisa to tell us her preferences. We can figure them out for ourselves by observing what she buys at various prices.

Also, the units in which we measure Lisa's preferences don't matter. Any arbitrary units will work. In this respect, utility is like temperature. Predictions about the freezing point of water don't depend on the temperature scale; and predictions about a household's consumption choice don't depend on the units of utility.

Lisa's Preferences In maximizing total utility by making the marginal utility per dollar equal for all goods, the units in which utility is measured do not matter.

You've seen that when Lisa maximizes her total utility, her marginal utility per dollar from soda, MU_S/P_S, equals her marginal utility per dollar from movies, MU_M/P_M. That is,

$$MU_S/P_S = MU_M/P_M.$$

Multiply both sides of this equation by the price of soda, P_S, to obtain

$$MU_S = MU_M \times (P_S/P_M).$$

This equation says that the marginal utility from soda, MU_S, is equal to the marginal utility from movies, MU_M, multiplied by the ratio of the price of soda, P_S, to the price of a movie, P_M.

The ratio P_S/P_M is the relative price of soda in terms of movies: It is the number of movies that must be forgone to get 1 case of soda. It is also the opportunity cost of soda. (See Chapter 2, p. 33 and Chapter 3, p. 56.)

For Lisa, when $P_M = \$8$ and $P_S = \$4$ we observe that in a month she goes to the movies twice and buys 6 cases of soda. So we know that her MU_S from 6 cases of soda equals her MU_M from 2 movies multiplied by $\$4/\$8$ or 0.5. That is, for Lisa, the marginal utility from 6 cases of soda equals one-half of the marginal utility from 2 movies.

If we observe the choices that Lisa makes at more prices, we can find more rows in her utility schedule. By her choices, Lisa reveals her preferences.

Units of Utility Don't Matter Lisa's marginal utility from 2 movies is a half of her marginal utility from 6 cases of soda. So if the marginal utility from the second movie is 40 units, then the marginal utility from the sixth case of soda is 20 units. But if we call the marginal utility from the second movie 50 units, then the marginal utility from the sixth case of soda is 25 units. The units of utility are arbitrary.

REVIEW QUIZ

1 Why does a consumer spend the entire budget?
2 What is the marginal utility per dollar and how is it calculated?
3 What two conditions are met when a consumer is maximizing utility?
4 Explain why equalizing the marginal utility per dollar for all goods maximizes utility.

You can work these questions in Study Plan 8.2 and get instant feedback.　MyEconLab

You now understand the marginal utility theory of consumer choices. Your next task is to see what the theory predicts.

Predictions of Marginal Utility Theory

We're now going to use marginal utility theory to make some predictions. You will see that marginal utility theory predicts the law of demand. The theory also predicts that a fall in the price of a substitute of a good decreases the demand for the good and that for a normal good, a rise in income increases demand. All these effects, which in Chapter 3 we simply assumed, are predictions of marginal utility theory.

To derive these predictions, we will study the effects of three events:

- A fall in the price of a movie
- A rise in the price of soda
- A rise in income

A Fall in the Price of a Movie

With the price of a movie at $8 and the price of soda at $4, Lisa is maximizing utility by seeing 2 movies and buying 6 cases of soda each month. Then, with no change in her $40 income and no change in the price of soda, the price of a movie falls from $8 to $4. How does Lisa change her buying plans?

Finding the New Quantities of Movies and Soda
You can find the effect of a fall in the price of a movie on the quantities of movies and soda that Lisa buys in a three-step calculation.

1. Determine the just-affordable combinations of movies and soda at the new prices.
2. Calculate the new marginal utilities per dollar from the good whose price has changed.
3. Determine the quantities of movies and soda that make their marginal utilities per dollar equal.

Affordable Combinations The lower price of a movie means that Lisa can afford more movies or more soda. Table 8.3 shows her new affordable combinations. In row *A*, if she continues to see 2 movies a month, she can now afford 8 cases of soda and in row *B*, if she continues to buy 6 cases of soda, she can now afford 4 movies. Lisa can afford any of the combinations shown in the rows of Table 8.3.

The next step is to find her new marginal utilities per dollar from movies.

New Marginal Utilities per Dollar from Movies A person's preferences don't change just because a price has changed. With no change in her preferences, Lisa's marginal utilities in Table 8.3 are the same as those in Table 8.1. But because the price of a movie has changed, the marginal utility *per dollar* from movies changes. In fact, with a halving of the price of a movie from $8 to $4, the marginal utility per dollar from movies has doubled.

The numbers in Table 8.3 show Lisa's new marginal utility per dollar from movies for each quantity of movies. The table also shows Lisa's marginal utility per dollar from soda for each quantity.

Equalizing the Marginal Utilities per Dollar You can see that if Lisa continues to see 2 movies a month and buy 6 cases of soda, her marginal utility per dollar from movies (row *A*) is 10 units and her marginal utility per dollar from soda (row *B*) is 5 units. Lisa is buying too much soda and too few movies. If she spends a dollar more on movies and a dollar less on soda, her total utility increases by 5 units (10 − 5).

If Lisa continues to buy 6 cases of soda and increases the number of movies to 4 (row *B*), her

TABLE 8.3   How a Change in the Price of Movies Affects Lisa's Choices

	Movies ($4 each)			Soda ($4 per case)		
	Quantity	Marginal utility	Marginal utility per dollar	Cases	Marginal utility	Marginal utility per dollar
	0	0		10	5	1.25
	1	50	12.50	9	7	1.75
A	2	40	**10.00**	8	10	2.50
	3	32	8.00	7	13	3.25
B	4	28	7.00	6	20	**5.00**
	5	26	6.50	5	22	5.50
C	6	24	**6.00**	4	24	**6.00**
	7	22	5.50	3	36	9.00
	8	20	5.00	2	48	12.00
	9	17	4.25	1	75	18.75
	10	16	4.00	0	0	

marginal utility per dollar from movies falls to 7 units, but her marginal utility per dollar from soda is 5 units. Lisa is still buying too much soda and seeing too few movies. If she spends a dollar more on movies and a dollar less on soda, her total utility increases by 2 units (7 − 5).

But if Lisa sees 6 movies and buys 4 cases of soda a month (row *C*), her marginal utility per dollar from movies (6 units) equals her marginal utility per dollar from soda and she is maximizing utility. If Lisa moves from this allocation of her budget in either direction, her total utility decreases.

Lisa's increased purchases of movies results from a substitution effect—she substitutes the now lower-priced movies for soda—and an income effect—she can afford more movies.

A Change in the Quantity Demanded Lisa's increase in the quantity of movies that she sees is a change in the quantity demanded. It is the change in the quantity of movies that she plans to see each month when the price of a movie changes and all other influences on buying plans remain the same. We illustrate a change in the quantity demanded by a movement along a demand curve.

Figure 8.4(a) shows Lisa's demand curve for movies. When the price of a movie is $8, Lisa sees 2 movies a month. When the price of a movie falls to $4, she sees 6 movies a month. Lisa moves downward along her demand curve for movies.

The demand curve traces the quantities that maximize utility at each price, with all other influences remaining the same. You can also see that utility-maximizing choices generate a downward-sloping demand curve. Utility maximization with diminishing marginal utility implies the law of demand.

A Change in Demand The decrease in the quantity of soda that Lisa buys is the change in the quantity of soda that she plans to buy at a given price of soda when the price of a movie changes. It is a change in her demand for soda. We illustrate a change in demand by a shift of a demand curve.

Figure 8.4(b) shows Lisa's demand curve for soda. The price of soda is fixed at $4 a case. When the price of a movie is $8, Lisa buys 6 cases of soda on demand curve D_0. When the price of a movie falls to $4, Lisa buys 4 cases of soda on demand curve D_1. The fall in the price of a movie decreases Lisa's demand for soda. Her demand curve for soda shifts leftward. For Lisa, soda and movies are substitutes.

FIGURE 8.4   A Fall in the Price of a Movie

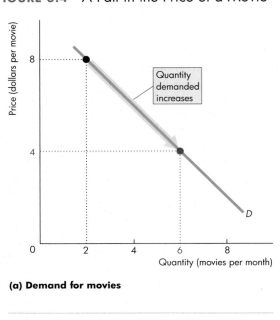

(a) Demand for movies

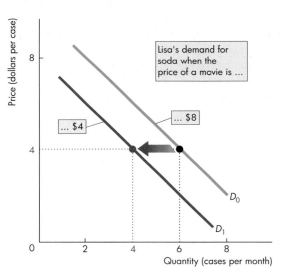

(b) Demand for soda

When the price of a movie falls and the price of soda remains the same, the quantity of movies demanded by Lisa increases, and in part (a), Lisa moves along her demand curve for movies. Also, when the price of a movie falls, Lisa's demand for soda decreases, and in part (b), her demand curve for soda shifts leftward. For Lisa, soda and movies are substitutes.

MyEconLab animation

A Rise in the Price of Soda

Now suppose that with the price of a movie at $4, the price of soda rises from $4 to $8 a case. How does this price change influence Lisa's buying plans? We find the answer by repeating the three-step calculation with the new price of soda.

Table 8.4 shows Lisa's new affordable combinations. In row *A*, if she continues to buy 4 cases of soda a month she can afford to see only 2 movies; and in row *B*, if she continues to see 6 movies a month, she can afford only 2 cases of soda.

Table 8.4 show Lisa's marginal utility per dollar from soda for each quantity of soda when the price is $8 a case. The table also shows Lisa's marginal utility per dollar from movies for each quantity.

If Lisa continues to buy 4 cases of soda (row *A*), her marginal utility per dollar from soda is 3. But she must cut the movies she sees to 2, which increases her marginal utility per dollar from movies to 10. Lisa is buying too much soda and too few movies. If she spends a dollar less on soda and a dollar more on movies, her utility increases by 7 units (10 − 3) .

But if Lisa sees 6 movies a month and cuts her soda to 2 cases (row *B*), her marginal utility per dollar from movies (6 units) equals her marginal utility per dollar from soda. She is maximizing utility.

Lisa's decreased purchases of soda results from an income effect—she can afford fewer cases and she buys fewer cases. But she continues to buy the same quantity of movies.

Lisa's Demand for Soda Now that we've calculated the effect of a change in the price of soda on Lisa's buying plans when income and the price of movies remain the same, we have found two points on her demand curve for soda: When the price of soda is $4 a case, Lisa buys 4 cases a month; and when the price of soda is $8 a case, she buys 2 cases a month.

Figure 8.5 shows these points on Lisa's demand curve for soda. It also shows the change in the quantity of soda demanded when the price of soda rises and all other influences on Lisa's buying plans remain the same.

In this example, Lisa continues to buy the same quantity of movies, but this outcome does not always occur. It is a consequence of Lisa's preferences. With different marginal utilities, she might have decreased or increased the quantity of movies that she sees when the price of soda changes.

You've seen that marginal utility theory predicts the law of demand—the way in which the quantity demanded of a good changes when its price changes. Next, we'll see how marginal utility theory predicts the effect of a change in income on demand.

TABLE 8.4 How a Change in the Price of Soda Affects Lisa's Choices

	Movies ($4 each)			Soda ($8 per case)		
	Quantity	Marginal utility	Marginal utility per dollar	Cases	Marginal utility	Marginal utility per dollar
	0	0		5	22	2.75
A	2	40	10.00	**4**	24	**3.00**
	4	28	7.00	3	36	4.50
B	6	24	**6.00**	2	48	**6.00**
	8	20	5.00	1	75	9.38
	10	16	4.00	0	0	

FIGURE 8.5 A Rise in the Price of Soda

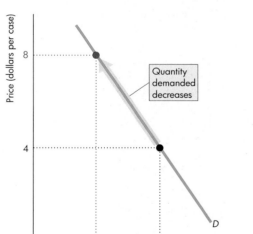

When the price of soda rises and the price of a movie and Lisa's income remain the same, the quantity of soda demanded by Lisa decreases. Lisa moves along her demand curve for soda.

MyEconLab animation

A Rise in Income

Suppose that Lisa's income increases from $40 to $56 a month and that the price of a movie is $4 and the price of soda is $4 a case. With these prices and with an income of $40 a month, Lisa sees 6 movies and buys 4 cases of soda a month (Table 8.3). How does the increase in Lisa's income from $40 to $56 change her buying plans?

Table 8.5 shows the calculations needed to answer this question. If Lisa continues to see 6 movies a month, she can now afford to buy 8 cases of soda (row A); if she continues to buy 4 cases of soda, she can now afford to see 10 movies (row C).

In row A, Lisa's marginal utility per dollar from movies is greater than her marginal utility per dollar from soda. She is buying too much soda and too few movies. In row C, Lisa's marginal utility per dollar from movies is less than her marginal utility per dollar from soda. She is buying too little soda and too many movies. But in row B, when Lisa sees 8 movies a month and buys 6 cases of soda, her marginal utility per dollar from movies equals that from soda. She is maximizing utility.

Figure 8.6 shows the effects of the rise in Lisa's income on her demand curves for movies and soda. The price of each good is $4. When Lisa's income

TABLE 8.5 Lisa's Choices with an Income of $56 a Month

	Movies ($4 each)			Soda ($4 per case)		
	Quantity	Marginal utility	Marginal utility per dollar	Cases	Marginal utility	Marginal utility per dollar
	4	28	7.00	10	5	1.25
	5	26	6.50	9	7	1.75
A	6	24	**6.00**	8	10	2.50
	7	22	5.50	7	13	3.25
B	8	20	**5.00**	6	20	**5.00**
	9	17	4.25	5	22	5.50
C	10	16	4.00	**4**	24	**6.00**

rises to $56 a month, she sees 2 more movies and buys 2 more cases of soda. Her demand curves for both movies and soda shift rightward—her demand for both movies and soda increases. With a larger income, the consumer always buys more of a *normal* good. For Lisa, movies and soda are normal goods.

FIGURE 8.6   The Effects of a Rise in Income

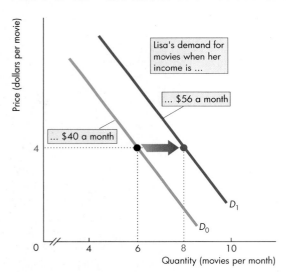

(a) Demand for movies

When Lisa's income increases, her demand for movies and her demand for soda increase. Lisa's demand curves for

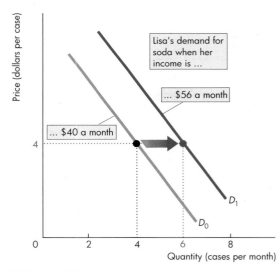

(b) Demand for soda

movies, in part (a), and for soda, in part (b), shift rightward. For Lisa, movies and soda are normal goods.

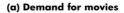

MyEconLab animation

The Paradox of Value

The price of water is low and the price of a diamond is high, but water is essential to life while diamonds are used mostly for decoration. How can valuable water be so cheap while a relatively useless diamond is so expensive? This so-called *paradox of value* has puzzled philosophers for centuries. Not until the theory of marginal utility had been developed could anyone give a satisfactory answer.

The Paradox Resolved The paradox is resolved by distinguishing between *total* utility and *marginal* utility. The total utility that we get from water is enormous. But remember, the more we consume of something, the smaller is its marginal utility.

We use so much water that its marginal utility—the benefit we get from one more glass of water or another 30 seconds in the shower—diminishes to a small value.

Diamonds, on the other hand, have a small total utility relative to water, but because we buy few diamonds, they have a high marginal utility.

When a household has maximized its total utility, it has allocated its income in the way that makes the marginal utility per dollar equal for all goods. That is, the marginal utility from a good divided by the price of the good is equal for all goods.

This equality of marginal utilities per dollar holds true for diamonds and water: Diamonds have a high price and a high marginal utility. Water has a low price and a low marginal utility. When the high marginal utility from diamonds is divided by the high price of a diamond, the result is a number that equals the low marginal utility from water divided by the low price of water. The marginal utility per dollar is the same for diamonds and water.

Value and Consumer Surplus Another way to think about the paradox of value and illustrate how it is resolved uses *consumer surplus*. Figure 8.7 explains the paradox of value by using this idea. The supply of water in part (a) is perfectly elastic at price P_W, so the quantity of water consumed is Q_W and the large green area shows the consumer surplus from water. The supply of diamonds in part (b) is perfectly inelastic at the quantity Q_D, so the price of a diamond is P_D and the small green area shows the consumer surplus from diamonds. Water is cheap, but brings a large consumer surplus; diamonds are expensive, but bring a small consumer surplus.

FIGURE 8.7   The Paradox of Value

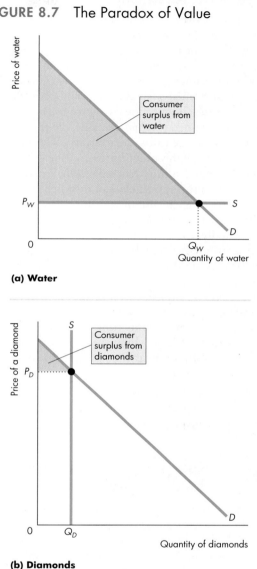

(a) Water

(b) Diamonds

Part (a) shows the demand for and supply of water. Supply is perfectly elastic at the price P_W. At this price, the quantity of water consumed is Q_W and the large green triangle shows consumer surplus. Part (b) shows the demand for and supply of diamonds. Supply is perfectly inelastic at the quantity Q_D. At this quantity, the price of a diamond is P_D and the small green triangle shows consumer surplus. Water is valuable—has a large consumer surplus—but cheap. Diamonds are less valuable than water—have a smaller consumer surplus—but are expensive.

MyEconLab animation

Temperature: An Analogy

Utility is similar to temperature—both are abstract concepts. You can't *observe* temperature. You can observe water turning to steam if it is hot enough or turning to ice if it is cold enough. You can also construct an instrument—a thermometer—that can help you to predict when such changes will occur. We call the scale on the thermometer *temperature* and we call the units of temperature *degrees*. But like the units of utility, these degree units are arbitrary. We can use Celsius units or Fahrenheit units or some other units.

The concept of utility helps us to make predictions about consumption choices in much the same way that the concept of temperature helps us to make predictions about physical phenomena.

Admittedly, marginal utility theory does not enable us to predict how buying plans change with the same precision that a thermometer enables us to predict when water will turn to ice or steam. But the theory provides important insights into buying plans and has some powerful implications. It helps us to understand why people buy more of a good or service when its price falls and why people buy more of most goods when their incomes increase. It also resolves the paradox of value.

We're going to end this chapter by looking at some new ways of studying individual economic choices and consumer behavior.

REVIEW QUIZ

1 When the price of a good falls and the prices of other goods and a consumer's income remain the same, explain what happens to the consumption of the good whose price has fallen and to the consumption of other goods.

2 Elaborate on your answer to the previous question by using demand curves. For which good does demand change and for which good does the quantity demanded change?

3 If a consumer's income increases and if all goods are normal goods, explain how the quantity bought of each good changes.

4 What is the paradox of value and how is the paradox resolved?

5 What are the similarities between utility and temperature?

You can work these questions in Study Plan 8.3 and get instant feedback.   MyEconLab

Economics in Action
Maximizing Utility from Recorded Music

In 2011, Americans spent $7 billion on recorded music, down from more than $14 billion in 1999. But the combined quantity of discs and downloads bought increased from 1.2 billion in 1999 to 1.8 billion in 2011 and the average price of a unit of recorded music fell from $12.60 to $3.89.

The average price fell because the mix of formats bought changed dramatically. In 1999, we bought 940 million CDs; in 2011, we bought only 241 million CDs and downloaded almost 1.5 billion music files. Figure 1 shows the longer history of the changing formats of recorded music.

The music that we buy isn't just one good—it is several goods. Singles and albums are different goods; downloads and discs are different goods; and downloads to a computer and downloads to a cell phone are different goods. There are five major categories and the table shows the quantities of each that we bought in 2011 (excluding DVDs and cassettes).

Format	Singles	Albums
	(millions in 2011)	
Disc	2	241
Download	1,306	105
Mobile	116	–

Source of data: Recording Industry Association of America.

Most people buy all their music in digital form, but many still buy physical CDs and some people buy both downloads and CDs.

We get utility from the singles and albums that we buy, and the more songs and albums we have, the more utility we get. But our marginal utility from songs and albums decreases as the quantity that we own increases.

We also get utility from convenience. A song that we can buy with a mouse click and play with the spin of a wheel is more convenient both to buy and to use than a song on a CD. The convenience of songs downloaded over the Internet means that, song for song, we get more utility from a song downloaded than we get from a song on a physical CD.

But most albums are still played at home on a CD player. So for most people, a physical CD is a more convenient medium for delivering an album. Album for album, people on average get more utility from a CD than from a download.

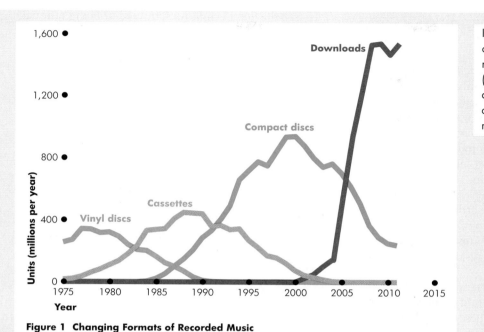

In the 1970s, recorded music came on vinyl discs. Cassettes gradually replaced vinyl, then compact discs (CDs) gradually replaced cassettes, and today, digital files downloaded to computers and mobile devices are replacing physical CDs.

Figure 1   Changing Formats of Recorded Music

Sources of data: U.S. Census Bureau, *The 2012 Statistical Abstract*, Table 1140; and the Recording Industry Association of America.

When we decide how many singles and albums to download and how many to buy on CD, we compare the marginal utility per dollar from each type of music in each format. We make the marginal utility per dollar from each type of music in each format equal, as the equations below show.

The market for single downloads has created an enormous consumer surplus. In 2011, 1,306 million singles were downloaded at an average price of $1.14. In the same year, 2 million singles were bought on a disc (either a CD or vinyl) at an average price of $4.76 a disc. If we assume that $4.76 is the most that anyone would pay for a single download (probably an underestimate), the demand curve for single downloads is that shown in Fig. 2.

With the average price of a single download at $1.14, consumer surplus (the area of the green triangle in Fig. 2) is $2.4 billion.

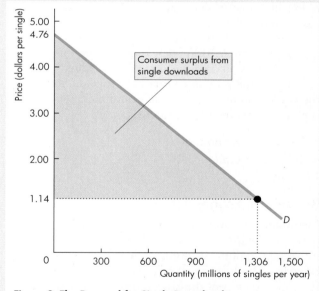

Figure 2   The Demand for Single Downloads

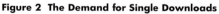

$$\frac{MU_{single\ downloads}}{P_{single\ downloads}} = \frac{MU_{album\ downloads}}{P_{album\ downloads}} = \frac{MU_{physical\ singles}}{P_{physical\ singles}} = \frac{MU_{physical\ albums}}{P_{physical\ albums}} = \frac{MU_{mobile}}{P_{mobile}}$$

$$\frac{MU_{single\ downloads}}{\$1.14} = \frac{MU_{album\ downloads}}{\$10.99} = \frac{MU_{physical\ singles}}{\$4.76} = \frac{MU_{physical\ albums}}{\$9.99} = \frac{MU_{mobile}}{\$2.39}$$

◤ New Ways of Explaining Consumer Choices

When William Stanley Jevons developed marginal utility theory in the 1860s, he would have loved to look inside people's brains and "see" their utility. But he believed that the human brain was the ultimate black box that could never be observed directly. For Jevons, and for most economists today, the purpose of marginal utility theory is to explain our *actions*, not what goes on inside our brains.

Economics has developed over the past 150 years with little help from and paying little attention to advances being made in psychology. Both economics and psychology seek to explain human behavior, but they have developed different ways of attacking the challenge.

A few researchers *have* paid attention to the potential payoff from exploring economic problems by using the tools of psychology. These researchers, some economists and some psychologists, think that marginal utility theory is based on a view of how people make choices that attributes too much to reason and rationality. They propose an alternative approach based on the methods of psychology.

Other researchers, some economists and some neuroscientists, are using new tools to look inside the human brain and open up Jevons' "black box."

This section provides a very brief introduction to these new and exciting areas of economics. We'll explore the two related research agendas:

■ Behavioral economics
■ Neuroeconomics

Behavioral Economics

Behavioral economics studies the ways in which limits on the human brain's ability to compute and implement rational decisions influences economic behavior—both the decisions that people make and the consequences of those decisions for the way markets work.

Behavioral economics starts with observed behavior. It looks for anomalies—choices that do not seem to be rational. It then tries to account for the anomalies by using ideas developed by psychologists that emphasize features of the human brain that limit rational choice.

In behavioral economics, instead of being rational utility maximizers, people are assumed to have three impediments that prevent rational choice: bounded rationality, bounded willpower, and bounded self-interest.

Bounded Rationality Bounded rationality is rationality that is limited by the computing power of the human brain. We can't always work out the rational choice.

For Lisa, choosing between movies and soda, it seems unlikely that she would have much trouble figuring out what to buy. But toss Lisa some uncertainty and the task becomes harder. She's read the reviews of "Ironman 2" on Fandango, but does she really want to see that movie? How much marginal utility will it give her? Faced with uncertainty, people might use rules of thumb, listen to the views of others, and make decisions based on gut instinct rather than on rational calculation.

Bounded Willpower Bounded willpower is the less-than-perfect willpower that prevents us from making a decision that we know, at the time of implementing the decision, we will later regret.

Lisa might be feeling particularly thirsty when she passes a soda vending machine. Under Lisa's rational utility-maximizing plan, she buys her soda at the discount store, where she gets it for the lowest possible price. Lisa has already bought her soda for this month, but it is at home. Spending $1 on a can now means giving up a movie later this month.

Lisa's rational choice is to ignore the temporary thirst and stick to her plan. But she might not possess the willpower to do so—sometimes she will and sometimes she won't.

Bounded Self-Interest Bounded self-interest is the limited self-interest that results in sometimes suppressing our own interests to help others.

A hurricane hits the Florida coast and Lisa, feeling sorry for the victims, donates $10 to a fund-raiser. She now has only $30 to spend on movies and soda this month. The quantities that she buys are not, according to her utility schedule, the ones that maximize her utility.

The main applications of behavioral economics are in two areas: finance, where uncertainty is a key factor in decision making, and savings, where the future is a key factor. But one behavior observed by behavioral economists is more general and might affect your choices. It is called the endowment effect.

The Endowment Effect   The endowment effect is the tendency for people to value something more highly simply because they own it. If you have allocated your income to maximize utility, then the price you would be willing to accept to give up something that you own (for example, your coffee mug) should be the same as the price you are willing to pay for an identical one.

In experiments, students seem to display the endowment effect: The price they are willing to pay for a coffee mug that is identical to the one they own is less than the price they would be willing to accept to give up the coffee mug that they own. Behavioral economists say that this behavior contradicts marginal utility theory.

Neuroeconomics

Neuroeconomics is the study of the activity of the human brain when a person makes an economic decision. The discipline uses the observational tools and ideas of neuroscience to obtain a better understanding of economic decisions.

Neuroeconomics is an experimental discipline. In an experiment, a person makes an economic decision and the electrical or chemical activity of the person's brain is observed and recorded using the same type of equipment that neurosurgeons use to diagnose brain disorders.

The observations provide information about which regions of the brain are active at different points in the process of making an economic decision.

Observations show that some economic decisions generate activity in the area of the brain (called the prefrontal cortex) where we store memories, analyze data, and anticipate the consequences of our actions. If people make rational utility-maximizing decisions, it is in this region of the brain that the decision occurs.

But observations also show that some economic decisions generate activity in the region of the brain (called the hippocampus) where we store memories of anxiety and fear. Decisions that are influenced by activity in this part of the brain might not be rational and be driven by fear or panic.

Neuroeconomists are also able to observe the amount of a brain hormone (called dopamine), the quantity of which increases in response to pleasurable events and decreases in response to disappointing events. These observations might one day enable neuroeconomists to actually measure utility and shine a bright light inside what was once believed to be the ultimate black box.

Controversy

The new ways of studying consumer choice that we've briefly described here are being used more widely to study business decisions and decisions in financial markets, and this type of research is surely going to become more popular.

But behavioral economics and neuroeconomics generate controversy. Most economists hold the view of Jevons that the goal of economics is to explain the decisions that we observe people making and not to explain what goes on inside people's heads.

Most economists would prefer to probe apparent anomalies more deeply and figure out why they are not anomalies after all.

Economists also point to the power of marginal utility theory and its ability to explain consumer choice and demand as well as resolve the paradox of value.

REVIEW QUIZ

1 Define behavioral economics.
2 What are the three limitations on human rationality that behavioral economics emphasizes?
3 Define neuroeconomics.
4 What do behavioral economics and neuroeconomics seek to achieve?

You can work these questions in Study Plan 8.4 and get instant feedback.   MyEconLab

◆ You have now completed your study of the marginal utility theory and some new ideas about how people make economic choices. You can see marginal utility theory in action once again in *Reading Between the Lines* on pp. 194–195, where it is used to compare the effects of a tax on or a ban on big cups of sugary soft drinks.

Influencing Consumer Choice for Sugary Drinks

Drinks Groups Sue Over NY "Supersize" Ban

Financial Times
October 12, 2012

The U.S. beverage industry is taking the administration of Michael Bloomberg, New York mayor, to court over its decision to ban sales of "supersized" sugary drinks.

Trade groups led by the American Beverage Association filed a lawsuit late on Friday in New York state court attempting to block the rule, which is set to be imposed next spring.

Last month, New York's board of health voted to approve a proposal made by Mr. Bloomberg in May that would prohibit restaurants, theaters, and stadiums from selling sugary drinks in portions bigger than 16 fl oz. ...

The lawsuit comes as the soda industry is locked in an increasingly contentious battle with regulators over labeling and taxation of their products. Industry groups are currently fighting soda tax proposals in two California cities and have successfully pushed back several other similar efforts. ...

Marc La Vorgna, a spokesman for Mr. Bloomberg, called the lawsuit baseless and suggested that the drinks industry would fail to stop the ban.

"For 100 years, major public health decisions—the posting of calorie counts, the ban of transfats, the sanitation of the sewage system, the fluoridation of the water system, and much more—have been left to a board of health professionals and it has benefited the health of New Yorkers," he said. "The mayor's plan to limit the size of sugary beverages—the leading contributor to the obesity epidemic—has spurred a long overdue national dialogue on obesity."

ESSENCE OF THE STORY

- New York City mayor Michael Bloomberg has banned the sale of sweetened drinks larger than 16 ounces at many venues.

- Two cities in California are considering placing a tax on sugar-sweetened beverages.

- Trade groups that sell these drinks are seeking court orders to block the ban and taxes.

- A spokesman for mayor Bloomberg says sugary drinks are the leading contributor to obesity and the ban is a public health measure like the sanitation system.

ECONOMIC ANALYSIS

- Concerned that people are choosing to consume more sugary soda than is healthy, New York mayor Michael Bloomberg wants to ban large serves and the City of Richmond, CA, is considering a 1-penny-per-ounce tax.

- Consumers choose to buy the quantity of sugary drinks that maximizes utility.

- To do so, they make the marginal utility per dollar for all other goods and services equal to the marginal utility per dollar for sugary drinks. That is:

$$\frac{MU_O}{P_O} = \frac{MU_S}{P_S}.$$

- Because of the way in which drinks are sold, there isn't a single price. The table shows some prices in St. Louis in June 2012.

Prices of Sugary Drinks

Size (ounces)	At the movies	At a 7-Eleven
20	4.00	1.09
32	4.50	1.29
44	5.00	1.49
52	5.50	1.69
104	[free refill]	

- These prices tell us that people who buy their drinks in big cups pay a lower price per ounce.

- Because a person who buys a 52-ounce cup gets a free refill, the price of the marginal ounce for that person is zero. With a price of zero, the buyer drinks the quantity at which marginal utility is also zero.

- The suggestions for decreasing the consumption of sugary drinks are ways of raising the price.

- A tax raises the price because the tax is added to the price received by the seller. A ban on large cups raises the price because the price per ounce is higher for small cups than for large cups. Both have a similar outcome.

- Faced with a higher price of sugary drinks, a consumer maximizes utility by consuming a smaller quantity of sugary drinks.

- The reason is that consumer equilibrium becomes

$$\frac{MU_O}{P_O} = \frac{MU_S}{(P_S + tax)}.$$

- When a tax is imposed, the price doesn't rise by the entire amount of the tax, but generally $P_S + tax$ is greater than the price before that tax was imposed.

- Because $P_S + tax$ is greater than P_S, MU_S must rise to restore the equality of the marginal utilities per dollar. But to increase MU_S, the quantity of sugary drinks consumed must decrease.

- Figure 1 illustrates and makes clear why consumption of sugary drinks decreases.

- Suppose that with no tax, the budget line is BL_0 and to make the marginal utilities per dollar equal, the consumer buys 60 ounces of drinks and 100 units of other goods and services per day.

- A tax raises the price to $P_S + tax$ and the budget line becomes steeper as BL_1.

- If the consumer continues to drink 60 ounces per day, the quantity of other items bought must fall to 50 units a day. MU_O rises and

$$\frac{MU_O}{P_O} > \frac{MU_S}{(P_S + tax)}.$$

- To restore maximum utility, the consumer buys a smaller quantity of sugary drinks, which increases MU_S, and a greater quantity of other goods, which decreases MU_O. A movement up along the budget line BL_1 shows these changes in quantities consumed.

- The consumer substitutes other goods and services for sugary drinks until

$$\frac{MU_O}{P_O} = \frac{MU_S}{(P_S + tax)}.$$

- At this point, the consumer is again maximizing utility.

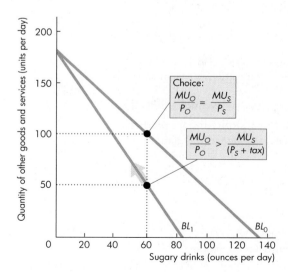

Figure 1 The Effect of a Tax

195

SUMMARY

Key Points

Consumption Choices (pp. 178–180)

- A household's consumption choices are determined by its consumption possibilities and preferences.
- A budget line defines a household's consumption possibilities.
- A household's preferences can be described by a utility schedule that lists the total utility and marginal utility derived from various quantities of goods and services consumed.
- The principle of diminishing marginal utility is that the marginal utility from a good or service decreases as consumption of the good or service increases.

Working Problems 1 to 5 will give you a better understanding of consumption choices.

Utility-Maximizing Choice (pp. 181–184)

- A consumer's objective is to maximize total utility.
- Total utility is maximized when all the available income is spent and when the marginal utility per dollar from all goods is equal.
- If the marginal utility per dollar for good A exceeds that for good B, total utility increases if the quantity purchased of good A increases and the quantity purchased of good B decreases.

Working Problems 6 to 11 will give you a better understanding of a consumer's utility-maximizing choice.

Predictions of Marginal Utility Theory (pp. 185–191)

- Marginal utility theory predicts the law of demand. That is, other things remaining the same, the higher the price of a good, the smaller is the quantity demanded of that good.
- Marginal utility theory also predicts that, other things remaining the same, an increase in the consumer's income increases the demand for a normal good.
- Marginal utility theory resolves the paradox of value.
- Total value is *total* utility or consumer surplus. But price is related to *marginal* utility.
- Water, which we consume in large amounts, has a high total utility and a large consumer surplus, but the price of water is low and the marginal utility from water is low.
- Diamonds, which we buy in small quantities, have a low total utility and a small consumer surplus, but the price of a diamond is high and the marginal utility from diamonds is high.

Working Problems 12 to 21 will give you a better understanding of the predictions of marginal utility theory.

New Ways of Explaining Consumer Choices (pp. 192–193)

- Behavioral economics studies limits on the ability of the human brain to compute and implement rational decisions.
- Bounded rationality, bounded willpower, and bounded self-interest are believed to explain some choices.
- Neuroeconomics uses the ideas and tools of neuroscience to study the effects of economic events and choices inside the human brain.

Working Problems 22 and 23 will give you a better understanding of the new ways of explaining consumer choices.

Key Terms

Behavioral economics, 192
Budget line, 178
Consumer equilibrium, 181
Diminishing marginal utility, 180

Marginal utility, 179
Marginal utility per dollar, 182
Neuroeconomics, 193
Preferences, 179

Total utility, 179
Utility, 179

STUDY PLAN PROBLEMS AND APPLICATIONS

MyEconLab   You can work Problems 1 to 23 in MyEconLab Chapter 8 Study Plan and get instant feedback.

Consumption Choices (Study Plan 8.1)

Jerry has $12 a week to spend on yogurt and magazines. The price of yogurt is $2, and the price of a magazine is $4.

1. List the combinations of yogurt and magazines that Jerry can afford. Draw a graph of Jerry's budget line with the quantity of magazines plotted on the *x*-axis.

2. Describe how Jerry's consumption possibilities change if, other things remaining the same, (i) the price of a magazine falls and (ii) Jerry's income increases.

Use the following data to work Problems 3 to 9.

Max enjoys windsurfing and snorkeling. Max has $35 a day to spend, and he can spend as much time as he likes on his leisure pursuits. The price of renting equipment for windsurfing is $10 an hour and for snorkeling is $5 an hour. The table shows the total utility Max gets from each activity.

Hours per day	Total utility from windsurfing	Total utility from snorkeling
1	120	40
2	220	76
3	300	106
4	360	128
5	396	140
6	412	150
7	422	158

3. Calculate Max's marginal utility from windsurfing at each number of hours per day. Does Max's marginal utility from windsurfing obey the principle of diminishing marginal utility?

4. Calculate Max's marginal utility from snorkeling at each number of hours per day. Does Max's marginal utility from snorkeling obey the principle of diminishing marginal utility?

5. Which does Max enjoy more: his 6th hour of windsurfing or his 6th hour of snorkeling?

Utility-Maximizing Choice (Study Plan 8.2)

6. Make a table that shows the various combinations of hours spent windsurfing and snorkeling that Max can afford.

7. In your table in Problem 6, add two columns and list Max's marginal utility per dollar from windsurfing and from snorkeling.

8. a. How many hours does Max windsurf and how many hours does he snorkel to maximize his utility?
   b. If Max spent a dollar more on windsurfing and a dollar less on snorkeling than in part (a), by how much would his total utility change?
   c. If Max spent a dollar less on windsurfing and a dollar more on snorkeling than in part (a), by how much would his total utility change?

9. Explain why, if Max equalized the marginal utility per hour from windsurfing and from snorkeling, he would *not* maximize his utility.

10. **Schools Get a Lesson in Lunch Line Economics**

    Sharp rises in the cost of milk, grain, and fresh fruits and vegetables are hitting cafeterias across the country, forcing cash-strapped schools to raise prices or serve more economical dishes. For example, Fairfax schools serve oranges —14¢ each—instead of grapes, which are 25¢ a serving.

    Source: *The Washington Post*, April 14, 2008

    Assume that a Fairfax school has a $14 daily fruit budget.
    a. How many oranges a day can the school afford to serve if it serves no grapes? How many servings of grapes can the school afford each day if it serves no oranges?
    b. If the school provides 50 oranges a day and maximizes utility, how many servings of grapes does it provide? If the marginal utility from an orange is 14 units, what is the marginal utility from a serving of grapes?

11. **Can Money Buy Happiness?**

    Whoever said money can't buy happiness isn't spending it right. There must be some connection, but once your basic human needs are met, does more money buy more happiness? An increase in income from $20,000 a year to $50,000 makes you twice as likely to be happy, but the payoff from more than $90,000 is slight.

    Source: CNN, July 18, 2006

a. What does the fundamental assumption of marginal utility theory suggest about the connection between money and happiness?

b. Explain why this news clip is consistent with marginal utility theory.

Predictions of Marginal Utility Theory

(Study Plan 8.3)

Use the data in Problem 3 to work Problems 12 to 16.

12. Max is offered a special deal: The price of renting windsurfing equipment is cut to $5 an hour. How many hours does Max spend windsurfing and how many hours does he spend snorkeling?

13. Draw Max's demand curve for rented windsurfing equipment. Over the price range from $5 to $10 an hour, is Max's demand for windsurfing equipment elastic or inelastic?

14. How does Max's demand for snorkeling equipment change when the price of windsurfing equipment falls? What is Max's cross elasticity of demand for snorkeling with respect to the price of windsurfing? Are windsurfing and snorkeling substitutes or complements for Max?

15. If Max's income increases from $35 to $55 a day, how does his demand for rented windsurfing equipment change? Is windsurfing a normal good or an inferior good for Max? Explain.

16. If Max's income increases from $35 to $55 a day, how does his demand for rented snorkeling equipment change? Is snorkeling a normal good or an inferior good for Max? Explain.

Use the following news clip to work Problems 17 and 18.

Compared to Other Liquids, Gasoline is Cheap

In 2008, when gasoline hit $4 a gallon, motorists complained, but they didn't complain about $1.59 for a 20-oz Gatorade and $18 for 16 mL of HP ink.

Source: *The New York Times*, May 27, 2008

The prices per gallon are $10.17 for Gatorade and $4,294.58 for printer ink.

17. a. What does marginal utility theory predict about the marginal utility per dollar from gasoline, Gatorade, and printer ink?

b. What do the prices per gallon tell you about the marginal utility from a gallon of gasoline, Gatorade, and printer ink?

18. a. What do the prices per unit reported in the news clip tell you about the marginal utility from a gallon of gasoline, a 20-oz bottle of Gatorade, and a cartridge of printer ink?

b. How can the paradox of value be used to explain why the fluids listed in the news clip might be less valuable than gasoline, yet far more expensive?

Use the following news clip to work Problems 19 to 21.

Exclusive Status: It's in the Bag; $52,500 Purses. 24 Worldwide. 1 in Washington.

Forget your Coach purse. Put away your Kate Spade. Even Hermes's famous Birkin bag seems positively discount. The Louis Vuitton Tribute Patchwork is this summer's ultimate status bag, ringing in at $52,500, and the company is offering only five for sale in North America and 24 worldwide.

Source: *The Washington Post*, August 21, 2007

19. Use marginal utility theory to explain the facts reported in the news clip.

20. If Louis Vuitton offered 500 Tribute Patchwork bags in North America and 2,400 worldwide, what do you predict would happen to the price that buyers would be willing to pay and what would happen to the consumer surplus?

21. If the Tribute Patchwork bag is copied and thousands are sold illegally, what do you predict would happen to the price that buyers would be willing to pay for a genuine bag and what would happen to the consumer surplus?

New Ways of Explaining Consumer Choices

(Study Plan 8.4)

Use the following news clip to work Problems 22 and 23.

Eating Away the Innings in Baseball's Cheap Seats

Baseball and gluttony, two of America's favorite pastimes, are merging and taking hold at Major League Baseball stadiums: all-you-can-eat seats. Some fans try to "set personal records" during their first game in the section, but by their second or third time in such seats they eat normally, just as they would at a game.

Source: *USA Today*, March 6, 2008

22. a. What conflict might exist between utility-maximization and setting "personal records" for eating?

b. What does the fact that fans eat less at subsequent games indicate about the marginal utility from ballpark food as the quantity consumed increases?

23. a. How can setting personal records for eating be reconciled with marginal utility theory?

b. Which ideas of behavioral economics are consistent with the information in the news clip?

ADDITIONAL PROBLEMS AND APPLICATIONS

MyEconLab   You can work these problems in MyEconLab if assigned by your instructor.

Consumption Choices

24. Tim buys 2 pizzas and sees 1 movie a week when he has $16 to spend, a movie ticket is $8, and a pizza is $4. Draw Tim's budget line. If the price of a movie ticket falls to $4, describe how Tim's consumption possibilities change.

25. Cindy has $70 a month to spend, and she can spend as much time as she likes playing golf and tennis. The price of an hour of golf is $10, and the price of an hour of tennis is $5. The table shows Cindy's marginal utility from each sport.

Hours per month	Marginal utility from golf	Marginal utility from tennis
1	80	40
2	60	36
3	40	30
4	30	10
5	20	5
6	10	2
7	6	1

Make a table that shows Cindy's affordable combinations of hours playing golf and tennis. If Cindy increases her expenditure to $100, describe how her consumption possibilities change.

Utility-Maximizing Choice

Use the information in Problem 25 to work Problems 26 and 27.

26. a. When Cindy has $70 to spend on golf and tennis, how many hours of golf and how many hours of tennis does she play to maximize her utility?
   b. Compared to part (a), if Cindy spent a dollar more on golf and a dollar less on tennis, by how much would her total utility change?
   c. Compared to part (a), if Cindy spent a dollar less on golf and a dollar more on tennis, by how much would her total utility change?

27. Explain why, if Cindy equalized the marginal utility per hour of golf and tennis, she would *not* maximize her utility.

Predictions of Marginal Utility Theory

28. Use the information in Problem 25. Cindy's tennis club raises its price of an hour of tennis to $10. The price of golf remains at $10 an hour and Cindy continues to spend $70 on tennis and golf.
   a. List the combinations of hours spent playing golf and tennis that Cindy can now afford.
   b. Along with the combinations in part (a), list Cindy's marginal utility per dollar from golf and from tennis.
   c. How many hours does Cindy now spend playing golf and how many hours does she spend playing tennis?

Use the information in Problems 25, 26, and 28 to work Problems 29 to 32.

29. Use your answers to Problems 26a and 28 to draw Cindy's demand curve for tennis. Over the price range of $5 to $10 an hour of tennis, is Cindy's demand for tennis elastic or inelastic?

30. Use your answers to Problems 26a and 28 to explain how Cindy's demand for golf changed when the price of an hour of tennis increased. What is Cindy's cross elasticity of demand for golf with respect to the price of tennis? Are tennis and golf substitutes or complements for Cindy?

31. Cindy loses her math tutoring job and the amount she has to spend on golf and tennis falls to $35 a month. How does Cindy's demand for golf change? For Cindy, is golf a normal good or an inferior good? Is tennis a normal good or an inferior good?

32. Cindy takes a Club Med vacation, the cost of which includes unlimited sports activities. With no extra charge for golf and tennis, Cindy allocates a total of 4 hours a day to these activities.
   a. How many hours does Cindy play golf and how many hours does she play tennis?
   b. What is Cindy's marginal utility from golf and from tennis?
   c. Why does Cindy equalize the marginal utilities rather than the marginal utility per dollar from golf and from tennis?

33. **Blu-Ray Format Expected to Dominate, but When?**

    Blu-ray stomped HD DVD to become the standard format for high-definition movie discs, but when will it claim victory over the old DVD? Buyers of $2,000, 40-inch TVs are the ones that will lead the charge. Everyone else will follow when the price falls. Blu-ray machine prices are now starting to drop and Wal-Mart Stores Inc. began stocking a $298 Magnavox model. That's cheaper than most alternatives, but a hefty price hike from a typical $50 DVD player.

    Source: CNN, June 2, 2008

    a. What does marginal utility theory predict about the marginal utility from a Magnavox Blu-ray machine compared to the marginal utility from a typical DVD player?

    b. What will have to happen to the marginal utility from a Blu-ray machine before it is able to "claim victory over the old DVD"?

34. Ben spends $50 a year on 2 bunches of flowers and $50 a year on 10,000 gallons of tap water. Ben is maximizing utility and his marginal utility from water is 0.5 unit per gallon.

    a. Are flowers or water more valuable to Ben?

    b. Explain how Ben's expenditure on flowers and water illustrates the paradox of value.

New Ways of Explaining Consumer Choices

Use the following news clip to work Problems 35 to 37.

Putting a Price on Human Life

Researchers at Stanford and the University of Pennsylvania estimated that a healthy human life is worth about $129,000. Using Medicare records on treatment costs for kidney dialysis as a benchmark, the authors tried to pinpoint the threshold beyond which ensuring another "quality" year of life was no longer financially worthwhile. The study comes amid debate over whether Medicare should start rationing health care on the basis of cost effectiveness.

Source: *Time*, June 9, 2008

35. Why might Medicare ration health care according to treatment that is "financially worthwhile" as opposed to providing as much treatment as is needed by a patient, regardless of costs?

36. What conflict might exist between a person's valuation of his or her own life and the rest of society's valuation of that person's life?

37. How does the potential conflict between self-interest and the social interest complicate setting a financial threshold for Medicare treatments?

Economics in the News

38. After you have studied *Reading Between the Lines* (pp. 194–195), answer the following questions.

    a. If big cups of sugary drinks are banned at restaurants, theaters, and stadiums:

       (i) How will the price of an ounce of sugary drink change?

       (ii) How will consumers respond to the change in price?

    b. If a tax is imposed on sugary drinks, how does

       (i) The marginal utility of a sugary drink change?

       (ii) The consumer surplus in the market for sugary drinks change?

39. **Five Signs You Have Too Much Money**

    When a bottle of water costs $38, it's hard not to agree that bottled water is a fool's drink. The drink of choice among image-conscious status seekers and high-end tee-totalers in L.A. is Bling H2O. It's not the water that accounts for the cost of the $38, but the "limited edition" bottle decked out in Swarovski crystals.

    Source: CNN, January 17, 2006

    a. Assuming that the price of a bottle of Bling H2O is $38 in all the major U.S. cities, what might its popularity in Los Angeles reveal about consumers' incomes or preferences in Los Angeles relative to other U.S. cities?

    b. Why might the marginal utility from a bottle of Bling H2O decrease more rapidly than the marginal utility from ordinary bottled water?

40. **How to Buy Happiness. Cheap**

    On any day, the rich tend to be a bit happier than the poor, but increases in average living standards don't seem to make people happier. The average American's income is up 80% since 1972, but the percentage describing themselves as "very happy" (roughly a third) hasn't changed. As living standards increase, most of us respond by raising our own standards: Things that once seemed luxuries now are necessities and we work harder to buy stuff that satisfies us less and less.

    Source: CNN, October 1, 2004

    According to the news clip,

    a. How do widespread increases in living standards influence total utility?

    b. How do total utility and marginal utility from consumption change over time?

9

POSSIBILITIES, PREFERENCES, AND CHOICES

After studying this chapter, you will be able to:

◆ Describe a household's budget line and show how it changes when prices or income change

◆ Use indifference curves to map preferences and explain the principle of diminishing marginal rate of substitution

◆ Predict the effects of changes in prices and income on consumption choices

The iPad has revolutionized the way we read magazines, books, and even recipes in the kitchen. Yet the magazine racks and bookstore shelves are still stuffed with traditional printed paper. Similarly, low-priced on-demand movies and DVD rentals have made it easier to watch a movie at home. Yet we're also going to movie theaters in ever-greater numbers.

In this chapter, we're going to study a model that explains the choices we make and applies it to choices about using new and old technologies. At the end of the chapter in *Reading Between the Lines*, we use the model to explain why e-books are taking off and replacing printed books.

Consumption Possibilities

Consumption choices are limited by income and by prices. A household has a given amount of income to spend and cannot influence the prices of the goods and services it buys. A household's **budget line** describes the limits to its consumption choices.

Let's look at Lisa's budget line.* Lisa has an income of $40 a month to spend. She buys two goods: movies and soda. The price of a movie is $8, and the price of soda is $4 a case.

Figure 9.1 shows alternative combinations of movies and soda that Lisa can afford. In row *A*, she sees no movies and buys 10 cases of soda. In row *F*, she sees 5 movies and buys no soda. Both of these combinations of movies and soda exhaust the $40 available. Check that the combination of movies and soda in each of the other rows also exhausts Lisa's $40 of income. The numbers in the table and the points *A* through *F* in the graph describe Lisa's consumption possibilities.

Divisible and Indivisible Goods Some goods—called divisible goods—can be bought in any quantity desired. Examples are gasoline and electricity. We can best understand household choice if we suppose that all goods and services are divisible. For example, Lisa can see half a movie a month on average by seeing one movie every two months. When we think of goods as being divisible, the consumption possibilities are not only the points *A* through *F* shown in Fig. 9.1, but also all the intermediate points that form the line running from *A* to *F*. This line is Lisa's budget line.

Affordable and Unaffordable Quantities Lisa's budget line is a constraint on her choices. It marks the boundary between what is affordable and what is unaffordable. She can afford any point on the line and inside it. She cannot afford any point outside the line. The constraint on her consumption depends on the prices and her income, and the constraint changes when the price of a good or her income changes. To see how, we use a budget equation.

---

* If you have studied Chapter 8 on marginal utility theory, you have already met Lisa. This tale of her thirst for soda and zeal for movies will sound familiar to you—up to a point. In this chapter, we're going to explore her budget line in more detail and use a different method for representing preferences—one that does not require the idea of utility.

FIGURE 9.1   The Budget Line

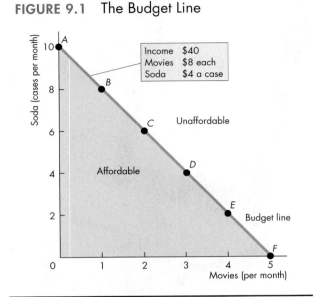

Income $40
Movies $8 each
Soda $4 a case

Consumption possibility	Movies (per month)	Soda (cases per month)
A	0	10
B	1	8
C	2	6
D	3	4
E	4	2
F	5	0

Lisa's budget line shows the boundary between what she can and cannot afford. The rows of the table list Lisa's affordable combinations of movies and soda when her income is $40, the price of soda is $4 a case, and the price of a movie is $8. For example, row *A* tells us that Lisa spends all of her $40 income when she buys 10 cases of soda and sees no movies. The figure graphs Lisa's budget line. Points *A* through *F* in the graph represent the rows of the table. For divisible goods, the budget line is the continuous line *AF*. To calculate the equation for Lisa's budget line, start with expenditure equal to income:

$$\$4Q_S + \$8Q_M = \$40.$$

Divide by $4 to obtain

$$Q_S + 2Q_M = 10.$$

Subtract $2Q_M$ from both sides to obtain

$$Q_S = 10 - 2Q_M.$$

MyEconLab animation

Budget Equation

We can describe the budget line by using a *budget equation*. The budget equation starts with the fact that

$$\text{Expenditure} = \text{Income}.$$

Expenditure is equal to the sum of the price of each good multiplied by the quantity bought. For Lisa,

$$\text{Expenditure} = (\text{Price of soda} \times \text{Quantity of soda})$$
$$+ (\text{Price of movie} \times \text{Quantity of movies}).$$

Call the price of soda P_S, the quantity of soda Q_S, the price of a movie P_M, the quantity of movies Q_M, and income Y. We can now write Lisa's budget equation as

$$P_S Q_S + P_M Q_M = Y.$$

Or, using the prices Lisa faces, $4 a case of soda and $8 a movie, and Lisa's income, $40, we get

$$\$4 Q_S + \$8 Q_M = \$40.$$

Lisa can choose any quantities of soda (Q_S) and movies (Q_M) that satisfy this equation. To find the relationship between these quantities, divide both sides of the equation by the price of soda (P_S) to get

$$Q_S + \frac{P_M}{P_S} \times Q_M = \frac{Y}{P_S}.$$

Now subtract the term (P_M/P_S) $\times Q_M$ from both sides of this equation to get

$$Q_S = \frac{Y}{P_S} - \frac{P_M}{P_S} \times Q_M.$$

For Lisa, income (Y) is $40, the price of a movie (P_M) is $8, and the price of soda (P_S) is $4 a case. So Lisa must choose the quantities of movies and soda to satisfy the equation

$$Q_S = \frac{\$40}{\$4} - \frac{\$8}{\$4} \times Q_M,$$

or

$$Q_S = 10 - 2Q_M.$$

To interpret the equation, look at the budget line in Fig. 9.1 and check that the equation delivers that budget line. First, set Q_M equal to zero. The budget equation tells us that Q_S, the quantity of soda, is Y/P_S, which is 10 cases. This combination of Q_M and Q_S is the one shown in row A of the table in Fig. 9.1. Next set Q_M equal to 5. Q_S now equals zero (row F of the table). Check that you can derive the other rows.

The budget equation contains two variables chosen by the household (Q_M and Q_S) and two variables that the household takes as given (Y/P_S and P_M/P_S). Let's look more closely at these variables.

Real Income A household's **real income** is its income expressed as a quantity of goods that the household can afford to buy. Expressed in terms of soda, Lisa's real income is Y/P_S. This quantity is the maximum quantity of soda that she can buy. It is equal to her money income divided by the price of soda. Lisa's money income is $40 and the price of soda is $4 a case, so her real income in terms of soda is 10 cases, which is shown in Fig. 9.1 as the point at which the budget line intersects the y-axis.

Relative Price A **relative price** is the price of one good divided by the price of another good. In Lisa's budget equation, the variable P_M/P_S is the relative price of a movie in terms of soda. For Lisa, P_M is $8 a movie and P_S is $4 a case, so P_M/P_S is equal to 2 cases of soda per movie. That is, to see 1 movie, Lisa must give up 2 cases of soda.

You've just calculated Lisa's opportunity cost of seeing a movie. Recall that the opportunity cost of an action is the best alternative forgone. For Lisa to see 1 more movie a month, she must forgo 2 cases of soda. You've also calculated Lisa's opportunity cost of soda. For Lisa to buy 2 more cases of soda a month, she must forgo seeing 1 movie. So her opportunity cost of 2 cases of soda is 1 movie.

The relative price of a movie in terms of soda is the magnitude of the slope of Lisa's budget line. To calculate the slope of the budget line, recall the formula for slope (see the Chapter 1 Appendix): Slope equals the change in the variable measured on the y-axis divided by the change in the variable measured on the x-axis as we move along the line. In Lisa's case (Fig. 9.1), the variable measured on the y-axis is the quantity of soda and the variable measured on the x-axis is the quantity of movies. Along Lisa's budget line, as soda decreases from 10 to 0 cases, movies increase from 0 to 5. So the magnitude of the slope of the budget line is 10 cases divided by 5 movies, or 2 cases of soda per movie. The magnitude of this slope is exactly the same as the relative price we've just calculated. It is also the opportunity cost of a movie.

A Change in Prices When prices change, so does the budget line. The lower the price of the good measured on the x-axis, other things remaining the same, the flatter is the budget line. For example, if the price of a movie falls from $8 to $4, real income

FIGURE 9.2   Changes in Prices and Income

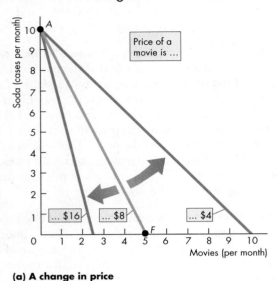

Price of a movie is ...

... $16   ... $8   ... $4

(a) A change in price

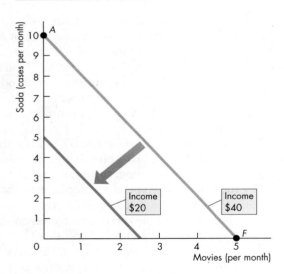

Income $20   Income $40

(b) A change in income

In part (a), the price of a movie changes. A fall in the price from $8 to $4 rotates the budget line outward and makes it flatter. A rise in the price from $8 to $16 rotates the budget line inward and makes it steeper.

In part (b), income falls from $40 to $20 while the prices of movies and soda remain the same. The budget line shifts leftward, but its slope does not change.

——— MyEconLab animation ———

in terms of soda does not change but the relative price of a movie falls. The budget line rotates outward and becomes flatter, as Fig. 9.2(a) illustrates. The higher the price of the good measured on the *x*-axis, other things remaining the same, the steeper is the budget line. For example, if the price of a movie rises from $8 to $16, the relative price of a movie increases. The budget line rotates inward and becomes steeper, as Fig. 9.2(a) illustrates.

A Change in Income A change in money income changes real income but does not change the relative price. The budget line shifts, but its slope does not change. An increase in money income increases real income and shifts the budget line rightward. A decrease in money income decreases real income and shifts the budget line leftward.

Figure 9.2(b) shows the effect of a change in money income on Lisa's budget line. The initial budget line when Lisa's income is $40 is the same as in Fig. 9.1. The new budget line shows how much Lisa can buy if her income falls to $20 a month. The two budget lines have the same slope because the relative price is the same. The new budget line is closer to the origin because Lisa's real income has decreased.

REVIEW QUIZ

1 What does a household's budget line show?
2 How does the relative price and a household's real income influence its budget line?
3 If a household has an income of $40 and buys only bus rides at $2 each and magazines at $4 each, what is the equation of the household's budget line?
4 If the price of one good changes, what happens to the relative price and the slope of the household's budget line?
5 If a household's money income changes and prices do not change, what happens to the household's real income and budget line?

You can work these questions in Study Plan 9.1 and get instant feedback.   MyEconLab

We've studied the limits to what a household can consume. Let's now learn how we can describe preferences and make a map that contains a lot of information about a household's preferences.

Preferences and Indifference Curves

You are going to discover a very cool idea: that of drawing a map of a person's preferences. A preference map is based on the intuitively appealing idea that people can sort all the possible combinations of goods into three groups: preferred, not preferred, and indifferent. To make this idea more concrete, let's ask Lisa to tell us how she ranks various combinations of movies and soda.

Figure 9.3 shows part of Lisa's answer. She tells us that she currently sees 2 movies and buys 6 cases of soda a month at point C. She then lists all the combinations of movies and soda that she says are just as acceptable to her as her current situation. When we plot these combinations of movies and soda, we get the green curve in Fig. 9.3(a). This curve is the key element in a preference map and is called an indifference curve.

An **indifference curve** is a line that shows combinations of goods among which a consumer is *indifferent*. The indifference curve in Fig. 9.3(a) tells us that Lisa is just as happy to see 2 movies and buy 6 cases of soda a month at point C as she is to have the combination of movies and soda at point G or at any other point along the curve.

Lisa also says that she prefers all the combinations of movies and soda above the indifference curve in Fig. 9.3(a)—the yellow area—to those on the indifference curve. And she prefers any combination on the indifference curve to any combination in the gray area below the indifference curve.

The indifference curve in Fig. 9.3(a) is just one of a whole family of such curves. This indifference curve appears again in Fig. 9.3(b), labeled I_1. The curves labeled I_0 and I_2 are two other indifference curves. Lisa prefers any point on indifference curve I_2 to any point on indifference curve I_1, and she prefers any point on I_1 to any point on I_0. We refer to I_2 as being a higher indifference curve than I_1 and I_1 as being higher than I_0.

A preference map is a series of indifference curves that resemble the contour lines on a map. By looking at the shape of the contour lines on a map, we can draw conclusions about the terrain. Similarly, by looking at the shape of the indifference curves, we can draw conclusions about a person's preferences.

Let's learn how to "read" a preference map.

FIGURE 9.3   A Preference Map

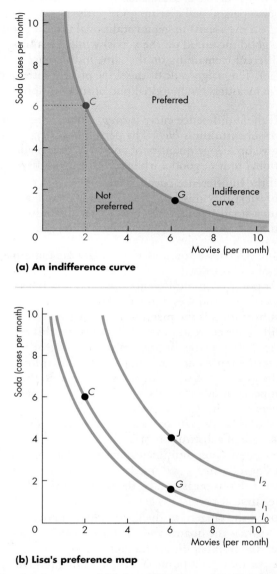

(a) An indifference curve

(b) Lisa's preference map

Part (a) shows one of Lisa's indifference curves. She is indifferent between point C (with 2 movies and 6 cases of soda) and all other points on the green indifference curve, such as G. She prefers points above the indifference curve (in the yellow area) to points on it, and she prefers points on the indifference curve to points below it (in the gray area). Part (b) shows three of the indifference curves—I_0, I_1, and I_2—in Lisa's preference map. She prefers point J to point C or G, and she prefers all the points on I_2 to those on I_1.

MyEconLab animation

Marginal Rate of Substitution

The **marginal rate of substitution** (*MRS*) is the rate at which a person will give up good *y* (the good measured on the *y*-axis) to get an additional unit of good *x* (the good measured on the *x*-axis) while remaining indifferent (remaining on the same indifference curve). The magnitude of the slope of an indifference curve measures the marginal rate of substitution.

- If the indifference curve is *steep*, the marginal rate of substitution is *high*. The person is willing to give up a large quantity of good *y* to get an additional unit of good *x* while remaining indifferent.
- If the indifference curve is *flat*, the marginal rate of substitution is *low*. The person is willing to give up a small amount of good *y* to get an additional unit of good *x* while remaining indifferent.

Figure 9.4 shows you how to calculate the marginal rate of substitution.

At point *C* on indifference curve I_1, Lisa buys 6 cases of soda and sees 2 movies. Her marginal rate of substitution is the magnitude of the slope of the indifference curve at point *C*. To measure this magnitude, place a straight line against, or tangent to, the indifference curve at point *C*. Along that line, as the quantity of soda decreases by 10 cases, the number of movies increases by 5—or 2 cases per movie. At point *C*, Lisa is willing to give up soda for movies at the rate of 2 cases per movie—a marginal rate of substitution of 2.

At point *G* on indifference curve I_1, Lisa buys 1.5 cases of soda and sees 6 movies. Her marginal rate of substitution is measured by the slope of the indifference curve at point *G*. That slope is the same as the slope of the tangent to the indifference curve at point *G*. Now, as the quantity of soda decreases by 4.5 cases, the number of movies increases by 9—or 1/2 case per movie. At point *G*, Lisa is willing to give up soda for movies at the rate of 1/2 case per movie—a marginal rate of substitution of 1/2.

As Lisa sees more movies and buys less soda, her marginal rate of substitution diminishes. Diminishing marginal rate of substitution is the key assumption about preferences. A **diminishing marginal rate of substitution** is a general tendency for a person to be willing to give up less of good *y* to get one more unit of good *x*, while at the same time remaining indifferent as the quantity of *x* increases. In Lisa's case, she is less willing to give up soda to see one more movie as the number of movies she sees increases.

FIGURE 9.4   The Marginal Rate of Substitution

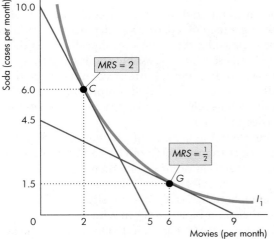

The magnitude of the slope of an indifference curve is called the marginal rate of substitution (*MRS*). The red line at point *C* tells us that Lisa is willing to give up 10 cases of soda to see 5 movies. Her marginal rate of substitution at point *C* is 10 divided by 5, which equals 2. The red line at point *G* tells us that Lisa is willing to give up 4.5 cases of soda to see 9 movies. Her marginal rate of substitution at point *G* is 4.5 divided by 9, which equals 1/2.

MyEconLab animation

Your Diminishing Marginal Rate of Substitution

Think about your own diminishing marginal rate of substitution. Imagine that in a week, you drink 10 cases of soda and see no movies. Most likely, you are willing to give up a lot of soda so that you can see just 1 movie. But now imagine that in a week, you buy 1 case of soda and see 6 movies. Most likely, you will now not be willing to give up much soda to see a seventh movie. As a general rule, the greater the number of movies you see, the smaller is the quantity of soda you are willing to give up to see one additional movie.

The shape of a person's indifference curves incorporates the principle of the diminishing marginal rate of substitution because the curves are bowed toward the origin. The tightness of the bend of an indifference curve tells us how willing a person is to substitute one good for another while remaining indifferent. Let's look at some examples that make this point clear.

Degree of Substitutability

Most of us would not regard movies and soda as being *close* substitutes, but they are substitutes. No matter how much you love soda, some increase in the number of movies you see will compensate you for being deprived of a can of soda. Similarly, no matter how much you love going to the movies, some number of cans of soda will compensate you for being deprived of seeing one movie. A person's indifference curves for movies and soda might look something like those for most ordinary goods and services shown in Fig. 9.5(a).

Close Substitutes Some goods substitute so easily for each other that most of us do not even notice which we are consuming. The different brands of marker pens and pencils are examples. Most people don't care which brand of these items they use or where they buy them. A marker pen from the campus bookstore is just as good as one from the local grocery store. You would be willing to forgo a pen from the campus store if you could get one more pen from the local grocery store. When two goods are perfect substitutes, their indifference curves are straight lines that slope downward, as Fig. 9.5(b) illustrates. The marginal rate of substitution is constant.

Complements Some goods do not substitute for each other at all. Instead, they are complements. The complements in Fig. 9.5(c) are left and right running shoes. Indifference curves of perfect complements are L-shaped. One left running shoe and one right running shoe are as good as one left shoe and two right shoes. Having two of each is preferred to having one of each, but having two of one and one of the other is no better than having one of each.

The extreme cases of perfect substitutes and perfect complements shown here don't often happen in reality, but they do illustrate that the shape of the indifference curve shows the degree of substitutability between two goods. The closer the two goods are to perfect substitutes, the closer the marginal rate of substitution is to being constant (a straight line), rather than diminishing (a curved line). Indifference

---

FIGURE 9.5   The Degree of Substitutability

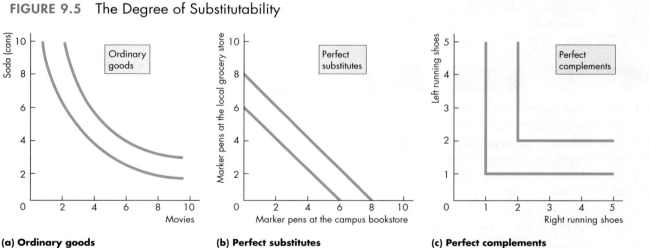

(a) Ordinary goods   **(b) Perfect substitutes**   **(c) Perfect complements**

The shape of the indifference curves reveals the degree of substitutability between two goods. Part (a) shows the indifference curves for two ordinary goods: movies and soda. To drink less soda and remain indifferent, one must see more movies. The number of movies that compensates for a reduction in soda increases as less soda is consumed. Part (b) shows the indifference curves for two perfect substitutes. For the consumer to remain indifferent, one fewer marker pen from the local grocery store must be replaced by one extra marker pen from the campus bookstore. Part (c) shows two perfect complements—goods that cannot be substituted for each other at all. Having two left running shoes with one right running shoe is no better than having one of each. But having two of each is preferred to having one of each.

MyEconLab animation

"With the pork I'd recommend an Alsatian
white or a Coke."

© The New Yorker Collection 1988
Robert Weber from cartoonbank.com. All Rights Reserved.

curves for poor substitutes are tightly curved and lie between the shapes of those shown in Figs. 9.5(a) and 9.5(c).

As you can see in the cartoon, according to the waiter's preferences, Coke and Alsatian white wine are perfect substitutes and each is a complement of pork. We hope the customers agree with him.

REVIEW QUIZ

1 What is an indifference curve and how does a preference map show preferences?
2 Why does an indifference curve slope downward and why is it bowed toward the origin?
3 What do we call the magnitude of the slope of an indifference curve?
4 What is the key assumption about a consumer's marginal rate of substitution?

You can work these questions in Study Plan 9.2 and get instant feedback.   MyEconLab

The two components of the model of household choice are now in place: the budget line and the preference map. We will now use these components to work out a household's choice and to predict how choices change when prices and income change.

Predicting Consumer Choices

We are now going to predict the quantities of movies and soda that Lisa chooses to buy. We're also going to see how these quantities change when a price changes or when Lisa's income changes. Finally, we're going to see how the *substitution effect* and the *income effect*, two ideas that you met in Chapter 3 (see p. 57), guarantee that for a normal good, the demand curve slopes downward.

Best Affordable Choice

When Lisa makes her best affordable choice of movies and soda, she spends all her income and is on her highest attainable indifference curve. Figure 9.6 illustrates this choice: The budget line is from Fig. 9.1 and the indifference curves are from Fig. 9.3(b). Lisa's best affordable choice is 2 movies and 6 cases of soda at point C—the *best affordable point*.

FIGURE 9.6   The Best Affordable Choice

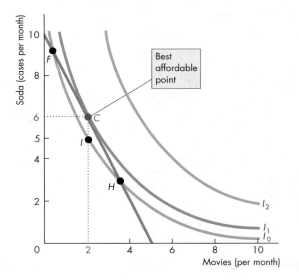

Lisa's best affordable choice is at point C, the point on her budget line and on her highest attainable indifference curve. At point C, Lisa's marginal rate of substitution between movies and soda (the magnitude of the slope of the indifference curve I_1) equals the relative price of movies and soda (the slope of the budget line).

———————— MyEconLab animation ————————

On the Budget Line The best affordable point is on the budget line. For every point inside the budget line, such as point *I*, there are points on the budget line that Lisa prefers. For example, she prefers all the points on the budget line between *F* and *H* to point *I*, so she chooses a point on the budget line.

On the Highest Attainable Indifference Curve Every point on the budget line lies on an indifference curve. For example, points *F* and *H* lie on the indifference curve I_0. By moving along her budget line from either *F* or *H* toward *C*, Lisa reaches points on ever-higher indifference curves that she prefers to points *F* or *H*. When Lisa gets to point *C*, she is on the highest attainable indifference curve.

Marginal Rate of Substitution Equals Relative Price At point *C*, Lisa's marginal rate of substitution between movies and soda (the magnitude of the slope of the indifference curve) is equal to the relative price of movies and soda (the magnitude of the slope of the budget line). Lisa's willingness to pay for a movie equals her opportunity cost of a movie.

Let's now see how Lisa's choices change when a price changes.

A Change in Price

The effect of a change in the price of a good on the quantity of the good consumed is called the **price effect**. We will use Fig. 9.7(a) to work out the price effect of a fall in the price of a movie. We start with the price of a movie at $8, the price of soda at $4 a case, and Lisa's income at $40 a month. In this situation, she buys 6 cases of soda and sees 2 movies a month at point *C*.

Now suppose that the price of a movie falls to $4. With a lower price of a movie, the budget line rotates outward and becomes flatter. The new budget line is the darker orange one in Fig. 9.7(a). For a refresher on how a price change affects the budget line, check back to Fig. 9.2(a).

Lisa's best affordable point is now point *J*, where she sees 6 movies and drinks 4 cases of soda. Lisa drinks less soda and watches more movies now that movies are cheaper. She cuts her soda purchases from 6 to 4 cases and increases the number of movies she sees from 2 to 6 a month. When the price of a movie falls and the price of soda and her income remain constant, Lisa substitutes movies for soda.

FIGURE 9.7   Price Effect and Demand Curve

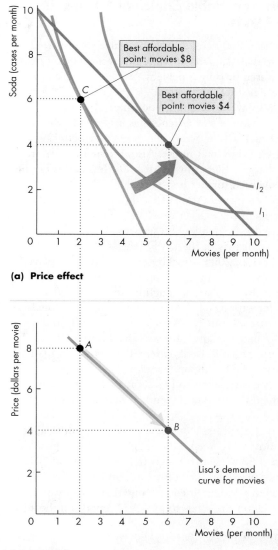

(a) Price effect

(b) Demand curve

Initially, Lisa's best affordable point is *C* in part (a). If the price of a movie falls from $8 to $4, Lisa's best affordable point is *J*. The move from *C* to *J* is the price effect.

At a price of $8 a movie, Lisa sees 2 movies a month, at point *A* in part (b). At a price of $4 a movie, she sees 6 movies a month, at point *B*. Lisa's demand curve for movies traces out her best affordable quantity of movies as the price of a movie varies.

MyEconLab animation

Economics in Action
Best Affordable Choice of Movies and DVDs

Between 2005 and 2012, box-office receipts rose by more than 20 percent while the average ticket price increased by only 6 percent. So people must have gone to the movies more often.

Why is movie-going booming? One answer is that the consumer's experience has improved. Movies in 3-D such as *Dr. Seuss' The Lorax* play better on the big screen than at home. Also, movie theaters are able to charge a higher price for 3-D films and other big hits, which further boosts receipts. But there is another answer, and at first thought an unlikely one: Events in the market for DVD rentals have impacted going to the movies. To see why, let's look at the recent history of the DVD rentals market.

Back in 2005, Blockbuster was the main player and the price of a DVD rental was around $4 a night. Redbox was a fledgling. It had started a year earlier with just 140 kiosks in selected McDonald's restaurants. But Redbox expanded rapidly and by 2007 had as many outlets as Blockbuster. In February 2008, Redbox rented 100 million DVDs at a price of $1 a night.

The easy access to DVDs at $1 a night transformed the markets for movie watching and the figure shows why.

A student has a budget of $40 a month to allocate to movies. To keep the story clear, we'll suppose that it cost $8 to go to a movie in both 2005 and 2012. The price of a DVD rental in 2005 was $4, so the student's budget line is the one that runs from 5 movies on the *y*-axis to 10 DVD rentals on the *x*-axis.

The student's best affordable point is 2 movies and 6 rentals a month.

In 2012, the price of a rental falls to $1 a night but the price of a movie ticket remains at $8. So the budget line rotates outward. The student's best affordable point is now at 3 movies and 16 rentals a month. (This student loves movies!)

Many other things changed between 2005 and 2012 that influenced the markets for movies and DVD rentals, but the fall in the price of a DVD rental was the biggest influence.

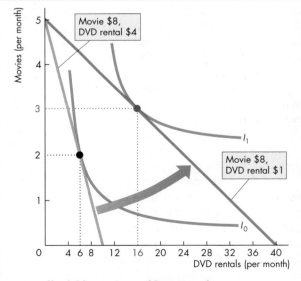

Best Affordable Movies and DVD Rentals

The Demand Curve In Chapter 3, we asserted that the demand curve slopes downward. We can now derive a demand curve from a consumer's budget line and indifference curves. By doing so, we can see that the law of demand and the downward-sloping demand curve are consequences of a consumer's choosing her or his best affordable combination of goods.

To derive Lisa's demand curve for movies, lower the price of a movie and find her best affordable point at different prices. We've just done this for two movie prices in Fig. 9.7(a). Figure 9.7(b) highlights these two prices and two points that lie on Lisa's demand curve for movies. When the price of a movie is $8, Lisa sees 2 movies a month at point A. When the price falls to $4, she increases the number of movies she sees to 6 a month at point B. The demand curve is made up of these two points plus all the other points that tell us Lisa's best affordable quantity of movies at each movie price, with the price of soda and Lisa's income remaining the same. As you can see, Lisa's demand curve for movies slopes downward—the lower the price of a movie, the more movies she sees. This is the law of demand.

Next, let's see how Lisa changes her purchases of movies and soda when her income changes.

A Change in Income

The effect of a change in income on buying plans is called the **income effect**. Let's work out the income effect by examining how buying plans change when income changes and prices remain constant. Figure 9.8 shows the income effect when Lisa's income falls. With an income of $40, the price of a movie at $4, and the price of soda at $4 a case, Lisa's best affordable point is J—she buys 6 movies and 4 cases of soda. If her income falls to $28, her best affordable point is K—she sees 4 movies and buys 3 cases of soda. When Lisa's income falls, she buys less of both goods. Movies and soda are normal goods.

The Demand Curve and the Income Effect A change in income leads to a shift in the demand curve, as shown in Fig. 9.8(b). With an income of $40, Lisa's demand curve for movies is D_0, the same as in Fig. 9.7(b). But when her income falls to $28, she plans to see fewer movies at each price, so her demand curve shifts leftward to D_1.

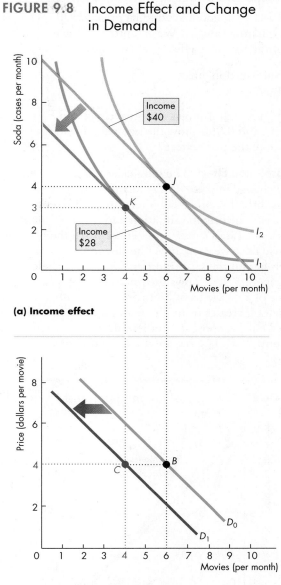

FIGURE 9.8 Income Effect and Change in Demand

(a) Income effect

(b) Demand curve for movies

A change in income shifts the budget line, changes the best affordable point, and changes demand.

In part (a), when Lisa's income decreases from $40 to $28, she sees fewer movies and buys less soda.

In part (b), when Lisa's income is $40, her demand curve for movies is D_0. When Lisa's income falls to $28, her demand curve for movies shifts leftward to D_1. For Lisa, going to the movies is a normal good. Her demand for movies decreases because she now sees fewer movies at each price.

MyEconLab animation

Substitution Effect and Income Effect

For a normal good, a fall in its price *always* increases the quantity bought. We can prove this assertion by dividing the price effect into two parts:

- Substitution effect
- Income effect

Figure 9.9(a) shows the price effect and Figs. 9.9(b) and 9.9(c) show the two parts into which we separate the price effect.

Substitution Effect The **substitution effect** is the effect of a change in price on the quantity bought when the consumer (hypothetically) remains indifferent between the original situation and the new one. To work out Lisa's substitution effect when the price of a movie falls, we must lower her income by enough to keep her on the same indifference curve as before.

Figure 9.9(a) shows the price effect of a fall in the price of a movie from $8 to $4. The number of movies increases from 2 to 6 a month. When the price falls, suppose (hypothetically) that we cut Lisa's income to $28. What's special about $28? It is the

income that is just enough, at the new price of a movie, to keep Lisa's best affordable point on the same indifference curve (I_1) as her original point C. Lisa's budget line is now the medium orange line in Fig. 9.9(b). With the lower price of a movie and a smaller income, Lisa's best affordable point is K. The move from C to K along indifference curve I_1 is the substitution effect of the price change. The substitution effect of the fall in the price of a movie is an increase in the quantity of movies from 2 to 4. The direction of the substitution effect never varies: When the relative price of a good falls, the consumer substitutes more of that good for the other good.

Income Effect To calculate the substitution effect, we gave Lisa a $12 pay cut. To calculate the income effect, we give Lisa back her $12. The $12 increase in income shifts Lisa's budget line outward, as shown in Fig. 9.9(c). The slope of the budget line does not change because both prices remain the same. This change in Lisa's budget line is similar to the one illustrated in Fig. 9.8. As Lisa's budget line shifts outward, her consumption possibilities expand and her best afford-

---

FIGURE 9.9   Substitution Effect and Income Effect

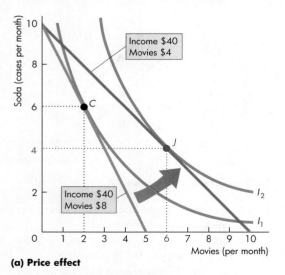

(a) Price effect

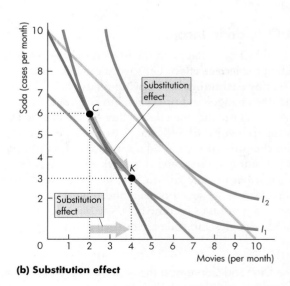

(b) Substitution effect

When the price of a movie falls from $8 to $4, Lisa moves from point C to point J in part (a). The price effect is an increase in the number of movies from 2 to 6 a month. This price effect is separated into a substitution effect in part (b) and an income effect in part (c).

To isolate the substitution effect, we confront Lisa with the new price but keep her on her original indifference curve, I_1. The substitution effect is the move from C to K along indifference curve I_1—an increase from 2 to 4 movies a month.

able point becomes *J* on indifference curve I_2. The move from *K* to *J* is the income effect of the price change.

As Lisa's income increases, she sees more movies. For Lisa, a movie is a normal good. For a normal good, the income effect *reinforces* the substitution effect. Because the two effects work in the same direction, we can be sure that the demand curve slopes downward. But some goods are inferior goods. What can we say about the demand for an inferior good?

Inferior Goods Recall that an *inferior good* is a good for which *demand decreases* when *income increases*. For an inferior good, the income effect is negative, which means that a lower price does not inevitably lead to an increase in the quantity demanded. The substitution effect of a fall in the price increases the quantity demanded, but the negative income effect works in the opposite direction and offsets the substitution effect to some degree. The key question is to what degree.

If the negative income effect *equals* the positive substitution effect, a fall in price leaves the quantity bought the same. When a fall in price leaves the quantity demanded unchanged, the demand curve is verti-

cal and demand is perfectly inelastic.

If the negative income effect *is smaller than* the positive substitution effect, a fall in price increases the quantity bought and the demand curve still slopes downward like that for a normal good. But the demand for an inferior good might be less elastic than that for a normal good.

If the negative income effect *exceeds* the positive substitution effect, a fall in the price *decreases* the quantity bought and the demand curve *slopes upward*. This case does not appear to occur in the real world.

You can apply the indifference curve model that you've studied in this chapter to explain the changes in the way we buy recorded music, see movies, and make all our other consumption choices. We allocate our budgets to make our best affordable choices. Changes in prices and incomes change our best affordable choices and change consumption patterns.

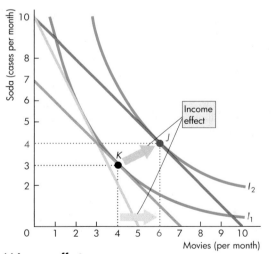

(c) Income effect

To isolate the income effect, we confront Lisa with the new price of movies but increase her income so that she can move from the original indifference curve, I_1, to the new one, I_2. The income effect is the move from *K* to *J*—an increase from 4 to 6 movies a month.

MyEconLab animation

◆ *Reading Between the Lines* on pp. 214–215 shows you how the theory of household choice explains why e-books are taking off and how people chose whether to buy their books in electronic or paper format.

In the chapters that follow, we study the choices that firms make in their pursuit of profit and how those choices determine the supply of goods and services and the demand for productive resources.

Paper Books Versus e-Books

Jumping on the e-Train

The Virginian-Pilot, Norfolk, VA
September 4, 2011

... "The whole book culture is changing ..."

The device at the bottom of this change is an 8-by-5-inch gadget on which you can read—and buy—books. e-readers, and tablets such as the iPad, can make reading a multimedia experience: Imagine reading a book on The Beatles while a video of them on "The Ed Sullivan Show" appears beside the text. It can also make bookstores a cemetery.

"We're seeing triple-digit percentage growth in e-books from last year," says Andi Sporkin for the Association of American Publishers.

"There is a massive change in this business due to e-book technology," says Mitch Kaplan, owner of the Coral Gables, Fla.-based Books & Books. "And it's happened faster than I could ever have imagined. A couple of years ago, e-books were maybe 2 percent of the business. Now we think it will be 25 percent by the end of the year, and there's no end in sight yet."

e-readers went on the market in the 1990s. High prices ($400 and up), clumsy technology, and a general skepticism about the technology relegated them to the fringe. Only in 2007, after the launch of the Amazon Kindle and the Sony Reader— which both used a new technology, e-ink, to make their text more booklike—did consumers get on board. Sales of e-books rocketed, from about $32 million in 2006 to $441 million in 2010, and are expected to top $1 billion this year. ...

ESSENCE OF THE STORY

- e-readers and tablets are changing book buying and reading.

- e-readers of the 1990s had high prices ($400 and up) and were clumsy.

- Today's e-readers use an e-ink technology and are more book-like.

- Sales of e-books increased from $32 million in 2006 to $441 million in 2010, to more than $1 billion in 2011—triple-digit percentage growth.

ECONOMIC ANALYSIS

- e-books are selling in rapidy growing numbers because of the choices that millions of consumers are making. One of these consumers is Andy.

- Andy loves reading, but he also enjoys music. And his budget for books and music is limited. So he must choose among the many alternative combinations of books and albums that he can afford.

- Figure 1 shows Andy's indifference curves for books (of all types) and albums.

- Andy's annual budget for albums and books is $600. The price of an album is $10, the price of a print book is $25, and the price of an e-book is $14.

- Figure 1 shows two budget lines: one if Andy buys print books and albums and another if he buys e-books and albums.

- In Fig. 1, the price of the most basic e-book reader is $200. Andy must spend this amount on a reader if he is to buy e-books, which leaves him with $400 for albums and e-books. If he buys 10 e-books, he can afford 26 albums [(10 × $14) + (26 × $10) = $400].

- If Andy buys print books and albums, he can afford 14 print books and 25 albums [(14 × $25) + (25 × $10) = $600].

- This combination is Andy's best affordable choice—14 print books and 25 albums shown at point A. Andy, doesn't buy e-books.

- Now the price of an e-book reader falls, and today Andy can buy the same basic reader that previously cost $200 for $80.

- Figure 2 shows what happens to Andy's budget line and his choices.

- If Andy buys print books and albums, nothing changes. He can still afford 14 print books and 25 albums [(14 × $25) + (25 × $10) = $600].

- But if he buys e-books, his situation has changed. After spending $80 on an e-book reader, Andy is left with $520 for albums and e-books. If he buys 14 e-books he can now afford 32 albums [(14 × $14) + (32 × $10) = $516 (he has $4 change)].

- Andy can now afford more albums if he buys the same number of books that he bought when the reader cost $200. But that's not Andy's best affordable combination of albums and books.

- The price of an e-book is lower than the price of a print book, so for Andy the relative price of a book has fallen and he can benefit by substituting books for albums.

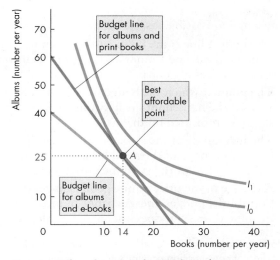

Figure 1 When the Price of a Reader is $200

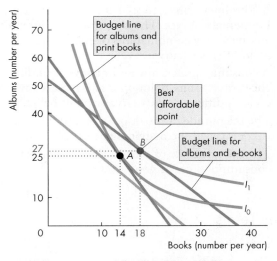

Figure 2 When the Price of a Reader is $80

- Andy moves along his budget line to the point at which his marginal rate of substitution of books for albums equals the relative price.

- This point occurs at B where Andy buys 18 e-books and 27 albums [(18 × $14) + (27 × $10) = $522 (he spends $2 less on gum)].

- The changing "book culture" is the consequence of Andy and other rational consumers responding to the incentive of a change in relative prices.

215

SUMMARY

Key Points

Consumption Possibilities (pp. 202–204)

- The budget line is the boundary between what a household can and cannot afford, given its income and the prices of goods.
- The point at which the budget line intersects the y-axis is the household's real income in terms of the good measured on that axis.
- The magnitude of the slope of the budget line is the relative price of the good measured on the x-axis in terms of the good measured on the y-axis.
- A change in the price of one good changes the slope of the budget line. A change in income shifts the budget line but does not change its slope.

Working Problems 1 to 10 will give you a better understanding of consumption possibilities.

Preferences and Indifference Curves (pp. 205–208)

- A consumer's preferences can be represented by indifference curves. The consumer is indifferent among all the combinations of goods that lie on an indifference curve.
- A consumer prefers any point above an indifference curve to any point on it and prefers any point on an indifference curve to any point below it.
- The magnitude of the slope of an indifference curve is called the marginal rate of substitution.
- The marginal rate of substitution diminishes as consumption of the good measured on the y-axis

decreases and consumption of the good measured on the x-axis increases.

Working Problems 11 to 15 will give you a better understanding of preferences and indifference curves.

Predicting Consumer Choices (pp. 208–213)

- A household consumes at its best affordable point. This point is on the budget line and on the highest attainable indifference curve and has a marginal rate of substitution equal to relative price.
- The effect of a price change (the price effect) can be divided into a substitution effect and an income effect.
- The substitution effect is the effect of a change in price on the quantity bought when the consumer (hypothetically) remains indifferent between the original choice and the new choice.
- The substitution effect always results in an increase in consumption of the good whose relative price has fallen.
- The income effect is the effect of a change in income on consumption.
- For a normal good, the income effect reinforces the substitution effect. For an inferior good, the income effect works in the opposite direction to the substitution effect.

Working Problems 16 to 20 will give you a better understanding of predicting consumer choices.

Key Terms

Budget line, 202	Indifference curve, 205	Relative price, 203
Diminishing marginal rate of substitution, 206	Marginal rate of substitution, 206	Substitution effect, 212
Income effect, 211	Price effect, 209	
	Real income, 203	

STUDY PLAN PROBLEMS AND APPLICATIONS

MyEconLab   You can work Problems 1 to 22 in MyEconLab Chapter 9 Study Plan and get instant feedback.

Consumption Possibilities (Study Plan 9.1)

Use the following information to work Problems 1 to 4.

Sara's income is $12 a week. The price of popcorn is $3 a bag, and the price of a smoothie is $3.

1. Calculate Sara's real income in terms of smoothies. Calculate her real income in terms of popcorn.

2. What is the relative price of smoothies in terms of popcorn? What is the opportunity cost of a smoothie?

3. Calculate the equation for Sara's budget line (with bags of popcorn on the left side).

4. Draw a graph of Sara's budget line with the quantity of smoothies on the x-axis. What is the slope of Sara's budget line? What determines its value?

Use the following information to work Problems 5 to 8.

Sara's income falls from $12 to $9 a week, while the price of popcorn is unchanged at $3 a bag and the price of a smoothie is unchanged at $3.

5. What is the effect of the fall in Sara's income on her real income in terms of smoothies?

6. What is the effect of the fall in Sara's income on her real income in terms of popcorn?

7. What is the effect of the fall in Sara's income on the relative price of a smoothie in terms of popcorn?

8. What is the slope of Sara's new budget line if it is drawn with smoothies on the x-axis?

Use the following information to work Problems 9 and 10.

Sara's income is $12 a week. The price of popcorn rises from $3 to $6 a bag, and the price of a smoothie is unchanged at $3.

9. What is the effect of the rise in the price of popcorn on Sara's real income in terms of smoothies and her real income in terms of popcorn?

10. What is the effect of the rise in the price of popcorn on the relative price of a smoothie in terms of popcorn? What is the slope of Sara's new budget line if it is drawn with smoothies on the x-axis?

Preferences and Indifference Curves (Study Plan 9.2)

11. Draw figures that show your indifference curves for the following pairs of goods:
    - Right gloves and left gloves
    - Coca-Cola and Pepsi
    - Tylenol and acetaminophen (the generic form of Tylenol)
    - Desktop computers and laptop computers
    - Strawberries and ice cream

For each pair, are the goods perfect substitutes, perfect complements, substitutes, complements, or unrelated?

12. Discuss the shape of the indifference curve for each of the following pairs of goods:
    - Orange juice and smoothies
    - Baseballs and baseball bats
    - Left running shoe and right running shoe
    - Eyeglasses and contact lenses

Explain the relationship between the shape of the indifference curve and the marginal rate of substitution as the quantities of the two goods change.

Use the following news clip to work Problems 13 and 14.

The Year in Medicine

Sudafed, used by allergy sufferers, contains as the active ingredient pseudoephedrine, which is widely used to make home-made methamphetamine. Allergy sufferers looking to buy Sudafed must now show photo ID and sign a logbook. The most common alternative, phenylephrine, isn't as effective as pseudoephedrine.

Source: *Time*, December 4, 2006

13. Sketch an indifference curve for Sudafed and phenylephrine that is consistent with this news clip. On your graph, identify combinations that allergy sufferers prefer, do not prefer, and are indifferent among.

14. Explain how the marginal rate of substitution changes as an allergy sufferer increases the consumption of Sudafed.

Use the following news clip to work Problems 15 and 16.

Gas Prices to Stunt Memorial Day Travel

With high gas prices, 12% of the people surveyed say that they have cancelled their Memorial Day road trip and 11% will take a trip near home. That may save consumers some money, but it will also likely hurt service stations, which will sell less gas and fewer snacks and hurt roadside hotels, which will have fewer rooms used and serve fewer meals.

Source: *MarketWatch*, May 22, 2008

15. Describe the degree of substitutability between Memorial Day trips and other trip-related goods and services and sketch a consumer's preference map that illustrates your description.

Predicting Consumer Choices (Study Plan 9.3)

16. a. Sketch a consumer's preference map between Memorial Day trips and other goods and services. Draw a consumer's budget line prior to the rise in the price of gasoline and mark the consumer's best affordable point.
    b. On your graph, show how the best affordable point changes when the price of gasoline rises.

Use the following information to work Problems 17 and 18.

Pam has made her best affordable choice of cookies and granola bars. She spends all of her weekly income on 30 cookies at $1 each and 5 granola bars at $2 each. Next week, she expects the price of a cookie to fall to 50¢ and the price of a granola bar to rise to $5.

17. a. Will Pam be able to buy and want to buy 30 cookies and 5 granola bars next week?
    b. Which situation does Pam prefer: cookies at $1 and granola bars at $2 or cookies at 50¢ and granola bars at $5?

18. a. If Pam changes how she spends her weekly income, will she buy more or fewer cookies and more or fewer granola bars?
    b. When the prices change next week, will there be an income effect, a substitution effect, or both at work?

Use the following information to work Problems 19 and 20.

Boom Time For "Gently Used" Clothes

Most retailers are blaming the economy for their poor sales, but one store chain that sells used name-brand children's clothes, toys, and furniture is boldly declaring that an economic downturn can actually be a boon for its business. Last year, the company took in $20 million in sales, up 5% from the previous year. Sales are already up 5% this year.

Source: CNN, April 17, 2008

19. a. According to the news clip, is used clothing a normal good or an inferior good?
    b. If the price of used clothing falls and income remains the same, explain how the quantity of used clothing bought changes.
    c. If the price of used clothing falls and income remains the same, describe the substitution effect and the income effect that occur.

20. a. Use a graph to illustrate a family's indifference curves for used clothing and other goods and services.
    b. In your graph in part (a), draw two budget lines to show the effect of a fall in income on the quantity of used clothing purchased.

Economics in the News (Study Plan 9.N)

Use the following information to work Problems 21 and 22.

Gas Prices Send Surge of Travelers to Mass Transit

With the price of gas approaching $4 a gallon, more commuters are abandoning their cars and taking the train or bus. It's very clear that a significant portion of the increase in transit use is directly caused by people who are looking for alternatives to paying $3.50 a gallon for gas. Some cities with long-established public transit systems, like New York and Boston, have seen increases in ridership of 5 percent, but the biggest surges—of 10 to 15 percent over last year—are occurring in many metropolitan areas in the Southwest where the driving culture is strongest and bus and rail lines are more limited.

Source: *The New York Times*, May 10, 2008

21. a. Sketch a graph of a preference map and a budget line to illustrate the best affordable combination of gasoline and public transit.
    b. On your graph show the effect of a rise in the price of gasoline on the quantities of gasoline and public transit services purchased.

22. If the gas price rise has been similar in all regions, compare the marginal rates of substitution in the Northeast and the Southwest. Explain how you have inferred the different marginal rates of substitution from the information in the news clip.

ADDITIONAL PROBLEMS AND APPLICATIONS

MyEconLab   You can work these problems in MyEconLab if assigned by your instructor.

Consumption Possibilities

Use the following information to work Problems 23 to 26.

Marc has a budget of $20 a month to spend on root beer and DVDs. The price of root beer is $5 a bottle, and the price of a DVD is $10.

23. What is the relative price of root beer in terms of DVDs and what is the opportunity cost of a bottle of root beer?

24. Calculate Marc's real income in terms of root beer. Calculate his real income in terms of DVDs.

25. Calculate the equation for Marc's budget line (with the quantity of root beer on the left side).

26. Draw a graph of Marc's budget line with the quantity of DVDs on the x-axis. What is the slope of Marc's budget line? What determines its value?

Use the following information to work Problems 27 to 30.

Amy has $20 a week to spend on coffee and cake. The price of coffee is $4 a cup, and the price of cake is $2 a slice.

27. Calculate Amy's real income in terms of cake. Calculate the relative price of cake in terms of coffee.

28. Calculate the equation for Amy's budget line (with cups of coffee on the left side).

29. If Amy's income increases to $24 a week and the prices of coffee and cake remain unchanged, describe the change in her budget line.

30. If the price of cake doubles while the price of coffee remains at $4 a cup and Amy's income remains at $20, describe the change in her budget line.

Use the following news clip to work Problems 31 and 32.

Gas Prices Straining Budgets

With gas prices rising, many people say they are staying in and scaling back spending to try to keep within their budget. They are driving as little as possible, cutting back on shopping and eating out, and reducing other discretionary spending.

Source: CNN, February 29, 2008

31. a. Sketch a budget line for a household that spends its income on only two goods: gasoline and restaurant meals. Identify the combinations of gasoline and restaurant meals that are affordable and those that are unaffordable.

    b. Sketch a second budget line to show how a rise in the price of gasoline changes the affordable and unaffordable combinations of gasoline and restaurant meals. Describe how the household's consumption possibilities change.

32. How does a rise in the price of gasoline change the relative price of a restaurant meal? How does a rise in the price of gasoline change real income in terms of restaurant meals?

Preferences and Indifference Curves

Use the following information to work Problems 33 and 34.

Rashid buys only books and CDs and the figure shows his preference map.

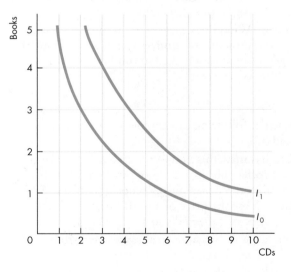

33. a. If Rashid chooses 3 books and 2 CDs, what is his marginal rate of substitution?

    b. If Rashid chooses 2 books and 6 CDs, what is his marginal rate of substitution?

34. Do Rashid's indifference curves display diminishing marginal rate of substitution? Explain why or why not.

35. **You May Be Paid More (or Less) Than You Think**

It's so hard to put a price on happiness, isn't it? But if you've ever had to choose between a job you like and a better-paying one that you like less, you probably wished some economist would tell you how much job satisfaction is worth. Trust in management is by far the biggest component to consider. Say you get a new boss and your trust in management goes up a bit (say, up 1 point on a 10-point scale). That's like getting a 36 percent pay raise. In other words, that increased level of trust will boost your level of overall satisfaction in life by about the same amount as a 36 percent raise would.

Source: CNN, March 29, 2006

a. Measure trust in management on a 10-point scale, measure pay on the same 10-point scale, and think of them as two goods. Sketch an indifference curve (with trust on the x-axis) that is consistent with the news clip.

b. What is the marginal rate of substitution between trust in management and pay according to this news clip?

c. What does the news clip imply about the principle of diminishing marginal rate of substitution? Is that implication likely to be correct?

Predicting Consumer Choices

Use the following information to work Problems 36 and 37.

Jim has made his best affordable choice of muffins and coffee. He spends all of his income on 10 muffins at $1 each and 20 cups of coffee at $2 each. Now the price of a muffin rises to $1.50 and the price of coffee falls to $1.75 a cup.

36. a. Will Jim now be able and want to buy 10 muffins and 20 coffees?

b. Which situation does Jim prefer: muffins at $1 and coffee at $2 a cup or muffins at $1.50 and coffee at $1.75 a cup?

37. a. If Jim changes the quantities that he buys, will he buy more or fewer muffins and more or less coffee?

b. When the prices change, will there be an income effect, a substitution effect, or both at work?

Use the following information to work Problems 38 to 40.

Sara's income is $12 a week. The price of popcorn is $3 a bag, and the price of cola is $1.50 a can. The figure shows Sara's preference map for popcorn and cola.

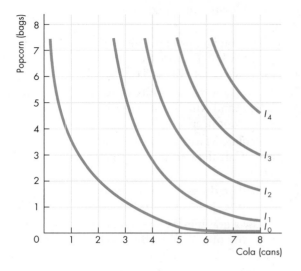

38. What quantities of popcorn and cola does Sara buy? What is Sara's marginal rate of substitution at the point at which she consumes?

39. Suppose that the price of cola rises to $3.00 a can and the price of popcorn and Sara's income remain the same. What quantities of cola and popcorn does Sara now buy? What are two points on Sara's demand curve for cola? Draw Sara's demand curve.

40. Suppose that the price of cola rises to $3.00 a can and the price of popcorn and Sara's income remain the same.

a. What is the substitution effect of this price change and what is the income effect of the price change?

b. Is cola a normal good or an inferior good? Explain.

Economics in the News

41. After you have studied *Reading Between the Lines* on pp. 214–215, answer the following questions.

a. How do you buy books?

b. Sketch your budget line for books and other goods.

c. Sketch your indifference curves for books and other goods.

d. Identify your best affordable point.

Making the Most of Life

UNDERSTANDING HOUSEHOLDS' CHOICES

The powerful forces of demand and supply shape the fortunes of families, businesses, nations, and empires in the same unrelenting way that the tides and winds shape rocks and coastlines. You saw in Chapters 3 through 7 how these forces raise and lower prices, increase and decrease quantities bought and sold, cause revenues to fluctuate, and send resources to their most valuable uses.

These powerful forces begin quietly and privately with the choices that each one of us makes. Chapters 8 and 9 probe these individual choices, offering two alternative approaches to explaining both consumption plans and the allocation of time. These explanations of consumption plans can also explain "non-economic" choices, such as whether to marry and how many children to have. In a sense, there are no non-economic choices. If there is scarcity, there must be choice, and economics studies all choices.

The earliest economists (Adam Smith and his contemporaries) did not have a very deep understanding of households' choices. It was not until the nineteenth century that progress was made in this area when Jeremy Bentham (below) introduced the concept of utility and applied it to the study of human choices. Today, Steven Levitt, whom you will meet on the following page, is one of the most influential students of human behavior.

Jeremy Bentham *(1748–1832), who lived in London, was the son and grandson of lawyers and was himself trained as a barrister. But Bentham rejected the opportunity to maintain the family tradition and, instead, spent his life as a writer, activist, and Member of Parliament in the pursuit of rational laws that would bring the greatest happiness to the greatest number of people.*

Bentham, whose embalmed body is preserved to this day in a glass cabinet in the University of London, was the first person to use the concept of utility to explain human choices. But in Bentham's day, the distinction between explaining and prescribing was not a sharp one, and Bentham was ready to use his ideas to tell people how they ought to behave. He was one of the first to propose pensions for the retired, guaranteed employment, minimum wages, and social benefits such as free education and free medical care.

> *"... It is the greatest happiness of the greatest number that is the measure of right and wrong."*
>
> **JEREMY BENTHAM**
> *Fragment on Government*

I think of economics as being primarily about a way of looking at the world and a set of tools for thinking clearly.

STEVEN D. LEVITT is William B. Ogden Distinguished Service Professor of Economics at the University of Chicago. Born in Minneapolis, he was an undergraduate at Harvard and a graduate student at MIT. Among his many honors, he was recently awarded the John Bates Clark Medal, given to the best economist under 40.

Professor Levitt has studied an astonishingly wide range of human choices and their outcomes. He has examined the effects of policing on crime, shown that real estate agents get a higher price when they sell their own homes than when they sell other people's, devised a test to detect cheating teachers, and studied the choices of drug dealers and gang members. Much of this research has been popularized in Freakonomics (Steven D. Levitt and Stephen J. Dubner, HarperCollins, 2005). What unifies this apparently diverse body of research is the use of natural experiments. Professor Levitt has an incredible ability to find just the right set of events and the data the events have generated to enable him to isolate the effect he's looking for.

Michael Parkin talked with Steven Levitt about his work and what economists have discovered about how people respond to incentives.

Why did you become an economist?

As a freshman in college, I took introductory economics. All the ideas made perfect sense to me—it was the way I naturally thought. My friends were befuddled. I thought, "This is the field for me!"

The idea of rational choice made at the margin lies at the heart of economics. Would you say that your work generally supports that idea or challenges it? Can you provide some examples?

I don't like the word "rational" in this context. I think economists model agents as being rational just for convenience. What really matters is whether people respond to incentives. My work very much supports the idea that humans in all types of circumstances respond strongly to incentives. I've seen it with drug dealers, auto thieves, sumo wrestlers, real estate agents, and elementary school teachers, just to name a few examples.

Drug dealers, for instance, want to make money, but they also want to avoid being arrested or even killed. In the data we have on drug sellers, we see that when the drug trade is more lucrative, dealers are willing to take greater risks of arrest to carve out a share of the market.... Sumo wrestlers, on the other hand, care mostly about their official ranking. Sometimes matches occur where one wrestler has more to lose or gain than the other wrestler. We find that sumo wrestlers make corrupt deals to make sure the wrestler who wins is the one who needs to win.

Why is an economist interested in crime and cheating?

I think of economics as being primarily about a way of looking at the world and a set of tools for thinking clearly. The topics you apply these tools to are unlimited. That is why I think economics has been so powerful. If you understand economics and use the tools wisely, you will be a better business person, doctor, public servant, parent.

*Read the full interview with Steven Levitt in MyEconLab.

10

ORGANIZING PRODUCTION

After studying this chapter, you will be able to:

◆ Explain the economic problem that all firms face

◆ Distinguish between technological efficiency and economic efficiency

◆ Define and explain the principal–agent problem

◆ Distinguish among different types of markets

◆ Explain why markets coordinate some economic activities and why firms coordinate others

In the fall of 1990, a British scientist named Tim Berners-Lee invented the World Wide Web, a remarkable idea that paved the way for the creation of thousands of profitable businesses such as Facebook, Twitter, Apple, and Google.

How do firms make their business decisions?

That's the question you study in this chapter. In *Reading Between the Lines* at the end of the chapter, we'll apply some of what you've learned and look at some of the choices made by Facebook and Google in an Internet advertising game.

◆ The Firm and Its Economic Problem

The 20 million firms in the United States differ in size and in the scope of what they do, but they all perform the same basic economic functions. Each **firm** is an institution that hires factors of production and organizes those factors to produce and sell goods and services. Our goal is to predict firms' behavior. To do so, we need to know a firm's goal and the constraints it faces. We start with the goal.

The Firm's Goal

When economists ask entrepreneurs what they are trying to achieve, they get many different answers. Some talk about making a high-quality product, others about business growth, others about market share, others about the job satisfaction of their workforce, and an increasing number today talk about social and environmental responsibility. All of these goals are pursued by firms, but they are not the fundamental goal: They are the means to that goal.

A firm's goal is to maximize profit. A firm that does not seek to maximize profit is either eliminated or taken over by a firm that does seek that goal.

What is the profit that a firm seeks to maximize? To answer this question, we'll look at Campus Sweaters, Inc., a small producer of knitted sweaters owned and operated by Cindy.

Accounting Profit

In 2012, Campus Sweaters received $400,000 for the sweaters it sold and paid out $80,000 for wool, $20,000 for utilities, $120,000 for wages, $5,000 for the lease of a computer, and $5,000 in interest on a bank loan. These expenses total $230,000, so the firm had a cash surplus of $170,000.

To measure the profit of Campus Sweaters, Cindy's accountant subtracted $20,000 for the depreciation of buildings and knitting machines from the $170,000 cash surplus. *Depreciation* is the fall in the value of a firm's capital. To calculate depreciation, accountants use Internal Revenue Service rules based on standards established by the Financial Accounting Standards Board. Using these rules, Cindy's accountant calculated that Campus Sweaters made a profit of $150,000 in 2012.

Economic Accounting

Accountants measure a firm's profit to ensure that the firm pays the correct amount of income tax and to show its investors how their funds are being used.

Economists measure a firm's profit to enable them to predict the firm's decisions, and the goal of these decisions is to maximize *economic profit*. **Economic profit** is equal to total revenue minus total cost, with total cost measured as the *opportunity cost of production*.

A Firm's Opportunity Cost of Production

The *opportunity cost* of any action is the highest-valued alternative forgone. The *opportunity cost of production* is the value of the best alternative use of the resources that a firm uses in production.

A firm's opportunity cost of production is the value of real alternatives forgone. We express opportunity cost in money units so that we can compare and add up the value of the alternatives forgone.

A firm's opportunity cost of production is the sum of the cost of using resources

- Bought in the market
- Owned by the firm
- Supplied by the firm's owner

Resources Bought in the Market A firm incurs an opportunity cost when it buys resources in the market. The amount spent on these resources is an opportunity cost of production because the firm could have bought different resources to produce some other good or service. For Campus Sweaters, the resources bought in the market are wool, utilities, labor, a leased computer, and a bank loan. The $230,000 spent on these items in 2012 could have been spent on something else, so it is an opportunity cost of producing sweaters.

Resources Owned by the Firm A firm incurs an opportunity cost when it uses its own capital. The cost of using capital owned by the firm is an opportunity cost of production because the firm could sell the capital that it owns and rent capital from another firm. When a firm uses its own capital, it implicitly rents it from itself. In this case, the firm's opportunity cost of using the capital it owns is called the **implicit rental rate** of capital. The implicit rental rate of capital has two components: economic depreciation and forgone interest.

Economic Depreciation Accountants measure *depreciation*, the fall in the value of a firm's capital, using formulas that are unrelated to the change in the market value of capital. **Economic depreciation** is the fall in the *market value* of a firm's capital over a given period. It equals the market price of the capital at the beginning of the period minus the market price of the capital at the end of the period.

Suppose that Campus Sweaters could have sold its buildings and knitting machines on January 1, 2012, for $400,000 and that it can sell the same capital on December 31, 2012, for $375,000. The firm's economic depreciation during 2012 is $25,000 ($400,000 – $375,000). This forgone $25,000 is an opportunity cost of production.

Forgone Interest The funds used to buy capital could have been used for some other purpose, and in their next best use, they would have earned interest. This forgone interest is an opportunity cost of production.

Suppose that Campus Sweaters used $300,000 of its own funds to buy capital. If the firm invested its $300,000 in bonds instead of a knitting factory (and rented the capital it needs to produce sweaters), it would have earned $15,000 a year in interest. This forgone interest is an opportunity cost of production.

Resources Supplied by the Firm's Owner A firm's owner might supply *both* entrepreneurship and labor.

Entrepreneurship The factor of production that organizes a firm and makes its decisions might be supplied by the firm's owner or by a hired entrepreneur. The return to entrepreneurship is profit, and the profit that an entrepreneur earns *on average* is called **normal profit**. Normal profit is the cost of entrepreneurship and is an opportunity cost of production.

If Cindy supplies entrepreneurial services herself, and if the normal profit she can earn on these services is $45,000 a year, this amount is an opportunity cost of production at Campus Sweaters.

Owner's Labor Services *In addition* to supplying entrepreneurship, the owner of a firm might supply labor but not take a wage. The opportunity cost of the owner's labor is the wage income forgone by not taking the best alternative job.

If Cindy supplies labor to Campus Sweaters, and if the wage she can earn on this labor at another firm is $55,000 a year, this amount of wages forgone is an opportunity cost of production at Campus Sweaters.

Economic Accounting: A Summary

Table 10.1 summarizes the economic accounting. Campus Sweaters' total revenue is $400,000; its opportunity cost of production is $370,000; and its economic profit is $30,000.

Cindy's personal income is the $30,000 of economic profit plus the $100,000 that she earns by supplying resources to Campus Sweaters.

Decisions

To achieve the objective of maximum economic profit, a firm must make five decisions:

1. What to produce and in what quantities
2. How to produce
3. How to organize and compensate its managers and workers
4. How to market and price its products
5. What to produce itself and buy from others

In all these decisions, a firm's actions are limited by the constraints that it faces. Your next task is to learn about these constraints.

TABLE 10.1   Economic Accounting

Item		Amount
Total Revenue		**$400,000**
Cost of Resources Bought in Market		
Wool	$80,000	
Utilities	20,000	
Wages	120,000	
Computer lease	5,000	
Bank interest	5,000	$230,000
Cost of Resources Owned by Firm		
Economic depreciation	$25,000	
Forgone interest	15,000	$40,000
Cost of Resources Supplied by Owner		
Cindy's normal profit	$45,000	
Cindy's forgone wages	55,000	$100,000
Opportunity Cost of Production		**$370,000**
Economic Profit		**$30,000**

The Firm's Constraints

Three features of a firm's environment limit the maximum economic profit it can make. They are

- Technology constraints
- Information constraints
- Market constraints

Technology Constraints Economists define technology broadly. A **technology** is any method of producing a good or service. Technology includes the detailed designs of machines and the layout of the workplace. It includes the organization of the firm. For example, the shopping mall is one technology for producing retail services. It is a different technology from the catalog store, which in turn is different from the downtown store.

It might seem surprising that a firm's profit is limited by technology because it seems that technological advances are constantly increasing profit opportunities. Almost every day, we learn about some new technological advance that amazes us. With computers that speak and recognize our own speech and cars that can find the address we need in a city we've never visited, we can accomplish more than ever.

Technology advances over time. But at each point in time, to produce more output and gain more revenue, a firm must hire more resources and incur greater costs. The increase in profit that a firm can achieve is limited by the technology available. For example, by using its current plant and workforce, Ford can produce some maximum number of cars per day. To produce more cars per day, Ford must hire more resources, which increases its costs and limits the increase in profit that it can make by selling the additional cars.

Information Constraints We never possess all the information we would like to have to make decisions. We lack information about both the future and the present. For example, suppose you plan to buy a new computer. When should you buy it? The answer depends on how the price is going to change in the future. Where should you buy it? The answer depends on the prices at hundreds of different computer stores. To get the best deal, you must compare the quality and prices in every store. But the opportunity cost of this comparison exceeds the cost of the computer!

A firm is constrained by limited information about the quality and efforts of its workforce, the current and future buying plans of its customers, and the plans of its competitors. Workers might make too little effort, customers might switch to competing suppliers, and a competitor might enter the market and take some of the firm's business.

To address these problems, firms create incentives to boost workers' efforts even when no one is monitoring them; conduct market research to lower uncertainty about customers' buying plans, and "spy" on each other to anticipate competitive challenges. But these efforts don't eliminate incomplete information and uncertainty, which limit the economic profit that a firm can make.

Market Constraints The quantity each firm can sell and the price it can obtain are constrained by its customers' willingness to pay and by the prices and marketing efforts of other firms. Similarly, the resources that a firm can buy and the prices it must pay for them are limited by the willingness of people to work for and invest in the firm. Firms spend billions of dollars a year marketing and selling their products. Some of the most creative minds strive to find the right message that will produce a knockout television advertisement. Market constraints and the expenditures firms make to overcome them limit the profit a firm can make.

REVIEW QUIZ

1 What is a firm's fundamental goal and what happens if the firm doesn't pursue this goal?
2 Why do accountants and economists calculate a firm's cost and profit in different ways?
3 What are the items that make opportunity cost differ from the accountant's measure of cost?
4 Why is normal profit an opportunity cost?
5 What are the constraints that a firm faces? How does each constraint limit the firm's profit?

You can work these questions in Study Plan 10.1 and get instant feedback.   MyEconLab

In the rest of this chapter and in Chapters 11 through 14, we study the choices that firms make. You're going to learn how we can predict a firm's decisions as those that maximize profit given the constraints the firm faces. We begin by taking a closer look at a firm's technology constraints.

Technological and Economic Efficiency

Microsoft employs a large workforce, and most Microsoft workers possess a large amount of human capital. But the firm uses a small amount of physical capital. In contrast, a coal-mining company employs a huge amount of mining equipment (physical capital) and almost no labor. Why? The answer lies in the concept of efficiency. There are two concepts of production efficiency: technological efficiency and economic efficiency. **Technological efficiency** occurs when the firm produces a given output by using the least amount of inputs. **Economic efficiency** occurs when the firm produces a given output at the least cost. Let's explore the two concepts of efficiency by studying an example.

Suppose that there are four alternative techniques for making TVs:

A. *Robot production.* One person monitors the entire computer-driven process.

B. *Production line.* Workers specialize in a small part of the job as the emerging TV passes them on a production line.

C. *Hand-tool production.* A single worker uses a few hand tools to make a TV.

D. *Bench production.* Workers specialize in a small part of the job but walk from bench to bench to perform their tasks.

Table 10.2 sets out the amounts of labor and capital required by each of these four methods to make 10 TVs a day.

Which of these alternative methods are technologically efficient?

Technological Efficiency

Recall that *technological efficiency* occurs when the firm produces a given output by using the least amount of inputs. Look at the numbers in the table and notice that method A uses the most capital and the least labor. Method C uses the most labor and the least capital. Method B and method D lie between the two extremes. They use less capital and more labor than method A and less labor but more capital than method C.

Compare methods B and D. Method D requires 100 workers and 10 units of capital to produce 10

TABLE 10.2   Four Ways of Making 10 TVs a Day

	Method	Quantities of inputs	
		Labor	Capital
A	Robot production	1	1,000
B	Production line	10	10
C	Hand-tool production	1,000	1
D	Bench production	100	10

TVs. Those same 10 TVs can be produced by method B with 10 workers and the same 10 units of capital. Because method D uses the same amount of capital and more labor than method B, method D is not technologically efficient.

Are any of the other methods not technologically efficient? The answer is no. Each of the other methods is technologically efficient. Method A uses more capital but less labor than method B, and method C uses more labor but less capital than method B.

Which of the methods are economically efficient?

Economic Efficiency

Recall that *economic efficiency* occurs when the firm produces a given output at the least cost.

Method D, which is technologically inefficient, is also economically inefficient. It uses the same amount of capital as method B but 10 times as much labor, so it costs more. A technologically inefficient method is never economically efficient.

One of the three technologically efficient methods is economically efficient. The other two are economically inefficient. But which method is economically efficient depends on factor prices.

In Table 10.3(a), the wage rate is $75 per day and the rental rate of capital is $250 per day. By studying Table 10.3(a), you can see that method B has the lowest cost and is the economically efficient method.

In Table 10.3(b), the wage rate is $150 a day and the rental rate of capital is $1 a day. Looking at Table 10.3(b), you can see that method A has the lowest cost and is the economically efficient method. In this case, capital is so cheap relative to labor that the

TABLE 10.3   The Costs of Different Ways of Making 10 TVs a Day

(a) Wage rate $75 per day; Capital rental rate $250 per day

Method	Inputs Labor	Capital	Labor cost ($75 per day)		Capital cost ($250 per day)		Total cost
A	1	1,000	$75	+	$250,000	=	$250,075
B	10	10	750	+	2,500	=	3,250
C	1,000	1	75,000	+	250	=	75,250

(b) Wage rate $150 per day; Capital rental rate $1 per day

Method	Inputs Labor	Capital	Labor cost ($150 per day)		Capital cost ($1 per day)		Total cost
A	1	1,000	$150	+	$1,000	=	$1,150
B	10	10	1,500	+	10	=	1,510
C	1,000	1	150,000	+	1	=	150,001

(c) Wage rate $1 per day; Capital rental rate $1,000 per day

Method	Inputs Labor	Capital	Labor cost ($1 per day)		Capital cost ($1,000 per day)		Total cost
A	1	1,000	$1	+	$1,000,000	=	$1,000,001
B	10	10	10	+	10,000	=	10,010
C	1,000	1	1,000	+	1,000	=	2,000

method that uses the most capital is the economically efficient method.

In Table 10.3(c), the wage rate is $1 a day and the rental rate of capital is $1,000 a day. You can see that method *C* has the lowest cost and is the economically efficient method. In this case, labor is so cheap relative to capital that the method that uses the most labor is the economically efficient method.

Economic efficiency depends on the relative costs of resources. The economically efficient method is the one that uses a smaller amount of the more expensive resource and a larger amount of the less expensive resource.

A firm that is not economically efficient does not maximize profit. Natural selection favors efficient firms and inefficient firms disappear. Inefficient firms go out of business or are taken over by firms that produce at lower costs.

REVIEW QUIZ

1 Is a firm technologically efficient if it uses the latest technology? Why or why not?
2 Is a firm economically inefficient if it can cut its costs by producing less? Why or why not?
3 Explain the key distinction between technological efficiency and economic efficiency.
4 Why do some firms use large amounts of capital and small amounts of labor while others use small amounts of capital and large amounts of labor?

You can work these questions in Study Plan 10.2 and get instant feedback.   MyEconLab

Next we study the information constraints that firms face and the wide array of organization structures these constraints generate.

▶ Information and Organization

Each firm organizes the production of goods and services using a combination of two systems:

- Command systems
- Incentive systems

Command Systems

A **command system** is a method of organizing production that uses a managerial hierarchy. Commands pass downward through the hierarchy, and information passes upward.

The military uses the purest form of command system. A commander-in-chief makes the big decisions about strategic goals. Beneath this highest level, generals organize their military resources. Beneath the generals, successively lower ranks organize smaller and smaller units but pay attention to ever-increasing degrees of detail. At the bottom of the hierarchy are the people who operate weapons systems.

Command systems in firms are not as rigid as those in the military, but they share some similar features. A chief executive officer (CEO) sits at the top of a firm's command system. Senior executives specialize in managing production, marketing, finance, and personnel. Beneath these senior managers are the people who supervise the day-to-day operations of the business and beneath them, the people who operate the firm's machines and who make and sell the firm's products.

Managers try to be well informed, but they almost always have incomplete information about what is happening in the divisions for which they are responsible. For this reason, firms also use incentive systems.

Incentive Systems

An **incentive system** is a method of organizing production that uses a market-like mechanism inside the firm. Instead of issuing commands, senior managers create compensation schemes to induce workers to perform in ways that maximize the firm's profit.

Incentive systems operate at all levels in a firm. The compensation plan of a CEO might include a share in the firm's profit, factory floor workers sometimes receive compensation based on the quantity they produce, and salespeople, who spend most of their working time alone, are induced to work hard by being paid a small salary and a large performance-related bonus.

The Principal–Agent Problem

The **principal–agent problem** is the problem of devising compensation rules that induce an *agent* to act in the best interest of a *principal*. For example, the stockholders of Texaco are *principals,* and the firm's managers are *agents.* The stockholders (the principals) must induce the managers (agents) to act in the stockholders' best interest. Similarly, Mark Zuckerberg (a principal) must induce the designers who are working on the next generation Facebook (agents) to work efficiently.

Agents, whether they are managers or workers, pursue their own goals and often impose costs on a principal. For example, the goal of stockholders of Citicorp (principals) is to maximize the firm's profit—its true profit, not some fictitious paper profit. But the firm's profit depends on the actions of its managers (agents), and they have their own goals. Perhaps a bank manager takes a customer to a ball game on the pretense that she is building customer loyalty, when in fact she is simply enjoying on-the-job leisure. This same manager is also a principal, and her tellers are agents. The manager wants the tellers to work hard and attract new customers so that she can meet her operating targets. But the workers slack off and take on-the-job leisure.

Coping with the Principal–Agent Problem

A principal must create incentives that induce each agent to work in the interests of the principal. Three ways of coping with the principal–agent problem are

- Ownership
- Incentive pay
- Long-term contracts

Ownership By assigning ownership (or part-ownership) of a business to managers or workers, it is sometimes possible to induce a job performance that increases a firm's profits. Part-ownership is quite common for senior managers but less common for workers. When United Airlines was running into problems a few years ago, it made most of its employees owners of the company.

Incentive Pay Incentive pay—pay related to performance—is very common. Incentives are based on a variety of performance criteria such as profits, production, or sales targets. Promoting an employee for good performance is another example of the use of incentive pay.

Long-Term Contracts Long-term contracts tie the long-term fortunes of managers and workers (agents) to the success of the principal(s)—the owner(s) of the firm. For example, a multiyear employment contract for a CEO encourages that person to take a long-term view and devise strategies that achieve maximum profit over a sustained period.

These three ways of coping with the principal–agent problem give rise to different types of business organization.

Types of Business Organization

The three main types of business organization are

- Proprietorship
- Partnership
- Corporation

Proprietorship A *proprietorship* is a firm with a single owner—a proprietor—who has unlimited liability. *Unlimited liability* is the legal responsibility for all the

---

◆ ECONOMICS IN THE NEWS

Principals and Agents Get It Wrong

JPMorgan Pay May Be Clawed Back

In May 2012, JPMorgan Chase announced that traders in London had incurred losses of $2 billion. CEO Jamie Dimon said the losses arose from a "flawed, complex, poorly reviewed, poorly executed, and poorly monitored" trading strategy. JPMorgan Chase's stock price fell on the news. One top executive took early retirement. JPMorgan executives and traders are compensated by results with bonus payments in cash and stock options. Dimon said "It's likely that there will be clawbacks" of compensation.

Sources: *AP, Bloomberg,* and *Reuters,* May/June, 2012

THE QUESTIONS

- Who are the principals and who are the agents?
- How did JPMorgan try to cope with its principal–agent problem?
- How, on the occasion reported here, how did JPMorgan get it wrong?
- What role did JPMorgan's share price play?

THE ANSWERS

- The JPMorgan stockholders are principals and Jamie Dimon is their agent.
- Jamie Dimon, as CEO, is a principal and the top executives are agents.
- JPMorgan top executives are principals, and the traders who incurred the losses are agents.
- JPMorgan tried to cope with the principal–agent problem by compensating agents with performance bonuses, profit shares through stock options, and with the possibility of clawbacks for poor performance.
- We don't know the details but based on what

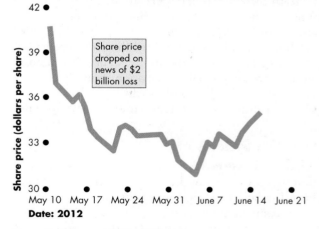

Figure 1 JPMorgan Share Price

Jamie Dimon said, it seems that the specific trading activities that incurred a $2 billion loss were complex and not properly understood either by the traders (the agents at the end of the line) or the managers who designed the trading activities.

- The fall in JPMorgan's stock price not only lowered the wealth of stockholders but also lowered the compensation of Jamie Dimon and the other executives compensated with stock options.

debts of a firm up to an amount equal to the entire personal wealth of the owner. Farmers, computer programmers, and artists are often proprietorships.

The proprietor makes management decisions, receives the firm's profits, and is responsible for its losses. Profits from a proprietorship are taxed at the same rate as other sources of the proprietor's personal income.

Partnership A *partnership* is a firm with two or more owners who have unlimited liability. Partners must agree on an appropriate management structure and on how to divide the firm's profits among themselves. The profits of a partnership are taxed as the personal income of the owners, but each partner is legally liable for all the debts of the partnership (limited only by the wealth of that individual partner). Liability for the full debts of the partnership is called *joint unlimited liability*. Most law firms are partnerships.

Corporation A *corporation* is a firm owned by one or more limited liability stockholders. *Limited liability* means that the owners have legal liability only for the value of their initial investment. This limi-

tation of liability means that if the corporation becomes bankrupt, its owners do not use their personal wealth to pay the corporation's debts.

Corporations' profits are taxed independently of stockholders' incomes. Stockholders pay a capital gains tax on the profit they earn when they sell a stock for a higher price than they paid for it. Corporate stocks generate capital gains when a corporation retains some of its profit and reinvests it in profitable activities. So retained earnings are taxed twice because the capital gains they generate are taxed. Dividend payments are also taxed but at a lower rate than other sources of income.

Pros and Cons of Different Types of Firms

The different types of business organization arise from firms trying to cope with the principal–agent problem. Each type has advantages in particular situations and because of its special advantages, each type continues to exist. Each type of business organization also has disadvantages.

Table 10.4 summarizes these and other pros and cons of the different types of firms.

TABLE 10.4 The Pros and Cons of Different Types of Firms

Type of Firm	Pros	Cons
Proprietorship	▪ Easy to set up ▪ Simple decision making ▪ Profits taxed only once as owner's income	▪ Bad decisions not checked; no need for consensus ▪ Owner's entire wealth at risk ▪ Firm dies with owner ▪ Cost of capital and labor is high relative to that of a corporation
Partnership	▪ Easy to set up ▪ Diversified decision making ▪ Can survive withdrawal of partner ▪ Profits taxed only once as owners' incomes	▪ Achieving consensus may be slow and expensive ▪ Owners' entire wealth at risk ▪ Withdrawal of partner may create capital shortage ▪ Cost of capital and labor is high relative to that of a corporation
Corporation	▪ Owners have limited liability ▪ Large-scale, low-cost capital available ▪ Professional management not restricted by ability of owners ▪ Perpetual life ▪ Long-term labor contracts cut labor costs	▪ Complex management structure can make decisions slow and expensive ▪ Retained profits taxed twice: as company profit and as stockholders' capital gains

Economics in Action

Types of Firms in the Economy

Three types of firms operate in the United States: proprietorships, partnerships, and corporations. Which type of firm dominates? Which produces most of the output of the U.S. economy?

Proprietorships Most Common Three quarters of the firms in the United States are proprietorships and they are mainly small businesses. Almost one fifth of the firms are corporations, and only a twentieth are partnerships (see Fig. 1).

Corporations Produce Most Corporations generate almost 90 percent of business revenue. Revenue is a measure of the value of production, so corporations produce most of the output in the U.S. economy.

Variety Across Industries In agriculture, forestry, and fishing, proprietorships generate about 40 percent of the total revenue. Proprietorships also generate a significant percentage of the revenue in services, construction, and retail trade. Partnerships account for a small percentage of revenue in all sectors and feature most in agriculture, forestry, and fishing, services, and mining. Corporations dominate all sectors and have the manufacturing industries almost to themselves.

Why do corporations dominate the business scene? Why do the other types of businesses survive? And why are proprietorships and partnerships more prominent in some sectors? The answers lie in the pros and cons of the different types of business organization. Corporations dominate where a large amount of capital is used; proprietorships dominate where flexibility in decision making is critical.

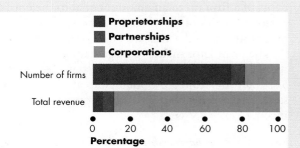

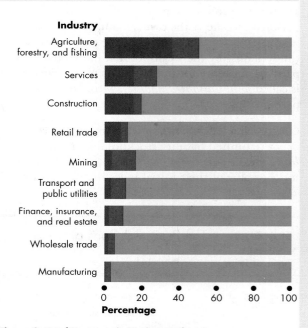

Figure 1 **Number of Firms and Total Revenue**

Figure 2 **Total Revenue in Various Industries**

Source of data: U.S. Bureau of the Census, *Statistical Abstract of the United States,* 2001.

REVIEW QUIZ

1 Explain the distinction between a command system and an incentive system.
2 What is the principal–agent problem? What are three ways in which firms try to cope with it?
3 What are the three types of firms? Explain the major advantages and disadvantages of each.

You can work these questions in Study Plan 10.3 and get instant feedback.   MyEconLab

You've now seen how technology constraints and information constraints influence the way firms operate. You've seen why some firms operate with a large amount of labor and human capital and a small amount of physical capital. You've also seen how firms use a mixture of command and incentive systems and employ different types of business organization to cope with the principal–agent problem.

Your next task is to look at the variety of market situations in which firms operate and classify the different market environments in which firms do business.

Markets and the Competitive Environment

The markets in which firms operate vary a great deal. Some are highly competitive, and profits in these markets are hard to come by. Some appear to be almost free from competition, and firms in these markets earn large profits. Some markets are dominated by fierce advertising campaigns in which each firm seeks to persuade buyers that it has the best products. And some markets display the character of a strategic game.

Economists identify four market types:

1. Perfect competition
2. Monopolistic competition
3. Oligopoly
4. Monopoly

Perfect competition arises when there are many firms, each selling an identical product, many buyers, and no restrictions on the entry of new firms into the industry. The many firms and buyers are all well informed about the prices of the products of each firm in the industry. The worldwide markets for wheat, corn, rice, and other grain crops are examples of perfect competition.

Monopolistic competition is a market structure in which a large number of firms compete by making similar but slightly different products. Making a product slightly different from the product of a competing firm is called **product differentiation**. Product differentiation gives a firm in monopolistic competition an element of market power. The firm is the sole producer of the particular version of the good in question. For example, in the market for pizzas, hundreds of firms make their own version of the perfect pizza. Each of these firms is the sole producer of a particular brand. Differentiated products are not necessarily different products. What matters is that consumers perceive them to be different. For example, different brands of potato chips and ketchup might be almost identical but be perceived by consumers to be different.

Oligopoly is a market structure in which a small number of firms compete. Computer software, airplane manufacture, and international air transportation are examples of oligopolistic industries. Oligopolies might produce almost identical products, such as the colas produced by Coke and Pepsi. Or they might produce differentiated products such as Boeing and Airbus aircraft.

Monopoly arises when there is one firm, which produces a good or service that has no close substitutes and in which the firm is protected by a barrier preventing the entry of new firms. In some places, the phone, gas, electricity, cable television, and water suppliers are local monopolies—monopolies restricted to a given location. Microsoft Corporation, the software developer that created Windows, the operating system for the personal computer, is an example of a global monopoly.

Perfect competition is the most extreme form of competition. Monopoly is the most extreme absence of competition. The other two market types fall between these extremes.

Many factors must be taken into account to determine which market structure describes a particular real-world market. One of these factors is the extent to which a small number of firms dominates the market. To measure this feature of markets, economists use indexes called measures of concentration. Let's look at these measures.

Measures of Concentration

Economists use two measures of concentration:

- The four-firm concentration ratio
- The Herfindahl-Hirschman Index

The Four-Firm Concentration Ratio The **four-firm concentration ratio** is the percentage of the value of sales accounted for by the four largest firms in an industry. The range of the concentration ratio is from almost zero for perfect competition to 100 percent for monopoly. This ratio is the main measure used to assess market structure.

Table 10.5 shows two calculations of the four-firm concentration ratio: one for tire makers and one for

printers. In this example, 14 firms produce tires. The largest four have 80 percent of the sales, so the four-firm concentration ratio is 80 percent. In the printing industry, with 1,004 firms, the largest four firms have only 0.5 percent of the sales, so the four-firm concentration ratio is 0.5 percent.

A low concentration ratio indicates a high degree of competition, and a high concentration ratio indicates an absence of competition. A monopoly has a concentration ratio of 100 percent—the largest (and only) firm has 100 percent of the sales. A four-firm concentration ratio that exceeds 60 percent is regarded as an indication of a market that is highly concentrated and dominated by a few firms in an oligopoly. A ratio of less than 60 percent is regarded as an indication of a competitive market.

The Herfindahl-Hirschman Index The **Herfindahl-Hirschman Index**—also called the HHI—is the square of the percentage market share of each firm summed over the largest 50 firms (or summed over all the firms if there are fewer than 50) in a market. For example, if there are four firms in a market and the market shares of the firms are 50 percent, 25 percent, 15 percent, and 10 percent, the Herfindahl-Hirschman Index is

$$HHI = 50^2 + 25^2 + 15^2 + 10^2 = 3,450.$$

TABLE 10.5 Calculating the Four-Firm Concentration Ratio

Tire makers		Printers	
Firm	**Sales** (millions of dollars)	**Firm**	**Sales** (millions of dollars)
Top, Inc.	200	Fran's	2.5
ABC, Inc.	250	Ned's	2.0
Big, Inc.	150	Tom's	1.8
XYZ, Inc.	100	Jill's	1.7
Largest 4 firms	700	Largest 4 firms	8.0
Other 10 firms	175	Other 1,000 firms	1,592.0
Industry	875	Industry	1,600.0

Four-firm concentration ratios:

Tire makers: $\frac{700}{875} \times 100 = 80$ percent

Printers: $\frac{8}{1,600} \times 100 = 0.5$ percent

Economics in Action
Concentration in the U.S. Economy

The U.S. Department of Commerce calculates and publishes data showing concentration ratios and the HHI for each industry in the United States. The bars in the figure show the four-firm concentration ratio and the number at the end of each bar is the HHI.

Chewing gum is one of the most concentrated industries. William Wrigley Jr. Company of Chicago employs 16,000 people and sells $5 billion worth of gum a year. It does have some competitors, but they have a very small market share.

Household laundry equipment, light bulbs, breakfast cereal, and motor vehicles are highly concentrated industries. They are oligopolies.

Pet food, cookies and crackers, computers, and soft drinks are moderately concentrated industries. They are examples of monopolistic competition.

Ice cream, milk, clothing, concrete blocks and bricks, and commercial printing have low concentration measures and are highly competitive industries.

Concentration measures are useful indicators of the degree of competition in a market, but they must be supplemented by other information to determine the structure of the market.

Newspapers and automobiles are examples of how the concentration measures give a misleading reading of the degree of competition. Most newspapers are local. They serve a single city or even a smaller area. So despite the low concentration measure, newspapers are concentrated in their own local areas. Automobiles are traded internationally and foreign cars are freely imported into the United States. Despite the high U.S. concentration measure, the automobile industry is competitive.

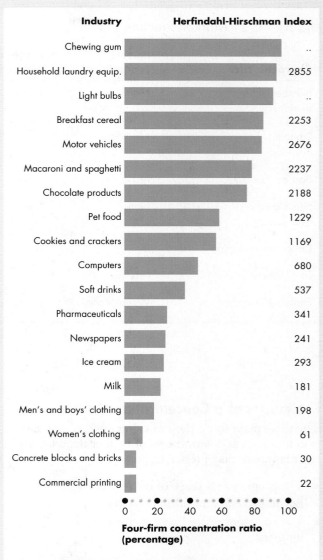

Concentration Measures in the United States

Source of data: Concentration Ratios in Manufacturing (Washington, D.C.: U.S. Department of Commerce,1996).

In perfect competition, the HHI is small. For example, if each of the largest 50 firms in an industry has a market share of 0.1 percent, then the HHI is $0.1^2 \times 50 = 0.5$. In a monopoly, the HHI is 10,000. The firm has 100 percent of the market: $100^2 = 10,000$.

The HHI became a popular measure of the degree of competition during the 1980s, when the Justice Department used it to classify markets. A market in which the HHI is less than 1,000 is regarded as being competitive. A market in which the HHI lies between 1,000 and 1,800 is regarded as being moderately competitive. But a market in which the HHI exceeds 1,800 is regarded as being uncompetitive. The Justice Department scrutinizes any merger of firms in a market in which the HHI exceeds 1,000 and is likely to challenge a merger if the HHI exceeds 1,800.

TABLE 10.6 Market Structure

Characteristics	Perfect competition	Monopolistic competition	Oligopoly	Monopoly
Number of firms in industry	Many	Many	Few	One
Product	Identical	Differentiated	Either identical or differentiated	No close substitutes
Barriers to entry	None	None	Moderate	High
Firm's control over price	None	Some	Considerable	Considerable or regulated
Concentration ratio	0	Low	High	100
HHI (approx. ranges)	Less than 100	101 to 1,800	More than 1,800	10,000
Examples	Wheat, corn	Food, clothing	Computer chips	Local water supply

Limitations of a Concentration Measure

The three main limitations of using only concentration measures as determinants of market structure are their failure to take proper account of

- The geographical scope of the market
- Barriers to entry and firm turnover
- The correspondence between a market and an industry

Geographical Scope of Market Concentration measures take a national view of the market. Many goods are sold in a *national* market, but some are sold in a *regional* market and some in a *global* one. The concentration measures for newspapers are low, indicating competition, but in most cities the newspaper industry is highly concentrated. The concentration measures for automobiles are high, indicating little competition, but the biggest three U.S. car makers compete with foreign car makers in a highly competitive global market.

Barriers to Entry and Firm Turnover Some markets are highly concentrated but entry is easy and the turnover of firms is large. For example, small towns have few restaurants, but no restrictions hinder a new restaurant from opening and many attempt to do so.

Also, a market with only a few firms might be competitive because of *potential entry*. The few firms in a market face competition from the many potential firms that will enter the market if economic profit opportunities arise.

Market and Industry Correspondence To calculate concentration ratios, the Department of Commerce classifies each firm as being in a particular industry. But markets do not always correspond closely to industries for three reasons.

First, markets are often narrower than industries. For example, the pharmaceutical industry, which has a low concentration ratio, operates in many separate markets for individual products—for example, measles vaccine and AIDS-fighting drugs. These drugs do not compete with each other, so this industry, which looks competitive, includes firms that are monopolies (or near monopolies) in markets for individual drugs.

Second, most firms make several products. For example, Westinghouse makes electrical equipment and, among other things, gas-fired incinerators and plywood. So this one firm operates in at least three separate markets, but the Department of Commerce classifies Westinghouse as being in the electrical goods and equipment industry. The fact that Westinghouse competes with other producers of plywood does not

Economics in Action
A Competitive Environment

How competitive are markets in the United States? Do most U.S. firms operate in competitive markets, in monopolistic competition, in oligopoly, or in monopoly markets?

The data needed to answer these questions are hard to get. The last attempt to answer the questions, in a study by William G. Shepherd, an economics professor at the University of Massachusetts at Amherst, covered the years from 1939 to 1980. The figure shows what he discovered.

In 1980, three quarters of the value of goods and services bought and sold in the United States was traded in markets that are essentially competitive—markets that have almost perfect competition or monopolistic competition. Monopoly and the dominance of a single firm accounted for about 5 percent of sales. Oligopoly, which is found mainly in manufacturing, accounted for about 18 percent of sales.

Over the period studied, the U.S. economy became increasingly competitive. The percentage of output sold by firms operating in competitive markets (blue bars) has expanded most, and has shrunk most in oligopoly markets (red bars).

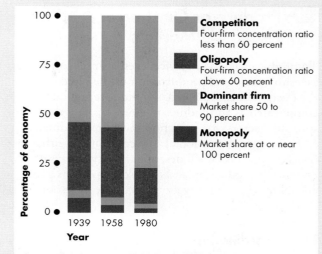

The Market Structure of the U.S. Economy

Source of data: William G. Shepherd, "Causes of Increased Competition in the U.S. Economy, 1939–1980," *Review of Economics and Statistics*, Vol 64, No 4 (November, 1982), pp. 613–626. © 1982 by the President and Fellows of Harvard College. Reprinted with permission.

But also during the past decades, the U.S. economy has become much more exposed to competition from the rest of the world. The data used by William G. Shepherd don't capture this international competition, so the data probably understate the degree of true competition in the U.S. economy.

show up in the concentration numbers for the plywood market.

Third, firms switch from one market to another depending on profit opportunities. For example, Motorola, which today produces cellular telephones and other communications products, has diversified from being a TV and computer chip maker. Motorola no longer produces TVs. Publishers of newspapers, magazines, and textbooks are today rapidly diversifying into Internet and multimedia products. These switches among markets show that there is much scope for entering and exiting a market, and so measures of concentration have limited usefulness.

Despite their limitations, concentration measures do provide a basis for determining the degree of competition in a market when they are combined with information about the geographical scope of the market, barriers to entry, and the extent to which large, multiproduct firms straddle a variety of markets.

REVIEW QUIZ

1 What are the four market types? Explain the distinguishing characteristics of each.
2 What are the two measures of concentration? Explain how each measure is calculated.
3 Under what conditions do the measures of concentration give a good indication of the degree of competition in a market?
4 Is the U.S. economy competitive? Is it becoming more competitive or less competitive?

You can work these questions in Study Plan 10.4 and get instant feedback.   MyEconLab

You now know the variety of market types and how we identify them. Our final question in this chapter is: What determines the things that firms decide to buy from other firms rather than produce for themselves?

◆ Produce or Outsource? Firms and Markets

To produce a good or service, even a simple one such as a shirt, factors of production must be hired and their activities coordinated. To produce a good as complicated as an iPhone, an enormous range of specialist factors of production must be coordinated.

Factors of production can be coordinated either by firms or markets. We'll describe these two ways of organizing production and then see why firms play a crucial role in achieving an efficient use of resources.

Firm Coordination

Firms hire labor, capital, and land, and by using a mixture of command systems and incentive systems (see p. 229) organize and coordinate their activities to produce goods and services.

Firm coordination occurs when you take your car to the garage for an oil change, brake check, and service. The garage owner hires a mechanic and tools and coordinates all the activities that get your car serviced. Firms also coordinate the production of cornflakes, golf clubs, and a host of other items.

Market Coordination

Markets coordinate production by adjusting prices and making the decisions of buyers and sellers of factors of production and components consistent.

Market coordination occurs to produce a rock concert. A promoter books a stadium, rents some stage equipment, hires some audio and video recording engineers and technicians, engages some rock groups, a superstar, a publicity agent, and a ticket agent. The promoter sells tickets to thousands of rock fans, audio rights to a recording company, and video and broadcasting rights to a television network. All these transactions take place in markets that coordinate the buying and selling of this huge variety of factors of production.

Outsourcing, buying parts or products from other firms, is another example of market coordination. Dell outsources the production of all the components of its computers. Automakers outsource the production of windshields, windows, transmission systems, engines, tires, and many other auto parts. Apple outsources the entire production of iPods, iPads, and iPhones.

Why Firms?

What determines whether a firm or a market coordinates a particular set of activities? How does a firm decide whether to buy an item from another firm or manufacture it itself? The answer is cost. Taking account of the opportunity cost of time as well as the costs of the other inputs, a firm uses the method that costs least. In other words, it uses the economically efficient method.

If a task can be performed at a lower cost by markets than by a firm, markets will do the job, and any attempt to set up a firm to replace such market activity will be doomed to failure.

Firms coordinate economic activity when a task can be performed more efficiently by a firm than by markets. In such a situation, it is profitable to set up a firm. Firms are often more efficient than markets as coordinators of economic activity because they can achieve

- Lower transactions costs
- Economies of scale
- Economies of scope
- Economies of team production

Transactions Costs Firms eliminate transactions costs. **Transactions costs** are the costs that arise from finding someone with whom to do business, of reaching an agreement about the price and other aspects of the exchange, and of ensuring that the terms of the agreement are fulfilled. Market transactions require buyers and sellers to get together and to negotiate the terms and conditions of their trading. Sometimes, lawyers have to be hired to draw up contracts. A broken contract leads to still more expense. A firm can lower such transactions costs by reducing the number of individual transactions undertaken.

Imagine getting your car fixed using market coordination. You hire a mechanic to diagnose the problems and make a list of the parts and tools needed to fix them. You buy the parts from several dealers, rent the tools from ABC Rentals, hire an auto mechanic, return the tools, and pay your bills. You can avoid all these transactions and the time they cost you by letting your local garage fix the car.

Economies of Scale When the cost of producing a unit of a good falls as its output rate increases, **economies of scale** exist. An automaker experiences economies of scale because as the scale of production increases, the firm can use cost-saving equipment and

Economics in Action
Apple Doesn't Make the iPhone!

Apple designed the iPhone and markets it, but Apple doesn't manufacture it. Why? Apple wants to produce the iPhone at the lowest possible cost. Apple achieves its goal by assigning the production task to more than 30 firms, some of which are listed in the table opposite. These 30 firms produce the components in Asia, Europe, and North America and then the components are assembled in its sleek, iconic case by Foxconn and Quanta in Taiwan.

Most electronic products—TVs, DVD players, iPods and iPads, and personal computers—are produced in a similar way to the iPhone with a combination of firm and market coordination. Hundreds of little-known firms compete fiercely to get their components into well-known consumer products.

Altus Technology	Taiwan
Balda	Germany
Broadcom	United States
Cambridge Silicon Radio	UK
Catcher	Taiwan
Cyntec	Taiwan
Delta Electronics	Taiwan
Epson	Japan
Foxconn	Taiwan
Infineon Technologies	Germany
Intel	United States
Largan Precision	Taiwan
Lite-On	Taiwan
Marvell	United States
Micron	United States
National Semiconductor	United States
Novatek	Taiwan
Primax	Taiwan
Quanta	Taiwan
Samsung	Korea
Sanyo	Japan
Sharp	Japan
Taiwan Semiconductor	Taiwan
TMD	Japan

highly specialized labor. An automaker that produces only a few cars a year must use hand-tool methods that are costly. Economies of scale arise from specialization and the division of labor that can be reaped more effectively by firm coordination rather than market coordination.

Economies of Scope A firm experiences **economies of scope** when it uses specialized (and often expensive) resources to produce a *range of goods and services*. For example, Toshiba uses its designers and specialized equipment to make the hard drive for the iPod. But it makes many different types of hard drives and other related products. As a result, Toshiba produces the iPod hard drive at a lower cost than a firm making only the iPod hard drive could achieve.

Economies of Team Production A production process in which the individuals in a group specialize in mutually supportive tasks is *team production*. Sports provide the best examples of team activity. In baseball, some team members specialize in pitching and others in fielding. In basketball, some team members specialize in defense and some in offense. The production of goods and services offers many examples of team activity. For example, production lines in a TV manufacturing plant work most efficiently when individual activity is organized in teams, each worker specializing in a few tasks. You can also think of an entire firm as being a team. The team has buyers of raw materials and other inputs, production workers, and salespeople. Each individual member of the team

specializes, but the value of the output of the team and the profit that it earns depend on the coordinated activities of all the team's members.

Because firms can economize on transactions costs, reap economies of scale and economies of scope, and organize efficient team production, it is firms rather than markets that coordinate most of our economic activity.

REVIEW QUIZ

1   What are the two ways in which economic activity can be coordinated?
2   What determines whether a firm or markets coordinate production?
3   What are the main reasons why firms can often coordinate production at a lower cost than markets can?

You can work these questions in Study Plan 10.5 and get instant feedback.   MyEconLab

◆ *Reading Between the Lines* on pp. 240–241 explores the market for Internet advertising. In the next four chapters, we continue to study firms and their decisions. In Chapter 11, we learn about the relationships between cost and output at different output levels. These relationships are common to all types of firms in all types of markets. We then turn to problems that are specific to firms in different types of markets.

Battling for Markets in Internet Advertising

Facebook Rolls Out Real-Time Ad Platform

Financial Times
September 14, 2012

Some of the world's largest advertising companies have signed up to Facebook's new real-time advertising platform, in a move that the social network hopes will bolster its revenue streams.

On Thursday, Facebook officially launched the platform, called Facebook Ad Exchange, or FBX, following months of testing. The system allows marketers to bid in real-time to buy ad impressions on the social networking site, and deliver their ads to users based on their immediate web-browsing habits, or linked to current events, such as sports results.

"Real-time marketing is getting to be a really important component of digital advertising," said Rebecca Lieb, an analyst with the Altimeter Group. "We'll see a lot of event-triggered marketing in the upcoming election cycle."

The ads use information gathered from computer browsing histories to target individual Facebook users, and the ad prices fluctuate as in auction-style bidding system. So a user who looks at shoes on a retail site could then see an ad for the same brand when clicking back to Facebook.

The capacity will help Facebook compete more directly with advertising rivals Google and Yahoo, which have long provided real-time bidding to advertisers. ...

Within one tenth of a second, the system notifies when an ad space is available, evaluates 2,000 data points to determine the most relevant ad, calculates a price and prompts the ad to appear.

The global real-time bidding sector is estimated to be worth some $3bn-$4bn, but industry observers expect this to reach as much as $20bn by 2015. ...

ESSENCE OF THE STORY

- Facebook is under pressure to generate advertising revenue.

- Real-time bidding is widely used for Internet advertising and its market share is growing rapidly.

- Facebook and Google are getting better at capturing user activity.

- A new Facebook system will target ads at the user's current interests.

- Advertisers will bid to get their ads in front of the right users.

ECONOMIC ANALYSIS

- Like all firms, Facebook and Google aim to maximize profit.

- Facebook provides social networking services and Google provides search services, a variety of other services, and with Google+ is offering a social networking service.

- Facebook and Google face constraints imposed by the market and technology.

- People who use social networks demand their services, and at the latest count Facebook and another 198 firms supply social networking services.

- People looking for information demand Internet search services, and Google and more than another 100 firms supply Internet search services.

- The equilibrium price of social networking services and of Internet search services is zero, and the equilibrium quantity of each is the quantity demanded at a zero price.

- Social network and Internet search providers enjoy economies of scope: They produce advertising services as well as their other service.

- Unlike social networking and search, Internet advertising is a big revenue and profit generator.

- Because the providers of social networking and search know a lot about their users, they can offer advertisers access to potential customers and charge a high price for this precision.

- Google has been enormously successful at delivering advertising based on a user's search activity, and its revenue has grown from almost zero in 2001 to $38 billion in 2011 (see Fig. 1). Google's profit in 2011 was almost $12 billion (see Fig. 2).

- Facebook is still learning how to tap its advertising potential and the news article describes its plans in 2012 to develop real-time bidding for advertising based on a user's browsing.

- Facebook's revenue is beginning to grow, but by 2011 it had reached only $4 billion (see Fig. 1).

- Providing a social networking service or search service doesn't guarantee success in generating advertising revenue and profit.

- Yahoo! is an example of a firm that hasn't performed as well as its owners would wish.

- As Google and Facebook have seen explosive growth in users and revenues, Yahoo! has struggled.

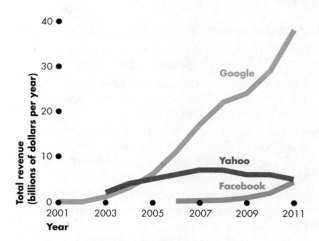

Figure 1 Total Revenue Comparison

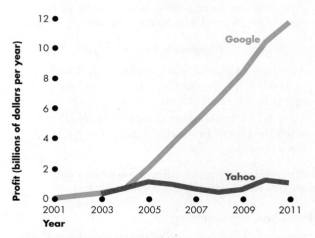

Figure 2 Profit Comparison

- Figure 1 shows that Yahoo's revenue peaked in 2008 and has been falling while Google's has soared and Facebook's has grown to almost equal that of Yahoo!.

- Figure 2 shows that Yahoo's profit has been flat while Google's has soared. (We don't know how much profit Facebook has made.)

- The data shown in Figs. 1 and 2 suggest that so far, Internet search is a more effective tool for generating revenue and profit than social networking. Perhaps Facebook's new revenue model will change that.

- The data also suggest that Facebook's and Google's expansion is tightening the market constraint that Yahoo! faces.

SUMMARY

Key Points

The Firm and Its Economic Problem (pp. 224–226)

- Firms hire and organize factors of production to produce and sell goods and services.
- A firm's goal is to maximize economic profit, which is total revenue minus total cost measured as the opportunity cost of production.
- A firm's opportunity cost of production is the sum of the cost of resources bought in the market, using the firm's own resources, and resources supplied by the firm's owner.
- Normal profit is the opportunity cost of entrepreneurship and is part of the firm's opportunity cost.
- Technology, information, and markets limit the economic profit that a firm can make.

Working Problems 1 and 2 will give you a better understanding of the firm and its economic problem.

Technological and Economic Efficiency (pp. 227–228)

- A method of production is technologically efficient when a firm uses the least amount of inputs to produce a given output.
- A method of production is economically efficient when the cost of producing a given output is as low as possible.

Working Problems 3 and 4 will give you a better understanding of technological and economic efficiency.

Information and Organization (pp. 229–232)

- Firms use a combination of command systems and incentive systems to organize production.
- Faced with incomplete information and uncertainty, firms induce managers and workers to per-

form in ways that are consistent with the firms' goals.
- Proprietorships, partnerships, and corporations use ownership, incentive pay, and long-term contracts to cope with the principal–agent problem.

Working Problems 5 to 8 will give you a better understanding of information and organization.

Markets and the Competitive Environment (pp. 233–237)

- In perfect competition, many sellers offer an identical product to many buyers and entry is free.
- In monopolistic competition, many sellers offer slightly different products to many buyers and entry is free.
- In oligopoly, a small number of sellers compete and barriers to entry limit the number of firms.
- In monopoly, one firm produces an item that has no close substitutes and the firm is protected by a barrier to entry that prevents the entry of competitors.

Working Problems 9 and 10 will give you a better understanding of markets and the competitive environment.

Produce or Outsource? Firms and Markets (pp. 238–239)

- Firms coordinate economic activities when they can perform a task more efficiently—at lower cost—than markets can.
- Firms economize on transactions costs and achieve the benefits of economies of scale, economies of scope, and economies of team production.

Working Problems 11 and 12 will give you a better understanding of firms and markets.

Key Terms

Command system, 229
Economic depreciation, 225
Economic efficiency, 227
Economic profit, 224
Economies of scale, 238
Economies of scope, 239
Firm, 224
Four-firm concentration ratio, 234
Herfindahl-Hirschman Index, 234
Implicit rental rate, 224
Incentive system, 229
Monopolistic competition, 233
Monopoly, 233
Normal profit, 225
Oligopoly, 233
Perfect competition, 233
Principal–agent problem, 229
Product differentiation, 233
Technological efficiency, 227
Technology, 226
Transactions costs, 238

STUDY PLAN PROBLEMS AND APPLICATIONS

MyEconLab   You can work Problems 1 to 13 in MyEconLab Chapter 10 Study Plan and get instant feedback.

The Firm and Its Economic Problem (Study Plan 10.1)

1. One year ago, Jack and Jill set up a vinegar-bottling firm (called JJVB). Use the following information to calculate JJVB's opportunity cost of production during its first year of operation:
   - Jack and Jill put $50,000 of their own money into the firm.
   - They bought equipment for $30,000.
   - They hired one employee to help them for an annual wage of $20,000.
   - Jack gave up his previous job, at which he earned $30,000, and spent all his time working for JJVB.
   - Jill kept her old job, which paid $30 an hour, but gave up 10 hours of leisure each week (for 50 weeks) to work for JJVB.
   - JJVB bought $10,000 of goods and services from other firms.
   - The market value of the equipment at the end of the year was $28,000.
   - Jack and Jill have a $100,000 home loan on which they pay interest of 6 percent a year.

2. Joe, who has no skills, no job experience, and no alternative employment, runs a shoeshine stand at the airport. Operators of other shoeshine stands earn $10,000 a year. Joe pays rent to the airport of $2,000 a year, and his total revenue from shining shoes is $15,000 a year. Joe spent $1,000 on a chair, polish, and brushes, using his credit card to buy them. The interest on a credit card balance is 20 percent a year. At the end of the year, Joe was offered $500 for his business and all its equipment. Calculate Joe's opportunity cost of production and his economic profit.

Technological and Economic Efficiency (Study Plan 10.2)

3. Alternative ways of laundering 100 shirts are

Method	Labor (hours)	Capital (machines)
A	1	10
B	5	8
C	20	4
D	50	1

   a. Which methods are technologically efficient?
   b. Which method is economically efficient if the

hourly wage rate and the implicit rental rate of capital are as follows:
   (i) Wage rate $1, rental rate $100?
   (ii) Wage rate $5, rental rate $50?
   (iii) Wage rate $50, rental rate $5?

4. **John Deere's Farm Team**
   Deere opened up the Pune [India] center in 2001. Deere's move was unexpected: Deere is known for its heavy-duty farm equipment and big construction gear whereas many of India's 300 million farmers still use oxen-pulled plows.
   Source: *Fortune*, April 14, 2008

   a. Why do many Indian farmers still use oxen-pulled plows? Are they efficient or inefficient? Explain.
   b. How might making John Deere farm equipment available to Indian farmers change the technology constraint they face?

Information and Organization (Study Plan 10.3)

5. **Here It Is. Now, You Design It!**
   The idea is that the most successful companies no longer invent new products and services on their own. They create them along with their customers, and they do it in a way that produces a unique experience for each customer. The important corollary is that no company owns enough resources—or can possibly own enough—to furnish unique experiences for each customer, so companies must organize a constantly shifting global web of suppliers and partners to do the job.
   Source: *Fortune*, May 26, 2008

   a. Describe this method of organizing and coordinating production: Does it use a command system or incentive system?
   b. How does this method of organizing and coordinating production help firms achieve lower costs?

6. **Rewarding Failure**
   Over the past 25 years CEO pay has risen faster than corporate profits, economic growth, or average wages. A more sensible alternative to the current compensation system would require CEOs to own a lot of company stock. If the stock is given to the boss, his salary and bonus should be docked to reflect its value. As for bonuses, they

should be based on improving a company's cash earnings relative to its cost of capital, not to manipulated measures like earnings per share. Bonuses should not be capped but be unavailable to the CEO for some period of years.

Source: *Fortune*, April 28, 2008

a. What is the economic problem that CEO compensation schemes are designed to solve?

b. How do the proposed changes to CEO compensation outlined in the news clip address the problem you described in part (a)?

Use the following news clip to work Problems 7 and 8.

Steps to Creating a Super Startup

Starting a business is a complicated and risky task. Just two-thirds of new small businesses survive at least two years, and only 44 percent survive at least four years. Most entrepreneurs start their businesses by dipping into their savings, borrowing from the family, and using the founder's credit cards. Getting a bank loan is tough unless you have assets—and that often means using your home as collateral.

Source: CNN, October 18, 2007

7. When starting a business, what are the risks identified in the news clip that are associated with a proprietorship?

8. How might (i) a partnership and (ii) a corporation help to overcome the risks identified in the news clip?

Markets and the Competitive Environment

(Study Plan 10.4)

9. Sales of the firms in the tattoo industry are

Firm	Sales (dollars per year)
Bright Spots	450
Freckles	325
Love Galore	250
Native Birds	200
Other 15 firms	800

Calculate the four-firm concentration ratio. What is the structure of the tattoo industry?

10. **GameStop Racks Up the Points**

No retailer has more cachet among gamers than GameStop. For now, only Wal-Mart has a larger market share—21.3% last year. GameStop's share was 21.1% last year, and may well overtake Wal-Mart this year. But if new women gamers prefer shopping at Target to GameStop, Wal-Mart and Target might erode GameStop's market share.

Source: *Fortune*, June 9, 2008

a. According to the news clip, what is the structure of the U.S. retail video-game market?

b. Estimate a range for the four-firm concentration ratio and the HHI for the game market in the United States based on the information provided in this news clip.

Produce or Outsource? Firms and Markets

(Study Plan 10.5)

11. American automakers buy auto parts from independent suppliers rather than produce the parts themselves. In the 1980s, Chrysler got about 70 percent of its auto parts from independent suppliers, while Ford got about 60 percent and General Motors got 25 percent. A decade earlier, the proportions were 50 percent at Chrysler, 5 percent at Ford, and 20 percent at General Motors.

Source: The Cato Institute Policy Analysis, 1987

a. Why did American automakers decide to outsource most of their parts production?

b. Explain why independent producers of auto parts are more efficient than the automakers.

12. Federal Express enters into contracts with independent truck operators who offer FedEx service and who are rewarded by the volume of packages they carry. Why doesn't FedEx buy more trucks and hire more drivers? What incentive problems might arise from this arrangement?

Economics in the News (Study Plan 10.N)

13. Lego, the Danish toymaker, incurred economic losses in 2003 and 2004 as it faced competition from low-cost copiers of its products and a fall in demand. In 2004, to restore profits, Lego fired 3,500 of its 8,000 workers; closed factories in Switzerland and the United States; opened factories in Eastern Europe and Mexico; and introduced performance-based pay for its managers. Lego returned to profit in 2005.

Based on **Picking Up the Pieces**,
The Economist, October 28, 2006

a. Describe the problems that Lego faced in 2003 and 2004, using the concepts of the three types of constraints that all firms face.

b. Which of the actions that Lego took to restore profits addressed an inefficiency? How did Lego seek to achieve economic efficiency?

c. Which of Lego's actions addressed an information and organization problem? How did Lego change the way in which it coped with the principal–agent problem?

d. In what type of market does Lego operate?

ADDITIONAL PROBLEMS AND APPLICATIONS

MyEconLab   You can work these problems in MyEconLab if assigned by your instructor.

The Firm and Its Economic Problem

Use the following information to work Problems 14 and 15.

Lee is a computer programmer who earned $35,000 in 2011. But on January 1, 2012, Lee opened a body board manufacturing business. At the end of the first year of operation, he submitted the following information to his accountant:

- He stopped renting out his cottage for $3,500 a year and used it as his factory. The market value of the cottage increased from $70,000 to $71,000.
- He spent $50,000 on materials, phone, etc.
- He leased machines for $10,000 a year.
- He paid $15,000 in wages.
- He used $10,000 from his savings account, which earns 5 percent a year interest.
- He borrowed $40,000 at 10 percent a year.
- He sold $160,000 worth of body boards.
- Normal profit is $25,000 a year.

14. Calculate Lee's opportunity cost of production and his economic profit.

15. Lee's accountant recorded the depreciation on his cottage during 2012 as $7,000. According to the accountant, what profit did Lee make?

16. In 2011, Toni taught music and earned $20,000. She also earned $4,000 by renting out her basement. On January 1, 2012, she quit teaching, stopped renting out her basement, and began to use it as the office for her new Web site design business. She took $2,000 from her savings account to buy a computer. During 2012, she paid $1,500 for the lease of a Web server and $1,750 for high-speed Internet service. She received a total revenue from Web site designing of $45,000 and earned interest at 5 percent a year on her savings account balance. Normal profit is $55,000 a year. At the end of 2012, Toni could have sold her computer for $500. Calculate Toni's opportunity cost of production and her economic profit in 2012.

17. **The Colvin Interview: Chrysler**

The key driver of profitability will be that the focus of the company isn't on profitability. Our focus is on the customer. If we can find a way to give customers what they want better than anybody else, then what can stop us?

Source: *Fortune*, April 14, 2008

a. In spite of what Chrysler's vice chairman and co-president claims, why is Chrysler's focus actually on profitability?

b. What would happen to Chrysler if it didn't focus on maximizing profit, but instead focused its production and pricing decisions to "give customers what they want"?

18. **Must Watches**

Stocks too volatile? Bonds too boring? Then try an alternative investment—one you can wear on your wrist. ... [The] typical return on a watch over five to ten years is roughly 10%. [One could] do better in an index fund, but ... what other investment is so wearable?

Source: *Fortune*, April 14, 2008

a. What is the cost of buying a watch?

b. What is the opportunity cost of owning a watch?

c. Does owning a watch create an economic profit opportunity?

Technological and Economic Efficiency

Use the following information to work Problems 19 and 20.

Four methods of completing a tax return and the time taken by each method are: with a PC, 1 hour; with a pocket calculator, 12 hours; with a pocket calculator and paper and pencil, 12 hours; and with a pencil and paper, 16 hours. The PC and its software cost $1,000, the pocket calculator costs $10, and the pencil and paper cost $1.

19. Which, if any, of the methods is technologically efficient?

20. Which method is economically efficient if the wage rate is

(i) $5 an hour?

(ii) $50 an hour?

(iii) $500 an hour?

21. **A Medical Sensation**

Hospitals are buying da Vinci surgical robots. Surgeons, sitting comfortably at a da Vinci console, can use various robotic attachments to perform even the most complex procedures.

Source: *Fortune*, April 28, 2008

a. Assume that performing a surgery with a surgical robot requires fewer surgeons and nurses.

Is using the surgical robot technologically efficient?

b. What additional information would you need to be able to say that switching to surgical robots is economically efficient for a hospital?

Information and Organization

22. Wal-Mart has more than 3,700 stores, more than one million employees, and total revenues of close to a quarter of a trillion dollars in the United States alone. Sarah Frey-Talley runs the family-owned Frey Farms in Illinois and supplies Wal-Mart with pumpkins and other fresh produce.

a. How does Wal-Mart coordinate its activities? Is it likely to use mainly a command system or also to use incentive systems? Explain.

b. How do you think Sarah Frey-Talley coordinates the activities of Frey Farms? Is she likely to use mainly a command system or also to use incentive systems? Explain.

c. Describe, compare, and contrast the principal–agent problems faced by Wal-Mart and Frey Farms. How might these firms cope with their principal–agent problems?

23. **Where Does Google Go Next?**

Google gives its engineers one day a week to work on whatever project they want. A couple of colleagues did what many of the young geniuses do at Google: They came up with a cool idea. At Google, you often end up with a laissez-faire mess instead of resource allocation.

Source: *Fortune*, May 26, 2008

a. Describe Google's method of organizing production with their software engineers.

b. What are the potential gains and opportunity costs associated with this method?

Markets and the Competitive Environment

24. Market shares of chocolate makers are

Firm	Market share (percent)
Truffles, Inc.	25
Magic, Inc.	20
Mayfair, Inc.	15
All Natural, Inc.	15
Gold, Inc.	15
Bond, Inc.	10

Calculate the Herfindahl-Hirschman Index. What is the structure of the chocolate industry?

Produce or Outsource? Firms and Markets

Use the following information to work Problems 25 to 27.

Two leading design firms, Astro Studios of San Francisco and Hers Experimental Design Laboratory, Inc. of Osaka, Japan, worked with Microsoft to design the Xbox 360 video game console. IBM, ATI, and SiS designed the Xbox 360's hardware. Three firms—Flextronics, Wistron, and Celestica—manufacture the Xbox 360 at their plants in China and Taiwan.

25. Describe the roles of market coordination and coordination by firms in the design, manufacture, and marketing of the Xbox 360.

26. a. Why do you think Microsoft works with a large number of other firms, rather than performing all the required tasks itself?

b. What are the roles of transactions costs, economies of scale, economies of scope, and economies of team production in the design, manufacture, and marketing of the Xbox?

27. Why do you think the Xbox is designed in the United States and Japan but built in China?

Economics in the News

28. After you have studied *Reading Between the Lines* on pp. 240–241, answer the following questions.

a. What products do Facebook and Google sell?

b. In what types of markets do Facebook and Google compete?

c. How do social networks and Internet search providers generate revenue?

d. What is special about social networking sites that make them attractive to advertisers?

e. What is special about Internet search providers that make them attractive to advertisers?

f. What technological changes might increase the profitability of social networks compared to Internet search providers?

29. **Long Reviled, Merit Pay Gains Among Teachers**

School districts in many states experiment with plans that compensate teachers partly based on classroom performance, rather than their years on the job and coursework completed. Working with mentors to improve their instruction and getting bonuses for raising student achievement encourages efforts to raise teaching quality.

Source: *The New York Times*, June 18, 2007

How does "merit pay" attempt to cope with the principal–agent problem in public education?

11

OUTPUT AND COSTS

After studying this chapter, you will be able to:

◆ Distinguish between the short run and the long run

◆ Explain and illustrate a firm's short-run product curves

◆ Explain and derive a firm's short-run cost curves

◆ Explain and derive a firm's long-run average cost curve

What do McDonald's and Campus Sweaters, a small (fictional) producer of knitwear that we'll study in this chapter, have in common? They must decide how much to produce, how many people to employ, and how much and what type of capital equipment to use. How do firms make these decisions?

We are going to answer these questions in this chapter and apply what we learn to the real-world costs of a grocery store checkout line. In *Reading Between the Lines*, we'll look at how recent decisions made by McDonald's in Ohio affect its production costs.

▶ Decision Time Frames

People who operate firms make many decisions, and all of their decisions are aimed at achieving one overriding goal: maximum attainable profit. But not all decisions are equally critical. Some decisions are big ones. Once made, they are costly (or impossible) to reverse. If such a decision turns out to be incorrect, it might lead to the failure of the firm. Other decisions are small. They are easily changed. If one of these decisions turns out to be incorrect, the firm can change its actions and survive.

The biggest decision that an entrepreneur makes is in what industry to establish a firm. For most entrepreneurs, their background knowledge and interests drive this decision. But the decision also depends on profit prospects—on the expectation that total revenue will exceed total cost.

Cindy has decided to set up Campus Sweaters. She has also decided the most effective method of organizing the firm. But she has not decided the quantity to produce, the factors of production to hire, or the price to charge for sweaters.

Decisions about the quantity to produce and the price to charge depend on the type of market in which the firm operates. Perfect competition, monopolistic competition, oligopoly, and monopoly all confront the firm with *different* problems. Decisions about *how* to produce a given output do not depend on the type of market in which the firm operates. *All* types of firms in *all* types of markets make similar decisions about how to produce.

The actions that a firm can take to influence the relationship between output and cost depend on how soon the firm wants to act. A firm that plans to change its output rate tomorrow has fewer options than one that plans to change its output rate six months or six years in the future.

To study the relationship between a firm's output decision and its costs, we distinguish between two decision time frames:

- The short run
- The long run

The Short Run

The **short run** is a time frame in which the quantity of at least one factor of production is fixed. For most firms, capital, land, and entrepreneurship are fixed factors of production and labor is the variable factor of production. We call the fixed factors of production the firm's *plant*: In the short run, a firm's plant is fixed.

For Campus Sweaters, the fixed plant is its factory building and its knitting machines. For an electric power utility, the fixed plant is its buildings, generators, computers, and control systems.

To increase output in the short run, a firm must increase the quantity of a variable factor of production, which is usually labor. So to produce more output, Campus Sweaters must hire more labor and operate its knitting machines for more hours a day. Similarly, an electric power utility must hire more labor and operate its generators for more hours a day.

Short-run decisions are easily reversed. The firm can increase or decrease its output in the short run by increasing or decreasing the amount of labor it hires.

The Long Run

The **long run** is a time frame in which the quantities of *all* factors of production can be varied. That is, the long run is a period in which the firm can change its *plant*.

To increase output in the long run, a firm can change its plant as well as the quantity of labor it hires. Campus Sweaters can decide whether to install more knitting machines, use a new type of machine, reorganize its management, or hire more labor. Long-run decisions are *not* easily reversed. Once a plant decision is made, the firm usually must live with it for some time. To emphasize this fact, we call the past expenditure on a plant that has no resale value a **sunk cost**. A sunk cost is irrelevant to the firm's current decisions. The only costs that influence its current decisions are the short-run cost of changing its labor inputs and the long-run cost of changing its plant.

◀ REVIEW QUIZ

1 Distinguish between the short run and the long run.
2 Why is a sunk cost irrelevant to a firm's current decisions?

You can work these questions in Study Plan 11.1 and get instant feedback.   MyEconLab

We're going to study costs in the short run and the long run. We begin with the short run and describe a firm's technology constraint.

Short-Run Technology Constraint

To increase output in the short run, a firm must increase the quantity of labor employed. We describe the relationship between output and the quantity of labor employed by using three related concepts:

1. Total product
2. Marginal product
3. Average product

These product concepts can be illustrated either by product schedules or by product curves. Let's look first at the product schedules.

Product Schedules

Table 11.1 shows some data that describe Campus Sweaters' total product, marginal product, and average product. The numbers tell us how the quantity of sweaters produced increases as Campus Sweaters employs more workers. The numbers also tell us about the productivity of the labor that Campus Sweaters employs.

Focus first on the columns headed "Labor" and "Total product." **Total product** is the maximum output that a given quantity of labor can produce. You can see from the numbers in these columns that as Campus Sweaters employs more labor, total product increases. For example, when 1 worker is employed, total product is 4 sweaters a day, and when 2 workers are employed, total product is 10 sweaters a day. Each increase in employment increases total product.

The **marginal product** of labor is the increase in total product that results from a one-unit increase in the quantity of labor employed, with all other inputs remaining the same. For example, in Table 11.1, when Campus Sweaters increases employment from 2 to 3 workers and does not change its capital, the marginal product of the third worker is 3 sweaters—total product increases from 10 to 13 sweaters.

Average product tells how productive workers are on average. The **average product** of labor is equal to total product divided by the quantity of labor employed. For example, in Table 11.1, the average product of 3 workers is 4.33 sweaters per worker— 13 sweaters a day divided by 3 workers.

If you look closely at the numbers in Table 11.1, you can see some patterns. As Campus Sweaters hires more labor, marginal product increases initially, and

TABLE 11.1   Total Product, Marginal Product, and Average Product

	Labor (workers per day)	Total product (sweaters per day)	Marginal product (sweaters per additional worker)	Average product (sweaters per worker)
A	0	0		
			 4	
B	1	4		4.00
			 6	
C	2	10		5.00
			 3	
D	3	13		**4.33**
			 2	
E	4	15		3.75
			 1	
F	5	16		3.20

Total product is the total amount produced. Marginal product is the change in total product that results from a one-unit increase in labor. For example, when labor increases from 2 to 3 workers a day (row C to row D), total product increases from 10 to 13 sweaters a day. The marginal product of going from 2 to 3 workers is 3 sweaters. Average product is total product divided by the quantity of labor employed. For example, the average product of 3 workers is 4.33 sweaters per worker (13 sweaters a day divided by 3 workers).

then begins to decrease. For example, marginal product increases from 4 sweaters a day for the first worker to 6 sweaters a day for the second worker and then decreases to 3 sweaters a day for the third worker. Average product also increases at first and then decreases. You can see the relationships between the quantity of labor hired and the three product concepts more clearly by looking at the product curves.

Product Curves

The product curves are graphs of the relationships between employment and the three product concepts you've just studied. They show how total product, marginal product, and average product change as employment changes. They also show the relationships among the three concepts. Let's look at the product curves.

Total Product Curve

Figure 11.1 shows Campus Sweaters' total product curve, *TP*, which is a graph of the total product schedule. Points *A* through *F* correspond to rows *A* through *F* in Table 11.1. To graph the entire total product curve, we vary labor by hours rather than whole days.

Notice the shape of the total product curve. As employment increases from zero to 1 worker a day, the curve becomes steeper. Then, as employment increases to 3, 4, and 5 workers a day, the curve becomes less steep.

The total product curve is similar to the *production possibilities frontier* (explained in Chapter 2). It separates the attainable output levels from those that are unattainable. All the points that lie above the curve are unattainable. Points that lie below the curve, in the orange area, are attainable, but they are inefficient—they use more labor than is necessary to produce a given output. Only the points *on* the total product curve are technologically efficient.

FIGURE 11.1 Total Product Curve

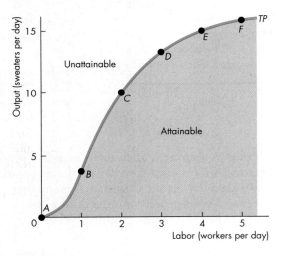

The total product curve, *TP*, is based on the data in Table 11.1. The total product curve shows how the quantity of sweaters produced changes as the quantity of labor employed changes. For example, 2 workers can produce 10 sweaters a day (point *C*). Points *A* through *F* on the curve correspond to the rows of Table 11.1. The total product curve separates attainable outputs from unattainable outputs. Points below the *TP* curve are inefficient.

—— MyEconLab animation ——

Marginal Product Curve

Figure 11.2 shows Campus Sweaters' marginal product of labor. Part (a) reproduces the total product curve from Fig. 11.1 and part (b) shows the marginal product curve, *MP*.

In part (a), the orange bars illustrate the marginal product of labor. The height of a bar measures marginal product. Marginal product is also measured by the slope of the total product curve. Recall that the slope of a curve is the change in the value of the variable measured on the *y*-axis—output—divided by the change in the variable measured on the *x*-axis—labor—as we move along the curve. A one-unit increase in labor, from 2 to 3 workers, increases output from 10 to 13 sweaters, so the slope from point *C* to point *D* is 3 sweaters per additional worker, the same as the marginal product we've just calculated.

Again varying the amount of labor in the smallest units possible, we can draw the marginal product curve shown in Fig. 11.2(b). The *height* of this curve measures the *slope* of the total product curve at a point. Part (a) shows that an increase in employment from 2 to 3 workers increases output from 10 to 13 sweaters (an increase of 3). The increase in output of 3 sweaters appears on the *y*-axis of part (b) as the marginal product of going from 2 to 3 workers. We plot that marginal product at the midpoint between 2 and 3 workers. Notice that the marginal product shown in Fig. 11.2(b) reaches a peak at 1.5 workers, and at that point, marginal product is 6 sweaters per additional worker. The peak occurs at 1.5 workers because the total product curve is steepest when employment increases from 1 worker to 2 workers.

The total product and marginal product curves differ across firms and types of goods. GM's product curves are different from those of PennPower, whose curves in turn are different from those of Campus Sweaters. But the shapes of the product curves are similar because almost every production process has two features:

- Increasing marginal returns initially
- Diminishing marginal returns eventually

Increasing Marginal Returns Increasing marginal returns occur when the marginal product of an additional worker exceeds the marginal product of the previous worker. Increasing marginal returns arise from increased specialization and division of labor in the production process.

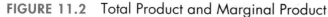

FIGURE 11.2   Total Product and Marginal Product

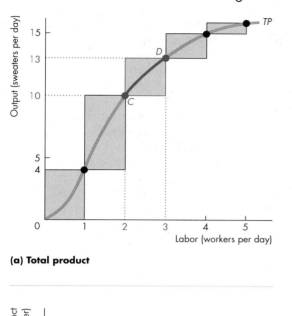

(a) Total product

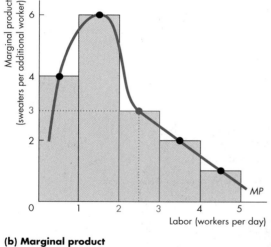

(b) Marginal product

Marginal product is illustrated by the orange bars. For example, when labor increases from 2 to 3 workers a day, marginal product is the orange bar whose height is 3 sweaters. (Marginal product is shown midway between the quantities of labor to emphasize that marginal product results from *changing* the quantity of labor.) The steeper the slope of the total product curve (*TP*) in part (a), the larger is marginal product (*MP*) in part (b). Marginal product increases to a maximum (in this example when 1.5 workers a day are employed) and then declines—diminishing marginal product.

MyEconLab animation

For example, if Campus Sweaters employs one worker, that person must learn all the aspects of sweater production: running the knitting machines, fixing breakdowns, packaging and mailing sweaters, buying and checking the type and color of the wool. All these tasks must be performed by that one person.

If Campus Sweaters hires a second person, the two workers can specialize in different parts of the production process and can produce more than twice as much as one worker. The marginal product of the second worker is greater than the marginal product of the first worker. Marginal returns are increasing.

Diminishing Marginal Returns Most production processes experience increasing marginal returns initially, but all production processes eventually reach a point of *diminishing* marginal returns. **Diminishing marginal returns** occur when the marginal product of an additional worker is less than the marginal product of the previous worker.

Diminishing marginal returns arise from the fact that more and more workers are using the same capital and working in the same space. As more workers are added, there is less and less for the additional workers to do that is productive. For example, if Campus Sweaters hires a third worker, output increases but not by as much as it did when it hired the second worker. In this case, after two workers are hired, all the gains from specialization and the division of labor have been exhausted. By hiring a third worker, the factory produces more sweaters, but the equipment is being operated closer to its limits. There are even times when the third worker has nothing to do because the machines are running without the need for further attention. Hiring more and more workers continues to increase output but by successively smaller amounts. Marginal returns are diminishing. This phenomenon is such a pervasive one that it is called a "law"—the law of diminishing returns. The **law of diminishing returns** states that

> As a firm uses more of a variable factor of production with a given quantity of the fixed factor of production, the marginal product of the variable factor eventually diminishes.

You are going to return to the law of diminishing returns when we study a firm's costs, but before we do that, let's look at the average product of labor and the average product curve.

Average Product Curve

Figure 11.3 illustrates Campus Sweaters' average product of labor and shows the relationship between average product and marginal product. Points *B* through *F* on the average product curve *AP* correspond to those same rows in Table 11.1. Average product increases from 1 to 2 workers (its maximum value at point *C*) but then decreases as yet more workers are employed. Notice also that average product is largest when average product and marginal product are equal. That is, the marginal product curve cuts the average product curve at the point of maximum average product. For the number of workers at which marginal product exceeds average product, average product is *increasing*. For the number of workers at which marginal product is less than average product, average product is *decreasing*.

The relationship between the average product and marginal product is a general feature of the relationship between the average and marginal values of any variable—even your grades.

FIGURE 11.3   Average Product

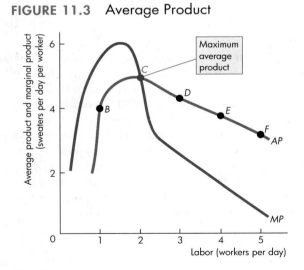

The figure shows the average product of labor and the connection between average product and marginal product. With 1 worker, marginal product exceeds average product, so average product is increasing. With 2 workers, marginal product equals average product, so average product is at its maximum. With more than 2 workers, marginal product is less than average product, so average product is decreasing.

—— MyEconLab animation ——

Economics in Action
How to Pull Up Your Average

Do you want to pull up your average grade? Then make sure that your grade this semester is better than your current average! This semester is your marginal semester. If your marginal grade exceeds your average grade (like the second semester in the figure), your average will rise. If your marginal grade equals your average grade (like the third semester in the figure), your average won't change. If your marginal grade is below your average grade (like the fourth semester in the figure), your average will fall.

The relationship between your marginal and average grades is exactly the same as that between marginal product and average product.

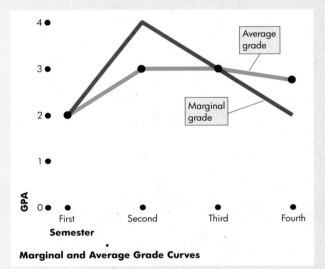

Marginal and Average Grade Curves

REVIEW QUIZ

1 Explain how the marginal product and average product of labor change as the labor employed increases (a) initially and (b) eventually.
2 What is the law of diminishing returns? Why does marginal product eventually diminish?
3 Explain the relationship between marginal product and average product.

You can work these questions in Study Plan 11.2 and get instant feedback.   MyEconLab

Campus Sweaters' product curves influence its costs, as you are now going to see.

Short-Run Cost

To produce more output in the short run, a firm must employ more labor, which means that it must increase its costs. We describe the relationship between output and cost by using three cost concepts:

- Total cost
- Marginal cost
- Average cost

Total Cost

A firm's **total cost** (*TC*) is the cost of *all* the factors of production it uses. We separate total cost into total *fixed* cost and total *variable* cost.

Total fixed cost (*TFC*) is the cost of the firm's fixed factors. For Campus Sweaters, total fixed cost includes the cost of renting knitting machines and *normal profit*, which is the opportunity cost of Cindy's entrepreneurship (see Chapter 10, p. 225). The quantities of fixed factors don't change as output changes, so total fixed cost is the same at all outputs.

Total variable cost (*TVC*) is the cost of the firm's variable factors. For Campus Sweaters, labor is the variable factor, so this component of cost is its wage bill. Total variable cost changes as output changes.

Total cost is the sum of total fixed cost and total variable cost. That is,

$$TC = TFC + TVC.$$

The table in Fig. 11.4 shows total costs. Campus Sweaters rents one knitting machine for $25 a day, so its *TFC* is $25. To produce sweaters, the firm hires labor, which costs $25 a day. *TVC* is the number of workers multiplied by $25. For example, to produce 13 sweaters a day, in row *D*, the firm hires 3 workers and *TVC* is $75. *TC* is the sum of *TFC* and *TVC*, so to produce 13 sweaters a day, *TC* is $100. Check the calculations in the other rows of the table.

Figure 11.4 shows Campus Sweaters' total cost curves, which graph total cost against output. The green *TFC* curve is horizontal because total fixed cost ($25 a day) does not change when output changes. The purple *TVC* curve and the blue *TC* curve both slope upward because to increase output, more labor must be employed, which increases total variable cost. Total fixed cost equals the vertical distance between the *TVC* and *TC* curves.

Let's now look at a firm's marginal cost.

FIGURE 11.4   Total Cost Curves

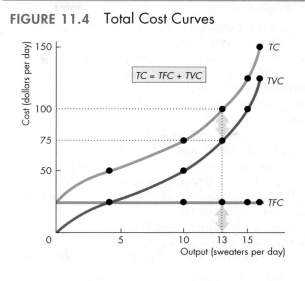

$$TC = TFC + TVC$$

	Labor (workers per day)	Output (sweaters per day)	Total fixed cost (*TFC*)	Total variable cost (*TVC*)	Total cost (*TC*)
				(dollars per day)	
A	0	0	25	0	25
B	1	4	25	25	50
C	2	10	25	50	75
D	**3**	**13**	**25**	**75**	**100**
E	4	15	25	100	125
F	5	16	25	125	150

Campus Sweaters rents a knitting machine for $25 a day, so this cost is the firm's total fixed cost. The firm hires workers at a wage rate of $25 a day, and this cost is its total variable cost. For example, in row *D*, Campus Sweaters employs 3 workers and its total variable cost is 3 × $25, which equals $75. Total cost is the sum of total fixed cost and total variable cost. For example, when Campus Sweaters employs 3 workers, total cost is $100—total fixed cost of $25 plus total variable cost of $75.

The graph shows Campus Sweaters' total cost curves. Total fixed cost is constant—the *TFC* curve is a horizontal line. Total variable cost increases as output increases, so the *TVC* curve and the *TC* curve increase as output increases. The vertical distance between the *TC* curve and the *TVC* curve equals total fixed cost, as illustrated by the two arrows.

MyEconLab animation

Marginal Cost

Figure 11.4 shows that total variable cost and total cost increase at a decreasing rate at small outputs but eventually, as output increases, total variable cost and total cost increase at an increasing rate. To understand this pattern in the change in total cost as output increases, we need to use the concept of *marginal cost.*

A firm's **marginal cost** is the increase in total cost that results from a one-unit increase in output. We calculate marginal cost as the increase in total cost divided by the increase in output. The table in Fig. 11.5 shows this calculation. When, for example, output increases from 10 sweaters to 13 sweaters, total cost increases from $75 to $100. The change in output is 3 sweaters, and the change in total cost is $25. The marginal cost of one of those 3 sweaters is ($25 ÷ 3), which equals $8.33.

Figure 11.5 graphs the marginal cost data in the table as the red marginal cost curve, *MC*. This curve is U-shaped because when Campus Sweaters hires a second worker, marginal cost decreases, but when it hires a third, a fourth, and a fifth worker, marginal cost successively increases.

At small outputs, marginal cost decreases as output increases because of greater specialization and the division of labor. But as output increases further, marginal cost eventually increases because of the *law of diminishing returns.* The law of diminishing returns means that the output produced by each additional worker is successively smaller. To produce an additional unit of output, ever more workers are required, and the cost of producing the additional unit of output—marginal cost—must eventually increase.

Marginal cost tells us how total cost changes as output increases. The final cost concept tells us what it costs, on average, to produce a unit of output. Let's now look at Campus Sweaters' average costs.

Average Cost

Three average costs of production are

1. Average fixed cost
2. Average variable cost
3. Average total cost

Average fixed cost (*AFC*) is total fixed cost per unit of output. **Average variable cost** (*AVC*) is total variable cost per unit of output. **Average total cost** (*ATC*) is total cost per unit of output. The average cost con-

cepts are calculated from the total cost concepts as follows:

$$TC = TFC + TVC.$$

Divide each total cost term by the quantity produced, *Q*, to get

$$\frac{TC}{Q} = \frac{TFC}{Q} + \frac{TVC}{Q},$$

or

$$ATC = AFC + AVC.$$

The table in Fig. 11.5 shows the calculation of average total cost. For example, in row *C*, output is 10 sweaters. Average fixed cost is ($25 ÷ 10), which equals $2.50, average variable cost is ($50 ÷ 10), which equals $5.00, and average total cost is ($75 ÷ 10), which equals $7.50. Note that average total cost is equal to average fixed cost ($2.50) plus average variable cost ($5.00).

Figure 11.5 shows the average cost curves. The green average fixed cost curve (*AFC*) slopes downward. As output increases, the same constant total fixed cost is spread over a larger output. The blue average total cost curve (*ATC*) and the purple average variable cost curve (*AVC*) are U-shaped. The vertical distance between the average total cost and average variable cost curves is equal to average fixed cost—as indicated by the two arrows. That distance shrinks as output increases because average fixed cost declines with increasing output.

Marginal Cost and Average Cost

The marginal cost curve (*MC*) intersects the average variable cost curve and the average total cost curve *at their minimum points.* When marginal cost is less than average cost, average cost is decreasing, and when marginal cost exceeds average cost, average cost is increasing. This relationship holds for both the *ATC* curve and the *AVC* curve. It is another example of the relationship you saw in Fig. 11.3 for average product and marginal product and in your average and marginal grades.

Why the Average Total Cost Curve Is U-Shaped

Average total cost is the sum of average fixed cost and average variable cost, so the shape of the *ATC* curve

FIGURE 11.5 Marginal Cost and Average Costs

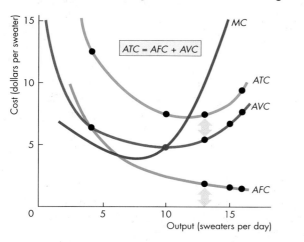

Marginal cost is calculated as the change in total cost divided by the change in output. When output increases from 4 to 10 sweaters, an increase of 6 sweaters, total cost increases by $25. Marginal cost is $25 ÷ 6, which is $4.17.

Each average cost concept is calculated by dividing the related total cost by output. When 10 sweaters are produced, AFC is $2.50 ($25 ÷ 10), AVC is $5 ($50 ÷ 10), and ATC is $7.50 ($75 ÷ 10).

The graph shows that the MC curve is U-shaped and intersects the AVC curve and the ATC curve at their minimum points. The average fixed cost curve (AFC) is downward sloping. The ATC curve and AVC curve are U-shaped. The vertical distance between the ATC curve and the AVC curve is equal to average fixed cost, as illustrated by the two arrows.

	Labor (workers per day)	Output (sweaters per day)	Total fixed cost (TFC)	Total variable cost (TVC)	Total cost (TC)	Marginal cost (MC) (dollars per additional sweater)	Average fixed cost (AFC)	Average variable cost (AVC)	Average total cost (ATC)
			(dollars per day)				(dollars per sweater)		
A	0	0	25	0	25		—	—	—
						.... 6.25			
B	1	4	25	25	50		6.25	6.25	12.50
						.... 4.17			
C	2	10	25	50	75		2.50	5.00	7.50
						.... 8.33			
D	3	13	25	75	100		1.92	5.77	7.69
						.......12.50			
E	4	15	25	100	125		1.67	6.67	8.33
						.......25.00			
F	5	16	25	125	150		1.56	7.81	9.38

MyEconLab animation

combines the shapes of the *AFC* and *AVC* curves. The U shape of the *ATC* curve arises from the influence of two opposing forces:

1. Spreading total fixed cost over a larger output
2. Eventually diminishing returns

When output increases, the firm spreads its total fixed cost over a larger output and so its average fixed cost decreases—its *AFC* curve slopes downward.

Diminishing returns means that as output increases, ever-larger amounts of labor are needed to produce an additional unit of output. So as output increases, average variable cost decreases initially but

eventually increases, and the *AVC* curve slopes upward. The *AVC* curve is U-shaped.

The shape of the *ATC* curve combines these two effects. Initially, as output increases, both average fixed cost and average variable cost decrease, so average total cost decreases. The *ATC* curve slopes downward.

But as output increases further and diminishing returns set in, average variable cost starts to increase. With average fixed cost decreasing more quickly than average variable cost is increasing, the *ATC* curve continues to slope downward. Eventually, average variable cost starts to increase more quickly than average fixed cost decreases, so average total cost starts to increase. The *ATC* curve slopes upward.

Cost Curves and Product Curves

The technology that a firm uses determines its costs. A firm's cost curves come directly from its product curves. You've used this link in the tables in which we have calculated total cost from the total product schedule and information about the prices of the factors of production. We're now going to get a clearer view of the link between the product curves and the cost curves. We'll look first at the link between total cost and total product and then at the links between the average and marginal product and cost curves.

Total Product and Total Variable Cost Figure 11.6 shows the links between the firm's total product curve, *TP*, and its total *variable* cost curve, *TVC*. The graph is a bit unusual in two ways. First, it measures two variables on the *x*-axis—labor and variable cost. Second, it graphs the *TVC* curve but with variable cost on the *x*-axis and output on the *y*-axis. The graph can show labor and cost on the *x*-axis because variable cost is proportional to labor. One worker costs $25 a day. Graphing output against labor gives the *TP* curve and graphing variable cost against output gives the *TVC* curve.

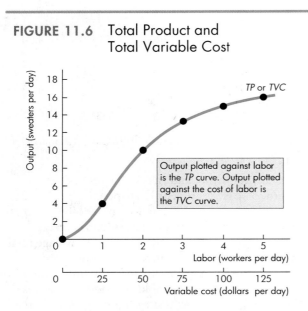

FIGURE 11.6   Total Product and Total Variable Cost

The figure shows the total product curve, *TP*, as a graph of output (sweaters per day) plotted against labor (workers per day). It also shows the total variable cost curve, *TVC*, as a graph of total variable cost (dollars per day) against output. The only difference between the *TVC* curve here and that in Fig. 11.4 is that we've switched the *x*-axis and *y*-axis.

—— MyEconLab animation ——

◆ ECONOMICS IN THE NEWS

Checkout Cost Curves

Welcome to More Self-Checkouts
Self-checkout is expanding. One estimate is that it will grow by 84 percent over the next five years. And new technologies will enable customers armed with smart phones to use apps that scan and pay for items in the aisles.

Source: MSNBC.com, July 22, 2011

DATA AND ASSUMPTIONS

A grocery store paid $20,000 to install 5 worker-operated checkout lines. With a life of 9 years and operating for 10 hours a day, these machines have an *implicit rental rate* of $1.00 an hour. Checkout clerks can be hired for $10 an hour. The total product schedule (checkouts per hour) for this store is:

Checkout clerks	1	2	3	4	5
Checkouts per hour	12	22	30	36	40

Another grocery store has converted to all self-checkout. It paid $100,000 to install a 5-line self-operated system. With a 5-year life and operating for 10 hours a day, the system has an *implicit rental rate* of $7.00 an hour. It hires checkout assistants to help customers at $10 an hour—the same wage as paid to checkout clerks. The total product schedule for this store is:

Checkout assistants	1	1	1	2
Checkouts per hour	12	22	30	36

That is, one checkout assistant can help shoppers check out up to a rate of 30 an hour and a second assistant can boost output to 36 an hour. (Shoppers using self-checkout aren't as quick as clerks, so the fastest rate at which this store can check out customers is 36 an hour.)

THE PROBLEM

■ Which checkout system has the lower average total cost (*ATC*)? Which system has the lower marginal cost (*MC*)? Sketch the *ATC* and *MC* curves for the two systems.

THE SOLUTION

■ Start with the worker-operated checkout system. Fixed cost is $1.00 per hour and variable cost is $10.00 per clerk. So the total cost schedule is:

Checkout clerks	1	2	3	4	5
Checkouts per hour	12	22	30	36	40
Total cost (*TC*) per hour	11	21	31	41	51

- Calculate *MC* as the change in *TC* divided by the change in output (change in number of checkouts) and calculate *ATC* as *TC* divided by output to get:

Checkouts per hour	12	22	30	36	40
Marginal cost (MC)	0.83	1.00	1.25	1.67	2.50
Average total cost (ATC)	0.92	0.95	1.03	1.14	1.28

- Figure 1 graphs the *MC* and *ATC* values at each output rate.

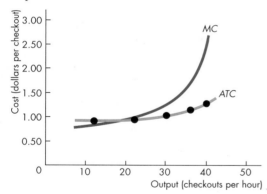

Figure 1   Operator Checkout

- Now do similar calculations for the self-checkout system. Fixed cost is $7.00 per hour and variable cost is $10.00 per clerk hour. So the total cost schedule is:

Checkout assistants	1	1	1	2
Checkouts per hour	12	22	30	36
Total cost (TC) per hour	17	17	17	27

- Calculate *MC* and *ATC* in the same way as before to get

Checkouts per hour	12	22	30	36
Marginal cost (MC)	0.83	0	0	1.67
Average total cost (ATC)	1.42	0.77	0.57	0.75

- Figure 2 graphs the *MC* and *ATC* values at each output rate.

- Figure 3 compares the *ATC* of the two systems. You can see that the self-checkout system has higher *ATC* at low output rates and lower *ATC* at higher output rates. The reason is that self-checkout has a higher fixed cost and lower variable cost than the worker-operated system.

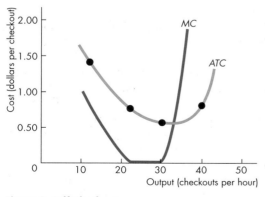

Figure 2   Self-Checkout

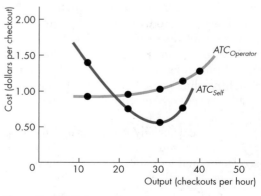

Figure 3   *ATC* Compared

Average and Marginal Product and Cost Figure 11.7 shows the links between the firm's average and marginal product curves and its average and marginal cost curves. The upper graph shows the average product curve, *AP*, and the marginal product curve, *MP*—like those in Fig. 11.3. The lower graph shows the average variable cost curve, *AVC*, and the marginal cost curve, *MC*—like those in Fig. 11.5.

As labor increases up to 1.5 workers a day (upper graph), output increases to 6.5 sweaters a day (lower graph). Marginal product and average product rise and marginal cost and average variable cost fall. At the point of maximum marginal product, marginal cost is at a minimum.

As labor increases from 1.5 workers to 2 workers a day, (upper graph) output increases from 6.5 sweaters to 10 sweaters a day (lower graph). Marginal product falls and marginal cost rises, but average product continues to rise and average variable cost continues to fall. At the point of maximum average product, average variable cost is at a minimum. As labor increases further, output increases. Average product diminishes and average variable cost increases.

Shifts in the Cost Curves

The position of a firm's short-run cost curves depends on two factors:

- Technology
- Prices of factors of production

Technology A technological change that increases productivity increases the marginal product and average product of labor. With a better technology, the same factors of production can produce more output, so the technological advance lowers the costs of production and shifts the cost curves downward.

For example, advances in robot production techniques have increased productivity in the automobile industry. As a result, the product curves of Chrysler, Ford, and GM have shifted upward and their cost curves have shifted downward. But the relationships between their product curves and cost curves have not changed. The curves are still linked in the way shown in Figs. 11.6 and 11.7.

Often, as in the case of robots producing cars, a technological advance results in a firm using more capital, a fixed factor, and less labor, a variable factor.

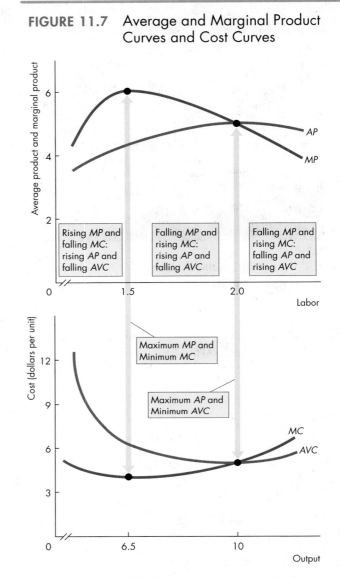

FIGURE 11.7 Average and Marginal Product Curves and Cost Curves

A firm's *MP* curve is linked to its *MC* curve. If, as the firm increases its labor from 0 to 1.5 workers a day, the firm's marginal product rises, its marginal cost falls. If marginal product is at a maximum, marginal cost is at a minimum. If, as the firm hires more labor, its marginal product diminishes, its marginal cost rises.

A firm's *AP* curve is linked to its *AVC* curve. If, as the firm increases its labor to 2 workers a day, its average product rises, its average variable cost falls. If average product is at a maximum, average variable cost is at a minimum. If, as the firm hires more labor, its average product diminishes, its average variable cost rises.

MyEconLab animation

TABLE 11.2   A Compact Glossary of Costs

Term	Symbol	Definition	Equation
Fixed cost		Cost that is independent of the output level; cost of a fixed factor of production	
Variable cost		Cost that varies with the output level; cost of a variable factor of production	
Total fixed cost	TFC	Cost of the fixed factors of production	
Total variable cost	TVC	Cost of the variable factors of production	
Total cost	TC	Cost of all factors of production	$TC = TFC + TVC$
Output (total product)	TP	Total quantity produced (output Q)	
Marginal cost	MC	Change in total cost resulting from a one-unit increase in total product	$MC = \Delta TC \div \Delta Q$
Average fixed cost	AFC	Total fixed cost per unit of output	$AFC = TFC \div Q$
Average variable cost	AVC	Total variable cost per unit of output	$AVC = TVC \div Q$
Average total cost	ATC	Total cost per unit of output	$ATC = AFC + AVC$

Another example is the use of ATMs by banks to dispense cash. ATMs, which are fixed capital, have replaced tellers, which are variable labor. Such a technological change decreases total cost but increases fixed costs and decreases variable cost. This change in the mix of fixed cost and variable cost means that at small outputs, average total cost might increase, while at large outputs, average total cost decreases.

Prices of Factors of Production An increase in the price of a factor of production increases the firm's costs and shifts its cost curves. How the curves shift depends on which factor price changes.

An increase in rent or some other component of *fixed* cost shifts the *TFC* and *AFC* curves upward and shifts the *TC* curve upward but leaves the *AVC* and *TVC* curves and the *MC* curve unchanged. For example, if the interest expense paid by a trucking company increases, the fixed cost of transportation services increases.

An increase in wages, gasoline, or another component of *variable* cost shifts the *TVC* and *AVC* curves upward and shifts the *MC* curve upward but leaves the *AFC* and *TFC* curves unchanged. For example, if

truck drivers' wages or the price of gasoline increases, the variable cost and marginal cost of transportation services increase.

You've now completed your study of short-run costs. All the concepts that you've met are summarized in a compact glossary in Table 11.2.

1 What relationships do a firm's short-run cost curves show?
2 How does marginal cost change as output increases (a) initially and (b) eventually?
3 What does the law of diminishing returns imply for the shape of the marginal cost curve?
4 What is the shape of the *AFC* curve and why does it have this shape?
5 What are the shapes of the *AVC* curve and the *ATC* curve and why do they have these shapes?

You can work these questions in Study Plan 11.3 and get instant feedback.   MyEconLab

◼◆ Long-Run Cost

We are now going to study the firm's long-run costs. In the long run, a firm can vary both the quantity of labor and the quantity of capital, so in the long run, all the firm's costs are variable.

The behavior of long-run cost depends on the firm's *production function*, which is the relationship between the maximum output attainable and the quantities of both labor and capital.

The Production Function

Table 11.3 shows Campus Sweaters' production function. The table lists total product schedules for four different quantities of capital. The quantity of capital identifies the plant size. The numbers for plant 1 are for a factory with 1 knitting machine—the case we've just studied. The other three plants have 2, 3, and 4 machines. If Campus Sweaters uses plant 2 with 2 knitting machines, the various amounts of labor can produce the outputs shown in the second column of the table. The other two columns show the outputs of yet larger quantities of capital. Each column of the table could be graphed as a total product curve for each plant.

Diminishing Returns Diminishing returns occur with each of the four plant sizes as the quantity of labor increases. You can check that fact by calculating the marginal product of labor in each of the plants with 2, 3, and 4 machines. With each plant size, as the firm increases the quantity of labor employed, the marginal product of labor (eventually) diminishes.

Diminishing Marginal Product of Capital Diminishing returns also occur with each quantity of labor as the quantity of capital increases. You can check that fact by calculating the marginal product of capital at a given quantity of labor. The *marginal product of capital* is the change in total product divided by the change in capital when the quantity of labor is constant—equivalently, the change in output resulting from a one-unit increase in the quantity of capital. For example, if Campus Sweaters has 3 workers and increases its capital from 1 machine to 2 machines, output increases from 13 to 18 sweaters a day. The marginal product of the second machine is 5 sweaters a day. If Campus Sweaters continues to employ 3 workers

TABLE 11.3   The Production Function

Labor (workers per day)	Output (sweaters per day)			
	Plant 1	Plant 2	Plant 3	Plant 4
1	4	10	13	15
2	10	15	18	20
3	13	18	22	24
4	15	20	24	26
5	16	21	25	27
Knitting machines (number)	**1**	**2**	**3**	**4**

The table shows the total product data for four quantities of capital (plant sizes). The greater the plant size, the larger is the output produced by any given quantity of labor. For a given plant size, the marginal product of labor diminishes as more labor is employed. For a given quantity of labor, the marginal product of capital diminishes as the quantity of capital used increases.

and increases the number of machines from 2 to 3, output increases from 18 to 22 sweaters a day. The marginal product of the third machine is 4 sweaters a day, down from 5 sweaters a day for the second machine.

Let's now see what the production function implies for long-run costs.

Short-Run Cost and Long-Run Cost

As before, Campus Sweaters can hire workers for $25 a day and rent knitting machines for $25 a day. Using these factor prices and the data in Table 11.3, we can calculate the average total cost and graph the ATC curves for factories with 1, 2, 3, and 4 knitting machines. We've already studied the costs of a factory with 1 machine in Figs. 11.4 and 11.5. In Fig. 11.8, the average total cost curve for that case is ATC_1. Figure 11.8 also shows the average total cost curve for a factory with 2 machines, ATC_2, with 3 machines, ATC_3, and with 4 machines, ATC_4.

You can see, in Fig. 11.8, that the plant size has a big effect on the firm's average total cost.

FIGURE 11.8   Short-Run Costs of Four Different Plants

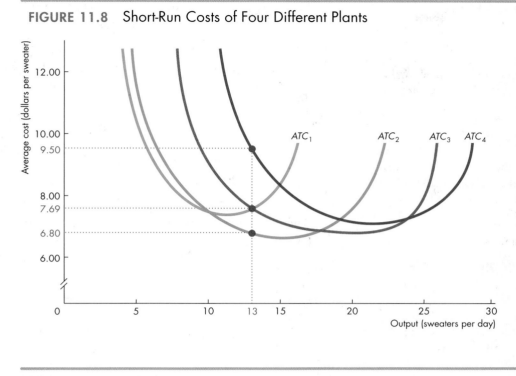

The figure shows short-run average total cost curves for four different quantities of capital at Campus Sweaters. The firm can produce 13 sweaters a day with 1 knitting machine on ATC_1 or with 3 knitting machines on ATC_3 for an average cost of $7.69 a sweater. The firm can produce 13 sweaters a day by using 2 machines on ATC_2 for $6.80 a sweater or by using 4 machines on ATC_4 for $9.50 a sweater.

If the firm produces 13 sweaters a day, the least-cost method of production, *the long-run method*, is with 2 machines on ATC_2.

In Fig. 11.8, two things stand out:

1. Each short-run ATC curve is U-shaped.
2. For each short-run ATC curve, the larger the plant, the greater is the output at which average total cost is at a minimum.

Each short-run ATC curve is U-shaped because, as the quantity of labor increases, its marginal product initially increases and then diminishes. This pattern in the marginal product of labor, which we examined in some detail for the plant with 1 knitting machine on pp. 254–255, occurs at all plant sizes.

The minimum average total cost for a larger plant occurs at a greater output than it does for a smaller plant because the larger plant has a higher total fixed cost and therefore, for any given output, a higher average fixed cost.

Which short-run ATC curve a firm operates on depends on the plant it has. In the long run, the firm can choose its plant and the plant it chooses is the one that enables it to produce its planned output at the lowest average total cost.

To see why, suppose that Campus Sweaters plans to produce 13 sweaters a day. In Fig. 11.8, with 1 machine, the average total cost curve is ATC_1 and the

average total cost of 13 sweaters a day is $7.69 a sweater. With 2 machines, on ATC_2, average total cost is $6.80 a sweater. With 3 machines, on ATC_3, average total cost is $7.69 a sweater, the same as with 1 machine. Finally, with 4 machines, on ATC_4, average total cost is $9.50 a sweater.

The economically efficient plant for producing a given output is the one that has the lowest average total cost. For Campus Sweaters, the economically efficient plant to use to produce 13 sweaters a day is the one with 2 machines.

In the long run, Cindy chooses the plant that minimizes average total cost. When a firm is producing a given output at the least possible cost, it is operating on its *long-run average cost curve*.

The **long-run average cost curve** is the relationship between the lowest attainable average total cost and output when the firm can change both the plant it uses and the quantity of labor it employs.

The long-run average cost curve is a planning curve. It tells the firm the plant and the quantity of labor to use at each output to minimize average cost. Once the firm chooses a plant, the firm operates on the short-run cost curves that apply to that plant.

The Long-Run Average Cost Curve

Figure 11.9 shows how a long-run average cost curve is derived. The long-run average cost curve *LRAC* consists of pieces of the four short-run *ATC* curves. For outputs up to 10 sweaters a day, average total cost is the lowest on ATC_1. For outputs between 10 and 18 sweaters a day, average total cost is the lowest on ATC_2. For outputs between 18 and 24 sweaters a day, average total cost is the lowest on ATC_3. And for outputs in excess of 24 sweaters a day, average total cost is the lowest on ATC_4. The piece of each *ATC* curve with the lowest average total cost is highlighted in dark blue in Fig. 11.9. This dark blue scallop-shaped curve made up of the pieces of the four *ATC* curves is the *LRAC* curve.

Economies and Diseconomies of Scale

Economies of scale are features of a firm's technology that make average total cost *fall* as output increases. When economies of scale are present, the *LRAC* curve slopes downward. In Fig. 11.9, Campus Sweaters has economies of scale for outputs up to 15 sweaters a day.

Greater specialization of both labor and capital is the main source of economies of scale. For example, if

GM produces 100 cars a week, each worker must perform many different tasks and the capital must be general-purpose machines and tools. But if GM produces 10,000 cars a week, each worker specializes in a small number of tasks, uses task-specific tools, and becomes highly proficient.

Diseconomies of scale are features of a firm's technology that make average total cost *rise* as output increases. When diseconomies of scale are present, the *LRAC* curve slopes upward. In Fig. 11.9, Campus Sweaters experiences diseconomies of scale at outputs greater than 15 sweaters a day.

The challenge of managing a large enterprise is the main source of diseconomies of scale.

Constant returns to scale are features of a firm's technology that keep average total cost constant as output increases. When constant returns to scale are present, the *LRAC* curve is horizontal.

Economies of Scale at Campus Sweaters The economies of scale and diseconomies of scale at Campus Sweaters arise from the firm's production function in Table 11.3. With 1 machine and 1 worker, the firm produces 4 sweaters a day. With 2 machines and 2 workers, total cost doubles but out-

---

FIGURE 11.9   Long-Run Average Cost Curve

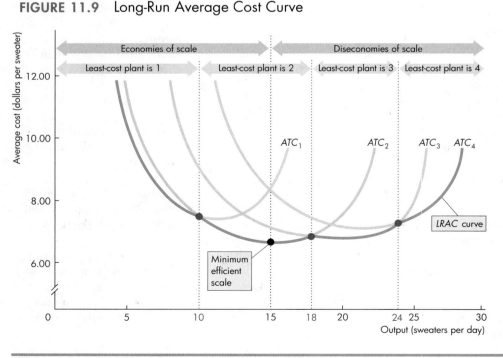

The long-run average cost curve traces the lowest attainable *ATC* when both labor and capital change. The green arrows highlight the output range over which each plant achieves the lowest *ATC*. Within each range, to change the quantity produced, the firm changes the quantity of labor it employs.

Along the *LRAC* curve, economies of scale occur if average cost falls as output increases; diseconomies of scale occur if average cost rises as output increases. Minimum efficient scale is the output at which average cost is lowest, 15 sweaters a day.

Economics in Action
Produce More to Cut Cost

Why do GM, Ford, and the other automakers have expensive equipment lying around that isn't fully used? You can answer this question with what you've learned in this chapter.

The basic answer is that auto production enjoys economies of scale. A larger output rate brings a lower long-run average cost—the firm's $LRAC$ curve slopes downward.

An auto producer's average total cost curves look like those in the figure. To produce 20 vehicles an hour, the firm installs the plant with the short-run average total cost curve ATC_1. The average cost of producing a vehicle is $20,000.

Producing 20 vehicles an hour doesn't use the plant at its lowest possible average total cost. If the firm could sell enough cars for it to produce 40 vehicles an hour, the firm could use its current plant and produce at an average cost of $15,000 a vehicle.

But if the firm planned to produce 40 vehicles an hour, it would not stick with its current plant. The firm would install a bigger plant with the short-run average total cost curve ATC_2, and produce 40 vehicles an hour for $10,000 a car.

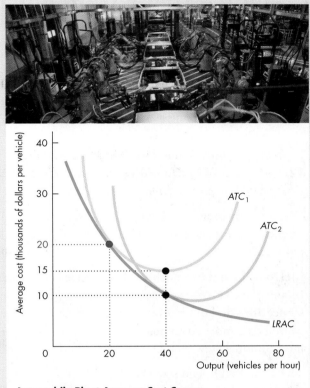

Automobile Plant Average Cost Curves

put more than doubles to 15 sweaters a day, so average cost decreases and Campus Sweaters experiences economies of scale. With 4 machines and 4 workers, total cost doubles again but output less than doubles to 26 sweaters a day, so average cost increases and the firm experiences diseconomies of scale.

Minimum Efficient Scale A firm's **minimum efficient scale** is the *smallest* output at which long-run average cost reaches its lowest level. At Campus Sweaters, the minimum efficient scale is 15 sweaters a day.

The minimum efficient scale plays a role in determining market structure. In a market in which the minimum efficient scale is small relative to market demand, the market has room for many firms, and the market is competitive. In a market in which the minimum efficient scale is large relative to market demand, only a small number of firms, and possibly only one firm, can make a profit and the market is either an oligopoly or monopoly. We will return to this idea in the next three chapters.

REVIEW QUIZ

1 What does a firm's production function show and how is it related to a total product curve?
2 Does the law of diminishing returns apply to capital as well as labor? Explain why or why not.
3 What does a firm's $LRAC$ curve show? How is it related to the firm's short-run ATC curves?
4 What are economies of scale and diseconomies of scale? How do they arise? What do they imply for the shape of the $LRAC$ curve?
5 What is a firm's minimum efficient scale?

You can work these questions in Study Plan 11.4 and get instant feedback.   MyEconLab

◆ *Reading Between the Lines* on pp. 264–265 applies what you've learned about a firm's cost curves. It looks at McDonald's cost curves and explains how increasing plant size can lower average total cost.

Expanding Capacity at McDonald's

McDonald's Rebuilds 12 Restaurants

Dayton Daily News
June 19, 2012

… Construction began last week of a new McDonald's restaurant … in Dayton, bringing to 12 the number of McDonald's restaurants across the Miami Valley scheduled for either a total rebuild or extensive renovations in 2012. …

"We are increasing the capacity to serve more customers more often," said Phil Saken, communications manager for the Ohio region of McDonald's—and that often requires more employees. …

McDonald's and its franchise owners have been aggressively rebuilding or improving their Miami Valley locations for several years in projects that modernize the restaurants' kitchens, service areas and dining rooms, and at most locations, create two drive-through lanes to accommodate more customers during peak times. The rebuilt restaurants usually require hiring additional crew members to accommodate the increased capacity. …

The Troy McDonald's at 1560 W. Main St., which closed March 31, was razed and rebuilt … employed 80 to 85 people when it closed, but will reopen with about 95 employees. …

The McDonald's locations that were built decades ago become inefficient in utilities, service, and operations, Herzog said. "We want to make these stores modern and attractive for customers," he said.

The new Keowee Street restaurant's seating capacity will grow by only a handful to 65, in part because Herzog said about 75 percent of his stores' sales are either drive-through or carry-out.

Employment at the Keowee location will grow slightly: "We've got about 60 to 65 employees now, and we'll probably go to 70 to 80 when we move into the new site," Herzog said.

ESSENCE OF THE STORY

- In 2012, McDonald's rebuilt or extensively renovated 12 restaurants in the Miami Valley, Ohio.

- The goal was to increase capacity to serve more customers.

- Capacity was increased by modernizing the kitchens, service areas, and dining rooms and by creating two drive-through lanes.

- In addition to increasing plant size, McDonald's planned to hire more workers—up from 80–85 to 95 employees in Troy and up from 60–65 to 70–80 at Keowee.

ECONOMIC ANALYSIS

- McDonald's is increasing its output in the Miami Valley.

- A firm can increase output with its existing plant by hiring more labor, or it can increase its plant size, or it can both increase its plant size and hire more labor.

- The decision turns on comparing costs and McDonald's has figured that it minimizes cost by increasing its plant size and hiring more labor.

- We don't know McDonald's actual costs (and they vary from one restaurant to another) but we can gain insight into the firm's decision with an example.

- The table shows an assumed total product schedule for a McDonald's restaurant. It also shows total cost (*TC*), marginal cost (*MC*), and average total cost, (*ATC*).

	Labor (workers per day)	Output (meals per day)	Total cost (*TC*) (dollars per day)	Marginal cost (*MC*)	Average total cost (*ATC*)
					(dollars per meal)
A	0	0	1,000		—
				. . . . . 2.00	
B	10	400	1,800		4.50
				. . . . . 1.33	
C	20	1,000	2,600		2.60
				. . . . . 2.67	
D	30	1,300	3,400		2.62
				. . . . . 4.00	
E	40	1,500	4,200		2.80
				. . . . . 8.00	
F	50	1,600	5,000		3.13

- Figure 1 graphs the marginal cost and average total cost curves.

- If McDonald's wants to increase production above 1,000 meals per day, marginal cost rises sharply and pulls upward the firm's average total cost.

- But if McDonald's replaces an old restaurant with a new one that has a greater capacity (a modern kitchen, expanded service area, more dining space, and two drive-through lanes), a given quantity of labor can produce a greater output.

- With a bigger capacity, fixed cost increases, so at low output levels, average total cost also increases. But at higher output levels average total cost decreases.

- Figure 2 shows McDonald's original *ATC* curve, ATC_0, and the new *ATC* curve for the new, larger, more modern restaurant, ATC_1.

- Increasing output in the larger plant avoids the sharply rising marginal cost and average total cost of the old restaurant.

- In this example, McDonald's can now hire more labor to operate the larger restaurant and average total cost falls as output increases above 1,000 meals per day.

- Figure 2 also shows McDonald's long-run average cost curve (*LRAC*).

- If the firm wants to expand output yet further and avoid the rising costs along ATC_1, it can build an even bigger restaurant and move along its long-run average cost curve.

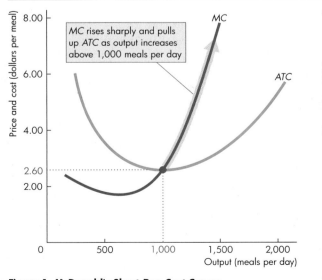

Figure 1 McDonald's Short-Run Cost Curves

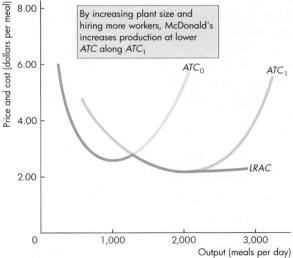

Figure 2 McDonald's Long-Run Cost Curves

Key Points

Decision Time Frames (p. 248)

- In the short run, the quantity of at least one factor of production is fixed and the quantities of the other factors of production can be varied.
- In the long run, the quantities of all factors of production can be varied.

Working Problems 1 and 2 will give you a better understanding of a firm's decision time frames.

Short-Run Technology Constraint (pp. 249–252)

- A total product curve shows the quantity a firm can produce with a given quantity of capital and different quantities of labor.
- Initially, the marginal product of labor increases as the quantity of labor increases, because of increased specialization and the division of labor.
- Eventually, marginal product diminishes because an increasing quantity of labor must share a fixed quantity of capital—the law of diminishing returns.
- Initially, average product increases as the quantity of labor increases, but eventually average product diminishes.

Working Problems 3 to 8 will give you a better understanding of a firm's short-run technology constraint.

Short-Run Cost (pp. 253–259)

- As output increases, total fixed cost is constant, and total variable cost and total cost increase.
- As output increases, average fixed cost decreases and average variable cost, average total cost, and marginal cost decrease at low outputs and increase at high outputs. These cost curves are U-shaped.

Working Problems 9 to 14 will give you a better understanding of a firm's short-run cost.

Long-Run Cost (pp. 260–263)

- A firm has a set of short-run cost curves for each different plant. For each output, the firm has one least-cost plant. The larger the output, the larger is the plant that will minimize average total cost.
- The long-run average cost curve traces out the lowest attainable average total cost at each output when both capital and labor inputs can be varied.
- With economies of scale, the long-run average cost curve slopes downward. With diseconomies of scale, the long-run average cost curve slopes upward.

Working Problems 15 to 20 will give you a better understanding of a firm's long-run cost.

Key Terms

Average fixed cost, 254	Economies of scale, 262	Short run, 248
Average product, 249	Law of diminishing returns, 251	Sunk cost, 248
Average total cost, 254	Long run, 248	Total cost, 253
Average variable cost, 254	Long-run average cost curve, 261	Total fixed cost, 253
Constant returns to scale, 262	Marginal cost, 254	Total product, 249
Diminishing marginal returns, 251	Marginal product, 249	Total variable cost, 253
Diseconomies of scale, 262	Minimum efficient scale, 263	

STUDY PLAN PROBLEMS AND APPLICATIONS

MyEconLab   You can work Problems 1 to 21 in MyEconLab Chapter 11 Study Plan and get instant feedback.

Decision Time Frames (Study Plan 11.1)

1. Which of the following news items involves a short-run decision and which involves a long-run decision? Explain.

   January 31, 2008: Starbucks will open 75 more stores abroad than originally predicted, for a total of 975.

   February 25, 2008: For three hours on Tuesday, Starbucks will shut down every single one of its 7,100 stores so that baristas can receive a refresher course.

   June 2, 2008: Starbucks replaces baristas with vending machines.

   July 18, 2008: Starbucks is closing 616 stores by the end of March.

2. **Maryland Farmers Turn from Tobacco to Flowers**

   Maryland tobacco farmers will be subsidized if they switch from growing tobacco to growing crops such as flowers and organic vegetables.
   Source: *The New York Times*, February 25, 2001

   a. How does offering farmers a payment to exit tobacco growing influence the opportunity cost of growing tobacco?

   b. What is the opportunity cost of using the equipment owned by a tobacco farmer?

Short-Run Technology Constraint (Study Plan 11.2)

Use the following table to work Problems 3 to 7. The table sets out Sue's Surfboards' total product schedule.

Labor (workers per week)	Output (surfboards per week)
1	30
2	70
3	120
4	160
5	190
6	210
7	220

3. Draw the total product curve.
4. Calculate the average product of labor and draw the average product curve.
5. Calculate the marginal product of labor and draw the marginal product curve.

6. a. Over what output range does Sue's Surfboards enjoy the benefits of increased specialization and division of labor?

   b. Over what output range does the firm experience diminishing marginal product of labor?

   c. Over what output range does the firm experience an increasing average product of labor but a diminishing marginal product of labor?

7. Explain how it is possible for a firm to experience simultaneously an increasing *average* product but a diminishing *marginal* product.

8. **Business Boot Camp**

   At a footwear company called Caboots, sales rose from $160,000 in 2000 to $2.3 million in 2006, but in 2007 sales dipped to $1.5 million. Joey and Priscilla Sanchez, who run Caboots, blame the decline partly on a flood that damaged the firm's office and sapped morale.
   Source: CNN, April 23, 2008

   If the Sanchezes are correct in their assumptions and the prices of footwear didn't change

   a. Explain the effect of the flood on the total product curve and marginal product curve at Caboots.

   b. Draw a graph to show the effect of the flood on the total product curve and marginal product curve at Caboots.

Short-Run Cost (Study Plan 11.3)

Use the following data to work Problems 9 to 13. Sue's Surfboards, in Problem 3, hires workers at $500 a week and its total fixed cost is $1,000 a week.

9. Calculate total cost, total variable cost, and total fixed cost of each output in the table. Plot these points and sketch the short-run total cost curves passing through them.

10. Calculate average total cost, average fixed cost, average variable cost, and marginal cost of each output in the table. Plot these points and sketch the short-run average and marginal cost curves passing through them.

11. Illustrate the connection between Sue's *AP*, *MP*, *AVC*, and *MC* curves in graphs like those in Fig. 11.7.

12. Sue's Surfboards rents a factory building. If the rent is increased by $200 a week and other things remain the same, how do Sue's Surfboards' short-run average cost curves and marginal cost curve change?

13. Workers at Sue's Surfboards negotiate a wage increase of $100 a week for each worker. If other things remain the same, explain how Sue's Surfboards' short-run average cost curves and marginal cost curve change.

14. **Grain Prices Go the Way of the Oil Price**

Every morning millions of Americans confront the latest trend in commodities markets at their kitchen table. Rising prices for crops have begun to drive up the cost of breakfast.

Source: *The Economist*, July 21, 2007

Explain how the rising price of crops affects the average total cost and marginal cost of producing breakfast cereals.

Long-Run Cost (Study Plan 11.4)

Use the table in Problem 3 and the following information to work Problems 15 and 16.

Sue's Surfboards buys a second plant and the output produced by each worker increases by 50 percent. The total fixed cost of operating each plant is $1,000 a week. Each worker is paid $500 a week.

15. Calculate the average total cost of producing 180 and 240 surfboards a week when Sue's Surfboards operates two plants. Graph these points and sketch the *ATC* curve.

16. a. To produce 180 surfboards a week, is it efficient to operate one or two plants?

    b. To produce 160 surfboards a week, is it efficient for Sue's to operate one or two plants?

Use the following table to work Problems 17 to 20. The table shows the production function of Jackie's Canoe Rides.

Labor (workers per day)	Output (rides per day)			
	Plant 1	Plant 2	Plant 3	Plant 4
10	20	40	55	65
20	40	60	75	85
30	65	75	90	100
40	75	85	100	110
Canoes	10	20	30	40

Jackie's pays $100 a day for each canoe it rents and $50 a day for each canoe operator it hires.

17. Graph the *ATC* curves for Plant 1 and Plant 2. Explain why these *ATC* curves differ.

18. Graph the *ATC* curves for Plant 3 and Plant 4. Explain why these *ATC* curves differ.

19. a. On Jackie's *LRAC* curve, what is the average cost of producing 40, 75, and 85 rides a week?

    b. What is Jackie's minimum efficient scale?

20. a. Explain how Jackie's uses its *LRAC* curve to decide how many canoes to rent.

    b. Does Jackie's production function feature economies of scale or diseconomies of scale?

21. **Airlines Seek Out New Ways to Save on Fuel as Costs Soar**

The financial pain of higher fuel prices is particularly acute for airlines because it is their single biggest expense. Airlines pump about 7,000 gallons into a Boeing 737 and about 60,000 gallons into the bigger 747 jet. Each generation of aircraft is more efficient: An Airbus A330 long-range jet uses 38 percent less fuel than the DC-10 it replaced, while the Airbus A319 medium-range jet is 27 percent more efficient than the DC-9 it replaced.

Source: *The New York Times*, June 11, 2008

a. Is the price of fuel a fixed cost or a variable cost for an airline?

b. Explain how an increase in the price of fuel changes an airline's total costs, average costs, and marginal cost.

c. Draw a graph to show the effects of an increase in the price of fuel on an airline's *TFC*, *TVC*, *AFC*, *AVC*, and *MC* curves.

d. Explain how a technological advance that makes an airplane engine more fuel efficient changes an airline's total product, marginal product, and average product.

e. Draw a graph to illustrate the effects of a more fuel-efficient aircraft on an airline's *TP*, *MP*, and *AP* curves.

f. Explain how a technological advance that makes an airplane engine more fuel efficient changes an airline's average variable cost, marginal cost, and average total cost.

g. Draw a graph to illustrate how a technological advance that makes an airplane engine more fuel efficient changes an airline's *AVC*, *MC*, and *ATC* curves.

ADDITIONAL PROBLEMS AND APPLICATIONS

MyEconLab   You can work these problems in MyEconLab if assigned by your instructor.

Decision Time Frames

22. **A Bakery on the Rise**

    Some 500 customers a day line up to buy Avalon's breads, scones, muffins, and coffee. Staffing and management are worries. Avalon now employs 35 and plans to hire 15 more. Its payroll will climb by 30 percent to 40 percent. The new CEO has executed an ambitious agenda that includes the move to a larger space, which will increase the rent from $3,500 to $10,000 a month.

    Source: CNN, March 24, 2008

    a. Which of Avalon's decisions described in the news clip is a short-run decision and which is a long-run decision?

    b. Why is Avalon's long-run decision riskier than its short-run decision?

23. **The Sunk-Cost Fallacy**

    You have good tickets to a basketball game an hour's drive away. There's a blizzard raging outside, and the game is being televised. You can sit warm and safe at home and watch it on TV, or you can bundle up, dig out your car, and go to the game. What do you do?

    Source: *Slate*, September 9, 2005

    a. What type of cost is your expenditure on tickets?

    b. Why is the cost of the ticket irrelevant to your current decision about whether to stay at home or go to the game?

Short-Run Technology Constraint

24. Terri runs a rose farm. One worker produces 1,000 roses a week; hiring a second worker doubles her total product; hiring a third worker doubles her output again; hiring a fourth worker increased her total product but by only 1,000 roses. Construct Terri's marginal product and average product schedules. Over what range of workers do marginal returns increase?

Short-Run Cost

25. Use the events described in the news clip in Problem 22. By how much will Avalon's short-run decision increase its total variable cost? By how much will Avalon's long-run decision increase its monthly total fixed cost? Sketch Avalon's short-run *ATC* curve before and after the events described in the news clip.

26. Bill's Bakery has a fire and Bill loses some of his cost data. The bits of paper that he recovers after the fire provide the information in the following table (all the cost numbers are dollars).

TP	AFC	AVC	ATC	MC
10	120	100	220	
				80
20	*A*	*B*	150	
				90
30	40	90	130	
				130
40	30	*C*	*D*	
				E
50	24	108	132	

    Bill asks you to come to his rescue and provide the missing data in the five spaces identified as *A*, *B*, *C*, *D*, and *E*.

    Use the following table to work Problems 27 and 28. ProPainters hires students at $250 a week to paint houses. It leases equipment at $500 a week. The table sets out its total product schedule.

Labor (students)	Output (houses painted per week)
1	2
2	5
3	9
4	12
5	14
6	15

27. If ProPainters paints 12 houses a week, calculate its total cost, average total cost, and marginal cost. At what output is average total cost a minimum?

28. Explain why the gap between ProPainters' total cost and total variable cost is the same no matter how many houses are painted.

29. **A Pepsi, a Business Decision**

    PepsiCo has done a deal with 300 small Mexican farmers close to their two factories to buy corn at a guaranteed price. PepsiCo saves transportation costs and the use of local farms assures it access to the type of corn best suited to its products and processes. "That gives us great leverage because corn prices don't fluctuate so much, but transportation costs do," said Pedro Padierna, president of PepsiCo in Mexico.

Source: *The New York Times*, February 21, 2011

a. How do fluctuations in the price of corn and in transportation costs influence PepsiCo's short-run cost curves?

b. How does the deal with the farmers to avoid fluctuations in costs benefit PepsiCo?

Long-Run Cost

Use the table in Problem 28 and the following information to work Problems 30 and 31.

If ProPainters doubles the number of students it hires and doubles the amount of equipment it leases, it experiences diseconomies of scale.

30. Explain how the *ATC* curve with one unit of equipment differs from that when ProPainters uses double the amount of equipment.

31. Explain what might be the source of the diseconomies of scale that ProPainters experiences.

Use the following information to work Problems 32 and 33.

The table shows the production function of Bonnie's Balloon Rides. Bonnie's pays $500 a day for each balloon it rents and $25 a day for each balloon operator it hires.

Labor (workers per day)	Output (rides per day)			
	Plant 1	Plant 2	Plant 3	Plant 4
10	6	10	13	15
20	10	15	18	20
30	13	18	22	24
40	15	20	24	26
50	16	21	25	27
Balloons (number)	1	2	3	4

32. Graph the *ATC* curves for Plant 1 and Plant 2. Explain why these *ATC* curves differ.

33. Graph the *ATC* curves for Plant 3 and Plant 4 Explain why these *ATC* curves differ.

34. a. On Bonnie's *LRAC* curve, what is the average cost of producing 18 rides and 15 rides a day?

b. Explain how Bonnie's uses its long-run average cost curve to decide how many balloons to rent.

Use the following news clip to work Problems 35 and 36.

Gap Will Focus on Smaller Scale Stores

Gap has too many stores that are 12,500 square feet.

The target store size is 6,000 square feet to 10,000 square feet, so Gap plans to combine previously separate concept stores. Some Gap body, adult, maternity, baby and kids stores will be combined in one store.

Source: CNN, June 10, 2008

35. Thinking of a Gap store as a production plant, explain why Gap is making a decision to reduce the size of its stores. Is Gap's decision a long-run decision or a short-run decision?

36. How might combining Gap's concept stores into one store help better take advantage of economies of scale?

Economics in the News

37. After you have studied *Reading Between the Lines* on pp. 264–265, answer the following questions.

a. Explain the distinction between the short run and the long run and identify when McDonald's would want to make each type of change.

b. Given the cost differences between the old and new restaurants described on p. 265, why would it ever be efficient to stick with an old restaurant?

c. Explain economies of scale. Does McDonald's reap economies of scale in the example on p. 265?

d. Draw a graph to illustrate McDonald's cost curves if it builds an even larger restaurant than the one whose costs are shown in Fig. 2 on p. 265.

38. **Starbucks Unit Brews Up Self-Serve Espresso Bars**

Coinstar has installed automated, self-serve espresso kiosks in grocery stores. Kiosks cost just under $40,000 each and Coinstar provides maintenance. The self-serve kiosk removes the labor costs of having a barista serve Starbucks' coffee, and store personnel refill the machine.

Source: MSNBC, June 1, 2008

a. What is Coinstar's total fixed cost of operating one self-serve kiosk? What are its variable costs of providing coffee at a self-serve kiosk?

b. Assume that a coffee machine operated by a barista costs less than $40,000. Explain how the fixed costs, variable costs, and total costs of barista-served and self-served coffee differ.

c. Sketch the marginal cost and average cost curves implied by your answer to part (b).

12

PERFECT COMPETITION

After studying this chapter, you will be able to:

- ◆ Define perfect competition
- ◆ Explain how a firm makes its output decision
- ◆ Explain how price and output are determined in perfect competition
- ◆ Explain why firms enter and leave a market
- ◆ Predict the effects of technological change in a competitive market
- ◆ Explain why perfect competition is efficient

A million "apps" have been created for smartphones and tablets. Most of these apps are the work of individuals in intense competition with each other. No single app writer can influence the price of an app, but each can and must decide how much to work and how many apps to produce.

In this chapter, we study producers who, like small app developers, are in intense competition—in *perfect competition*.

At the end of the chapter, in *Reading Between the Lines*, we apply the perfect competition model to the highly competitive market in apps.

What Is Perfect Competition?

The firms that you study in this chapter face the force of raw competition. We call this extreme form of competition perfect competition. **Perfect competition** is a market in which

- Many firms sell identical products to many buyers.
- There are no restrictions on entry into the market.
- Established firms have no advantage over new ones.
- Sellers and buyers are well informed about prices.

Farming, fishing, wood pulping and paper milling, the manufacture of paper cups and shopping bags, grocery and fresh flower retailing, photo finishing, lawn services, plumbing, painting, dry cleaning, and laundry services are all examples of highly competitive industries.

How Perfect Competition Arises

Perfect competition arises if the minimum efficient scale of a single producer is small relative to the market demand for the good or service. In this situation, there is room in the market for many firms. A firm's *minimum efficient scale* is the smallest output at which long-run average cost reaches its lowest level. (See Chapter 11, p. 263.)

In perfect competition, each firm produces a good that has no unique characteristics, so consumers don't care which firm's good they buy.

Price Takers

Firms in perfect competition are price takers. A **price taker** is a firm that cannot influence the market price because its production is an insignificant part of the total market.

Imagine that you are a wheat farmer in Kansas. You have a thousand acres planted—which sounds like a lot. But compared to the millions of acres in Colorado, Oklahoma, Texas, Nebraska, and the Dakotas, as well as the millions more in Canada, Argentina, Australia, and Ukraine, your thousand acres are a drop in the ocean. Nothing makes your wheat any better than any other farmer's, and all the buyers of wheat know the price at which they can do business.

If the market price of wheat is $4 a bushel, then that is the highest price you can get for your wheat. Ask for $4.10 and no one will buy from you. Offer it for $3.90 and you'll be sold out in a flash and have given away 10¢ a bushel. You take the market price.

Economic Profit and Revenue

A firm's goal is to maximize *economic profit*, which is equal to total revenue minus total cost. Total cost is the *opportunity cost* of production, which includes *normal profit*. (See Chapter 10, p. 225.)

A firm's **total revenue** equals the price of its output multiplied by the number of units of output sold (price × quantity). **Marginal revenue** is the change in total revenue that results from a one-unit increase in the quantity sold. Marginal revenue is calculated by dividing the change in total revenue by the change in the quantity sold.

Figure 12.1 illustrates these revenue concepts. In part (a), the market demand curve, D, and market supply curve, S, determine the market price. The market price is $25 a sweater. Campus Sweaters is just one of many producers of sweaters, so the best it can do is to sell its sweaters for $25 each.

Total Revenue Total revenue is equal to the price multiplied by the quantity sold. In the table in Fig. 12.1, if Campus Sweaters sells 9 sweaters, its total revenue is $225 (9 × $25).

Figure 12.1(b) shows the firm's total revenue curve (TR), which graphs the relationship between total revenue and the quantity sold. At point A on the TR curve, the firm sells 9 sweaters and has a total revenue of $225. Because each additional sweater sold brings in a constant amount—$25—the total revenue curve is an upward-sloping straight line.

Marginal Revenue Marginal revenue is the change in total revenue that results from a one-unit increase in quantity sold. In the table in Fig. 12.1, when the quantity sold increases from 8 to 9 sweaters, total revenue increases from $200 to $225, so marginal revenue is $25 a sweater.

Because the firm in perfect competition is a price taker, the change in total revenue that results from a one-unit increase in the quantity sold equals the market price. *In perfect competition, the firm's marginal revenue equals the market price.* Figure 12.1(c) shows the firm's marginal revenue curve (MR) as the horizontal line at the market price.

Demand for the Firm's Product The firm can sell any quantity it chooses at the market price. So the demand curve for the firm's product is a horizontal line at the market price, the same as the firm's marginal revenue curve.

FIGURE 12.1   Demand, Price, and Revenue in Perfect Competition

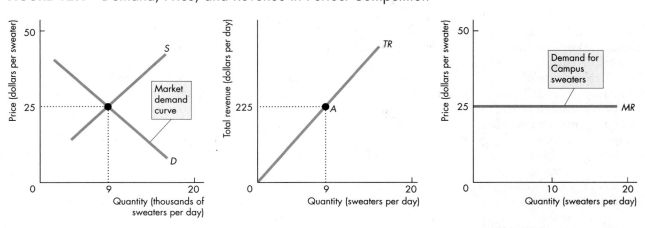

(a) Sweater market   **(b) Campus Sweaters' total revenue**   **(c) Campus Sweaters' marginal revenue**

Quantity sold (Q) (sweaters per day)	Price (P) (dollars per sweater)	Total revenue (TR = P × Q) (dollars)	Marginal revenue (MR = ΔTR/ΔQ) (dollars per additional sweater)
8	25	200	
			 25
9	25	225	
			 25
10	25	250	

In part (a), market demand and market supply determine the market price (and quantity). Part (b) shows the firm's total revenue curve (*TR*). Point *A* corresponds to the second row of the table—Campus Sweaters sells 9 sweaters at $25 a sweater, so total revenue is $225. Part (c) shows the firm's marginal revenue curve (*MR*). This curve is also the demand curve for the firm's sweaters. The demand for sweaters from Campus Sweaters is perfectly elastic at the market price of $25 a sweater.

MyEconLab animation

A horizontal demand curve illustrates a perfectly elastic demand, so the demand for the firm's product is perfectly elastic. A sweater from Campus Sweaters is a *perfect substitute* for a sweater from any other factory. But the *market* demand for sweaters is *not* perfectly elastic: Its elasticity depends on the substitutability of sweaters for other goods and services.

The Firm's Decisions

The goal of the competitive firm is to maximize economic profit, given the constraints it faces. To achieve its goal, a firm must decide

1. How to produce at minimum cost
2. What quantity to produce
3. Whether to enter or exit a market

You've already seen how a firm makes the first decision. It does so by operating with the plant that minimizes long-run average cost—by being on its

long-run average cost curve. We'll now see how the firm makes the other two decisions. We start by looking at the firm's output decision.

REVIEW QUIZ

1 Why is a firm in perfect competition a price taker?
2 In perfect competition, what is the relationship between the demand for the firm's output and the market demand?
3 In perfect competition, why is a firm's marginal revenue curve also the demand curve for the firm's output?
4 What decisions must a firm make to maximize profit?

You can work these questions in Study Plan 12.1 and get instant feedback.   *MyEconLab*

◆ The Firm's Output Decision

A firm's cost curves (total cost, average cost, and marginal cost) describe the relationship between its output and costs (see pp. 253–259). And a firm's revenue curves (total revenue and marginal revenue) describe the relationship between its output and revenue (pp. 272–273). From the firm's cost curves and revenue curves, we can find the output that maximizes the firm's economic profit.

Figure 12.2 shows how to do this for Campus Sweaters. The table lists the firm's total revenue and total cost at different outputs, and part (a) of the figure shows the firm's total revenue curve, *TR*, and total cost curve, *TC*. These curves are graphs of numbers in the first three columns of the table.

Economic profit equals total revenue minus total cost. The fourth column of the table in Fig. 12.2 shows the economic profit made by Campus Sweaters, and part (b) of the figure graphs these numbers as its economic profit curve, *EP*.

Campus Sweaters maximizes its economic profit by producing 9 sweaters a day: Total revenue is $225, total cost is $183, and economic profit is $42. No other output rate achieves a larger profit.

At outputs of less than 4 sweaters and more than 12 sweaters a day, Campus Sweaters would incur an economic loss. At either 4 or 12 sweaters a day, Campus Sweaters would make zero economic profit, called a *break-even point*.

FIGURE 12.2   Total Revenue, Total Cost, and Economic Profit

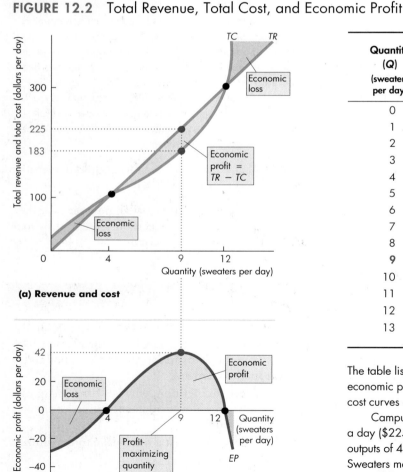

(a) Revenue and cost

(b) Economic profit and loss

Quantity (Q) (sweaters per day)	Total revenue (TR) (dollars)	Total cost (TC) (dollars)	Economic profit (TR − TC) (dollars)
0	0	22	−22
1	25	45	−20
2	50	66	−16
3	75	85	−10
4	100	100	0
5	125	114	11
6	150	126	24
7	175	141	34
8	200	160	40
9	**225**	**183**	**42**
10	250	210	40
11	275	245	30
12	300	300	0
13	325	360	−35

The table lists Campus Sweaters' total revenue, total cost, and economic profit. Part (a) graphs the total revenue and total cost curves and part (b) graphs economic profit.

Campus Sweaters makes maximum economic profit, $42 a day ($225 − $183), when it produces 9 sweaters a day. At outputs of 4 sweaters and 12 sweaters a day, Campus Sweaters makes zero economic profit—these are break-even points. At outputs less than 4 sweaters and greater than 12 sweaters a day, Campus Sweaters incurs an economic loss.

Marginal Analysis and the Supply Decision

Another way to find the profit-maximizing output is to use marginal analysis, which compares marginal revenue, *MR*, with marginal cost, *MC*. As output increases, the firm's marginal revenue is constant but its marginal cost eventually increases.

If marginal revenue exceeds marginal cost (*MR* > *MC*), then the revenue from selling one more unit exceeds the cost of producing it and an increase in output increases economic profit. If marginal revenue is less than marginal cost (*MR* < *MC*), then the revenue from selling one more unit is less than the cost of producing that unit and a *decrease* in output *increases* economic profit. If marginal revenue equals marginal cost (*MR* = *MC*), then the revenue from selling one more unit equals the cost incurred to produce that unit. Economic profit is maximized and either an increase or a decrease in output decreases economic profit.

Figure 12.3 illustrates these propositions. If Campus Sweaters increases its output from 8 sweaters to 9 sweaters a day, marginal revenue ($25) exceeds marginal cost ($23), so by producing the 9th sweater economic profit increases by $2 from $40 to $42 a day. The blue area in the figure shows the increase in economic profit when the firm increases production from 8 to 9 sweaters per day.

If Campus Sweaters increases its output from 9 sweaters to 10 sweaters a day, marginal revenue ($25) is less than marginal cost ($27), so by producing the 10th sweater, economic profit decreases. The last column of the table shows that economic profit decreases from $42 to $40 a day. The red area in the figure shows the economic loss that arises from increasing production from 9 to 10 sweaters a day.

Campus Sweaters maximizes economic profit by producing 9 sweaters a day, the quantity at which marginal revenue equals marginal cost.

A firm's profit-maximizing output is its quantity supplied at the market price. The quantity supplied at a price of $25 a sweater is 9 sweaters a day. If the price were higher than $25 a sweater, the firm would increase production. If the price were lower than $25 a sweater, the firm would decrease production. These profit-maximizing responses to different market prices are the foundation of the law of supply:

> Other things remaining the same, the higher the market price of a good, the greater is the quantity supplied of that good.

FIGURE 12.3   Profit-Maximizing Output

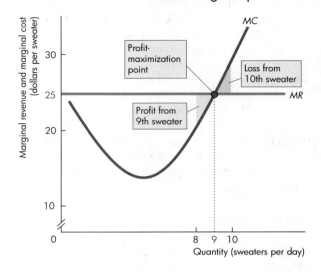

Quantity (Q) (sweaters per day)	Total revenue (TR) (dollars)	Marginal revenue (MR) (dollars per additional sweater)	Total cost (TC) (dollars)	Marginal cost (MC) (dollars per additional sweater)	Economic profit (TR − TC) (dollars)
7	175		141		34
		 25		 19	
8	200		160		40
		 25		. . . 23	
9	**225**		**183**		**42**
		 25		 27	
10	250		210		40
		 25		 35	
11	275		245		30

The firm maximizes profit by producing the output at which marginal revenue equals marginal cost and marginal cost is increasing. The table and figure show that marginal cost equals marginal revenue and economic profit is maximized when Campus Sweaters produces 9 sweaters a day.

The table shows that if Campus Sweaters increases output from 8 to 9 sweaters, marginal cost is $23, which is less than the marginal revenue of $25. If output increases from 9 to 10 sweaters, marginal cost is $27, which exceeds the marginal revenue of $25. If marginal revenue exceeds marginal cost, an increase in output increases economic profit. If marginal revenue is less than marginal cost, an increase in output decreases economic profit. If marginal revenue equals marginal cost, economic profit is maximized.

MyEconLab animation

Temporary Shutdown Decision

You've seen that a firm maximizes profit by producing the quantity at which marginal revenue (price) equals marginal cost. But suppose that at this quantity, price is less than average total cost. In this case, the firm incurs an economic loss. Maximum profit is a loss (a minimum loss). What does the firm do?

If the firm expects the loss to be permanent, it goes out of business. But if it expects the loss to be temporary, the firm must decide whether to shut down temporarily and produce no output, or to keep producing. To make this decision, the firm compares the loss from shutting down with the loss from producing and takes the action that minimizes its loss.

Loss Comparisons A firm's economic loss equals total fixed cost, *TFC*, plus total variable cost minus total revenue. Total variable cost equals average variable cost, *AVC*, multiplied by the quantity produced, *Q*, and total revenue equals price, *P*, multiplied by the quantity *Q*. So

$$\text{Economic loss} = TFC + (AVC - P) \times Q.$$

If the firm shuts down, it produces no output ($Q = 0$). The firm has no variable costs and no revenue but it must pay its fixed costs, so its economic loss equals total fixed cost.

If the firm produces, then in addition to its fixed costs, it incurs variable costs. But it also receives revenue. Its economic loss equals total fixed cost—the loss when shut down—plus total variable cost minus total revenue. If total variable cost exceeds total revenue, this loss exceeds total fixed cost and the firm shuts down. Equivalently, if average variable cost *exceeds* price, this loss exceeds total fixed cost and the firm *shuts down*.

The Shutdown Point A firm's **shutdown point** is the price and quantity at which it is indifferent between producing and shutting down. The shutdown point occurs at the price and the quantity at which average variable cost is a minimum. At the shutdown point, the firm is minimizing its loss and its loss equals total fixed cost. If the price falls below minimum average variable cost, the firm shuts down temporarily and continues to incur a loss equal to total fixed cost. At prices above minimum average variable cost but below average total cost, the firm produces the loss-minimizing output and incurs a loss, but a loss that is less than total fixed cost.

Figure 12.4 illustrates the firm's shutdown decision and the shutdown point that we've just described for Campus Sweaters.

The firm's average variable cost curve is *AVC* and the marginal cost curve is *MC*. Average variable cost has a minimum of $17 a sweater when output is 7 sweaters a day. The *MC* curve intersects the *AVC* curve at its minimum. (We explained this relationship in Chapter 11; see pp. 254–255.)

The figure shows the marginal revenue curve *MR* when the price is $17 a sweater, a price equal to minimum average variable cost. Marginal revenue equals marginal cost at 7 sweaters a day, so this quantity maximizes economic profit (minimizes economic loss). The *ATC* curve shows that the firm's average total cost of producing 7 sweaters a day is $20.14 a sweater. The firm incurs a loss equal to $3.14 a sweater on 7 sweaters a day, so its loss is $22 a day. The table in Fig. 12.3 shows that Campus Sweaters' loss equals its total fixed cost.

FIGURE 12.4   The Shutdown Decision

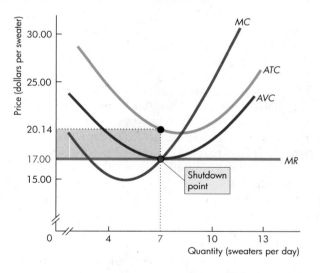

The shutdown point is at minimum average variable cost. At a price below minimum average variable cost, the firm shuts down and produces no output. At a price equal to minimum average variable cost, the firm is indifferent between shutting down and producing no output or producing the output at minimum average variable cost. Either way, the firm minimizes its economic loss and incurs a loss equal to total fixed cost.

MyEconLab animation

The Firm's Supply Curve

A perfectly competitive firm's supply curve shows how its profit-maximizing output varies as the market price varies, other things remaining the same. The supply curve is derived from the firm's marginal cost curve and average variable cost curves. Figure 12.5 illustrates the derivation of the supply curve.

When the price *exceeds* minimum average variable cost (more than $17), the firm maximizes profit by producing the output at which marginal cost equals price. If the price rises, the firm increases its output—it moves up along its marginal cost curve.

When the price is *less than* minimum average variable cost (less than $17 a sweater), the firm maximizes profit by temporarily shutting down and producing no output. The firm produces zero output at all prices below minimum average variable cost.

When the price *equals* minimum average variable cost, the firm maximizes profit *either* by temporarily shutting down and producing no output *or* by producing the output at which average variable cost is a minimum—the shutdown point, *T*. The firm never produces a quantity between zero and the quantity at the shutdown point *T* (a quantity greater than zero and less than 7 sweaters a day).

The firm's supply curve in Fig. 12.5(b) runs along the *y*-axis from a price of zero to a price equal to minimum average variable cost, jumps to point *T*, and then, as the price rises above minimum average variable cost, follows the marginal cost curve.

FIGURE 12.5   A Firm's Supply Curve

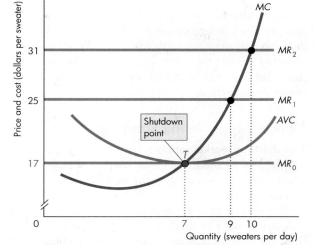

(a) Marginal cost and average variable cost

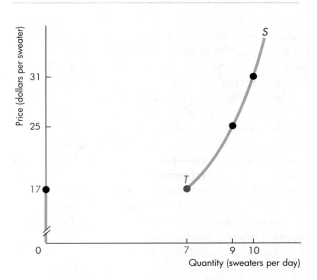

(b) Campus Sweaters' short-run supply curve

Part (a) shows the firm's profit-maximizing output at various market prices. At $25 a sweater, it produces 9 sweaters, and at $17 a sweater, it produces 7 sweaters. At all prices below $17 a sweater, Campus Sweaters produces nothing. Its shutdown point is *T*. Part (b) shows the firm's supply curve—the quantity of sweaters it produces at each price. Its supply curve is made up of the marginal cost curve at all prices above minimum average variable cost and the vertical axis at all prices below minimum average variable cost.

— MyEconLab animation —

◆ REVIEW QUIZ

1   Why does a firm in perfect competition produce the quantity at which marginal cost equals price?

2   What is the lowest price at which a firm produces an output? Explain why.

3   What is the relationship between a firm's supply curve, its marginal cost curve, and its average variable cost curve?

You can work these questions in Study Plan 12.2 and get instant feedback.   MyEconLab

So far, we've studied a single firm in isolation. We've seen that the firm's profit-maximizing decision depends on the market price, which it takes as given. How is the market price determined? Let's find out.

Output, Price, and Profit in the Short Run

To determine the price and quantity in a perfectly competitive market, we need to know how market demand and market supply interact. We start by studying a perfectly competitive market in the short run. The short run is a situation in which the number of firms is fixed.

Market Supply in the Short Run

The **short-run market supply curve** shows the quantity supplied by all the firms in the market at each price when each firm's plant and the number of firms remain the same.

You've seen how an individual firm's supply curve is determined. The market supply curve is derived from the individual supply curves. The quantity supplied by the market at a given price is the sum of the quantities supplied by all the firms in the market at that price.

Figure 12.6 shows the supply curve for the competitive sweater market. In this example, the market consists of 1,000 firms exactly like Campus Sweaters. At each price, the quantity supplied by the market is 1,000 times the quantity supplied by a single firm.

The table in Fig. 12.6 shows the firm's and the market's supply schedules and how the market supply curve is constructed. At prices below $17 a sweater, every firm in the market shuts down; the quantity supplied by the market is zero. At $17 a sweater, each firm is indifferent between shutting down and producing nothing or operating and producing 7 sweaters a day. Some firms will shut down, and others will supply 7 sweaters a day. The quantity supplied by each firm is *either* 0 or 7 sweaters, and the quantity supplied by the market is *between* 0 (all firms shut down) and 7,000 (all firms produce 7 sweaters a day each).

The market supply curve is a graph of the market supply schedules and the points on the supply curve *A* through *D* represent the rows of the table.

To construct the market supply curve, we sum the quantities supplied by all the firms at each price. Each of the 1,000 firms in the market has a supply schedule like Campus Sweaters. At prices below $17 a sweater, the market supply curve runs along the *y*-axis. At $17 a sweater, the market supply curve is horizontal—supply is perfectly elastic. As the price

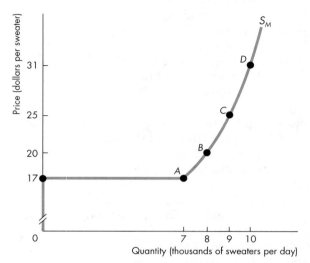

FIGURE 12.6   Short-Run Market Supply Curve

	Price (dollars per sweater)	Quantity supplied by Campus Sweaters (sweaters per day)	Quantity supplied by market (sweaters per day)
A	17	0 or 7	0 to 7,000
B	20	8	8,000
C	25	9	9,000
D	31	10	10,000

The market supply schedule is the sum of the supply schedules of all the individual firms. A market that consists of 1,000 identical firms has a supply schedule similar to that of one firm, but the quantity supplied by the market is 1,000 times as large as that of the one firm (see the table). The market supply curve is S_M. Points A, B, C, and D correspond to the rows of the table. At the shutdown price of $17 a sweater, each firm produces either 0 or 7 sweaters a day and the quantity supplied by the market is between 0 and 7,000 sweaters a day. The market supply is perfectly elastic at the shutdown price.

MyEconLab animation

rises above $17 a sweater, each firm increases its quantity supplied and the quantity supplied by the market increases by 1,000 times that of one firm.

Short-Run Equilibrium

Market demand and short-run market supply determine the market price and market output. Figure 12.7(a) shows a short-run equilibrium. The short-run supply curve, S, is the same as S_M in Fig. 12.6. If the market demand curve is D_1, the market price is $20 a sweater. Each firm takes this price as given and produces its profit-maximizing output, which is 8 sweaters a day. Because the market has 1,000 identical firms, the market output is 8,000 sweaters a day.

A Change in Demand

Changes in demand bring changes to short-run market equilibrium. Figure 12.7(b) shows these changes.

If demand increases and the demand curve shifts rightward to D_2, the market price rises to $25 a sweater. At this price, each firm maximizes profit by increasing its output to 9 sweaters a day. The market output increases to 9,000 sweaters a day.

If demand decreases and the demand curve shifts leftward to D_3, the market price falls to $17. At this price, each firm maximizes profit by decreasing its output. If each firm produces 7 sweaters a day, the market output decreases to 7,000 sweaters a day.

If the demand curve shifts farther leftward than D_3, the market price remains at $17 a sweater because the market supply curve is horizontal at that price. Some firms continue to produce 7 sweaters a day, and others temporarily shut down. Firms are indifferent between these two activities, and whichever they choose, they incur an economic loss equal to total fixed cost. The number of firms continuing to produce is just enough to satisfy the market demand at a price of $17 a sweater.

Profits and Losses in the Short Run

In short-run equilibrium, although the firm produces the profit-maximizing output, it does not necessarily end up making an economic profit. It might do so, but it might alternatively break even or incur an economic loss. Economic profit (or loss) per sweater is price, P, minus average total cost, ATC. So economic profit (or loss) is $(P - ATC) \times Q$. If price

FIGURE 12.7   Short-Run Equilibrium

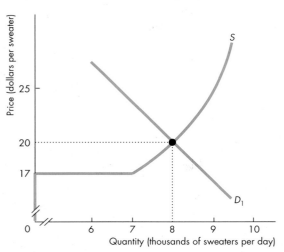

(a) Equilibrium

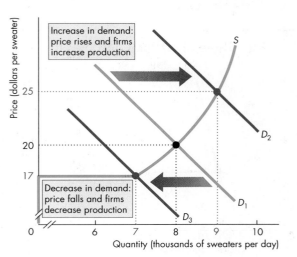

(b) Change in equilibrium

In part (a), the market supply curve is S and the market demand curve is D_1. The market price is $20 a sweater. At this price, each firm produces 8 sweaters a day and the market produces 8,000 sweaters a day.

In part (b), if the market demand increases to D_2, the price rises to $25 a sweater. Each firm produces 9 sweaters a day and market output is 9,000 sweaters. If market demand decreases to D_3, the price falls to $17 a sweater and each firm decreases its output. If each firm produces 7 sweaters a day, the market output is 7,000 sweaters a day.

MyEconLab animation

equals average total cost, a firm breaks even—the entrepreneur makes normal profit. If price exceeds average total cost, a firm makes an economic profit. If price is less than average total cost, a firm incurs an economic loss. Figure 12.8 shows these three possible short-run profit outcomes for Campus Sweaters. These outcomes correspond to the three different levels of market demand that we've just examined.

Three Possible Short-Run Outcomes

Figure 12.8(a) corresponds to the situation in Fig. 12.7(a) where the market demand is D_1. The equilibrium price of a sweater is $20 and the firm produces 8 sweaters a day. Average total cost is $20 a sweater. Price equals average total cost (ATC), so the firm breaks even (makes zero economic profit).

Figure 12.8(b) corresponds to the situation in Fig. 12.7(b) where the market demand is D_2. The equilibrium price of a sweater is $25 and the firm produces 9 sweaters a day. Here, price exceeds average total cost, so the firm makes an economic profit. Its economic profit is $42 a day, which equals $4.67 per sweater ($25.00 − $20.33) multiplied by 9, the

profit-maximizing number of sweaters produced. The blue rectangle shows this economic profit. The height of that rectangle is profit per sweater, $4.67, and the length is the quantity of sweaters produced, 9 a day. So the area of the rectangle is economic profit of $42 a day.

Figure 12.8(c) corresponds to the situation in Fig. 12.7(b) where the market demand is D_3. The equilibrium price of a sweater is $17. Here, the price is less than average total cost, so the firm incurs an economic loss. Price and marginal revenue are $17 a sweater, and the profit-maximizing (in this case, loss-minimizing) output is 7 sweaters a day. Total revenue is $119 a day (7 × $17). Average total cost is $20.14 a sweater, so the economic loss is $3.14 per sweater ($20.14 − $17.00). This loss per sweater multiplied by the number of sweaters is $22. The red rectangle shows this economic loss. The height of that rectangle is economic loss per sweater, $3.14, and the length is the quantity of sweaters produced, 7 a day. So the area of the rectangle is the firm's economic loss of $22 a day. If the price dips below $17 a sweater, the firm temporarily shuts down and incurs an economic loss equal to total fixed cost.

FIGURE 12.8   Three Short-Run Outcomes for the Firm

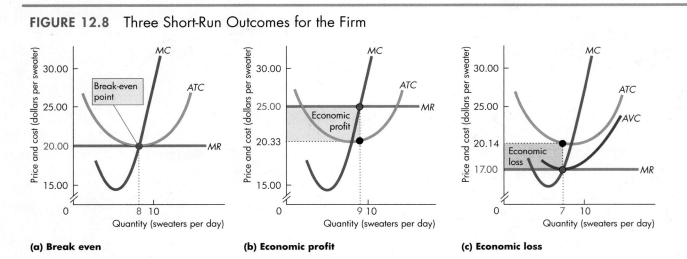

(a) Break even   **(b) Economic profit**   **(c) Economic loss**

In the short run, the firm might break even (make zero economic profit), make an economic profit, or incur an economic loss. In part (a), the price equals minimum average total cost. At the profit-maximizing output, the firm breaks even and makes zero economic profit. In part (b), the market price is $25 a sweater. At the profit-maximizing output,

the price exceeds average total cost and the firm makes an economic profit equal to the area of the blue rectangle. In part (c), the market price is $17 a sweater. At the profit-maximizing output, the price is below minimum average total cost and the firm incurs an economic loss equal to the area of the red rectangle.

MyEconLab animation

Economics in Action
Production Cutback and Temporary Shutdown

The high price of gasoline and anxiety about unemployment and future incomes brought a decrease in the demand for luxury goods including high-end motorcycles such as Harley-Davidsons.

Harley-Davidson's profit-maximizing response to the decrease in demand was to cut production and lay off workers. Some of the production cuts and lay-offs were temporary and some were permanent.

Harley-Davidson's bike production plant in York County, Pennsylvania, was temporarily shut down in the summer of 2008 because total revenue was insufficient to cover total variable cost.

The firm also permanently cut its workforce by 300 people. This permanent cut was like that at Campus Sweaters when the market demand for sweaters decreased from D_1 to D_3 in Fig. 12.7(b).

◆ Output, Price, and Profit in the Long Run

In short-run equilibrium, a firm might make an economic profit, incur an economic loss, or break even. Although each of these three situations is a short-run equilibrium, only one of them is a long-run equilibrium. The reason is that in the long run, firms can enter or exit the market.

Entry and Exit

Entry occurs in a market when new firms come into the market and the number of firms increases. Exit occurs when existing firms leave a market and the number of firms decreases.

Firms respond to economic profit and economic loss by either entering or exiting a market. New firms enter a market in which existing firms are making an economic profit. Firms exit a market in which they are incurring an economic loss. Temporary economic profit and temporary economic loss don't trigger entry and exit. It's the prospect of persistent economic profit or loss that triggers entry and exit.

Entry and exit change the market supply, which influences the market price, the quantity produced by each firm, and its economic profit (or loss).

If firms enter a market, supply increases and the market supply curve shifts rightward. The increase in supply lowers the market price and eventually eliminates economic profit. When economic profit reaches zero, entry stops.

If firms exit a market, supply decreases and the market supply curve shifts leftward. The market price rises and economic loss decreases. Eventually, economic loss is eliminated and exit stops.

To summarize:

■ New firms enter a market in which existing firms are making an economic profit.

■ As new firms enter a market, the market price falls and the economic profit of each firm decreases.

■ Firms exit a market in which they are incurring an economic loss.

■ As firms leave a market, the market price rises and the economic loss incurred by the remaining firms decreases.

■ Entry and exit stop when firms make zero economic profit.

A Closer Look at Entry

The sweater market has 800 firms with cost curves like those in Fig. 12.9(a). The market demand curve is D, the market supply curve is S_1, and the price is $25 a sweater in Fig. 12.9(b). Each firm produces 9 sweaters a day and makes an economic profit.

This economic profit is a signal for new firms to enter the market. As entry takes place, supply increases and the market supply curve shifts rightward toward S^*. As supply increases with no change in demand, the market price gradually falls from $25 to $20 a sweater. At this lower price, each firm makes zero economic profit and entry stops.

Entry results in an increase in market output, but each firm's output *decreases*. Because the price falls, each firm moves down its supply curve and produces less. Because the number of firms increases, the market produces more.

A Closer Look at Exit

The sweater market has 1,200 firms with cost curves like those in Fig. 12.9(a). The market demand curve is D, the market supply curve is S_2, and the price is $17 a sweater in Fig. 12.9(b). Each firm produces 7 sweaters a day and incurs an economic loss.

This economic loss is a signal for firms to exit the market. As exit takes place, supply decreases and the market supply curve shifts leftward toward S^*. As supply decreases with no change in demand, the market price gradually rises from $17 to $20 a sweater. At this higher price, losses are eliminated, each firm makes zero economic profit, and exit stops.

Exit results in a decrease in market output, but each firm's output *increases*. Because the price rises, each firm moves up its supply curve and produces more. Because the number of firms decreases, the market produces less.

FIGURE 12.9   Entry, Exit, and Long-Run Equilibrium

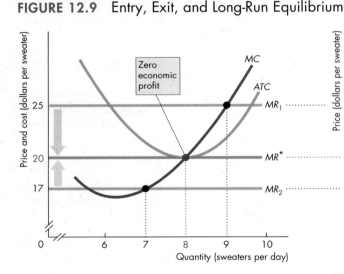

(a) Campus Sweaters

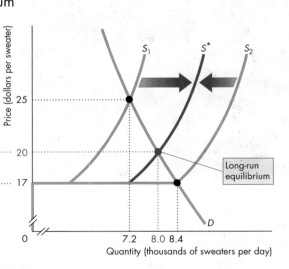

(b) The sweater market

Each firm has cost curves like those of Campus Sweaters in part (a). The market demand curve is D in part (b).

When the market supply curve in part (b) is S_1, the price is $25 a sweater. In part (a), each firm produces 9 sweaters a day and makes an economic profit. Profit triggers the entry of new firms and as new firms enter, the market supply curve shifts rightward, from S_1 toward S^*. The price falls from $25 to $20 a sweater, and the quantity produced increases from 7,200 to 8,000 sweaters. Each firm decreases its output to 8

sweaters a day and its economic profit falls to zero.

When the market supply curve is S_2, the price is $17 a sweater. In part (a), each firm produces 7 sweaters a day and incurs an economic loss. Loss triggers exit and as firms exit, the market supply curve shifts leftward, from S_2 toward S^*. The price rises from $17 to $20 a sweater, and the quantity produced decreases from 8,400 to 8,000 sweaters. Each firm increases its output from 7 to 8 sweaters a day and its economic profit rises to zero.

MyEconLab animation

Economics in Action
Entry and Exit

An example of entry and falling prices occurred during the 1980s and 1990s in the personal computer market. When IBM introduced its first PC in 1981, IBM had little competition. The price was $7,000 (about $16,850 in today's money) and IBM made a large economic profit selling the new machine.

Observing IBM's huge success, new firms such as Gateway, NEC, Dell, and a host of others entered the market with machines that were technologically identical to IBM's. In fact, they were so similar that they came to be called "clones." The massive wave of entry into the personal computer market increased the market supply and lowered the price. The economic profit for all firms decreased.

Today, a $400 computer is vastly more powerful than its 1981 ancestor that cost 42 times as much.

The same PC market that saw entry during the 1980s and 1990s has seen some exit more recently. In 2001, IBM, the firm that first launched the PC, announced that it was exiting the market. The intense competition from Gateway, NEC, Dell, and others that entered the market following IBM's lead has lowered the price and eliminated the economic profit. So IBM now concentrates on servers and other parts of the computer market.

IBM exited the PC market because it was incurring economic losses. Its exit decreased market supply and made it possible for the remaining firms in the market to make zero economic profit.

International Harvester, a manufacturer of farm equipment, provides another example of exit. For decades, people associated the name "International Harvester" with tractors, combines, and other farm machines. But International Harvester wasn't the only maker of farm equipment. The market became intensely competitive, and the firm began to incur economic losses. Now the firm has a new name, Navistar International, and it doesn't make tractors any more. After years of economic losses and shrinking revenues, it got out of the farm-machine business in 1985 and started to make trucks.

International Harvester exited because it was incurring an economic loss. Its exit decreased supply and made it possible for the remaining firms in the market to break even.

Long-Run Equilibrium

You've now seen how economic profit induces entry, which in turn eliminates the profit. You've also seen how economic loss induces exit, which in turn eliminates the loss.

When economic profit and economic loss have been eliminated and entry and exit have stopped, a competitive market is in *long-run equilibrium*.

You've seen how a competitive market adjusts toward its long-run equilibrium. But a competitive market is rarely *in* a state of long-run equilibrium. Instead, it is constantly and restlessly evolving toward long-run equilibrium. The reason is that the market is constantly bombarded with events that change the constraints that firms face.

Markets are constantly adjusting to keep up with changes in tastes, which change demand, and changes in technology, which change costs.

In the next sections, we're going to see how a competitive market reacts to changing tastes and technology and how the market guides resources to their highest-valued use.

REVIEW QUIZ

1 What triggers entry in a competitive market? Describe the process that ends further entry.
2 What triggers exit in a competitive market? Describe the process that ends further exit.

You can work these questions in Study Plan 12.4 and get instant feedback.   MyEconLab

Changes in Demand and Supply as Technology Advances

The arrival of high-speed Internet service increased the demand for personal computers and the demand for music and movie downloads. At the same time, the arrival of these technologies decreased the demand for the retail services of record stores.

What happens in a competitive market when the demand for its product changes? The perfect competition model can answer this questions.

An Increase in Demand

Producers of computer components are in long-run equilibrium making zero economic profit when the arrival of the high-speed Internet brings an increase in the demand for computers and the components from which they are built. The equilibrium price of a component rises and producers make economic profits. New firms start to enter the market. Supply

increases and the price stops rising and then begins to fall. Eventually, enough firms have entered for the supply and the increased demand to be in balance at a price that enables the firms in the market to return to zero economic profit—long-run equilibrium.

Figure 12.10 illustrates. In the market in part (a), demand is D_0, supply is S_0, price is P_0 and market output is Q_0. At the firm in part (b), profit is maximized with marginal revenue, MR_0, equal to marginal cost, MC, at output q_0. Economic profit is zero.

Market demand increases and the demand curve shifts rightward to D_1, in Fig. 12.10(a). The price rises to P_1, and the quantity supplied increases from Q_0 to Q_1 as the market moves up along its short-run supply curve S_0. In Fig. 12.10(b), the firm maximizes profit by producing q_1, where marginal revenue MR_1 equals MC. The market is now in short-run equilibrium in which each firm makes an economic profit.

The economic profit brings entry and short-run supply increases—the market supply curve starts to shift rightward. The increase in supply lowers the

---

FIGURE 12.10   An Increase in Demand

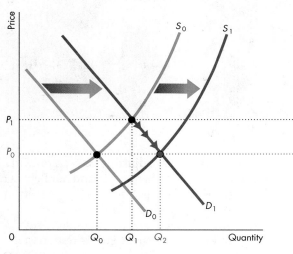

(a) Market

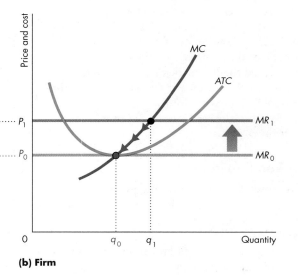

(b) Firm

A market starts out in long-run competitive equilibrium. Part (a) shows the market demand curve D_0, the market supply curve S_0, the market price P_0, and the equilibrium quantity Q_0. Each firm sells its output at the price P_0, so its marginal revenue curve is MR_0 in part (b). Each firm produces q_0 and makes zero economic profit.

Market demand increases from D_0 to D_1 in part (a) and the market price rises to P_1. Each firm maximizes profit by increasing its output to q_1 in part (b), and the market output

increases to Q_1 in part (a). Firms now make economic profits. New firms enter the market, and as they do so, the market supply curve gradually shifts rightward, from S_0 toward S_1. This shift gradually lowers the market price from P_1 back to P_0. While the price is above P_0, firms make economic profits, so new firms keep entering the market. Once the price has returned to P_0, each firm makes zero economic profit and there is no incentive for firms to enter. Each firm produces q_0, and the market output is Q_2.

price and firms decrease output—move down along their marginal cost or supply curve in Fig. 12.10(b).

Eventually, entry shifts the supply curve to S_1 in Fig. 12.10(a). The market price has returned to its original level, P_0. At this price, each firm produces q_0, the same as the quantity produced before the increase in demand. Market output is Q_2 in a long-run equilibrium.

The difference between the initial long-run equilibrium and the new long-run equilibrium is the number of firms in the market. An increase in demand has increased the number of firms. In the process of moving from the initial equilibrium to the new one, each firm makes an economic profit.

A Decrease in Demand

A *decrease* in demand triggers a similar response to the one you've just studied but in the opposite direction. A decrease in demand brings a lower price, economic losses, and exit. Exit decreases supply, which raises the price to its original level and economic profit returns to zero in a new long-run equilibrium. *Economics in the News* below looks at an example.

◆ ECONOMICS IN THE NEWS

Record Stores Exit

Iconic Central Texas Record Store Set to Close
Bobby Barnard opened Sundance Records & Tapes in San Marcos in 1977. But the customers stopped coming, so in 2012 this oldest continually operating music store in Central Texas closed its doors.

Source: Associated Press, March 28, 2012

THE PROBLEM

Provide a graphical analysis to explain why Sundance exited the market and the effects of exit on the market for record store services.

THE SOLUTION

- With demand D_0 and supply S_0, Q_0 customers are served at a price P_0 in part (a) of Fig. 1.
- With marginal revenue MR_0 and marginal cost MC, a record store serves q_0 customers in long-run equilibrium in part (b) of Fig. 1.

- Demand decreases to D_1, the price falls to P_1, and marginal revenue falls to MR_1. Customers decrease to q_1 (and Q_1) and stores incur economic losses.
- Faced with economic loss, Sundance and other stores exit and the market supply decreases to S_1.
- The decrease in supply raises the price and firms remaining return to zero economic profit.

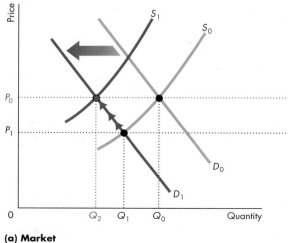

(a) Market

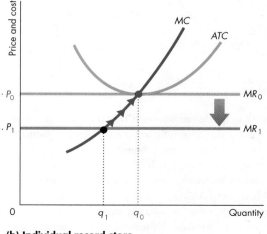

(b) Individual record store

Figure 1   The Market for Record Store Services

Technological Advances Change Supply

We've studied the effects of technological change on demand and to isolate those effects we've kept the individual firm's cost curves unchanged. But new technologies also lower production costs. We now study those effects of advancing technology.

Starting from a long-run equilibrium, when a new technology becomes available that lowers production costs, the first firms to use it make economic profit. But as more firms begin to use the new technology, market supply increases and the price falls. At first, new-technology firms continue to make positive economic profits, so more enter. But firms that continue to use the old technology incur economic losses. Why? Initially they were making zero economic profit and now with the lower price they incur economic losses. So old-technology firms exit.

Eventually, all the old-technology firms have exited and enough new-technology firms have entered to increase the market supply to a level that lowers the price to equal the minimum average total cost using the new technology. In this situation, all the firms, all of which are now new-technology firms, are making zero economic profit.

Figure 12.11 illustrates the process that we've just described. Part (a) shows the market demand and supply curves and market equilibrium. Part (b) shows the cost and revenue curves for a firm using the original old technology. Initially these are the only firms. Part (c) shows the cost and revenue curves for a firm using a new technology after it becomes available.

In part (a), the demand curve is D and initially the supply curve is S_0, so the price is P_0 and the equilibrium quantity is Q_0.

In part (b), marginal revenue is MR_0 and each firm produces q_0 where MR_0 equals MC_{Old}. Economic profit is zero and firms are producing at minimum average total cost on the curve ATC_{Old}.

When a new technology becomes available, average total cost and marginal cost of production fall, and firms that use the new technology produce with the average total cost curve ATC_{New} and marginal cost curve MC_{New} in part (c).

When one firm adopts the new technology, it is too small to influence supply, so the price remains at P_0 and the firm makes an economic profit. But economic profit brings entry of new-technology firms. Market supply increases and the price falls.

FIGURE 12.11   A Technological Advance Lowers Production Costs

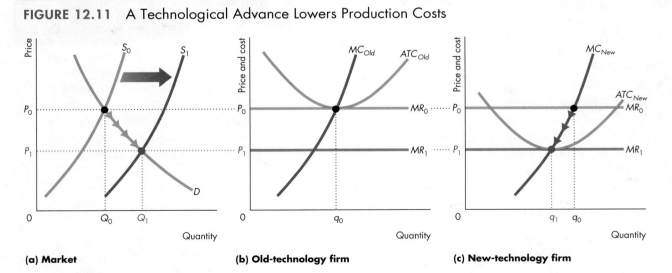

(a) Market

(b) Old-technology firm

(c) New-technology firm

In part (a), the demand curve is D and initially the supply curve is S_0. The price is P_0 and the equilibrium quantity is Q_0. In part (b), marginal revenue is MR_0 and each firm produces q_0 where MR_0 equals MC_{Old}. Economic profit is zero.

A new technology becomes available with lower costs of ATC_{New} and MC_{New} in part (c). A firm that uses this technology produces q_0 where MR_0 equals MC_{New}.

As more firms use this technology, market supply

increases and the price falls. With price below P_0 and above P_1, old-technology firms incur economic losses and exit and new-technology firms make economic profits and new firms enter the market.

In the new long-run equilibrium, the old-technology firms have gone. New-technology firms increase the market supply to S_1. The price falls to P_1, marginal revenue is MR_1, and each firm produces q_1 where MR_1 equals MC_{New}.

◆ ECONOMICS IN THE NEWS

The Falling Cost of Sequencing DNA

Company Announces Low-Cost DNA Decoding Machine

Life Technologies Corp. announced it has developed a $149,000 machine that can decode a person's DNA in a day, at a long-sought price goal of $1,000, making a person's genome useful for medical care.

Source: *USA Today*, January 11, 2012

SOME DATA

The graph shows how the cost of sequencing a person's entire genome has fallen. Life Technologies (in the news clip) is one of around 40 firms competing to develop a machine that can lower that cost from the current $5,000 to $1,000 or less. Many dozens of firms operate DNA sequencing machines and sell their services in a competitive market.

THE QUESTIONS

- What are the competitive markets in the news clip?
- Are any of these markets in long-run equilibrium?
- Are any firms in these markets likely to be making an economic profit?
- Are any of the firms in these markets likely to be incurring an economic loss?
- Are these markets likely to be experiencing entry, exit, or both? If both, which is likely to be greater?
- Who gains from the advances in DNA sequencing technology in the short run and in the long run: producers, consumers, or both?

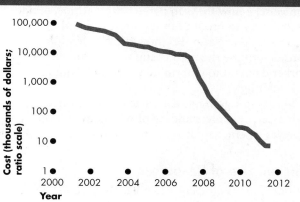

Figure 1 Cost per Genome

Source of data: National Human Genome Research Institute.

THE ANSWERS

- The markets are for DNA sequencing machines and for DNA sequencing services.
- With massive ongoing technological change, neither market is likely to be in long-run equilibrium.
- Firms using the latest technology are likely to be making economic profit.
- Firms using the older technology are likely to be incurring economic loss.
- New-technology firms are entering and old-technology firms are exiting, but with falling prices, there is more entry than exit.
- In the short run, firms gain from higher profit and consumers gain from the lower price. In the long run, economic profit will be zero but consumers will continue to gain from the low price.

With price below P_0, old-technology firms incur an economic loss and exit. With price above P_1, new-technology firms make an economic profit and enter. When a new long-run equilibrium is achieved, the old-technology firms have gone. The number of new-technology firms that have entered have shifted the supply curve to S_1. The price is P_1, marginal revenue is MR_1, and each firm in Fig. 12.11(c) produces q_1 using the new technology where MR_1 equals MC_{New}.

Technological change brings only temporary gains to producers. But the lower prices and better products that technological advances bring are permanent gains for consumers.

◆ REVIEW QUIZ

Describe what happens to output, price, and economic profit in the short run and in the long run in a competitive market following:

1 An increase in demand.
2 A decrease in demand.
3 The adoption of a new technology that lowers production costs.

You can work these questions in Study Plan 12.5 and get instant feedback.   MyEconLab

▶ Competition and Efficiency

You've seen how firms in perfect competition decide the quantity to produce in the short run and in the long run. You've also seen how these individual decisions determine the market supply that interacts with market demand to determine the equilibrium price and quantity.

We're now going to use what you've learned to gain a deeper understanding of why competition achieves an efficient allocation of resources.

Efficient Use of Resources

Resource use is efficient when we produce the goods and services that people value most highly (see Chapter 2, pp. 35–37, and Chapter 5, p. 108). If it is possible to make someone better off without anyone else becoming worse off, resources are *not* being used efficiently. For example, suppose we produce a computer that no one wants and no one will ever use and, at the same time, some people are clamoring for more video games. If we produce fewer computers and reallocate the unused resources to produce more video games, some people will be better off and no one will be worse off. So the initial resource allocation was inefficient.

We can test whether resources are allocated efficiently by comparing marginal social benefit and marginal social cost. In the computer and video games example, the marginal social benefit of a video game exceeds its marginal social cost; the marginal social cost of a computer exceeds its marginal social benefit. So by producing fewer computers and more video games, we move resources toward a higher-valued use.

Choices, Equilibrium, and Efficiency

We can use what you have learned about the decisions of consumers and firms and equilibrium in a competitive market to describe an efficient use of resources.

Choices Consumers allocate their budgets to get the most value possible out of them. We derive a consumer's demand curve by finding how the best budget allocation changes as the price of a good changes. So consumers get the most value out of their resources at all points along their demand curves. If the people who consume a good or service are the

only ones who benefit from it, then the market demand curve measures the benefit to the entire society and is the marginal social benefit curve.

Competitive firms produce the quantity that maximizes profit. We derive the firm's supply curve by finding the profit-maximizing quantity at each price. So firms get the most value out of their resources at all points along their supply curves. If the firms that produce a good or service bear all the costs of producing it, then the market supply curve measures the marginal cost to the entire society and the market supply curve is the marginal social cost curve.

Equilibrium and Efficiency Resources are used efficiently when marginal social benefit equals marginal social cost. Competitive equilibrium achieves this efficient outcome because, with no externalities, price equals marginal social benefit for consumers, and price equals marginal social cost for producers.

The gains from trade are the sum of consumer surplus and producer surplus. The gains from trade for consumers are measured by *consumer surplus*, which is the area below the demand curve and above the price paid. (See Chapter 5, p. 109.) The gains from trade for producers are measured by *producer surplus*, which is the area above the supply curve and below the price received. (See Chapter 5, p. 111.) The total gains from trade equals *total surplus*—the sum of consumer surplus and producer surplus. When the market for a good or service is in equilibrium, the gains from trade are maximized.

Efficiency in the Sweater Market Figure 12.12 illustrates the efficiency of perfect competition in the sweater market. Part (a) shows the market, and part (b) shows Campus Sweaters.

In part (a), consumers get the most value from their budgets at all points on the market demand curve, $D = MSB$. Producers get the most value from their resources at all points on the market supply curve, $S = MSC$. At the equilibrium quantity and price, marginal social benefit equals marginal social cost, and resources are allocated efficiently. Consumer surplus is the green area, producer surplus is the blue area, and *total surplus* (the sum of producer surplus and consumer surplus) is maximized.

In part (b), at the equilibrium price Campus Sweaters (and every other firm) makes zero economic profit and each firm has the plant that enables it to produce at the lowest possible average total cost.

FIGURE 12.12 Efficiency of Perfect Competition

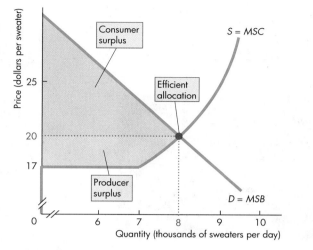

(a) The sweater market

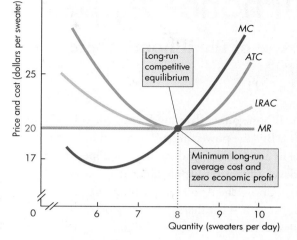

(b) Campus Sweaters

In part (a), market demand, *D*, and market supply, *S*, determine the equilibrium price and quantity. Consumers have made the best available choices on the demand curve, and firms are producing at least cost on the supply curve.

Marginal social benefit, *MSB*, equals marginal social cost, *MSC*, so resources are used efficiently. In part (b) Campus Sweaters produces at the lowest possible long-run average total cost and makes zero economic profit.

MyEconLab animation

Consumers are as well off as possible because the good cannot be produced at a lower cost and the price equals that least possible cost.

When firms in perfect competition are away from long-run equilibrium, either entry or exit moves the market toward the situation depicted in Fig. 12.12. During this process, the market is efficient because marginal social benefit equals marginal social cost. But it is only in long-run equilibrium that economic profit is driven to zero and consumers pay the lowest feasible price.

◆ You've now completed your study of perfect competition. *Reading Between the Lines* on pp. 290–291 gives you an opportunity to use what you have learned to understand the market for smartphone and tablet computer "apps."

Although many markets approximate the model of perfect competition, many do not. In Chapter 13, we study markets at the opposite extreme of market power: monopoly. Then in the following chapters we'll study markets that lie between perfect competi-

tion and monopoly. In Chapter 14, we study monopolistic competition and in Chapter 15, we study oligopoly. When you have completed this study, you'll have a tool kit that will enable you to understand the variety of real-world markets.

REVIEW QUIZ

1 State the conditions that must be met for resources to be allocated efficiently.
2 Describe the choices that consumers make and explain why consumers are efficient on the market demand curve.
3 Describe the choices that producers make and explain why producers are efficient on the market supply curve.
4 Explain why resources are used efficiently in a competitive market.

You can work these questions in Study Plan 12.6 and get instant feedback.   MyEconLab

Perfect Competition in iPhone "Apps"

Because of the iPhone, There Is an App for That

GigaOM
June 29, 2012

... The iPhone only offered web apps when it debuted in 2007. But the powerful hardware and unique user interface lit a fire of demand among developers for a software development kit. Apple obliged a year later and also introduced the App Store, kicking off the modern mobile app era. That market is now worth $8.5 billion and is expected to grow to $46 billion in 2016.

As we celebrate the five-year anniversary of the iPhone's launch on Friday, the true impact of the device can't be measured without talking about the era of mobile apps it spawned, creating success stories like Instagram, Angry Birds, Foursquare, and many others. Suddenly, "apps" became an easy way of understanding software, opening up opportunities to thousands of eager developers who could sell directly to a fast growing base of users. And that has in turn changed the way people compute, weaning them off of PCs to smaller devices: first smartphones, and now tablets. ...

Apple's App Store now boasts 650,000 apps, including 225,000 for the iPad. Apple users have downloaded 30 billion apps from the App Store, generating $5 billion in revenue for developers after Apple's 30 percent cut. To be sure, there were mobile apps prior to the iPhone, but they were either found on third-party app stores or they were controlled by carriers, which chose which apps got to appear on phones sold for their networks.

ESSENCE OF THE STORY

- The iPhone has created opportunities for thousands of "apps" developers who can sell directly to a fast growing base of users.

- The mobile app market had total revenue of $8.5 billion in 2012 and is expected to grow to $46 billion in 2016.

- Apple's App Store offers 650,000 "apps," including 225,000 for the iPad.

- Apple users have downloaded 30 billion "apps" from the App Store, generating $5 billion in revenue for developers after Apple's 30 percent cut.

ECONOMIC ANALYSIS

- The iPhone, iPad, and Android smartphones and tablet computers have created a large demand for apps.

- Although apps are not like corn or sweaters and come in thousands of varieties, the market for apps is highly competitive and we can use the perfect competition model to explain what is happening in that market.

- In 2007, the market for apps didn't exist. There was no supply and almost no demand.

- The market began to operate in 2008, when the first app developers got to work using a software development kit made available by Apple.

- During 2009 through 2012, the number of iPhones and Android smartphones increased dramatically. By 2012, 218 million iPhones and 400 million Android phones had been sold.

- The increase in the number of devices in use increased the demand for apps.

- Thousands of developers, most of them individuals, saw a profit opportunity and got to work creating apps. Their entry into the market increased the supply of apps.

- But the demand for apps kept growing and despite the entry of more developers, profit opportunities remained.

- Figure 1 illustrates the market for apps. In 2011, the demand for apps was D_0 and the supply was S_0. The equilibrium price was P_0 and the quantity was Q_0.

- Figure 2 illustrates the cost and revenue curves of an individual app developer. With marginal revenue MR and marginal cost MC, the developer maximizes profit by producing an app that sells q_0 units. Average total cost of an app (on the ATC curve) is less than the price, so the developer makes an economic profit.

- Economic profit brings entry, so in Fig. 1, supply increases in 2012 to S_1. But the demand for apps also keeps increasing and in 2012 the demand curve is D_1.

- The equilibrium quantity increases to Q_1, and this quantity is produced by an increased number of developers—each producing q_0 units and each continuing to make an economic profit.

- The developer's cost curves in Fig. 2 are unchanged, but as development tools improve, development costs will fall and the cost curves will shift downward, which will further increase supply.

- At some future date, market supply will increase by enough to eliminate economic profit and the market for apps will be in long-run equilibrium. That date is unknown but likely to be a long way off.

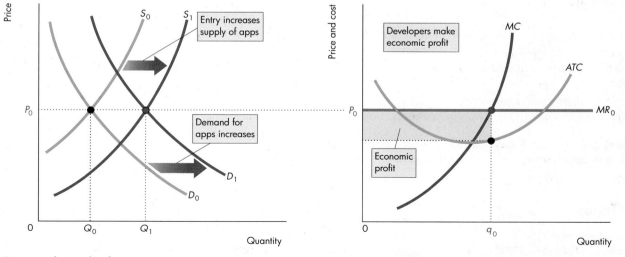

Figure 1 The Market for Apps

Figure 2 An Individual App Developer

291

SUMMARY

Key Points

What Is Perfect Competition? (pp. 272–273)

- In perfect competition, many firms sell identical products to many buyers; there are no restrictions on entry; sellers and buyers are well informed about prices.
- A perfectly competitive firm is a price taker.
- A perfectly competitive firm's marginal revenue always equals the market price.

Working Problems 1 to 3 will give you a better understanding of perfect competition.

The Firm's Output Decision (pp. 274–277)

- The firm produces the output at which marginal revenue (price) equals marginal cost.
- In short-run equilibrium, a firm can make an economic profit, incur an economic loss, or break even.
- If price is less than minimum average variable cost, the firm temporarily shuts down.
- At prices below minimum average variable cost, a firm's supply curve runs along the y-axis; at prices above minimum average variable cost, a firm's supply curve is its marginal cost curve.

Working Problems 4 to 7 will give you a better understanding of a firm's output decision.

Output, Price, and Profit in the Short Run (pp. 278–281)

- The market supply curve shows the sum of the quantities supplied by each firm at each price.
- Market demand and market supply determine price.
- A firm might make a positive economic profit, a zero economic profit, or incur an economic loss.

Working Problems 8 and 9 will give you a better understanding of output, price, and profit in the short run.

Output, Price, and Profit in the Long Run (pp. 281–283)

- Economic profit induces entry and economic loss induces exit.
- Entry increases supply and lowers price and profit. Exit decreases supply and raises price and profit.
- In long-run equilibrium, economic profit is zero. There is no entry or exit.

Working Problems 10 and 11 will give you a better understanding of output, price, and profit in the long run.

Changes in Demand and Supply as Technology Advances (pp. 284–287)

- A permanent increase in demand leads to a larger market output and a larger number of firms. A permanent decrease in demand leads to a smaller market output and a smaller number of firms.
- New technologies lower the cost of production, increase supply, and in the long run lower the price and increase the quantity.

Working Problems 12 to 16 will give you a better understanding of changes in demand and supply as technology advances.

Competition and Efficiency (pp. 288–289)

- Resources are used efficiently when we produce goods and services in the quantities that people value most highly.
- Perfect competition achieves an efficient allocation. In long-run equilibrium, consumers pay the lowest possible price and marginal social benefit equals marginal social cost.

Working Problems 17 and 18 will give you a better understanding of competition and efficiency.

Key Terms

Marginal revenue, 272

Perfect competition, 272

Price taker, 272

Short-run market supply curve, 278

Shutdown point, 276

Total revenue, 272

STUDY PLAN PROBLEMS AND APPLICATIONS

MyEconLab   You can work Problems 1 to 18 in MyEconLab Chapter 12 Study Plan and get instant feedback.

What Is Perfect Competition? (Study Plan 12.1)

Use the following information to work Problems 1 to 3.

Lin's makes fortune cookies that are identical to those made by dozens of other firms, and there is free entry in the fortune cookie market. Buyers and sellers are well informed about prices.

1. In what type of market does Lin's operate? What determines the price of fortune cookies and what determines Lin's marginal revenue from fortune cookies?

2. a. If fortune cookies sell for $10 a box and Lin's offers its cookies for sale at $10.50 a box, how many boxes does it sell?
   b. If fortune cookies sell for $10 a box and Lin's offers its cookies for sale at $9.50 a box, how many boxes does it sell?

3. What is the elasticity of demand for Lin's fortune cookies and how does it differ from the elasticity of the market demand for fortune cookies?

The Firm's Output Decision (Study Plan 12.2)

Use the following table to work Problems 4 to 6. Pat's Pizza Kitchen is a price taker. Its costs are

Output (pizzas per hour)	Total cost (dollars per hour)
0	10
1	21
2	30
3	41
4	54
5	69

4. Calculate Pat's profit-maximizing output and economic profit if the market price is
   (i) $14 a pizza.
   (ii) $12 a pizza.
   (iii) $10 a pizza.

5. What is Pat's shutdown point and what is Pat's economic profit if it shuts down temporarily?

6. Derive Pat's supply curve.

7. The market for paper is perfectly competitive and there are 1,000 firms that produce paper. The table sets out the market demand schedule for paper.

Price (dollars per box)	Quantity demanded (thousands of boxes per week)
3.65	500
5.20	450
6.80	400
8.40	350
10.00	300
11.60	250
13.20	200

Each producer of paper has the following costs when it uses its least-cost plant:

Output (boxes per week)	Marginal cost (dollars per additional box)	Average variable cost	Average total cost
		(dollars per box)	
200	6.40	7.80	12.80
250	7.00	7.00	11.00
300	7.65	7.10	10.43
350	8.40	7.20	10.06
400	10.00	7.50	10.00
450	12.40	8.00	10.22
500	20.70	9.00	11.00

   a. What is the market price of paper?
   b. What is the market's output?
   c. What is the output produced by each firm?
   d. What is the economic profit made or economic loss incurred by each firm?

Output, Price, and Profit in the Short Run
(Study Plan 12.3)

8. In Problem 7, as more and more computer users read documents online rather than print them, the market demand for paper decreases and in the short run the demand schedule becomes

Price (dollars per box)	Quantity demanded (thousands of boxes per week)
2.95	500
4.13	450
5.30	400
6.48	350
7.65	300
8.83	250
10.00	200
11.18	150

If each firm producing paper has the costs set out in Problem 7, what is the market price and the economic profit or loss of each firm in the short run?

9. **Fuel Prices Could Squeeze Cheap Flights**

Airlines are having difficulty keeping prices low, especially as fuel prices keep rising. Airlines have raised fares to make up for the fuel costs. American Airlines increased its fuel surcharge by $20 a round-trip, which Delta, United Airlines, and Continental matched.

Source: CNN, June 12, 2008

a. Explain how an increase in fuel prices might cause an airline to change its output (number of flights) in the short run.

b. Draw a graph to show the increase in fuel prices on an airline's output in the short run.

c. Explain why an airline might incur an economic loss in the short run as fuel prices rise.

Output, Price, and Profit in the Long Run

(Study Plan 12.4)

10. The pizza market is perfectly competitive, and all pizza producers have the same costs as Pat's Pizza Kitchen in Problem 4.

a. At what price will some firms exit the pizza market in the long run?

b. At what price will firms enter the pizza market in the long run?

11. In Problem 7, in the long run,

a. Do firms have an incentive to enter or exit the paper market?

b. If firms do enter or exit the market, explain how the economic profit or loss of the remaining paper producers will change.

c. What is the long-run equilibrium market price and the quantity of paper produced? What is the number of firms in the market?

Changes in Demand and Supply as Technology Advances (Study Plan 12.5)

12. If in the long run, the market demand for paper remains the same as in Problem 8, what is the long-run equilibrium price of paper, the market output, and the economic profit or loss of each firm?

13. Explain and illustrate graphically how the growing world population is influencing the world market for wheat and a representative individual wheat farmer.

14. Explain and illustrate graphically how the market for vacation air travel has been affected by the introduction of low-cost budget airlines.

Use the following news clip to work Problems 15 and 16.

Coors Brewing Expanding Plant

Coors Brewing Co. of Golden will expand its Virginia packaging plant at a cost of $24 million. The addition will accommodate a new production line, which will bottle beer faster. Coors Brewing employs 470 people at its Virginia plant. The expanded packaging line will add another eight jobs.

Source: *Denver Business Journal*, January 6, 2006

15. a. How will Coors' expansion change its marginal cost curve and short-run supply curve?

b. What does this expansion decision imply about the point on Coors' *LRAC* curve at which the firm was before the expansion?

16. a. If other breweries follow the lead of Coors, what will happen to the market price of beer?

b. How will the adjustment that you have described in part (a) influence the economic profit of Coors and other beer producers?

Competition and Efficiency (Study Plan 12.6)

17. In a perfectly competitive market in long-run equilibrium, can consumer surplus be increased? Can producer surplus be increased? Can a consumer become better off by making a substitution away from this market?

18. **Never Pay Retail Again**

Not only has scouring the Web for the best possible price become standard protocol before buying a big-ticket item, but more consumers are employing creative strategies for scoring hot deals. Comparison shopping, haggling and swapping discount codes are all becoming mainstream marks of savvy shoppers. Online shoppers can check a comparison service like Price Grabber before making a purchase.

Source: CNN, May 30, 2008

a. Explain the effect of the Internet on the degree of competition in the market.

b. Explain how the Internet influences market efficiency.

ADDITIONAL PROBLEMS AND APPLICATIONS

MyEconLab   You can work these problems in MyEconLab if assigned by your instructor.

What Is Perfect Competition?

Use the following news clip to work Problems 19 to 21.

Money in the Tank

Two gas stations stand on opposite sides of the road: Rutter's Farm Store and Sheetz gas station. Rutter's doesn't even have to look across the highway to know when Sheetz changes its price for a gallon of gas. When Sheetz raises the price, Rutter's pumps are busy. When Sheetz lowers prices, there's not a car in sight. Both gas stations survive but each has no control over the price.

Source: *The Mining Journal*, May 24, 2008

19. In what type of market do these gas stations operate? What determines the price of gasoline and the marginal revenue from gasoline?

20. Describe the elasticity of demand that each of these gas stations faces.

21. Why does each of these gas stations have so little control over the price of the gasoline it sells?

The Firm's Output Decision

22. The figure shows the costs of Quick Copy, one of many copy shops near campus.

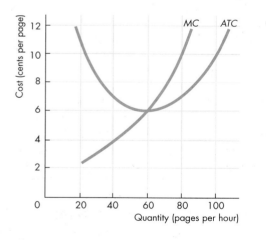

If the market price of copying is 10¢ a page, calculate Quick Copy's

a. Profit-maximizing output.

b. Economic profit.

23. The market for smoothies is perfectly competitive. The following table sets out the market demand schedule.

Price (dollars per smoothie)	Quantity demanded (smoothies per hour)
1.90	1,000
2.00	950
2.20	800
2.91	700
4.25	550
5.25	400
5.50	300

Each of the 100 producers of smoothies has the following costs when it uses its least-cost plant:

Output (smoothies per hour)	Marginal cost (dollars per additional smoothie)	Average variable cost	Average total cost
		(dollars per smoothie)	
3	2.50	4.00	7.33
4	2.20	3.53	6.03
5	1.90	3.24	5.24
6	2.00	3.00	4.67
7	2.91	2.91	4.34
8	4.25	3.00	4.25
9	8.00	3.33	4.44

a. What is the market price of a smoothie?

b. What is the market quantity of smoothies?

c. How many smoothies does each firm sell?

d. What is the economic profit made or economic loss incurred by each firm?

24. **Cadillac Plant Shuts Down Temporarily, Future Uncertain**

Delta Truss in Cadillac [Michigan] is shutting down and temporarily discontinuing truss production. Workers fear this temporary shutdown will become permanent, but the firm announced that it anticipates that production will resume when the spring business begins.

Source: *9&10 News*, February 18, 2008

a. Explain how the shutdown decision will affect Delta Truss' *TFC*, *TVC*, and *TC*.

b. Under what conditions would this shutdown decision maximize Delta Truss' economic profit (or minimize its loss)?

c. Under what conditions will Delta Truss start producing again?

Output, Price, and Profit in the Short Run

25. Big Drops in Prices for Crops Make It Tough Down on the Farm

Grain prices have fallen roughly 50 percent from earlier this year. With better-than-expected crop yields, world grain production this year will rise 5 percent from 2007 to a record high.

Source: *USA Today*, October 23, 2008

Why did grain prices fall in 2008? Draw a graph to show that short-run effect on an individual farmer's economic profit.

Output, Price, and Profit in the Long Run

26. In Problem 23, do firms enter or exit the market in the long run? What is the market price and the equilibrium quantity in the long run?

27. In Problem 24, under what conditions will Delta Truss exit the market?

28. Exxon Mobil Selling All Its Retail Gas Stations

Exxon Mobil is not alone among Big Oil exiting the retail gas business, a market where profits have gotten tougher as crude oil prices have risen. Gas station owners say they're struggling to turn a profit because while wholesale gasoline prices have risen sharply, they've been unable to raise pump prices fast enough to keep pace.

Source: *Houston Chronicle*, June 12, 2008

a. Is Exxon Mobil making a shutdown or exit decision in the retail gasoline market?

b. Under what conditions will this decision maximize Exxon Mobil's economic profit?

c. How might Exxon Mobil's decision affect the economic profit of other gasoline retailers?

Changes in Demand and Supply as Technology Advances

29. Another DVD Format, but It's Cheaper

New Medium Enterprises claims that its new system, HD VMD, is equal to Blu-ray's but at $199 it's cheaper than the $300 Blu-ray player. The Blu-ray Disc Association says New Medium will fail because it believes that Blu-ray technology will always be more expensive. But mass production will cut the cost of a Blu-ray player to $90.

Source: *The New York Times*, March 10, 2008

a. Explain how technological change in Blu-ray production might support the prediction of lower prices in the long run. Illustrate your explanation with a graph.

b. Even if Blu-ray prices do drop to $90 in the long run, why might the HD VMD still end up being less expensive at that time?

Competition and Efficiency

30. In a perfectly competitive market, each firm maximizes its profit by choosing only the quantity to produce. Regardless of whether the firm makes an economic profit or incurs an economic loss, the short-run equilibrium is efficient. Is the statement true? Explain why or why not.

Economics in the News

31. After you have studied *Reading Between the Lines* on pp. 290–291, answer the following questions.

a. What are the features of the market for apps that make it competitive?

b. Does the information provided in the news article suggest that the app market is in long-run equilibrium? Explain why or why not.

c. How would an advance in development technology that lowered a developer's costs change the market supply and the developer's marginal revenue, marginal cost, average total cost, and economic profit?

d. Illustrate your answer to part (c) with an appropriate graphical analysis.

32. Cell Phone Sales Hit 1 Billion Mark

More than 1.15 billion mobile phones were sold worldwide in 2007, a 16 percent increase in a year. Emerging markets, especially China and India, provided much of the growth as many people bought their first phone. Carolina Milanesi, research director for mobile devices at Gartner, reported that in mature markets, such as Japan and Western Europe, consumers' appetite for feature-laden phones was met with new models packed with TV tuners, global positioning satellite functions, touch screens, and cameras.

Source: CNET News, February 27, 2008

a. Explain the effects of the increase in global demand for cell phones on the market for cell phones and on an individual cell-phone producer in the short run.

b. Draw a graph to illustrate your explanation in part (a).

c. Explain the long-run effects of the increase in global demand for cell phones on the market for cell phones.

13

MONOPOLY

After studying this chapter, you will be able to:

◆ Explain how monopoly arises

◆ Explain how a single-price monopoly determines its output and price

◆ Compare the performance and efficiency of single-price monopoly and competition

◆ Explain how price discrimination increases profit

◆ Explain how monopoly regulation influences output, price, economic profit, and efficiency

Google and Microsoft are big players in the markets for Web search and advertising and for computer operating systems, markets that are obviously not perfectly competitive.

In this chapter, we study markets dominated by one big firm. We call such a market *monopoly*. We study the performance and the efficiency of monopoly and compare it with perfect competition.

In *Reading Between the Lines* at the end of the chapter, we look at the remarkable success of Google and ask whether Google is serving the social interest or violating the U.S. antitrust law.

Monopoly and How It Arises

A **monopoly** is a market with a single firm that produces a good or service with no close substitutes and that is protected by a barrier that prevents other firms from entering that market.

How Monopoly Arises

Monopoly arises for two key reasons:

- No close substitutes
- Barrier to entry

No Close Substitutes If a good has a close substitute, even though only one firm produces it, that firm effectively faces competition from the producers of the substitute. A monopoly sells a good or service that has no good substitutes. Tap water and bottled water are close substitutes for drinking, but tap water has no effective substitutes for showering or washing a car and a local public utility that supplies tap water is a monopoly.

Barrier to Entry A constraint that protects a firm from potential competitors is called a **barrier to entry**. The three types of barrier to entry are

- Natural
- Ownership
- Legal

Natural Barrier to Entry A natural barrier to entry creates a **natural monopoly**: a market in which economies of scale enable one firm to supply the entire market at the lowest possible cost. The firms that deliver gas, water, and electricity to our homes are examples of natural monopoly.

Figure 13.1 illustrates a natural monopoly. The market demand curve for electric power is *D*, and the long-run average cost curve is *LRAC*. Economies of scale prevail over the entire length of the *LRAC* curve. At a price of 5 cents per kilowatt-hour, the quantity demanded is 4 million kilowatt-hours and one firm can produce that quantity at a cost of 5 cents per kilowatt-hour. If two firms shared the market equally, it would cost each of them 10 cents per kilowatt-hour to produce a total of 4 million kilowatt-hours.

Ownership Barrier to Entry An ownership barrier to entry occurs if one firm owns a significant portion of a key resource. An example of this type of monopoly occurred during the last century when De Beers con-

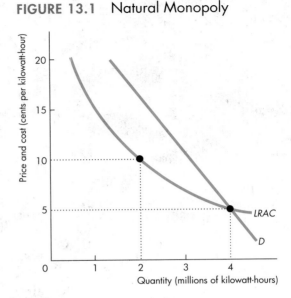

FIGURE 13.1   Natural Monopoly

The market demand curve for electric power is *D*, and the long-run average cost curve is *LRAC*. Economies of scale exist over the entire *LRAC* curve. One firm can distribute 4 million kilowatt-hours at a cost of 5 cents a kilowatt-hour. This same total output costs 10 cents a kilowatt-hour with two firms. One firm can meet the market demand at a lower cost than two or more firms can. The market is a natural monopoly.

MyEconLab animation

trolled up to 90 percent of the world's supply of diamonds. (Today, its share is only 65 percent.)

Legal Barrier to Entry A legal barrier to entry creates a **legal monopoly**: a market in which competition and entry are restricted by the granting of a public franchise, government license, patent, or copyright.

A *public franchise* is an exclusive right granted to a firm to supply a good or service. An example is the U.S. Postal Service, which has the exclusive right to carry first-class mail. A *government license* controls entry into particular occupations, professions, and industries. Examples of this type of barrier to entry occur in medicine, law, dentistry, schoolteaching, architecture, and many other professional services. Licensing does not always create a monopoly, but it does restrict competition.

A *patent* is an exclusive right granted to the inventor of a product or service. A *copyright* is an exclusive right granted to the author or composer of a literary, musical, dramatic, or artistic work. Patents and copyrights are valid for a limited time period that varies from country to country. In the United States, a patent is valid for 20 years. Patents encourage the *invention* of new products and production methods. They also stimulate *innovation*—the use of new inventions—by encouraging inventors to publicize their discoveries and offer them for use under license. Patents have stimulated innovations in areas as diverse as soybean seeds, pharmaceuticals, memory chips, and video games.

Economics in Action
Information-Age Monopolies

Information-age technologies have created four big natural monopolies—firms with large plant costs but almost zero marginal cost, so they experience economies of scale.

These firms are: Microsoft, with 92 percent of personal computers using a version of Windows and 54 percent using Internet Explorer for Web browsing; Google, which performs 83 percent of Internet searches; Facebook, with 64 percent of the social media market; and eBay, with 62 percent of the Internet auction market.

These same information-age technologies have also destroyed monopolies. FedEx, UPS, the fax machine, and e-mail have weakened the monopoly of the U.S. Postal Service; and the satellite dish has weakened cable television monopolies.

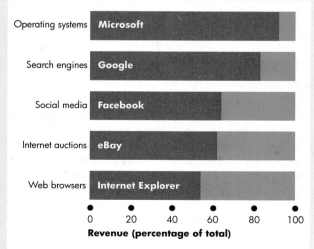

Market Shares

Monopoly Price-Setting Strategies

A major difference between monopoly and competition is that a monopoly sets its own price. In doing so, the monopoly faces a market constraint: To sell a larger quantity, the monopoly must set a lower price. There are two monopoly situations that create two pricing strategies:

- Single price
- Price discrimination

Single Price A **single-price monopoly** is a firm that must sell each unit of its output for the same price to all its customers. De Beers sells diamonds (of a given size and quality) for the same price to all its customers. If it tried to sell at a low price to some customers and at a higher price to others, only the low-price customers would buy from De Beers. Others would buy from De Beers' low-price customers. De Beers is a *single-price* monopoly.

Price Discrimination When a firm practices **price discrimination**, it sells different units of a good or service for different prices. Many firms price discriminate. Microsoft sells its Windows and Office software at different prices to different buyers. Computer manufacturers who install the software on new machines, students and teachers, governments, and businesses all pay different prices. Pizza producers offer a second pizza for a lower price than the first one. These are examples of *price discrimination*.

When a firm price discriminates, it looks as though it is doing its customers a favor. In fact, it is charging the highest possible price for each unit sold and making the largest possible profit.

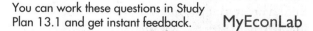
REVIEW QUIZ

1 How does monopoly arise?
2 How does a natural monopoly differ from a legal monopoly?
3 Distinguish between a price-discriminating monopoly and a single-price monopoly.

You can work these questions in Study Plan 13.1 and get instant feedback.   MyEconLab

We start with a single-price monopoly and see how it makes its decisions about the quantity to produce and the price to charge to maximize its profit.

A Single-Price Monopoly's Output and Price Decision

To understand how a single-price monopoly makes its output and price decision, we must first study the link between price and marginal revenue.

Price and Marginal Revenue

Because in a monopoly there is only one firm, the demand curve facing the firm is the market demand curve. Let's look at Bobbie's Barbershop, the sole supplier of haircuts in Cairo, Nebraska. The table in Fig. 13.2 shows the market demand schedule. At a price of $20, Bobbie sells no haircuts. The lower the price, the more haircuts per hour she can sell. For example, at $12, consumers demand 4 haircuts per hour (row E).

Total revenue (TR) is the price (P) multiplied by the quantity sold (Q). For example, in row D, Bobbie sells 3 haircuts at $14 each, so total revenue is $42. *Marginal revenue* ($MR$) is the change in total revenue (ΔTR) resulting from a one-unit increase in the quantity sold. For example, if the price falls from $16 (row C) to $14 (row D), the quantity sold increases from 2 to 3 haircuts. Total revenue increases from $32 to $42, so the change in total revenue is $10. Because the quantity sold increases by 1 haircut, marginal revenue equals the change in total revenue and is $10. Marginal revenue is placed between the two rows to emphasize that marginal revenue relates to the *change* in the quantity sold.

Figure 13.2 shows the market demand curve and marginal revenue curve (MR) and also illustrates the calculation we've just made. Notice that at each level of output, marginal revenue is less than price—the marginal revenue curve lies below the demand curve. Why is marginal revenue *less* than price? It is because when the price is lowered to sell one more unit, two opposing forces affect total revenue. The lower price results in a revenue loss, and the increased quantity sold results in a revenue gain. For example, at a price of $16, Bobbie sells 2 haircuts (point C). If she lowers the price to $14, she sells 3 haircuts and has a revenue gain of $14 on the third haircut. But she now receives only $14 on the first two haircuts—$2 less than before. As a result, she loses $4 of revenue on the first 2 haircuts. To calculate marginal revenue, she must deduct this amount from the revenue gain of $14. So her marginal revenue is $10, which is less than the price.

FIGURE 13.2   Demand and Marginal Revenue

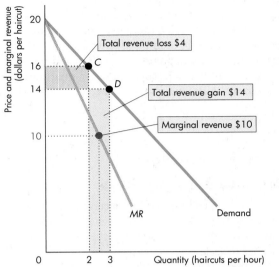

Price (P) (dollars per haircut)	Quantity demanded (Q) (haircuts per hour)	Total revenue (TR = P × Q) (dollars)	Marginal revenue (MR = ΔTR/ΔQ) (dollars per haircut)
A 20	0	0	
			18
B 18	1	18	
			14
C 16	2	32	
			10
D 14	3	42	
			6
E 12	4	48	
			2
F 10	5	50	

The table shows the demand schedule. Total revenue (*TR*) is price multiplied by quantity sold. For example, in row *C*, the price is $16 a haircut, Bobbie sells 2 haircuts, and total revenue is $32. Marginal revenue (*MR*) is the change in total revenue that results from a one-unit increase in the quantity sold. For example, when the price falls from $16 to $14 a haircut, the quantity sold increases from 2 to 3, an increase of 1 haircut, and total revenue increases by $10. Marginal revenue is $10. The demand curve and the marginal revenue curve, *MR*, are based on the numbers in the table and illustrate the calculation of marginal revenue when the price falls from $16 to $14 a haircut.

Marginal Revenue and Elasticity

A single-price monopoly's marginal revenue is related to the *elasticity of demand* for its good. The demand for a good can be *elastic* (the elasticity is greater than 1), *inelastic* (the elasticity is less than 1), or *unit elastic* (the elasticity is equal to 1). Demand is *elastic* if a 1 percent fall in the price brings a greater than 1 percent increase in the quantity demanded. Demand is *inelastic* if a 1 percent fall in the price brings a less than 1 percent increase in the quantity demanded. Demand is *unit elastic* if a 1 percent fall in the price brings a 1 percent increase in the quantity demanded. (See Chapter 4, pp. 84–86.)

If demand is elastic, a fall in the price brings an increase in total revenue—the revenue gain from the increase in quantity sold outweighs the revenue loss from the lower price—and marginal revenue is *positive*. If demand is inelastic, a fall in the price brings a decrease in total revenue—the revenue gain from the increase in quantity sold is outweighed by the revenue loss from the lower price—and marginal revenue is *negative*. If demand is unit elastic, total revenue does not change—the revenue gain from the increase in the quantity sold offsets the revenue loss from the lower price—and marginal revenue is *zero*. (See Chapter 4, p. 88.)

Figure 13.3 illustrates the relationship between marginal revenue, total revenue, and elasticity. As the price gradually falls from $20 to $10 a haircut, the quantity demanded increases from 0 to 5 haircuts an hour. Over this output range, marginal revenue is positive in part (a), total revenue increases in part (b), and the demand for haircuts is elastic. As the price falls from $10 to $0 a haircut, the quantity of haircuts demanded increases from 5 to 10 an hour. Over this output range, marginal revenue is negative in part (a), total revenue decreases in part (b), and the demand for haircuts is inelastic. When the price is $10 a haircut, marginal revenue is zero in part (a), total revenue is at a maximum in part (b), and the demand for haircuts is unit elastic.

In Monopoly, Demand Is Always Elastic   The relationship between marginal revenue and elasticity of demand that you've just discovered implies that a profit-maximizing monopoly never produces an output in the inelastic range of the market demand curve. If it did so, it could charge a higher price, produce a smaller quantity, and increase its profit. Let's now look at a monopoly's price and output decision.

FIGURE 13.3   Marginal Revenue and Elasticity

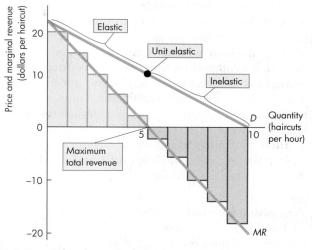

(a) Demand and marginal revenue curves

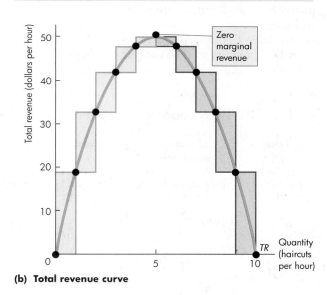

(b) Total revenue curve

In part (a), the demand curve is *D* and the marginal revenue curve is *MR*. In part (b), the total revenue curve is *TR*. Over the range 0 to 5 haircuts an hour, a price cut increases total revenue, so marginal revenue is positive—as shown by the blue bars. Demand is elastic. Over the range 5 to 10 haircuts an hour, a price cut decreases total revenue, so marginal revenue is negative—as shown by the red bars. Demand is inelastic. At 5 haircuts an hour, total revenue is maximized and marginal revenue is zero. Demand is unit elastic.

MyEconLab animation

Price and Output Decision

A monopoly sets its price and output at the levels that maximize economic profit. To determine this price and output level, we need to study the behavior of both cost and revenue as output varies. A monopoly faces the same types of technology and cost constraints as a competitive firm, so its costs (total cost, average cost, and marginal cost) behave just like those of a firm in perfect competition. And a monopoly's revenues (total revenue, price, and marginal revenue) behave in the way we've just described.

Table 13.1 provides information about Bobbie's costs, revenues, and economic profit, and Fig. 13.4 shows the same information graphically.

Maximizing Economic Profit You can see in Table 13.1 and Fig. 13.4(a) that total cost (*TC*) and total revenue (*TR*) both rise as output increases, but *TC* rises at an increasing rate and *TR* rises at a decreasing rate. Economic profit, which equals *TR* minus *TC*, increases at small output levels, reaches a maximum, and then decreases. The maximum profit ($12) occurs when Bobbie sells 3 haircuts for $14 each. If she sells 2 haircuts for $16 each or 4 haircuts for $12 each, her economic profit will be only $8.

Marginal Revenue Equals Marginal Cost You can see Bobbie's marginal revenue (*MR*) and marginal cost (*MC*) in Table 13.1 and Fig. 13.4(b).

When Bobbie increases output from 2 to 3 haircuts, *MR* is $10 and *MC* is $6. *MR* exceeds *MC* by $4 and Bobbie's profit increases by that amount. If Bobbie increases output yet further, from 3 to 4 haircuts, *MR* is $6 and *MC* is $10. In this case, *MC* exceeds *MR* by $4, so profit decreases by that amount. When *MR* exceeds *MC*, profit increases if output increases. When *MC* exceeds *MR*, profit increases if output *decreases*. When *MC* equals *MR*, profit is maximized.

Figure 13.4(b) shows the maximum profit as price (on the demand curve *D*) minus average total cost (on the *ATC* curve) multiplied by the quantity produced—the blue rectangle.

Maximum Price the Market Will Bear Unlike a firm in perfect competition, a monopoly influences the price of what it sells. But a monopoly doesn't set the price at the maximum *possible* price. At the maximum possible price, the firm would be able to sell only one unit of output, which in general is less than the profit-maximizing quantity. Rather, a monopoly produces the profit-maximizing quantity and sells that quantity for the highest price it can get.

TABLE 13.1 A Monopoly's Output and Price Decision

Price (P) (dollars per haircut)	Quantity demanded (Q) (haircuts per hour)	Total revenue (TR = P × Q) (dollars)	Marginal revenue (MR = ΔTR/ΔQ) (dollars per haircut)	Total cost (TC) (dollars)	Marginal cost (MC = ΔTC/ΔQ) (dollars per haircut)	Profit (TR − TC) (dollars)
20	0	0		20		−20
			18		1	
18	1	18		21		−3
			14		3	
16	2	32		24		+8
			10		6	
14	3	42		30		+12
			6		10	
12	4	48		40		+8
			2		15	
10	5	50		55		−5

This table gives the information needed to find the profit-maximizing output and price. Total revenue (TR) equals price multiplied by the quantity sold. Profit equals total revenue minus total cost (TC). Profit is maximized when 3 haircuts are sold at a price of $14 each. Total revenue is $42, total cost is $30, and economic profit is $12 ($42 − $30).

FIGURE 13.4   A Monopoly's Output and Price

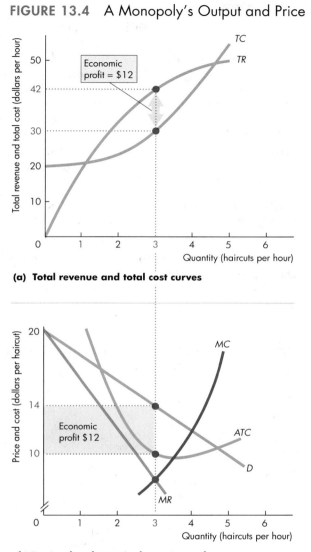

(a) Total revenue and total cost curves

(b) Demand and marginal revenue and cost curves

In part (a), economic profit is the vertical distance equal to total revenue (*TR*) minus total cost (*TC*) and it is maximized at 3 haircuts an hour.

In part (b), economic profit is maximized when marginal cost (*MC*) equals marginal revenue (*MR*). The profit-maximizing output is 3 haircuts an hour. The price is determined by the demand curve (*D*) and is $14 a haircut. The average total cost of a haircut is $10, so economic profit, the blue rectangle, is $12—the profit per haircut ($4) multiplied by 3 haircuts.

── MyEconLab animation ──

All firms maximize profit by producing the output at which marginal revenue equals marginal cost. For a competitive firm, price equals marginal revenue, so price also equals marginal cost. For a monopoly, price exceeds marginal revenue, so price also exceeds marginal cost.

A monopoly charges a price that exceeds marginal cost, but does it always make an economic profit? In Fig. 13.4(b), Bobbie produces 3 haircuts an hour. Her average total cost is $10 (on the *ATC* curve) and her price is $14 (on the *D* curve), so her profit per haircut is $4 ($14 minus $10). Bobbie's economic profit is shown by the area of the blue rectangle, which equals the profit per haircut ($4) multiplied by the number of haircuts (3), for a total of $12.

If firms in a perfectly competitive market make a positive economic profit, new firms enter. That does *not* happen in monopoly. Barriers to entry prevent new firms from entering the market, so a monopoly can make a positive economic profit and might continue to do so indefinitely. Sometimes that economic profit is large, as in the international diamond business.

Bobbie makes a positive economic profit. But suppose that Bobbie's landlord increases the rent on her salon. If Bobbie pays an additional $12 an hour for rent, her fixed cost increases by $12 an hour. Her marginal cost and marginal revenue don't change, so her profit-maximizing output remains at 3 haircuts an hour. Her profit decreases by $12 an hour to zero. If Bobbie's salon rent increases by more than $12 an hour, she incurs an economic loss. If this situation were permanent, Bobbie would go out of business.

◆ REVIEW QUIZ

1 What is the relationship between marginal cost and marginal revenue when a single-price monopoly maximizes profit?

2 How does a single-price monopoly determine the price it will charge its customers?

3 What is the relationship between price, marginal revenue, and marginal cost when a single-price monopoly is maximizing profit?

4 Why can a monopoly make a positive economic profit even in the long run?

You can work these questions in Study Plan 13.2 and get instant feedback.   MyEconLab

Single-Price Monopoly and Competition Compared

Imagine a market that is made up of many small firms operating in perfect competition. Then imagine that a single firm buys out all these small firms and creates a monopoly.

What will happen in this market? Will the price rise or fall? Will the quantity produced increase or decrease? Will economic profit increase or decrease? Will either the original competitive situation or the new monopoly situation be efficient?

These are the questions we're now going to answer. First, we look at the effects of monopoly on the price and quantity produced. Then we turn to the questions about efficiency.

Comparing Price and Output

Figure 13.5 shows the market we'll study. The market demand curve is D. The demand curve is the same regardless of how the industry is organized. But the supply side and the equilibrium are different in monopoly and competition. First, let's look at the case of perfect competition.

Perfect Competition Initially, with many small perfectly competitive firms in the market, the market supply curve is S. This supply curve is obtained by summing the supply curves of all the individual firms in the market.

In perfect competition, equilibrium occurs where the supply curve and the demand curve intersect. The price is P_C, and the quantity produced by the industry is Q_C. Each firm takes the price P_C and maximizes its profit by producing the output at which its own marginal cost equals the price. Because each firm is a small part of the total industry, there is no incentive for any firm to try to manipulate the price by varying its output.

Monopoly Now suppose that this industry is taken over by a single firm. Consumers do not change, so the market demand curve remains the same as in the case of perfect competition. But now the monopoly recognizes this demand curve as a constraint on the price at which it can sell its output. The monopoly's marginal revenue curve is MR.

The monopoly maximizes profit by producing the quantity at which marginal revenue equals marginal cost. To find the monopoly's marginal cost curve, first

recall that in perfect competition, the market supply curve is the sum of the supply curves of the firms in the industry. Also recall that each firm's supply curve is its marginal cost curve (see Chapter 12, p. 277). So when the market is taken over by a single firm, the competitive market's supply curve becomes the monopoly's marginal cost curve. To remind you of this fact, the supply curve is also labeled MC.

The output at which marginal revenue equals marginal cost is Q_M. This output is smaller than the competitive output Q_C. And the monopoly charges the price P_M, which is higher than P_C. We have established that

> Compared to a perfectly competitive market, a single-price monopoly produces a smaller output and charges a higher price.

We've seen how the output and price of a monopoly compare with those in a competitive market. Let's now compare the efficiency of the two types of market.

FIGURE 13.5   Monopoly's Smaller Output and Higher Price

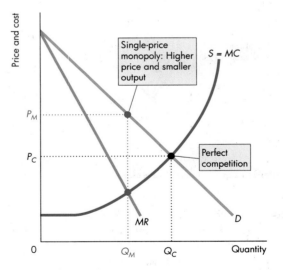

A competitive market produces the quantity Q_C at price P_C. A single-price monopoly produces the quantity Q_M at which marginal revenue equals marginal cost and sells that quantity for the price P_M. Compared to perfect competition, a single-price monopoly produces a smaller output and charges a higher price.

—— MyEconLab animation ——

Efficiency Comparison

Perfect competition (with no externalities) is efficient. Figure 13.6(a) illustrates the efficiency of perfect competition and serves as a benchmark against which to measure the inefficiency of monopoly. Along the demand and marginal social benefit curve ($D = MSB$), consumers are efficient. Along the supply curve and marginal social cost curve ($S = MSC$), producers are efficient. In competitive equilibrium, the price is P_C, the quantity is Q_C, and marginal social benefit equals marginal social cost.

Consumer surplus is the green triangle under the demand curve and above the equilibrium price (see Chapter 5, p. 109). *Producer surplus* is the blue area above the supply curve and below the equilibrium price (see Chapter 5, p. 111). Total surplus (consumer surplus and producer surplus) is maximized.

Also, in long-run competitive equilibrium, entry and exit ensure that each firm produces its output at the minimum possible long-run average cost.

To summarize: At the competitive equilibrium, marginal social benefit equals marginal social cost; total surplus is maximized; firms produce at the lowest possible long-run average cost; and resource use is efficient.

Figure 13.6(b) illustrates the inefficiency of monopoly and the sources of that inefficiency. A monopoly produces Q_M and sells its output for P_M. The smaller output and higher price drive a wedge between marginal social benefit and marginal social cost and create a *deadweight loss*. The gray triangle shows the deadweight loss and its magnitude is a measure of the inefficiency of monopoly.

Consumer surplus shrinks for two reasons. First, consumers lose by having to pay more for the good. This loss to consumers is a gain for monopoly and increases the producer surplus. Second, consumers lose by getting less of the good, and this loss is part of the deadweight loss.

Although the monopoly gains from a higher price, it loses some producer surplus because it produces a smaller output. That loss is another part of the deadweight loss.

A monopoly produces a smaller output than perfect competition and faces no competition, so it does not produce at the lowest possible long-run average cost. As a result, monopoly damages the consumer interest in three ways: A monopoly produces less, increases the cost of production, and raises the price by more than the increased cost of production.

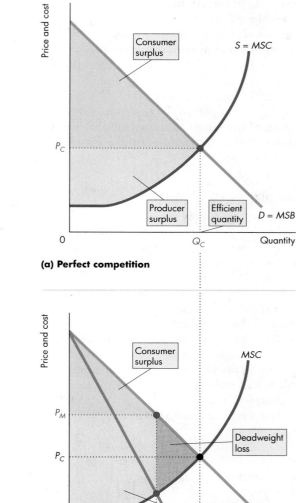

FIGURE 13.6   Inefficiency of Monopoly

(a) Perfect competition

(b) Monopoly

In perfect competition in part (a), output is Q_C and the price is P_C. Marginal social benefit (MSB) equals marginal social cost (MSC); total surplus, the sum of consumer surplus (the green triangle) and producer surplus (the blue area), is maximized; and in the long run, firms produce at the lowest possible average cost. Monopoly in part (b) produces Q_M and raises the price to P_M. Consumer surplus shrinks, the monopoly gains, and a deadweight loss (the gray triangle) arises.

——— MyEconLab animation ———

Redistribution of Surpluses

You've seen that monopoly is inefficient because marginal social benefit exceeds marginal social cost and there is deadweight loss—a social loss. But monopoly also brings a *redistribution* of surpluses.

Some of the lost consumer surplus goes to the monopoly. In Fig. 13.6, the monopoly takes the difference between the higher price, P_M, and the competitive price, P_C, on the quantity sold, Q_M. So the monopoly takes that part of the consumer surplus. This portion of the loss of consumer surplus is not a loss to society. It is redistribution from consumers to the monopoly producer.

Rent Seeking

You've seen that monopoly creates a deadweight loss and is inefficient. But the social cost of monopoly can exceed the deadweight loss because of an activity called rent seeking. Any surplus—consumer surplus, producer surplus, or economic profit—is called **economic rent**. The pursuit of wealth by capturing economic rent is called **rent seeking**.

You've seen that a monopoly makes its economic profit by diverting part of consumer surplus to itself—by converting consumer surplus into economic profit. So the pursuit of economic profit by a monopoly is rent seeking. It is the attempt to capture consumer surplus.

Rent seekers pursue their goals in two main ways. They might

- Buy a monopoly
- Create a monopoly

Buy a Monopoly To rent seek by buying a monopoly, a person searches for a monopoly that is for sale at a lower price than the monopoly's economic profit. Trading of taxicab licenses is an example of this type of rent seeking. In some cities, taxicabs are regulated. The city restricts both the fares and the number of taxis that can operate so that operating a taxi results in economic profit. A person who wants to operate a taxi must buy a license from someone who already has one. People rationally devote time and effort to seeking out profitable monopoly businesses to buy. In the process, they use up scarce resources that could otherwise have been used to produce goods and services. The value of this lost production is part of the social cost of monopoly. The amount paid for a monopoly is not a social cost because the payment is just a transfer of an existing producer surplus from the buyer to the seller.

Create a Monopoly Rent seeking by creating a monopoly is mainly a political activity. It takes the form of lobbying and trying to influence the political process. Such influence might be sought by making campaign contributions in exchange for legislative support or by indirectly seeking to influence political outcomes through publicity in the media or more direct contacts with politicians and bureaucrats. An example of a monopoly created in this way is the government-imposed restrictions on the quantities of textiles that may be imported into the United States. Another is a regulation that limits the number of oranges that may be sold in the United States. These are regulations that restrict output and increase price.

This type of rent seeking is a costly activity that uses up scarce resources. Taken together, firms spend billions of dollars lobbying Congress, state legislators, and local officials in the pursuit of licenses and laws that create barriers to entry and establish a monopoly.

Rent-Seeking Equilibrium

Barriers to entry create monopoly. But there is no barrier to entry into rent seeking. Rent seeking is like perfect competition. If an economic profit is available, a new rent seeker will try to get some of it. And competition among rent seekers pushes up the price that must be paid for a monopoly, to the point at which the rent seeker makes zero economic profit by operating the monopoly. For example, competition for the right to operate a taxi in New York City leads to a price of more than $100,000 for a taxi license, which is sufficiently high to eliminate the economic profit made by a taxi operator.

Figure 13.7 shows a rent-seeking equilibrium. The cost of rent seeking is a fixed cost that must be added to a monopoly's other costs. Rent seeking and rent-seeking costs increase to the point at which no economic profit is made. The average total cost curve, which includes the fixed cost of rent seeking, shifts upward until it just touches the demand curve. Economic profit is zero. It has been lost in rent seeking.

Consumer surplus is unaffected, but the deadweight loss from monopoly is larger. The deadweight loss now includes the original deadweight loss triangle plus the lost producer surplus, shown by the enlarged gray area in Fig. 13.7.

FIGURE 13.7   Rent-Seeking Equilibrium

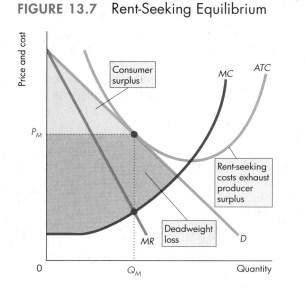

With competitive rent seeking, a single-price monopoly uses all its economic profit to maintain its monopoly. The firm's rent-seeking costs are fixed costs. They add to total fixed cost and to average total cost. The *ATC* curve shifts upward until, at the profit-maximizing price, the firm breaks even.

———— MyEconLab animation ————

REVIEW QUIZ

1 Why does a single-price monopoly produce a smaller output and charge more than the price that would prevail if the market were perfectly competitive?
2 How does a monopoly transfer consumer surplus to itself?
3 Why is a single-price monopoly inefficient?
4 What is rent seeking and how does it influence the inefficiency of monopoly?

You can work these questions in Study Plan 13.3 and get instant feedback.   MyEconLab

So far, we've considered only a single-price monopoly. But many monopolies do not operate with a single price. Instead, they price discriminate. Let's now see how a price-discriminating monopoly works.

Price Discrimination

You encounter *price discrimination*—selling a good or service at a number of different prices—when you travel, go to the movies, get your hair cut, visit an art museum or theme park, or buy pizza. These are all examples of firms with market power, setting the prices of an identical good or service at different levels for different customers.

Not all price *differences* are price *discrimination*: they reflect differences in production costs. For example, real-time meters for electricity enable power utilities to charge a different price at peak-load times than during the night. But it costs more per kilowatt-hour to generate electricity at peak-load times so this price difference reflects production cost differences and is not price discrimination.

At first sight, price discrimination appears to be inconsistent with profit maximization. Why would a movie theater allow children to see movies at a discount? Why would a hairdresser charge students and senior citizens less? Aren't these firms losing profit by being nice to their customers? The answer, as you are about to discover, is that price discrimination is profitable: It increases economic profit.

But to be able to price discriminate, the firm must sell a product that cannot be resold; and it must be possible to identify and separate different buyer types.

Two Ways of Price Discriminating

Firms price discriminate in two broad ways. They discriminate:

■ Among groups of buyers
■ Among units of a good

Discriminating Among Groups of Buyers People differ in the value they place on a good—their marginal benefit and willingness to pay. Some of these differences are correlated with features such as age, employment status, and other easily distinguished characteristics. When such a correlation is present, firms can profit by price discriminating among the different groups of buyers.

For example, salespeople and other business travelers know that a face-to-face sales meeting with a customer might bring a large and profitable order. So for these travelers, the marginal benefit from a trip is large and the price that such a traveler is willing to pay for a trip is high. In contrast, for a leisure traveler, any of several different trips and even no trip at all are options. So for leisure travelers, the marginal benefit of a trip is small and the price that such a traveler is willing to pay for a trip is low. Because the price that business travelers are willing to pay exceeds what leisure travelers are willing to pay, it is possible for an airline to price discriminate between these two groups and increase its profit. We'll return to this example of price discrimination below.

Discriminating Among Units of a Good Everyone experiences diminishing marginal benefit so if all the units of the good are sold for a single price, buyers end up with a consumer surplus equal to the value they get from each unit minus the price paid for it.

A firm that price discriminates by charging a buyer one price for a single item and a lower price for a second or third item can capture some of the consumer surplus. Buy one pizza and get a second one for a lower price is an example of this type of price discrimination.

Increasing Profit and Producer Surplus

By getting buyers to pay a price as close as possible to their maximum willingness to pay, a monopoly captures the consumer surplus and converts it into producer surplus. And more producer surplus means more economic profit.

To see why more producer surplus means more economic profit, recall some definitions. With total revenue TR and total cost TC,

$$\text{Economic profit} = TR - TC.$$

Producer surplus is total revenue minus the area under the marginal cost curve. But the area under the marginal cost curve is total *variable* cost, TVC. So producer surplus equals total revenue minus TVC, or

$$\text{Producer surplus} = TR - TVC.$$

You can see that the difference between economic profit and producer surplus is the same as the difference between TC and TVC. But TC minus TVC equals total *fixed* cost, TFC. So

$$\text{Economic profit} = \text{Producer surplus} - TFC.$$

For a given level of total fixed cost, anything that increases producer surplus also increases economic profit.

Let's now see how price discrimination works by looking at a price-discriminating airline.

A Price-Discriminating Airline

Inter-City Airlines has a monopoly on passenger flights between two cities. Figure 13.8 shows the market demand curve, D, for travel on this route. It also shows Inter-City Airline's marginal revenue curve, MR, and marginal cost curve, MC. Inter-City's marginal cost is a constant $40 per trip. (It is easier to see how price discrimination works for a firm with constant marginal cost.)

Single-Price Profit Maximization As a single-price monopoly, Inter-City maximizes profit by producing the quantity of trips at which MR equals MC, which is 8,000 trips a week, and charging $120 a trip. With a marginal cost of $40 a trip, producer surplus is $80 a trip, and Inter-City's producer surplus is $640,000 a week, shown by the area of the blue rectangle. Inter-City's customers enjoy a consumer surplus shown by the area of the green triangle.

FIGURE 13.8   A Single Price of Air Travel

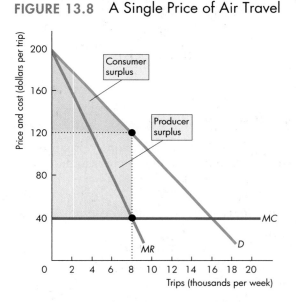

Inter-City Airlines has a monopoly on an air route with a market demand curve D. Inter-City's marginal cost, MC, is $40 per trip. As a single-price monopoly, Inter-City's marginal revenue curve is MR. Profit is maximized by selling 8,000 trips a week at $120 a trip. Producer surplus is $640,000 a week—the blue rectangle—and Inter-City's customers enjoy a consumer surplus—the green triangle.

——— MyEconLab animation ———

Discrimination Between Two Types of Travelers

Inter-City surveys its customers and discovers that they are all business travelers. It also surveys people who are *not* its customers and discovers that they are mainly people who travel for leisure. These people travel by bus or car, but would travel by air at a low fare. Inter-City would like to attract some of these travelers and knows that to do so, it must offer a fare below the current $120 a trip. How can it do that?

Inter-City digs more deeply into its survey results and discovers that its current customers always plan their travel less than two weeks before departure. In contrast, the people who travel by bus or car know their travel plans at least two weeks ahead of time.

Inter-City sees that it can use what it has discovered about its current and potential new customers to separate the two types of travelers into two markets: one market for business travel and another for leisure travel.

Figure 13.9 shows Inter-City's two markets. Part (a), the market for business travel, is the same as Fig. 13.8. Part (b) shows the market for leisure travel. No leisure traveler is willing to pay the business fare of $120 a trip, so at that price, the quantity demanded in part (b) is zero. The demand curve D_L is the demand for travel on this route after satisfying the demand of business travelers. Inter-City's marginal cost remains at $40 a trip, so its marginal revenue curve is MR_L. Inter-City maximizes profit by setting the leisure fare at $80 a trip and attracting 4,000 leisure travelers a week. Inter-City's producer surplus increases by $160,000 a week—the area of the blue rectangle in Fig. 13.9(b) and leisure travelers enjoy a consumer surplus—the area of the green triangle.

Inter-City announces its new fare schedule: no restrictions, $120 and 14-day advance purchase, $80. Inter-City increases its passenger count by 50 percent and increases its producer surplus by $160,000.

FIGURE 13.9   Price Discrimination

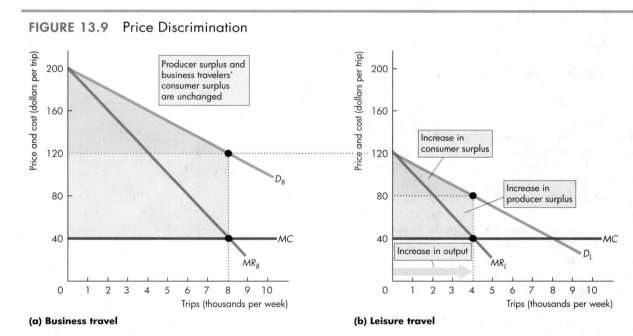

(a) Business travel

Inter-City separates its market into two types of travel: business travel with no restrictions in part (a) and leisure travel that requires a 14-day advance purchase in part (b). For business travel, the profit-maximizing price is $120 a trip with 8,000 trips a week. For leisure travel, the profit-maximizing price is $80 a trip with 4,000 trips a week.

(b) Leisure travel

Inter-City continues to make the same producer surplus on business travel as it did with a single price and business travelers continue to enjoy the same consumer surplus. But in part (b), Inter-City sells 4,000 trips to leisure travelers, which increases its producer surplus—the blue rectangle—and increases consumer surplus—the green triangle.

MyEconLab animation

Discrimination Among Several Types of Travelers

Pleased with the success of its price discrimination between business and leisure travelers, Inter-City sees that it might be able to profit even more by dividing its customers into a larger number of types. So it does another customer survey, which reveals that some business travelers are willing to pay $160 for a fully-refundable, unrestricted ticket while others are willing to pay only $120 for a nonrefundable ticket. So applying the same principles as it used to discriminate between business and leisure travelers, Inter-City now discriminates between business travelers who want a refundable ticket and those who want a non-refundable ticket.

Another survey of leisure travelers reveals that they fall into two goups: those who are able to plan 14 days ahead and others who can plan 21 days ahead. So Inter-City discriminates between these two groups with two fares: an $80 and a $60 fare.

By offering travelers four different fares, the airline increases its producer surplus and increases its economic profit. But why only four fares? Why not keep looking for ever more traveler types and offer even more fares?

Perfect Price Discrimination

Firms try to capture an ever larger part of consumer surplus by devising a host of special conditions, each one of which appeals to a tiny segment of the market but at the same time excludes others from taking advantage of a lower price. The more consumer surplus a firm is able to capture, the closer it gets to the extreme case called **perfect price discrimination**, which occurs if a firm can sell each unit of output for the highest price someone is willing to pay for it. In this extreme (hypothetical) case consumer surplus is eliminated and captured as producer surplus.

With perfect price discrimination, something special happens to marginal revenue—the market demand curve becomes the marginal revenue curve. The reason is that when the monopoly cuts the price to sell a larger quantity, it sells only the marginal unit at the lower price. All the other units continue to be sold for the highest price that each buyer is willing to pay. So for the perfect price discriminator, marginal revenue *equals* price and the market demand curve becomes the monopoly's marginal revenue curve.

With marginal revenue equal to price, Inter-City can obtain even greater producer surplus by increasing output up to the point at which price (and marginal revenue) equals marginal cost.

So Inter-City seeks new travelers who will not pay as much as $60 a trip but who will pay more than $40, its marginal cost. Inter-City offers a variety of vacation specials at different low fares that appeal only to new travelers. Existing customers continue to pay the higher fares and some, with further perks and frills that have no effect on cost, are induced to pay fares going all the way up to $200 a trip.

With all these special conditions and fares, Inter-City increases its output to the quantity demanded at marginal cost, extracts the entire consumer surplus on that quantity, and maximizes economic profit.

Figure 13.10 shows the outcome with perfect price discrimination and compares it with the single-price monopoly outcome. The range of business-class fares extract the entire consumer surplus from this group. The new leisure-class fares going down to $40 a trip attract an additional 8,000 travelers and take the entire consumer surplus of leisure travelers. Inter-City makes the maximum possible economic profit.

FIGURE 13.10   Perfect Price Discrimination

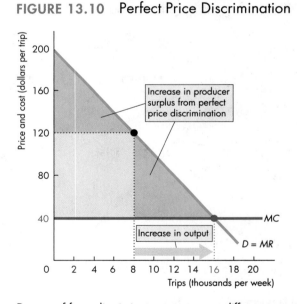

Dozens of fares discriminate among many different types of business travelers, and many new low fares with restrictions appeal to leisure travelers. With perfect price discrimination, the market demand curve becomes Inter-City's marginal revenue curve. Producer surplus is maximized when the lowest fare equals marginal cost. Inter-City sells 16,000 trips and makes the maximum possible economic profit.

——— MyEconLab animation ———

Would it bother you to hear how little I paid for this flight?

From William Hamilton, "Voodoo Economics," © 1992 by The Chronicle Publishing Company, p. 3. Reprinted with permission of Chronicle Books.

Efficiency and Rent Seeking with Price Discrimination

With perfect price discrimination, output increases to the point at which price equals marginal cost. This output is identical to that of perfect competition. Perfect price discrimination pushes consumer surplus to zero but increases the monopoly's producer surplus to equal the total surplus in perfect competition. With perfect price discrimination, no deadweight loss is created, so perfect price discrimination achieves efficiency.

> The more perfectly the monopoly can price discriminate, the closer its output is to the competitive output and the more efficient is the outcome.

But the outcomes of perfect competition and perfect price discrimination differ. First, the distribution of the total surplus is not the same. In perfect competition, total surplus is shared by consumers and producers, while with perfect price discrimination, the monopoly takes it all. Second, because the monopoly takes all the total surplus, rent seeking is profitable.

People use resources in pursuit of economic rent, and the bigger the rents, the more resources are used in pursuing them. With free entry into rent seeking, the long-run equilibrium outcome is that rent seekers use up the entire producer surplus.

Real-world airlines are as creative as Inter-City Airlines, as you can see in the cartoon! Disney Corporation is creative too in extracting consumer surplus, as Economics in Action shows.

We next study some key monopoly policy issues.

Economics in Action
Attempting Perfect Price Discrimination

If you want to spend a day at Disney World in Orlando, it will cost you $94.79. You can spend a second consecutive day for an extra $92.65. A third day will cost you $70.29. But for a fourth day, you'll pay only $14.91 and for a fifth day, $12.78. For more days all the way up to 10, you'll pay only $10.65 a day. The Disney Corporation hopes that it has read your willingness to pay correctly and not left you with too much consumer surplus.

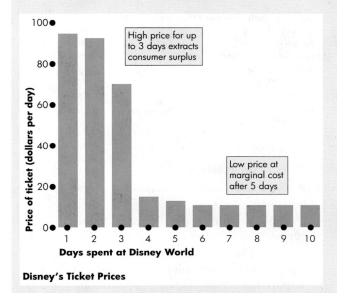

Disney's Ticket Prices

REVIEW QUIZ

1 What is price discrimination and how is it used to increase a monopoly's profit?
2 Explain how consumer surplus changes when a monopoly price discriminates.
3 Explain how consumer surplus, economic profit, and output change when a monopoly perfectly price discriminates.
4 What are some of the ways that real-world airlines price discriminate?

You can work these questions in Study Plan 13.4 and get instant feedback.   MyEconLab

◆ ECONOMICS IN THE NEWS

Microsoft Monopoly

Microsoft Windows 8 to Go on Sale in October

Microsoft announced that its Windows 8 operating system will be released in October 2012, three years after Windows 7 went public. Windows 8 will be available in 109 languages across 231 markets worldwide.

Source: AFP, July 9, 2012

SOME DATA

Microsoft Windows 7 Versions and U.S. Prices

Version	Price
Full from Microsoft	299.99
Upgrade from Microsoft	199.99
Full from Amazon	136.48
Full from Mission Softs (OEM)	77.50
Student from Microsoft	64.95

Microsoft sold 240 million Windows 7 licenses per year and at different prices in different national markets.

THE QUESTIONS

- Is Microsoft a monopoly?
- Is Microsoft a natural monopoly or a legal monopoly?
- Does Microsoft price discriminate or do the different prices of Windows reflect cost differences?
- Sketch a demand curve for Windows, Microsoft's marginal cost curve, and the distribution of the total surplus between consumers and Microsoft.

THE ANSWERS

- Microsoft controls 92 percent of the market for computer operating systems, and almost 100 percent of the non-Apple market, which makes it an effective monopoly.
- Microsoft is a natural monopoly. It has large fixed costs and almost zero marginal cost, so its long-run average cost curve (*LRAC*) slopes downward and economies of scale are achieved when the *LRAC* curve intersects the demand curve.
- Microsoft sells Windows for a number of different prices to different market segments and the marginal cost of a Windows license is the same for all market segments, so Microsoft is a price-discriminating monopoly.

- The figure illustrates the demand curve, *D*, and marginal cost curve, *MC*, for Windows licenses.
- Using the U.S. prices in the data table, the figure shows how Microsoft converts consumer surplus into producer surplus by price discriminating.
- Because Microsoft also price discriminates among its different national markets, it gains even more producer surplus than the figure illustrates.

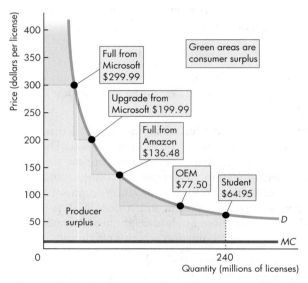

Microsoft Grabs Consumer Surplus

Windows 8 will have many more foreign language versions than Windows 7 and greater scope for price discrimination.

Monopoly Regulation

Natural monopoly presents a dilemma. With economies of scale, it produces at the lowest possible cost. But with market power, it has an incentive to raise the price above the competitive price and produce too little—to operate in the self-interest of the monopolist and not in the social interest.

Regulation—rules administered by a government agency to influence prices, quantities, entry, and other aspects of economic activity in a firm or industry—is a possible solution to this dilemma.

To implement regulation, the government establishes agencies to oversee and enforce the rules. For example, the Surface Transportation Board regulates prices on interstate railroads, some trucking and bus lines, and water and oil pipelines. By the 1970s, almost a quarter of the nation's output was produced by regulated industries (far more than just natural monopolies) and a process of deregulation began.

Deregulation is the process of removing regulation of prices, quantities, entry, and other aspects of economic activity in a firm or industry. During the past 30 years, deregulation has occurred in domestic air transportation, telephone service, interstate trucking, and banking and financial services. Cable TV was deregulated in 1984, re-regulated in 1992, and deregulated again in 1996.

Regulation is a possible solution to the dilemma presented by natural monopoly but not a guaranteed solution. There are two theories about how regulation actually works: the *social interest theory* and the *capture theory*.

The **social interest theory** is that the political and regulatory process relentlessly seeks out inefficiency and introduces regulation that eliminates deadweight loss and allocates resources efficiently.

The **capture theory** is that regulation serves the self-interest of the producer, who captures the regulator and maximizes economic profit. Regulation that benefits the producer but creates a deadweight loss gets adopted because the producer's gain is large and visible while each individual consumer's loss is small and invisible. No individual consumer has an incentive to oppose the regulation but the producer has a big incentive to lobby for it.

We're going to examine efficient regulation that serves the social interest and see why it is not a simple matter to design and implement such regulation.

Efficient Regulation of a Natural Monopoly

A cable TV company is a *natural monopoly*—it can supply the entire market at a lower price than two or more competing firms can. Cox Communications, based in Atlanta, provides cable TV to households in 20 states. The firm has invested heavily in satellite receiving dishes, cables, and control equipment and so has large fixed costs. These fixed costs are part of the firm's average total cost. Its average total cost decreases as the number of households served increases because the fixed cost is spread over a larger number of households.

Unregulated, Cox produces the quantity that maximizes profit. Like all single-price monopolies, the profit-maximizing quantity is less than the efficient quantity, and underproduction results in a deadweight loss.

How can Cox be regulated to produce the efficient quantity of cable TV service? The answer is by being regulated to set its price equal to marginal cost, known as the **marginal cost pricing rule**. The quantity demanded at a price equal to marginal cost is the efficient quantity—the quantity at which marginal benefit equals marginal cost.

Figure 13.11 illustrates the marginal cost pricing rule. The demand curve for cable TV is *D*. Cox's marginal cost curve is *MC*. That marginal cost curve is (assumed to be) horizontal at $10 per household per month—that is, the cost of providing each additional household with a month of cable programming is $10. The efficient outcome occurs if the price is regulated at $10 per household per month with 10 million households served.

But there is a problem: At the efficient output, average total cost exceeds marginal cost, so a firm that uses marginal cost pricing incurs an economic loss. A cable TV company that is required to use a marginal cost pricing rule will not stay in business for long. How can the firm cover its costs and, at the same time, obey a marginal cost pricing rule?

There are two possible ways of enabling the firm to cover its costs: price discrimination and a two-part price (called a *two-part tariff*).

For example, Verizon offers plans at a fixed monthly price that give access to the cell-phone network and unlimited free calls. The price of a call (zero) equals Verizon's marginal cost of a call. Similarly, a cable TV operator can charge a one-time connection fee that covers its fixed cost and then charge a monthly fee equal to marginal cost.

FIGURE 13.11   Regulating a Natural Monopoly

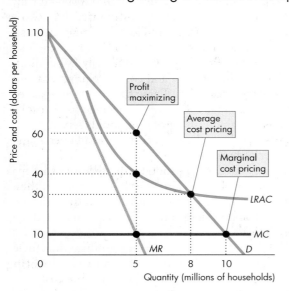

A natural monopoly cable TV supplier faces the demand curve *D*. The firm's marginal cost is constant at $10 per household per month, as shown by the curve labeled *MC*. The long-run average cost curve is *LRAC*.

Unregulated, as a profit-maximizer, the firm serves 5 million households at a price of $60 a month. An efficient marginal cost pricing rule sets the price at $10 a month. The monopoly serves 10 million households and incurs an economic loss. A second-best average cost pricing rule sets the price at $30 a month. The monopoly serves 8 million households and earns zero economic profit.

——————— MyEconLab animation ———————

Second-Best Regulation of a Natural Monopoly

A natural monopoly cannot always be regulated to achieve an efficient outcome. Two possible ways of enabling a regulated monopoly to avoid an economic loss are

- Average cost pricing
- Government subsidy

Average Cost Pricing   The **average cost pricing rule** sets price equal to average total cost. With this rule the firm produces the quantity at which the average

total cost curve cuts the demand curve. This rule results in the firm making zero economic profit—breaking even. But because for a natural monopoly average total cost exceeds marginal cost, the quantity produced is less than the efficient quantity and a deadweight loss arises.

Figure 13.11 illustrates the average cost pricing rule. The price is $30 a month and 8 million households get cable TV.

Government Subsidy   A government subsidy is a direct payment to the firm equal to its economic loss. To pay a subsidy, the government must raise the revenue by taxing some other activity. You saw in Chapter 6 that taxes themselves generate deadweight loss.

And the Second-Best Is …   Which is the better option, average cost pricing or marginal cost pricing with a government subsidy? The answer depends on the relative magnitudes of the two deadweight losses. Average cost pricing generates a deadweight loss in the market served by the natural monopoly. A subsidy generates deadweight losses in the markets for the items that are taxed to pay for the subsidy. The smaller deadweight loss is the second-best solution to regulating a natural monopoly. Making this calculation in practice is too difficult and average cost pricing is generally preferred to a subsidy.

Implementing average cost pricing presents the regulator with a challenge because it is not possible to be sure what a firm's costs are. So regulators use one of two practical rules:

- Rate of return regulation
- Price cap regulation

Rate of Return Regulation   Under **rate of return regulation**, a firm must justify its price by showing that its return on capital doesn't exceed a specified target rate. This type of regulation can end up serving the self-interest of the firm rather than the social interest. The firm's managers have an incentive to inflate costs by spending on items such as private jets, free baseball tickets (disguised as public relations expenses), and lavish entertainment. Managers also have an incentive to use more capital than the efficient amount. The rate of return on capital is regulated but not the total return on capital, and the greater the amount of capital, the greater is the total return.

Price Cap Regulation For the reason that we've just examined, rate of return regulation is increasingly being replaced by price cap regulation. A **price cap regulation** is a price ceiling—a rule that specifies the highest price the firm is permitted to set. This type of regulation gives a firm an incentive to operate efficiently and keep costs under control. Price cap regulation has become common for the electricity and telecommunications industries and is replacing rate of return regulation.

To see how a price cap works, let's suppose that the cable TV operator is subject to this type of regulation. Figure 13.12 shows that without regulation, the firm maximizes profit by serving 5 million households and charging a price of $60 a month. If a price cap is set at $30 a month, the firm is permitted to sell

FIGURE 13.12 Price Cap Regulation

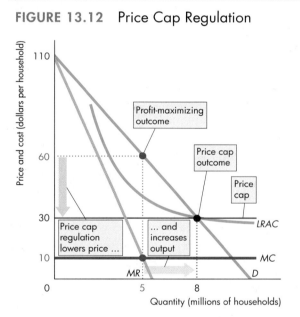

A natural monopoly cable TV supplier faces the demand curve *D*. The firm's marginal cost is constant at $10 per household per month, as shown by the curve labeled *MC*. The long-run average cost curve is *LRAC*.

Unregulated, the firm serves 5 million households at a price of $60 a month. A price cap sets the maximum price at $30 a month. The firm has an incentive to minimize cost and serve the quantity of households that demand service at the price cap. The price cap regulation lowers the price and increases the quantity.

—————— MyEconLab animation ——————

any quantity it chooses at that price or at a lower price. At 5 million households, the firm now incurs an economic loss. It can decrease the loss by increasing output to 8 million households. To increase output above 8 million households, the firm would have to lower the price and again it would incur a loss. So the profit-maximizing quantity is 8 million households—the same as with average cost pricing.

Notice that a price cap lowers the price and increases output. This outcome is in sharp contrast to the effect of a price ceiling in a competitive market that you studied in Chapter 6 (pp. 128–130). The reason is that in a monopoly, the unregulated equilibrium output is less than the competitive equilibrium output, and the price cap regulation replicates the conditions of a competitive market.

In Fig. 13.12, the price cap delivers average cost pricing. In practice, the regulator might set the cap too high. For this reason, price cap regulation is often combined with *earnings sharing regulation*—a regulation that requires firms to make refunds to customers when profits rise above a target level.

◆ REVIEW QUIZ

1 What is the pricing rule that achieves an efficient outcome for a regulated monopoly? What is the problem with this rule?

2 What is the average cost pricing rule? Why is it not an efficient way of regulating monopoly?

3 What is a price cap? Why might it be a more effective way of regulating monopoly than rate of return regulation?

4 Compare the consumer surplus, producer surplus, and deadweight loss that arise from average cost pricing with those that arise from profit-maximization pricing and marginal cost pricing.

You can work these questions in Study Plan 13.5 and get instant feedback.   **MyEconLab**

◆ You've now completed your study of monopoly. *Reading Between the Lines* on pp. 316–317 looks at Google's dominant position in the market for Internet search advertising.

In the next chapter, we study markets that lie between the extremes of perfect competition and monopoly and that blend elements of the two.

Is Google Misusing Monopoly Power?

Data Show Google Abuses Search Role, Group Contends

http://www.sfgate.com
June 3, 2010

Consumer Watchdog continues to push its case that Google Inc.'s behavior necessitates antitrust scrutiny, releasing a report Wednesday that alleges that the company is abusing its dominance in online search to direct users to its own services.

The study, which will be sent to U.S. and European antitrust regulators, cites online traffic data that the Santa Monica group claims shows the Mountain View Internet giant seized large portions of market share in areas like online maps, video and comparison shopping after its search engine began highlighting links to its products in results.

Google called the report's methodology and premise flawed and said its practices are designed to benefit users.

"Our goal is to give users the info they're seeking as quickly as possible," a spokesman said in a statement. "Sometimes that means showing a map, a streaming audio link, or an answer to a question at the top of the page if we think that's what users want. We strive to deliver what we think is the most relevant result from a variety of content types, and if we're not giving users the information they want then other sources of information are always one click away."

Google doubled its market share in online video to nearly 80 percent since 2007, the year in which the company began returning high or prominent links to videos from its YouTube subsidiary in search results, according to the report by Consumer Watchdog's Inside Google project.

. . .

ESSENCE OF THE STORY

- Consumer Watchdog says that Google should be scrutinized by U.S. and European antitrust regulators because it is abusing its dominant position in online search by directing users to its own services.

- The claim is that Google has grown a large market share in online maps, video, and comparison shopping because its search engine highlights links to these products in search results.

- Google says its goal is to give users the information they are seeking, in the format required, as quickly as possible.

- Google's market share in online video has doubled to nearly 80 percent since 2007, when it began returning links to YouTube videos.

ECONOMIC ANALYSIS

- Google began selling advertisements associated with search keywords in 2000.

- Google sells keywords based on a combination of willingness-to-pay and the number of clicks an advertisement receives, with bids starting at 5 cents per click.

- Google has steadily improved its search engine and refined and simplified its interface with both searchers and advertisers to make searches more powerful and advertising more effective.

- Figure 1 shows Google's extraordinary success in terms of its revenue, cost, and profit.

- Google could have provided a basic search engine with none of the features of today's Google.

- If Google had followed this strategy, people seeking information would have used other search engines and advertisers would have been willing to pay low prices for Google ads.

- Google would have faced the market described in Fig. 2 and earned a small economic profit.

- Instead, Google improved its search and the effectiveness of advertising. The demand for Google ads increased.

- By selling keywords to the highest bidder, Google is able to achieve perfect price discrimination.

- Figure 3 shows the consequences of Google's successful strategy. With perfect price discrimination, Google's producer surplus is maximized. Google produces the efficient quantity of search and advertising by accepting ads as long as price exceeds marginal cost.

- Google does not appear to be acting against the social interest: There is no antitrust case to answer.

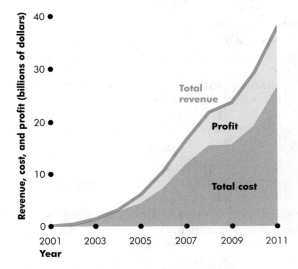

Figure 1 Google's Revenue, Cost, and Profit

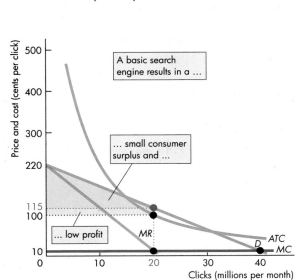

Figure 2 Basic Search Engine

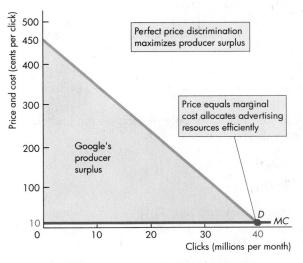

Figure 3 Google with AdWords and Other Features

317

SUMMARY

Key Points

Monopoly and How It Arises (pp. 298–299)

- A monopoly is a market with a single supplier of a good or service that has no close substitutes and in which barriers to entry prevent competition.
- Barriers to entry may be legal (public franchise, license, patent, or copyright), ownership (one firm controls a resource), or natural (created by economies of scale).
- A monopoly might be able to price discriminate when there is no resale possibility.
- Where resale is possible, a firm charges one price.

Working Problems 1 to 4 will give you a better understanding of monopoly and how it arises.

A Single-Price Monopoly's Output and Price Decision (pp. 300–303)

- A monopoly's demand curve is the market demand curve and a single-price monopoly's marginal revenue is less than price.
- A monopoly maximizes profit by producing the output at which marginal revenue equals marginal cost and by charging the maximum price that consumers are willing to pay for that output.

Working Problems 5 to 9 will give you a better understanding of a single-price monopoly's output and price decision.

Single-Price Monopoly and Competition Compared (pp. 304–307)

- A single-price monopoly charges a higher price and produces a smaller quantity than a perfectly competitive market.
- A single-price monopoly restricts output and creates a deadweight loss.

- The total loss that arises from monopoly equals the deadweight loss plus the cost of the resources devoted to rent seeking.

Working Problems 10 to 12 will give you a better understanding of the comparison of single-price monopoly and perfect competition.

Price Discrimination (pp. 307–312)

- Price discrimination converts consumer surplus into economic profit.
- Perfect price discrimination extracts the entire consumer surplus; each unit is sold for the maximum price that each consumer is willing to pay; the quantity produced is the efficient quantity.
- Rent seeking with perfect price discrimination might eliminate the entire consumer surplus and producer surplus.

Working Problems 13 to 16 will give you a better understanding of price discrimination.

Monopoly Regulation (pp. 313–315)

- Monopoly regulation might serve the social interest or the interest of the monopoly (the monopoly captures the regulator).
- Price equal to marginal cost achieves efficiency but results in economic loss.
- Price equal to average cost enables the firm to cover its cost but is inefficient.
- Rate of return regulation creates incentives for inefficient production and inflated cost.
- Price cap regulation with earnings sharing regulation can achieve a more efficient outcome than rate of return regulation.

Working Problems 17 to 19 will give you a better understanding of monopoly regulation.

Key Terms

Average cost pricing rule, 314	Marginal cost pricing rule, 313	Rate of return regulation, 314
Barrier to entry, 298	Monopoly, 298	Regulation, 313
Capture theory, 313	Natural monopoly, 298	Rent seeking, 306
Deregulation, 313	Perfect price discrimination, 310	Single-price monopoly, 299
Economic rent, 306	Price cap regulation, 315	Social interest theory, 313
Legal monopoly, 298	Price discrimination, 299	

STUDY PLAN PROBLEMS AND APPLICATIONS

MyEconLab   You can work problems 1 to 19 in MyEconLab Chapter 13 Study Plan and get instant feedback.

Monopoly and How It Arises (Study Plan 13.1)

Use the following information to work Problems 1 to 3.
The United States Postal Service has a monopoly on non-urgent First Class Mail and the exclusive right to put mail in private mailboxes. Pfizer Inc. makes LIPITOR, a prescription drug that lowers cholesterol. Cox Communications is the sole provider of cable television service in some parts of San Diego.

1. a. What are the substitutes, if any, for the goods and services described above?
    b. What are the barriers to entry, if any, that protect these three firms from competition?

2. Which of these three firms, if any, is a natural monopoly? Explain your answer and draw a graph to illustrate it.

3. a. Which of these three firms, if any, is a legal monopoly? Explain your answer.
    b. Which of these three firms are most likely to be able to profit from price discrimination and which are most likely to sell their good or service for a single price?

4. **Barbie's Revenge: Brawl over Doll Is Heading to Trial**

    Four years ago, Mattel Inc. exhorted its executives to help save Barbie from a new doll clique called the Bratz. With its market share dropping at a "chilling rate," Barbie needed to be more "aggressive, revolutionary, and ruthless." Mattel has gone to court and is trying to seize ownership of the Bratz line, which Mattel accuses of stealing the idea for the pouty-lipped dolls with the big heads.

    Source: *The Wall Street Journal*, May 23, 2008

    a. Before Bratz entered the market, what type of monopoly did Mattel Inc. possess in the market for "the pouty-lipped dolls with the big heads"?
    b. What is the barrier to entry that Mattel might argue should protect it from competition in the market for Barbie dolls?
    c. Explain how the entry of Bratz dolls might be expected to change the demand for Barbie dolls.

A Single-Price Monopoly's Output and Price Decision (Study Plan 13.2)

Use the following table to work Problems 5 to 9.
Minnie's Mineral Springs, a single-price monopoly, faces the market demand schedule:

Price (dollars per bottle)	Quantity demanded (bottles per hour)
10	0
8	1
6	2
4	3
2	4
0	5

5. a. Calculate Minnie's total revenue schedule.
    b. Calculate its marginal revenue schedule.

6. a. Draw a graph of the market demand curve and Minnie's marginal revenue curve.
    b. Why is Minnie's marginal revenue less than the price?

7. a. At what price is Minnie's total revenue maximized?
    b. Over what range of prices is the demand for water from Minnie's Mineral Springs elastic?

8. Why will Minnie not produce a quantity at which the market demand for water is inelastic?

9. Minnie's Mineral Springs faces the market demand schedule in Problem 5 and has the following total cost schedule:

Quantity produced (bottles per hour)	Total cost (dollars)
0	1
1	3
2	7
3	13
4	21
5	31

    a. Calculate Minnie's profit-maximizing output and price.
    b. Calculate the economic profit.

Single-Price Monopoly and Competition Compared

(Study Plan 13.3)

Use the following news clip to work Problems 10 to 12.

Zoloft Faces Patent Expiration

Pfizer's antidepressant Zoloft, with $3.3 billion in 2005 sales, loses patent protection on June 30. When a brand name drug loses its patent, both the price of the drug and the dollar value of its sales each tend to drop 80 percent over the next year, as competition opens to a host of generic drugmakers. The real winners are the patients and the insurers, who pay much lower prices. The Food and Drug Administration insists that generics work identically to brand-names.

Source: *CNN*, June 15, 2006

10. a. Assume that Pfizer has a monopoly in the antidepressant market and that Pfizer cannot price discriminate. Use a graph to illustrate the market price and quantity of Zoloft sold.

    b. On your graph, identify consumer surplus, producer surplus, and deadweight loss.

11. How might you justify protecting Pfizer from competition with a legal barrier to entry?

12. a. Explain how the market for an antidepressant drug changes when a patent expires.

    b. Draw a graph to illustrate how the expiration of the Zoloft patent will change the price and quantity in the market for antidepressants.

    c. Explain how consumer surplus, producer surplus, and deadweight loss change with the expiration of the Zoloft patent.

Price Discrimination (Study Plan 13.4)

Use the following news clip to work Problems 13 and 14.

The Saturday-Night Stay Requirement Is on Its Final Approach

The Saturday-night stay—the requirement that airlines instituted to ensure that business travelers pay an outrageous airfare if he or she wants to go home for the weekend—has gone the way of the dodo bird. Experts agree that low-fare carriers, such as Southwest, are the primary reason major airlines are adopting more consumer-friendly fare structures, which include the elimination of the Saturday-night stay, the introduction of one-way and walk-up fares, and the general restructuring of fares.

Source: *Los Angeles Times*, August 15, 2004

13. Explain why the opportunity for price discrimination exists for air travel. How does an airline profit from price discrimination?

14. Describe the change in price discrimination in the market for air travel when discount airlines entered the market and explain the effect of discount airlines on the price and the quantity of air travel.

Use the following information to work Problems 15 and 16.

La Bella Pizza can produce a pizza for a marginal cost of $2. Its standard price is $15 a pizza. It offers a second pizza for $5. It also distributes coupons that give a $5 rebate on a standard-priced pizza.

15. How can La Bella Pizza make a larger economic profit with this range of prices than it could if it sold every pizza for $15? Use a graph to illustrate your answer.

16. How might La Bella Pizza make even more economic profit? Would La Bella Pizza then be more efficient than it would be if it charged $15 for each pizza?

Monopoly Regulation (Study Plan 13.5)

Use the following information to work Problems 17 to 19.

The figure shows a situation similar to that of Calypso U.S. Pipeline, a firm that operates a natural gas distribution system in the United States. Calypso is a natural monopoly that cannot price discriminate.

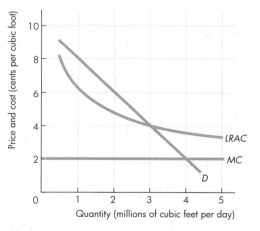

What quantity will Calypso produce, what price will it charge, what is the total surplus, and what is the deadweight loss if Calypso is

17. An unregulated profit-maximizing firm?

18. Regulated to make zero economic profit?

19. Regulated to be efficient?

ADDITIONAL PROBLEMS AND APPLICATIONS

MyEconLab   You can work these problems in MyEconLab if assigned by your instructor.

Monopoly and How It Arises

Use the following list, which gives some information about seven firms, to answer Problems 20 and 21.

- Coca-Cola cuts its price below that of Pepsi-Cola in an attempt to increase its market share.
- A single firm, protected by a barrier to entry, produces a personal service that has no close substitutes.
- A barrier to entry exists, but the good has some close substitutes.
- A firm offers discounts to students and seniors.
- A firm can sell any quantity it chooses at the going price.
- The government issues Nike an exclusive license to produce golf balls.
- A firm experiences economies of scale even when it produces the quantity that meets the entire market demand.

20. In which of the seven cases might monopoly arise?
21. Which of the seven cases are natural monopolies and which are legal monopolies? Which can price discriminate, which cannot, and why?

A Single-Price Monopoly's Output and Price Decision

Use the following information to work Problems 22 to 26.

Hot Air Balloon Rides is a single-price monopoly. Columns 1 and 2 of the table set out the market demand schedule and columns 2 and 3 set out the total cost schedule:

Price (dollars per ride)	Quantity demanded (rides per month)	Total cost (dollars per month)
220	0	80
200	1	160
180	2	260
160	3	380
140	4	520
120	5	680

22. Construct Hot Air's total revenue and marginal revenue schedules.
23. Draw a graph of the market demand curve and Hot Air's marginal revenue curve.
24. Find Hot Air's profit-maximizing output and price and calculate the firm's economic profit.

25. If the government imposes a tax on Hot Air's profit, how do its output and price change?
26. If instead of taxing Hot Air's profit, the government imposes a sales tax on balloon rides of $30 a ride, what are the new profit-maximizing quantity, price, and economic profit?
27. The figure illustrates the situation facing the publisher of the only newspaper containing local news in an isolated community.

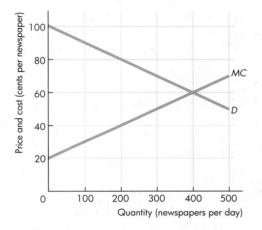

a. On the graph, mark the profit-maximizing quantity and price and the publisher's total revenue per day.
b. At the price charged, is the demand for this newspaper elastic or inelastic? Why?

Single-Price Monopoly and Competition Compared

28. Show on the graph in Problem 27 the consumer surplus from newspapers and the deadweight loss created by the monopoly. Explain why this market might encourage rent seeking.
29. If the newspaper market in Problem 27 were perfectly competitive, what would be the quantity, price, consumer surplus, and producer surplus? Mark each on the graph.
30. **Telecoms Look to Grow by Acquisition**
   Multibillion-dollar telecommunications mergers show how global cellular powerhouses are scouting for growth in emerging economies while consolidating in their own, crowded backyards. France Télécom offered to buy TeliaSonera, a Swedish-Finnish telecommunications operator, but

within hours, TeliaSonera rejected the offer as too low. Analysts said higher bids—either from France Télécom or others—could persuade TeliaSonera to accept a deal. In the United States, Verizon Wireless agreed to buy Alltel for $28.1 billion—a deal that would make the company the biggest mobile phone operator in the United States. A combination of France Télécom and TeliaSonera would create the world's fourth-largest mobile operator, smaller only than China Mobile, Vodafone, and Telefónica of Spain.

Source: *International Herald Tribune*, June 5, 2008

a. Explain the rent-seeking behavior of global telecommunications companies.

b. Explain how mergers may affect the efficiency of the telecommunications market.

Price Discrimination

31. **AT&T Moves Away from Unlimited-Data Pricing**

AT&T said it will eliminate its $30 unlimited data plan as the crush of data use from the iPhone has hurt call quality. AT&T is introducing new plans costing $15 a month for 200 megabytes of data traffic or $25 a month for 2 gigabytes. AT&T says those who exceed 2 gigabytes of usage will pay $10 a month for each additional gigabyte. AT&T hopes that these plans will attract more customers.

Source: *The Wall Street Journal*, June 2, 2010

a. Explain why AT&T's new plans might be price discrimination.

b. Draw a graph to illustrate the original plan and the new plans.

Monopoly Regulation

32. **iSurrender**

In 2008, getting your hands the new iPhone meant signing a two-year AT&T contract. Some markets, because of the costs of being a player, tend toward either a single firm or a small number of firms. Everyone hoped the wireless market would be different. A telephone monopoly has been the norm for most of American telecommunication history, except for what may turn out to have been a brief experimental period from 1984 through 2012 or so. It may be that telephone monopolies in America are a national tradition.

Source: *Slate*, June 10, 2008

a. How did AT&T, the exclusive provider of wireless service for the iPhone in 2008, influence the wireless telecommunication market?

b. Explain why the wireless market might "tend toward either a single firm or a small number of firms." Why might this justify allowing a regulated monopoly to exist in this market?

Economics in the News

33. After you have studied *Reading Between the Lines* on pp. 316–317, answer the following questions.

a. Why does Consumer Watchdog say that Google needs to be investigated? Do you agree? Explain why or why not.

b. Explain why it would be inefficient to regulate Google to make it charge the same price per keyword click to all advertisers.

c. Explain why selling keywords to the highest bidder can lead to an efficient allocation of advertising resources.

34. **F.C.C. Planning Rules to Open Cable Market**

The Federal Communications Commission (F.C.C.) is setting new regulations to open the cable television market to independent programmers and rival video services. The new rules will make it easier for small independent programmers to lease access to cable channels and the size of the nation's largest cable companies will be capped at 30 percent of the market.

Source: *The New York Times*, November 10, 2007

a. What barriers to entry exist in the cable television market?

b. Are high cable prices evidence of monopoly power?

c. Draw a graph to illustrate the effects of the F.C.C.'s new regulations on the price, quantity, total surplus, and deadweight loss.

35. **Antitrust Inquiry Launched into Intel**

Intel, the world's largest chipmaker, holds 80 percent of the microprocessor market. Advanced Micro Devices complains that Intel stifles competition, but Intel says that the 42.4 percent fall in prices between 2000 and 2007 shows that this industry is fiercely competitive.

Source: *The Washington Post*, June 7, 2008

a. Is Intel a monopoly in the chip market?

b. Evaluate the argument made by Intel that the fall in prices "shows that this industry is fiercely competitive."

14

MONOPOLISTIC COMPETITION

After studying this chapter, you will be able to:

◆ Define and identify monopolistic competition

◆ Explain how a firm in monopolistic competition determines its price and output in the short run and the long run

◆ Explain why advertising costs are high and why firms in monopolistic competition use brand names

The online shoe store shoebuy.com lists athletic shoes made by 56 producers in 40 categories. Athletic shoe producers compete, but each has a monopoly on its own special kind of shoe—the market is an example of monopolistic competition.

The model of monopolistic competition helps us to understand the competition that we see every day in the markets for athletic shoes and many other goods.

Reading Between the Lines, at the end of this chapter, applies the monopolistic competition model to the market for smartphones as new entrants take market share from the Apple iPhone.

◆ What Is Monopolistic Competition?

You have studied perfect competition, in which a large number of firms produce at the lowest possible cost, make zero economic profit, and are efficient. You've also studied monopoly, in which a single firm restricts output, produces at a higher cost and price than in perfect competition, and is inefficient.

Most real-world markets are competitive but not perfectly competitive, because firms in these markets have some power to set their prices, as monopolies do. We call this type of market *monopolistic competition*.

Monopolistic competition is a market structure in which

- A large number of firms compete.
- Each firm produces a differentiated product.
- Firms compete on product quality, price, and marketing.
- Firms are free to enter and exit the industry.

Large Number of Firms

In monopolistic competition, as in perfect competition, the industry consists of a large number of firms. The presence of a large number of firms has three implications for the firms in the industry.

Small Market Share In monopolistic competition, each firm supplies a small part of the total industry output. Consequently, each firm has only limited power to influence the price of its product. Each firm's price can deviate from the average price of other firms by only a relatively small amount.

Ignore Other Firms A firm in monopolistic competition must be sensitive to the average market price of the product, but the firm does not pay attention to any one individual competitor. Because all the firms are relatively small, no one firm can dictate market conditions, and so no one firm's actions directly affect the actions of the other firms.

Collusion Impossible Firms in monopolistic competition would like to be able to conspire to fix a higher price—called *collusion*. But because the number of firms in monopolistic competition is large, coordination is difficult and collusion is not possible.

Product Differentiation

A firm practices **product differentiation** if it makes a product that is slightly different from the products of competing firms. A differentiated product is one that is a close substitute but not a perfect substitute for the products of the other firms. Some people are willing to pay more for one variety of the product, so when its price rises, the quantity demanded of that variety decreases, but it does not (necessarily) decrease to zero. For example, Adidas, Asics, Diadora, Etonic, Fila, New Balance, Nike, Puma, and Reebok all make differentiated running shoes. If the price of Adidas running shoes rises and the prices of the other shoes remain constant, Adidas sells fewer shoes and the other producers sell more. But Adidas shoes don't disappear unless the price rises by a large enough amount.

Competing on Quality, Price, and Marketing

Product differentiation enables a firm to compete with other firms in three areas: product quality, price, and marketing.

Quality The quality of a product is the physical attributes that make it different from the products of other firms. Quality includes design, reliability, the service provided to the buyer, and the buyer's ease of access to the product. Quality lies on a spectrum that runs from high to low. Some firms—such as Dell Computer Corp.—offer high-quality products. They are well designed and reliable, and the customer receives quick and efficient service. Other firms offer a lower-quality product that is poorly designed, that might not work perfectly, and that is not supported by effective customer service.

Price Because of product differentiation, a firm in monopolistic competition faces a downward-sloping demand curve. So, like a monopoly, the firm can set both its price and its output. But there is a tradeoff between the product's quality and price. A firm that makes a high-quality product can charge a higher price than a firm that makes a low-quality product.

Marketing Because of product differentiation, a firm in monopolistic competition must market its product. Marketing takes two main forms: advertising and packaging. A firm that produces a high-quality product wants to sell it for a suitably high price. To be able to do so, it must advertise and package its product in a way that convinces buyers that they are getting the higher quality for which they are paying a higher price. For example, pharmaceutical companies advertise and package their brand-name drugs to persuade buyers that these items are superior to the lower-priced generic alternatives. Similarly, a low-quality producer uses advertising and packaging to persuade buyers that although the quality is low, the low price more than compensates for this fact.

Entry and Exit

Monopolistic competition has no barriers to prevent new firms from entering the industry in the long run. Consequently, a firm in monopolistic competition cannot make an economic profit in the long run. When existing firms make an economic profit, new firms enter the industry. This entry lowers prices and eventually eliminates economic profit. When firms incur economic losses, some firms leave the industry in the long run. This exit increases prices and eventually eliminates the economic loss.

In long-run equilibrium, firms neither enter nor leave the industry and the firms in the industry make zero economic profit.

Examples of Monopolistic Competition

Economics in Action below shows 10 industries that are good examples of monopolistic competition. These industries have a large number of firms, which is shown in parentheses. In the market for audio and video equipment, the largest 4 firms produce only 30 percent of the industry's total sales and the largest 20 firms produce 75 percent of total sales. The number on the right is the Herfindahl-Hirschman Index (see Chapter 10, p. 235). Producers of clothing, jewelry, computers, and sporting goods operate in monopolistic competition.

REVIEW QUIZ

1 What are the distinguishing characteristics of monopolistic competition?
2 How do firms in monopolistic competition compete?
3 Provide some examples of industries near your school that operate in monopolistic competition (excluding those in the figure below).

You can work these questions in Study Plan 14.1 and get instant feedback.   MyEconLab

Economics in Action
Monopolistic Competition Today

These ten industries operate in monopolistic competition. The number of firms in the industry is shown in parentheses after the name of the industry. The red bars show the percentage of industry sales by the largest 4 firms. The green bars show the percentage of industry sales by the next 4 largest firms, and the blue bars show the percentage of industry sales by the next 12 largest firms. So the entire length of the combined red, green, and blue bars shows the percentage of industry sales by the largest 20 firms. The Herfindahl-Hirschman Index is shown on the right.

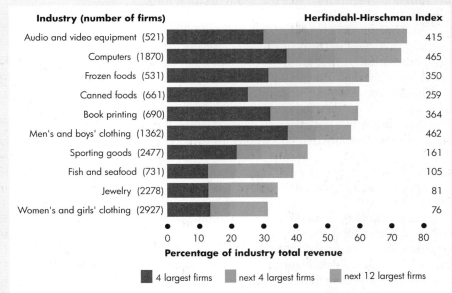

Industry (number of firms)	Herfindahl-Hirschman Index
Audio and video equipment (521)	415
Computers (1870)	465
Frozen foods (531)	350
Canned foods (661)	259
Book printing (690)	364
Men's and boys' clothing (1362)	462
Sporting goods (2477)	161
Fish and seafood (731)	105
Jewelry (2278)	81
Women's and girls' clothing (2927)	76

Percentage of industry total revenue

■ 4 largest firms   ■ next 4 largest firms   ■ next 12 largest firms

Measures of Concentration

Source of data: U.S. Census Bureau.

▶ Price and Output in Monopolistic Competition

Suppose you've been hired by VF Corporation, the firm that owns Nautica Clothing Corporation, to manage the production and marketing of Nautica jackets. Think about the decisions that you must make at Nautica. First, you must decide on the design and quality of jackets and on your marketing program. Second, you must decide on the quantity of jackets to produce and the price at which to sell them.

We'll suppose that Nautica has already made its decisions about design, quality, and marketing and now we'll concentrate on the output and pricing decision. We'll study quality and marketing decisions in the next section.

For a given quality of jackets and marketing activity, Nautica faces given costs and market conditions. Given its costs and the demand for its jackets, how does Nautica decide the quantity of jackets to produce and the price at which to sell them?

The Firm's Short-Run Output and Price Decision

In the short run, a firm in monopolistic competition makes its output and price decision just like a monopoly firm does. Figure 14.1 illustrates this decision for Nautica jackets.

The demand curve for Nautica jackets is *D*. This demand curve tells us the quantity of Nautica jackets demanded at each price, given the prices of other jackets. It is not the demand curve for jackets in general.

The *MR* curve shows the marginal revenue curve associated with the demand curve for Nautica jackets. It is derived just like the marginal revenue curve of a single-price monopoly that you studied in Chapter 13.

The *ATC* curve and the *MC* curve show the average total cost and the marginal cost of producing Nautica jackets.

Nautica's goal is to maximize its economic profit. To do so, it produces the output at which marginal revenue equals marginal cost. In Fig. 14.1, this output is 125 jackets a day. Nautica charges the price that buyers are willing to pay for this quantity, which is determined by the demand curve. This price is $75 per jacket. When Nautica produces 125 jackets a day, its average total cost is $25 per jacket and it makes an economic profit of $6,250 a day ($50 per jacket mul-

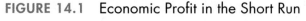

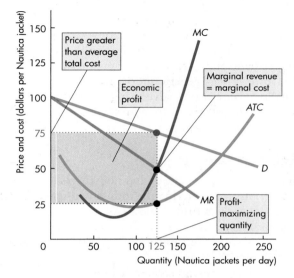

FIGURE 14.1   Economic Profit in the Short Run

Nautica maximizes profit by producing the quantity at which marginal revenue equals marginal cost, 125 jackets a day, and charging the price of $75 a jacket. This price exceeds the average total cost of $25 a jacket, so the firm makes an economic profit of $50 a jacket. The blue rectangle illustrates economic profit, which equals $6,250 a day ($50 a jacket multiplied by 125 jackets a day).

MyEconLab animation

tiplied by 125 jackets a day). The blue rectangle shows Nautica's economic profit.

Profit Maximizing Might Be Loss Minimizing

Figure 14.1 shows that Nautica is making a large economic profit. But such an outcome is not inevitable. A firm might face a level of demand for its product that is too low for it to make an economic profit.

Excite@Home was such a firm. Offering high-speed Internet service over the same cable that provides television, Excite@Home hoped to capture a large share of the Internet portal market in competition with AOL, MSN, and a host of other providers.

Figure 14.2 illustrates the situation facing Excite@Home in 2001. The demand curve for its portal service is *D*, the marginal revenue curve is *MR*, the average total cost curve is *ATC*, and the marginal cost curve is *MC*. Excite@Home maximized profit—

FIGURE 14.2 Economic Loss in the Short Run

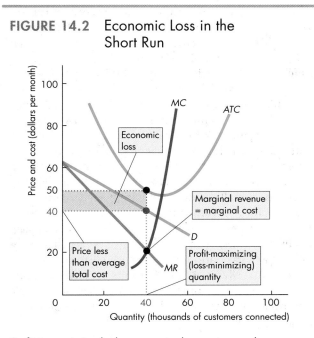

Profit is maximized where marginal revenue equals marginal cost. The loss-minimizing quantity is 40,000 customers. The price of $40 a month is less than the average total cost of $50 a month, so the firm incurs an economic loss of $10 a customer. The red rectangle illustrates economic loss, which equals $400,000 a month ($10 a customer multiplied by 40,000 customers).

———— MyEconLab animation ————

equivalently, it minimized its loss—by producing the output at which marginal revenue equals marginal cost. In Fig. 14.2, this output is 40,000 customers. Excite@Home charged the price that buyers were willing to pay for this quantity, which was determined by the demand curve and which was $40 a month. With 40,000 customers, Excite@Home's average total cost was $50 per customer, so it incurred an economic loss of $400,000 a month ($10 a customer multiplied by 40,000 customers). The red rectangle shows Excite@Home's economic loss.

So far, the firm in monopolistic competition looks like a single-price monopoly. It produces the quantity at which marginal revenue equals marginal cost and then charges the price that buyers are willing to pay for that quantity, as determined by the demand curve. The key difference between monopoly and monopolistic competition lies in what happens next when firms either make an economic profit or incur an economic loss.

Long Run: Zero Economic Profit

A firm like Excite@Home is not going to incur an economic loss for long. Eventually, it goes out of business. Also, there is no restriction on entry into monopolistic competition, so if firms in an industry are making economic profit, other firms have an incentive to enter that industry.

As the Gap and other firms start to make jackets similar to those made by Nautica, the demand for Nautica jackets decreases. The demand curve for Nautica jackets and the marginal revenue curve shift leftward. As these curves shift leftward, the profit-maximizing quantity and price fall.

Figure 14.3 shows the long-run equilibrium. The demand curve for Nautica jackets and the marginal revenue curve have shifted leftward. The firm produces 75 jackets a day and sells them for $25 each. At this output level, average total cost is also $25 per jacket.

FIGURE 14.3 Output and Price in the Long Run

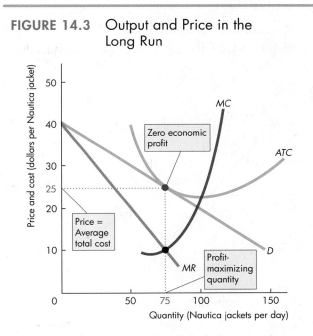

Economic profit encourages entry, which decreases the demand for each firm's product. When the demand curve touches the ATC curve at the quantity at which MR equals MC, the market is in long-run equilibrium. The output that maximizes profit is 75 jackets a day, and the price is $25 per jacket. Average total cost is also $25 per jacket, so economic profit is zero.

———— MyEconLab animation ————

So Nautica is making zero economic profit on its jackets. When all the firms in the industry are making zero economic profit, there is no incentive for new firms to enter.

If demand is so low relative to costs that firms incur economic losses, exit will occur. As firms leave an industry, the demand for the products of the remaining firms increases and their demand curves shift rightward. The exit process ends when all the firms in the industry are making zero economic profit.

Monopolistic Competition and Perfect Competition

Figure 14.4 compares monopolistic competition and perfect competition and highlights two key differences between them:

- Excess capacity
- Markup

Excess Capacity A firm has **excess capacity** if it produces less than its **efficient scale**, which is the quantity at which average total cost is a minimum—the quantity at the bottom of the U-shaped *ATC* curve. In Fig. 14.4, the efficient scale is 100 jackets a day. Nautica in part (a) produces 75 Nautica jackets a day and has *excess capacity* of 25 jackets a day. But if all jackets are alike and are produced by firms in perfect competition, each firm in part (b) produces 100 jackets a day, which is the efficient scale. Average total cost is the lowest possible only in *perfect* competition.

You can see the excess capacity in monopolistic competition all around you. Family restaurants (except for the truly outstanding ones) almost always have some empty tables. You can always get a pizza delivered in less than 30 minutes. It is rare that every pump at a gas station is in use with customers waiting in line. Many real estate agents are ready to help you find or sell a home. These industries are examples of monopolistic competition. The firms have excess

---

FIGURE 14.4   Excess Capacity and Markup

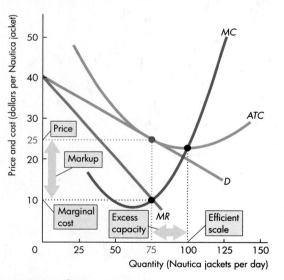

(a) Monopolistic competition

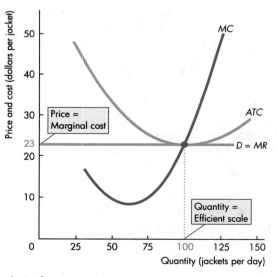

(b) Perfect competition

The efficient scale is 100 jackets a day. In monopolistic competition in the long run, because the firm faces a downward-sloping demand curve for its product, the quantity produced is less than the efficient scale and the firm has excess capacity. Price exceeds marginal cost by the amount of the markup.

In contrast, because in perfect competition the demand for each firm's product is perfectly elastic, the quantity produced in the long run equals the efficient scale and price equals marginal cost. The firm produces at the least possible cost and there is no markup.

 MyEconLab animation

capacity. They could sell more by cutting their prices, but they would then incur losses.

Markup A firm's **markup** is the amount by which price exceeds marginal cost. Figure 14.4(a) shows Nautica's markup. In perfect competition, price always equals marginal cost and there is no markup. Figure 14.4(b) shows this case. In monopolistic competition, buyers pay a higher price than in perfect competition and also pay more than marginal cost.

Is Monopolistic Competition Efficient?

Resources are used efficiently when marginal social benefit equals marginal social cost. Price equals marginal social benefit and the firm's marginal cost equals marginal social cost (assuming there are no external benefits or costs). So if the price of a Nautica jacket exceeds the marginal cost of producing it, the quantity of Nautica jackets produced is less than the efficient quantity. And you've just seen that in long-run equilibrium in monopolistic competition, price *does* exceed marginal cost. So is the quantity produced in monopolistic competition less than the efficient quantity?

Making the Relevant Comparison Two economists meet in the street, and one asks the other, "How is your husband?" The quick reply is "Compared to what?" This bit of economic wit illustrates a key point: Before we can conclude that something needs fixing, we must check out the available alternatives.

The markup that drives a gap between price and marginal cost in monopolistic competition arises from product differentiation. It is because Nautica jackets are not quite the same as jackets from Banana Republic, CK, Diesel, DKNY, Earl Jackets, Gap, Levi's, Ralph Lauren, or any of the other dozens of producers of jackets that the demand for Nautica jackets is not perfectly elastic. The only way in which the demand for jackets from Nautica might be perfectly elastic is if there is only one kind of jacket and all firms make it. In this situation, Nautica jackets are indistinguishable from all other jackets. They don't even have identifying labels.

If there was only one kind of jacket, the total benefit of jackets would almost certainly be less than it is with variety. People value variety—not only because it enables each person to select what he or she likes best but also because it provides an external benefit. Most of us enjoy seeing variety in the choices of oth-

ers. Contrast a scene from the China of the 1960s, when everyone wore a Mao tunic, with the China of today, where everyone wears the clothes of their own choosing. Or contrast a scene from the Germany of the 1930s, when almost everyone who could afford a car owned a first-generation Volkswagen Beetle, with the world of today with its enormous variety of styles and types of automobiles.

If people value variety, why don't we see infinite variety? The answer is that variety is costly. Each different variety of any product must be designed, and then customers must be informed about it. These initial costs of design and marketing—called setup costs—mean that some varieties that are too close to others already available are just not worth creating.

The Bottom Line Product variety is both valued and costly. The efficient degree of product variety is the one for which the marginal social benefit of product variety equals its marginal social cost. The loss that arises because the quantity produced is less than the efficient quantity is offset by the gain that arises from having a greater degree of product variety. So compared to the alternative—product uniformity—monopolistic competition might be efficient.

◆ REVIEW QUIZ

1 How does a firm in monopolistic competition decide how much to produce and at what price to offer its product for sale?

2 Why can a firm in monopolistic competition make an economic profit only in the short run?

3 Why do firms in monopolistic competition operate with excess capacity?

4 Why is there a price markup over marginal cost in monopolistic competition?

5 Is monopolistic competition efficient?

You can work these questions in Study Plan 14.2 and get instant feedback.   MyEconLab

---

You've seen how the firm in monopolistic competition determines its output and price in both the short run and the long run when it produces a given product and undertakes a *given* marketing effort. But how does the firm choose its product quality and marketing effort? We'll now study these decisions.

▶ Product Development and Marketing

When Nautica made its price and output decision that we've just studied, it had already made its product quality and marketing decisions. We'll now look at these decisions and see how they influence the firm's output, price, and economic profit.

Innovation and Product Development

The prospect of new firms entering the industry keeps firms in monopolistic competition on their toes! To enjoy economic profits, they must continually seek ways of keeping one step ahead of imitators—other firms who imitate the success of profitable firms.

One major way of trying to maintain economic profit is for a firm to seek out new products that will provide it with a competitive edge, even if only temporarily. A firm that introduces a new and differentiated product faces a demand that is less elastic and is able to increase its price and make an economic profit. Eventually, imitators will make close substitutes for the innovative product and compete away the economic profit arising from an initial advantage. So to restore economic profit, the firm must again innovate.

Profit-Maximizing Product Innovation The decision to innovate and develop a new or improved product is based on the same type of profit-maximizing calculation that you've already studied.

Innovation and product development are costly activities, but they also bring in additional revenues. The firm must balance the cost and revenue at the margin.

The marginal dollar spent on developing a new or improved product is the marginal cost of product development. The marginal dollar that the new or improved product earns for the firm is the marginal revenue of product development. At a low level of product development, the marginal revenue from a better product exceeds the marginal cost. At a high level of product development, the marginal cost of a better product exceeds the marginal revenue.

When the marginal cost and marginal revenue of product development are equal, the firm is undertaking the profit-maximizing amount of product development.

Efficiency and Product Innovation Is the profit-maximizing amount of product innovation also the efficient amount? Efficiency is achieved if the marginal social benefit of a new and improved product equals its marginal social cost.

The marginal social benefit of an innovation is the increase in price that consumers are willing to pay for it. The marginal social cost is the amount that the firm must pay to make the innovation. Profit is maximized when marginal *revenue* equals marginal cost. But in monopolistic competition, marginal revenue is less than price, so product innovation is probably not pushed to its efficient level.

Monopolistic competition brings many product innovations that cost little to implement and are purely cosmetic, such as improved packaging or a new scent in laundry powder. Even when there is a truly improved product, it is never as good as the consumer would like and for which the consumer is willing to pay a higher price. For example, "The Legend of Zelda: Twilight Princess" is regarded as an almost perfect and very cool game, but users complain that it isn't quite perfect. It is a game whose features generate a marginal revenue equal to the marginal cost of creating them.

Advertising

A firm with a differentiated product needs to ensure that its customers know how its product is different from the competition. A firm also might attempt to create a consumer perception that its product is different, even when that difference is small. Firms use advertising and packaging to achieve this goal.

Advertising Expenditures Firms in monopolistic competition incur huge costs to ensure that buyers appreciate and value the differences between their own products and those of their competitors. So a large proportion of the price that we pay for a good covers the cost of selling it, and this proportion is increasing. Advertising in newspapers and magazines and on radio, television, and the Internet is the main selling cost. But it is not the only one. Selling costs include the cost of shopping malls that look like movie sets, glossy catalogs and brochures, and the salaries, airfares, and hotel bills of salespeople.

Advertising expenditures affect the profits of firms in two ways: They increase costs, and they change demand. Let's look at these effects.

Economics in Action
The Cost of Selling a Pair of Shoes

When you buy a pair of running shoes that cost you $70, you're paying $9 for the materials from which the shoes are made, $2.75 for the services of the Malaysian worker who made the shoes, and $5.25 for the production and transportation services of a manufacturing firm in Asia and a shipping company. These numbers total $17. You pay $3 to the U.S. government in import duty. So we've now accounted for a total of $20. Where did the other $50 go? It is the cost of advertising, retailing, and other sales and distribution services.

The selling costs associated with running shoes are not unusual. Almost everything that you buy includes a selling cost component that exceeds one half of the total cost. Your clothing, food, electronic items, DVDs, magazines, and even your textbooks cost more to sell than they cost to manufacture.

Advertising costs are only a part, and often a small part, of total selling costs. For example, Nike spends about $4 on advertising per pair of running shoes sold.

For the U.S. economy as a whole, there are some 20,000 advertising agencies, which employ more than 200,000 people and have sales of $45 billion. These numbers are only part of the total cost of advertising because firms have their own internal advertising departments, the costs of which we can only guess.

But the biggest part of selling costs is not the cost of advertising. It is the cost of retailing services. The retailer's selling costs (and economic profit) are often as much as 50 percent of the price you pay.

| Raw materials $9 | Production costs $8 | Import duty $3 | Selling costs $50 |

Selling Costs and Total Cost Selling costs are fixed costs and they increase the firm's total cost. So like the fixed cost of producing a good, advertising costs per unit decrease as the quantity produced increases.

Figure 14.5 shows how selling costs change a firm's average total cost. The blue curve shows the average total cost of production. The red curve shows the firm's average total cost of production plus advertising. The height of the red area between the two curves shows the average fixed cost of advertising. The *total* cost of advertising is fixed. But the *average* cost of advertising decreases as output increases.

Figure 14.5 shows that if advertising increases the quantity sold by a large enough amount, it can lower average total cost. For example, if the quantity sold increases from 25 jackets a day with no advertising to 100 jackets a day with advertising, average total cost falls from $60 to $40 a jacket. The reason is that although the *total* fixed cost has increased, the greater fixed cost is spread over a greater output, so average total cost decreases.

FIGURE 14.5   Selling Costs and Total Cost

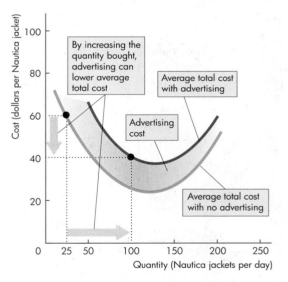

Selling costs such as the cost of advertising are fixed costs. When added to the average total cost of production, selling costs increase average total cost by a greater amount at small outputs than at large outputs. If advertising enables sales to increase from 25 jackets a day to 100 jackets a day, average total cost *falls* from $60 to $40 a jacket.

MyEconLab animation

Selling Costs and Demand Advertising and other selling efforts change the demand for a firm's product. But how? Does demand increase or does it decrease? The most natural answer is that advertising increases demand. By informing people about the quality of its products or by persuading people to switch from the products of other firms, a firm might expect to increase the demand for its own products.

But all firms in monopolistic competition advertise, and all seek to persuade customers that they have the best deal. If advertising enables a firm to survive, the number of firms in the market might increase. And to the extent that the number of firms does increase, advertising *decreases* the demand faced by any one firm. It also makes the demand for any one firm's product more elastic. So advertising can end up not only lowering average total cost but also lowering the markup and the price.

Figure 14.6 illustrates this possible effect of advertising. In part (a), with no advertising, the demand for Nautica jackets is not very elastic. Profit is maxi-

mized at 75 jackets per day, and the markup is large. In part (b), advertising, which is a fixed cost, increases average total cost from ATC_0 to ATC_1 but leaves marginal cost unchanged at MC. Demand becomes much more elastic, the profit-maximizing quantity increases, and the markup shrinks.

Using Advertising to Signal Quality

Some advertising, like the Roger Federer Rolex watch ad in glossy magazines or the huge number of dollars that Coke and Pepsi spend, seems hard to understand. There doesn't seem to be any concrete information about a watch in a tennis player's smile. And surely everyone knows about Coke and Pepsi. What is the gain from pouring millions of dollars into advertising these well-known colas?

One answer is that advertising is a signal to the consumer of a high-quality product. A **signal** is an action taken by an informed person (or firm) to send a message to uninformed people. Think about two colas:

FIGURE 14.6   Advertising and the Markup

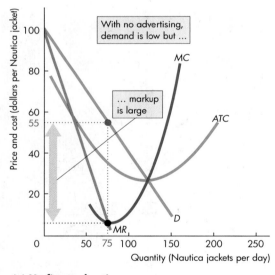

(a) No firms advertise

(b) All firms advertise

If no firms advertise, demand for each firm's product is low and not very elastic. The profit-maximizing output is small, the markup is large, and the price is high.

Advertising increases average total cost and shifts the ATC curve upward from ATC_0 to ATC_1. If all firms advertise, the demand for each firm's product becomes more elastic. Output increases, the price falls, and the markup shrinks.

MyEconLab animation

Coke and Oke. Oke knows that its cola is not very good and that its taste varies a lot depending on which cheap batch of unsold cola it happens to buy each week. So Oke knows that while it could get a lot of people to try Oke by advertising, they would all quickly discover what a poor product it is and switch back to the cola they bought before. Coke, in contrast, knows that its product has a high-quality consistent taste and that once consumers have tried it, there is a good chance they'll never drink anything else. On the basis of this reasoning, Oke doesn't advertise but Coke does. And Coke spends a lot of money to make a big splash.

Cola drinkers who see Coke's splashy ads know that the firm would not spend so much money advertising if its product were not truly good. So consumers reason that Coke is indeed a really good product. The flashy expensive ad has signaled that Coke is really good without saying anything about Coke.

Notice that if advertising is a signal, it doesn't need any specific product information. It just needs to be expensive and hard to miss. That's what a lot of advertising looks like. So the signaling theory of advertising predicts much of the advertising that we see.

Brand Names

Many firms create and spend a lot of money promoting a brand name. Why? What benefit does a brand name bring to justify the sometimes high cost of establishing it?

The basic answer is that a brand name provides information to consumers about the quality of a product, and is an incentive to the producer to achieve a high and consistent quality standard.

To see how a brand name helps the consumer, think about how you use brand names to get information about quality. You're on a road trip, and it is time to find a place to spend the night. You see roadside advertisements for Holiday Inn, Joe's Motel, and Annie's Driver's Stop. You know about Holiday Inn because you've stayed in it before. You've also seen their advertisements and know what to expect. You have no information at all about Joe's and Annie's. They might be better than the lodgings you do know about, but without that knowledge, you're not going to try them. You use the brand name as information and stay at Holiday Inn.

This same story explains why a brand name provides an incentive to achieve high and consistent quality. Because no one would know whether Joe's and Annie's were offering a high standard of service, they

have no incentive to do so. But equally, because everyone expects a given standard of service from Holiday Inn, a failure to meet a customer's expectation would almost surely lose that customer to a competitor. So Holiday Inn has a strong incentive to deliver what it promises in the advertising that creates its brand name.

Efficiency of Advertising and Brand Names

To the extent that advertising and brand names provide consumers with information about the precise nature of product differences and product quality, they benefit the consumer and enable a better product choice to be made. But the opportunity cost of the additional information must be weighed against the gain to the consumer.

The final verdict on the efficiency of monopolistic competition is ambiguous. In some cases, the gains from extra product variety offset the selling costs and the extra cost arising from excess capacity. The tremendous varieties of books, magazines, clothing, food, and drinks are examples of such gains. It is less easy to see the gains from being able to buy a brand-name drug with the identical chemical composition to that of a generic alternative, but many people willingly pay more for the brand-name alternative.

REVIEW QUIZ

1 How, other than by adjusting price, do firms in monopolistic competition compete?

2 Why might product innovation and development be efficient and why might it be inefficient?

3 Explain how selling costs influence a firm's cost curves and its average total cost.

4 Explain how advertising influences the demand for a firm's product.

5 Are advertising and brand names efficient?

You can work these questions in Study Plan 14.3 and get instant feedback.   MyEconLab

◆ Monopolistic competition is one of the most common market structures that you encounter in your daily life. *Reading Between the Lines* on pp. 334–335 applies the model of monopolistic competition to the market for smartphones and shows why you can expect continual innovation and the introduction of new phones from Apple and other smartphone producers.

Product Differentiation and Entry in the Market for Smartphones

Samsung Set to Unveil iPhone Challenger

Financial Times
May 1, 2012

If Apple were to challenge its smartphone competitors to a contest with its all-conquering iPhone 4S, Samsung's Galaxy S would probably be the model thrown into the arena to compete.

A new, third version of the Galaxy S will be unveiled in Earls Court, London, on Thursday amid speculation that it could be the official phone for the 2012 Olympics, which Samsung is sponsoring. ...

It estimated that the two companies provided 60 percent of the 139m smartphones shipped worldwide, up from 46 percent in the previous quarter. Samsung "may now have established a firm lead" with 47m units to Apple's 35m, Juniper said; although analysts have widely different estimates of Samsung sales, which are not specified by the company.

Apple still leads in handset revenues though, according to Juniper, with sales of $22.7bn in the first quarter compared with about $17bn for Samsung, including the Korean company's non-smartphones, or feature phones.

Samsung has produced a wide variety of smartphones running Android, Windows Phone, and its own Bada operating systems. Screen sizes have varied wildly, ranging as big as the 5.3in Galaxy Note, a smartphone/tablet hybrid equipped with a stylus. In contrast, Apple has stuck to a 3.5in screen size since the iPhone's debut and sales are focused on the latest 4S model, although the 4 and 3GS versions continue to be available. ...

ESSENCE OF THE STORY

- A new version of Samsung's Galaxy S is a serious challenger to the iPhone 4S.
- An estimated 139m smartphones were shipped worldwide in the first quarter of 2012, up 46 percent from the previous quarter.
- Samsung is estimated to have shipped 47 million units and Apple 35 million iPhones, which together represent 60 percent of the total.
- Total revenue estimates for the first quarter 2012 are $22.7 billion for Apple and $17 billion (not all smartphones) for Samsung.
- Samsung has produced a wider variety of smartphones than Apple.

ECONOMIC ANALYSIS

- Apple sold its first iPhone in 2007 and brought the more powerful 4S version to market in 2011.

- By creating a substantially differentiated product, Apple was able to generate a great deal of interest in smartphones throughout the world.

- In the first year and a quarter, Apple sold an average of 1 million iPhones per quarter.

- But Apple soon had competitors as a host of other smartphones using Google's Android operating system hit the market.

- To remain competitive, Apple introduced ever more powerful versions of the iPhone. And the competitors' smartphones kept getting better too.

- The monopolistic competition model explains what is happening in the smartphone market.

- Figure 1 shows the market for Apple's first iPhone. (The numbers are assumptions.)

- Because Apple's iPhone differs from other cell phones and has features that users value, the demand curve, *D*, and marginal revenue curve, *MR*, provide a large short-run profit opportunity.

- The marginal cost curve is *MC* and the average total cost curve is *ATC*. Apple maximizes its economic profit by producing the quantity at which marginal revenue equals marginal cost, which in this example is 1 million iPhones per quarter.

- This quantity of iPhones can be sold for $400 each.

- The blue rectangle shows Apple's economic profit.

- Because this market is profitable, entry takes place. Samsung and others (such as HTC, Motorola, LG, and Nokia) enter the smartphone market.

- Figure 2 shows the consequences of entry.

- The demand for the iPhone decreases as the market is shared with the other phones.

- Apple's profit-maximizing price for the iPhone falls, and in the long run, economic profit is eliminated.

- With zero economic profit, Apple has an incentive to develop an even better differentiated phone and start the cycle described here again, making an economic profit with a new phone in the short run.

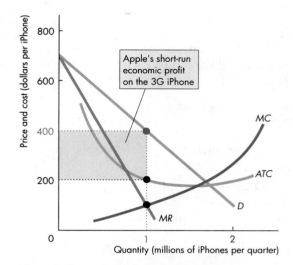

Figure 1 Economic Profit in the Short Run

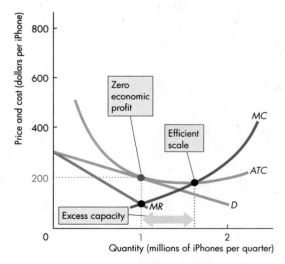

Figure 2 Zero Economic Profit in the Long Run

- The iPhone 4S launched in 2011 and the iPhone 5 launched in 2012 are examples of Apple's response to the competition from Samsung (and others) described in the news article.

SUMMARY

Key Points

What Is Monopolistic Competition? (pp. 324–325)

- Monopolistic competition occurs when a large number of firms compete with each other on product quality, price, and marketing.

Working Problems 1 and 2 will give you a better understanding of what monopolistic competition is.

Price and Output in Monopolistic Competition (pp. 326–329)

- Each firm in monopolistic competition faces a downward-sloping demand curve and produces the profit-maximizing quantity.
- Entry and exit result in zero economic profit and excess capacity in long-run equilibrium.

Working Problems 3 to 12 will give you a better understanding of price and output in monopolistic competition.

Product Development and Marketing (pp. 330–333)

- Firms in monopolistic competition innovate and develop new products.
- Advertising expenditures increase total cost, but average total cost might fall if the quantity sold increases by enough.
- Advertising expenditures might increase demand, but demand might decrease if competition increases.
- Whether monopolistic competition is inefficient depends on the value we place on product variety.

Working Problems 13 to 18 will give you a better understanding of product development and marketing.

Key Terms

Efficient scale, 328	Markup, 329	Product differentiation, 324
Excess capacity, 328	Monopolistic competition, 324	Signal, 332

STUDY PLAN PROBLEMS AND APPLICATIONS

MyEconLab   You can work Problems 1 to 19 in MyEconLab Chapter 14 Study Plan and get instant feedback.

What Is Monopolistic Competition? (Study Plan 14.1)

1. Which of the following items are sold by firms in monopolistic competition? Explain your selections.
   - Cable television service
   - Wheat
   - Athletic shoes
   - Soda
   - Toothbrushes
   - Ready-mix concrete

2. The four-firm concentration ratio for audio equipment makers is 30 and for electric lamp makers it is 89. The HHI for audio equipment makers is 415 and for electric lamp makers it is 2,850. Which of these markets is an example of monopolistic competition?

Price and Output in Monopolistic Competition

(Study Plan 14.2)

Use the following information to work Problems 3 and 4.

Sara is a dot.com entrepreneur who has established a Web site at which people can design and buy sweatshirts. Sara pays $1,000 a week for her Web server and Internet connection. The sweatshirts that her customers design are made to order by another firm, and Sara pays this firm $20 a sweatshirt. Sara has no other costs. The table sets out the demand schedule for Sara's sweatshirts.

Price (dollars per sweatshirt)	Quantity demanded (sweatshirts per week)
0	100
20	80
40	60
60	40
80	20
100	0

3. Calculate Sara's profit-maximizing output, price, and economic profit.

4. a. Do you expect other firms to enter the Web sweatshirt business and compete with Sara?
   b. What happens to the demand for Sara's sweatshirts in the long run? What happens to Sara's economic profit in the long run?

Use the following figure, which shows the situation facing a producer of running shoes, to work Problems 5 to 10.

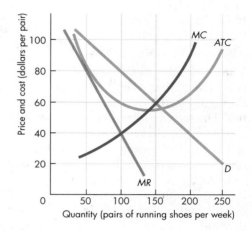

5. What quantity does the firm produce, what price does it charge, and what is its economic profit or economic loss?

6. In the long run, how does the number of firms producing running shoes change?

7. In the long run, how does the price of running shoes and the quantity the firm produces change? What happens to the market output?

8. Does the firm have excess capacity in the long run? If the firm has excess capacity in the long run, why doesn't it decrease its capacity?

9. In the long run, compare the price of a pair of running shoes and the marginal cost of producing the pair.

10. Is the market for running shoes efficient or inefficient in the long run? Explain your answer.

11. **Wake Up and Smell the Coffee**
    Every change that Starbucks made over the past few years—automated espresso machines, pre-ground coffee, drive-throughs, fewer soft chairs and less carpeting—was made for a reason: to smooth operations or boost sales. Those may have been the right choices at the time, but together they ultimately diluted the coffee-centric experience. By 2008, Starbucks experienced a drop in traffic as customers complained that in pursuing rapid growth, the company has strayed too far from its roots. Starbucks will once again grind beans in its stores for drip coffee, give free

drip refills, and provide two hours of wi-fi. The company will roll out its new sleek, low-rise espresso machine that makes baristas more visible.

Source: *Time*, April 7, 2008

a. Explain how Starbucks' past attempts to maximize profits ended up eroding product differentiation.

b. Explain how Starbucks' new plan intends to increase economic profit.

12. **The Shoe That Won't Quit**

I finally decided to take the plunge and buy a pair of Uggs, but when I got around to shopping for my Uggs, the style that I wanted was sold out. The scarcity factor was not a glitch in the supply chain, but rather a carefully calibrated strategy by Ugg's parent Deckers Outdoor that is one of the big reasons behind the brand's success. Deckers tightly controls distribution to ensure that supply does not outstrip demand. If Deckers ever opened up the supply of Uggs to meet demand, sales would shoot up like a rocket, but they'd come back down just as fast.

Source: *Fortune*, June 5, 2008

a. Explain why Deckers intentionally restricts the quantity of Uggs that the firm sells.

b. Draw a graph to illustrate how Deckers maximizes the economic profit from Uggs.

Product Development and Marketing (Study Plan 14.3)

Use the following information to work Problems 13 to 16.

Suppose that Tommy Hilfiger's marginal cost of a jacket is a constant $100 and the total fixed cost at one of its stores is $2,000 a day. This store sells 20 jackets a day, which is its profit-maximizing number of jackets. Then the stores nearby start to advertise their jackets. The Tommy Hilfiger store now spends $2,000 a day advertising its jackets, and its profit-maximizing number of jackets sold jumps to 50 a day.

13. a. What is this store's average total cost of a jacket sold before the advertising begins?

b. What is this store's average total cost of a jacket sold after the advertising begins?

14. a. Can you say what happens to the price of a Tommy Hilfiger jacket? Why or why not?

b. Can you say what happens to Tommy's markup? Why or why not?

c. Can you say what happens to Tommy's economic profit? Why or why not?

15. How might Tommy Hilfiger use advertising as a signal? How is a signal sent and how does it work?

16. How does having a brand name help Tommy Hilfiger to increase its economic profit?

Use the following news clip to work Problems 17 and 18.

Food's Next Billion-Dollar Brand?

While it's not the biggest brand in margarine, Smart Balance has an edge on its rivals in that it's made with a patented blend of vegetable and fruit oils that has been shown to help improve consumers' cholesterol levels. Smart Balance sales have skyrocketed while overall sales for margarine have stagnated. It remains to be seen if Smart Balance's healthy message and high price will resound with consumers.

Source: *Fortune*, June 4, 2008

17. How do you expect advertising and the Smart Balance brand name will affect Smart Balance's ability to make a positive economic profit?

18. Are long-run economic profits a possibility for Smart Balance? In long-run equilibrium, will Smart Balance have excess capacity or a markup?

Economics in the News (Study Plan 14.N)

19. **Computer Makers Prepare to Stake Bigger Claim in Phones**

Emboldened by Apple's success with its iPhone, many PC makers and chip companies are charging into the mobile-phone business, promising new devices that can pack the horsepower of standard computers into palm-size packages—devices that handle the full glory of the Internet, power two-way video conferences, and stream high-definition movies to your TV. It is a development that spells serious competition for established cell-phone makers and phone companies.

Source: *The New York Times*, March 15, 2009

a. Draw a graph of the cost curves and revenue curves of a cell-phone company that makes a positive economic profit in the short run.

b. If cell-phone companies start to include the popular features introduced by PC makers, explain how this decision will affect their profit in the short run.

c. What do you expect to happen to the cell-phone company's economic profit in the long run, given the information in the news clip?

d. Draw a graph to illustrate your answer to part (c).

ADDITIONAL PROBLEMS AND APPLICATIONS

MyEconLab   You can work these problems in MyEconLab if assigned by your instructor.

What Is Monopolistic Competition?

20. Which of the following items are sold by firms in monopolistic competition? Explain your selection.
    - Orange juice
    - Canned soup
    - PCs
    - Chewing gum
    - Breakfast cereals
    - Corn

21. The HHI for automobiles is 2,350, for sporting goods it is 161, for batteries it is 2,883, and for jewelry it is 81. Which of these markets is an example of monopolistic competition?

Price and Output in Monopolistic Competition

Use the following information to work Problems 22 and 23.

Lorie teaches singing. Her fixed costs are $1,000 a month, and it costs her $50 of labor to give one class. The table shows the demand schedule for Lorie's singing lessons.

Price (dollars per lesson)	Quantity demanded (lessons per month)
0	250
50	200
100	150
150	100
200	50
250	0

22. Calculate Lorie's profit-maximizing output, price, and economic profit.

23. a. Do you expect other firms to enter the singing lesson business and compete with Lorie?

    b. What happens to the demand for Lorie's lessons in the long run? What happens to Lorie's economic profit in the long run?

Use the figure in the next column, which shows the situation facing Mike's Bikes, a producer of mountain bikes, to work Problems 24 to 28. The demand and costs of other mountain bike producers are similar to those of Mike's Bikes.

24. What quantity does the firm produce and what is its price? Calculate the firm's economic profit or economic loss.

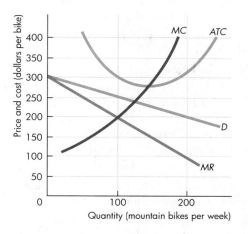

25. What will happen to the number of firms producing mountain bikes in the long run?

26. a. How will the price of a mountain bike and the number of bikes produced by Mike's Bikes change in the long run?

    b. How will the quantity of mountain bikes produced by all firms change in the long run?

27. Is there any way for Mike's Bikes to avoid having excess capacity in the long run?

28. Is the market for mountain bikes efficient or inefficient in the long run? Explain your answer.

Use the following news clip to work Problems 29 and 30.

Groceries for the Gourmet Palate

No food, it seems, is safe from being repackaged to look like an upscale product. Samuel Adams' $120 Utopias, in a ridiculous copper-covered 24-oz. bottle meant to resemble an old-fashioned brew kettle, is barely beer. It's not carbonated like a Bud, but aged in oak barrels like scotch. It has a vintage year, like a Bordeaux, is light, complex, and free of any alcohol sting, despite having six times as much alcohol content as a regular can of brew.

Source: *Time*, April 14, 2008

29. a. Explain how Samuel Adams has differentiated its Utopias to compete with other beer brands in terms of quality, price, and marketing.

    b. Predict whether Samuel Adams produces at, above, or below the efficient scale in the short run.

30. a. Predict whether the $120 price tag on the Utopias is at, above, or below marginal cost:

(i) In the short run.

(ii) In the long run.

b. Do you think that Samuel Adams' Utopias makes the market for beer inefficient?

Use the following news clip to work Problems 31 and 32.

Swinging for Female Golfers

One of the hottest areas of innovation is in clubs for women, who now make up nearly a quarter of the 24 million golfers in the United States. Callaway and Nike, two of the leading golf-equipment manufacturers, recently released new clubs designed for women.

Source: *Time*, April 21, 2008

31. a. How are Callaway and Nike attempting to maintain economic profit?

b. Draw a graph to illustrate the cost curves and revenue curves of Callaway or Nike in the market for golf clubs for women.

c. Show on your graph in part (b) the short-run economic profit.

32. a. Explain why the economic profit that Callaway and Nike make on golf clubs for women is likely to be temporary.

b. Draw a graph to illustrate the cost curves and revenue curves of Callaway or Nike in the market for golf clubs for women in the long run. Mark the firm's excess capacity.

Product Development and Marketing

Use the following information to work Problems 33 to 35.

Bianca bakes delicious cookies. Her total fixed cost is $40 a day, and her average variable cost is $1 a bag. Few people know about Bianca's Cookies, and she is maximizing her profit by selling 10 bags a day for $5 a bag. Bianca thinks that if she spends $50 a day on advertising, she can increase her market share and sell 25 bags a day for $5 a bag.

33. If Bianca's advertising works as she expects, can she increase her economic profit by advertising?

34. If Bianca advertises, will her average total cost increase or decrease at the quantity produced?

35. If Bianca advertises, will she continue to sell her cookies for $5 a bag or will she change her price?

Use the following news clip to work Problems 36 and 37.

A Thirst for More Champagne

Champagne exports have tripled in the past 20 years. That poses a problem for northern France, where the bubbly hails from—not enough grapes. So French

authorities have unveiled a plan to extend the official Champagne grape-growing zone to cover 40 new villages. This revision has provoked debate. The change will take several years to become effective. In the meantime the vineyard owners whose land values will jump markedly if the changes are finalized certainly have reason to raise a glass.

Source: *Fortune*, May 12, 2008

36. a. Why is France so strict about designating the vineyards that can use the Champagne label?

b. Explain who most likely opposes this plan.

37. Assuming that vineyards in these 40 villages are producing the same quality of grapes with or without this plan, why will their land values "jump markedly" if this plan is approved?

38. **Under Armour's Big Step Up**

Under Armour, the red-hot athletic-apparel brand, has joined Nike, Adidas, and New Balance as a major player in the market for athletic footwear. Under Armour plans to revive the long-dead cross-training category. But will young athletes really spend $100 for a cross training shoe to lift weights in?

Source: *Time*, May 26, 2008

What factors influence Under Armour's ability to make an economic profit in the cross-training shoe market?

Economics in the News

39. After you have studied *Reading Between the Lines* on pp. 334–335, answer the following questions.

a. Describe the cost curves (*MC* and *ATC*) and the marginal revenue and demand curves for the iPhone when Apple first introduced it.

b. How do you think the creation of the iPhone influenced the demand for older generation cell phones?

c. Explain the effects of the introduction of the iPhone 5 on Samsung and other firms in the market for smartphones.

d. Draw a graph to illustrate your answer to part (c).

e. Explain the effect on Apple of the decisions by Samsung and others to bring their own smartphones to market.

f. Draw a graph to illustrate your answer to part (e).

g. Do you think the market for smartphones is efficient? Explain your answer.

h. Do you predict that producers of smartphones have excess capacity? Explain your answer.

15

OLIGOPOLY

After studying this chapter, you will be able to:

◆ Define and identify oligopoly

◆ Use game theory to explain how price and output are determined in oligopoly

◆ Use game theory to explain other strategic decisions

◆ Describe the antitrust laws that regulate oligopoly

The chip in your laptop was made by Intel or AMD; the battery in your TV remote was made by Duracell or Energizer; and the airplane that takes you on a long-distance trip was made by Boeing or the European firm Airbus.

How does a market work when only two or a handful of firms compete? To answer this question, we use the model of oligopoly.

At the end of the chapter, in *Reading Between the Lines*, we'll look at the market for ferry service in Singapore and see how Batam Fast and Penguin battle to maximize profit.

◆ What Is Oligopoly?

Oligopoly, like monopolistic competition, lies between perfect competition and monopoly. The firms in oligopoly might produce an identical product and compete only on price, or they might produce a differentiated product and compete on price, product quality, and marketing. **Oligopoly** is a market structure in which

- Natural or legal barriers prevent the entry of new firms.
- A small number of firms compete.

Barriers to Entry

Natural or legal barriers to entry can create oligopoly. You saw in Chapter 13 how economies of scale and demand form a natural barrier to entry that can create a *natural monopoly*. These same factors can create a *natural oligopoly*.

Figure 15.1 illustrates two natural oligopolies. The demand curve, D (in both parts of the figure), shows the demand for taxi rides in a town. If the average

total cost curve of a taxi company is ATC_1 in part (a), the market is a natural **duopoly**—an oligopoly market with two firms. You can probably see some examples of duopoly where you live. Some cities have only two taxi companies, two car rental firms, two copy centers, or two college bookstores.

The lowest price at which the firm would remain in business is $10 a ride. At that price, the quantity of rides demanded is 60 a day, the quantity that can be provided by just two firms. There is no room in this market for three firms. But if there were only one firm, it would make an economic profit and a second firm would enter to take some of the business and economic profit.

If the average total cost curve of a taxi company is ATC_2 in part (b), the efficient scale of one firm is 20 rides a day. This market is large enough for three firms.

A legal oligopoly arises when a legal barrier to entry protects the small number of firms in a market. A city might license two taxi firms or two bus companies, for example, even though the combination of demand and economies of scale leaves room for more than two firms.

FIGURE 15.1   Natural Oligopoly

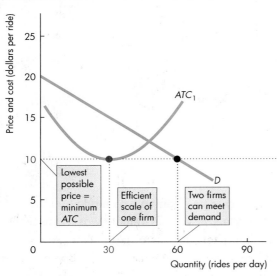

(a) Natural duopoly

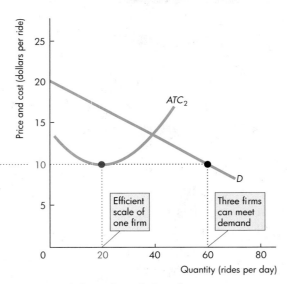

(b) Natural oligopoly with three firms

The lowest possible price is $10 a ride, which is the minimum average total cost. When a firm produces 30 rides a day, the efficient scale, two firms can satisfy the market demand. This natural oligopoly has two firms—a natural duopoly.

When the efficient scale of one firm is 20 rides per day, three firms can satisfy the market demand at the lowest possible price. This natural oligopoly has three firms.

Economics in Action
Oligopoly Today

These markets are oligopolies. Although in some of them, the number of firms (in parentheses) is large, the share of the market held by the 4 largest firms (the red bars) is close to 100 percent.

The most concentrated markets—cigarettes, glass bottles and jars, washing machines and dryers, and batteries, are dominated by just one or two firms.

If you want to buy a battery for your TV remote or toothbrush, you'll find it hard to avoid buying a Duracell or an Energizer.

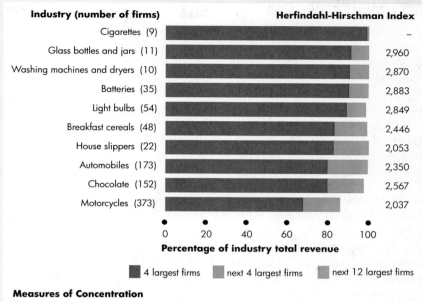

Industry (number of firms)	Herfindahl-Hirschman Index
Cigarettes (9)	–
Glass bottles and jars (11)	2,960
Washing machines and dryers (10)	2,870
Batteries (35)	2,883
Light bulbs (54)	2,849
Breakfast cereals (48)	2,446
House slippers (22)	2,053
Automobiles (173)	2,350
Chocolate (152)	2,567
Motorcycles (373)	2,037

Percentage of industry total revenue

■ 4 largest firms   ■ next 4 largest firms   ■ next 12 largest firms

Measures of Concentration
Source of data: U.S. Census Bureau.

Small Number of Firms

Because barriers to entry exist, oligopoly consists of a small number of firms, each of which has a large share of the market. Such firms are interdependent, and they face a temptation to cooperate to increase their joint economic profit.

Interdependence With a small number of firms in a market, each firm's actions influence the profits of all the other firms. When Penny Stafford opened her coffee shop in Bellevue, Washington, a nearby Starbucks coffee shop took a hit. Within days, Starbucks began to attract Penny's customers with enticing offers and lower prices. Starbucks survived but Penny eventually went out of business. Penny Stafford and Starbucks were interdependent.

Temptation to Cooperate When a small number of firms share a market, they can increase their profits by forming a cartel and acting like a monopoly. A **cartel** is a group of firms acting together—colluding—to limit output, raise price, and increase economic profit. Cartels are illegal, but they do operate in some markets. But for reasons that you'll discover in this chapter, cartels tend to break down.

Examples of Oligopoly

Economics in Action above shows some examples of oligopoly. The dividing line between oligopoly and monopolistic competition is hard to pin down. As a practical matter, we identify oligopoly by looking at concentration ratios, the Herfindahl-Hirschman Index, and information about the geographical scope of the market and barriers to entry. The HHI that divides oligopoly from monopolistic competition is generally taken to be 1,000. An HHI below 1,000 is usually an example of monopolistic competition, and a market in which the HHI exceeds 1,000 is usually an example of oligopoly.

◀ REVIEW QUIZ

1 What are the two distinguishing characteristics of oligopoly?
2 Why are firms in oligopoly interdependent?
3 Why do firms in oligopoly face a temptation to collude?
4 Can you think of some examples of oligopolies that you buy from?

You can work these questions in Study Plan 15.1 and get instant feedback.   MyEconLab

▶ Oligopoly Games

Economists think about oligopoly as a game between two or a few players, and to study oligopoly markets they use game theory. **Game theory** is a set of tools for studying *strategic behavior*—behavior that takes into account the expected behavior of others and the recognition of mutual interdependence. Game theory was invented by John von Neumann in 1937 and extended by von Neumann and Oskar Morgenstern in 1944 (p. 367). Today, it is one of the major research fields in economics.

Game theory seeks to understand oligopoly as well as other forms of economic, political, social, and even biological rivalries by using a method of analysis specifically designed to understand games of all types, including the familiar games of everyday life (see Talking with Thomas Hubbard on p. 368). To lay the foundation for studying oligopoly games, we first think about the features that all games share.

What Is a Game?

What is a game? At first thought, the question seems silly. After all, there are many different games. There are ball games and parlor games, games of chance and games of skill. But what is it about all these different activities that makes them games? What do all these games have in common? All games share four common features:

- Rules
- Strategies
- Payoffs
- Outcome

We're going to look at these features of games by playing a game called "the prisoners' dilemma." The prisoners' dilemma game displays the essential features of many games, including oligopoly games, and it gives a good illustration of how game theory works and generates predictions.

The Prisoners' Dilemma

Art and Bob have been caught red-handed stealing a car. Facing airtight cases, they will receive a sentence of two years each for their crime. During his interviews with the two prisoners, the district attorney begins to suspect that he has stumbled on the two people who were responsible for a multimillion-dollar bank robbery some months earlier. But this is just a suspicion. He has no evidence on which he can convict them of the greater crime unless he can get them to confess. But how can he extract a confession? The answer is by making the prisoners play a game. The district attorney makes the prisoners play the following game.

Rules Each prisoner (player) is placed in a separate room and cannot communicate with the other prisoner. Each is told that he is suspected of having carried out the bank robbery and that

> If both of them confess to the larger crime, each will receive a sentence of 3 years for both crimes.

> If he alone confesses and his accomplice does not, he will receive only a 1-year sentence while his accomplice will receive a 10-year sentence.

Strategies In game theory, **strategies** are all the possible actions of each player. Art and Bob each have two possible actions:

1. Confess to the bank robbery.
2. Deny having committed the bank robbery.

Because there are two players, each with two strategies, there are four possible outcomes:

1. Both confess.
2. Both deny.
3. Art confesses and Bob denies.
4. Bob confesses and Art denies.

Payoffs Each prisoner can work out his *payoff* in each of these situations, and we can tabulate the four possible payoffs for each of the prisoners in what is called a payoff matrix for the game. A **payoff matrix** is a table that shows the payoffs for every possible action by each player for every possible action by each other player.

Table 15.1 shows a payoff matrix for Art and Bob. The squares show the payoffs for each prisoner—the red triangle in each square shows Art's and the blue triangle shows Bob's. If both prisoners confess (top left), each gets a prison term of 3 years. If Bob confesses but Art denies (top right), Art gets a 10-year sentence and Bob gets a 1-year sentence. If Art confesses and Bob denies (bottom left), Art gets a 1-year sentence and Bob gets a 10-year sentence. Finally, if both of them deny (bottom right), neither can be convicted of the bank robbery charge but both are sentenced for the car theft—a 2-year sentence.

Outcome The choices of both players determine the outcome of the game. To predict that outcome, we use an equilibrium idea proposed by John Nash of Princeton University (who received the Nobel Prize for Economic Science in 1994 and was the subject of the 2001 movie *A Beautiful Mind*). In **Nash equilibrium**, player *A* takes the best possible action given the action of player *B* and player *B* takes the best possible action given the action of player *A*.

In the case of the prisoners' dilemma, the Nash equilibrium occurs when Art makes his best choice given Bob's choice and when Bob makes his best choice given Art's choice.

To find the Nash equilibrium, we compare all the possible outcomes associated with each choice and eliminate those that are dominated—that are not as good as some other choice. Let's find the Nash equilibrium for the prisoners' dilemma game.

Finding the Nash Equilibrium Look at the situation from Art's point of view. If Bob confesses (top row), Art's best action is to confess because in that case, he is sentenced to 3 years rather than 10 years. If Bob denies (bottom row), Art's best action is still to confess because in that case, he receives 1 year rather than 2 years. So Art's best action is to confess.

Now look at the situation from Bob's point of view. If Art confesses (left column), Bob's best action is to confess because in that case, he is sentenced to 3 years rather than 10 years. If Art denies (right column), Bob's best action is still to confess because in that case, he receives 1 year rather than 2 years. So Bob's best action is to confess.

Because each player's best action is to confess, each does confess, each goes to jail for 3 years, and the district attorney has solved the bank robbery. This is the Nash equilibrium of the game.

The Nash equilibrium for the prisoners' dilemma is called a **dominant-strategy equilibrium**, which is an equilibrium in which the best strategy of each player is to cheat (confess) *regardless of the strategy of the other player*.

The Dilemma The dilemma arises as each prisoner contemplates the consequences of his decision and puts himself in the place of his accomplice. Each knows that it would be best if both denied. But each also knows that if he denies it is in the best interest of the other to confess. So each considers whether to deny and rely on his accomplice to deny or to confess

TABLE 15.1 Prisoners' Dilemma Payoff Matrix

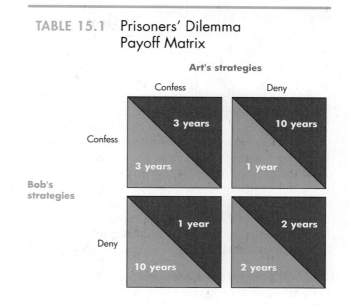

Each square shows the payoffs for the two players, Art and Bob, for each possible pair of actions. In each square, the red triangle shows Art's payoff and the blue triangle shows Bob's. For example, if both confess, the payoffs are in the top left square. The equilibrium of the game is for both players to confess and each gets a 3-year sentence.

hoping that his accomplice denies but expecting him to confess. The dilemma leads to the equilibrium of the game.

A Bad Outcome For the prisoners, the equilibrium of the game, with each confessing, is not the best outcome. If neither of them confesses, each gets only 2 years for the lesser crime. Isn't there some way in which this better outcome can be achieved? It seems that there is not, because the players cannot communicate with each other. Each player can put himself in the other player's place, and so each player can figure out that there is a best strategy for each of them. The prisoners are indeed in a dilemma. Each knows that he can serve 2 years *only* if he can trust the other to deny. But each prisoner also knows that it is *not* in the best interest of the other to deny. So each prisoner knows that he must confess, thereby delivering a bad outcome for both.

The firms in an oligopoly are in a similar situation to Art and Bob in the prisoners' dilemma game. Let's see how we can use this game to understand oligopoly.

An Oligopoly Price-Fixing Game

We can use game theory and a game like the prisoners' dilemma to understand price fixing, price wars, and other aspects of the behavior of firms in oligopoly. We'll begin with a price-fixing game.

To understand price fixing, we're going to study the special case of duopoly—an oligopoly with two firms. Duopoly is easier to study than oligopoly with three or more firms, and it captures the essence of all oligopoly situations. Somehow, the two firms must share the market. And how they share it depends on the actions of each. We're going to describe the costs of the two firms and the market demand for the item they produce. We're then going to see how game theory helps us to predict the prices charged and the quantities produced by the two firms in a duopoly.

Cost and Demand Conditions Two firms, Trick and Gear, produce switchgears. They have identical costs. Figure 15.2(a) shows their average total cost curve (*ATC*) and marginal cost curve (*MC*). Figure 15.2(b) shows the market demand curve for switchgears (*D*). The two firms produce identical switchgears, so one firm's switchgear is a perfect substitute for the other's, and the market price of each firm's product is identical. The quantity demanded depends on that price—the higher the price, the smaller is the quantity demanded.

This industry is a natural duopoly. Two firms can produce this good at a lower cost than either one firm or three firms can. For each firm, average total cost is at its minimum when production is 3,000 units a week. When price equals minimum average total cost, the total quantity demanded is 6,000 units a week, and two firms can just produce that quantity.

Collusion We'll suppose that Trick and Gear enter into a collusive agreement. A **collusive agreement** is an agreement between two (or more) producers to form a cartel to restrict output, raise the price, and increase profits. Such an agreement is illegal in the United States and is undertaken in secret. The strategies that firms in a cartel can pursue are to

- Comply
- Cheat

A firm that complies carries out the agreement. A firm that cheats breaks the agreement to its own benefit and to the cost of the other firm.

Because each firm has two strategies, there are four possible combinations of actions for the firms:

1. Both firms comply.
2. Both firms cheat.
3. Trick complies and Gear cheats.
4. Gear complies and Trick cheats.

FIGURE 15.2   Costs and Demand

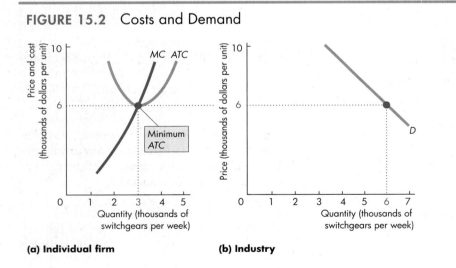

(a) Individual firm

(b) Industry

The average total cost curve for each firm is *ATC*, and the marginal cost curve is *MC* (part a). Minimum average total cost is $6,000 a unit, and it occurs at a production of 3,000 units a week.

Part (b) shows the market demand curve. At a price of $6,000, the quantity demanded is 6,000 units per week. The two firms can produce this output at the lowest possible average cost. If the market had one firm, it would be profitable for another to enter. If the market had three firms, one would exit. There is room for only two firms in this industry. It is a natural duopoly.

Colluding to Maximize Profits Let's work out the payoffs to the two firms if they collude to make the maximum profit for the cartel by acting like a monopoly. The calculations that the two firms perform are the same calculations that a monopoly performs. (You can refresh your memory of these calculations by looking at Chapter 13, pp. 302–303.) The only thing that the firms in duopoly must do beyond what a monopoly does is to agree on how much of the total output each of them will produce.

Figure 15.3 shows the price and quantity that maximize industry profit for the duopoly. Part (a) shows the situation for each firm, and part (b) shows the situation for the industry as a whole. The curve labeled MR is the industry marginal revenue curve. This marginal revenue curve is like that of a single-price monopoly (Chapter 13, p. 300). The curve labeled MC_I is the industry marginal cost curve if each firm produces the same quantity of output. This curve is constructed by adding together the outputs of the two firms at each level of marginal cost. Because the two firms are the same size, at each level of marginal cost, the industry output is twice the output of one firm. The curve MC_I in part (b) is twice as far to the right as the curve MC in part (a).

To maximize industry profit, the firms in the duopoly agree to restrict output to the rate that makes the industry marginal cost and marginal revenue equal. That output rate, as shown in part (b), is 4,000 units a week. The demand curve shows that the highest price for which the 4,000 switchgears can be sold is $9,000 each. Trick and Gear agree to charge this price.

To hold the price at $9,000 a unit, production must be 4,000 units a week. So Trick and Gear must agree on output rates for each of them that total 4,000 units a week. Let's suppose that they agree to split the market equally so that each firm produces 2,000 switchgears a week. Because the firms are identical, this division is the most likely.

The average total cost (ATC) of producing 2,000 switchgears a week is $8,000, so the profit per unit is $1,000 and economic profit is $2 million (2,000 units × $1,000 per unit). The economic profit of each firm is represented by the blue rectangle in Fig. 15.3(a).

We have just described one possible outcome for a duopoly game: The two firms collude to produce the monopoly profit-maximizing output and divide that output equally between themselves. From the industry point of view, this solution is identical to a monopoly. A duopoly that operates in this way is indistinguishable from a monopoly. The economic profit that is made by a monopoly is the maximum total profit that can be made by the duopoly when the firms collude.

But with price greater than marginal cost, either firm might think of trying to increase profit by cheating on the agreement and producing more than the agreed amount. Let's see what happens if one of the firms does cheat in this way.

FIGURE 15.3   Colluding to Make Monopoly Profits

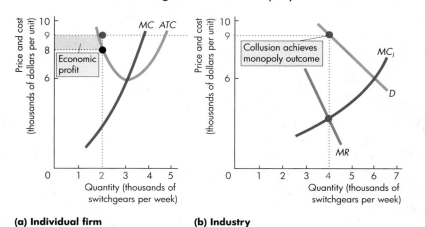

(a) Individual firm

(b) Industry

The industry marginal cost curve, MC_I in part (b), is the horizontal sum of the two firms' marginal cost curves, MC in part (a). The industry marginal revenue curve is MR. To maximize profit, the firms produce 4,000 units a week (the quantity at which marginal revenue equals marginal cost). They sell that output for $9,000 a unit. Each firm produces 2,000 units a week. Average total cost is $8,000 a unit, so each firm makes an economic profit of $2 million (blue rectangle)—2,000 units multiplied by $1,000 profit a unit.

MyEconLab animation

One Firm Cheats on a Collusive Agreement   To set the stage for cheating on their agreement, Trick convinces Gear that demand has decreased and that it cannot sell 2,000 units a week. Trick tells Gear that it plans to cut its price so that it can sell the agreed 2,000 units each week. Because the two firms produce an identical product, Gear matches Trick's price cut but still produces only 2,000 units a week.

In fact, there has been no decrease in demand. Trick plans to increase output, which it knows will lower the price, and Trick wants to ensure that Gear's output remains at the agreed level.

Figure 15.4 illustrates the consequences of Trick's cheating. Part (a) shows Gear (the complier); part (b) shows Trick (the cheat); and part (c) shows the industry as a whole. Suppose that Trick increases output to 3,000 units a week. If Gear sticks to the agreement to produce only 2,000 units a week, total output is now 5,000 a week, and given demand in part (c), the price falls to $7,500 a unit.

Gear continues to produce 2,000 units a week at a cost of $8,000 a unit and incurs a loss of $500 a unit, or $1 million a week. This economic loss is shown by the red rectangle in part (a). Trick produces 3,000 units a week at a cost of $6,000 a unit. With a price

of $7,500, Trick makes a profit of $1,500 a unit and therefore an economic profit of $4.5 million. This economic profit is the blue rectangle in part (b).

We've now described a second possible outcome for the duopoly game: One of the firms cheats on the collusive agreement. In this case, the industry output is larger than the monopoly output and the industry price is lower than the monopoly price. The total economic profit made by the industry is also smaller than the monopoly's economic profit. Trick (the cheat) makes an economic profit of $4.5 million, and Gear (the complier) incurs an economic loss of $1 million. The industry makes an economic profit of $3.5 million. This industry profit is $0.5 million less than the economic profit that a monopoly would make, but it is distributed unevenly. Trick makes a bigger economic profit than it would under the collusive agreement, while Gear incurs an economic loss.

A similar outcome would arise if Gear cheated and Trick complied with the agreement. The industry profit and price would be the same, but in this case, Gear (the cheat) would make an economic profit of $4.5 million and Trick (the complier) would incur an economic loss of $1 million.

Let's next see what happens if both firms cheat.

FIGURE 15.4   One Firm Cheats

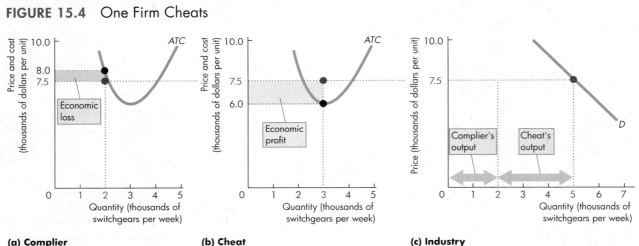

(a) Complier   **(b) Cheat**   **(c) Industry**

One firm, shown in part (a), complies with the agreement and produces 2,000 units. The other firm, shown in part (b), cheats on the agreement and increases its output to 3,000 units a week. Given the market demand curve, shown in part (c), and with a total production of 5,000 units a week,

the price falls to $7,500 a unit. At this price, the complier in part (a) incurs an economic loss of $1 million ($500 per unit × 2,000 units), shown by the red rectangle. In part (b), the cheat makes an economic profit of $4.5 million ($1,500 per unit × 3,000 units), shown by the blue rectangle.

MyEconLab animation

Both Firms Cheat Suppose that both firms cheat and that each firm behaves like the cheating firm that we have just analyzed. Each tells the other that it is unable to sell its output at the going price and that it plans to cut its price. But because both firms cheat, each will propose a successively lower price. As long as price exceeds marginal cost, each firm has an incentive to increase its production—to cheat. Only when price equals marginal cost is there no further incentive to cheat. This situation arises when the price has reached $6,000. At this price, marginal cost equals price. Also, price equals minimum average total cost. At a price less than $6,000, each firm incurs an economic loss. At a price of $6,000, each firm covers all its costs and makes zero economic profit. Also, at a price of $6,000, each firm wants to produce 3,000 units a week, so the industry output is 6,000 units a week. Given the demand conditions, 6,000 units can be sold at a price of $6,000 each.

Figure 15.5 illustrates the situation just described. Each firm, in part (a), produces 3,000 units a week, and its average total cost is a minimum ($6,000 per unit). The market as a whole, in part (b), operates at the point at which the market demand curve (D) intersects the industry marginal cost curve (MC_I). Each firm has lowered its price and increased its output to try to gain an advantage over the other firm. Each has pushed this process as far as it can without incurring an economic loss.

We have now described a third possible outcome of this duopoly game: Both firms cheat. If both firms cheat on the collusive agreement, the output of each firm is 3,000 units a week and the price is $6,000 a unit. Each firm makes zero economic profit.

The Payoff Matrix Now that we have described the strategies and payoffs in the duopoly game, we can summarize the strategies and the payoffs in the form of the game's payoff matrix. Then we can find the Nash equilibrium.

Table 15.2 sets out the payoff matrix for this game. It is constructed in the same way as the payoff matrix for the prisoners' dilemma in Table 15.1. The squares show the payoffs for the two firms—Gear and Trick. In this case, the payoffs are profits. (For the prisoners' dilemma, the payoffs were losses.)

The table shows that if both firms cheat (top left), they achieve the perfectly competitive outcome—each firm makes zero economic profit. If both firms comply (bottom right), the industry makes the monopoly profit and each firm makes an economic profit of $2 million. The top right and bottom left squares show the payoff if one firm cheats while the other complies. The firm that cheats makes an economic profit of $4.5 million, and the one that complies incurs a loss of $1 million.

Nash Equilibrium in the Duopolists' Dilemma The duopolists have a dilemma like the prisoners' dilemma. Do they comply or cheat? To answer this question, we must find the Nash equilibrium.

FIGURE 15.5   Both Firms Cheat

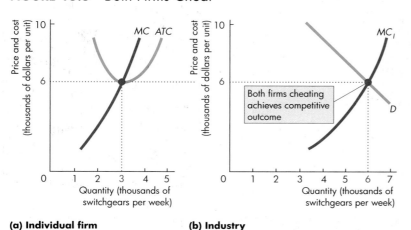

(a) Individual firm   (b) Industry

If both firms cheat by increasing production, the collusive agreement collapses. The limit to the collapse is the competitive equilibrium. Neither firm will cut its price below $6,000 (minimum average total cost) because to do so will result in losses. In part (a), each firm produces 3,000 units a week at an average total cost of $6,000. In part (b), with a total production of 6,000 units, the price falls to $6,000. Each firm now makes zero economic profit. This output and price are the ones that would prevail in a competitive industry.

TABLE 15.2   Duopoly Payoff Matrix

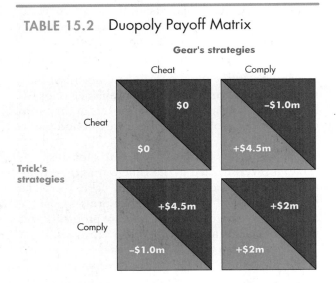

Each square shows the payoffs from a pair of actions. For example, if both firms comply with the collusive agreement, the payoffs are recorded in the bottom right square. The red triangle shows Gear's payoff, and the blue triangle shows Trick's. In Nash equilibrium, both firms cheat.

Look at things from Gear's point of view. Gear reasons as follows: Suppose that Trick cheats. If I comply, I will incur an economic loss of $1 million. If I also cheat, I will make zero economic profit. Zero is better than *minus* $1 million, so I'm better off if I cheat. Now suppose Trick complies. If I cheat, I will make an economic profit of $4.5 million, and if I comply, I will make an economic profit of $2 million. A $4.5 million profit is better than a $2 million profit, so I'm better off if I cheat. So regardless of whether Trick cheats or complies, it pays Gear to cheat. Cheating is Gear's best strategy.

Trick comes to the same conclusion as Gear because the two firms face an identical situation. So both firms cheat. The Nash equilibrium of the duopoly game is that both firms cheat. And although the industry has only two firms, they charge the same price and produce the same quantity as those in a competitive industry. Also, as in perfect competition, each firm makes zero economic profit.

Economics in Action (opposite) and *Economics in the News* (p. 353) look at some other prisoners' dilemma games. But not all games are prisoners' dilemmas, as you'll now see.

Economics in Action
A Game in the Market for Tissues

Anti-Viral Kleenex and Puffs Plus Lotion didn't get developed because Kimberly-Clark (Kleenex) and P&G (Puffs) were thinking about helping you cope with a miserable cold. These new style tissues and other innovations in the quality of facial tissues are the product of a costly research and development (R&D) game.

The table below illustrates the game (with hypothetical numbers). Each firm can spend either $25 million or nothing on R&D. If neither firm spends, Kimberly-Clark makes an economic profit of $70 million and P&G of $30 million (bottom right). If each firm spends on R&D, Kimberly-Clark's economic profit is $45 million and P&G's is $5 million (top left). The other parts of the matrix show the economic profits for each when one spends on R&D and the other doesn't.

Confronted with these payoffs, Kimberly-Clark sees that it gets a bigger profit if it spends on R&D regardless of what P&G does. P&G reaches the same conclusion: It, too, gets a bigger profit by spending on R&D regardless of what Kimberly-Clark does.

Because R&D is the best strategy for both players, it is the Nash equilibrium—a *dominant-strategy Nash equilibrium*.

The outcome of this game is that both firms conduct R&D. They make less profit than they would if they could collude to achieve the cooperative outcome of no R&D. But you get a better Kleenex or Puffs tissue.

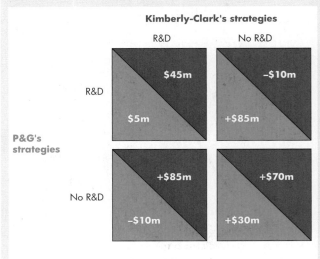

Kleenex Versus Puffs: An R&D Game

A Game of Chicken

The Nash equilibrium for the prisoners' dilemma is unique: both players cheat (confess). Not all games have a unique equilibrium, and one that doesn't is a game called "chicken."

An Example of the Game of Chicken A graphic, if disturbing, version of "chicken" has two cars racing toward each other. The first driver to swerve and avoid a crash is the "chicken." The payoffs are a big loss for both if no one "chickens out;" zero for both if both "chicken out;" and zero for the chicken and a gain for the one who stays the course. If player 1 swerves, player 2's best strategy is to stay the course; and if player 1 stays the course, player 2's best strategy is to swerve.

An Economic Example of Chicken An economic game of chicken can arise when research and development (R&D) creates a new technology that cannot be kept secret or patented, so both firms benefit from the R&D of either firm. The chicken in this case is the firm that does the R&D.

Suppose, for example, that either Apple or Nokia spends $9 million developing a new touch-screen technology that both would end up being able to use regardless of which of them developed it.

Table 15.3 illustrates a payoff matrix for the game that Apple and Nokia play. Each firm has two strategies: Do the R&D ("chicken out") or do not do the R&D. Each entry shows the additional profit (the profit from the new technology minus the cost of the research), given the strategies adopted.

If neither firm does the R&D, each makes zero additional profit. If both firms conduct the R&D, each firm makes an additional $5 million. If one of the firms does the R&D ("chickens out"), the chicken makes $1 million and the other firm makes $10 million. Confronted with these payoffs the two firms calculate their best strategies. Nokia is better off doing R&D if Apple does no R&D. Apple is better off doing R&D if Nokia does no R&D. There are two Nash equilibrium outcomes: Only one of them does the R&D, but we can't predict which one.

You can see that an outcome with no firm doing R&D isn't a Nash equilibrium because one firm would be better off doing it. Also both firms doing R&D isn't a Nash equilibrium because one firm would be better off *not* doing it. To decide *which* firm does the R&D, the firms might toss a coin, called a mixed strategy.

TABLE 15.3   An R&D Game of Chicken

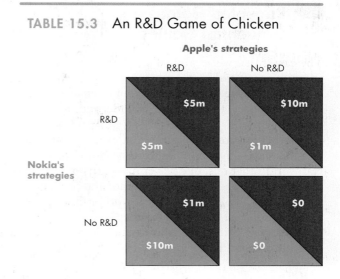

If neither firm does the R&D, their payoffs are in the bottom right square. When one firm "chickens out" and does the R&D while the other does no R&D, their payoffs are in the top right and bottom left squares. When both "chicken out" and do the R&D, the payoffs are in the top left square. The red triangle shows Apple's payoff, and the blue triangle shows Nokia's. The equilibrium for this R&D game of chicken is for only one firm to undertake the R&D. We cannot tell which firm will do the R&D and which will not.

REVIEW QUIZ

1 What are the common features of all games?
2 Describe the prisoners' dilemma game and explain why the Nash equilibrium delivers a bad outcome for both players.
3 Why does a collusive agreement to restrict output and raise the price create a game like the prisoners' dilemma?
4 What creates an incentive for firms in a collusive agreement to cheat and increase output?
5 What is the equilibrium strategy for each firm in a duopolists' dilemma and why do the firms not succeed in colluding to raise the price and profits?
6 Describe the payoffs for an R&D game of chicken and contrast them with the payoffs in a prisoners' dilemma game.

You can work these questions in Study Plan 15.2 and get instant feedback.   MyEconLab

▶ Repeated Games and Sequential Games

The games that we've studied are played just once. In contrast, many real-world games are played repeatedly. This feature of games turns out to enable real-world duopolists to cooperate, collude, and make a monopoly profit.

Another feature of the games that we've studied is that the players move simultaneously. But in many real-world situations, one player moves first and then the other moves—the play is sequential rather than simultaneous. This feature of real-world games creates a large number of possible outcomes.

We're now going to examine these two aspects of strategic decision making.

A Repeated Duopoly Game

If two firms play a game repeatedly, one firm has the opportunity to penalize the other for previous "bad" behavior. If Gear cheats this week, perhaps Trick will cheat next week. Before Gear cheats this week, won't it consider the possibility that Trick will cheat next week? What is the equilibrium of this game?

Actually, there is more than one possibility. One is the Nash equilibrium that we have just analyzed. Both players cheat, and each makes zero economic profit forever. In such a situation, it will never pay one of the players to start complying unilaterally because to do so would result in a loss for that player and a profit for the other. But a **cooperative equilibrium** in which the players make and share the monopoly profit is possible.

A cooperative equilibrium might occur if cheating is punished. There are two extremes of punishment. The smallest penalty is called "tit for tat." A *tit-for-tat strategy* is one in which a player cooperates in the current period if the other player cooperated in the previous period, but cheats in the current period if the other player cheated in the previous period. The most severe form of punishment is called a trigger strategy. A *trigger strategy* is one in which a player cooperates if the other player cooperates but plays the Nash equilibrium strategy forever thereafter if the other player cheats.

In the duopoly game between Gear and Trick, a tit-for-tat strategy keeps both players cooperating and making monopoly profits. Let's see why with an example.

Table 15.4 shows the economic profit that Trick and Gear will make over a number of periods under two alternative sequences of events: colluding and cheating with a tit-for-tat response by the other firm.

If both firms stick to the collusive agreement in period 1, each makes an economic profit of $2 million. Suppose that Trick contemplates cheating in period 1. The cheating produces a quick $4.5 million economic profit and inflicts a $1 million economic loss on Gear. But a cheat in period 1 produces a response from Gear in period 2. If Trick wants to get back into a profit-making situation, it must return to the agreement in period 2 even though it knows that Gear will punish it for cheating in period 1. So in period 2, Gear punishes Trick and Trick cooperates. Gear now makes an economic profit of $4.5 million, and Trick incurs an economic loss of $1 million. Adding up the profits over two periods of play, Trick would have made more profit by cooperating—$4 million compared with $3.5 million.

What is true for Trick is also true for Gear. Because each firm makes a larger profit by sticking with the collusive agreement, both firms do so and the monopoly price, quantity, and profit prevail.

In reality, whether a cartel works like a one-play game or a repeated game depends primarily on the

---

TABLE 15.4   Cheating with Punishment

Period of play	Collude		Cheat with tit-for-tat	
	Trick's profit (millions of dollars)	Gear's profit (millions of dollars)	Trick's profit (millions of dollars)	Gear's profit (millions of dollars)
1	2	2	4.5	−1.0
2	2	2	−1.0	4.5
3	2	2	2.0	2.0
4	•	•	•	•

If duopolists repeatedly collude, each makes a profit of $2 million per period of play. If one player cheats in period 1, the other player plays a tit-for-tat strategy and cheats in period 2. The profit from cheating can be made for only one period and must be paid for in the next period by incurring a loss. Over two periods of play, the best that a duopolist can achieve by cheating is a profit of $3.5 million, compared to an economic profit of $4 million by colluding.

◆ ECONOMICS IN THE NEWS

Airbus Versus Boeing

Boeing Strikes Back in Single-Aisle Market

Airbus and Boeing are in fierce competition in the narrow-body passenger jet market. Airbus got moving first with its A320neo for which it has 1,400 orders. Boeing responded with the 737 Max for which it had 549 orders in mid-2012 and an aim for 1,000 orders by the end of 2012.

Boeing rejected suggestions that it was in a price war with Airbus over the A320neo and 737 Max but confirmed it would woo some airline customers of its European rival.

Source: *Financial Times*, July 9, 2012

SOME DATA

Aircraft	List price
Airbus Neo	$96.7 million
Boeing Max	$96.0 million

ASSUMPTIONS

Assume that the performance and operating costs of the A320neo and the Max are identical.

At list prices, Airbus and Boeing can get another 200 orders each and make $3 billion each in economic profit.

At discounted prices, Airbus and Boeing can get another 225 orders each and make $1 billion each in economic profit.

If one of them holds the list price and the other discounts, the discounter can get 450 new orders and makes $2 billion and the other will get no new orders.

THE QUESTIONS

- In what type of market are Airbus and Boeing competing?
- How did moving first benefit Airbus?
- Given the assumptions above, will the airplane producers discount their prices or stick to the list prices? To answer this question, set out the payoff matrix for the game that Airbus and Boeing are playing and find the Nash equilibrium.
- If the game could be played repeatedly, how might the strategies and equilibrium change?

THE ANSWERS

- Airbus and Boeing are a duopoly.
- By moving first, Airbus had a temporary monopoly and was able to grab a large market share.

- The table illustrates the payoff matrix for the game between Airbus and Boeing.
- The outcome is a dominant-strategy Nash equilibrium. Both firms discount their prices and get 225 new orders each. If one firm held the list price, the other would discount and take the 450 new orders.
- If the game could be played repeatedly, the discounter could be punished and a cooperative equilibrium would arise in which neither discounts.

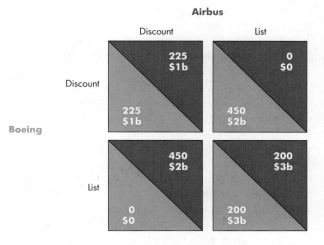

Duopoly Game: Market for Airplanes

Are the A320neo and Max in a price war?

number of players and the ease of detecting and punishing cheating. The larger the number of players, the harder it is to maintain a cartel.

Games and Price Wars A repeated duopoly game can help us understand real-world behavior and, in particular, price wars. Some price wars can be interpreted as the implementation of a tit-for-tat strategy. But the game is a bit more complicated than the one we've looked at because the players are uncertain about the demand for the product.

Playing a tit-for-tat strategy, firms have an incentive to stick to the monopoly price. But fluctuations in demand lead to fluctuations in the monopoly price, and sometimes, when the price changes, it might seem to one of the firms that the price has fallen because the other has cheated. In this case, a price war will break out. The price war will end only when each firm is satisfied that the other is ready to cooperate again. There will be cycles of price wars and the restoration of collusive agreements. Fluctuations in the world price of oil might be interpreted in this way.

Some price wars arise from the entry of a small number of firms into an industry that had previously been a monopoly. Although the industry has a small number of firms, the firms are in a prisoners' dilemma and they cannot impose effective penalties for price cutting. The behavior of prices and outputs in the computer chip industry during 1995 and 1996 can be explained in this way. Until 1995, the market for Pentium chips for IBM-compatible computers was dominated by one firm, Intel Corporation, which was able to make maximum economic profit by producing the quantity of chips at which marginal cost equaled marginal revenue. The price of Intel's chips was set to ensure that the quantity demanded equaled the quantity produced. Then in 1995 and 1996, with the entry of a small number of new firms, the industry became an oligopoly. If the firms had maintained Intel's price and shared the market, together they could have made economic profits equal to Intel's profit. But the firms were in a prisoners' dilemma, so prices fell toward the competitive level.

Let's now study a sequential game. There are many such games, and the one we'll examine is among the simplest. It has an interesting implication and it will give you the flavor of this type of game. The sequential game that we'll study is an entry game in a contestable market.

A Sequential Entry Game in a Contestable Market

If two firms play a sequential game, one firm makes a decision at the first stage of the game and the other makes a decision at the second stage.

We're going to study a sequential game in a **contestable market**—a market in which firms can enter and leave so easily that firms in the market face competition from *potential* entrants. Examples of contestable markets are routes served by airlines and by barge companies that operate on the major waterways. These markets are contestable because firms could enter if an opportunity for economic profit arose and could exit with no penalty if the opportunity for economic profit disappeared.

If the Herfindahl-Hirschman Index (p. 234) is used to determine the degree of competition, a contestable market appears to be uncompetitive. But a contestable market can behave as if it were perfectly competitive. To see why, let's look at an entry game for a contestable air route.

A Contestable Air Route Agile Air is the only firm operating on a particular route. Demand and cost conditions are such that there is room for only one airline to operate. Wanabe Inc. is another airline that could offer services on the route.

We describe the structure of a sequential game by using a *game tree* like that in Fig. 15.6. At the first stage, Agile Air must set a price. Once the price is set and advertised, Agile can't change it. That is, once set, Agile's price is fixed and Agile can't react to Wanabe's entry decision. Agile can set its price at either the monopoly level or the competitive level.

At the second stage, Wanabe must decide whether to enter or to stay out. Customers have no loyalty (there are no frequent-flyer programs) and they buy from the lowest-price firm. So if Wanabe enters, it sets a price just below Agile's and takes all the business.

Figure 15.6 shows the payoffs from the various decisions (Agile's in the red triangles and Wanabe's in the blue triangles).

To decide on its price, Agile's CEO reasons as follows: Suppose that Agile sets the monopoly price. If Wanabe enters, it earns 90 (think of all payoff numbers as thousands of dollars). If Wanabe stays out, it earns nothing. So Wanabe will enter. In this case Agile will lose 50.

Now suppose that Agile sets the competitive price. If Wanabe stays out, it earns nothing, and if it enters,

FIGURE 15.6   Agile Versus Wanabe: A Sequential Entry Game in a Contestable Market

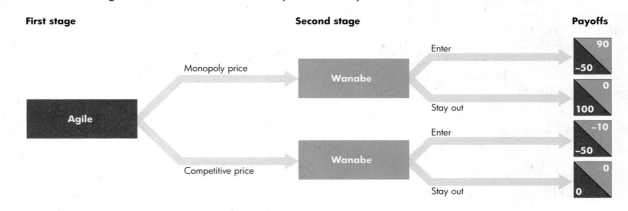

If Agile sets the monopoly price, Wanabe makes 90 (thousand dollars) by entering and earns nothing by staying out. So if Agile sets the monopoly price, Wanabe enters.

If Agile sets the competitive price, Wanabe earns nothing if it stays out and incurs a loss if it enters. So if Agile sets the competitive price, Wanabe stays out.

MyEconLab animation

it loses 10, so Wanabe will stay out. In this case, Agile will make zero economic profit.

Agile's best strategy is to set its price at the competitive level and make zero economic profit. The option of earning 100 by setting the monopoly price with Wanabe staying out is not available to Agile. If Agile sets the monopoly price, Wanabe enters, undercuts Agile, and takes all the business.

In this example, Agile sets its price at the competitive level and makes zero economic profit. A less costly strategy, called **limit pricing**, sets the price at the highest level that inflicts a loss on the entrant. Any loss is big enough to deter entry, so it is not always necessary to set the price as low as the competitive price. In the example of Agile and Wanabe, at the competitive price, Wanabe incurs a loss of 10 if it enters. A smaller loss would still keep Wanabe out.

This game is interesting because it points to the possibility of a monopoly behaving like a competitive industry and serving the social interest without regulation. But the result is not general and depends on one crucial feature of the setup of the game: At the second stage, Agile is locked in to the price set at the first stage.

If Agile could change its price in the second stage, it would want to set the monopoly price if Wanabe stayed out—100 with the monopoly price beats zero with the competitive price. But Wanabe can figure out what Agile would do, so the price set at the first stage

has no effect on Wanabe. Agile sets the monopoly price and Wanabe might either stay out or enter.

We've looked at two of the many possible repeated and sequential games, and you've seen how these types of games can provide insights into the complex forces that determine prices and profits.

◆ REVIEW QUIZ

1 If a prisoners' dilemma game is played repeatedly, what punishment strategies might the players employ and how does playing the game repeatedly change the equilibrium?

2 If a market is contestable, how does the equilibrium differ from that of a monopoly?

You can work these questions in Study Plan 15.3 and get instant feedback.   MyEconLab

So far, we've studied oligopoly with unregulated market power. Firms like Trick and Gear are free to collude to maximize their profit with no concern for the consumer or the law.

But when firms collude to achieve the monopoly outcome, they also have the same effects on efficiency and the social interest as monopoly. Profit is made at the expense of consumer surplus and a deadweight loss arises. Your next task is to see how U.S. antitrust law limits market power.

 **Antitrust Law**

Antitrust law is the law that regulates oligopolies and prevents them from becoming monopolies or behaving like monopolies. Two government agencies cooperate to enforce the antitrust laws: the Federal Trade Commission and the Antitrust Division of the U.S. Department of Justice.

The Antitrust Laws

The two main antitrust laws are

- The Sherman Act, 1890
- The Clayton Act, 1914

The Sherman Act The Sherman Act made it a felony to create or attempt to create a monopoly or a cartel.

During the 1880s, lawmakers and the general public were outraged and disgusted by the practices of some of the big-name leaders of American business. The actions of J.P. Morgan, John D. Rockefeller, and W.H. Vanderbilt led to them being called the "robber barons." It turns out that the most lurid stories of the actions of these great American capitalists were not of their creation of monopoly power to exploit consumers but of their actions to damage each other.

Nevertheless, monopolies that damaged the consumer interest did emerge. For example, John D. Rockefeller had a virtual monopoly in the market for oil.

Table 15.5 summarizes the two main provisions of the Sherman Act. Section 1 of the act is precise:

TABLE 15.5   The Sherman Act of 1890

Section 1:

Every contract, combination in the form of trust or otherwise, or conspiracy, in restraint of trade or commerce among the several States, or with foreign nations, is hereby declared to be illegal.

Section 2:

Every person who shall monopolize, or attempt to monopolize, or combine or conspire with any other person or persons, to monopolize any part of the trade or commerce among the several States, or with foreign nations, shall be deemed guilty of a felony.

Conspiring with others to restrict competition is illegal. But Section 2 is general and imprecise. Just what is an "attempt to monopolize"?

The Clayton Act The Clayton Act, which was passed in response to a wave of mergers that occurred at the beginning of the twentieth century, provided the answer to the question left dangling by the Sherman Act: It defined the "attempt to monopolize." The Clayton Act supplemented the Sherman Act and strengthened and clarified the antitrust law.

When Congress passed the Clayton Act, it also established the Federal Trade Commission, the federal agency charged with the task of preventing monopoly practices that damage the consumer interest.

Two amendments to the Clayton Act—the Robinson-Patman Act of 1936 and the Celler-Kefauver Act of 1950—outlaw specific practices and provide even greater precision to the antitrust law. Table 15.6 describes these practices and summarizes the main provisions of these three acts.

TABLE 15.6   The Clayton Act and Its Amendments

Clayton Act	1914
Robinson-Patman Act	1936
Celler-Kefauver Act	1950

These acts prohibit the following practices *only if* they substantially lessen competition or create monopoly:

1. Price discrimination
2. Contracts that require other goods to be bought from the same firm (called *tying arrangements*)
3. Contracts that require a firm to buy all its requirements of a particular item from a single firm (called *requirements contracts*)
4. Contracts that prevent a firm from selling competing items (called *exclusive dealing*)
5. Contracts that prevent a buyer from reselling a product outside a specified area (called *territorial confinement*)
6. Acquiring a competitor's shares or assets
7. Becoming a director of a competing firm

Price Fixing Always Illegal

Colluding with competitors to fix the price is *always* a violation of the antitrust law. If the Justice Department can prove the existence of a price fixing cartel, also called a *horizontal price fixing agreement*, defendants can offer no acceptable excuse.

The predictions of the effects of price fixing that you saw in the previous sections of this chapter provide the reasons for the unqualified attitude toward price fixing. A duopoly cartel can maximize profit and behave like a monopoly. To achieve the monopoly outcome, the cartel restricts production and fixes the price at the monopoly level. The consumer suffers because consumer surplus shrinks. And the outcome is inefficient because a deadweight loss arises.

It is for these reasons that the law declares that all price fixing is illegal. No excuse can justify the practice.

Other antitrust practices are more controversial and generate debate among lawyers and economists. We'll examine three of these practices.

Three Antitrust Policy Debates

The three practices that we'll examine are

- Resale price maintenance
- Tying arrangements
- Predatory pricing

Resale Price Maintenance Most manufacturers sell their products to the final consumer indirectly through a wholesale and retail distribution system. **Resale price maintenance** occurs when a distributor agrees with a manufacturer to resell a product *at or above a specified minimum price*.

A resale price maintenance agreement, also called a *vertical price fixing agreement*, is *not* illegal under the Sherman Act provided it is not anticompetitive. Nor is it illegal for a manufacturer to refuse to supply a retailer who doesn't accept guidance on what the minimum price should be.

In 2007, the Supreme Court ruled that a handbag manufacturer could impose a minimum retail price on a Dallas store, Kay's Kloset. Since that ruling, many manufacturers have imposed minimum retail prices. The practice is judged on a case-by-case basis.

Does resale price maintenance create an inefficient or efficient use of resources? Economists can be found on both sides of this question.

Inefficient Resale Price Maintenance Resale price maintenance is inefficient if it enables dealers to charge the monopoly price. By setting and enforcing the resale price, the manufacturer might be able to achieve the monopoly price.

Efficient Resale Price Maintenance Resale price maintenance might be efficient if it enables a manufacturer to induce dealers to provide the efficient standard of service. Suppose that SilkySkin wants shops to demonstrate the use of its new unbelievable moisturizing cream in an inviting space. With resale price maintenance, SilkySkin can offer all the retailers the same incentive and compensation. Without resale price maintenance, a cut-price drug store might offer SilkySkin products at a low price. Buyers would then have an incentive to visit a high-price shop for a product demonstration and then buy from the low-price shop. The low-price shop would be a free rider (like the consumer of a public good in Chapter 16, p. 375), and an inefficient level of service would be provided.

SilkySkin could pay a fee to retailers that provide good service and leave the resale price to be determined by the competitive forces of supply and demand. But it might be too costly for SilkySkin to monitor shops and ensure that they provide the desired level of service.

Tying Arrangements A **tying arrangement** is an agreement to sell one product only if the buyer agrees to buy another, different product. With tying, the only way the buyer can get the one product is to also buy the other product. Microsoft has been accused of tying Internet Explorer and Windows. Textbook publishers sometimes tie a Web site and a textbook and force students to buy both. (You can't buy the book you're now reading, new, without the Web site. But you can buy the Web site access without the book, so these products are not tied.)

Could textbook publishers make more money by tying a book and access to a Web site? The answer is sometimes but not always. Suppose that you and other students are willing to pay $80 for a book and $20 for access to a Web site. The publisher can sell these items separately for these prices or bundled for $100. The publisher does not gain from bundling.

But now suppose that you and only half of the students are willing to pay $80 for a book and $20 for a Web site and the other half of the students are willing to pay $80 for a Web site and $20 for a book. Now if the two items are sold separately, the publisher can charge $80 for the book and $80 for the Web site. Half the students buy the book but not the Web site, and the other half buy the Web site but not the book. But if the book and Web site are bundled for $100, everyone buys the bundle and the publisher makes an extra $20 per student. In this case, bundling has enabled the publisher to price discriminate.

There is no simple, clear-cut test of whether a firm is engaging in tying or whether, by doing so, it has increased its market power and profit and created inefficiency.

Predatory Pricing **Predatory pricing** is setting a low price to drive competitors out of business with the intention of setting a monopoly price when the competition has gone. John D. Rockefeller's Standard Oil Company was the first to be accused of this practice in the 1890s, and it has been claimed often in antitrust cases since then. Predatory pricing is an attempt to create a monopoly and as such it is illegal under Section 2 of the Sherman Act.

It is easy to see that predatory pricing is an idea, not a reality. Economists are skeptical that predatory pricing occurs. They point out that a firm that cuts its price below the profit-maximizing level loses during the low-price period. Even if it succeeds in driving its competitors out of business, new competitors will enter as soon as the price is increased, so any potential gain from a monopoly position is temporary. A high and certain loss is a poor exchange for a temporary and uncertain gain. No case of predatory pricing has been definitively found.

Economics in Action
The United States Versus Microsoft

In 1998, the Antitrust Division of the U.S. Department of Justice along with the Departments of Justice of a number of states charged Microsoft, the world's largest producer of software for personal computers, with violations of both sections of the Sherman Act.

A 78-day trial followed that pitched two prominent MIT economics professors against each other, Franklin Fisher for the government and Richard Schmalensee for Microsoft.

The Case Against Microsoft The claims against Microsoft were that it

- Possessed monopoly power
- Used predatory pricing and tying arrangements
- Used other anticompetitive practices

It was claimed that with 80 percent of the market for PC operating systems, Microsoft had excessive monopoly power. This monopoly power arose from two barriers to entry: economies of scale and network economies. Microsoft's average total cost falls as production increases (economies of scale) because the fixed cost of developing an operating system such as Windows is large while the marginal cost of producing one copy of Windows is small. Further, as the number of Windows users increases, the range of Windows applications expands (network economies), so a potential competitor would need to produce not only a competing operating system but also an entire range of supporting applications as well.

When Microsoft entered the Web browser market with its Internet Explorer, it offered the browser for a zero price. This price was viewed as predatory pricing. Microsoft integrated Internet Explorer with Windows so that anyone who uses this operating system would not need a separate browser such as Netscape Navigator. Microsoft's competitors claimed that this practice was an illegal tying arrangement.

Microsoft's Response Microsoft challenged all these claims. It said that Windows was vulnerable to competition from other operating systems such as Linux and Apple's Mac OS and that there was a permanent threat of competition from new entrants.

Microsoft claimed that integrating Internet Explorer with Windows provided a single, unified product of greater consumer value like a refrigerator with a chilled water dispenser or an automobile with a CD player.

The Outcome The court agreed that Microsoft was in violation of the Sherman Act and ordered that it be broken into two firms: an operating systems producer and an applications producer. Microsoft successfully appealed this order. In the final judgment, though, Microsoft was ordered to disclose to other software developers details of how its operating system works, so that they could compete effectively against Microsoft. In the summer of 2002, Microsoft began to comply with this order.

Economics in Action
FTC Takes the Fizz out of Soda Mergers

The FTC used its HHI guidelines to block proposed mergers in the market for soft drinks. PepsiCo wanted to buy 7-Up and Coca-Cola wanted to buy Dr Pepper. The market for carbonated soft drinks is highly concentrated. Coca-Cola had a 39 percent share, PepsiCo had 28 percent, Dr Pepper was next with 7 percent, followed by 7-Up with 6 percent. One other producer, RJR, had a 5 percent market share. So the five largest firms in this market had an 85 percent market share.

The PepsiCo and 7-Up merger would have increased the HHI by more than 300 points. The Coca-Cola and Dr Pepper merger would have increased it by more than 500 points, and both mergers together would have increased the index by almost 800 points.

The FTC decided that increases in the HHI of these magnitudes were not in the social interest and blocked the mergers. The figures summarize the HHI guideline and HHIs in the soft drinks market.

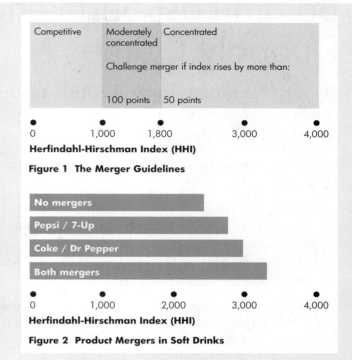

Figure 1 The Merger Guidelines

Figure 2 Product Mergers in Soft Drinks

Mergers and Acquisitions

Mergers, which occur when two or more firms agree to combine to create one larger firm, and *acquisitions*, which occur when one firm buys another firm, are common events. Mergers occurred when Chrysler and the German auto producer Daimler-Benz combined to form DaimlerChrysler and when the Belgian beer producer InBev bought the U.S. brewing giant Anheuser-Busch and created a new combined company, Anheuser-Busch InBev. An acquisition occurred when Rupert Murdoch's News Corp bought Myspace.

The mergers and acquisitions that occur don't create a monopoly. But two (or more) firms might be tempted to try to merge so that they can gain market power and operate like a monopoly. If such a situation arises, the Federal Trade Commission (FTC) takes an interest in the move and stands ready to block the merger. To determine which mergers it will examine and possibly block, the FTC uses guidelines, one of which is the Herfindahl-Hirschman Index (HHI) (see Chapter 10, pp. 234–235).

A market in which the HHI is less than 1,000 is regarded as competitive. An index between 1,000 and 1,800 indicates a moderately concentrated market, and a merger in this market that would increase the index by 100 points is challenged by the FTC. An index above 1,800 indicates a concentrated market, and a merger in this market that would increase the index by 50 points is challenged. You can see an application of these guidelines in *Economics in Action* above.

REVIEW QUIZ

1 What are the two main antitrust laws and when were they enacted?
2 When is price fixing not a violation of the antitrust laws?
3 What is an attempt to monopolize an industry?
4 What are resale price maintenance, tying arrangements, and predatory pricing?
5 Under what circumstances is a merger unlikely to be approved?

You can work these questions in Study Plan 15.4 and get instant feedback.   **MyEconLab**

◆ Oligopoly is a market structure that you often encounter in your daily life. *Reading Between the Lines* on pp. 360–361 looks at a game played in the market for ferry service in Singapore.

Batam Fast and Penguin in a Duopoly Game

Ferry Operators Fined for Anti-Competitive Behavior

The Business Times Singapore
July 19, 2012

TWO ferry operators have found themselves in hot water for engaging in anti-competitive behaviour.

Batam Fast Ferry Pte Ltd and Penguin Ferry Services Pte Ltd were levied penalties of $172,906 and $113,860 respectively by the Competition Commission of Singapore (CCS) yesterday for infringing the Competition Act. The two companies are the only operators serving the routes between Harbour Front Centre and Sekupang, and between Singapore and Batam Centre, and are thus a duopoly.

The CCS said the operators had infringed a competitive act by exchanging and providing sensitive and confidential price information on ferry tickets sold to corporate clients and travel agents for these routes between 2007 and 2009.

For instance, there were examples of email messages which were blind copied ("BCC") from one ferry operator to the other regarding confidential price information sent to clients, as well as instances of price verification between the ferry operators when clients asked for quotes for the purchase of ferry tickets.

The CCS noted that in a "concentrated market like the duopoly", such undertakings are "particularly restrictive of competition" as they reduce the already limited competition in such a market structure by eliminating the uncertainty of competitor prices that drives competition.

ESSENCE OF THE STORY

- Legal action was taken against two ferry operators in Singapore engaging in anti-competitive behavior.

- The two operators are the only firms serving Singapore and an Indonesian city, and they are a duopoly.

- Both operators were found guilty of exchanging confidential information on ticket prices.

- The Competition Commission of Singapore (CCS) noted that the undertakings of both firms had limited competition in the market.

ECONOMIC ANALYSIS

- The ferry routes between Singapore and Sekupang, and Singapore and Batam, are operated by only two firms: Batam Fast Ferry and Penguin Ferry.

- The market for these ferry routes is an example of duopoly.

- Each firm can set a low price for its ferry tickets or a high price. And the profit that results for each firm depends on its own price and on the price set by the other firm.

- Competition between Batam Fast and Penguin Ferry can be interpreted as a duopoly game.

- Table 1 shows the payoff matrix for the game played by the two ferry operators. The numbers, in Singapore dollars (S$) of profit, are hypothetical.

- Batam Fast reasons as follows. If Penguin sets a low price, we will make a larger profit by also setting a low price (S$5 million versus S$2 million). If Penguin sets a high price, we will again make a larger profit by setting a low price (S$10 million versus S$8 million).

- Batam Fast concludes that its best strategy is to set a low price independent of Penguin's price.

- Penguin Ferry reasons in a similar way. If Batam sets a low price, we will make a larger profit by also setting a low price (S$5 million versus S$2 million). If Batam sets a high price, we will again make a larger profit by setting a low price (S$10 million versus S$8 million).

- Penguin Ferry concludes that its best strategy is to set a low price independent of Batam's price.

- The two ferry operators are in a prisoners' dilemma.

- The game they play is a prisoners' dilemma with a dominant-strategy equilibrium.

- The Nash equilibrium of the game is for both firms to set a low price.

- If the firms were able to collude, operate as a cartel, and set a high price, each would gain S$3 million (S$8 million versus S$5 million).

- Because both firms understand the benefit of setting a high price, they colluded by exchanging pricing information.

- Because collusion is against the antitrust law, both firms were fined by the Competition Commission of Singapore for infringing a Competition Act.

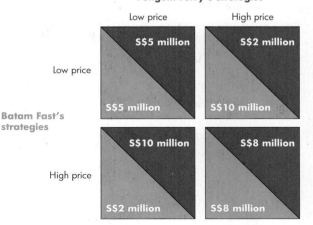

Penguin Ferry's strategies

	Low price	High price
Low price	S$5 million / S$5 million	S$2 million / S$10 million
High price	S$10 million / S$2 million	S$8 million / S$8 million

Batam Fast's strategies

Table 1 Penguin Ferry and Batam Fast in a Prisoners' Dilemma

SUMMARY

Key Points

What Is Oligopoly? (pp. 342–343)

■ Oligopoly is a market in which a small number of firms compete.

Working Problems 1 to 3 will give you a better understanding of what oligopoly is.

Oligopoly Games (pp. 344–351)

■ Oligopoly is studied by using game theory, which is a method of analyzing strategic behavior.

■ In a prisoners' dilemma game, two prisoners acting in their own self-interest harm their joint interest.

■ An oligopoly (duopoly) price-fixing game is a prisoners' dilemma in which the firms might collude or cheat.

■ In Nash equilibrium, both firms cheat and output and price are the same as in perfect competition.

■ Firms' decisions about advertising and R&D can be studied by using game theory.

Working Problems 4 to 7 will give you a better understanding of oligopoly games.

Repeated Games and Sequential Games (pp. 352–355)

■ In a repeated game, a punishment strategy can produce a cooperative equilibrium in which price and output are the same as in a monopoly.

■ In a sequential contestable market game, a small number of firms can behave like firms in perfect competition.

Working Problem 8 will give you a better understanding of repeated and sequential games.

Antitrust Law (pp. 356–359)

■ The first antitrust law, the Sherman Act, was passed in 1890, and the law was strengthened in 1914 when the Clayton Act was passed and the Federal Trade Commission was created.

■ All price-fixing agreements are violations of the Sherman Act, and no acceptable excuse exists.

■ Resale price maintenance might be efficient if it enables a producer to ensure the efficient level of service by distributors.

■ Tying arrangements can enable a monopoly to price discriminate and increase profit, but in many cases, tying would not increase profit.

■ Predatory pricing is unlikely to occur because it brings losses and only temporary potential gains.

■ The Federal Trade Commission uses guidelines such as the Herfindahl-Hirschman Index to determine which mergers to investigate and possibly block.

Working Problems 9 to 11 will give you a better understanding of antitrust law.

Key Terms

Antitrust law, 356
Cartel, 343
Collusive agreement, 346
Contestable market, 354
Cooperative equilibrium, 352
Dominant-strategy equilibrium, 345

Duopoly, 342
Game theory, 344
Limit pricing, 355
Nash equilibrium, 345
Oligopoly, 342
Payoff matrix, 344

Predatory pricing, 358
Resale price maintenance, 357
Strategies, 344
Tying arrangement, 357

STUDY PLAN PROBLEMS AND APPLICATIONS

MyEconLab   You can work Problems 1 to 12 in MyEconLab Chapter 15 Study Plan and get instant feedback.

What Is Oligopoly? (Study Plan 15.1)

1. Two firms make most of the chips that power a PC: Intel and Advanced Micro Devices. What makes the market for PC chips a duopoly? Sketch the market demand curve and cost curves that describe the situation in this market and that prevent other firms from entering.

2. **Sparks Fly for Energizer**

   Energizer is gaining market share against competitor Duracell and its profit is rising despite the sharp rise in the price of zinc, a key battery ingredient.

   Source: www.businessweek.com, August 2007

   In what type of market are batteries sold? Explain your answer.

3. **Oil City**

   In the late 1990s, Reliance spent $6 billion to build a world-class oil refinery at Jamnagar, India. Now Reliance is more than doubling the size of the facility, which will make it the world's biggest producer of gasoline —1.2 million gallons of gasoline per day, or about 5% of global capacity. Reliance plans to sell the gasoline in the United States and Europe where it's too expensive and politically difficult to build new refineries. The bulked-up Jamnagar will be able to move the market and Singapore traders expect a drop in fuel prices as soon as it's going at full steam.

   Source: *Fortune*, April 28, 2008

   a. Explain why the news clip implies that the global market for gasoline is not perfectly competitive.
   b. What barriers to entry might limit competition in this market and give a firm such as Reliance power to influence the market price?

Oligopoly Games (Study Plan 15.2)

4. Consider a game with two players who cannot communicate, and in which each player is asked a question. The players can answer the question honestly or lie. If both answer honestly, each receives $100. If one player answers honestly and the other lies, the liar receives $500 and the honest player gets nothing. If both lie, then each receives $50.

   a. Describe the strategies and payoffs of this game.
   b. Construct the payoff matrix.
   c. What is the equilibrium of this game?
   d. Compare this game to the prisoners' dilemma. Are the two games similar or different? Explain.

Use the following information to work Problems 5 and 6.

Soapy Inc. and Suddies Inc. are the only producers of soap powder. They collude and agree to share the market equally. If neither firm cheats on the agreement, each makes $1 million profit. If either firm cheats, the cheat makes a profit of $1.5 million, while the complier incurs a loss of $0.5 million. If both cheat, they break even. Neither firm can monitor the other's actions.

5. a. What are the strategies in this game?
   b. Construct the payoff matrix for this game.

6. a. What is the equilibrium of this game if it is played only once?
   b. Is the equilibrium a dominant-strategy equilibrium? Explain.

7. **The World's Largest Airline**

   On May 3, 2010, United Airlines and Continental Airlines announced a $3 billion merger that would create the world's biggest airline. The deal was completed in a remarkably short three weeks, and would give the airlines the muscle to fend off low-cost rivals at home and to take on foreign carriers abroad. For consumers, the merger could eventually result in higher prices although the new company does not intend to raise fares. One of the rationales for airline mergers is to cut capacity.

   Source: *The New York Times*, June 7, 2010

   a. Explain how this airline merger might increase air travel prices.
   b. Explain how this airline merger might lower air travel production costs.
   c. Explain how cost savings arising from a cut in capacity might get passed on to travelers and might boost producers' profits. Which do you predict will happen from this airline merger and why?

Repeated Games and Sequential Games

(Study Plan 15.3)

8. If Soapy Inc. and Suddies Inc. repeatedly play the duopoly game that has the payoffs described in Problem 5, on each round of play:
   a. What now are the strategies that each firm might adopt?
   b. Can the firms adopt a strategy that gives the game a cooperative equilibrium?
   c. Would one firm still be tempted to cheat in a cooperative equilibrium? Explain your answer.

Antitrust Law (Study Plan 15.4)

9. **Price Cuts Seen for Apple's New iPhone**
   AT&T plans to sell the new iPhone for $200. The lower-priced phone would give AT&T an attractive weapon to win new subscribers.
   AT&T's revenue is an average of $95 a month from each iPhone customer, nearly twice the average of its conventional cell phone user. AT&T has a revenue-sharing agreement with Apple that requires it to give Apple 25% of its iPhone customers' monthly payments.
   AT&T offers a $200 subsidy to customers who lock into the carrier for two years. It's a small investment for AT&T for a large return. After giving Apple its cut of the revenue, AT&T receives between $70 and $75 a month per iPhone user, totaling more than $1,700 over the life of the two-year contract.
   Source: *Fortune*, June 2, 2008
   a. How does this arrangement between AT&T and Apple regarding the iPhone affect competition in the market for cell-phone service?
   b. Does the iPhone arrangement between AT&T and Apple violate U.S. antitrust laws? Explain.

10. **Congress Examines Giant Airline Merger**
    Congress examined a proposed merger between Delta Airlines and Northwest Airlines that would discourage competition, reduce service, and result in higher fares. Delta claims that the merger would not limit competition because the carriers primarily serve different geographic regions. Witnesses scheduled to testify before the House Subcommittee were likely to focus on whether the merger would result in lower airfares or reduced competition.
    Source: CNN, May 14, 2008

    Explain the guidelines that the Federal Trade Commission uses to evaluate mergers and why it might permit or block this merger.

11. **AT&T's New Pricing Takes Smartphones to the Masses**
    AT&T, the second largest U.S. wireless carrier and only operator offering the iPhone, plans to attract average consumers to sign up for data service by cutting its prices: A $15 a month plan for 200 megabytes of data; $25 a month plan for 2 gigabytes of data. Verizon Wireless, the largest U.S. wireless operator, wouldn't comment on AT&T's new pricing plans. But if history is any indication, it won't take long before Verizon, operator of the HTC Incredible, a smartphone that looks very similar to an iPhone, begins offering tiered data service.
    Source: Cnet News, June 3, 2010
    a. Describe the basis of the competition between AT&T and Verizon.
    b. Is AT&T likely to be using predatory pricing?
    c. If a price war develops in the market for data services, who benefits most?

Economics in the News (Study Plan 15.N)

12. **Starbucks Sued for Trying to Sink Competition**
    Penny Stafford, owner of the Seattle-based Belvi Coffee and Tea Exchange Inc. filed the lawsuit, which contends that Starbucks exploited its monopoly power. Starbucks used predatory practices such as offering to pay leases that exceeded market value if the building owner would refuse to allow competitors into the same building; having its employees offer free coffee samples in front of her store to lure away customers; and offering to buy out competitors at below-market prices and threatening to open nearby stores if the offer is rejected.
    Source: CNN, September 26, 2006
    a. Explain how Starbucks is alleged to have violated U.S. antitrust laws in Seattle.
    b. Explain why it is unlikely that Starbucks might use predatory pricing to permanently drive out competition.
    c. What information would you need that is not provided in the news clip to decide whether Starbucks had practiced predatory pricing?
    d. Sketch the situation facing Belvi Coffee and Tea Exchange Inc. when the firm closed.

ADDITIONAL PROBLEMS AND APPLICATIONS

MyEconLab   You can work these problems in MyEconLab if assigned by your instructor.

What Is Oligopoly?

13. **An Energy Drink with a Monster of a Stock**

    The $5.7 billion energy-drink category, in which Monster holds the No. 2 position behind industry leader Red Bull, has slowed down as copycat brands jostle for shelf space. Over the past five years Red Bull's market share in dollar terms has gone from 91 percent to well under 50 percent and much of that loss has been Monster's gain.

    Source: *Fortune*, December 25, 2006

    a. Describe the structure of the energy-drink market. How has that structure changed over the past few years?

    b. If Monster and Red Bull formed a cartel, how would the price charged for energy drinks and the profits made change?

Oligopoly Games

Use the following information to work Problems 14 and 15.

Bud and Wise are the only two producers of aniseed beer, a New Age product designed to displace root beer. Bud and Wise are trying to figure out how much of this new beer to produce. They know:

  (i)   If they both produce 10,000 gallons a day, they will make the maximum attainable joint economic profit of $200,000 a day, or $100,000 a day each.

  (ii) If either firm produces 20,000 gallons a day while the other produces 10,000 gallons a day, the one that produces 20,000 gallons will make an economic profit of $150,000 and the other will incur an economic loss of $50,000.

  (iii) If both produce 20,000 gallons a day, each firm will make zero economic profit.

14. Construct a payoff matrix for the game that Bud and Wise must play.

15. Find the Nash equilibrium of the game that Bud and Wise play.

16. **Asian Rice Exporters to Discuss Cartel**

    The Asian rice-exporting nations planned to discuss a proposal that they form a cartel. Ahead of the meeting, the countries said that the purpose of the rice cartel would be to contribute to ensuring food stability, not just in an individual country but also to address food shortages in the region and the world. The cartel will not hoard rice and raise prices when there are shortages.

    The Philippines says that it is a bad idea. It will create an oligopoly, and the cartel could price the grain out of reach for millions of people.

    Source: CNN, May 6, 2008

    a. Assuming the rice-exporting nations become a profit-maximizing colluding oligopoly, explain how they would influence the global market for rice and the world price of rice.

    b. Assuming the rice-exporting nations become a profit-maximizing colluding oligopoly, draw a graph to illustrate their influence on the global market for rice.

    c. Even in the absence of international antitrust laws, why might it be difficult for this cartel to successfully collude? Use the ideas of game theory to explain.

17. Suppose that Mozilla and Microsoft each develop their own versions of an amazing new Web browser that allows advertisers to target consumers with great precision. Also, the new browser is easier and more fun to use than existing browsers. Each firm is trying to decide whether to sell the browser or to give it away. What are the likely benefits from each action? Which action is likely to occur?

18. Why do Coca-Cola and PepsiCo spend huge amounts on advertising? Do they benefit? Does the consumer benefit? Explain your answer by constructing a game to illustrate the choices Coca-Cola and PepsiCo make.

Use the following information to work Problems 19 and 20.

Microsoft with Xbox 360, Nintendo with Wii, and Sony with PlayStation 3 are slugging it out in the market for the latest generation of video game consoles. Xbox 360 was the first to market; Wii has the lowest price; PS3 uses the most advanced technology and has the highest price.

19. a. Thinking of the competition among these firms in the market for consoles as a game, describe the firms' strategies concerning design, marketing, and price.

    b. What, based on the information provided, turned out to be the equilibrium of the game?

20. Can you think of reasons why the three consoles are so different?

Repeated Games and Sequential Games

21. If Bud and Wise in Problem 15 play the game repeatedly, what is the equilibrium of the game?

22. Agile Airlines' profit on a route on which it has a monopoly is $10 million a year. Wanabe Airlines is considering entering the market and operating on this route. Agile warns Wanabe to stay out and threatens to cut the price so that if Wanabe enters it will make no profit. Wanabe determines that the payoff matrix for the game in which it is engaged with Agile is shown in the table.

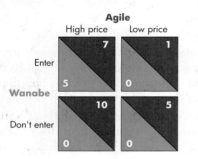

Agile

	High price	Low price
Enter	7 / 5	1 / 0
Don't enter	10 / 0	5 / 0

Does Wanabe believe Agile's assertion? Does Wanabe enter or not? Explain.

23. **Oil Trading Probe May Uncover Manipulation**

Amid soaring oil prices the Commodity Futures Trading Commission (CFTC) is looking into manipulation of the oil market—withholding oil in an attempt to drive prices higher. The CFTC has found such evidence in the past and it's likely it will find evidence again. But it is unlikely that a single player acting alone would be able to run the price up from $90 to $135.

Source: CNN, May 30, 2008

What type of market does the news clip imply best describes the U.S. oil market?

Antitrust Law

Use the following news clip to work Problems 24 and 25.

Gadgets for Sale ... or Not

How come the prices of some gadgets, like the iPod, are the same no matter where you shop? No, the answer isn't that Apple illegally manages prices. In reality, Apple uses an accepted retail strategy called minimum advertised price to discourage resellers from discounting. The minimum advertised price (MAP) is the absolute lowest price of a product that resellers can advertise. MAP is usually enforced through marketing subsidies offered by a manufacturer to its resellers that keep the price at or above the

MAP. Stable prices are important to the company that is both a manufacturer and a retailer. If Apple resellers advertised the iPod below cost, they could squeeze the Apple Stores out of their own markets. The downside to the price stability is that by limiting how low sellers can go, MAP keeps prices artificially high (or at least higher than they might otherwise be with unfettered price competition).

Source: *Slate*, December 22, 2006

24. a. Describe the practice of resale price maintenance that violates the Sherman Act.

    b. Describe the MAP strategy used by Apple and explain how it differs from a resale price maintenance agreement that would violate the Sherman Act.

25. Why might the MAP strategy be against the social interest and benefit only the producer?

Economics in the News

26. After you have studied *Reading Between the Lines* on pp. 360–361, answer the following questions.

    a. What is the dominant strategy for both firms?

    b. Why is collusion necessary for both firms to earn higher profits?

    c. Is the Nash equilibrium outcome beneficial to consumers? If so, why is this so?

    d. Based on the payoff matrix on p. 361, what is the maximum fine each firm is willing to pay for collusion to be more profitable than the Nash equilibrium outcome?

27. **Boeing and Airbus Predict Asian Sales Surge**

Airlines in the Asia-Pacific region are emerging as the biggest customers for aircraft makers Boeing and Airbus. The two firms predict that over the next 20 years, more than 8,000 planes worth up to $1.2 trillion will be sold there.

Source: BBC News, February 3, 2010

    a. In what type of market are big airplanes sold?

    b. Thinking of competition between Boeing and Airbus as a game, what are the strategies and the payoffs?

    c. Set out a hypothetical payoff matrix for the game you've described in part (b). What is the equilibrium of the game?

    d. Do you think the market for big airplanes is efficient? Explain and illustrate your answer.

Managing Change and Limiting Market Power

PART FOUR

Our economy is constantly changing. Every year, new goods appear and old ones disappear. New firms are born, and old ones die. This process of change is initiated and managed by firms operating in markets.

When a new product appears, just one or two firms sell it: Apple and IBM were the only producers of personal computers; Microsoft was (and almost still is) the only producer of the PC operating system; Intel was the only producer of the PC chip. These firms had enormous power to determine the quantity to produce and the price of their products.

In many markets, entry eventually brings competition. Even with just two rivals, the industry changes its face in a dramatic way. *Strategic interdependence* is capable of leading to an outcome like perfect competition.

With the continued arrival of new firms in an industry, the market becomes competitive. But in most markets, the competition isn't perfect: it becomes *monopolistic competition* with each firm selling its own differentiated product.

Often, an industry that is competitive becomes less so as the bigger and more successful firms in the industry begin to swallow up the smaller firms, either by driving them out of business or by acquiring their assets. Through this process, an industry might return to oligopoly or even monopoly. You can see such a movement in the auto and banking industries today.

By studying firms and markets, we gain a deeper understanding of the forces that allocate resources and begin to see the invisible hand at work.

John von Neumann *was one of the great minds of the twentieth century. Born in Budapest, Hungary, in 1903, Johnny, as he was known, showed early mathematical brilliance. He was 25 when he published the article that changed the social sciences and began a flood of research on* **game theory**—*a flood that has not subsided. In that article, von Neumann proved that in a zero-sum game (such as sharing a pie), there exists a best strategy for each player.*

Von Neumann did more than invent game theory: He also invented and built the first practical computer, and he worked on the Manhattan Project, which developed the atomic bomb during World War II.

Von Neumann believed that the social sciences would progress only if they used their own mathematical tools, not those of the physical sciences.

"Real life consists of bluffing, of little tactics of deception, of asking yourself what is the other man going to think I mean to do."

JOHN VON NEUMANN, told to Jacob Bronowski (in a London taxi) and reported in *The Ascent of Man*

THOMAS HUBBARD is the John L. and Helen Kellogg Distinguished Professor of Management and Strategy at the Kellogg School of Management, Northwestern University and a research fellow at the National Bureau of Economic Research.

Professor Hubbard is an empirical economist. His work is driven by data. The central problems that unify much of his work are the limits to information and the fact that information is costly to obtain. Professor Hubbard studies the ways in which information problems influence the organization of firms; the extent to which firms make or buy what they sell; and the structure and performance of markets.

His work appears in the leading journals such as the *American Economic Review*, the *Quarterly Journal of Economics*, and the *Rand Journal of Economics*. He is a co-editor of the *Journal of Industrial Economics*.

Michael Parkin talked with Thomas Hubbard about his research and what we learn from it about the choices that firms make and their implications for market structure and performance.

Professor Hubbard, you have made important contributions to our understanding of outsourcing: whether a firm will make it or buy it. Can you summarize what economists know about this issue?

If there is one thing that Coase (Ronald Coase, see p. 415) taught us about the boundaries of the firm, it is that when thinking about whether to do something internally or to outsource it, a very useful starting point is to make the decision on a transaction-by-transaction basis.

The way I like to think about it is to boil it down to the theory of markets and incentives. Markets provide strong incentives but not necessarily good incentives. So when you outsource something, you rely on a market mechanism rather than on something within a firm that is less than a market mechanism. By outsourcing, you expose people to a strong market incentive. Now that can be good, and it is good most of the time. Strong market incentives get people to do things that the market rewards. Market rewards are generally quite valuable, but in some circumstances what the market rewards isn't

> Markets provide strong incentives but not necessarily good incentives.

what the buyer would want to reward. So there's a tradeoff. Strong incentives are sometimes good and sometimes bad. Therefore, keeping things inside the firm provides a weaker incentive. Sometimes that is good.

Can you provide an example?

Think about McDonald's. McDonald's is not one firm. It is many firms because a lot of the outlets are owned and managed by franchisees and some are owned and managed internally by McDonald's.

McDonald's thinks about whether to run one of its restaurants itself or to franchise it out. One thing that it has in mind is that if it franchises it out, then the franchisor is going to be exposed to very strong market incentives. Now under some circumstances this is great. The franchisee treats the business as if he owns it. So the good part about it is the franchisee works hard to try to develop his business.

But a flip side to the franchisee's treating the business as his own is that it can be harmful for the McDonald's brand.

*Read the full interview with Thomas Hubbard in **MyEconLab**.

16

PUBLIC CHOICES
AND PUBLIC GOODS

After studying this chapter, you will be able to:

◆ Explain why some choices are *public* choices and how they are made in a political marketplace

◆ Explain how the free-rider problem arises and how the quantity of public goods is determined

◆ Explain why goods with external benefits lead to inefficient underproduction and how public choices can achieve allocative efficiency

Fighting a Colorado wildfire, providing schools and colleges, policing neighborhoods and highways, operating the courts: Governments do all these things. But why? Why not private firms? And do governments do an efficient job, or are they too big? These are the questions we study in this chapter.

We illustrate the principles of public choice by looking at the provision of education and health care, and in *Reading Between the Lines* at the end of the chapter, we look at the *2010 Affordable Care Act*—Obamacare.

◆ Public Choices

All economic choices are made by individuals, but some choices are *private* and some are *public*. A *private choice* is a decision that has consequences for only the person making it. Decisions to buy (demand) or to sell (supply) goods and services in competitive markets are examples of private choices. At the market equilibrium price, these choices are consistent and one person's decision to buy or sell a little bit more or a little bit less has an imperceptible effect on the outcome.

A **public choice** is a decision that has consequences for many people and perhaps for an entire society. Decisions by political leaders and senior public servants about price and quantity regulations, taxes, international trade policy, and government spending are examples of public choices.

You studied the consequences of some public choices in Chapter 6 where you saw how price ceilings and price floors prevent voluntary exchanges even though marginal social benefit exceeds marginal social cost; you also saw how taxes drive a wedge between marginal social benefit and marginal social cost. In Chapter 7, you saw how tariffs and import quotas restrict international trade. All of these public choices result in scarce resources being used inefficiently—they create deadweight loss.

Why do governments do things that create inefficiency? Aren't they supposed to make things better? If governments make things worse, why do they exist? Why aren't the successful societies those that have no government? The economic theory of government explains both why governments exist and why they do a less-than-perfect job.

Why Governments Exist

Governments exist for three major reasons. First, they establish and maintain property rights. Second, they provide nonmarket mechanisms for allocating scarce resources. Third, they implement arrangements that redistribute income and wealth.

Property rights are the fundamental foundation of the market economy. By establishing property rights and the legal system that enforces them, governments enable markets to function. In many situations, markets function well and allocate scarce resources efficiently. But sometimes the market results in inefficiency—market failure (see Chapter 5, pp. 114–115).

When market failure occurs, too many of some things and too few of some other things are produced. Choices made in the pursuit of self-interest have not served the social interest. By reallocating resources, it is possible to make some people better off while making no one worse off.

The market economy also delivers a distribution of income and wealth that most people regard as unfair. Equity requires some redistribution.

Replacing markets with government resource-allocation decisions is no simple matter. Just as there can be market failure, there can also be government failure. **Government failure** is a situation in which government actions lead to inefficiency—to either underprovision or overprovision.

Government failure can arise because government is made up of many individuals, each with their own economic objectives. Public choices are the outcome of the choices made by these individuals. To analyse these choices, economists have developed a public choice theory of the political marketplace.

Public Choice and the Political Marketplace

Four groups of decision makers, shown in Fig. 16.1, interact in the political marketplace. They are

- Voters
- Firms
- Politicians
- Bureaucrats

Voters Voters evaluate politicians' policy proposals, benefit from public goods and services, and pay some of the taxes. In the economic model of public choice, voters support the politicians whose policy proposals make them better off and express their demand for public goods and services by voting, helping in political campaigns, lobbying, and making campaign contributions.

Firms Firms also evaluate politicians' policy proposals, benefit from public goods and services, and pay some of the taxes. Although firms don't vote, they do make campaign contributions and are a major source of funds for political parties. Firms also engage in lobbying activity to persuade politicians to propose policies that benefit them.

Politicians Politicians are the elected persons in the federal, state, and local governments—from the President of the United States to the Superintendent

FIGURE 16.1   The Political Marketplace

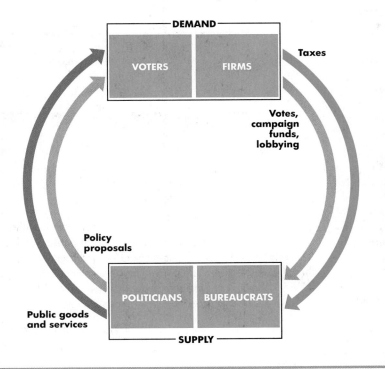

Voters express their demand for policies with their votes.

Voters and firms express their demand for policies with campaign contributions and by lobbying.

Politicians express their supply of policies with proposals that they hope will attract enough votes to get them elected and keep them in office. Politicians also set the taxes paid by voters and firms.

Bureaucrats provide public goods and services and try to get the largest possible budget for their departments.

A political equilibrium balances all these public choices.

MyEconLab animation

of Yuma, Arizona, School District One. Federal and state politicians form coalitions—political parties—to develop policy proposals, which they present to voters in the hope of attracting majority support. Politicians also direct bureaucrats in the delivery of public goods and services and other policy actions. The goal of a politician is to get elected and to remain in office. Votes to a politician are like profit to a firm.

Bureaucrats Bureaucrats are the public servants who work in government departments. They administer tax collection, the delivery of public goods and services, and the administration of rules and regulations.

The self-interest of a bureaucrat is best served when the budget of her or his department is maximized. The bigger the budget of a department, the greater is the prestige of its chief and the greater are the opportunities for promotion for people further down the bureaucratic ladder. So all the members of a department have an interest in maximizing the department's budget. This economic assumption doesn't imply that bureaucrats do a poor job. Rather it implies that, in doing what they perceive to be a good job, they take care of their own self-interest too.

Political Equilibrium

Voters, firms, politicians, and bureaucrats make their economic choices to achieve their own self-interest. Public choices, like private choices, are constrained by what is feasible. Each person's public choices are also constrained by the public choices of others.

The balance of forces in the political marketplace determines the outcome of all the public choices that people make. In a **political equilibrium** the choices of voters, firms, politicians, and bureaucrats are all compatible and no group can see a way of improving its position by making a different choice.

Ideally, the political equilibrium will achieve allocative efficiency and serve the social interest, but such an outcome is not guaranteed, as you'll see later in this chapter.

We make public choices because some situations just don't permit private choices. The core of the reason we can't always make private choices is that some goods and services (and some factors of production) have a public nature—they are *public* goods and services.

Your next task is to see exactly what we mean by a *public* good or service.

What is a Public Good?

To see what makes a good a *public* good, we distinguish between two features of all goods: the extent to which people can be *excluded* from consuming them and the extent to which one person's consumption *rivals* someone else's consumption.

Excludable   A good is **excludable** if it is possible to prevent someone from enjoying its benefits. Brink's security services, East Point Seafood's fish, and a U2 concert are examples. People must pay to benefit from them.

A good is **nonexcludable** if it is impossible (or extremely costly) to prevent anyone from benefiting from it. The services of the LAPD, fish in the Pacific Ocean, and a concert on network television are examples. When an LAPD cruiser enforces the speed limit, everyone on the highway benefits; anyone with a boat can fish in the ocean; and anyone with a TV can watch a network broadcast.

Rival   A good is **rival** if one person's use of it decreases the quantity available for someone else. A Brink's truck can't deliver cash to two banks at the same time. A fish can be consumed only once.

A good is **nonrival** if one person's use of it does not decrease the quantity available for someone else. The services of the LAPD and a concert on network television are nonrival. One person's benefit doesn't lower the benefit of others.

A Fourfold Classification

Figure 16.2 classifies goods, services, and resources into four types.

Private Goods   A **private good** is both rival and excludable. A can of Coke and a fish on East Point Seafood's farm are examples of private goods.

Public Goods   A **public good** is both nonrival and nonexcludable. A public good simultaneously benefits everyone, and no one can be excluded from its benefits. National defense is the best example of a public good.

Common Resources   A **common resource** is rival and nonexcludable. A unit of a common resource can be used only once, but no one can be prevented from using what is available. Ocean fish are a common resource. They are rival because a fish taken by one person isn't available for anyone else, and they are

FIGURE 16.2   Fourfold Classification of Goods

	Private goods	Common resources
Rival	Food and drink Car House	Fish in ocean Atmosphere National parks
	Natural monopoly goods	Public goods
Nonrival	Internet Cable television Bridge or tunnel	National defense The law Air traffic control
	Excludable	Nonexcludable

A private good is one for which consumption is rival and from which consumers can be excluded. A public good is one for which consumption is nonrival and from which it is impossible to exclude a consumer. A common resource is one that is rival but nonexcludable. A good that is nonrival but excludable is produced by a natural monopoly.

MyEconLab animation

nonexcludable because it is difficult to prevent people from catching them.

Natural Monopoly Goods   A **natural monopoly good** is nonrival and excludable. When buyers can be excluded if they don't pay but the good is nonrival, marginal cost is zero. The fixed cost of producing such a good is usually high, so economies of scale exist over the entire range of output for which there is a demand (see p. 298). An iTunes song and cable television are examples of natural monopoly goods.

Mixed Goods and Externalities

Some goods don't fit neatly into the four-fold classification of Fig. 16.2. They are mixed goods. A **mixed good** is a private good the production or consumption of which creates an externality. An **externality** is a cost (external cost) or a benefit (external benefit) that arises from the production or consumption of a private good and that falls on someone other than its producer or consumer. A **negative externality** imposes a cost and a **positive externality** provides a benefit.

We'll look at some examples of mixed goods with externalities and study those with positive externalities later in this chapter and those with negative externalities in Chapter 17.

Economics in Action
Is a Lighthouse a Public Good?

Built on Little Brewster Island in 1716 to guide ships into and out of the Boston Harbor, Boston Lighthouse was the first light station in North America.

For two centuries, economists used the lighthouse as an example of a public good. No one can be prevented from seeing its warning light—*nonexcludable*—and one person seeing its light doesn't prevent someone else from doing so too—*nonrival*.

Ronald Coase, who won the 1991 Nobel Prize for ideas he first developed when he was an undergraduate at the London School of Economics, discovered that before the nineteenth century, lighthouses in England were built and operated by private corporations that earned profits by charging tolls on ships docking at nearby ports. A ship that refused to pay the lighthouse toll was *excluded* from the port.

So the benefit arising from the services of a lighthouse is *excludable*. Because the services provided by a lighthouse are nonrival but excludable, a lighthouse is an example of a natural monopoly good and not a public good.

Mixed Goods with External Benefits Two of the things that have the greatest impact on your welfare, your education and health care, are mixed goods with external benefits.

Think about a flu vaccination. It is *excludable* because it would be possible to sell vaccinations and exclude those not willing to pay from benefiting from them. A flu vaccination is also *rival* because providing one person with a vaccination means one fewer available for everyone else. A flu vaccination is a private good, but it creates an externality.

If you decide to get a flu vaccination, you benefit from a lower risk of getting infected in the coming flu season. But if you avoid the flu, your neighbor who didn't get vaccinated has a better chance of avoiding it too. A flu vaccination brings a benefit to others, so it is a *mixed good* with an external benefit.

The external benefit of a flu vaccination is like a public good. It is nonexcludable because everyone with whom you come into contact benefits. You can't selectively benefit only your friends! And it is nonrival—protecting one person from the flu does not diminish the protection for others.

Your education is another example of a mixed good with external benefits. If all education was organized by private schools and universities, those not willing or able to pay would be excluded, and one person's place in a class would rival another's. So education is a private good.

But your being educated brings benefits to others. It brings benefits to your friends who enjoy your sharp, educated wit and it brings benefits to the community in which you live because well-educated people with a strong sense of fellowship and responsibility toward others make good neighbors. These external benefits are like a public good. You can't selectively decide who benefits from your good neighborliness and one person's enjoyment of your good behavior doesn't rival someone else's. So education is a mixed good with an external benefit.

Mixed Goods with External Costs Mixed goods with external costs have become a huge political issue in recent years. The main ones are electricity and transportation (road, rail, and air) produced by burning hydrocarbon fuels—coal, oil, and natural gas.

Electricity and transportation are excludable and rival—they are private goods. But when you use electricity or travel by car, bus, train, or airplane, carbon dioxide and other chemicals pour into the atmosphere. This consequence of consuming a private good creates an external cost and is a public bad. (A "bad" is the opposite of a good.) No one can be excluded from bearing the external cost and one person's discomfort doesn't rival another's. Electricity and transportation are mixed goods with external costs.

Other private goods that generate external costs include logging and the clearing of forests, which destroy the habitat of wildlife and influence the amount of carbon dioxide in the atmosphere; smoking cigarettes in a confined space, which imposes a health risk on others; and driving under the influence of alcohol, which increases the risk of accident and injury for others.

Inefficiencies that Require Public Choices

Public goods, mixed goods, common resources, and natural monopoly goods all create inefficiency problems that require public choices. Public choices must be made to

- Provide public goods and mixed goods
- Conserve common resources
- Regulate natural monopoly

Provide Public Goods and Mixed Goods Because no one can be excluded from enjoying the benefits of a public good, no one has an incentive to pay for their share of it. Even people with a social conscience have no incentive to pay because one person's enjoyment of a public good doesn't lower the enjoyment of others—it is nonrival.

If private firms tried to produce and sell public goods to consumers, they wouldn't remain in business for very long. The market economy would fail to deliver the efficient quantity of those goods. For example, there would be too little national defense, police services and law enforcement, courts and judges, storm-water and sewage disposal services.

Mixed goods pose a less extreme problem. The market economy would underprovide mixed goods with external benefits because their producers and consumers don't take the external benefits into account when they make their own choices. The market economy would overprovide mixed goods with

external costs because their producers and consumers don't take the external costs into account when they make their own choices.

Conserve Common Resources Because no one can be excluded from enjoying the benefits of a common resource, no one has an incentive to pay for their share of it or to conserve it for future enjoyment.

If boat owners are left to catch as much Southern Bluefin tuna as they wish, the stock will deplete and eventually the species will vanish. The market economy would overproduce tuna while stocks lasted and then underproduce as stocks ran out.

This problem, called the *tragedy of the commons*, requires public choices to limit the overuse and eventual destruction of common resources.

Regulate Natural Monopoly When people can be excluded from enjoying the benefits of a good if they don't pay for it, and when the good is nonrival, the marginal cost of producing it is zero. A natural monopoly can produce such a good at the lowest cost. But as Chapter 13 explains, when one firm serves a market, that firm maximizes profit by producing too little of the good.

You studied the regulation of natural monopoly in Chapter 13. This chapter and the next one study the other two public choices that must be made. In this chapter, we'll focus on the underprovision of public goods and mixed goods with external benefits. Chapter 17 studies mixed goods with external costs and conserving common resources.

REVIEW QUIZ

1 List three main reasons why governments exist.
2 Describe the political marketplace. Who demands, who supplies, and what is the political equilibrium?
3 Distinguish among public goods, private goods, common resources, natural monopoly goods, and mixed goods.
4 What are the problems that arise from public goods, common resources, natural monopoly goods, and mixed goods?

You can work these questions in Study Plan 16.1 and get instant feedback.   MyEconLab

Providing Public Goods

Why do governments provide firefighting services? Why don't the people of California buy brush firefighting services from Firestorm, a private firm that competes for our dollars in the marketplace in the same way that McDonald's does? The answer is that firefighting is a public good. It is nonexcludable and nonrival and it has a free-rider problem.

The Free-Rider Problem

A free rider enjoys the benefits of a good or service without paying for it. Because a public good is provided for everyone to use and no one can be excluded from its benefits, no one has an incentive to pay his or her share of the cost. Everyone has an incentive to free ride. The **free-rider problem** is that the economy would provide an inefficiently small quantity of a public good. Marginal social benefit from the public good would exceed its marginal social cost and a deadweight loss would arise.

Let's look at the marginal social benefit and marginal social cost of a public good.

Marginal Social Benefit from a Public Good

Lisa and Max (the only people in a society) value fire-fighting airplanes. Figure 16.3(a) and 16.3(b) graph their marginal benefits from the airplanes as MB_L for Lisa and MB_M for Max. The marginal benefit from a public good (like that from a private good) diminishes as the quantity of the good increases.

Figure 16.3(c) shows the marginal *social* benefit curve, *MSB*. Because everyone gets the same quantity of a public good, its marginal social benefit curve is the sum of the marginal benefits of all the individuals at each *quantity*—it is the *vertical* sum of the individual marginal benefit curves. So the curve *MSB* is the marginal social benefit curve for the economy made up of Lisa and Max. For each airplane, Lisa's marginal benefit is added to Max's marginal benefit.

Contrast the *MSB* curve for a public good with that of a private good. To obtain the economy's *MSB* curve for a private good, we sum the *quantities demanded* by all the individuals at each *price*—we sum the individual marginal benefit curves *horizontally* (see Chapter 5, pp. 108–109).

FIGURE 16.3   Benefits of a Public Good

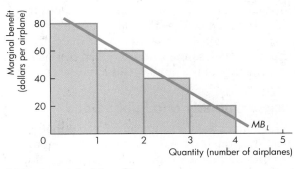

(a) Lisa's marginal benefit

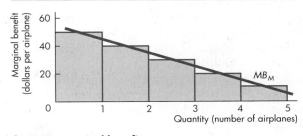

(b) Max's marginal benefit

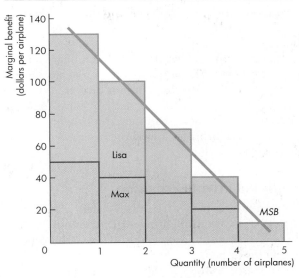

(c) Economy's marginal social benefit

The marginal social benefit at each quantity of the public good is the sum of the marginal benefits of all individuals. The marginal benefit curves are MB_L for Lisa and MB_M for Max. The economy's marginal social benefit curve is *MSB*.

━━━ MyEconLab animation ━━━

Marginal Social Cost of a Public Good

The marginal social cost of a public good is determined in exactly the same way as that of a private good—see Chapter 5, p. 110. The principle of increasing marginal cost applies to the marginal cost of a public good, so the marginal social cost increases as the quantity of the public good increases.

Efficient Quantity of a Public Good

To determine the efficient quantity of a public good, we use the principles that you learned in Chapter 5. The efficient quantity is that at which marginal social benefit equals marginal social cost.

Figure 16.4 shows the marginal social benefit curve, *MSB*, and the marginal social cost curve, *MSC*, for firefighting airplanes. (We'll now think of society as consisting of Lisa and Max and the other 39 million Californians.)

If marginal social benefit exceeds marginal social cost, as it does with 2 airplanes, resources can be used more efficiently by increasing the number of airplanes. The extra benefit exceeds the extra cost. If marginal social cost exceeds marginal social benefit, as it does with 4 airplanes, resources can be used more efficiently by decreasing the number of airplanes. The cost saving exceeds the loss of benefit.

If marginal social benefit equals marginal social cost, as it does with 3 airplanes, resources are allocated efficiently. Resources cannot be used more efficiently because to provide more than 3 airplanes increases cost by more than the extra benefit, and to provide fewer airplanes lowers the benefit by more than the cost saving.

Inefficient Private Provision

Could a private firm—Firestorm—deliver the efficient quantity of firefighting airplanes? Most likely it couldn't, because no one would have an incentive to buy his or her share of the airplanes. Everyone would reason as follows: The number of airplanes provided by Firestorm is not affected by my decision to pay my share or not. But my own private consumption will be greater if I free ride and do not pay my share of the cost of the airplanes. If I don't pay, I enjoy the same level of fire protection and I can buy more private goods. I will spend my money on private goods and free ride on fire protection. Such reasoning is the free-rider problem. If

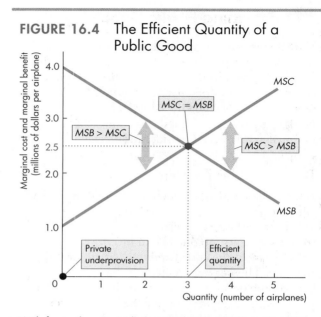

FIGURE 16.4   The Efficient Quantity of a Public Good

With fewer than 3 airplanes, marginal social benefit, *MSB*, exceeds marginal social cost, *MSC*. With more than 3 airplanes, *MSC* exceeds *MSB*. Only with 3 airplanes is *MSC* equal to *MSB* and the number of airplanes is efficient.

—— MyEconLab animation ——

everyone reasons the same way, Firestorm has no revenue and so provides no airplanes. Because the efficient number of airplanes is 3, private provision is inefficient.

Efficient Public Provision

The outcome of the political process might be efficient or inefficient. We look first at an efficient outcome. There are two political parties: Fears and Hopes. They agree on all issues except the number of firefighting airplanes: The Fears want 4, and the Hopes want 2. Both parties want to get elected, so they run a voter survey and discover the marginal social benefit curve of Fig. 16.5. They also consult with airplane producers to establish the marginal cost curve. The parties then do a "what-if" analysis. If the Fears propose 4 airplanes and the Hopes propose 2, the voters will be equally unhappy with both parties. Compared to the efficient quantity, the Hopes want an underprovision of 1 airplane and the Fears want an overprovision of 1 airplane. The deadweight losses are equal and the election would be too close to call.

Contemplating this outcome, the Fears realize that they are too fearful to get elected. They figure that, if they scale back to 3 airplanes, they will win the election if the Hopes stick with 2. The Hopes reason in a similar way and figure that, if they increase the number of airplanes to 3, they can win the election if the Fears propose 4.

So they both propose 3 airplanes. The voters are indifferent between the parties, and each party receives 50 percent of the vote. But regardless of which party wins the election, 3 airplanes are provided and this quantity is efficient. Competition in the political place results in the efficient provision of a public good.

The Principle of Minimum Differentiation The **principle of minimum differentiation** is the tendency for competitors (including political parties) to make themselves similar to appeal to the maximum number of clients or voters. This principle describes the behavior of political parties. It also explains why fast-food restaurants cluster in the same block. For example, if Domino's opens a new pizza outlet, it is likely that Pizza Hut will soon open nearby.

FIGURE 16.5   An Efficient Political Outcome

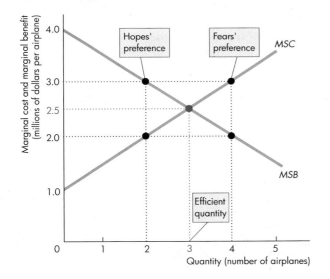

The Hopes would like to provide 2 airplanes and the Fears would like to provide 4 airplanes. The political outcome is 3 airplanes because unless each party proposes 3 airplanes, the other party will beat it in an election.

_____ MyEconLab animation _____

Economics in Action
Fighting Colorado's Wildfires

The 2012 wildfire season was extreme. Colorado had its worst season in a decade with major fires that devastated communities in and around Colorado Springs. And across the Western states, close to half a million acres (780 square miles) of land were burned.

Wildfires are natural and vital for the ecosystem, but some fires are started by human action, and some both human-made and naturally occurring fires, like the 2012 fires in Colorado, burn close to where people live. So protection against wildfires is a vital *public good*.

But not all fire protection services are *produced* by government. *Private* wildfire service contractors supply around 40 percent of wildfire suppression services. So fighting wildfires is an example of a public good that is *provided* by government and paid for with tax revenues, but in part *produced* by private firms.

Firestorm Wildfire Suppression Inc. is one such firm. Operating from Chico, CA, Firestorm hires and trains firefighters and produces firefighting services to maximize its profit. To achieve this goal, the firm must produce firefighting services at the lowest possible cost.

But if Firestorm (and its competitors) tried to sell their services to each individual homeowner in the wildfire regions, they wouldn't get enough revenue to remain in business. There would be a free-rider problem. The free-rider problem is avoided because governments buy the services of Firestorm.

For the political process to deliver the efficient outcome, voters must be well informed, evaluate the alternatives, and vote in the election. Political parties must be well informed about voter preferences. As the next section shows, we can't expect to achieve this outcome.

Inefficient Public Overprovision

If competition between two political parties is to deliver the efficient quantity of a public good, bureaucrats must cooperate and help to achieve this outcome. But bureaucrats might have a different idea and end up frustrating rather than facilitating an efficient outcome. Their actions might bring *government failure*.

Objective of Bureaucrats   Bureaucrats want to maximize their department's budget because a bigger budget brings greater status and more power. So the Emergency Services Department's objective is to maximize the budget for firefighting airplanes.

Figure 16.6 shows the outcome if the bureaucrats are successful in the pursuit of their goal. They might try to persuade the politicians that 3 airplanes cost more than the originally budgeted amount; or they might press their position more strongly and argue for more than 3 airplanes. In Fig. 16.6, the Emergency Services Department persuades the politicians to provide 4 airplanes.

Why don't the politicians block the bureaucrats? Won't overproviding airplanes cost future votes? It will if voters are well informed and know what is best for them. But voters might not be well informed, and well-informed interest groups might enable the bureaucrats to achieve their objective and overcome the objections of the politicians.

Rational Ignorance   A principle of the economic analysis of public choices is that it is rational for a voter to be ignorant about an issue unless that issue has a perceptible effect on the voter's economic welfare. Each voter knows that he or she can make virtually no difference to the fire protection policy of the government of California and that it would take an enormous amount of time and effort to become even moderately well informed about alternative fire-protection technologies. Rationally uninformed voters enable bureaucrats and special interest groups to overprovide public goods.

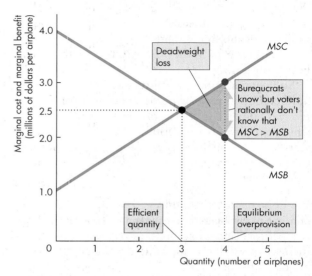

FIGURE 16.6   Bureaucratic Overprovision

Well-informed bureaucrats want to maximize their budget and rationally ignorant voters enable the bureaucrats to go some way toward achieving their goal. A public good might be inefficiently overprovided with a deadweight loss.

—— MyEconLab animation ——

REVIEW QUIZ

1   What is the free-rider problem? Why do free riders make the private provision of a public good inefficient?
2   Under what conditions will competition among politicians for votes result in an efficient provision of a public good?
3   How do rationally ignorant voters and budget-maximizing bureaucrats prevent the political marketplace from delivering the efficient quantity of a public good?
4   Explain why public choices might lead to the overprovision rather than the underprovision of a public good.

You can work these questions in Study Plan 16.2 and get instant feedback.   MyEconLab

You've seen how the political marketplace provides public goods and why it might *over*provide them. Your next task is to see how the political marketplace provides mixed goods that bring external benefits.

Positive Externalities: Education and Health Care

Most of the goods and services provided by governments are *mixed* goods, not *public* goods. The two mixed goods with external benefits on which most is spent are education and health care. We're going to look at how governments influence the provision of these items. We're also going to look at possible improvements on the current arrangements.

To keep our explanation clear, we'll focus first on the market for college education. We'll then apply the lessons we learn to the market for health care.

We begin our study of the provision of mixed goods by distinguishing between private benefits and social benefits.

Private Benefits and Social Benefits

A *private benefit* is a benefit that the consumer of a good or service receives. For example, expanded job opportunities and a higher income are private benefits of a college education.

Marginal benefit is the benefit from an *additional unit* of a good or service. So **marginal private benefit** (*MB*) is the benefit that the consumer of a good or service receives from an additional unit of it. When one additional student attends college, the benefit that student receives is the marginal private benefit from college education.

The *external benefit* from a good or service is the benefit that someone other than the consumer of the good or service receives. College graduates generate many external benefits. On average, they are better citizens, have lower crime rates, and are more tolerant of the views of others. They enable the success of high-quality newspapers and television channels, music, theater, and other organized social activities that bring benefits to many other people.

A **marginal external benefit** is the benefit from an additional unit of a good or service that people *other than its consumer* enjoy. The benefit that your friends and neighbors get from your college education is the marginal external benefit of your college education.

Marginal social benefit (*MSB*) is the marginal benefit enjoyed by society—by the consumer of a good or service (marginal private benefit) and by others (the marginal external benefit). That is,

$$MSB = MB + \text{Marginal external benefit.}$$

Figure 16.7 shows an example of the relationship between marginal private benefit, marginal external benefit, and marginal social benefit. The marginal benefit curve, *MB*, describes the marginal private benefit enjoyed by the people who receive a college education. Marginal private benefit decreases as the number of students enrolled in college increases.

In the example in Fig. 16.7, when 15 million students enroll in college, the marginal external benefit is $15,000 per student per year. The marginal social benefit curve, *MSB*, is the sum of marginal private benefit and marginal external benefit at each number of students. For example, when 15 million students a year enroll in college, the marginal private benefit is $10,000 per student and the marginal external benefit is $15,000 per student, so the marginal social benefit is $25,000 per student.

When people make schooling decisions, they ignore its external benefits and consider only its private benefits. So if education were provided by private schools

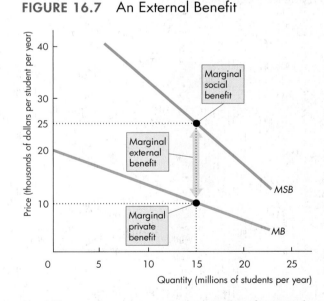

FIGURE 16.7   An External Benefit

The *MB* curve shows the marginal private benefit enjoyed by the people who receive a college education. The *MSB* curve shows the sum of marginal private benefit and marginal external benefit. When 15 million students attend college, the marginal private benefit is $10,000 per student, the marginal external benefit is $15,000 per student, and the marginal social benefit is $25,000 per student.

MyEconLab animation

that charged full-cost tuition, there would be too few college graduates.

Figure 16.8 illustrates this private underprovision. The supply curve is the marginal social cost curve, $S = MSC$. The demand curve is the marginal *private* benefit curve, $D = MB$. Market equilibrium occurs at a tuition of $15,000 per student per year and 7.5 million students per year. At this equilibrium, the marginal social benefit of $38,000 per student exceeds the marginal social cost by $23,000 per student. Too few students are enrolled in college. The efficient number is 15 million per year, where marginal social benefit equals marginal social cost. The gray triangle shows the deadweight loss created.

To get closer to producing the efficient quantity of a mixed good with an external benefit, we make public choices, through governments, to modify the market outcome.

Government Actions in the Market for a Mixed Good with External Benefits

To encourage more students to enroll in college—to achieve an efficient quantity of college education—students must be confronted with a lower market price and the taxpayer must somehow pay for the costs not covered by what the student pays.

Figure 16.9 illustrates an efficient outcome. With marginal social cost curve MSC and marginal social benefit curve MSB, the efficient number of college students is 15,000. The marginal *private* benefit curve MB, tells us that 15,000 students will enroll only if the tuition is $10,000 per year. But the marginal social cost of 15,000 students is $25,000 per year. To enable the marginal social cost to be paid, taxpayers must pay the balance of $15,000 per student per year.

FIGURE 16.8 Inefficiency with an External Benefit

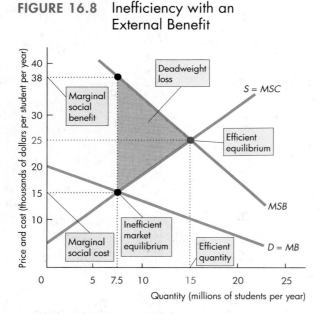

The market demand curve is the marginal private benefit curve, $D = MB$. The supply curve is the marginal social cost curve, $S = MSC$. Market equilibrium at a tuition of $15,000 a year and 7.5 million students is inefficient because marginal social benefit exceeds marginal social cost. The efficient quantity is 15 million students. A deadweight loss arises (gray triangle) because too few students enroll in college.

FIGURE 16.9 An Efficient Outcome with an External Benefit

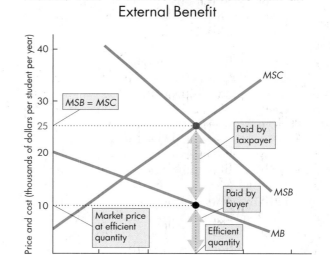

The efficient number of college students is 15 million, where marginal social benefit equals marginal social cost. With the demand and marginal private benefit curve, $D = MB$, the price at which the efficient number will enroll is $10,000 per year. If students pay this price, the taxpayer must somehow pay the rest, which equals the marginal external cost at the efficient quantity—$15,000 per student per year.

Three devices that governments can use to achieve a more efficient allocation of resources in the presence of external benefits are

- Public production
- Private subsidies
- Vouchers

Public Production With **public production**, a good or service is produced by a public authority that receives its revenue from the government. The education services produced by state universities and colleges and public schools are examples of public production.

In the example in Fig. 16.9, efficient public production occurs if public colleges receive funds from government equal to $15,000 per student per year, charge tuition of $10,000 per student per year, and enroll 15 million students.

Private Subsidies A **subsidy** is a payment that the government makes to private producers. By making the subsidy depend on the level of output, the government can induce private decision makers to consider external benefits when they make their choices.

In the example in Fig. 16.9, efficient private provision would occur if private colleges received a government subsidy of $15,000 per student per year. This subsidy reduces the colleges' costs and would make their marginal cost equal to $10,000 per student at the efficient quantity. Tuition of $10,000 would cover this cost, and the subsidy of $15,000 per student would cover the balance of the cost.

Vouchers A **voucher** is a token that the government provides to households, which they can use to buy specified goods or services. Food stamps are examples of vouchers. The vouchers (food stamps) can be spent only on food and are designed to improve the diet and health of extremely poor families.

School vouchers have been advocated as a means of improving the quality of education and are used in Washington, D.C. A school voucher allows parents to choose the school their children will attend and to use the voucher to pay part of the cost. The school cashes the vouchers to pay its bills. A voucher could be provided to a college student in a similar way, and although technically not a voucher, a federal Pell Grant has a similar effect.

Because vouchers can be spent only on a specified item, they increase the willingness to pay for that item and so increase the demand for it.

Efficient provision of college education occurs if the government provides a voucher to each student with a value equal to the marginal external benefit at the efficient number of students. In the example in Fig. 16.9, the efficient number of students is 15 million and the voucher is valued at $15,000 per student. Each student pays $10,000 tuition and gives the college a $15,000 voucher. The colleges receive $25,000 per student, which equals their marginal cost.

Bureaucratic Inefficiency and Government Failure

You've seen three government actions that achieve an efficient provision of a mixed good with an external benefit. In each case, if the government estimates the marginal external benefit correctly and makes marginal social benefit equal to marginal social cost, the outcome is efficient.

Does the comparison that we've just made mean that pubic provision, subsidized private provision, and vouchers are equivalent? It does not. And the reason lies in something that you've already encountered in your study of public goods earlier in this chapter—the behavior of bureaucrats combined with rational ignorance that leads to government failure.

Problems with Public Production Public colleges and schools are operated by a bureaucracy and are subject to the same problems as the provision of public goods. Bureaucrats seek to maximize their budgets, which brings inefficient overspending.

In the case of colleges and schools, overspending doesn't mean *overprovision*. Just the opposite: People complain about *underprovision*. The overspending is budget padding and waste.

Education bureaucrats incur costs that exceed the minimum efficient cost. They might hire more assistants than the number needed to do their work efficiently; give themselves sumptuous offices; get generous expense allowances; build schools in the wrong places where land costs are too high.

Economists have compared the costs of private and public schools and have found that the costs per student of public schools are on the order of *three times* the costs of comparable private schools (see Talking with Carolyn Hoxby on p. 416.)

But bureaucracy can be limited and public production made more efficient. Charter schools (see *Economics in Action* on p. 382) are showing one way of cutting costs even while improving quality.

Problems with Private Subsidies Subsidizing private producers might overcome some of the problems created by public production. A private producer has an incentive to produce at minimum cost and avoid the budget padding of a bureaucratic producer. But two problems arise with private subsidies.

First, the subsidy budget must be allocated by a bureau. A national, state, or local department of education must lobby for its own budget and allocate this budget between school subsidies and its own administration costs. To the extent that the bureaucrats succeed in maximizing their own adminstration budget, they siphon off resources from schools and a problem similar to that of public production arises.

Second, it is in the self-interest of subsidized producers to maximize their subsidy. These producers might even spend some of the subsidy they receive lobbying for an even bigger one.

So subsidized private provision is unlikely to achieve an efficient allocation of resources. What about the third method: vouchers?

Are Vouchers the Solution? Vouchers have four advantages over the other two approaches:

1. Vouchers can be used with public production, private provision, or competition between the two.
2. Governments can set the value of vouchers and the total voucher budget to overcome bureaucratic overprovision and budget padding.
3. Vouchers spread the public contribution thinly across millions of consumers, so no one consumer has an interest in wasting part of the value received in lobbying for overprovision.
4. By giving the buying power to the final consumer, producers must compete for business and provide a high standard of service at the lowest attainable cost.

For these four reasons, vouchers are popular with economists. But they are controversial and opposed by most education administrators and teachers.

In *The Economics of School Choice,* a book edited by Caroline M. Hoxby, economists study the effect of school choice on student achievement and school productivity and show how vouchers can be designed to achieve their goals while avoiding their potential pitfalls. Caroline Hoxby is confident that she can design a voucher that best achieves any educational and school performance objective.

Economics in Action
Education Quality and Cost: Charter Schools

The three methods of achieving efficient education have similar effects on the *quantity* of education but different effects on its *quality* and its *cost*. And education quality has become a big issue with international league tables showing U.S. students performing worse on standardized math and science tests than same-age students in more than 20 other countries.

In an attempt to improve quality of education and at the same time contain costs, many states are setting up charter schools.

A *charter school* is a public school, so it is funded like a regular public school. What makes a charter school an unusual public school is that it is free to make its own education policy.

Around 4,000 charter schools in 40 states and teaching more than 1 million students are in operation today. When the demand for places in a charter school exceeds the supply, students are chosen by lottery. This method of selection provides rich data for testing the performance of charter schools.

Are charter schools succeeding? Success has two dimensions: educational standards attained and cost per student.

Charter schools perform well on both dimensions. They achieve higher standards and cost less. Charter school students achieve better test scores in math and reading than equivalent students who apply to but randomly don't get into a charter school.

Charter schools also achieve this higher standard at lower cost. For example, in New York, cost per student in charter schools is 18 percent less than in regular public schools.

La Cima Elementary Charter School, Brooklyn, New York

Health-Care Services

Health care is two distinct products: health insurance that pays health-care bills, and health-care services, which are the services of physicians, specialists, nurses, other professionals, and hospitals.

Left to competitive markets with no government intervention, both health insurance and health-care services would be underprovided because each product is an example of a mixed good with external benefits. So all the principles and potential solutions that you've studied in the context of education apply to the health-care markets.

Health-Care Externalities

The external benefits from health care arise in three ways. The most direct and simple is avoiding spreading infectious diseases. A flu shot is a private good but one with external benefits. People who get a flu shot protect themselves and everyone with whom they come into contact. So the marginal social benefit of flu shots exceeds the marginal private benefit and without one of the three methods of dealing with a positive externality, too few people will get a flu shot.

A second external benefit is similar to that from education. It is more pleasant to live and work with healthy neighbors than with people who are sick and frequently not showing up for work or social events.

A third, and for many people overriding, external benefit is that of living in a society that treats older, poor, and sick people with compassion and respect and provides them with access to affordable health care.

Alternative Solutions to Providing Health Care

Because of its special features, no country leaves the delivery of health care to the private market economy. Every country spends a large percentage of its income on the public provision of health care. *Economics in Action* shows the amounts spent per person in the United States and 11 other countries. Countries spend their public health-care dollars in different ways, some using *public production* and some *private production*.

Public Provision and Public Production

In many countries, Canada and the United Kingdom are examples, doctors, nurses, and hospitals receive most (and in some cases all) their incomes from government. Government pays the bills and produces the health-care services. This method of delivering health-care limits patient choice but contains costs by setting the

Economics in Action
U.S. Health-Care Expenditures in Global Perspective

The best U.S. health care is the best in the world. But it is costly. Americans spend 17.6 percent of income—$8,200 per person per year—on health care, which is *more than double* the average spent in other rich countries. And the cost is projected to rise as the U.S. population ages and the "baby boom" generation retires.

The figure below compares U.S. health-care costs with those of 11 other countries, some rich and some not so rich. Even rich countries such as Canada, Germany, and France spend barely a half as much, per person, on their health care as Americans do. And health outcomes—life expectancy and quality of health—in these other rich countries are as good as or better than those in the United States.

Another feature of U.S. health-care expenditure is its very large public component. Government expenditure per person on health care in the United States is the third highest in the world. It is exceeded only by that of Switzerland and the Netherlands. It exceeds that in Canada, where private health care is illegal, and in Germany and France, where there is a greater acceptance of high taxes and big government than in the United States.

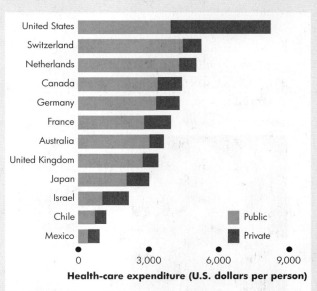

Health-Care Expenditures in 12 Countries

◆ AT ISSUE

Is Obamacare the Solution to U.S. Health-Care Problems?

The *Affordable Care Act* (Obamacare) was signed into law in March 2010 and became the subject of a Supreme Court challenge for its mandating the purchase of health insurance. The Supreme Court ruled in June 2012 that the Act is constitutional and that the penalty for not buying health insurance is just a tax.

The Act remains controversial, and alternative solutions to the health-care problem have been proposed. So, *is* Obamacare the solution?

Yes

- When the Supreme Court ruled that the *Affordable Care Act* is constitutional, the White House issued a *Fact Sheet*, restating the President's view of the benefits of his health-care reforms.

- The *Fact Sheet* says the *Affordable Care Act* keeps health-care costs low, promotes prevention, and holds insurance companies accountable.

- The Act ends the unchecked power of insurance companies to cancel policies, to deny coverage of children with pre-existing conditions, or to charge women a higher price than men.

- It makes preventive care such as mammograms and wellness visits for seniors free of charge.

- It helps seniors and people with disabilities to buy prescription drugs that were previously not covered.

- Very importantly, it makes quality, affordable, private health-insurance plans available for those currently uninsured.

- It makes middle-class families and small businesses eligible for health-insurance tax credits.

- The Supreme Court ruling ensures that everyone contributes to and is covered by health insurance.

No

- Laurence Kotlikoff, an economics professor at Boston University, says Obamacare has no effective mechanism for containing costs.

- Given the demographic changes that we know are coming, the health-care budget will balloon.

- In Professor Kotlikoff's *Medical Security System*, Medicare, Medicaid, and employer-based health-care insurance are replaced with an affordable Basic Plan that provides universal private health insurance and creates incentives to improve health and deliver health-care services efficiently.

- An Independent Panel of doctors defines the coverage of the Basic Plan that insurance companies must offer.

- Each year, each American gets a voucher to buy a Basic Plan from an insurance company of their choice.

- The voucher's value equals the expected cost of covering the person, which is determined by health indicators held in electronic medical records. (Example: An 80-year-old diabetic might get a $70,000 voucher while a healthy 14-year-old girl might get a $3,000 voucher.)

- The total value of vouchers does not exceed 10 percent of total U.S. income—an amount equal to that spent on the replaced Medicare and Medicaid and the tax breaks to employer-provided health plans.

- Public expenditure on health care grows as income grows, and the Independent Panel adds procedures and technologies covered by the Basic Plan but at a slower pace than in the current system.

Professor Laurence J. Kotlikoff of Boston University; author of *The Healthcare Fix* and creator of *Medicare Part C for All*.

budget and the number of physicians, nurses, and hospital beds to supply.

Patients access services at a zero (or low) price and, because the quantity demanded exceeds the quantity supplied, services are allocated first-come, first-served (see Chapter 5, pp. 106–107) with long wait-times for treatment.

This "solution" to the provision of health care is inefficient. Some people who are waiting in a long line are willing to pay more than the cost of the attention their health problem needs—marginal benefit exceeds marginal cost. Others get service even if their marginal benefit is less than marginal cost. Lots of deadweight-loss triangles are created.

Defenders of the system say that inefficiencies are small and worth accepting because the outcome is fair as everyone has equal access to services. But it isn't exactly true that everyone has equal access. Some people are better at playing the system than others and are able to jump the line.

Public Provision and Private Production In the United States, most health-care services are produced by private doctors and hospitals that receive their incomes from both governments and private health-insurance companies. The health-insurance companies in turn receive their income from employers and individual contributors.

Despite the enormous expenditure on health care, until the 2010 Affordable Care Act becomes fully effective, 47 million people have no health insurance and a further 25 million have too little insurance.

Of those who do have health insurance, nearly 40 million are covered by the government's Medicare and Medicaid programs. These programs are in effect an open-ended commitment of public funds to the health care of the aged (Medicare) and those too poor to buy private health care (Medicaid). In 2035, when those born in 1955 turn 80, benefits under these programs will cost an estimated $50,000 per person per year. Benefits on these programs alone will cost more than 18 percent of the value of the nation's total production.

You can see that health care in the United States faces two problems: underprovision because private choices don't value all the external benefits; and overexpenditure because private health-care producers decide how much to produce and then collect fees for their services from the government.

The Affordable Care Act addresses the first of these problems by requiring everyone to be insured and by creating a new Pre-Existing Condition Insurance Plan financed partly by the government.

But the act does little to address the problem of overexpenditure, and this problem is extremely serious. It is so serious that without massive change, the present open-ended health-care programs will bankrupt the United States.

At Issue (opposite) looks at one part of the debate between supporters of the 2010 Act and an economist who proposes a market-based health-care voucher solution.

Sytems Compared Comparing health-care arrangements across countries is difficult because lifestyle, diet, and exercise as well as health-care services contribute to the health of a population and it is hard to isolate the effects of health care alone.

Nonetheless, the health-care delivery systems of Canada and the United Kingdom, while inefficient and possibly unfair, deliver health outcomes that in most respects are similar to those of the United States. Health care is more costly in the United States than it is in the rest of the world for two main reasons: U.S. doctors' remuneratio and pharmaceutical prices are higher; and the volume of high-tech diagnostic tests using CT scanners and MRI equipment vastly exceeds that of other countries.

REVIEW QUIZ

1 What is special about education and health care that makes them mixed goods with external benefits?

2 Why would the market economy produce too little education and health care?

3 How might public production, private subsidies, and vouchers achieve an efficient provision of a mixed good with external benefits?

4 What are the key differences among public production, private subsidies, and vouchers?

5 Why do economists generally favor vouchers rather than public production or subsidies to achieve an efficient outcome?

You can work these questions in Study Plan 16.3 and get instant feedback.   MyEconLab

◆ *Reading Between the Lines* on pp. 386–387 looks at the effects of the 2010 Act and some of the problems that it brings.

Reforming Health Care

Protective Net for All Residents; Q&A Legislation Details

Financial Times
March 22, 2010

What would the U.S. health-care bill do?

Offer or subsidize health-care coverage for 32m people, a tenth of the population, who are uninsured; mandate that every U.S. and legal resident receive minimal coverage.

Beginning in 2014, people who are out of work, self-employed, or working for companies that do not offer insurance could buy coverage from "health exchanges" in which private insurers would offer different kinds of plans.

About 19m people would be eligible for financial subsidies to help pay for insurance. If individuals refused to buy insurance coverage, they would be subject to a tax penalty.

How much would it cost and who is paying for it?

The non-partisan Congressional Budget Office estimates the bill would cost $940 billion over 10 years. This is expected to be paid for through tax on the wealthy and health-related industries, including a tax on so-called "Cadillac" insurance plans that would raise $32 billion over 10 years. The bill would also create a Medicare (the health-care scheme for the elderly) commission that would have power to impose steep cuts in payments. Individuals making more than $200,000 a year, or couples making more than $250,000 a year, would pay higher taxes on Medicare and face a new 3.8 percent tax on dividends, interest, and other unearned income. The tax would take effect in January 2013. The CBO estimates the health-care bill would reduce the U.S. deficit by $138 billion over 10 years. ...

ESSENCE OF THE STORY

- Over the first ten years, health-care reform will cost $940 billion.

- Coverage will expand to 32 million Americans who are currently uninsured.

- New taxes will pay for the plan and cut the budget deficit.

- Medicaid will expand to cover about 19 million low-income people.

- Except for some low-income families, everyone will be required to buy health insurance and will face penalties if they refuse to do so.

ECONOMIC ANALYSIS

- Health care in the United States faces two problems: 1) *Underprovision* because private choices leave too many families and individuals without health insurance; 2) *Overexpenditure* on public programs because the government pays for the quantity that patients demand and doctors supply.

- The health-care reform of 2010 (the Patient Protection and Affordable Care Act of 2010) addresses the first problem. It expands the scope of government provision of health care by covering more families and individuals and by improving the health-care insurance of those already covered. (The news article describes some of the details of the Act.)

- The 2010 Act notes the problem of cost containment but does little to address the main source of overexpenditure: Medicare and Medicaid.

- Medicare and Medicaid remain under the new plan, and Medicaid will be expanded to cover more people.

- Figure 1 shows how Medicare and Medicaid overprovide services to those covered by the programs. The quantity provided is the quantity demanded by patients and supplied by doctors at a zero (or almost zero) price.

- Because the price is zero, marginal benefit, *MB*, is also zero.

- Doctors and hospitals negotiate fees with the government that equal marginal cost, which also equals marginal social cost, *MSC*.

- Marginal social cost, shown by the *MSC* curve, exceeds the (zero) marginal benefit. In this example, *MSC* is $25,000 per patent per year at the quantity provided.

- Medicare and Medicaid services would be provided efficiently if marginal social cost, *MSC*, equaled marginal social benefit, *MSB*.

- With overprovision, a deadweight loss arises shown by the gray triangle.

- Expenditure on Medicare and Medicaid equals the fee per unit of service multiplied by the quantity provided. Figure 2 illustrates this expenditure.

- The white rectangle shows what expenditure would be with the efficient quantity. The purple area shows the overexpenditure. Total expenditure is the sum of these areas and equals $25,000 × 30 million.

- As the population gets older and as treatment techniques become more sophisticated and more conditions can be treated, the *MB* curve shifts rightward.

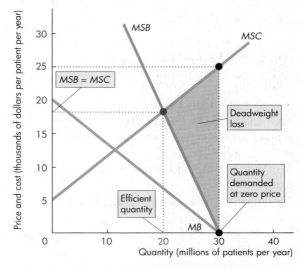

Figure 1 Overprovision of Medicare and Medicaid

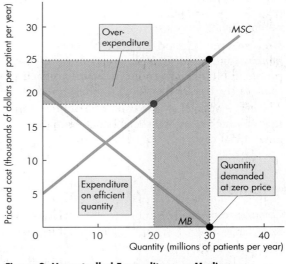

Figure 2 Uncontrolled Expenditure on Medicare and Medicaid

- The quantity of health-care services provided by Medicare and Medicaid increases and the expenditure on these programs grows.

- A health-care voucher program like that explained for education is one way (and possibly the only effective way) of achieving an efficient provision of Medicare and Medicaid and of containing their cost.

SUMMARY

Key Points

Public Choices (pp. 370–374)

- Governments establish and maintain property rights, provide nonmarket mechanisms for allocating scarce resources, and redistribute income and wealth.
- Public choice theory explains how voters, firms, politicians, and bureaucrats interact in the political marketplace and why government failure might occur.
- A private good is a good or service that is rival and excludable.
- A public good is a good or service that is nonrival and nonexcludable.
- A mixed good is a private good that creates an external benefit or external cost.

Working Problems 1 to 6 will give you a better understanding of public choices.

Providing Public Goods (pp. 375–378)

- Because a public good is a good or service that is *nonrival* and *nonexcludable*, it creates a *free-rider* problem: No one has an incentive to pay their share of the cost of providing a public good.
- The efficient level of provision of a public good is that at which marginal social benefit equals marginal social cost.

- Competition between political parties can lead to the efficient scale of provision of a public good.
- Bureaucrats who maximize their budgets and voters who are rationally ignorant can lead to the inefficient overprovision of a public good—government failure.

Working Problems 7 to 15 will give you a better understanding of providing public goods.

Positive Externalities: Education and Health Care (pp. 379–385)

- Mixed goods provide external benefits—benefits that are received by people other than the consumer of a good or service.
- Marginal social benefit equals marginal private benefit plus marginal external benefit.
- External benefits arise from education and health care.
- Vouchers provided to households can achieve a more efficient provision of education and health care than public production or subsidies to private producers.
- U.S. expenditure per person on health care is more than double that of other rich countries and U.S. public expenditure exceeds that of other countries, but U.S. health outcomes are similar to those in other countries.

Working Problems 16 to 20 will give you a better understanding of providing mixed goods with external benefits.

Key Terms

Common resource, 372
Excludable, 372
Externality, 372
Free-rider problem, 375
Government failure, 370
Marginal external benefit, 379
Marginal private benefit, 379
Marginal social benefit, 379
Mixed good, 372

Natural monopoly good, 372
Negative externality, 372
Nonexcludable, 372
Nonrival, 372
Political equilibrium, 371
Positive externality, 372
Principle of minimum differentiation, 377
Private good, 372

Public choice, 370
Public good, 372
Public production, 381
Rival, 372
Subsidy, 381
Voucher, 381

STUDY PLAN PROBLEMS AND APPLICATIONS

MyEconLab   You can work Problems 1 to 20 in MyEconLab Chapter 16 Study Plan and get instant feedback.

Public Choices (Study Plan 16.1)

1. Classify each of the following items as excludable, nonexcludable, rival, or nonrival.
   - A Big Mac
   - Brooklyn Bridge
   - A view of the Statue of Liberty
   - A tsunami warning system

2. Classify each of the following items as a public good, a private good, a natural monopoly good, or a common resource.
   - Highway control services
   - City sidewalks
   - U.S. Postal Service
   - FedEx courier service

3. Classify the following services for computer owners with an Internet connection as rival, nonrival, excludable, or nonexcludable.
   - eBay
   - A mouse
   - A Twitter page
   - MyEconLab Web site

4. Classify each of the following items as a public good, a private good, a mixed good, or a common resource.
   - Georges Banks' cod stock
   - A courtside seat at the U.S. Open (tennis)
   - A well-stocked buffet that promises the most bang for your buck
   - The Mississippi River

5. Explain which of the following events creates an external benefit or an external cost:
   - A huge noisy crowd gathers outside the lecture room
   - Your neighbor grows beautiful flowers on his apartment deck.
   - A fire alarm goes off accidently in the middle of a lecture.
   - Your instructor offers a free tutorial after class.

6. **Wind Farm Off Cape Cod Clears Hurdle**

   The nation's first offshore wind farm with 130 turbines will be built 5 miles off the coast. Wind turbines are noisy, stand 440 feet tall, can be seen from the coast, and will produce power for 75 percent of nearby homes.

   Source: *The New York Times*, January 16, 2009

   List the externalities created by this wind farm.

Providing Public Goods (Study Plan 16.2)

7. For each of the following goods, explain whether there is a free-rider problem. If there is no such problem, how is it avoided?
   - July 4th fireworks display
   - Interstate 81 in Virginia
   - Wireless Internet access in hotels
   - The public library in your city

8. The table sets out the marginal benefits that Terri and Sue receive from police officers on duty on the college campus:

Police officers on duty (number per night)	Marginal benefit Terri (dollars per police officer)	Sue (dollars per police officer)
1	18	22
2	14	18
3	10	14
4	6	10
5	2	6

   a. If the police officers are provided by the city government, is the presence of the police on-campus a private good or a public good?

   b. Suppose that Terri and Sue are the only students on the campus at night. Draw a graph to show the marginal social benefit from on-campus police officers on duty at night.

9. For each of the following goods and services, explain whether there is a free-rider problem. If there is no such problem, how is it avoided?
   - National hurricane warning system
   - Ambulance service
   - Road safety signs
   - The U.S. Coast Guard

10. **Vaccination Dodgers**

    Doctors struggle to eradicate polio worldwide, but one of the biggest problems is persuading parents to vaccinate their children. Since the discovery of the vaccine, polio has been eliminated from Europe and the law requires everyone to be vaccinated. People who refuse to be vaccinated are "free riders."

    Source: *USA Today*, March 12, 2008

    Explain why someone who has not opted out on medical or religious grounds and refuses to be vaccinated is a "free rider."

Use the following figure to work Problems 11 to 13. The figure provides information about a waste disposal system that a city of 1 million people is considering installing.

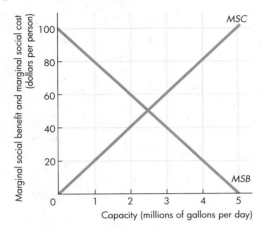

11. What is the efficient capacity of the waste disposal system? How much will each person have to pay in taxes for the city to install the efficient capacity?
12. What is the political equilibrium if voters are well informed?
13. What is the political equilibrium if voters are rationally ignorant and bureaucrats achieve the highest attainable budget?

Use the data on a mosquito control program in the following table to work Problems 14 and 15.

Quantity (square miles sprayed per day)	Marginal social cost	Marginal social benefit
	(thousands of dollars per day)	
1	2	10
2	4	8
3	6	6
4	8	4
5	10	2

14. What quantity of spraying would a private mosquito control program provide? What is the efficient quantity of spraying? In a single-issue election on the quantity of spraying, what quantity would the winner of the election provide?
15. If the government sets up a Department of Mosquito Control and appoints a bureaucrat to run it, would mosquito spraying most likely be underprovided, overprovided, or provided at the efficient quantity?

Providing Mixed Goods with External Benefits

(Study Plan 16.3)

Use the following figure, which shows the marginal private benefit from college education, to work Problems 16 to 19.

The marginal cost of a college education is a constant $6,000 per student per year. The marginal external benefit from a college education is a constant $4,000 per student per year.

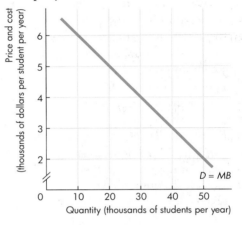

16. What is the efficient number of students? If all colleges are private, how many people enroll in college and what is the tuition?
17. If the government decides to provide public colleges, what tuition will these colleges charge to achieve the efficient number of students? How much will taxpayers have to pay?
18. If the government decides to subsidize private colleges, what subsidy will achieve the efficient number of college students?
19. If the government offers vouchers to those who enroll at a college and no subsidy, what is the value of the voucher that will achieve the efficient number of students?

20. **Tuition Hikes, not Loan Access, Should Frighten Students**

The real danger during a recession is a hike in tuition, not a cut in student loans. In past recessions, states have cut funding for colleges and increased tuition. The Cato Institute says a better policy would be for states to maintain the subsidies to colleges and increase their deficits.

Source: *USA Today*, October 22, 2008

If government cuts the subsidy to colleges, why will tuition rise and the number of students enrolled decrease? Why is it a better policy for government to maintain the subsidy to colleges?

ADDITIONAL PROBLEMS AND APPLICATIONS

MyEconLab   You can work these problems in MyEconLab if assigned by your instructor.

Public Choices

21. Classify each of the following items as excludable, nonexcludable, rival, or nonrival.
    - Homeland security
    - A Starbucks coffee
    - A view of the Liberty Bell
    - The Appalachian Trail
    - A google search

22. Classify each of the following items as a public good, a private good, a natural monopoly good, a common resource, or a mixed good.
    - Measles vaccinations
    - Tuna in the Pacific Ocean
    - Air service in the United States
    - Local storm-water system

23. Consider each of the following activities or events and say for each one whether it creates an externality. If so, say whether it creates an external benefit or external cost and whether the externality arises from production or consumption.
    - Airplanes take off from LaGuardia Airport during the U.S. Open tennis tournament, which is taking place nearby.
    - A sunset over the Pacific Ocean
    - An increase in the number of people who are studying for graduate degrees
    - A person wears strong perfume to class.

24. Classify each of the following goods as a private good, a public good, or a mixed good and say whether it creates an external benefit, external cost, or neither.
    - Chewing gum
    - The Santa Monica freeway at peak travel time
    - The New York City subway
    - A skateboard
    - The Santa Monica beach

Providing Public Goods

Use the following news clip to work Problems 25 and 26.

"Free Riders" Must be Part of Health Debate

President Obama insists that "the reason people don't have health insurance isn't because they don't want it, it's because they can't afford it." There are 47 million uninsured people in the United States. Of these, 16 percent earn more than $75,000 a year and 15 percent earn between $50,000 and $75,000 a year. About 16 percent of those who received "free" medical care in 2004 had incomes at least four times the federal poverty level.

Source: *Los Angeles Times*, March 4, 2008

25. Explain why government-subsidized health-care services can create a free-rider problem.

26. Explain the evidence the news clip presents to contradict the argument that "the reason people don't have health insurance isn't because they don't want it, it's because they can't afford it."

27. The table sets out the marginal benefits that Sam and Nick receive from the town's street lighting:

Number of street lights	Marginal benefit	
	Sam	Nick
	(dollars per street light)	
1	10	12
2	8	9
3	6	6
4	4	3
5	2	0

  a. Is the town's street lighting a private good or a public good?

  b. Suppose that Sam and Nick are the only residents of the town. Draw a graph to show the marginal social benefit from the town's street lighting.

28. What is the principle of diminishing marginal benefit? In Problem 27, does Sam's, Nick's, the society's marginal benefit diminish faster?

Use the following news clip to work Problems 29 and 30.

A Bridge Too Far Gone

The gas taxes paid for much of America's post-war freeway system. Now motorists pay about one-third in gas taxes to drive a mile as they did in the 1960s. Yet raising such taxes is politically tricky. This would matter less if private cash was flooding into infrastructure, or if new ways were being found to control demand. Neither is happening, and private companies building toll roads brings howls of outrage.

Source: *The Economist*, August 9, 2007

29. Why is it "politically tricky" to raise gas taxes to finance infrastructure?

30. What in this news clip points to a distinction between public *production* of a public good and

public *provision*? Give examples of three public goods that are *produced* by private firms but *provided* by government and paid for with taxes.

Providing Mixed Goods with External Benefits

Use the following information and figure to work Problems 31 and 34.

The marginal cost of educating a student is a constant $4,000 a year and the figure shows the students' marginal benefit curve. Suppose that college education creates a marginal external benefit of a constant $2,000 per student per year.

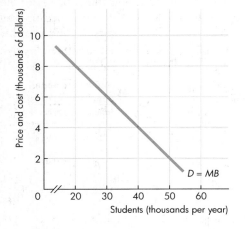

31. If all colleges are private and the market for education is competitive, how many students enroll, what is the tuition, and what is the deadweight loss created?

32. If the government decides to provide public colleges, what tuition will these colleges charge to achieve the efficient number of students? How much will taxpayers have to pay?

33. If the government decides to subsidize private colleges, what subsidy will achieve the efficient number of college students?

34. If the government offers vouchers to those who enroll at a college and no subsidy, what is the value of the voucher that will achieve the efficient number of students?

35. **My Child, My Choice**
    Fully vaccinating all U.S. children born in a given year saves 33,000 lives, prevents 14 million infections, and saves $10 billion in medical costs. Part of the reason is that vaccinations protect not only the kids that receive the shots but also those who can't receive them—such as newborns and cancer patients with suppressed immune systems.
    Source: *Time*, June 2, 2008

a. Describe the private benefits and external benefits of vaccinations and explain why a private market for vaccinations would produce an inefficient outcome.

b. Draw a graph to illustrate a private market for vaccinations and show the deadweight loss.

c. Explain how government intervention could achieve an efficient quantity of vaccinations and draw a graph to illustrate this outcome.

Economics in the News

36. After you have studied *Reading Between the Lines* on pp. 386–387, answer the following questions:

a. What are the two major problems confronting the provision of health-care services in the United States?

b. How is it possible for the two problems you've identified to occur together?

c. Why might a voucher system be superior to the current method of providing health-care services?

d. Compare the main features of the 2010 health-care reform with the plan suggested by Laurence Kotlikoff on p. 385.

e. Which plan would be better and why?

37. **Who's Hiding Under Our Umbrella?**
    Students of the Cold War learn that, to deter possible Soviet aggression, the United States placed a "strategic umbrella" over NATO Europe and Japan, with the United States providing most of their national security. Under President Ronald Reagan, the United States spent 6 percent of total income on defense, whereas the Europeans spent only 2 to 3 percent and the Japanese spent only 1 percent, although all faced a common enemy. Thus the U.S. taxpayer paid a disproportionate share of the overall defense spending, whereas NATO Europe and Japan spent more on consumer goods or saved
    Source: *International Herald Tribune*, January 30, 2008

a. Explain the free-rider problem described in this news clip.

b. Does the free-rider problem in international defense mean that the world has too little defense against aggression?

c. How do nations try to overcome the free-rider problem among nations?

17

EXTERNALITIES AND THE ENVIRONMENT

After studying this chapter, you will be able to:

◆ Explain why external costs bring market failure and too much pollution and how property rights and public choices might achieve an efficient outcome

◆ Explain the tragedy of the commons and its possible solutions

How can we use less coal, natural gas, and oil to reduce the air pollution and global warming we're causing? What can we do to conserve the ocean's fish stocks and save endangered species from extinction?

These questions arise because some of our choices impose costs on others—external costs—that we don't think about when we make those choices. How can we be made to take these costs into account?

In *Reading Between the Lines* at the end of the chapter, you will see one answer: a carbon tax to counter global warming and climate change.

◆ Negative Externalities: Pollution

Every time we take an airplane trip, we leave a carbon footprint and pollute the air. Can each one of us be relied upon to make decisions in the social interest when they affect air quality and the climate? Must governments change the incentives we face so that our self-interested choices are also in the social interest? How can governments change incentives? How can we encourage the use of technologies that improve air quality and lessen climate change?

These questions (first posed in Chapter 1, p. 7) arise because energy produced from coal, oil, and natural gas has negative externalities—*external costs*.

Air pollution and climate change are just two of a broader class of negative externalities that arise from economic activity. Industrial processes, fertilizers, and garbage disposal all pollute the air, rivers, lakes, and land, and these individual areas of pollution interact through the ecosystem.

The principles that you learn in this chapter apply to all these types of pollution and more broadly to all economic activities that bring external costs.

We focus on air quality and climate change both as examples and as vitally important issues and begin with a review of the sources of these problems and the negative externalities they bring.

Sources and Consequences of Air Pollution

The problems of local air quality and the global problem of climate change are related but are distinct problems that present their own challenges.

Local air quality is influenced by more than 180 airborne substances which, in sufficiently large concentrations, can damage human health. But the six most important ones are carbon monoxide, lead, nitrogen dioxide, ground level ozone, particulate matter, and sulfur dioxide. In the United States, the trend in these pollutants is strongly downward (see *Economics in Action* on the next page).

Global temperature is influenced by human emissions of greenhouse gasses, of which the most important is carbon dioxide (CO_2). Less important greenhouse gasses include methane and nitrous oxide.

CO_2 emission is a global phenomenon and problem. The United States and China each account for about one-quarter of the CO_2 poured into the global atmosphere in a year. Some of this additional CO_2 is taken up by the oceans or by vegetation on land, so the amount in the atmosphere changes by the emissions minus the net amount removed.

More CO_2 is emitted than removed, so the amount in the atmosphere is rising as you can see in *Economics in Action* on the next page.

Electric power utilities, highway vehicles, and industrial processes are the main sources of both local air pollution and global CO_2 emissions.

The effects of pollution mean that production and consumption decisions impose costs that are not taken fully into account when decisions are made. You are now going to see how economists analyze these decisions and solve pollution problems.

Production and Pollution: How Much?

To see what determines the amount of pollution and external cost, we begin by distinguishing between the private cost and the social cost of production.

A *private cost* of production is a cost that is borne by the producer of a good or service. *Marginal cost* is the cost of producing an *additional unit* of a good or service. So **marginal private cost** (*MC*) is the cost of producing an additional unit of a good or service that is borne by its producer.

An *external cost* is a cost of producing a good or service that is *not* borne by the producer but borne by other people. A **marginal external cost** is the cost of producing an additional unit of a good or service that falls on people other than the producer.

Marginal social cost (*MSC*) is the marginal cost incurred by the producer and by everyone else on whom the cost falls—by society. It is the sum of marginal private cost and marginal external cost. That is,

$$MSC = MC + \text{Marginal external cost.}$$

We express costs in dollars, but we must always remember that a cost is an opportunity cost—something real, such as clean air or a clean river, is given up to get something.

Valuing an External Cost Economists use market prices to put a dollar value on the external cost of pollution. For example, suppose that there are two similar rivers, one polluted and the other clean. Ten identical homes are built along the side of each river. The homes on the clean river rent for $2,000 per month, and those on the polluted river rent for $1,500 per month. If the pollution is the only detectable difference between the two rivers and the two locations, the rent difference of $500 per month is the pollution cost per home. With 10 homes on the side of a polluted river, the external cost of pollution is $5,000 per month.

Economics in Action
Opposing Trends: Success and Failure

The trends in local U.S. air quality and global greenhouse gas concentrations are starkly opposing. The concentrations of air pollutants in U.S. cities is decreasing, as it has done so for the past 30 years. In contrast, the concentration of greenhouse gases (mainly carbon dioxide) in the global atmosphere is increasing and posing an ever more urgent problem.

Air Pollution Trends

Figure 1 shows the trends in the concentrations of the six main pollutants of the air in the United States between 1980 and 2010. The concentrations of all these pollutants decreased.

The Clean Air Act has brought regulations that cut emissions of carbon monoxide, volatile organic compounds, oxides of nitrogen, sulfur dioxide, and particulate matter to around 64 percent of their 1980 levels. And economic actions that you will learn about in this chapter have almost eliminated lead from highway vehicles and industrial processes.

These reductions in air pollution are even more impressive seen against the trends in economic activity. Between 1980 and 2010, total production in the United States increased by 124 percent, vehicle miles traveled increased by 95 percent, and the population increased by 36 percent.

Global CO_2 and Temperature Trends

Figure 2 shows the global trends in carbon dioxide (CO_2) concentration and temperature.

Both trends are starkly upward. CO_2 concentration has increased by almost 40 percent since 1850, and global temperature has been rising for more than 100 years.

Scientists agree that the scale on which we burn fossil fuels is the major source of the rising CO_2 trend. There is more uncertainty about the effect of the increase in CO_2 on global temperature, but the consensus is that the effect is significant.

Stopping the rising CO_2 trend requires joint action by the governments of every nation. But a binding agreement among nations to reduce greenhouse gas emissions, the *Kyoto Protocol*, excluded the major developing countries and the United States refused to ratify it. You will see in this chapter why global warming is a much harder problem to solve than reducing air pollution in the United States.

Figure 1 U.S. Air Pollution Trends

Source of data: United States Environmental Protection Agency.

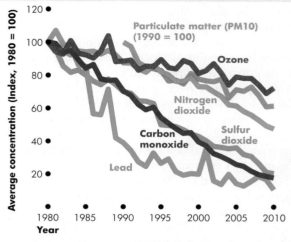

Los Angeles still has a smoggy dawn on some days

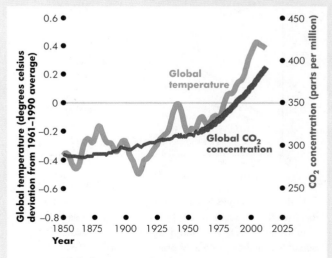

Figure 2 Global Warming Trends

Sources of data: Temperature: Met Office Hadley Centre (combined land and oceans); CO_2: Scripps Institution of Oceanography, Mauna Loa Observatory, Hawaii, data since 1960 and ice-core estimates before 1960.

External Cost and Output Figure 17.1 shows an example of the relationship between output and cost in a paint industry that pollutes rivers. The marginal cost curve, *MC*, describes the marginal private cost borne by the paint producers, which increases as the quantity of paint produced increases.

If a firm pollutes a river, it imposes an external cost borne by other users of the river. Pollution and its marginal external cost increase with the amount of paint produced.

The marginal social cost curve, *MSC*, is found by adding marginal external cost to marginal private cost. So a point on the *MSC* curve shows the sum of the marginal private cost and marginal external cost at a given level of output.

For example, if 3 million gallons of paint per month are produced, marginal private cost is $1.00 per gallon, marginal external cost is 75¢ per gallon, and marginal social cost is $1.75 per gallon.

Let's now see how much paint gets produced and how much pollution gets created.

Equilibrium and Amount of Pollution Equilibrium in the market for paint determines the amount of pollution. Figure 17.2 has the same *MC* and *MSC* curves as Fig. 17.1 and also has a market demand and marginal social benefit curve, *D = MSB*. Equilibrium occurs at a price of $1.00 per gallon and 3 million gallons per month. This equilibrium is one with *inefficient overproduction* (Chapter 5, p. 114) because marginal social cost at $1.75 per gallon exceeds marginal social benefit at $1.00 per gallon. The efficient equilibrium occurs where marginal social benefit *equals* marginal social cost at 2 million gallons of paint per month. Too much paint is produced, too much pollution is created, and the area of the deadweight loss triangle measures the society's loss.

If some method can be found to get paint factories to create less pollution and eliminate the deadweight loss, everyone—the owners of paint factories and the residents of the riverside homes—can gain.

FIGURE 17.2 Inefficiency with an External Cost

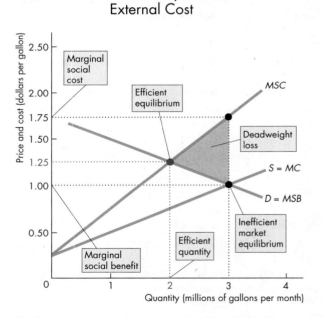

The factories' marginal private cost curve is the market supply curve, *S = MC*. The market demand curve is the marginal social benefit curve, *D = MSB*. The market equilibrium occurs at a price of $1.00 per gallon and 3 million gallons per month. This outcome is inefficient because marginal social cost exceeds marginal social benefit. The efficient quantity of paint is 2 million gallons per month. The gray triangle shows the deadweight loss created by the pollution.

FIGURE 17.1 An External Cost

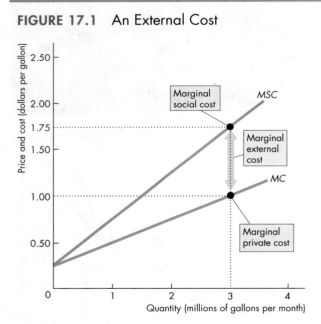

The *MC* curve shows the marginal private cost borne by the factories that produce paint. The *MSC* curve shows the sum of marginal private cost and marginal external cost. When output is 3 million gallons of paint per month, marginal private cost is $1.00 per gallon, marginal external cost is 75¢ per gallon, and marginal social cost is $1.75 per gallon.

— MyEconLab animation —

— MyEconLab animation —

So, what can be done to fix the inefficiency that arises from an external cost? Three approaches are available and we will examine each of them. They are

- Establish property rights
- Mandate clean technology
- Tax or price pollution

Establish Property Rights

Property rights are legally established titles to the ownership, use, and disposal of factors of production and goods and services that are enforceable in the courts. Establishing property rights where they do not currently exist can confront producers with the costs of their actions and provide the incentives that allocate resources efficiently.

To see how property rights work, suppose that the paint producers have property rights on a river and the homes alongside it—they *own* the river and the homes. The rental income that the paint producers are able to make on the homes depends on the amount of pollution they create. Using the earlier example, people are willing to pay a rent of $2,000 a month to live alongside a pollution-free river but only $1,500 a month to live with the pollution created by producing 3 million gallons of paint per month.

The forgone rental income from homes alongside a polluted river is an opportunity cost of producing paint. The paint producers must now decide how to respond to this cost. There are two possible responses:

- Use an abatement technology
- Produce less and pollute less

Use an Abatement Technology An **abatement technology** is a production technology that reduces or prevents pollution. The catalytic converter in every U.S. car is an example of an abatement technology. Its widespread adoption (with lead-free gasoline) has dramatically reduced pollution from highway vehicles and helped to achieve the trends in U.S. air quality shown on p. 395.

Abatement technologies exist to eliminate or reduce pollution from electricity generation and many industrial processes, including the manufacture of paint.

Produce Less and Pollute Less An alternative to incurring the cost of using an abatement technology is to use the polluting technology but cut production, reduce pollution, and get a higher income from renting homes by the river. The decision turns on cost: Firms will choose the least-cost alternative.

Efficient Market Equilibrium Figure 17.3 illustrates the efficient market outcome. With property rights in place, the paint producers face the pollution costs or the abatement costs, whichever is lower. The *MSC* curve includes the cost of producing paint plus *either* the cost of abatement *or* the cost of pollution (forgone rent), whichever is lower. This curve, labeled $S = MC = MSC$, is now the market supply curve.

Market equilibrium occurs at a price of $1.25 per gallon and 2 million gallons of paint per month. This outcome is efficient.

If the forgone rent is less than the abatement cost, the factories will still create some pollution, but it will be the efficient quantity. If the abatement cost is lower than the forgone rent, the factories will stop polluting. But they will produce the efficient quantity because marginal cost includes the abatement cost.

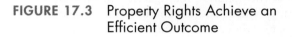

FIGURE 17.3   Property Rights Achieve an Efficient Outcome

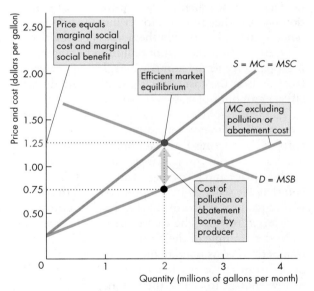

With property rights, the marginal cost curve that excludes pollution and abatement costs shows only part of the producers' marginal cost. The marginal cost of producing paint now includes the cost of pollution—the external cost—or the cost of abatement. So the market supply curve is $S = MC = MSC$. Market equilibrium occurs at a price of $1.25 per gallon and 2 million gallons of paint per month. Marginal social cost equals marginal social benefit, so the outcome is efficient.

MyEconLab animation

The Coase Theorem Does it matter whether the polluter or the victim of the pollution owns the resource that might be polluted? Until 1960, everyone thought that it did matter. But in 1960, Ronald Coase (see p. 415) had a remarkable insight that we now call the Coase theorem.

The **Coase theorem** is the proposition that if property rights exist and the transactions costs of enforcing them are low, then private transactions are efficient and it doesn't matter who has the property rights.

Application of the Coase Theorem Suppose that instead of the paint factories owning the homes, the residents own their homes and the river. Now the factories must pay a fee to the homeowners for the right to dump their waste. The greater the quantity of waste dumped into the river, the more the factories must pay. So again, the factories face the opportunity cost of the pollution they create. The quantity of paint produced and the amount of waste dumped are the same whoever owns the homes and the river. If the factories own them, they bear the cost of pollution because they receive a lower income from home rents. If the residents own the homes and the river, the factories bear the cost of pollution because they must pay a fee to the homeowners. In both cases, the factories bear the cost of their pollution and dump the efficient amount of waste into the river.

The Coase solution works only when transactions costs are low. **Transactions costs** are the opportunity costs of conducting a transaction. For example, when you buy a house, you pay an agent to help you find the best place and a lawyer to run checks that assure you that the seller owns the property and that after you've paid for it, the ownership has been properly transferred to you. These costs are transactions costs.

In the example of the homes alongside a river, the transactions costs that are incurred by a small number of paint factories and a few homeowners might be low enough to enable them to negotiate the deals that produce an efficient outcome. But in many situations, transactions costs are so high that it would be inefficient to incur them. In these situations, the Coase solution is not available.

Mandate Clean Technology

When property rights are too difficult to define and enforce, public choices are made. Regulation is a government's most likely response.

Most countries regulate what may be dumped in rivers and lakes and emitted into the atmosphere. The environmental resources of the United States are heavily regulated.

An example of environmental regulation is the Clean Air Act of 1970 and its later amendments, which give the Environmental Protection Agency (EPA) the authority to issue regulations that limit emissions and achieve defined air quality standards.

The EPA has issued thousands of regulations that require chemical plants, utilities, and steel mills to adopt best-practice pollution abatement technologies and limit their emissions of specified air pollutants. Other regulations have been issued that govern road vehicle emission limits, which must be met by the vehicle manufacturers.

In 2007, the Supreme Court ruled that the EPA has authority to regulate greenhouse gas emissions.

Although direct regulation can and has reduced emissions and improved air quality, economists are generally skeptical about this approach. Abatement is not always the least-cost solution. Also, government agencies are not well placed to find the cost-minimizing solution to a pollution problem. Individual firms seeking to minimize cost and maximize profit and responding to price signals are more likely to achieve an efficient outcome. We'll now examine these other approaches to pollution.

Tax or Cap and Price Pollution

Governments use two main methods of confronting polluters with the costs of their decisions:

- Taxes
- Cap-and-trade

Taxes Governments can use taxes as an incentive for producers to cut back the pollution they create. Taxes used in this way are called **Pigovian taxes**, in honor of Arthur Cecil Pigou, the British economist who first worked out this method of dealing with external costs during the 1920s.

By setting the tax equal to the marginal external cost (or marginal abatement cost if it is lower), firms can be made to behave in the same way as they would if they bore the cost of the externality directly.

To see how government actions can change the outcome in a market with external costs, let's return to the example of paint factories and the river. Assume that the government has assessed the marginal external cost of pollution accurately and imposes a tax on the factories that exactly equals this cost. The producers are now confronted with the social cost of their actions. The market equilibrium is one in which price equals marginal social cost—an efficient outcome.

Figure 17.4 illustrates the effects of a Pigovian tax on paint factory pollution. The curve $D = MSB$ is the market demand and the marginal social benefit curve. The curve MC is the marginal cost curve. The tax equals the marginal external cost of the pollution. We add this tax to the marginal private cost to find the market supply curve, the curve labeled $S = MC + tax = MSC$. This curve is the market supply curve because it tells us the quantity supplied at each price, given the factories' marginal cost and the tax they must pay. This curve is also the marginal social cost curve because the pollution tax has been set equal to the marginal external cost.

Demand and supply now determine the market equilibrium price at $1.25 per gallon and a quantity of 2 million gallons of paint a month. At this quantity of paint production, the marginal social cost is $1.25 and the marginal social benefit is $1.25, so the market outcome is efficient. The factories incur a marginal private cost of 75¢ per gallon and pay a pollution tax of 50¢ per gallon. The government collects tax revenue of $1 million per month.

Cap-and-Trade A cap is an upper limit. You've met the idea of a government imposing an upper limit before when you learned about production quotas (Chapter 6, p. 139), and import quotas (Chapter 7, p. 160). A cap is a quota—a pollution quota.

A government that uses this method must first estimate the efficient quantity of pollution and set the overall cap at that level.

Just like a production or import quota, a pollution quota or cap must somehow be allocated to individual firms (and possibly even households). In an efficient allocation of pollution quotas, each firm has the same marginal social cost. So to make an efficient allocation of the cap across firms, the government would need to know each firm's marginal production cost and marginal abatement cost.

A Pigovian tax achieves an efficient allocation of pollution across firms because each firm chooses how much to produce and pollute taking the tax into account, and produces the quantity at which marginal social cost equals price. Because all firms face the same market price, they also incur the same marginal social cost.

FIGURE 17.4 A Pollution Tax to Achieve an Efficient Outcome

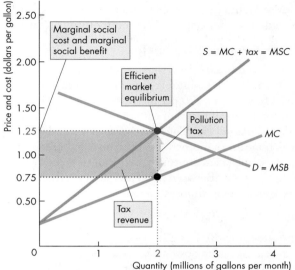

When the government imposes a pollution tax equal to the marginal external cost of pollution, the market supply curve becomes the marginal private cost curve, MC, plus the tax—the curve $S = MC + tax$. Market equilibrium occurs at a price of $1.25 per gallon and a quantity of 2 million gallons of paint per month. This equilibrium is efficient because marginal social cost equals marginal social benefit. The purple rectangle shows the government's tax revenue.

MyEconLab animation

The government solves the allocation problem by making an initial distribution of the cap across firms and allowing them to trade in a market for pollution permits. Firms that have a low marginal abatement cost sell permits and make big cuts in pollution. Firms that have a high marginal abatement cost buy permits and make smaller cuts or perhaps even no cuts in pollution.

The market in permits determines the equilibrium price of pollution and each firm, confronted with that price, maximizes profit by setting its marginal pollution cost or marginal abatement cost, whichever is lower, equal to the market price of a permit.

By confronting polluters with a price of pollution, trade in pollution permits can achieve the same efficient outcome as a Pigovian tax.

Economics in Action
Taxing Carbon Emissions

British Columbia, Australia, and the United Kingdom are making their carbon footprints smaller.

British Columbia's Carbon Tax

Introduced in 2008 at $10 per metric ton of carbon emitted, British Columbia's tax increased each year to its final rate of $30 per metric ton in 2012. The tax applies to all forms of carbon emission from coal, oil, and natural gas. The tax is revenue-neutral, which means that other taxes, personal and corporate income taxes, are cut by the amount raised by the carbon tax. Between 2008 and 2010, carbon emissions fell by almost 5 percent.

Australia's Carbon Tax

Introduced in 2012 at $23 per metric ton of carbon emitted, Australia's carbon tax is set to rise through 2015 and then become a market-determined price. Australia has exclued gasoline from the carbon tax, but the gasoline price in Australia is higher than in British Columbia because of a high excise tax.

U.K. Tax on Gasoline

The United Kingdom doesn't call its gasoline tax a carbon tax, but it has the same effect on drivers. The figure shows the U.K. price of gasoline compared with that in three other countries. The enormous differences arise almost entirely from tax differences.

An effect of these price differences is that cars in the United Kingdom get an average of 38 miles per gallon while in the United States, the average is 23 miles per gallon. A high gas tax cuts carbon emissions by inducing people to drive smaller cars and to drive less.

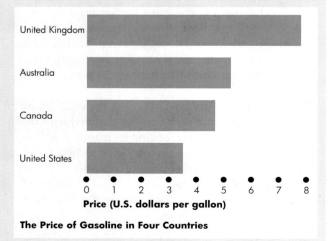

The Price of Gasoline in Four Countries

Coping with Global Externalities

The United States has made its own air cleaner by adopting the measures you've just seen. But one country, even the country with the world's largest economy that represents 20 percent of the value of global production, can't solve the problem of global warming and climate change alone. Coping with this problem requires public choices at a *global* level, which are much harder to make.

A lower CO_2 concentration in the world's atmosphere is a global *public good*. And like all public goods, it brings a *free-rider problem* (see Chapter 16, p. 375). Without a mechanism to compel participation in a global carbon reduction program, countries have an incentive to leave the task to others.

Not only is carbon reduction hampered by free riders but it also faces *carbon leakage*—a tendency for non-participants in carbon reduction to increase emissions.

The only major attempt at international coordination of carbon reduction is the Kyoto Protocol, signed in 1997 by only 37 countries, unratified by the United States, and renounced by Canada. This agreement ends in December 2012.

But some governments have set an example and introduced a carbon tax. Among them are the Canadian province of British Columbia and Australia. Also, some countries such as the United Kingdom have the equivalent of a partial carbon tax on gasoline (see *Economics in Action*).

At Issue on the next page summarizes two views about what needs to happen next to limit carbon emissions.

REVIEW QUIZ

1 What is the distinction between private cost and social cost?
2 How do external costs prevent a competitive market from allocating resources efficiently?
3 How can external costs be eliminated by assigning property rights?
4 How do taxes, pollution charges, and cap-and-trade work to reduce emissions?

You can work these questions in Study Plan 17.1 and get instant feedback.   MyEconLab

Your next task is to study common resources and the arrangements that can achieve their efficient use.

◆ AT **ISSUE**

Should We Be Doing More to Reduce Carbon Emissions?

Economists agree that tackling the global warming problem requires changes in the incentives that people face. The cost of carbon-emitting activities must rise and the cost of clean-energy technologies must fall.

Disagreement centers on *how* to change incentives. Should more countries set targets for cutting carbon emissions at a faster rate and introduce a carbon tax or emissions charges or cap-and-trade to cut emissions? Should clean energy research and development be subsidized?

Yes: *The Stern Review*

- Confronting emitters with a tax or price on carbon imposes low present costs for high future benefits.

- The cost of reducing greenhouse gas emissions to safe levels can be kept to 1 percent of global income each year.

- The future benefits are incomes at least 5 percent and possibly 20 percent higher than they will be with inaction every year forever.

- Climate change is a global problem that requires an international coordinated response.

- Unlike most taxes, which bring deadweight loss, a carbon tax eliminates (or reduces) deadweight loss.

- Strong, deliberate policy action is required to change the incentives that emitters face.

- Policy actions should include:

  1. Emissions limits and emissions trading
  2. Increased subsidies for energy research and development, including the development of low-cost clean technology for generating electricity
  3. Reduced deforestation and research into new drought and flood-resilient crop varieties

No: **The Copenhagen Consensus**

- Confronting emitters with a tax or price on carbon imposes high present costs and low future benefits.

- Unless the entire world signs onto an emissions reduction program, free riders will increase their emissions and carbon leakage will occur.

- A global emissions reduction program and carbon tax would lower living standards in the rich countries and slow the growth rate of living standards in developing countries.

- Technology is already advancing and the cost of cleaner energy is falling.

- Fracking technology has vastly expanded the natural gas deposits that can be profitably exploited and replacing coal with gas halves the carbon emissions from electricity generation.

- Free-market price signals will allocate resources to the development of new technologies that stop and eventually reverse the upward trend in greenhouse gasses.

Economist Nicholas Stern, principal author of *The Stern Review on the Economics of Climate Change*. Greenhouse gas emission is "the greatest market failure the world has ever seen."

To avoid the risk of catastrophic climate change, the upward CO_2 trend must be stopped.

Bjørn Lomborg, President of the Copenhagen Consensus and author of *The Skeptical Environmentalist*. "For little environmental benefit, we could end up sacrificing growth, jobs, and opportunities for the big majority, especially in the developing world."

◆ The Tragedy of the Commons

Overgrazing the pastures around a village in Middle Ages England, and overfishing the Southern Bluefin tuna, Pacific Yellowfin tuna, Atlantic cod, and Minke whales during the recent past are tragedies of the commons. Other current tragedies are the destruction of tropical rainforests in Africa and the Amazon basin of South America.

The **tragedy of the commons** is the overuse of a common resource that arises when its users have no incentive to conserve it and use it sustainably and efficiently.

To study the tragedy of the commons and its possible remedies, we'll focus on one of the recent and current tragedies – overfishing and depleting the stock of tuna. You're about to discover that there are two problems that give rise to the tragedy of the commons:

- Unsustainable use of a common resource
- Inefficient use of a common resource

Unsustainable Use of a Common Resource

Many common resources are renewable—they replenish themselves by the birth and growth of new members of the population. Fish, trees and the fertile soil are all examples of this type of resource. At any given time, there is a stock of the resource and a rate at which it is being used.

A common resource is being used *unsustainably* if its rate of use persistently decreases its stock. A common resource is being used *sustainably* if its rate of use is less than or equal to its rate of renewal so that the stock available either grows or remains constant.

Focusing on the example of fish, a species is being used unsustainably if the catch persistently decreases the stock and it is being used sustainably if the catch is less than or equal to the rate of renewal of the fish population.

The sustainable catch depends on the stock and in the way illustrated in Fig. 17.5 by the sustainable catch curve, *SCC*.

Along the *SCC* curve, with a small stock of fish the quantity of new fish born is also small, so the sustainable catch is small.

With a large stock of fish many fish are born but they must compete with each other for food, so only a few survive to reproduce and to grow large enough to catch, and again the sustainable catch is small.

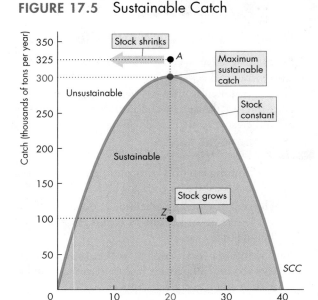

FIGURE 17.5   Sustainable Catch

As the fish stock increases (on the x-axis), the sustainable catch (on the y-axis) increases to a maximum. As the stock increases further, the fish must compete for food and the sustainable catch falls. If the catch exceeds the sustainable catch, such as at point A, the fish stock diminishes. If the catch is less than the sustainable catch, such as at point Z, the fish stock increases.

MyEconLab animation

Between a small and a large stock is a stock of fish that maximizes the sustainable catch. In Fig. 17.5, this stock is 20 million tons and the maximum sustainable catch is 300,000 tons per year.

The maximum sustainable catch arises from a balancing of the birth of new fish from the stock and the availability of food to sustain the fish population. If the quantity of fish caught is less than the sustainable catch, at a point such as Z, the fish stock grows. If the quantity caught equals the sustainable catch, at any point on the *SCC*, the fish stock remains constant and is available for future generations of fishers in the same quantity that is available today.

But if the quantity caught exceeds the sustainable catch, at a point such as A, the fish stock shrinks and, unchecked, eventually falls to zero.

You now understand the problem of using a common renewable natural resource sustainably. But another problem is using it efficiently.

Inefficient Use of a Common Resource

In an unregulated market, even if the catch is sustainable, it will be bigger than the efficient catch: over-fishing occurs. And most likely, the catch will not be sustainable. Why does overfishing occur? The answer is that fishers face only their own private cost and don't face the cost they impose on others—the external cost. The social cost of fishing combines the private cost and the external cost. Let's examine these costs.

Marginal Private Cost The *marginal private cost* of catching fish is the cost incurred by keeping a boat and crew at sea for long enough to increase the catch by one ton. Keeping a fishing boat at sea eventually runs into *diminishing marginal returns* (see Chapter 11, p. 251). As the crew gets tired, the storage facilities get overfull, and the boat's speed is cut to conserve fuel, the catch per hour decreases. The cost of keeping the boat at sea for an additional hour is constant, so the marginal cost of catching fish increases as the quantity caught increases.

You've just seen that the *principle of increasing marginal cost* applies to catching fish just as it applies to other production activities: Marginal private cost increases as the quantity of fish caught increases.

The marginal private cost of catching fish determines an indiviual fisher's supply of fish. A profit-maximizing fisher is willing to supply the quantity at which the market price of fish covers the marginal private cost. And the market supply is the sum of the quantities supplied by each individual fisher.

Marginal External Cost The marginal external cost of catching fish is the cost per additional ton that one fisher's production imposes on all other fishers. This additional cost arises because one fisher's catch decreases the remaining stock, which in turn decreases the renewal rate of the stock and makes it harder for others to find and catch fish.

Marginal external cost also increases as the quantity of fish caught increases. If the quantity of fish caught is so large that it drives the species to near extinction, the marginal external cost becomes infinitely large.

Marginal Social Cost The *marginal social cost* of catching fish is the marginal private cost plus the marginal external cost. Because both components of marginal social cost increase as the quantity caught increases, marginal social cost also increases with the quantity of fish caught.

Marginal Social Benefit and Demand The marginal social benefit from fish is the price that consumers are willing to pay for an additional pound of fish. Marginal social benefit decreases as the quantity of fish consumed increases, so the market demand curve, which is also the marginal social benefit curve, slopes downward.

Overfishing Equilibrium Figure 17.6 illustrates over-fishing and how it arises. The market demand curve for fish is the marginal social benefit curve, *MSB*. The market supply curve is the marginal *private* cost curve, *MC*. Market equilibrium occurs at the inter-section point of these two curves. The equilibrium quantity is 800,000 tons of fish per year and the equi-librium price is $10 per pound. At this market equi-librium, overfishing occurs.

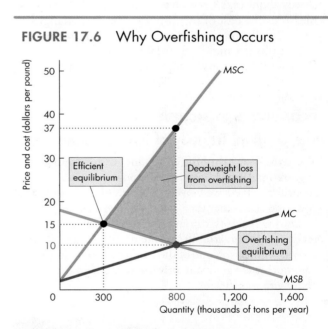

FIGURE 17.6 Why Overfishing Occurs

The market supply curve is the marginal private cost curve, *MC*. The market demand curve is the marginal social bene-fit curve, *MSB*. Market equilibrium occurs at a quantity of 800,000 tons per year and a price of $10 per pound.

The marginal social cost curve is *MSC* and at the mar-ket equilibrium there is overfishing—marginal social cost exceeds marginal social benefit.

The quantity at which *MSC* equals *MSB* is the efficient quantity, 300,000 tons per year. The area of the gray trian-gle measures the deadweight loss from overfishing.

Figure 17.6 illustrates why overfishing occurs. At the market equilibrium quantity, marginal social benefit (and willingness to pay) is $10 per pound, but the marginal social cost ($37 per pound) exceeds this amount. The marginal external cost is the cost of running down the fish stock.

Efficient Equilibrium What is the efficient use of a common resource? It is the use of the resource that makes the marginal social benefit from the resource equal to the marginal social cost of using it.

In Fig. 17.6, the efficient quantity of fish is 300,000 tons per year—the quantity that makes marginal social cost (on the *MSC* curve) equal to marginal social benefit (on the *MSB* curve). At this quantity, the marginal catch of each individual fisher costs society what people are willing to pay for it.

Deadweight Loss from Overfishing Deadweight loss measures the cost of overfishing. The gray triangle in Fig. 17.6 illustrates this loss. It is the marginal social cost minus the marginal social benefit from all the fish caught in excess of the efficient quantity.

Achieving an Efficient Outcome

Defining the conditions under which a common resource is used efficiently is easier than delivering those conditions. To use a common resource efficiently, it is necessary to design an incentive mechanism that confronts the users of the resource with the marginal *social* consequences of their actions. The same principles apply to common resources as those that you met earlier in this chapter when you studied the external cost of pollution.

The three main methods that might be used to achieve the efficient use of a common resource are

- Property rights
- Production quotas
- Individual transferable quotas (ITQs)

Property Rights A common resource that no one owns and that anyone is free to use contrasts with *private property*, which is a resource that *someone* owns and has an incentive to use in the way that

Economics in Action
The Original Tragedy of the Commons

The term "tragedy of the commons" comes from 14th-century England, where areas of rough grassland surrounding villages were overgrazed and the quantity of cows and sheep that they could feed kept falling.

During the 16th century, the price of wool increased, sheep farming became profitable, and sheep owners wanted to control the land they used. So the commons were gradually privatized and land use became more efficient.

One of Today's Tragedies of the Commons

Before 1970, Atlantic cod was abundant, despite the fact that it had been fished for many centuries and was a major food source for the first European settlers in North America. By 1620, there were more than 1,000 fishing boats catching large quantities of cod in the northwest Atlantic off the coast of what is now New England and Newfoundland. During these years, cod were huge fish, typically weighing in at more than 220 pounds and measuring 3–6 feet in length.

Most of the fishing during these years was done using lines and productivity was low. But low productivity limited the catch and enabled cod to be caught sustainably over hundreds of years.

The situation changed dramatically during the 1960s with the introduction of high-efficiency nets (called trawls, seines, and gill nets), sonar technology to find fish concentrations, and large ships with efficient processing and storage facilities. These technological advances brought soaring cod harvests. In less than a decade, cod landings increased from less than 300,000 tons a year to 800,000 tons.

This volume of cod could not be taken without a serious collapse in the remaining stock and by the 1980s it became vital to regulate cod fishing. But regulation was of limited success and stocks continued to

maximizes its value. One way of overcoming the tragedy of the commons is to convert a common resource to private property. By assigning private property rights to what was previously a common resource, its owner faces the same conditions as society faces. It doesn't matter who owns the resource. The users of the resource will be confronted with the full cost of using it because they either own it or pay a fee to the owner for permission to use it.

When private property rights over a resource are established and enforced, the *MSC* curve becomes the marginal *private* cost curve, and the use of the resource is efficient.

Figure 17.7 illustrates an efficient outcome with property rights. The supply curve $S = MC = MSC$ and the demand curve $D = MSB$ determine the equilibrium price and quantity. The price equals both marginal social benefit and marginal social cost and the quantity is efficient.

The private property solution to the tragedy of the commons *is* available in some cases. It was the solution to the original tragedy of the commons in

decline. In 1992, a total ban on cod fishing in the North Atlantic stabilized the population but at a very low level. Two decades of ban have enabled the species to repopulate, and it is now hoped that one day cod fishing will return but at a low and sustainable rate.

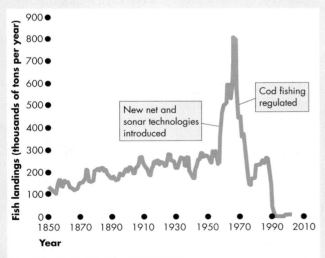

The Atlantic Cod Catch: 1850–2005

Source of data for graph: Millennum Ecosystem Assessment.
Source of information: Codfishes—Atlantic cod and its fishery,
http://science.jrank.org/

FIGURE 17.7   Property Rights Achieve an Efficient Outcome

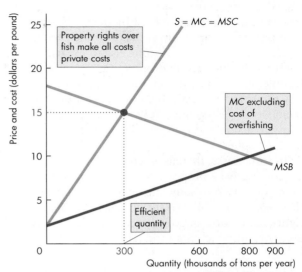

With private property rights, fishers pay the owner of the fish stock for permission to fish and they face the full social cost of their actions. The marginal cost includes the external cost, so the market supply curve is the marginal private cost and the marginal social cost curves, $S = MC = MSC$.

Market equilibrium occurs at $15 per pound and at that price, the quantity caught is 300,000 tons per year. At this quantity, marginal social cost equals marginal social benefit, and the quantity of fish caught is efficient.

The property rights convert the fish stock from a common resource to a private resource and it is used efficiently.

_____ MyEconLab animation _____

England's Middle Ages. It is also a solution that has been used to prevent overuse of the airwaves that carry cell-phone services. The right to use this space (called the frequency spectrum) has been auctioned by governments to the highest bidders. The owner of each part of the spectrum is the only one permitted to use it (or to license someone else to use it).

But assigning private property rights is not always feasible. It would be difficult to assign private property rights to the oceans because the cost of enforcing them would be too high. It would be even more costly to assign and protect private property rights to the atmosphere.

In some cases, there is an emotional objection to assigning private property rights. Critics of it have a moral objection to someone owning a resource that they regard as public. In the absence of property rights, some form of government intervention is used, one of which is a production quota.

Production Quota

A *production quota* is an upper limit to the quantity of a good that may be produced in a specified period. Each individual producer is allocated a quota.

You studied the effects of a production quota in Chapter 6 (pp. 139–140) and learned that a quota can drive a wedge between marginal social benefit and marginal social cost and create deadweight loss. In that earlier example, the market was efficient without a quota. But in the case of common resources, the market overuses the resource and produces an inefficient quantity. A production quota in this market brings a move toward a more efficient outcome.

Figure 17.8 shows a production quota that achieves an efficient outcome. The quota limits the catch (production) to 300,000 tons, the efficient quantity at which marginal social benefit, *MSB*, equals marginal social cost, *MSC*. If everyone sticks to their own quota, the outcome is efficient. But implementing a production quota has two problems.

First, it is in every fisher's self-interest to catch more fish than the quantity permitted under the quota. The reason is that price exceeds marginal private cost, so by catching more fish, a fisher gets a higher income. If enough fishers break the quota, overfishing and the tragedy of the commons remain.

Second, marginal cost is not, in general, the same for all producers—as we're assuming here. Efficiency requires that the quota be allocated to the producers with the lowest marginal cost. But bureaucrats who allocate quotas do not have information about the mar-

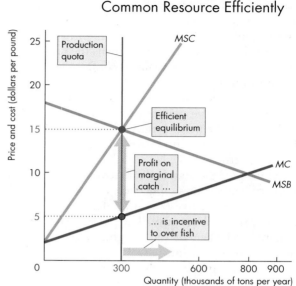

FIGURE 17.8   A Production Quota to Use a Common Resource Efficiently

A quota of 300,000 tons limits production to this quantity, raises the price to $15 per pound, and lowers marginal cost to $5 per pound. A fisher who cheats and produces more than the alloted quota increases his profit by $10 per pound. If all (or most) fishers cheat, production exceeds the quota and there is a return to overfishing.

MyEconLab animation

ginal cost of individual producers. Even if they tried to get this information, producers would have an incentive to lie about their costs so as to get a bigger quota.

So where producers are difficult, or very costly, to monitor or where marginal cost varies across producers, a production quota cannot achieve an efficient outcome.

Individual Transferable Quotas   Where producers are difficult to monitor or where marginal cost varies across producers, a more sophisticated quota system can be effective. It is an **individual transferable quota (ITQ)**, which is a production limit that is assigned to an individual who is then free to transfer (sell) the quota to someone else. A market in ITQs emerges and ITQs are traded at their market price. (Cap-and-trade to limit pollution is an ITQ for pollution).

The market price of an ITQ is the highest price that someone is willing to pay for one. That price is marginal social benefit minus marginal cost. The price of an ITQ will rise to this level because fishers who don't have a quota would be willing to pay this amount to get one.

A fisher with an ITQ could sell it for the market price, so by not selling the ITQ the fisher incurs an opportunity cost. The marginal cost of fishing, which now includes the opportunity cost of the ITQ, equals the marginal social benefit from the efficient quantity.

Figure 17.9 illustrates how ITQs work. Each fisher receives an allocation of ITQs and the total catch permitted by the ITQs is 300,000 tons per year. Fishers trade ITQs: Those with low marginal cost buy ITQs from those with high marginal cost and the market price of an ITQ settles at $10 per pound of fish. The marginal private cost of fishing now becomes the original marginal private cost, MC, plus the cost of the ITQ. The marginal private cost curve shifts upward from MC to MC + price of ITQ and each fisher is confronted with the marginal *social* cost of fishing. No one has an incentive to exceed the quota because to do so would send marginal cost above price and result in a loss on the marginal catch. The outcome is efficient.

FIGURE 17.9   ITQs to Use a Common Resource Efficiently

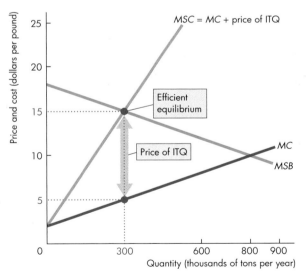

ITQs are issued on a scale that keeps output at the efficient level. The market price of an ITQ equals the marginal social benefit minus marginal cost. Because each user of the common resource faces the opportunity cost of using the resource, self-interest achieves the social interest.

—— MyEconLab animation ——

Economics in Action
ITQs Work

Iceland introduced the first ITQs in 1984 to conserve its stocks of lobster. In 1986, New Zealand and a bit later Australia introduced ITQs to conserve fish stocks in the South Pacific and Southern Oceans. The evidence from these countries suggests that ITQs work well.

ITQs help maintain fish stocks, but they also reduce the size of the fishing industry. This consequence of ITQs puts them against the self-interest of fishers. In all countries, the fishing industry opposes restrictions on its activities, but in Australia and New Zealand, the opposition is not strong enough to block ITQs.

In the United States the opposition has been harder to overcome and in 1996, Congress passed the Sustainable Fishing Act that put a moratorium on ITQs. This moratorium was lifted in 2004 and since then, ITQs have been applied to 28 fisheries from the Gulf of Alaska to the Gulf of Mexico. Economists have studied the effects of ITQs extensively and agree that they work. ITQs offer an effective tool for achieving an efficient use of the stock of ocean fish.

REVIEW QUIZ

1 What is the tragedy of the commons? Give two examples, including one from your state.
2 Describe the conditions under which a common resource is used efficiently.
3 Review three methods that might achieve the efficient use of a common resource and explain the obstacles to efficiency.

You can work these questions in Study Plan 17.2 and get instant feedback.   MyEconLab

◆ *Reading Between the Lines* on pp. 408–409 looks at how Australia's carbon tax is changing the incentives faced by airlines.

The next two chapters examine the third big question of economics: For whom are goods and services produced? We examine the markets for factors of production and discover how factor incomes and the distribution of income are determined.

A Carbon Tax at Work

Virgin Expands Its Green Fuel Options

The Australian
December 14, 2011

Virgin Australia has entered an agreement with another biofuel company to investigate the feasibility of producing aviation fuel using a proprietary Australian technology that turns biological waste into oil. The airline has signed a memorandum of understanding with Licella to look at a technology called catalytic hydrothermal reaction (CAT-HTR) which can turn biomass into refineryready biocrude in 30 minutes.

Licella and joint venture partner Norske Skog Australasia have the exclusive global licence to CAT-HTR technology, which can use biomass feedstocks such as forestry residue and agricultural waste to produce biocrude that can be dropped into an existing refinery.

The biocrude is expected to have life-cycle emissions that are 60 percent less than fossil fuels. They have already been working with New Zealand Trade and Enterprise and Air New Zealand on the technology and hope to build a large-scale production facility capable of producing 500,000 barrels a year in either Australia or New Zealand.

Both Virgin and Qantas are looking at several possibilities to source biofuel and Virgin already has an iron in the fire with a project to convert mallee tree biomass to biofuel.

Virgin Australia group executive of operations Sean Donohue said the Licella process was a global first that offered a cleaner, faster, and more cost effective way to process biomass.

"Virgin Australia's strategy on sustainable aviation fuel is to work with a range of stake holders across the industry—we know there will be no "magic bullet" and that creating financially viable biofuel will involve a range of feedstocks and processes," he said. . . .

ESSENCE OF THE STORY

- Two Australian airlines, Virgin Australia and Qantas, are investing in technology to convert biomass into aviation fuel.

- The technology, called CAT-HTR, uses biomass waste in existing refineries.

- The new fuel is expected to have carbon emissions that are 60 percent less than fossil fuel.

ECONOMIC ANALYSIS

- Why are two Australian airlines planning to change their fuel sources?

- Australia's carbon tax and a carbon tax imposed by the European Union are providing an incentive for airlines to make this switch.

- Figure 1 shows the market for air transport before a carbon tax is imposed.

- The market demand curve is D. The airlines use aviation fuel made from oil, the cost of which is part of their marginal cost, and the supply curve is $MC_{oil} = S_0$.

- The equilibrium price is $250 per trip and 20,000 passengers per month are carried.

- Carbon emissions bring a marginal external cost and the marginal social cost is MSC. Overproduction of air travel occurs and creates a deadweight loss.

- Figure 2 shows what happens when a carbon tax is imposed.

- The carbon tax is a Pigovian tax equal to marginal external cost of carbon emissions.

- The supply curve becomes $MC_{oil} + tax = S_1$, and the equilibrium quantity decreases to 15,000 passengers per month, the efficient quantity.

- But airlines now pay the carbon tax and their producer surplus shrinks.

- Constantly seeking ways to increase producer surplus, the airlines discover a new clean biofuel that can be produced using CAT-HTR technology.

- The cost of the biofuel is greater than that of oil-based fuel but less than the cost of oil-based fuel plus the carbon tax.

- The new fuel cuts carbon emissions and we will assume that it is exempt from the carbon tax. An airline that uses the fuel has a higher marginal cost but a lower tax bill.

- Figure 3 shows what happens when the airlines switch to the new fuel.

- The marginal cost curve becomes MC_{bio} and this curve becomes the new market supply curve, S_1.

- The equilibrium quantity is 19,000 passengers per month and the price is $255 per trip.

- Producer surplus increases to almost the level before the carbon tax was imposed.

- In this example, the carbon tax ends up generating no tax revenue but it reduces carbon emissions.

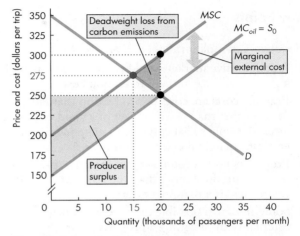

Figure 1 Before the Carbon Tax

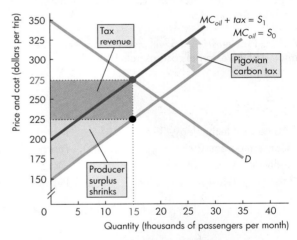

Figure 2 The Carbon Tax Shrinks Producer Surplus

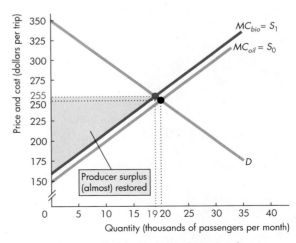

Figure 3 New Biofuel Restores Producer Surplus

409

SUMMARY

Key Points

Negative Externalities: Pollution (pp. 394–401)

- A competitive market would produce too much of a good that has external production costs.
- External costs are costs of production that fall on people other than the producer of a good or service. Marginal social cost equals marginal private cost plus marginal external cost.
- Producers take account only of marginal private cost and produce more than the efficient quantity when there is a marginal external cost.
- Sometimes it is possible to overcome a negative externality by assigning a property right.
- When property rights cannot be assigned, governments might overcome externalities by using taxes or cap-and-trade.

Working Problems 1 to 15 will give you a better understanding of the external costs of pollution.

The Tragedy of the Commons (pp. 402–407)

- Common resources create a problem that is called the tragedy of the commons—no one has a private incentive to conserve the resources and use them at an efficient rate.
- A common resource is used to the point at which the marginal private benefit equals the marginal cost.
- A common resource might be used efficiently by creating a private property right, setting a quota, or issuing individual transferable quotas.

Working Problems 16 to 22 will give you a better understanding of the tragedy of the commons.

Key Terms

Abatement technology, 397	Marginal external cost, 394	Property rights, 397
Coase theorem, 398	Marginal private cost, 394	Tragedy of the commons, 402
Individual transferable	Marginal social cost, 394	Transactions costs, 398
quota (ITQ), 406	Pigovian taxes, 398	

STUDY PLAN PROBLEMS AND APPLICATIONS

MyEconLab   You can work Problems 1 to 22 in MyEconLab Chapter 17 Study Plan and get instant feedback.

Negative Externalities: Pollution (Study Plan 17.1)

Use the following figure to work Problems 1 to 5.
The figure illustrates the market for cotton. Consider a small town surrounded by a large cotton farm. Suppose that the cotton grower sprays the plants with chemicals to control insects and the chemical waste flows into the river passing through the town. The marginal social cost of producing the cotton is double the marginal private cost.

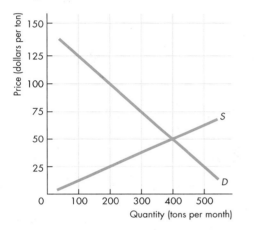

1. If no one owns the river and the town takes no action to control the waste, what is the quantity of cotton and the deadweight loss created?

2. a. Suppose that the town owns the river and makes the cotton grower pay the cost of pollution. How much cotton is produced and what does the farmer pay the town per ton of cotton produced?

   b. Suppose that the cotton grower owns the river and rents it to the town. How much cotton is produced and how is the rent paid by the town to the grower (per ton of cotton produced) influenced by cotton growing?

   c. Compare the quantities of cotton produced in parts (a) and (b) and explain the relationship between these quantities.

3. Suppose that no one owns the river and that the city introduces a pollution tax. What is the tax per ton of cotton produced that achieves an efficient outcome?

4. Compare the outcomes when property rights exist and when the pollution tax achieves the efficient amount of waste.

5. Suppose that no one owns the river and that the government issues two marketable pollution permits: one to the cotton grower and one to the city. Each permit allows the same amount of pollution of the river, and the total pollution created is the efficient amount.

   What is the quantity of cotton produced and what is the market price of a pollution permit? Who buys and who sells a permit?

Use the following news clip to work Problems 6 to 8.

As the developing countries turn to the mining industry to secure their economic futures, indigenous peoples and peasant farmers in Panama are trying to stop the development of a gold mine and the world's last major copper reserve, which would strip thousands of hectares of rainforest, deplete and contaminate water supplies, and displace communities that have lived in the area for centuries.

Source: npr, June 14, 2012

6. List the negative externalites mentioned in the news clip.

7. How would the outcome be changed if the indigenous communities had property rights over the resources?

8. Which of the public choice methods might be used to achieve an efficient allocation of resources in this situation?

Use the following news clip to work Problems 9 to 11.

Bag Revolution

Thin plastic shopping bags aren't biodegradable. Americans use about 110 billion bags a year. In 2007, San Francisco required large retailers to offer only compostable or reusable bags. In all, 28 U.S. cities have proposed laws restricting the use of plastic bags.

Source: *Fortune*, May 12, 2008

9. Describe the externality that arises from plastic bags. Draw a graph to illustrate how plastic bags create deadweight loss.

10. a. In July 2008, Seattle imposed a tax of 20¢ per bag from grocery, drug, and convenience stores. Explain the effects of Seattle's policy on the use of plastic bags.

    b. Draw a graph to illustrate Seattle's policy and show the change in the deadweight loss that arises from this policy.

11. In 2010, California banned plastic shopping bags. The Governor said that the ban "will be a great victory for our environment." Explain why a complete ban might be inefficient.

Use the following news clip to work Problems 12 to 14.

The Year in Medicine: Cell Phones

Talking on a hands-free cell phone while driving might seem safe, but people who used hands-free cell phones in simulation trials exhibited slower reaction times and took longer to hit the brakes than drivers who weren't otherwise distracted. Data from real-life driving tests show that cell-phone use rivals drowsy driving as a major cause of accidents.

Source: *Time*, December 4, 2006

12. Explain the external costs that arise from using a cell phone while driving and why the market for cell-phone service creates a deadweight loss.

13. Draw a graph to illustrate how a deadweight loss arises from the use of cell phones.

14. Explain how government intervention might improve the efficiency of cell-phone use.

15. **Pollution Rules Squeeze Strawberry Crop**

Last year, Ventura County farmers harvested nearly 12,000 acres of strawberries valued at more than $323 million. To comply with the federal Clean Air Act, growers must use 50 percent less pesticide. It is estimated that strawberry output will fall by 60 percent.

Source: *USA Today*, February 29, 2008

Explain how a limit on pesticide will change the efficiency of the strawberry industry. Would a cap-and-trade scheme be more efficient?

Tragedy of the Commons (Study Plan 17.2)

Use the following figure to work Problems 16 to 18. The figure shows the market for North Atlantic tuna.

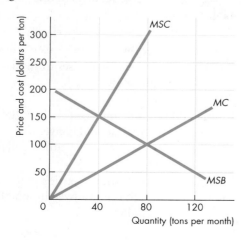

16. a. What is the quantity of tuna that fishers catch and the price of tuna? Is the tuna stock being used efficiently? Explain why or why not.

    b. What would be the price of tuna, if the stock of tuna is used efficiently?

17. With a quota of 40 tons a month for the tuna fishing industry, what is the equilibrium price of tuna and the quantity of tuna that fishers catch? Is the equilibrium an overfishing equilibrium?

18. If the government issues ITQs to individual fishers that limit the total catch to the efficient quantity, what is the market price of an ITQ?

19. **Whaling "Hurts Tourist Industry"**

The World Society for the Protection of Animals reported that whale watching is more economically significant and sustainable to people and communities than whaling. The global annual whale-watching industry is a $1.25 billion business enjoyed by over 10 million people in more than 90 countries.

Source: BBC, June 2, 2009

Describe the tradeoff facing communities in whaling areas. How might a whale-watching industry avoid the tragedy of the commons?

Use the following information to work Problems 20 to 22.

A natural spring runs under land owned by ten people. Each person has the right to sink a well and can take water from the spring at a constant marginal cost of $5 per gallon. The table sets out the external cost and the social benefit of water.

Quantity of water (gallons per day)	Marginal external cost (dollars per gallon)	Marginal social benefit (dollars per gallon)
10	1	10
20	2	9
30	3	8
40	4	7
50	5	6
60	6	5
70	7	4

20. On a graph mark the market equilibrium and show the efficient quantity of water taken.

21. If the government sets a quota on the total amount of water such that the spring is used efficiently, what would that quota be?

22. If the government issues ITQs that limit the total amount of water taken to the efficient quantity, what is the market price of an ITQ?

ADDITIONAL PROBLEMS AND APPLICATIONS

MyEconLab   You can work these problems in MyEconLab if assigned by your instructor.

Negative Externalities: Pollution

23. Betty and Anna work at the same office in Philadelphia. They both must attend a meeting in Pittsburgh, so they decide to drive to the meeting together. Betty is a cigarette smoker and her marginal benefit from smoking a package of cigarettes a day is $40. Cigarettes are $6 a pack. Anna dislikes cigarette smoke, and her marginal benefit from a smoke-free environment is $50 a day. What is the outcome if

    a. Betty drives her car with Anna as a passenger?

    b. Anna drives her car with Betty as a passenger?

Use the following information and the figure, which illustrates the market for a pesticide with no government intervention, to work Problems 24 to 27.

When factories produce pesticide, they also create waste, which they dump into a lake on the outskirts of the town. The marginal external cost of the waste is equal to the marginal private cost of producing the pesticide (that is, the marginal social cost of producing the pesticide is double the marginal private cost).

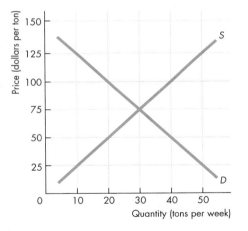

24. What is the quantity of pesticide produced if no one owns the lake and what is the efficient quantity of pesticide?

25. If the residents of the town own the lake, what is the quantity of pesticide produced and how much do residents of the town charge the factories to dump waste?

26. If the pesticide factories own the lake, how much pesticide is produced?

27. If no one owns the lake and the government levies a pollution tax, what is the tax that achieves the efficient outcome?

Use the following table to work Problems 28 to 30. The first two columns of the table show the demand schedule for electricity from a coal burning utility; the second and third columns show the utility's cost of producing electricity. The marginal external cost of the pollution created equals the marginal cost.

Price (cents per kilowatt)	Quantity (kilowatts per day)	Marginal cost (cents per kilowatt)
4	500	10
8	400	8
12	300	6
16	200	4
20	100	2

28. With no government action to control pollution, what is the quantity of electricity produced, the price of electricity, and the marginal external cost of the pollution generated?

29. With no government action to control pollution, what is the marginal social cost of the electricity generated and the deadweight loss created?

30. If the government levies a pollution tax such that the utility produces the efficient quantity, what is the price of electricity, the tax levied, and the government's tax revenue per day?

Use the following news clip to work Problems 31 to 33.

America's Most Polluted Lake Finally Comes Clean

Onondaga Lake in Syracuse, N.Y., is called America's most polluted lake as raw sewage and industrial dumping made fishing and swimming impossible. Using environmental laws and the courts, industrial dumping has stopped, Onondaga County has agreed to upgrade its sewage-treatment plant, suck up toxic mud containing mercury, and build an underground barrier wall to keep contaminated groundwater from seeping into the lake. Fishing and swimming will return.

Source: npr, July 31, 2012

31. Describe the externalities at Onondaga Lake and draw a graph to illustrate the inefficiency arising from them.

32. Which of the alternative methods for achieving an efficient use of resources in the face of pollution were used to clean up Onondaga Lake?

33. Draw a graph to explain and illustrate the situation at Onondaga Lake when allocative efficiency is achieved.

34. Shale Gas Boom Helps Slash U.S. Emissions

U.S. carbon emissions fell in the past year as coal generation decreased by 19 percent and gas generation increased by 38 percent. A gas-fired plant produces half the CO_2 emissions of a coal-fired one, but the use of shale gas is the subject of a heated environmental debate in which critics allege that it contaminated groundwater.

Source: *Financial Times*, May 23, 2012

How does the switch from coal generation to gas generation change the external cost of and deadweight loss from generating electricity? Draw a graph to illustrate your answer.

The Tragedy of the Commons

35. If hikers and other visitors were required to pay a fee to use the Appalachian Trail,
    a. Would the use of this common resource be more efficient?
    b. Would it be even more efficient if the most popular spots along the trail had the highest prices?
    c. Why do you think we don't see more market solutions to the tragedy of the commons?

Use the following figure to work Problems 36 to 38.

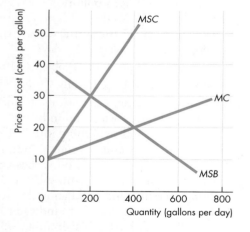

A spring runs under a village. Everyone can sink a well on her or his land and take water from the spring. The figure shows the marginal social benefit from and the marginal cost of taking water.

36. What is the quantity of water taken and what is the private cost of the water taken?

37. What is the efficient quantity of water taken and the marginal social cost at the efficient quantity?

38. If the village council sets a quota on the total amount of water such that the spring is used effi-

ciently, what would be the quota and the market value of the water taken per day?

39. Polar Ice Cap Shrinks Further and Thins

With the warming of the planet, the polar ice cap is shrinking and the Arctic Sea is expanding. As the ice cap shrinks further, more and more underwater mineral resources will become accessible. Many countries are staking out territorial claims to parts of the polar region.

Source: *The Wall Street Journal*, April 7, 2009

Explain how ownership of these mineral resources will influence the amount of damage done to the Arctic Sea and its wildlife.

Economics in the News

40. After you have studied *Reading Between the Lines* on pp. 408–409, answer the following questions:
    a. What are the marginal private costs of and marginal private benefits from using biofuel rather than fuel made from oil?
    b. What are the marginal social costs of and marginal social benefits from using biofuel rather than fuel made from oil?
    c. How does a carbon tax help to achieve an efficient quantity of air transport?
    d. Why might a carbon tax end up generating almost no tax revenue?

41. Where the Tuna Roam

To the first settlers, the Great Plains posed the same problem as the oceans today: a vast, open area where there seemed to be no way to protect animals. But animals thrived once the settlers divvied up the land and devised ways to protect their livestock. Today, the oceans are much like an open range. Fishermen catch as much as they can this year, even if they are overfishing. They figure any fish they don't take for themselves will just be taken by someone else.

Source: *The New York Times*, November 4, 2006

    a. What are the similarities between the problems faced by the earliest settlers in the West and today's fishers?
    b. Can the tragedy of the commons in the oceans be eliminated in the same manner used by the early settlers on the plains?
    c. How can ITQs change the short-term outlook of fishers to a long-term outlook?

We, the People, …

PART FIVE

Thomas Jefferson knew that creating a government of the people, by the people, and for the people was a huge enterprise and one that could easily go wrong. Creating a constitution that made despotic and tyrannical rule impossible was relatively easy. The founding fathers did their best to practice sound economics. They designed a sophisticated system of incentives—of carrots and sticks—to make the government responsive to public opinion and to limit the ability of individual self-interests to gain at the expense of the majority. But they were not able to create a constitution that effectively blocks the ability of special interest groups to capture the consumer and producer surpluses that result from specialization and exchange.

We have created a system of government to deal with four market failures: (1) monopoly; (2) externalities; (3) public goods; and (4) common resources.

Government might help cope with these market failures, but as the founding fathers knew well, government does not eliminate the pursuit of self-interest. Voters, politicians, and bureaucrats pursue their self-interest, sometimes at the expense of the social interest, and instead of market failure, we get government failure.

Many economists have thought long and hard about the problems discussed in this part. But none has had as profound an effect on our ideas in this area as Ronald Coase.

Ronald Coase *(1910–), was born in England and educated at the London School of Economics, where he was deeply influenced by his teacher, Arnold Plant, and by the issues of his youth: communist central planning versus free markets.*

Professor Coase has lived in the United States since 1951. He first visited America as a 20-year-old on a traveling scholarship during the depths of the Great Depression. It was on this visit, and before he had completed his bachelor's degree, that he conceived the ideas that 60 years later were to earn him the 1991 Nobel Prize for Economic Science.

Ronald Coase discovered and clarified the significance of transactions costs and property rights for the functioning of the economy. He has revolutionized the way we think about property rights and externalities and has opened up the growing field of law and economics.

"The question to be decided is: Is the value of fish lost greater or less than the value of the product which contamination of the stream makes possible?"

RONALD H. COASE
The Problem of Social Cost

CAROLINE M. HOXBY is the Allie S. Freed Professor of Economics at Harvard University. Born in Cleveland, Ohio, she was an undergraduate at Harvard and a graduate student at Oxford and MIT.

Professor Hoxby is a leading student of the economics of education. She has written many articles on this topic and has published books entitled *The Economics of School Choice* and *College Choices* (both University of Chicago Press, 2003 and 2004, respectively). She is Program Director of the Economics of Education Program at the National Bureau of Economic Research, serves on several other national boards that study education issues, and has advised or provided testimony to several state legislatures and the United States Congress.

Michael Parkin talked with Caroline Hoxby about her work and the progress that economists have made in understanding how the financing and the provision of education influence the quality of education and the equality of access to it.

Why did you decide to become an economist?

I've wanted to be an economist from about the age of 13. That was when I took my first class in economics (an interesting story in itself) and discovered that all of the thoughts swimming around in my head belonged to a "science" and there was an entire body of people who understood this science—a lot better than I did, anyway. I can still recall reading *The Wealth of Nations* for the first time; it was a revelation.

What drew you to study the economics of education?

We all care about education, perhaps because it is the key means by which opportunity is (or should be) extended to all in the United States. Also, nearly everyone now acknowledges that highly developed countries like the United States rely increasingly on education as the engine of economic growth. Thus, one reason I was drawn to education is its importance. However, what primarily drew me was that education issues were so clearly begging for economic analysis and that there was so little of it. I try hard to understand educational institutions and problems, but I insist on bringing economic logic to bear on educational issues.

What can economists say about the alternative methods of financing education? Is there a voucher solution that could work?

There is definitely a voucher solution that could work because vouchers are inherently an extremely flexible policy. ...

> Economists should say to policy makers: "Tell me your goals; I'll design you a voucher."

Any well-designed voucher system will give schools an incentive to compete. However, when designing vouchers, we can also build in remedies for a variety of educational problems. Vouchers can be used to ensure that disabled children get the funding they need and the program choices they need.

Compared to current school finance programs, vouchers can do a better job of ensuring that low-income families have sufficient funds to invest in the child's education. Well-designed vouchers can encourage schools to make their student bodies socio-economically diverse.

Economists should say to policy makers: "Tell me your goals; I'll design you a voucher."

*Read the full interview with Caroline Hoxby in MyEconLab.

18

MARKETS FOR FACTORS OF PRODUCTION

After studying this chapter, you will be able to:

◆ Describe the anatomy of factor markets

◆ Explain how the value of marginal product determines the demand for a factor of production

◆ Explain how wage rates and employment are determined and how labor unions influence labor markets

◆ Explain how capital and land rental rates and natural resource prices are determined

Wage rates are lower in China than in Europe and the United States, but wage rates in China are rising. Why? What determines the wage rates that people earn? Why do some jobs pay high wage rates and others low wage rates? And why is the number of jobs in some industries expanding and in other industries shrinking?

In this chapter, we study labor markets along with the markets for capital and natural resources. In *Reading Between the Lines* at the end of the chapter we look at some trends in the market for labor in China.

The Anatomy of Factor Markets

The four factors of production are

- Labor
- Capital
- Land (natural resources)
- Entrepreneurship

Let's take a brief look at the anatomy of the markets in which these factors of production are traded.

Markets for Labor Services

Labor services are the physical and mental work effort that people supply to produce goods and services. A labor market is a collection of people and firms who trade labor services. The price of labor services is the wage rate.

Some labor services are traded day by day. These services are called *casual labor*. People who pick fruit and vegetables often just show up at a farm and take whatever work is available that day. But most labor services are traded on a job contract.

Most labor markets have many buyers and many sellers and are competitive. In these markets, supply and demand determine the wage rate and quantity of labor employed. Jobs expand when demand increases and jobs disappear when demand decreases.

In some labor markets, a labor union operates like a monopoly on the supply-side of the labor market. In this type of labor market, a bargaining process between the union and the employer determines the wage rate.

We'll study both competitive labor markets and labor unions in this chapter.

Markets for Capital Services

Capital consists of the tools, instruments, machines, buildings, and other constructions that have been produced in the past and that businesses now use to produce goods and services. These physical objects are themselves goods—capital goods. Capital goods are traded in goods markets, just as bottled water and toothpaste are. The price of a dump truck, a capital good, is determined by supply and demand in the market for dump trucks. This market is not a market for capital services.

A market for *capital services* is a *rental market*—a market in which the services of capital are hired.

An example of a market for capital services is the vehicle rental market in which Avis, Budget, Hertz,

U-Haul, and many other firms offer automobiles and trucks for hire. The price in a capital services market is a *rental rate*.

Most capital services are not traded in a market. Instead, a firm buys capital and uses it itself. The services of the capital that a firm owns and operates have an implicit price that arises from depreciation and interest costs (see Chapter 10, pp. 224–225). You can think of this price as the implicit rental rate of capital. Firms that buy capital and use it themselves are *implicitly* renting the capital to themselves.

Markets for Land Services and Natural Resources

Land consists of all the gifts of nature—natural resources. The market for land as a factor of production is the market for the *services of land*—the use of land. The price of the services of land is a rental rate.

Most natural resources, such as farm land, can be used repeatedly. But a few natural resources are non-renewable. **Nonrenewable natural resources** are resources that can be used only once. Examples are oil, natural gas, and coal. The prices of nonrenewable natural resources are determined in global *commodity markets* and are called *commodity prices*.

Entrepreneurship

Entrepreneurial services are not traded in markets. Entrepreneurs receive the profit or bear the loss that results from their business decisions.

REVIEW QUIZ

1 What are the factors of production and their prices?
2 What is the distinction between capital and the services of capital?
3 What is the distinction between the price of capital equipment and the rental rate of capital?

You can work these questions in Study Plan 18.1 and get instant feedback.   MyEconLab

---

The rest of this chapter explores the influences on the demand and supply of factors of production. We begin by studying the demand for a factor of production.

The Demand for a Factor of Production

The demand for a factor of production is a **derived demand**—it is derived from the demand for the goods and services that the labor produces. You've seen, in Chapters 10 through 15, how a firm determines its profit-maximizing output. The quantities of factors of production demanded are a consequence of the firm's output decision. A firm hires the quantities of factors of production that produce the firm's profit-maximizing output.

To decide the quantity of a factor of production to hire, a firm compares the cost of hiring an additional unit of the factor with its value to the firm. The cost of hiring an additional unit of a factor of production is the factor price. The value to the firm of hiring one more unit of a factor of production is called the factor's **value of marginal product**. We calculate the value of marginal product as the price of a unit of output multiplied by the marginal product of the factor of production.

To study the demand for a factor of production, we'll use labor as the example. But what you learn here about the demand for labor applies to the demand for all factors of production.

Value of Marginal Product

Table 18.1 shows you how to calculate the value of the marginal product of labor at Angelo's Bakery.

The first two columns show Angelo's total product schedule—the number of loaves per hour that each quantity of labor can produce. The third column shows the marginal product of labor—the change in total product that results from a one-unit increase in the quantity of labor employed. (See Chapter 11, pp. 249–252 for a refresher on product schedules.)

Angelo can sell bread at the going market price of $2 a loaf. Given this information, we can calculate the value of marginal product (fourth column). It equals price multiplied by marginal product. For example, the marginal product of hiring the second worker is 6 loaves. Each loaf sold brings in $2, so the value of the marginal product of the second worker is $12 (6 loaves at $2 each).

A Firm's Demand for Labor

The value of the marginal product of labor tells us what an additional worker is worth to a firm. It tells us the revenue that the firm earns by hiring one more worker. The wage rate tells us what an additional worker costs a firm.

The value of the marginal product of labor and the wage rate together determine the quantity of labor demanded by a firm. Because the value of marginal product decreases as the quantity of labor employed increases, there is a simple rule for maximizing profit: Hire the quantity of labor at which the value of marginal product equals the wage rate.

If the value of marginal product of labor exceeds the wage rate, a firm can increase its profit by hiring

---

TABLE 18.1   Value of Marginal Product at Angelo's Bakery

	Quantity of labor (L) (workers)	Total product (TP) (loaves per hour)	Marginal product ($MP = \Delta TP / \Delta L$) (loaves per worker)	Value of marginal product ($VMP = MP \times P$) (dollars per worker)
A	0	0		
			7	14
B	1	7		
			6	12
C	2	13		
			5	10
D	3	18		
			4	8
E	4	22		
			3	6
F	5	25		

The value of the marginal product of labor equals the price of the product multiplied by marginal product of labor. If Angelo's hires 2 workers, the marginal product of the second worker is 6 loaves (in the third column). The price of a loaf is $2, so the value of the marginal product of the second worker is $2 a loaf multiplied by 6 loaves, which is $12 (in fourth column).

one more worker. If the wage rate exceeds the value of marginal product of labor, a firm can increase its profit by firing one worker. But if the wage rate equals the value of the marginal product of labor, the firm cannot increase its profit by changing the number of workers it employs. The firm is making the maximum possible profit. So

> The quantity of labor demanded by a firm is the quantity at which the value of the marginal product of labor equals the wage rate.

A Firm's Demand for Labor Curve

A firm's demand for labor curve is derived from its value of marginal product curve. Figure 18.1 shows these two curves. Figure 18.1(a) shows the value of marginal product curve at Angelo's Bakery. The blue bars graph the numbers in Table 18.1. The curve labeled *VMP* is Angelo's value of marginal product curve.

If the wage rate falls and other things remain the same, a firm hires more workers. Figure 18.1(b) shows Angelo's demand for labor curve.

Suppose the wage rate is $10 an hour. You can see in Fig.18.1(a) that if Angelo hires 2 workers, the value of the marginal product of labor is $12 an hour. At a wage rate of $10 an hour, Angelo makes a profit of $2 an hour on the second worker. If Angelo hires a third worker, the value of the marginal product of that worker is $10 an hour. So on this third worker, Angelo breaks even.

If Angelo hired 4 workers, his profit would fall. The fourth worker generates a value of marginal product of only $8 an hour but costs $10 an hour, so Angelo does not hire the fourth worker. When the wage rate is $10 an hour, the quantity of labor demanded by Angelo is 3 workers.

Figure 18.1(b) shows Angelo's demand for labor curve, *D*. At $10 an hour, the quantity of labor demanded by Angelo is 3 workers. If the wage rate increased to $12 an hour, Angelo would decrease the quantity of labor demanded to 2 workers. If the wage rate decreased to $8 an hour, Angelo would increase the quantity of labor demanded to 4 workers.

A change in the wage rate brings a change in the quantity of labor demanded and a movement along the demand for labor curve.

A change in any other influence on a firm's labor-hiring plans changes the demand for labor and shifts the demand for labor curve.

FIGURE 18.1   The Demand for Labor at Angelo's Bakery

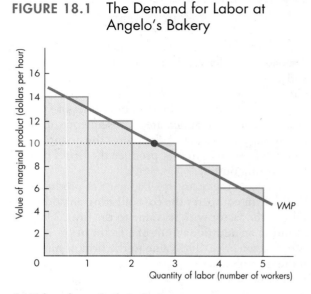

(a) Value of marginal product

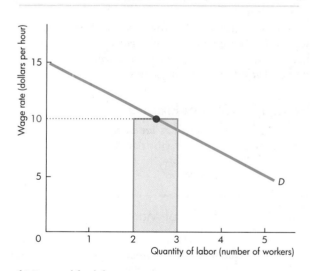

(b) Demand for labor

Angelo's Bakery can sell any quantity of bread at $2 a loaf. The blue bars in part (a) represent the firm's value of marginal product of labor (based on Table 18.1). The line labeled *VMP* is the firm's value of marginal product curve. Part (b) shows Angelo's demand for labor curve. Angelo hires the quantity of labor that makes the value of marginal product equal to the wage rate. The demand for labor curve slopes downward because the value of marginal product diminishes as the quantity of labor employed increases.

———————————— MyEconLab animation ————

Changes in a Firm's Demand for Labor

A firm's demand for labor depends on

- The price of the firm's output
- The prices of other factors of production
- Technology

The Price of the Firm's Output The higher the price of a firm's output, the greater is the firm's demand for labor. The price of output affects the demand for labor through its influence on the value of marginal product of labor. A higher price for the firm's output increases the value of the marginal product of labor. A change in the price of a firm's output leads to a shift in the firm's demand for labor curve. If the price of the firm's output increases, the demand for labor increases and the demand for labor curve shifts rightward.

For example, if the price of bread increased to $3 a loaf, the value of the marginal product of Angelo's fourth worker would increase from $8 an hour to $12 an hour. At a wage rate of $10 an hour, Angelo would now hire 4 workers instead of 3.

The Prices of Other Factors of Production If the price of using capital decreases relative to the wage rate, a firm substitutes capital for labor and increases the quantity of capital it uses. Usually, the demand for labor will decrease when the price of using capital falls. For example, if the price of a bread-making machine falls, Angelo might decide to install one machine and lay off a worker. But the demand for labor could increase if the lower price of capital led to a sufficiently large increase in the scale of production. For example, with cheaper machines available, Angelo might install a machine and hire more labor to operate it. This type of factor substitution occurs in the long run when the firm can change the size of its plant.

Technology New technologies decrease the demand for some types of labor and increase the demand for other types. For example, if a new automated bread-making machine becomes available, Angelo might install one of these machines and fire most of his workforce—a decrease in the demand for bakery workers. But the firms that manufacture and service automated bread-making machines hire more labor, so there is an increase in the demand for this type of labor. An event similar to this one occurred during the 1990s when the introduction of electronic

telephone exchanges decreased the demand for telephone operators and increased the demand for computer programmers and electronics engineers.

Table 18.2 summarizes the influences on a firm's demand for labor.

TABLE 18.2   A Firm's Demand for Labor

The Law of Demand

(Movements along the demand curve for labor)

The quantity of labor demanded by a firm

Decreases if:	Increases if:
■ The wage rate increases	■ The wage rate decreases

Changes in Demand

(Shifts in the demand curve for labor)

A firm's demand for labor

Decreases if:	Increases if:
■ The price of the firm's output decreases	■ The price of the firm's output increases
■ The price of a substitute for labor falls	■ The price of a substitute for labor rises
■ The price of a complement of labor rises	■ The price of a complement of labor falls
■ A new technology or new capital decreases the marginal product of labor	■ A new technology or new capital increases the marginal product of labor

---

◢ REVIEW QUIZ

1. What is the value of marginal product of labor?
2. What is the relationship between the value of marginal product of labor and the marginal product of labor?
3. How is the demand for labor derived from the value of marginal product of labor?
4. What are the influences on the demand for labor?

You can work these questions in Study Plan 18.2 and get instant feedback.   **MyEconLab**

◢ Labor Markets

Labor services are traded in many different labor markets. Examples are markets for bakery workers, van drivers, crane operators, computer support specialists, air traffic controllers, surgeons, and economists. Some of these markets, such as the market for bakery workers, are local. They operate in a given urban area. Some labor markets, such as the market for air traffic controllers, are national. Firms and workers search across the nation for the right match of worker and job. And some labor markets are global, such as the market for superstar hockey, basketball, and soccer players.

We'll look at a local market for bakery workers as an example. First, we'll look at a *competitive* labor market. Then, we'll see how monopoly elements can influence a labor market.

A Competitive Labor Market

A competitive labor market is one in which many firms demand labor and many households supply labor.

Market Demand for Labor Earlier in the chapter, you saw how an individual firm decides how much labor to hire. The market demand for labor is derived from the demand for labor by individual firms. We determine the market demand for labor by adding together the quantities of labor demanded by all the firms in the market at each wage rate. (The market demand for a good or service is derived in a similar way—see Chapter 5, pp. 108–109.)

Because each firm's demand for labor curve slopes downward, the market demand for labor curve also slopes downward.

The Market Supply of Labor The market supply of labor is derived from the supply of labor decisions made by individual households.

Individual's Labor Supply Decision People can allocate their time to two broad activities: labor supply and leisure. (Leisure is a catch-all term. It includes all activities other than supplying labor.) For most people, leisure is more fun than work so to induce them to work they must be offered a wage.

Think about the labor supply decision of Jill, one of the workers at Angelo's Bakery. Let's see how the wage rate influences the quantity of labor she is willing to supply.

Reservation Wage Rate Jill enjoys her leisure time, and she would be pleased if she didn't have to spend her time working at Angelo's Bakery. But Jill wants to earn an income, and as long as she can earn a wage rate of at least $5 an hour, she's willing to work. This wage is called her *reservation wage*. At any wage rate above her reservation wage, Jill supplies some labor.

The wage rate at Angelo's is $10 an hour, and at that wage rate, Jill chooses to work 30 hours a week. At a wage rate of $10 an hour, Jill regards this use of her time as the best available. Figure 18.2 illustrates.

Backward-Bending Labor Supply Curve If Jill were offered a wage rate between $5 and $10 an hour, she would want to work fewer hours. If she were offered a wage rate above $10 an hour, she would want to work more hours, but only up to a point. If Jill could

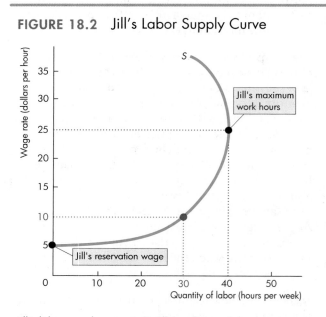

FIGURE 18.2   Jill's Labor Supply Curve

Jill's labor supply curve is S. Jill supplies no labor at wage rates below her reservation wage of $5 an hour. As the wage rate rises above $5 an hour, the quantity of labor that Jill supplies increases to a maximum of 40 hours a week at a wage rate of $25 an hour. As the wage rate rises above $25 an hour, Jill supplies a decreasing quantity of labor: her labor supply curve bends backward. The income effect on the demand for leisure dominates the substitution effect.

MyEconLab animation

earn $25 an hour, she would be willing to work 40 hours a week (and earn $1,000 a week). But at a wage rate above $25 an hour, with the goods and services that Jill can buy for $1,000, her priority would be a bit more leisure time. So if the wage rate increased above $25 an hour, Jill would cut back on her work hours and take more leisure. Jill's labor supply curve eventually bends backward.

Jill's labor supply decisions are influenced by a substitution effect and an income effect.

Substitution Effect At wage rates below $25 an hour, the higher the wage rate Jill is offered, the greater is the quantity of labor that she supplies. Jill's wage rate is her *opportunity cost of leisure*. If she quits work an hour early to catch a movie, the cost of that extra hour of leisure is the wage rate that Jill forgoes. The higher the wage rate, the less willing Jill is to forgo the income and take the extra leisure time. This tendency for a higher wage rate to induce Jill to work longer hours is a *substitution effect*.

Income Effect The higher Jill's wage rate, the higher is her income. A higher income, other things remaining the same, induces Jill to increase her demand for most goods and services. Leisure is one of those goods. Because an increase in income creates an increase in the demand for leisure, it also creates a decrease in the quantity of labor supplied.

Market Supply Curve The market supply curve shows the quantity of labor supplied by all households in a particular job market. It is found by adding together the quantities of labor supplied by all households to a given job market at each wage rate, so the greater the number of households (the greater is the working-age population), the greater is the market supply of labor.

Despite the fact that an individual's labor supply curve eventually bends backward, the market supply curve of labor slopes upward. The higher the wage rate for bakery workers, the greater is the quantity of bakery workers supplied in that labor market.

One reason why the market supply curve doesn't bend backward is that different households have different reservation wage rates and different wage rates at which their labor supply curves bend backward.

Also, along a supply curve in a particular job market, the wage rates available in other job markets remain the same. For example, along the supply curve of bakers, the wage rates of salespeople and all other types of labor are constant.

Let's now look at labor market equilibrium.

Competitive Labor Market Equilibrium Labor market equilibrium determines the wage rate and employment. In Fig. 18.3, the market demand curve for bakery workers is D and the market supply curve of bakery workers is S. The equilibrium wage rate is $10 an hour, and the equilibrium quantity is 300 bakery workers. If the wage rate exceeded $10 an hour, there would be a surplus of bakery workers. More people would be looking for jobs in bakeries than firms were willing to hire. In such a situation, the wage rate would fall as firms found it easy to hire people at a lower wage rate. If the wage rate were less than $10 an hour, there would be a shortage of bakery workers. Firms would not be able to fill all the positions they had available. In this situation, the wage rate would rise as firms found it necessary to offer higher wages to attract labor. Only at a wage rate of $10 an hour are there no forces operating to change the wage rate.

FIGURE 18.3   The Market for Bakery Workers

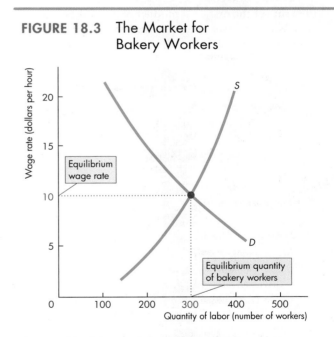

A competitive labor market coordinates firms' and households' plans. The market is in equilibrium—the quantity of labor demanded equals the quantity supplied at a wage rate of $10 an hour when 300 workers are employed. If the wage rate exceeds $10 an hour, the quantity supplied exceeds the quantity demanded and the wage rate will fall. If the wage rate is below $10 an hour, the quantity demanded exceeds the quantity supplied and the wage rate will rise.

MyEconLab animation

Economics in Action
Wage Rates in the United States

In 2011, the average wage rate in the United States was a bit less than $20 an hour. The figure shows the *average hourly wage rates* for twenty jobs selected from the more than 700 jobs for which the Bureau of Labor Statistics reports wage rate data.

You can see that a general internist, on average, earns 10 times as much per hour as a fast-food worker and more than twice as much as an economist. Remember that these numbers are averages. Some doctors earn much more and some earn less than the average general internist.

Many more occupations earn a wage rate below the national average than above it. Most of the occupations that earn more than the national average require a college degree and postgraduate training.

Earning differences are explained by differences in the value of the marginal product of the skills in the various occupations and in market power.

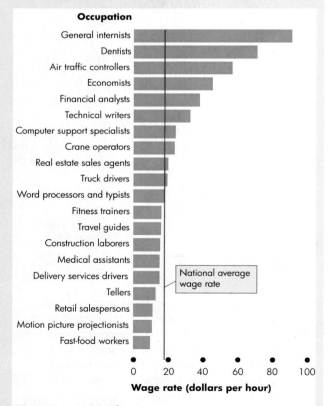

Wage Rates in 20 Jobs
Source of data: Bureau of Labor Statistics.

Differences and Trends in Wage Rates

You can use what you've learned about labor markets to explain some of the differences in wage rates across occupations and the trends in wage rates.

Wage rates are unequal, and *Economics in Action* on this page shows a sample of the inequality in wages in 2011. The differences in wage rates across occupations—including college professors and basketball coaches—are driven by differences in demand and supply in labor markets. The highest wage rates are earned in occupations where the value of marginal product is highest and where few people have the ability and training to perform the job.

Rising Wage Rates Wage rates increase over time and trend upward. The reason is that the value of marginal product of labor also increases over time. Technological change and the new types of capital that it brings make workers more productive. With greater labor productivity, the demand for labor increases, which increases the wage rate. Even jobs in which physical productivity doesn't increase experience increases in the *value* of marginal product. Child care is an example. A child-care worker can't care for an increasing number of children, but an increasing number of parents who earn high wages are willing to hire child-care workers. The *value* of marginal product of these workers increases, so the demand for their services increases, and so does their wage rate.

Increased Wage Inequality In recent years wage inequality has increased. High wage rates have increased more rapidly than the low ones, and some low wage rates have stagnated or even fallen. The reasons are complex and not fully understood, but the best explanation is that there is an interaction between technology and education.

The new information technologies of the 1990s and 2000s made well-educated, skilled workers more productive, so it raised their wage rates. For example, the computer created the jobs and increased the wage rates of computer programmers and electronic engineers.

These same technologies destroyed some low-skilled jobs. For example, the ATM took the jobs and lowered the wage rate of bank tellers, and automatic telephones took the jobs of telephone operators.

Another reason for increased inequality is that globalization has brought increased competition for low-skilled workers and at the same time opened global markets for high-skilled workers.

◆ ECONOMICS IN THE NEWS

College Major and Job Prospects

The Most Valuable College Major
Which college major is most likely to land you a well-paying job right out of school? Katie Bardaro, an economist at PayScale, a compensation research firm, says biomedical engineering is your best bet. The median salary starts at $53,800 and by mid-career reaches $84,700 and keeps rising. The median salary for all biomedical engineers in 2012 was $88,000.

Some other science and engineering jobs pay more but don't have as good an outlook for jobs growth. The Bureau of Labor Statistics projects that the number of jobs for biomedical engineers will increase from today's 20,000 to 32,000 in 2020—an increase of more than 60 percent. In contrast, the working-age population will increase by only 8 percent by 2020.

Sources: The Bureau of Labor Statistics and
Forbes, May 15, 2012

THE QUESTIONS

- Why is the number of jobs for biomedical engineering graduates increasing?
- What determines the demand for biomedical engineers and why might it be increasing?
- What determines the supply of biomedical engineers and why might it be increasing?
- What determines whether the wage rate of biomedical engineers will rise?
- Provide a graphical illustration of the market for biomedical engineers in 2012 and 2020.

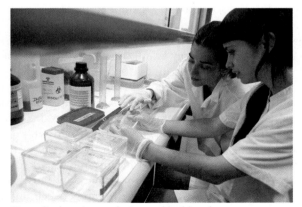

Biomedical engineers design and build replacement parts for the human body.

THE ANSWERS

- The number of jobs for biomedical engineers is growing because *both* demand for and supply of biomedical engineers are increasing.
- The demand for biomedical engineers is *derived* from the demand for biomedical products. The demand for replacement parts for the human body is increasing because technological advances are creating new and improved products.
- The supply of biomedical engineers is determined by the working-age population and the number of people who decide to major in the subject. The supply is increasing because the working-age population is increasing and good job prospects are attracting a larger percentage of people to study biomedical engineering.
- The wage rate of biomedical engineers will rise if the demand for their services increases faster than supply.
- The figure illustrates the market for biomedical engineers in 2012 and in 2020.
- Demand is expected to increase from D_{12} to D_{20}.
- Supply is expected to increase from S_{12} to S_{20}.
- The increase in demand is much greater than the increase in supply.
- The equilibrium quantity (the number of jobs) increases from 20,000 in 2012 to 32,000 in 2020.
- Because demand increases by more than supply, the equilibrium wage rate rises. (The 2020 wage rate is an assumption.)

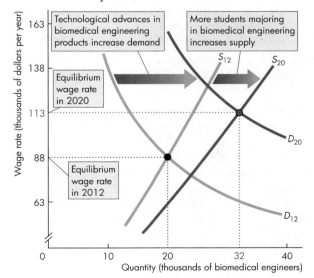

The Market for Biomedical Engineers in 2012 and 2020

A Labor Market with a Union

A **labor union** is an organized group of workers that aims to increase the wage rate and influence other job conditions. Let's see what happens when a union enters a competitive labor market.

Influences on Labor Supply One way of raising the wage rate is to decrease the supply of labor. In some labor markets, a union can restrict supply by controlling entry into apprenticeship programs or by influencing job qualification standards. Markets for skilled workers, doctors, dentists, and lawyers are the easiest ones to control in this way.

If there is an abundant supply of nonunion labor, a union can't decrease supply. For example, in the market for farm labor in southern California, the flow of nonunion labor from Mexico makes it difficult for a union to control the supply.

On the demand side of the labor market, the union faces a tradeoff: The demand for labor curve slopes downward, so restricting supply to raise the wage rate costs jobs. For this reason, unions also try to influence the demand for union labor.

Influences on Labor Demand A union tries to increase the demand for the labor of its members in four main ways:

1. Increasing the value of marginal product of its members by organizing and sponsoring training schemes and apprenticeship programs, and by professional certification.
2. Lobbying for import restrictions and encouraging people to buy goods made by unionized workers.
3. Supporting minimum wage laws, which increase the cost of employing low-skilled labor and lead firms to substitute high-skilled union labor for low-skilled nonunion labor.
4. Lobbying for restrictive immigration laws to decrease the supply of foreign workers.

Labor Market Equilibrium with a Union Figure 18.4 illustrates what happens to the wage rate and employment when a union successfully enters a competitive labor market. With no union, the demand curve is D_C, the supply curve is S_C, the wage rate is $10 an hour, and 300 workers have jobs.

Now a union enters this labor market. First, look at what happens if the union has sufficient control over the supply of labor to be able to restrict supply

FIGURE 18.4   A Union Enters a Competitive Labor Market

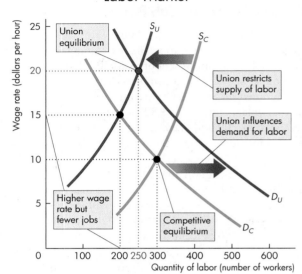

In a competitive labor market, the demand curve is D_C and the supply curve is S_C. The wage rate is $10 an hour and 300 workers are employed. If a union decreases the supply of labor and the supply of labor curve shifts to S_U, the wage rate rises to $15 an hour and employment decreases to 200 workers. If the union can also increase the demand for labor and shift the demand for labor curve to D_U, the wage rate rises to $20 an hour and 250 workers are employed.

——— **MyEconLab** animation ———

below its competitive level—to S_U. If that is all the union is able to do, employment falls to 200 workers and the wage rate rises to $15 an hour.

Suppose now that the union is also able to increase the demand for labor to D_U. The union can get an even bigger increase in the wage rate and with a smaller fall in employment. By maintaining the restricted labor supply at S_U, the union increases the wage rate to $20 an hour and achieves an employment level of 250 workers.

Because a union restricts the supply of labor in the market in which it operates, the union's actions spill over into nonunion markets. Workers who can't get union jobs must look elsewhere for work. This action increases the supply of labor in nonunion markets and lowers the wage rate in those markets. This spillover effect further widens the gap between union and nonunion wages.

Monopsony in the Labor Market Not all labor markets in which unions operate are competitive. Rather, some are labor markets in which the employer possesses market power and the union enters to try to counteract that power.

A market in which there is a single buyer is called a **monopsony**. A monopsony labor market has one employer. In some parts of the country, managed health-care organizations are the major employer of health-care professionals. In some communities, Wal-Mart is the main employer of salespeople. These firms have monopsony power.

A monopsony acts on the buying side of a market in a similar way to a monopoly on the selling side. The firm maximizes profit by hiring the quantity of labor that makes the marginal cost of labor equal to the value of marginal product of labor and by paying the lowest wage rate at which it can attract this quantity of labor.

Figure 18.5 illustrates a monopsony labor market. Like all firms, a monopsony faces a downward-sloping value of marginal product curve, *VMP*, which is its demand for labor curve, *D*—the curve labeled *VMP* = *D* in the figure.

What is special about monopsony is the marginal cost of labor. For a firm in a competitive labor market, the marginal cost of labor is the wage rate. For a monopsony, the marginal cost of labor exceeds the wage rate. The reason is that being the only buyer in the market, the firm faces an upward-sloping supply of labor curve—the curve *S* in the figure.

To attract one more worker, the monopsony must offer a higher wage rate. But it must pay this higher wage rate to all its workers, so the marginal cost of a worker is the wage rate plus the increased wage bill that arises from paying all the workers the higher wage rate.

The supply curve is now the average cost of labor curve and the relationship between the supply curve and the marginal cost of labor curve, *MCL,* is similar to that between a monopoly's demand curve and marginal revenue curve (see p. 300). The relationship between the supply curve and the *MCL* curve is also similar to that between a firm's average cost curve and marginal cost curve (see pp. 258–259).

To find the profit-maximizing quantity of labor to hire, the monopsony sets the marginal cost of labor equal to the value of marginal product of labor. In Fig. 18.5, this outcome occurs when the firm employs 100 workers.

To hire 100 workers, the firm must pay $10 an hour (on the supply of labor curve). Each worker is paid $10 an hour, but the value of marginal product of labor is $20 an hour, so the firm makes an economic profit of $10 an hour on the marginal worker.

If the labor market in Fig. 18.5 were competitive, the equilibrium wage rate and employment would be determined by the demand and supply curves. The wage rate would be $15 an hour, and 150 workers would be employed. So compared with a competitive labor market, a monopsony pays a lower wage rate and employs fewer workers.

A Union and a Monopsony A union is like a monopoly. If the union (monopoly seller) faces a monopsony buyer, the situation is called **bilateral monopoly**. An example of bilateral monopoly is the Writers Guild of America that represents film, television, and radio

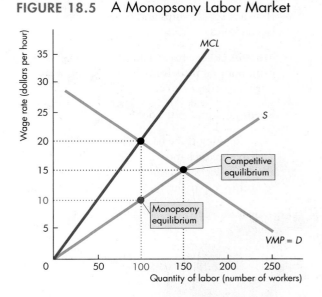

FIGURE 18.5   A Monopsony Labor Market

A monopsony is a market structure in which there is a single buyer. A monopsony in the labor market has a value of marginal product curve *VMP* and faces a labor supply curve *S*. The marginal cost of labor curve is *MCL*. Making the marginal cost of labor equal to the value of marginal product maximizes profit. The monopsony hires 100 hours of labor and pays the lowest wage rate for which that quantity of labor will work, which is $10 an hour.

MyEconLab animation

◆ AT ISSUE

Monopoly Power for Evil or Good?

The standard view of economists is that monopoly is bad. It prevents resources from being used efficiently, and on any criterion of fairness or equity, monopoly is unfair. It fails to serve the social interest.

We normally think of a monopoly as a big firm that gouges its customers. But a surprising monopoly (and monopsony) has attracted attention—the National Collegiate Athletic Association (NCAA).

Does the NCAA do a good job at efficiently allocating the talents of college athletes and providing those athletes with a fair return for their efforts?

The standard economist's view is that the NCAA doesn't serve the social interest. But there is a contrarian view.

Let's look at both sides of this argument.

The Standard View

Robert Barro expresses the standard economist view. While acknowledging that the NCAA has boosted the productivity of college sports programs, he says that the NCAA monopoly:

- Suppresses financial competition in college sports.

- Restricts scholarships and other payments to college athletes.

- Prevents college basketball players who come from poor families from accumulating wealth during a college career.

- Keeps poor students poor.

- Despite doing these bad things, the NCAA manages to convince most people that the bad guys are the colleges that violate NCAA rules by attempting to pay their athletes competitive wages.

The contenders for best monopoly in America include the Post Office, Microsoft, and the NCAA. And the winner is ... the NCAA.

Robert Barro, "The Best Little Monopoly in America", *BusinessWeek*, December 9, 2002

A Contrarian View

Richard B. McKenzie of the University of California, Irvine, and Dwight R. Lee of the University of Georgia, in their book, *In Defense of Monopoly: How Market Power Fosters Creative Production*, (University of Michigan Press, 2008) say the NCAA:

- Helps its members to cooperate to everyone's benefit.

- Has enabled healthy growth of college athletics over the past 50 years.

- Has generated economic profits for member schools.

- Does not lower student athletes' wages.

- Has stimulated the demand for student athletes and increased their wages and employment opportunities.

- Permitting NCAA colleges to pay athletes competitive wages is misguided.

The Kentucky Wildcats celebrate their victory at the 2012 NCAA National Championship

writers, and an employers' alliance that represents CBS, MGM, NBC, and other entertainment companies. Every three years, the Writers Guild and the employers' alliance negotiate a pay deal.

In bilateral monopoly, the outcome is determined by bargaining, which depends on the costs that each party can inflict on the other. The firm can shut down temporarily and lock out its workers, and the workers can shut down the firm by striking. Each party estimates the other's strength and what it will lose if it does not agree to the other's demands.

Usually, an agreement is reached without a strike or a lockout. The threat is usually enough to bring the bargaining parties to an agreement. When a strike or lockout does occur, it is because one party has misjudged the costs each party can inflict on the other. Such an event occurred in November 2007 when the writers and entertainment producers failed to agree on a compensation deal. A 100-day strike followed that ended up costing the entertainment industry an estimated $2 billion.

In the example in Fig. 18.5, if the union and employer are equally strong, and each party knows the strength of the other, they will agree to split the gap between $10 (the wage rate on the supply curve) and $20 (the wage rate on the demand curve) and agree to a wage rate of $15 an hour.

You've now seen that in a monopsony, a union can bargain for a higher wage rate without sacrificing jobs. A similar outcome can arise in a monopsony labor market when a minimum wage law is enforced. Let's look at the effect of a minimum wage.

Monopsony and the Minimum Wage In a competitive labor market, a minimum wage that exceeds the equilibrium wage decreases employment (see Chapter 6, pp. 131–132). In a monopsony labor market, a minimum wage can increase both the wage rate and employment. Let's see how.

Figure 18.6 shows a monopsony labor market without a union. The wage rate is $10 an hour and 100 workers are employed.

A minimum wage law is passed that requires employers to pay at least $15 an hour. The monopsony now faces a perfectly elastic supply of labor at $15 an hour up to 150 workers (along the minimum wage line). To hire more than 150 workers, a wage rate above $15 an hour must be paid (along the supply curve). Because the wage rate is $15 an hour up to 150 workers, so is the marginal cost of labor $15 an hour up to 150 workers. To maximize profit, the monopsony sets the marginal cost of labor equal to the value of marginal product of

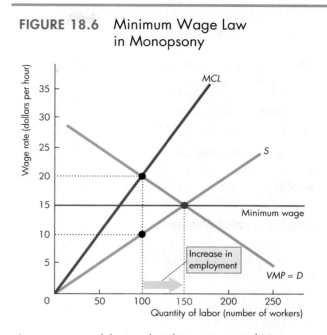

FIGURE 18.6   Minimum Wage Law in Monopsony

In a monopsony labor market, the wage rate is $10 an hour and 100 workers are hired. If a minimum wage law increases the wage rate to $15 an hour, the wage rate rises to this level and employment increases to 150 workers.

———— MyEconLab animation ————

labor (on the demand curve). That is, the monopsony hires 150 workers and pays $15 an hour. The minimum wage law has succeeded in raising the wage rate and increasing the number of workers employed.

REVIEW QUIZ

1 What determines the amount of labor that households plan to supply?
2 How are the wage rate and employment determined in a competitive labor market?
3 How do labor unions influence wage rates?
4 What is a monopsony and why is a monopsony able to pay a lower wage rate than a firm in a competitive labor market?
5 How is the wage rate determined when a union faces a monopsony?
6 What is the effect of a minimum wage law in a monopsony labor market?

You can work these questions in Study Plan 18.3 and get instant feedback.   MyEconLab

Capital and Natural Resource Markets

The markets for capital and land can be understood by using the same basic ideas that you've seen when studying a competitive labor market. But markets for nonrenewable natural resources are different. We'll now examine three groups of factor markets:

- Capital rental markets
- Land rental markets
- Nonrenewable natural resource markets

Capital Rental Markets

The demand for capital is derived from the *value of marginal product of capital*. Profit-maximizing firms hire the quantity of capital services that makes the value of marginal product of capital equal to the *rental rate of capital*. The *lower* the rental rate of capital, other things remaining the same, the *greater* is the quantity of capital demanded. The supply of capital responds in the opposite way to the rental rate. The *higher* the rental rate, other things remaining the same, the *greater* is the quantity of capital supplied. The equilibrium rental rate makes the quantity of capital demanded equal to the quantity supplied.

Figure 18.7 illustrates the rental market for tower cranes—capital used to construct high-rise buildings. The value of marginal product and the demand curve is *VMP* = *D*. The supply curve is *S*. The equilibrium rental rate is $1,000 per day and 100 tower cranes are rented.

Rent-Versus-Buy Decision Some capital services are obtained in a rental market like the market for tower cranes. And like tower cranes, many of the world's large airlines rent their airplanes. But not all capital services are obtained in a rental market. Instead, firms buy the capital equipment that they use. You saw in Chapter 10 (pp. 224–225) that the cost of the services of the capital that a firm owns and operates itself is an implicit rental rate that arises from depreciation and interest costs. Firms that buy capital *implicitly* rent the capital to themselves.

The decision to obtain capital services in a rental market rather than buy capital and rent it implicitly is made to minimize cost. The firm compares the cost of explicitly renting the capital and the cost of buying and implicitly renting it. This decision is the same as

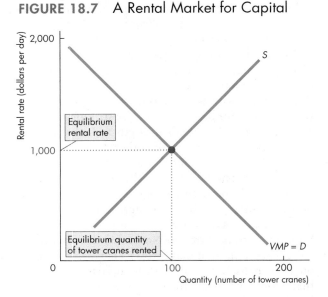

FIGURE 18.7 A Rental Market for Capital

The value of marginal product of tower cranes, *VMP*, determines the demand, *D*, for tower crane rentals. With the supply curve, *S*, the equilibrium rental rate is $1,000 a day and 100 cranes are rented.

MyEconLab animation

the one that a household makes in deciding whether to rent or buy a home.

To make a rent-versus-buy decision, a firm must compare a cost incurred in the *present* with a stream of rental costs incurred over some *future* period. The Mathematical Note (pp. 436–437) explains how to make this comparison by calculating the *present value* of a future amount of money. If the *present value* of the future rental payments of an item of capital equipment exceeds the cost of buying the capital, the firm will buy the equipment. If the *present value* of the future rental payments of an item of capital equipment is less than the cost of buying the capital, the firm will rent (or lease) the equipment.

Land Rental Markets

The demand for land is based on the same factors as the demand for labor and the demand for capital—the *value of marginal product of land*. Profit-maximizing firms rent the quantity of land at which the value of marginal product of land is equal to the *rental rate of land*. The *lower* the rental rate, other things remaining the same, the *greater* is the quantity of land demanded.

But the supply of land is special: Its quantity is fixed, so the quantity supplied cannot be changed by people's decisions. The supply of each particular block of land is perfectly inelastic.

The equilibrium rental rate makes the quantity of land demanded equal to the quantity available. Figure 18.8 illustrates the market for a 10-acre block of land on 42nd Street in New York City. The quantity supplied is fixed and the supply curve is *S*. The value of marginal product and the demand curve is *VMP* = *D*. The equilibrium rental rate is $1,000 an acre per day.

The rental rate of land is high in New York because the willingness to pay for the services produced by that land is high, which in turn makes the *VMP* of land high. A Big Mac costs more at McDonald's on 42nd Street, New York, than at McDonald's on Jefferson Avenue, St. Louis, but not because the rental rate of land is higher in New York. The rental rate of land is higher in New York because of the greater willingness to pay for a Big Mac (and other goods and services) in New York.

FIGURE 18.8   A Rental Market for Land

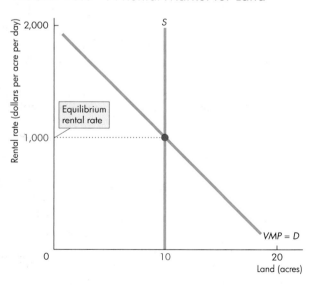

The value of marginal product of a 10-acre block, *VMP*, determines the rental demand, *D*, for this land. With the supply curve *S*, the block rents for $10,000 a day.

———— MyEconLab animation ————

Nonrenewable Natural Resource Markets

The nonrenewable natural resources are oil, gas, and coal. Burning one of these fuels converts it to energy and other by-products, and the used resource cannot be re-used. The natural resources that we use to make metals are also nonrenewable, but they can be used again, at some cost, by recycling them.

Oil, gas, and coal are traded in global commodity markets. The price of a given grade of crude oil is the same in New York, London, and Singapore. Traders, linked by telephone and the Internet, operate these markets around the clock every day of the year.

Demand and supply determine the prices and the quantities traded in these commodity markets. We'll look at the influences on demand and supply by considering the global market for crude oil.

The Demand for Oil The two key influences on the demand for oil are

1. The *value of marginal product* of oil
2. The expected future price of oil

The value of marginal product of oil is the *fundamental* influence on demand. It works in exactly the same way for a nonrenewable resource as it does for any other factor of production. The greater the quantity of oil used, the smaller is the value of marginal product of oil. Diminishing value of marginal product makes the demand curve slope downward. The lower the price, the greater is the quantity demanded.

The higher the expected future price of oil, the greater is the present demand for oil. The expected future price is a *speculative* influence on demand. Oil in the ground and oil in storage tanks are inventories that can be held or sold. A trader might plan to buy oil to hold now and to sell it later for a profit. Instead of buying oil to hold and sell later, the trader could buy a bond and earn interest. The interest forgone is the opportunity cost of holding the oil. If the price of oil is expected to rise by a bigger percentage than the interest rate, a trader will hold oil and incur the opportunity cost. In this case, the return from holding oil exceeds the return from holding bonds.

The Supply of Oil The three key influences on the supply of oil are

1. The known oil reserves
2. The scale of current oil production facilities
3. The expected future price of oil

Known oil reserves are the oil that has been discovered and can be extracted with today's technology. This quantity increases over time because advances in technology enable ever-less accessible sources to be discovered. The greater the size of known reserves, the greater is the supply of oil. But this influence on supply is small and indirect. It operates by changing the expected distant future price of oil. Even a major new discovery of oil would have a negligible effect on current supply of oil.

The scale of current oil production facilities is the *fundamental* influence on the supply of oil. Producing oil is like any production activity: It is subject to increasing marginal cost. The increasing marginal cost of extracting oil means that the supply curve of oil slopes upward. The higher the price of oil, the greater is the quantity supplied. When new oil wells are sunk or when new faster pumps are installed, the supply of oil increases. When existing wells run dry, the supply of oil decreases. Over time, the factors that increase supply are more powerful than those that decrease supply, so changes in the scale of current oil production facilities increase the supply of oil.

Speculative forces based on expectations about the future price also influence the supply of oil. The *higher* the expected future price of oil, the *smaller* is the present supply of oil. A trader with an oil inventory might plan to sell now or to hold and sell later. You've seen that interest forgone is the opportunity cost of holding the oil. If the price of oil is expected to rise by a bigger percentage than the interest rate, it is profitable to incur the opportunity cost of holding oil rather than selling it immediately.

The Equilibrium Price of Oil

The demand for oil and the supply of oil determine the equilibrium price and quantity traded. Figure 18.9 illustrates the market equilibrium.

The value of marginal product of oil, *VMP*, is the *fundamental determinant of demand*, and the marginal cost of extraction, *MC*, is the *fundamental determinant of supply*. Together, they determine the *market fundamentals price*.

If expectations about the future price are also based on fundamentals, the equilibrium price is the market fundamentals price. But if expectations about the future price of oil depart from what the market fundamentals imply, *speculation* can drive a wedge between the equilibrium price and the market fundamentals price.

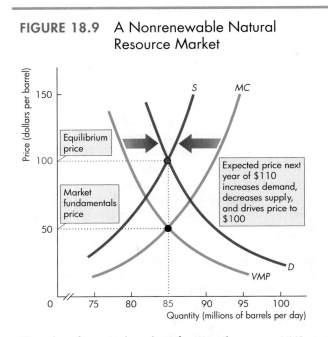

FIGURE 18.9   A Nonrenewable Natural Resource Market

The value of marginal product of a natural resource, *VMP*, and the marginal cost of extraction, *MC*, determine the *market fundamentals* price. Demand, *D*, and supply, *S*, which determine the equilibrium price, are influenced by the expected future price. Speculation can bring a gap between the market fundamentals price and the equilibrium price.

———————————————— MyEconLab animation ————————————————

The Hotelling Principle Harold Hotelling, an economist at Columbia University, had an incredible idea: Traders expect the price of a nonrenewable natural resource to rise at a rate equal to the interest rate. We call this idea the **Hotelling principle**. Let's see why it is correct.

You've seen that the interest rate is the opportunity cost of holding an oil inventory. If the price of oil is expected to rise at a rate that exceeds the interest rate, it is profitable to hold a bigger inventory. Demand increases, supply decreases, and the price rises. If the interest rate exceeds the rate at which the price of oil is expected to rise, it is not profitable to hold an oil inventory. Demand decreases, supply increases, and the price falls. But if the price of oil is expected to rise at a rate equal to the interest rate, holding an inventory of oil is just as good as holding bonds. Demand and supply don't change and the price does not change. Only when the price of oil is expected to rise at a rate equal to the interest rate is the price at its equilibrium.

Economics in Action
The World and U.S. Markets for Oil

The world produced about 87 million barrels of oil in 2011 and the price shot upward from $70 in 2010 to $100 in 2011.

Although the United States imports almost three quarters of its oil from other countries, much of it comes from close to home. Figure 1 provides the details: Only 14 percent of the U.S. oil supply comes from the Middle East and more than one third comes from Canada, Mexico, and other Western Hemisphere nations.

Even if the United States produced all its own oil, it would still face a fluctuating global price. U.S. producers would not willingly sell to U.S. buyers for a price below the world price. So energy independence doesn't mean an independent oil price.

The Hotelling principle tells us that we must expect the price of oil to rise at a rate equal to the interest rate. But expecting the price to rise at a rate equal to the interest rate doesn't mean that the price will rise at this rate. As you can see in Fig. 2, the price of oil over the past 50 or so years has not followed the path predicted by the Hotelling principle.

The forces that influence expectations are not well understood. The expected future price of oil depends on its expected future rate of use and the rate of discovery of new sources of supply. One person's expectation about a future price also depends on guesses about other people's expectations. These guesses can change abruptly and become self-reinforcing. When

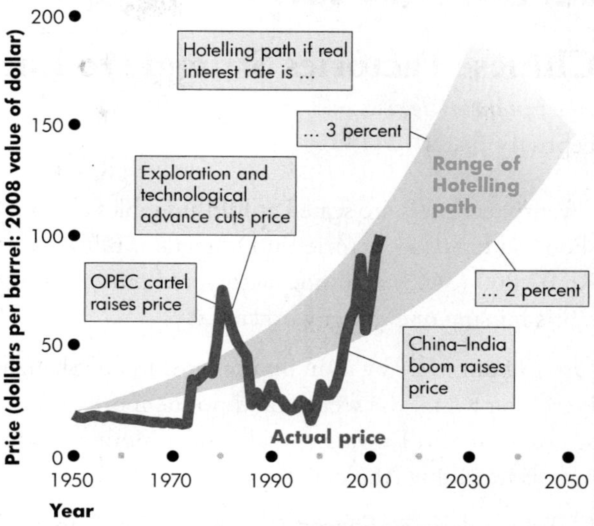

Figure 2 The Price of Oil and Its Hotelling Path

Source of data: U.S. Energy Information Administration.

the expected future price of oil changes for whatever reason, demand and supply change, and so does the price. Prices in speculative markets are always volatile.

REVIEW QUIZ

1 What determines demand and supply in rental markets for capital and land?
2 What determines the demand for a nonrenewable natural resource?
3 What determines the supply of a nonrenewable natural resource?
4 What is the market fundamentals price and how might it differ from the equilibrium price?
5 Explain the Hotelling principle.

You can work these questions in Study Plan 18.4 and get instant feedback.   **MyEconLab**

◆ *Reading Between the Lines* on pp. 434–435 examines the wage and employment trends in labor markets in China.

The next chapter looks more closely at the distribution of income and its trends. The chapter also looks at the efforts by governments to redistribute income and modify the market outcome.

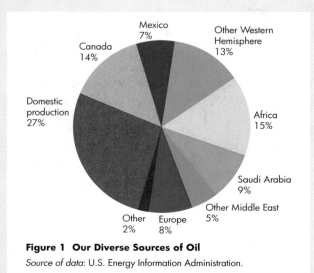

Figure 1 Our Diverse Sources of Oil

Source of data: U.S. Energy Information Administration.

Labor Markets in China

Chinese Factories Struggle to Lure Workers

The Financial Times
February 17, 2012

Twenty recruiters are seated at fold-up tables along a canal that separates two rows of shoe and handbag factories in Dongguan. Billboards tout monthly wages of Rmb1,800 to Rmb2,800 ($445) at a shoe factory and more at a technology company, but the alfresco job fair is missing one thing: workers. …

Just an hour away by train on the outskirts of Shenzhen, the special economic zone bordering Hong Kong, the scene could not be more different. 1,000 workers queue for interviews at Foxconn, the Taiwanese maker of computers and mobile phones for a host of western brands including Apple.

Monthly salaries at Foxconn are higher than apparel factories—from Rmb2,400 to Rmb3,500 including overtime—but for many young Chinese, the cachet of working on computers is the real draw. …

China's labor market—just like the country—is diverse. Electronics companies are not facing big worker shortages. On the coast of Fujian province, for example, TPV Technology, a Chinese TV manufacturer which last year bought Philips' HDTV business, says hiring is right on track.

But in Zhongshan, a southern Chinese factoryville like Dongguan where companies make everything from lighting fixtures to shoes, the local government this week said many factories were delaying reopening because the area was short of tens of thousands of workers. …

To lure workers from competitors, many Chinese employers are offering incentives such as dormitories with air-conditioners, a guaranteed hot water supply, and better food in the canteen. In Dongguan, a sign-on bonus of Rmb400 to Rmb600 has also become widespread, but employers still complain of being understaffed. …

ESSENCE OF THE STORY

- The demand for labor is increasing in China.
- In areas where technology firms operate, the top wage rate is Rmb3,500 per month.
- In areas dominated by light manufacturing (such as apparel factories), the top wage rate is Rmb2,800 per month.
- Educated workers prefer to work in interesting technology jobs.
- Light manufacturing firms are facing labor shortages, so they are raising wage rates and non-wage benefits.

ECONOMIC ANALYSIS

- An increase in the demand for goods produced in China has increased the value of marginal product (*VMP*) of Chinese workers and increased the demand for their labor.

- The *VMP* of labor has increased most in technology firms and least in light manufacturing firms such as apparel producers.

- Because the *VMP* of labor and the demand for labor have increased most in technology firms, wage rates have increased more in those firms than in firms that produce apparel and other light manufactured goods.

- Technology jobs, which are attractive to workers because they are more interesting and have better career paths, have become even more attractive because wage rates are now higher in these jobs.

- Figures 1 and 2 illustrate these events in the markets for technology workers and apparel workers.

- In the market for technology workers in Fig. 1, initially the demand for labor is LD_0, the supply of labor is LS_0, and the wage rate is Rmb2,000 per month.

- When the *VMP* of labor increases, the demand for labor increases and the demand curve shifts rightward to LD_1. Population growth increases the supply of labor but by a much smaller amount than the increase in demand. The supply curve shifts rightward to LS_1.

- The wage rate rises to Rmb3,500 per month and the quantity of labor employed in technology jobs increases.

- In the market for apparel workers in Fig. 2, initially demand is LD_0, supply is LS_0, and the wage rate is Rmb2,000 per month. (We're assuming the same starting wage rate in both sectors for simplicity.)

- The demand for apparel labor increases and the demand curve shifts rightward to LD_1. But the supply of apparel labor *decreases* and the supply curve shifts leftward to LS_1. The reason for the decrease in supply is the widening wage gap between technology jobs and apparel jobs. Workers leave the apparel market to seek jobs in the technology market.

- With an increase in demand and decrease in supply, the wage rate rises.

- But at the time of the news article, the wage rate had not reached its equilibrium level. We know this fact because apparel producers (and other producers of light manufactures) could not hire all the labor they demanded at the current wage rate.

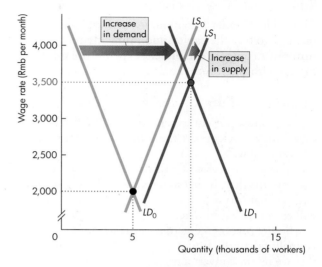

Figure 1 The Market for Technology Workers

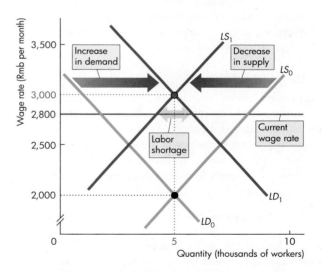

Figure 2 The Market for Apparel Workers

- The double-headed arrow shows the shortage of labor.

- But market forces will keep raising the wage rate of apparel workers until the labor shortage disappears.

- An ongoing increase in the *VMP* of technology workers at a faster pace than that of apparel workers will result in the process we've just described persisting.

435

MATHEMATICAL NOTE
Present Value and Discounting

Rent-Versus-Buy Decision

To decide whether to rent an item of capital equipment or to buy the capital and implicitly rent it, a firm must compare the present expenditure on the capital with the future rental cost of the capital.

Comparing Current and Future Dollars

To compare a present expenditure with a future expenditure, we convert the future expenditure to its "present value."

The **present value** of a future amount of money is the amount that, if invested today, will grow to be as large as that future amount when the interest that it will earn is taken into account.

So the present value of a future amount of money is smaller than the future amount. The calculation that we use to convert a future amount of money to its present value is called **discounting**.

The easiest way to understand discounting and present value is to first consider its opposite: How a present value grows to a future amount of money because of *compound interest*.

Compound Interest

Compound interest is the interest on an initial investment plus the interest on the interest that the investment has previously earned. Because of compound interest, a present amount of money (a present value) grows into a larger future amount. The future amount is equal to the present amount (present value) plus the interest it will earn in the future. That is,

Future amount = Present value + Interest income.

The interest in the first year is equal to the present value multiplied by the interest rate, r, so

Amount after 1 year = Present value + ($r \times$ Present value).

or

Amount after 1 year = Present value $\times (1 + r)$.

If you invest $100 today and the interest rate is 10 percent a year ($r = 0.1$), 1 year from today you will have $110—the original $100 plus $10 interest.

Check that the above formula delivers that answer:

$$\$100 \times 1.1 = \$110.$$

If you leave this $110 invested to earn 10 percent during a second year, at the end of that year you will have

Amount after 2 years = Present value $\times (1 + r)^2$.

With the numbers of the previous example, you invest $100 today at an interest rate of 10 percent a year ($r = 0.1$). After 1 year, you will have $110—the original $100 plus $10 interest. And after 2 years, you will have $121. In the second year, you earned $10 on your initial $100 plus $1 on the $10 interest that you earned in the first year.

Check that the above formula delivers that answer:

$$\$100 \times (1.1)^2 = \$100 \times 1.21 = \$121.$$

If you leave your $100 invested for n years, it will grow to

Amount after n years = Present value $\times (1 + r)^n$.

With an interest rate of 10 percent a year, your $100 will grow to $195 after 7 years ($n = 7$)—almost double the present value of $100.

Discounting a Future Amount

We have just calculated future amounts 1 year, 2 years, and n years in the future, knowing the present value and the interest rate. To calculate the present value of these future amounts, we just work backward.

To find the present value of an amount 1 year in the future, we divide the future amount by $(1 + r)$. That is,

$$\text{Present value} = \frac{\text{Amount of money one year in future}}{(1 + r)}.$$

Let's check that we can use the present value formula by calculating the present value of $110 1 year from now when the interest rate is 10 percent a year.

You'll be able to guess that the answer is $100 because we just calculated that $100 invested today at 10 percent a year becomes $110 in one year. So the present value of $110 to be received 1 year from today is $100. But let's use the formula. Putting the numbers into the above formula, we have

$$\text{Present value} = \frac{\$110}{(1 + 0.1)}$$

$$= \frac{\$110}{1.1} = \$100.$$

To calculate the present value of an amount of money 2 years in the future, we use the formula:

$$\text{Present value} = \frac{\text{Amount of money two years in future}}{(1 + r)^2}$$

Use this formula to calculate the present value of $121 to be received 2 years from now at an interest rate of 10 percent a year. With these numbers, the formula gives

$$\text{Present value} = \frac{\$121}{(1 + 0.1)^2}$$

$$= \frac{\$121}{(1.1)^2}$$

$$= \frac{\$121}{1.21}$$

$$= \$100.$$

We can calculate the present value of an amount of money n years in the future by using the general formula

$$\text{Present value} = \frac{\text{Amount of money } n \text{ years in future}}{(1 + r)^n}$$

For example, if the interest rate is 10 percent a year, $100 to be received 10 years from now has a present value of $38.55. That is, if $38.55 is invested today at 10 percent a year it will accumulate to $100 in 10 years.

Present Value of a Sequence of Future Amounts

You've seen how to calculate the present value of an amount of money to be received 1 year, 2 years, and n years in the future. Most practical applications of present value calculate the present value of a sequence of future amounts of money that are spread over several years. An airline's payment of rent for the lease of airplanes is an example.

To calculate the present value of a sequence of amounts over several years, we use the formula you have learned and apply it to each year. We then sum the present values for all the years to find the present value of the sequence of amounts.

For example, suppose that a firm expects to pay $100 a year for each of the next 5 years and the interest rate is 10 percent a year ($r = 0.1$). The present value (PV) of these five payments of $100 each is calculated by using the following formula:

$$PV = \frac{\$100}{1.1} + \frac{\$100}{1.1^2} + \frac{\$100}{1.1^3} + \frac{\$100}{1.1^4} + \frac{\$100}{1.1^5},$$

which equals

$$PV = \$90.91 + \$82.64 + \$75.13 + \$68.30 + \$62.09$$
$$= \$379.07.$$

You can see that the firm pays $500 over 5 years. But because the money is paid in the future, it is not worth $500 today. Its present value is only $379.07. And the farther in the future the money is paid, the smaller is its present value. The $100 paid 1 year in the future is worth $90.91 today, but the $100 paid 5 years in the future is worth only $62.09 today.

The Decision

If this firm could lease a machine for 5 years at $100 a year or buy the machine for $500, it would jump at leasing. Only if the firm could buy the machine for less than $379.07 would it want to buy.

Many personal and business decisions turn on calculations like the one you've just made. A decision to buy or rent an apartment, to buy or lease a car, and to pay off a student loan or let the loan run another year can all be made using the above calculation.

SUMMARY

Key Points

The Anatomy of Factor Markets (p. 418)

- The factor markets are: job markets for labor; rental markets (often implicit rental markets) for capital and land; and global commodity markets for nonrenewable natural resources.
- The services of entrepreneurs are not traded on a factor market.

Working Problem 1 will give you a better understanding of the anatomy of factor markets.

The Demand for a Factor of Production
(pp. 419–421)

- The value of marginal product determines the demand for a factor of production.
- The value of marginal product decreases as the quantity of the factor employed increases.
- The firm employs the quantity of each factor of production that makes the value of marginal product equal to the factor price.

Working Problems 2 to 8 will give you a better understanding of the demand for a factor of production.

Labor Markets (pp. 422–429)

- The value of marginal product of labor determines the demand for labor. A rise in the wage rate brings a decrease in the quantity demanded.
- The quantity of labor supplied depends on the wage rate. At low wage rates, a rise in the wage rate increases the quantity supplied. Beyond a high enough wage rate, a rise in the wage rate decreases the quantity supplied—the supply curve eventually bends backward.

- Demand and supply determine the wage rate in a competitive labor market.
- A labor union can raise the wage rate by restricting the supply or increasing the demand for labor.
- A monopsony can lower the wage rate below the competitive level.
- A union or a minimum wage in a monopsony labor market can raise the wage rate without a fall in employment.

Working Problems 9 to 11 will give you a better understanding of labor markets.

Capital and Natural Resource Markets (pp. 430–433)

- The value of marginal product of capital (and land) determines the demand for capital (and land).
- Firms make a rent-versus-buy decision by choosing the option that minimizes cost.
- The supply of land is inelastic and the demand for land determines the rental rate.
- The demand for a nonrenewable natural resource depends on the value of marginal product and on the expected future price.
- The supply of a nonrenewable natural resource depends on the known reserves, the cost of extraction, and the expected future price.
- The price of nonrenewable natural resources can differ from the market fundamentals price because of speculation based on expectations about the future price.
- The price of a nonrenewable natural resource is expected to rise at a rate equal to the interest rate.

Working Problems 12 to 17 will give you a better understanding of capital and natural resource markets.

Key Terms

Bilateral monopoly, 427
Compound interest, 436
Derived demand, 419
Discounting, 436

Hotelling principle, 432
Labor union, 426
Monopsony, 427

Nonrenewable natural
  resources, 418
Present value, 436
Value of marginal product, 419

STUDY PLAN PROBLEMS AND APPLICATIONS

MyEconLab   You can work Problems 1 to 18 in Chapter 18 Study Plan and get instant feedback.

The Anatomy of Factor Markets (Study Plan 18.1)

1. Tim is opening a new online store. He plans to hire two people to key in the data at $10 an hour. Tim is also considering buying or leasing some new computers. The purchase price of a computer is $900 and after three years it is worthless. The annual cost of leasing a computer is $450.

   a. In which factor markets does Tim operate?

   b. What is the price of the capital equipment and the rental rate of capital?

The Demand for a Factor of Production

(Study Plan 18.2)

Use the following data to work Problems 2 to 7. Wanda owns a fish store. She employs students to sort and pack the fish. Students can pack the following amounts of fish:

Number of students	Quantity of fish (pounds)
1	20
2	50
3	90
4	120
5	145
6	165
7	180
8	190

The fish market is competitive and the price of fish is 50¢ a pound. The market for packers is competitive and their market wage rate is $7.50 an hour.

2. Calculate the marginal product of the students and draw the marginal product curve.

3. Calculate the value of marginal product of labor and draw the value of marginal product curve.

4. a. Find Wanda's demand for labor curve.

   b. How many students does Wanda employ?

Use the following additional information to work Problems 5 and 6.

The market price of fish falls to 33.33¢ a pound, but the packers' wage rate remains at $7.50 an hour.

5. a. How does the students' marginal product change?

   b. How does the value of marginal product of labor change?

6. a. How does Wanda's demand for labor change?

   b. What happens to the number of students that Wanda employs?

7. At Wanda's fish store, packers' wages increase to $10 an hour, but the price of fish remains at 50¢ a pound.

   a. What happens to the value of marginal product of labor?

   b. What happens to Wanda's demand for labor curve?

   c. How many students does Wanda employ?

8. **British Construction Activity Falls**

   Construction activity in Britain declined in June at the fastest rate in 11 years. A major home builder was unable to raise more capital—both signs of worsening conditions in the battered housing industry. Employment of construction labor declined in June after 23 months of growth. Average house prices fell 0.9 percent in June, the eighth consecutive month of declines, leaving the average 6.3 percent below June 2007.

   Source: *Forbes*, July 2, 2008

   a. Explain how a fall in house prices influences the market for construction labor.

   b. On a graph illustrate the effect of falling house prices in the market for construction labor.

Labor Markets (Study Plan 18.3)

Use the following news clip to work Problems 9 to 11.

In Modern Rarity, Workers Form Union at Small Chain

In New York's low-income neighborhoods, labor unions have virtually no presence. But after a year-long struggle, 95 workers at a chain of 10 sneaker stores have formed a union. After months of negotiations, the two sides signed a three-year contract that sets the wage rate at $7.25 an hour.

Source: *The New York Times*, February 5, 2006

9. Why are labor unions scarce in New York's low-income neighborhoods?

10. Who wins from this union contract? Who loses?

11. How can this union try to change the demand for labor?

Capital and Natural Resource Markets

(Study Plan 18.4)

12. Classify the following items as a nonrenewable natural resource, a renewable natural resource, or not a natural resource. Explain your answers.

    a. Trump Tower

    b. Lake Michigan

    c. Coal in a West Virginia coal mine

    d. The Internet

    e. Yosemite National Park

    f. Power generated by wind turbines

13. **Land Prices Reflect High Commodity Prices**

    As their family grows, the Steens are finding it more difficult for the next generation to stay in ranching. "The problem is they don't create any more land," Steen said. As the prices for cattle, corn, and other commodities climb, so does the value of land in South Dakota.

    Source: *Rapid City Journal*, January 30, 2012

    a. Why does the price of land in South Dakota keep rising? In your answer include a discussion of the demand for and supply of land.

    b. Use a graph to show why the price of land in South Dakota has increased over the past decade.

    c. Is the supply of land in South Dakota perfectly inelastic?

14. In the news clip in Problem 8,

    a. Explain how a fall in house prices influences the market for construction equipment leases.

    b. Draw a graph to illustrate the effect of a fall in house prices in the market for construction equipment leases.

Use the following news clip to work Problems 15 and 16.

Intensive Farming: Ecologically Sustainable?

According to the European Commission, global agricultural production needs to be doubled by 2050 to feed the world. But at the same time, it says this will have to be done with less water and fewer pesticides and greenhouse gas emissions, amid growing competition for land.

Source: euractiv.com, August 16, 2011

15. a. Is farmland a renewable or nonrenewable resource?

    b. Explain how the growing demand for farm products will affect the market for land and draw a graph to illustrate your answer.

16. How might farmers meet the growing demand for farm products without having to use a greater quantity of farmland?

17. **Copter Crisis**

    Helicopters are in short supply these days. You could blame a rise in military spending, a jump in disaster relief, even crowded airports pushing executives into private travel. But the fastest growth is coming from the offshore oil-and-gas industry, where helicopters are the only way to ferry crews to and from rigs and platforms. Hundred-dollar oil has pushed producers to work existing fields harder and to open new deep-sea wells in Brazil, India, and Alaska. The number of rigs and platforms has grown by 13% over the past decade. Oil companies are facing a two-year backlog in orders for the Sikorsky S92, a favorite of the oil industry, and a 40% rise in prices for used models.

    Source: *Fortune*, May 12, 2008

    a. Explain how high oil prices influence the market for helicopter leases and services (such as the Sikorsky S92).

    b. What happens to the value of marginal product of a helicopter as a firm leases or buys additional helicopters?

Mathematical Note (Study Plan 18.MN)

18. Keshia is opening a new bookkeeping service. She is considering buying or leasing some new laptop computers. The purchase price of a laptop is $1,500 and after three years it is worthless. The annual lease rate is $550 per laptop. The value of marginal product of one laptop is $700 a year. The value of marginal product of a second laptop is $625 a year. The value of marginal product of a third laptop is $575 a year. And the value of marginal product of a fourth laptop is $500 a year.

    a. How many laptops will Keshia lease or buy?

    b. If the interest rate is 4 percent a year, will Keshia lease or buy her laptops?

    c. If the interest rate is 6 percent a year, will Keshia lease or buy her laptops?

ADDITIONAL PROBLEMS AND APPLICATIONS

MyEconLab   You can work these problems in MyEconLab if assigned by your instructor.

The Anatomy of Factor Markets

19. Venus is opening a tennis school. She plans to hire a marketing graduate to promote and manage the school at $20 an hour. Venus is also considering buying or leasing a new tennis ball machine. The purchase price of the machine is $1,000 and after three years it is worthless. The annual cost of leasing the machine is $500.
    a. In which factor markets does Venus operate?
    b. What is the price of the capital equipment and the rental rate of capital?

The Demand for a Factor of Production

Use the following data to work Problems 20 to 23.
Kaiser's Ice Cream Parlor hires workers to produce milk shakes. The market for milk shakes is perfectly competitive, and the price of a milk shake is $4. The labor market is competitive, and the wage rate is $40 a day. The table shows the workers' total product schedule.

Number of workers	Quantity produced (milk shakes per day)
1	7
2	21
3	33
4	43
5	51
6	55

20. Calculate the marginal product of hiring the fourth worker and the fourth worker's value of marginal product.

21. How many workers will Kaiser's hire to maximize its profit and how many milk shakes a day will Kaiser's produce?

22. If the price of a milk shake rises to $5, how many workers will Kaiser's hire?

23. Kaiser's installs a new machine for making milk shakes that increases the productivity of workers by 50 percent. If the price of a milk shake remains at $4 and the wage rises to $48 a day, how many workers does Kaiser's hire?

24. **Detroit Oil Refinery Expansion Approved**
    Marathon Oil Saturday started work on a $1.9 billion expansion of its gasoline refinery in Detroit. Marathon will employ 800 construction workers and add 135 permanent jobs to the existing 480 workers at the refinery.
    Source: *United Press International*, June 21, 2008
    a. Explain how rising gasoline prices influence the market for refinery labor.
    b. Draw a graph to illustrate the effects of rising gasoline prices on the market for refinery labor.

Labor Markets

Use the following news clip to work Problems 25 to 28.

Miner Sacks 17,000 Workers Over Pay Dispute
Impala Platinum has sacked 17,000 South African miners at its Rustenburg mine because they took part in an illegal strike. The miners refused to have their union negotiate in the two-week pay dispute with the world's second largest platinum producer. Mining provides a quarter of all jobs in Rustenburg.
Source: abc.com.au, February 3, 2012

25. How would the wage rate and employment for the Rustenburg miners be determined in a competitive market?

26. a. Explain how it is possible that the mine workers were being paid less than the wage that would be paid in a competitive labor market.
    b. What would be the effect of a minimum wage law in the market for miners?

27. a. Explain how a miners' union would attempt to counteract Impala Mine's wage offers.
    b. Is it possible that the union officials might be acting in their own interest and not in the interest of the miners?

28. If the market for labor in mining is competitive, explain the potential effect of a union on the wage rate. Draw a graph to illustrate your answer.

Use the following news clip to work Problems 29 to 32.

The New War over Wal-Mart
Today, Wal-Mart employs more people—1.7 million—than any other private employer in the world. With size comes power: Wal-Mart's prices are lower and United Food and Commercial Workers International

Union argues that Wal-Mart's wages are also lower than its competitors. Last year, the workers at a Canadian outlet joined the union and Wal-Mart immediately closed the outlet. But does Wal-Mart behave any worse than its competitors? When it comes to payroll, Wal-Mart's median hourly wage tracks the national median wage for general retail jobs.

Source: *The Atlantic*, June 2006

29. a. Assuming that Wal-Mart has market power in a labor market, explain how the firm could use that market power in setting wages.
    b. Draw a graph to illustrate how Wal-Mart might use labor market power to set wages.

30. a. Explain how a union of Wal-Mart's employees would attempt to counteract Wal-Mart's wage offers (a bilateral monopoly).
    b. Explain the response by the Canadian Wal-Mart to the unionization of employees.

31. Based upon evidence presented in this article, does Wal-Mart function as a monopsony in labor markets, or is the market for retail labor more competitive? Explain.

32. If the market for retail labor is competitive, explain the potential effect of a union on the wage rates. Draw a graph to illustrate your answer.

Capital and Natural Resource Markets

33. New technology has allowed oil to be pumped from much deeper offshore oil fields than before. For example, 28 deep ocean rigs operate in the deep waters of the Gulf of Mexico.
    a. What effect do you think deep ocean sources have had on the world oil price?
    b. Who will benefit from drilling for oil in the Gulf of Mexico? Explain your answer.

34. Water is a natural resource that is plentiful in Canada but not plentiful in Arizona.
    a. If Canadians start to export bulk water to Arizona, what do you predict will be the effect on the price of bulk water?
    b. Will Canada eventually run out of water?
    c. Do you think the Hotelling principle applies to Canada's water? Explain why or why not.

Use the following news clip to work Problems 35 and 36.

Gas Prices Create Land Rush

There is a land rush going on across Pennsylvania, but buyers aren't interested in the land itself. Buyers are interested in what lies beneath the earth's surface—mineral rights to natural gas deposits. Record high natural gas prices have already pushed up drilling activity across the state, but drilling companies have discovered a new technology that will enable deep gas-bearing shale to be exploited. Development companies, drilling companies, and speculators have been trying to lease mineral rights from landowners. The new drilling techniques might recover about 10 percent of those reserves, and that would ring up at a value of $1 trillion.

Source: *Erie Times-News*, June 15, 2008

35. a. Is natural gas a renewable or nonrenewable resource? Explain.
    b. Explain why the demand for land in Pennsylvania has increased.

36. a. If companies are responding to the higher prices for natural gas by drilling right now wherever they can, what does that imply about their assumptions about the future price of natural gas in relation to current interest rates?
    b. What could cause the price of natural gas to fall in the future?

Economics in the News

37. After you have studied *Reading Between the Lines* on pp. 434–435, answer the following questions.
    a. The analysis assumes that the increase in the demand for technology workers is greater than that of apparel workers. Can you think of reasons why this might be the case?
    b. The analysis shows a decreasing wage gap between the two sectors, due to the movement of workers from the apparel sector into the technology sector. Do you expect wage rates in the two sectors to eventually equalize? Can you think of supply-related reasons why the gap might continue in favor of technology wage rates?
    c. The analysis assumes that workers are free to move across regions. In China, it is not uncommon for the government to restrict labor's spatial mobility. How would this practise affect the wage rates in each of the two sectors?
    d. What do you expect will happen in the long run to the demand for technology workers relative to that of apparel workers?

19

ECONOMIC INEQUALITY

After studying this chapter, you will be able to:

◆ Describe the distributions of income and wealth and the trends in economic inequality in the United States

◆ Describe the distribution of income and the trends in inequality in selected countries and the world

◆ Explain the sources of economic inequality and its trends

◆ Describe the scale of government income redistribution in the United States

Extreme poverty and extreme wealth exist side by side in every major city, even in the rich United States. How does the distribution of income in the United States compare with that in other countries? Are the rich getting richer and the poor getting poorer?

In this chapter, we study economic inequality—its extent, its sources, and the things governments do to make it less extreme. We end, in *Reading Between the Lines*, by looking at Egypt's attempts to redistribute income by subsidizing food and fuel.

◆ Economic Inequality in the United States

The most commonly used measure of economic inequality is the distribution of annual income. The Census Bureau defines income as **money income**, which equals *market income* plus cash payments to households by government. **Market income** equals wages, interest, rent, and profit earned in factor markets, before paying income taxes.

The Distribution of Income

Figure 19.1 shows the distribution of annual income across the 121 million households in the United States in 2011. Note that the *x*-axis measures household income and the *y*-axis is percentage of households.

The most common household income, called the *mode* income, was received by the 6 percent of the households whose incomes fell between $20,000 and $25,000. The value of $22,000 marked on the figure is an estimate.

The middle level of household income in 2011, called the *median* income, was $50,054. Fifty percent of households have an income that exceeds the median and fifty percent have an income below the median.

The average household money income in 2011, called the *mean* income, was $69,677. This number equals total household income, about $8.4 trillion, divided by the 121 million households. You can see in Fig. 19.1 that the mode is less than the median and that the median is less than the mean. This feature of the distribution of income tells us that there are more households with low incomes than with high incomes. It also tells us that some of the high incomes are very high.

The income distribution in Fig. 19.1 is called a *positively skewed* distribution, which means that it has a long tail of high values. This distribution contrasts with the bell that describes the distribution of people's heights. In a bell-shaped distribution, the mean, median, and mode are all equal.

Another way of looking at the distribution of income is to measure the percentage of total income received by each given percentage of households. Data are reported for five groups—called *quintiles* or fifth shares—each consisting of 20 percent of households.

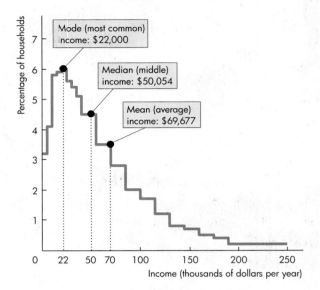

FIGURE 19.1   The Distribution of Income in the United States in 2011

The distribution of income is positively skewed. The mode (most common) income is less than the median (middle) income, which in turn is less than the mean (average) income. The distribution shown here ends at $250,000 because data above that level are not available, but the distribution goes up to several million dollars a year.

Source of data: DeNavas-Walt, Carmen, Bernadette D. Proctor, and Jessica C. Smith, U.S. Census Bureau, Current Population Reports, P60–243, Income, Poverty, and Health Insurance Coverage in the United States: 2011, U.S. Government Printing Office, Washington, DC, 2012.

—— MyEconLab animation ——

Figure 19.2 shows the distribution based on these shares in 2011. The poorest 20 percent of households received 3.2 percent of total income; the second poorest 20 percent received 8.4 percent of total income; the middle 20 percent received 14.3 percent of total income; the next highest 20 percent received 23.0 percent of total income; and the highest 20 percent received 51.1 percent of total income.

The distribution of income in Fig. 19.1 and the quintile shares in Fig. 19.2 tell us that income is distributed unequally. But we need a way of comparing the distribution of income in different periods and using different measures. A clever graphical tool called the *Lorenz curve* enables us to make such comparisons.

Economic Inequality in the United States

FIGURE 19.2   U.S. Quintile Shares in 2011

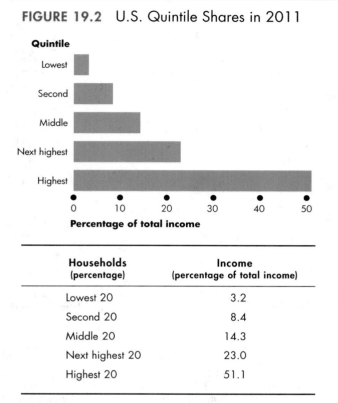

In 2011, the poorest 20 percent of households received 3.2 percent of total income; the second poorest 20 percent received 8.4 percent; the middle 20 percent received 14.3 percent; the next highest 20 percent received 23.0 percent; and the highest 20 percent received 51.1 percent.

Source of data: See Fig. 19.1.

———————— MyEconLab animation ————————

The Income Lorenz Curve

The income **Lorenz curve** graphs the cumulative percentage of income against the cumulative percentage of households. Figure 19.3 shows the income Lorenz curve using the quintile shares from Fig. 19.2. The table shows the percentage of income of each quintile group. For example, row *A* tells us that the lowest quintile of households receives 3.2 percent of total income. The table also shows the *cumulative* percentages of households and income. For example, row *B* tells us that the lowest two quintiles (lowest 40 percent) of households receive 11.6 percent of total income (3.2 percent for the lowest quintile plus 8.4 percent for the next lowest).

FIGURE 19.3   The Income Lorenz Curve in 2011

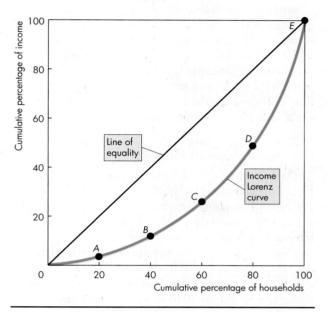

	Households		Income	
	Percentage	Cumulative percentage	Percentage	Cumulative percentage
A	Lowest 20	20	3.2	3.2
B	Second 20	40	8.4	11.6
C	Middle 20	60	14.3	25.9
D	Next highest 20	80	23.0	48.9
E	Highest 20	100	51.1	100.0

The cumulative percentage of income is graphed against the cumulative percentage of households. Points *A* through *E* on the Lorenz curve correspond to the rows of the table. If incomes were distributed equally, each 20 percent of households would receive 20 percent of total income and the Lorenz curve would fall along the line of equality. The Lorenz curve shows that income is unequally distributed.

Source of data: See Fig. 19.1.

———————— MyEconLab animation ————————

The Lorenz curve provides a direct visual clue about the degree of income inequality by comparing it with the line of equality. This line, identified in Fig. 19.3, shows what the Lorenz curve would be if everyone had the same level of income.

If income were distributed equally across all the households, each quintile would receive 20 percent of total income and the cumulative percentages of income received would equal the cumulative percentages of households, so the Lorenz curve would be the straight line labeled "Line of equality."

The actual distribution of income shown by the curve labeled "Income Lorenz curve" can be compared with the line of equality. The closer the Lorenz curve is to the line of equality, the more equal is the distribution of income.

The Distribution of Wealth

The distribution of wealth provides another way of measuring economic inequality. A household's **wealth** is the value of the things that it owns at a *point in time*. In contrast, income is the amount that the household receives over a given *period of time*.

Figure 19.4 shows the Lorenz curve for wealth in the United States in 2010 (the most recent year for which we have wealth distribution data). The median household wealth in 2010 was $77,300. Wealth is extremely unequally distributed, and for this reason, the data are grouped by five unequal groups of households. The poorest 25 percent of households have no wealth and the next poorest 25 percent own only 1.1 percent of total wealth (row B' in the table in Fig. 19.4). Even the third richest 25 percent own oly 8.5 percent of total wealth. The richest 25 percent of households own 90.4 percent of wealth, and within this wealthiest group the richest 10 percent of households own 74.5 percent of total wealth.

Figure 19.4 shows the income Lorenz curve (from Fig. 19.3) alongside the wealth Lorenz curve. You can see that the Lorenz curve for wealth is much farther away from the line of equality than is the Lorenz curve for income, which means that the distribution of wealth is much more unequal than the distribution of income.

Wealth or Income?

We've seen that wealth is much more unequally distributed than is income. Which distribution provides the better description of the degree of inequality? To answer this question, we need to think about the connection between wealth and income.

Wealth is a stock of assets, and income is the flow of earnings that results from the stock of wealth. Suppose that a person owns assets worth

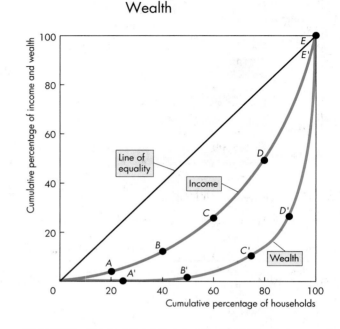

FIGURE 19.4   Lorenz Curves for Income and Wealth

	Households		Wealth	
	Percentage	Cumulative percentage	Percentage	Cumulative percentage
A' Lowest 25	25		0.0	0.0
B' Next 25	50		1.1	1.1
C' Next 25	75		8.5	9.6
D' Next 15	90		15.9	25.5
E' Highest 10	100		74.5	100.0

The cumulative percentage of wealth is graphed against the cumulative percentage of households. Points A' through E' on the Lorenz curve for wealth correspond to the rows of the table. By comparing the Lorenz curves for income and wealth, we can see that wealth is distributed much more unequally than is income.

Sources of data: For the income distribution data, see Fig. 19.1. The Wealth distribution data are calculated from the Federal Reserve Board's Survey of Consumer Finances for 2010, reported in Jesse Bricker, Arthur B. Kennickell, Kevin B. Moore, and John Sabelhaus, with assistance from Samuel Ackerman, Robert Argento, Gerhard Fries, and Richard A. Windle, "Changes in U.S. Family Finances from 2007 to 2010: Evidence from the Survey of Consumer Finances," *Federal Reserve Bulletin*, June 2012, Vol. 98, No. 2.

MyEconLab animation

$1 million—has a wealth of $1 million. If the rate of return on assets is 5 percent a year, then this person receives an income of $50,000 a year from those assets. We can describe this person's economic condition by using either the wealth of $1 million or the income of $50,000. When the rate of return is 5 percent a year, $1 million of wealth equals $50,000 of income in perpetuity. Wealth and income are just different ways of looking at the same thing.

But in Fig. 19.4, the distribution of wealth is more unequal than the distribution of income. Why? It is because the wealth data do not include the value of human capital, while the income data measure income from all wealth, including human capital.

Think about Lee and Peter, two people with equal income and equal wealth. Lee's wealth is human capital and his entire income is from employment. Peter's wealth is in the form of investments in stocks and bonds and his entire income is from these investments.

When a Census Bureau agent interviews Lee and Peter in a national income and wealth survey, their incomes are recorded as being equal, but Lee's wealth is recorded as zero, while Peter's wealth is recorded as the value of his investments. Peter looks vastly more wealthy than Lee in the survey data.

Because the national survey of wealth excludes human capital, the income distribution is a more accurate measure of economic inequality than the wealth distribution.

Annual or Lifetime Income and Wealth?

A typical household's income changes over its life cycle. Income starts out low, grows to a peak when the household's workers reach retirement age, and then falls after retirement. Also, a typical household's wealth changes over time. Like income, it starts out low, grows to a peak at the point of retirement, and falls after retirement.

Think about three households with identical lifetime incomes, one young, one middle-aged, and one retired. The middle-aged household has the highest income and wealth, the retired household has the lowest, and the young household falls in the middle. The distributions of annual income and wealth in a given year are unequal, but the distributions of lifetime income and wealth are equal.

The data on inequality share the bias that you've just seen. Inequality in annual income and wealth data overstates lifetime inequality because households are at different stages in their life cycles.

Trends in Inequality

To see trends in the income distribution, we use a measure called the Gini ratio. The **Gini ratio** equals the area between the Lorenz curve and the line of equality divided by the entire area beneath the line of equality. The more the Lorenz curve bows away from the line of equality, the larger is the Gini ratio. And the larger the Gini ratio, the greater is the degree of income inequality. If income is equally distributed, the Lorenz curve is the same as the line of equality, so the Gini ratio is zero. If most people have an income close to zero and a few people have very large incomes, the Gini ratio is close to 1.

Figure 19.5 shows the U.S. Gini ratio from 1971 to 2011. You can see that the Gini ratio has steadily increased, which means that incomes have become less equal.

FIGURE 19.5   The U.S. Gini Ratio: 1971–2011

Measured by the Gini ratio, the distribution of income in the United States became more unequal from 1971 to 2011. The percentage of income earned by the richest households increased through these years. Changes in definitions make the numbers before and after 1992 and before and after 2000 not comparable. Despite the breaks in the data, the trends are still visible.

Source of data: See Fig. 19.1.

————————— MyEconLab animation ——

Economics in Action

The Rich Get Richer, but School Still Pays

American incomes have been getting steadily more unequal, and in 2011 more than 30 percent of Americans told the Gallup poll that they think incomes are too unequal. Twenty years earlier, in 1991, only 21 percent of Americans thought there were too many rich people.

A key feature of rising inequality is the trend in the incomes of the super rich. Emmanuel Saez of the University of California, Berkeley, used tax returns data to get the numbers graphed in Fig. 1.

After decades of a falling share, starting in 1981, the share of income received by the richest one percent began a steady climb. By 2010 (the latest year in the database), the richest 1 percent were earning 17.4 percent of the nation's income.

The bottom quintile gets 3.4 percent of total income, so an average household in the top 1 percent receives more than 100 times the average income of a household in the lowest quintile.

Movie stars, sports stars, and the CEOs of large corporations are among the super rich. People who scratch out a living doing seasonal work on farms earn the lowest incomes. Aside from these extremes, what are the characteristics of the people who earn high

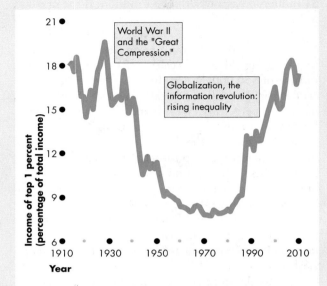

Figure 1 The Income Shares of the Top One Percent

Source of data: Alvaredo, Facundo, Anthony B. Atkinson, Thomas Piketty and Emmanuel Saez, The World Top Incomes Database, http://g-mond.parisschoolofeconomics.eu/topincomes, 12/08/2012.

incomes and the people who earn low incomes? Figure 2 below answers this question. (The data are for 2011, but the patterns are persistent).

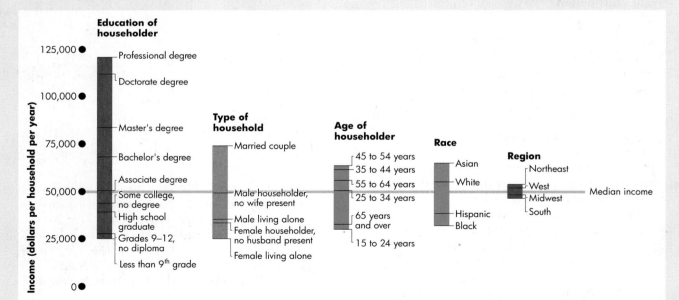

Figure 2 The Distribution of Income by Selected Household Characteristics

Source of data: See Fig. 19.1.

Education A postgraduate education is the main source of a high income. A person with a professional degree (such as a medical or law degree) earns, on average, $121,000—more than double the median income. Just completing high school raises a person's income by more than $12,000 a year; and getting a bachelor's degree adds another $30,000 a year. The average income of people who have not completed 9th grade is $26,000—less than half the median income.

Type of Household Married couples earn more, on average, than people who live alone. A married couple earns about $74,000. In contrast, men who live alone earn about $50,000, and women who live alone earn only $34,000.

Age of Householder Households with the oldest and youngest householders have lower incomes than do those with middle-aged householders. When the householder is aged between 45 and 54, household income averages $64,000. And when the householder is aged between 35 and 44, household income averages $62,000. When the householder is aged between 15 and 24, average household income is $30,000. And for householders over 65, the average household income is $33,000.

Race and Ethnicity White Americans have an average income of $55,000, while black Americans have an average income of $33,000. People of Hispanic origin are a bit better off, with an average income of $39,000. Asians are best off with an average income of $65,000.

Region People who live in the West and Northeast earn more, on average, than people who live in the Midwest and the South. While the region does make a difference, its magnitude is small compared to the dominating effect of education.

The bottom line: School pays and so does marriage.

Poverty

Households at the bottom of the income distribution are so poor that they are considered to be living in poverty. **Poverty** is a situation in which a household's income is too low to be able to buy the quantities of food, shelter, and clothing that are deemed necessary. This concept of poverty is relative: People are poor compared to what is regarded as normal or average, and so poor that their situation is regarded as a problem that needs attention.

A different poverty concept is *absolute poverty*—poverty so extreme that it challenges survival. For millions of people living in Africa and Asia, poverty is absolute. The poorest struggle to survive on incomes of less than $400 a year.

Official U.S. Poverty Measure In the United States, the poverty level is calculated each year by the Social Security Administration. In 2012, the poverty level for a four-person household was an income of $23,050. Other income levels apply to households of different sizes.

Amount of Poverty About 46 million Americans—15 percent of the population—live in households that have incomes below the poverty level. The incidence of poverty varies by race, age, work experience, physical ability, and household status.

We'll look at each of these influences on poverty.

Race The poverty rate among white Americans is 13 percent compared to 25 percent for Hispanic-origin Americans and 28 percent of black Americans.

But the absolute number of white Americans in poverty, 31 million, is greater than the number of minority households—11 million black and 13 million Hispanic.

Age Poverty rates are 22 percent for children, 14 percent for people aged 18 to 64, and 9 percent for seniors aged 65 and over.

Work Experience Americans with a job, either full time or part time, are much less likely to be living in poverty than those without a job. The poverty rate for those with jobs is 7 percent and for those without jobs is 33 percent.

Physical Ability People with disabilities experience a very high poverty rate—29 percent. These people often have no jobs and no easy access to care.

Household Status More than 28 percent of households in which the householder is a female with no husband present have incomes below the poverty level.

The overall poverty rate and the averages for the groups we've just examined have increased during the past few years following a major economic recession. But aside from this recent upturn in the poverty rate, it has been remarkably constant.

Economics in Action

Is the American Dream Still Alive?

The "American Dream" is that with hard work and fair play, everyone can expect to be rewarded with a better and rising standard of living. Is this idea alive and well today?

Of the several ways in which we might test whether the dream is still alive, the one that we'll examine here is the mobility that occurs up and down the income distribution. Can households in the middle, lower, and bottom quintiles move up to a higher quintile?

The graphs, which show data for 2007 to 2009, provide an answer to this question. Part (a) shows that about a quarter of the households in the middle quintile moved up to higher quintiles and a few moved up two quintiles to the highest. Some households in the second and lowest quintiles also moved up two, three, and even four quintiles.

But by the definition of an income distribution, for all the movements up there must be some movements down. Top quintile households don't have a permanent right to be at the top. And as you can see in the graph, close to one fifth of the highest quintile moved down one quintile and a few, bringing the total down-

ward movement to about a quarter of households, even moved all the way to the bottom quintile.

Part (b) shows that a majority of households remained in the same quintile, and at both extremes more remained than moved. A majority of the middle quintile moved, but in roughly equal numbers in both directions.

So what do these data say about the dream? It is alive for some: It is possible to move up the income ladder. But it is also possible to move down. There is two-way mobility for American households.

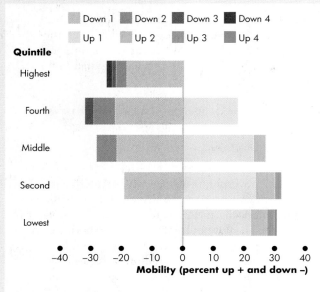

(a) Income mobility
Income Mobility and Immobility 2007–2009

Sources of data: See Fig. 19.4.

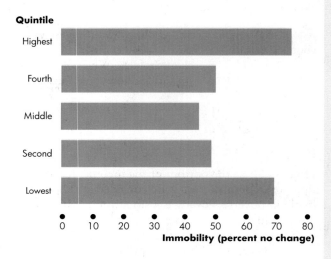

(b) Income immobility

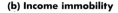

REVIEW QUIZ

1 Which is distributed more unequally, income or wealth? Why? Which is the better measure?

2 How has the distribution of income changed in the past few decades?

3 What are the main characteristics of high-income and low-income households?

4 What is poverty and how does its incidence vary across the races?

5 How much mobility has there been through the income quintiles since 2007?

You can work these questions in Study Plan 19.1 and get instant feedback.   MyEconLab

Inequality in the World Economy

Which countries have the greatest economic inequality and which have the least and the greatest equality? Where does the United States rank? Is it one of the most equal or most unequal or somewhere in the middle? And how much inequality is there in the world as a whole when we consider the entire world as a single global economy?

We'll answer these questions by first looking at the income distribution in a selection of countries and then by examining features of the global distribution of income.

Income Distributions in Selected Countries

By inspecting the income distribution data for every country, we can compare the degree of income inequality and identify the countries with the most inequality and those with the least inequality.

Figure 19.6 summarizes some extremes and shows where the United States lies in the range of degrees of income inequality.

Look first at the numbers in the table. They tell us that in Brazil and South Africa, the poorest 20 percent of households receive only 2 percent of total income while the highest 20 percent receive 65 percent of total income. An average person in the highest quintile receives 32.5 times the income of an average person in the lowest quintile.

Contrast these numbers with those for Finland and Sweden. In these countries, the poorest 20 percent receive 8 percent of total income and the highest 20 percent receive 35 percent. So an average person in the highest quintile receives 4.4 times the income of an average person in the lowest quintile.

The numbers for the United States lie between these extremes with an average person in the highest quintile receiving just under 10 times the amount received by an average person in the lowest quintile.

Brazil and South Africa are extremes not matched in any other major country or region. Inequality is large in these countries because they have a relatively small but rich European population and a large and relatively poor indigenous population.

Finland and Sweden are extremes, but they are not unusual. Income distributions similar to these are found in many European countries in which governments pursue aggressive income redistribution policies.

We look next at the global income distribution.

FIGURE 19.6 Lorenz Curves Compared

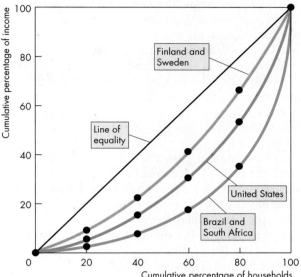

Households (percentage)	Percentage of total income[1]		
	Brazil and South Africa	United States	Finland and Sweden
Lowest 20	2	5	8
Second 20	5	10	14
Middle 20	10	16	20
Next highest 20	18	22	23
Highest 20	65	47	35

The table shows the percentages of total income received by each quintile. The figure shows the cumulative percentage of income graphed against the cumulative percentage of households. The data and the Lorenz curves show that income is distributed most unequally in Brazil and South Africa and least unequally in Finland and Sweden. The degree of income inequality in the United States lies between these extremes.

Sources of data: Brazil, South Africa, Finland, and Sweden, Klaus W. Deininger and Lyn Squire, Measuring Income Inequality Database, World Bank, http://go.worldbank.org/. United States, See Fig. 19.1.

[1] The data are based on income *after* redistribution. See pp. 457–459 for an account of income redistribution in the United States.

————— MyEconLab animation —————

Global Inequality and Its Trends

The global distribution of income is much more unequal than the distribution within any one country. The reason is that many countries, especially in Africa and Asia, are in a pre-industrial stage of economic development and are poor, while industrial countries such as the United States are rich. When we look at the distribution of income across the entire world population that goes from the low income of the poorest African to the high income of the richest American, we observe a very large degree of inequality.

To put some raw numbers on this inequality, start with the poorest. Measured in the value of the U.S. dollar in 2005, a total of 3 billion people or 50 percent of the world population live on $2.50 a day or less. Another 2 billion people or 30 percent of the world population live on more than $2.50 but less than $10 a day. So 5 billion people or 80 percent of the world population live on $10 a day or less.

In contrast, in the rich United States, the *average* person has an income of $115 per day and an average person in the highest income quintile has an income of $460 a day.

So the average American earns 46 times the income of one of the world's 3 billion poorest people and more than 11.5 times the income of 80 percent of the people who live in developing economies. An American with the average income in the highest quintile earns 184 times that of the world's poorest people but only 15 times that of an average bottom quintile American.

World Gini Ratio We can compare world inequality with U.S. inequality by comparing Gini ratios. You saw that the U.S. Gini ratio in 2009 was about 0.47. The world Gini ratio is about 0.61. Recalling the interpretation of the Gini ratio in terms of the Lorenz curve, the world Lorenz curve lies much farther from the line of equality than the U.S. Lorenz curve.

World Trend You saw (in Fig. 19.5 on p. 447) that incomes have become more unequal in the United States—the Gini ratio has increased. The same trends are found in most economies. Increased income inequality is a big issue in two of the world's largest and poor nations, China and India. In these two economies, urban middle classes are getting richer at a faster pace than the rural farmers.

Despite greater inequality within countries, the world is becoming *less* unequal. Figure 19.7 shows

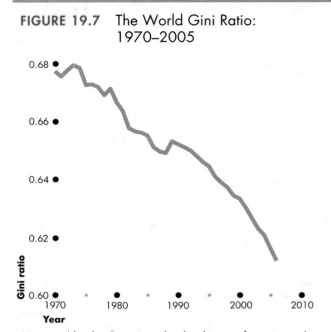

FIGURE 19.7   The World Gini Ratio: 1970–2005

Measured by the Gini ratio, the distribution of income in the entire world became more equal between 1970 and 2005.

Source of data: Xavier Sala-i-Martin and Maxim Pinkovskiy, "Parametric estimations of the world distribution of income," 22 January 2010, http://www.voxeu.org/article/parametric-estimations-world-distribution-income.

——————— MyEconLab animation ———————

this trend toward less inequality as measured by the world Gini ratio. How can the world income distribution become less unequal while individual countries become more unequal? The answer is that average incomes in poorer countries are rising much faster than average incomes in rich countries. While the gap between rich and poor is widening within countries, it is narrowing across countries.

REVIEW QUIZ

1 In which countries are incomes distributed most unequally and least unequally?
2 Which income distribution is more unequal and why: the income distribution in the United States or in the entire world?
3 How can incomes become *more* unequally distributed within countries and *less* unequally distributed across countries?

You can work these questions in Study Plan 19.2 and get instant feedback.   MyEconLab

The Sources of Economic Inequality

We've described some key facts about economic inequality and its trends and our task now is to explain those facts. We began this task in Chapter 18 by learning about the forces that influence demand and supply in the markets for labor, capital, and land. We're now going to deepen our understanding of these forces.

Inequality arises from unequal labor market outcomes and from unequal ownership of capital. We'll begin by looking at labor markets and three features of them that contribute to differences in income:

- Human capital
- Discrimination
- Contests among superstars

Human Capital

A clerk in a law firm earns less than a tenth of the amount earned by the attorney he assists. An operating room assistant earns less than a tenth of the amount earned by the surgeon with whom she works. A bank teller earns less than a tenth of the amount earned by the bank's CEO. Some of the differences in these earnings arise from differences in human capital.

To see the influence of human capital on labor incomes, consider the example of a law clerk and the attorney he assists. (The same reasoning can be applied to an operating room assistant and surgeon, or a bank teller and bank CEO.)

Demand, Supply, and Wage Rates An attorney performs many tasks that a law clerk cannot perform. Imagine an untrained law clerk cross-examining a witness in a complicated trial. The tasks that the attorney performs are valued highly by her clients who willingly pay for her services. Using a term that you learned in Chapter 18, an attorney has a *high value of marginal product*, and a higher value of marginal product than her law clerk. But you also learned in Chapter 18 that the value of marginal product of labor determines (is the same as) the demand for labor. So, because an attorney has a higher value of marginal product, the demand for attorney services is greater than the demand for law-clerk services.

To become an attorney, a person must acquire human capital. But human capital is costly to acquire. This cost—an opportunity cost—includes expenditures on tuition and textbooks. It also includes forgone earnings during the years spent in college and law school. It might also include low earnings doing on-the-job training in a law office during the summer.

Because the human capital needed to supply attorney services is costly to acquire, a person's willingness to supply these services reflects this cost. The supply of attorney services is smaller than the supply of law-clerk services.

The demand for and supply of each type of labor determine the wage rate that each type of labor earns. Attorneys earn a higher wage rate than law clerks because the demand for attorneys is greater and the supply of attorneys is smaller. The gap between the wage rates reflects the higher value of marginal product of an attorney (demand) and the cost of acquiring human capital (supply).

Trends in Wage Inequality You've seen that high-income households have earned an increasing share of total income while low-income households have earned a decreasing share: The distribution of income in the United States has become more unequal. Technological change and globalization are two possible sources of this increased inequality.

Technological Change Information technologies such as computers and laser scanners are *substitutes* for low-skilled labor: They perform tasks that previously were performed by low-skilled labor. The introduction of these technologies has lowered the marginal product and the demand for low-skilled labor. These same technologies require high-skilled labor to design, program, and run them. High-skilled labor and the information technologies are *complements*. So the introduction of these technologies has increased the marginal product and demand for high-skilled labor.

Figure 19.8 illustrates the effects on wages and employment. The supply of low-skilled labor in part (a) and that of high-skilled labor in part (b) are S, and initially, the demand in each market is D_0. The low-skill wage rate is \$5 an hour, and the high-skill wage rate is \$10 an hour. The demand for low-skilled labor decreases to D_1 in part (a) and the demand for high-skilled labor increases to D_1 in part (b). The low-skill wage rate falls to \$4 an hour and the high-skill wage rate rises to \$15 an hour.

Globalization The entry of China and other developing countries into the global economy has low-

FIGURE 19.8   Explaining the Trend in Income Distribution

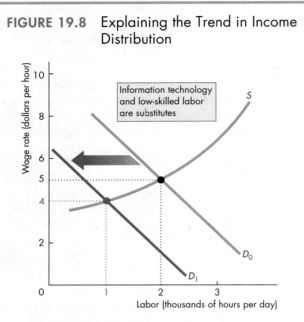

(a) A decrease in demand for low-skilled labor

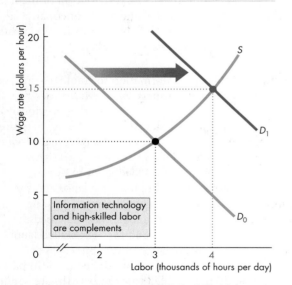

(b) An increase in demand for high-skilled labor

Low-skilled labor in part (a) and information technologies are substitutes. Advances in information technology decrease the demand for low-skilled labor and lower its wage rate. High-skilled labor in part (b) and information technologies are complements. Advances in information technology increase the demand for high-skilled labor and raise its wage rate.

————— MyEconLab animation —————

ered the prices of many manufactured goods. Lower prices for the firm's output lowers the value of marginal product of the firm's workers and decreases the demand for their labor. A situation like that in Fig. 19.8(a) occurs. The wage rate falls, and employment shrinks.

At the same time, the growing global economy increases the demand for services that employ high-skilled workers, and the value of marginal product and the demand for high-skilled labor increases. A situation like that in Fig. 19.8(b) occurs. The wage rate rises, and employment opportunities for high-skilled workers expand.

Discrimination

Human capital differences can explain some of the economic inequality that we observe. Discrimination is another possible source of inequality.

Suppose that black females and white males have identical abilities as investment advisors. If everyone is free of race and sex prejudice, the market determines the same wage rate for both groups. But if customers are prejudiced against women and minorities, this prejudice is reflected in the wage rates—white men earn more than black women.

Counteracting Forces Economists disagree about whether prejudice actually causes wage differentials, and one line of reasoning implies that it does not. In the above example, customers who buy from white men pay a higher service charge for investment advice than do the customers who buy from black women. This price difference acts as an incentive to encourage people who are prejudiced to buy from the people against whom they are prejudiced. This force could be strong enough to eliminate the effects of discrimination altogether. Suppose, as is true in manufacturing, that a firm's customers never meet its workers. If such a firm discriminates against women or minorities, it can't compete with firms who hire these groups because its costs are higher than those of the nonprejudiced firms. Only firms that do not discriminate survive in a competitive industry.

Whether because of discrimination or from some other source, women and visible minorities do earn lower incomes than white males. Another possible source of lower wage rates of women arises from differences in the relative degree of specialization of women and men.

Differences in the Degree of Specialization Couples must choose how to allocate their time between working for a wage and doing jobs in the home, such as cooking, cleaning, shopping, organizing vacations, and, most important, bearing and raising children. Let's look at the choices of Bob and Sue.

Bob might specialize in earning an income and Sue in taking care of the home. Or Sue might specialize in earning an income and Bob in taking care of the home. Or both of them might earn an income and share home production jobs.

The allocation they choose depends on their preferences and on their earning potential. The choice of an increasing number of households is for each person to diversify between earning an income and doing some household chores. But in most households, Bob will specialize in earning an income and Sue will both earn an income and bear a larger share of the task of running the home. With this allocation, Bob will probably earn more than Sue. If Sue devotes time and effort to ensuring Bob's mental and physical well-being, the quality of Bob's market labor will be higher than it would be if he were diversified. If the roles were reversed, Sue would be able to supply market labor that earns more than Bob's.

To test whether the degree of specialization accounts for earnings differences between the sexes, economists have compared the incomes of never-married men and women. They have found that, on the average, with equal amounts of human capital, the wages of these two groups are the same.

Contests Among Superstars

The differences in income that arise from differences in human capital are important and affect a large proportion of the population. But human capital differences can't account for some of the really large income differences.

The super rich—those in the top one percent of the income distribution whose income share has been rising—earn vastly more than can be explained by human capital differences. What makes a person super rich?

A clue to the answer is provided by thinking about the super rich in tennis and golf. What makes tennis players and golfers special is that their earnings depend on where they finish in a tournament. When Serena Williams won the U.S. Open Tennis Championship in 2012, she received $1,900,000. The runner-up in this event, Victoria Azarenka

received $950,000. So Serena earned double the amount earned by Victoria. And she earned 83 times the amount received by the players who lost in the first round of the tournament.

It is true that Serena Williams has a lot of human capital. She practices hard and long and is a remarkable athlete. But anyone who is good enough to get into a tennis Grand Slam tournament is similarly well equipped with human capital and has spent a similar number of long hours in training and practice. It isn't human capital that explains the differences in earnings. It is the tournament and the prize differences that accounts for the large differences in earnings.

But three questions jump out: First, why do we reward superstar tennis players (and golfers) with prizes for winning a contest? Second, why are the prizes so different? And third, do the principles that apply on the tennis court (and golf course) apply more generally?

Why Prizes for a Contest? The answer to this question (which was noted in Chapter 5, see p. 106) is that contests with prizes do a good job of allocating scarce resources efficiently when the efforts of the participants are hard to monitor and reward directly. There is only one winner, but many people work hard in an attempt to be that person. So a great deal of diligent effort is induced by a contest.

Why Are Prizes So Different? The prizes need to be substantially different to induce enough effort. If the winner received 10 percent more than the runner up, the gain from being the winner would be insufficient to encourage anyone to work hard enough. Someone would win but no one would put in much effort. Tennis matches would be boring, golf scores would be high, and no one would be willing to pay to see these sports. Big differences are necessary to induce a big enough effort to generate the quality of performance that people are willing to pay to see.

Does the Principle Apply More Generally? Winner-takes-all isn't confined to tennis and golf. Movie stars, superstars in baseball, basketball, football, and ice hockey, and top corporate executives can all be viewed as participants in contests that decide the winners. The prize for the winner is an income at least double that of the runner up and many multiples of the incomes of those who drop out earlier in the tournament.

Do Contests Among Superstars Explain the Trend?
Contests among superstars can explain large differences in incomes. But can contests explain the trend toward greater inequality with an increasing share of total income going to the super rich as shown on p. 448?

An idea first suggested by University of Chicago economist Sherwin Rosen suggests that a winner-takes-all contest can explain the trend. The key is that globalization has increased the market reach of the winner and increased the spread between the winner and the runners-up.

Global television audiences now watch all the world's major sporting events and the total revenue generated by advertising spots during these events has increased. Competition among networks and cable and satellite television distributors has increased the fees that event organizers receive. And to attract the top star performers, prize money has increased and the winner gets the biggest share of the prize pot.

So the prizes in sports have become bigger and the share of income going to the "winner" has increased.

A similar story can be told about superstars and the super rich in business. As the cost of doing business on a global scale has fallen, more and more businesses have become global in their reach. Not only are large multinational corporations sourcing their inputs from far afield and selling in every country, they are also recruiting their top executives from a global talent pool. With a larger source of talent, and a larger total revenue, firms must make the "prize"—the reward for the top job—more attractive to compete for the best managers.

We've examined some sources of inequality in the labor market. Let's now look at the way inequality arises from unequal ownership of capital.

Unequal Wealth

You've seen that wealth inequality—excluding human capital—is much greater than income inequality. This greater wealth inequality arises from two sources: life-cycle saving patterns and transfers of wealth from one generation to the next.

Life-Cycle Saving Patterns Over a family's life cycle, wealth starts out at zero or perhaps less than zero. A student who has financed education all the way through graduate school might have lots of human capital and an outstanding student loan of $60,000. This person has negative wealth. Gradually loans get

paid off and a retirement fund is accumulated. At the point of retiring from full-time work, the family has maximum wealth. Then, during its retirement years, the family spends its wealth. This life-cycle pattern means that much of the wealth is owned by people in their sixties.

Intergenerational Transfers Some households inherit wealth from the previous generation. Some save more than enough on which to live during retirement and transfer wealth to the next generation. But these intergenerational transfers of wealth do not always increase wealth inequality. If a generation that has a high income saves a large part of that income and leaves wealth to a succeeding generation that has a lower income, this transfer decreases the degree of inequality. But one feature of intergenerational transfers of wealth leads to increased inequality: wealth concentration through marriage.

Marriage and Wealth Concentration People tend to marry within their own socioeconomic class—a phenomenon called *assortative mating*. In everyday language, "like attracts like." Although there is a good deal of folklore that "opposites attract," perhaps such Cinderella tales appeal to us because they are so rare in reality. Wealthy people seek wealthy partners.

Because of assortative mating, wealth becomes more concentrated in a small number of families and the distribution of wealth becomes more unequal.

REVIEW QUIZ

1 What role does human capital play in accounting for income inequality?
2 What role might discrimination play in accounting for income inequality?
3 What role might contests among superstars play in accounting for income inequality?
4 How might technological change and globalization explain trends in the distribution of income?
5 Does inherited wealth make the distribution of income less equal or more equal?

You can work these questions in Study Plan 19.3 and get instant feedback.   MyEconLab

Next, we're going to see how taxes and government programs redistribute income and decrease the degree of economic inequality.

▶ Income Redistribution

The three main ways in which governments in the United States redistribute income are

- Income taxes
- Income maintenance programs
- Subsidized services

Income Taxes

Income taxes may be progressive, regressive, or proportional. A **progressive income tax** is one that taxes income at an average rate that increases as income increases. A **regressive income tax** is one that taxes income at an average rate that decreases as income increases. A **proportional income tax** (also called a *flat-rate income tax*) is one that taxes income at a constant average rate, regardless of the level of income.

The income tax rates that apply in the United States are composed of two parts: federal and state taxes. Some cities, such as New York City, also have an income tax. There is variety in the detailed tax arrangements in the individual states, but the tax system, at both the federal and state levels, is progressive. The poorest working households receive money from the government through an earned income tax credit. Successively higher-income households pay 10 percent, 15 percent, 25 percent, 28 percent, 33 percent, and 35 percent of each additional dollar earned.

Income Maintenance Programs

Three main types of programs redistribute income by making direct payments (in cash, services, or vouchers) to people in the lower part of the income distribution. They are

- Social Security programs
- Unemployment compensation
- Welfare programs

Social Security Programs   The main Social Security program is OASDHI—Old Age, Survivors, Disability, and Health Insurance. Monthly cash payments to retired or disabled workers or their surviving spouses and children are paid for by compulsory payroll taxes on both employers and employees. In 2010, total Social Security expenditure was budgeted at

$736 billion, and the standard monthly Social Security check for a married couple was a bit more than $1,892 in 2010.

The other component of Social Security is Medicare, which provides hospital and health insurance for the elderly and disabled.

Unemployment Compensation   To provide an income to unemployed workers, every state has established an unemployment compensation program. Under these programs, a tax is paid that is based on the income of each covered worker and such a worker receives a benefit when he or she becomes unemployed. The details of the benefits vary from state to state.

Welfare Programs   The purpose of welfare is to provide incomes for people who do not qualify for Social Security or unemployment compensation. They are

1. Supplementary Security Income (SSI) program, designed to help the neediest elderly, disabled, and blind people

2. Temporary Assistance for Needy Households (TANF) program, designed to help households that have inadequate financial resources

3. Food Stamp program, designed to help the poorest households obtain a basic diet

4. Medicaid, designed to cover the costs of medical care for households receiving help under the SSI and TANF programs

Subsidized Services

A great deal of redistribution takes place in the United States through the provision of subsidized services—services provided by the government at prices below the cost of production. The taxpayers who consume these goods and services receive a transfer in kind from the taxpayers who do not consume them. The two most important areas in which this form of redistribution takes place are health care and education—both kindergarten through grade 12 and college and university.

In 2011–2012, students enrolled in the University of California system paid annual tuition and fees of $13,200. The cost of providing a year's education at the University of California was probably about $36,000. So households with a member enrolled in one of these institutions received a benefit from the government of $22,800 a year.

Economics in Action

Income Redistribution: Only the Richest Pay

A household's *market income* tells us what a household earns in the absence of government redistribution. You've seen that market income is *not* the official basis for measuring the distribution of income that we've used in this chapter. The Census Bureau's measure is *money income* (market income plus cash transfers from the government). But market income is the correct starting point for measuring the scale of income redistribution.

We begin with market income and then subtract taxes and add the amounts received in benefits. The result is the distribution of income after taxes and benefits. The data available on benefits exclude the value of subsidized services such as college, so the resulting distribution might understate the total amount of redistribution from the rich to the poor.

The figures show the scale of redistribution in 2001, the most recent year for which the Census Bureau has provided these data. In Fig. 1, the blue Lorenz curve describes the market distribution of income and the green Lorenz curve shows the distribution of income after all taxes and benefits, including Medicaid and Medicare benefits. (The Lorenz curve based on money income in Fig. 19.3 lies between these two curves.)

The distribution after taxes and benefits is less unequal than is the market distribution. The lowest 20 percent of households received only 0.9 percent of market income but 4.6 percent of income after taxes and benefits. The highest 20 percent of households received 55.6 percent of market income, but only 46.7 percent of income after taxes and benefits.

Figure 2 highlights the percentage of total income redistributed among the five groups. The share of total income received by the lowest 60 percent of households increased. The share received by the fourth quintile barely changed. And the share received by the highest quintile fell by 8.9 percent.

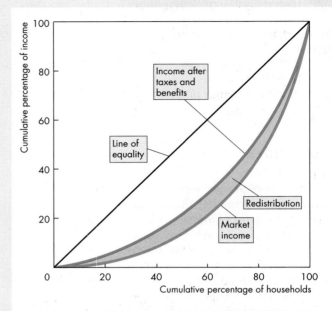

Figure 1 Income Distribution Before and After Redistribution

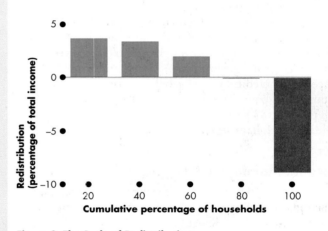

Figure 2 The Scale of Redistribution

Source of data: U.S. Bureau of the Census, "Income Poverty, and Health Insurance Coverage in the United States: 2007," *Current Population Reports*, P-60-235 (Washington, DC: U.S. Government Printing Office, 2008).

Government provision of health-care services has grown to the scale of private provision. Programs such as Medicaid and Medicare bring high-quality and high-cost health care to millions of people who earn too little to buy such services themselves.

The Big Tradeoff

The redistribution of income creates what has been called the **big tradeoff**, a tradeoff between equity and efficiency. The big tradeoff arises because redistribution uses scarce resources and weakens incentives.

A dollar collected from a rich person does not translate into a dollar received by a poor person. Some of it gets used up in the process of redistribution. Tax-collecting agencies such as the Internal Revenue Service and welfare-administering agencies (as well as tax accountants and lawyers) use skilled labor, computers, and other scarce resources to do their work. The bigger the scale of redistribution, the greater is the opportunity cost of administering it.

But the cost of collecting taxes and making welfare payments is a small part of the total cost of redistribution. A bigger cost arises from the inefficiency (deadweight loss) of taxes and benefits. Greater equality can be achieved only by taxing productive activities such as work and saving. Taxing people's income from their work and saving lowers the after-tax income they receive. This lower after-tax income makes them work and save less, which in turn results in smaller output and less consumption not only for the rich who pay the taxes but also for the poor who receive the benefits.

It is not only taxpayers who face weaker incentives to work. Benefit recipients also face weaker incentives. In fact, under the welfare arrangements that prevailed before the 1996 reforms, the weakest incentives to work were those faced by households that benefited from welfare. When a welfare recipient got a job, benefits were withdrawn and eligibility for programs such as Medicaid ended, so the household in effect paid a tax of more than 100 percent on its earnings. This arrangement locked poor households in a welfare trap.

So the agencies that determine the scale and methods of income redistribution must pay close attention to the incentive effects of taxes and benefits. Let's close this chapter by looking at one way in which lawmakers are tackling the big tradeoff today.

A Major Welfare Challenge Young women who have not completed high school, have a child (or children), live without a partner, and more likely are black or Hispanic are among the poorest people in the United States today. They and their children present a major welfare challenge.

First, their numbers are large. In 2011, there were 16 million single-mother families. This number is 13 percent of families. In 2009 (the most recent year with census data), single mothers were owed $35 billion in child support and 30 percent of the women received no support from their children's fathers.

The long-term solution to the problem these women face is education and job training—acquiring human capital. The short-term solutions are enforcing child support payments by absent fathers and former spouses and providing welfare.

Welfare must be designed to minimize the disincentive to pursue the long-term goal of becoming self-supporting. The current welfare program in the United States tries to walk this fine line.

Passed in 1996, the Personal Responsibility and Work Opportunities Reconciliation Act strengthened the Office of Child Support Enforcement and increased the penalties for nonpayment of support. The act also created the Temporary Assistance for Needy Households (TANF) program. TANF is a block grant paid to the states, which administer payments to individuals. It is not an open-ended entitlement program. An adult member of a household that is receiving assistance must either work or perform community service, and there is a five-year limit for assistance.

REVIEW QUIZ

1 How do governments in the United States redistribute income?

2 Describe the scale of redistribution in the United States.

3 What is one of the major welfare challenges today and how is it being tackled in the United States?

You can work these questions in Study Plan 19.4 and get instant feedback.   MyEconLab

◆ We've examined the scale and rising trend of economic inequality. *Reading Between the Lines* on pp. 460–461 looks at an example of government subsidies intended to benefit the poor that end up benefiting the rich.

The next chapter focuses on some problems for the market economy that arise from uncertainty and incomplete information. But unlike the cases we studied in Chapters 16 and 17, this time the market does a good job of coping with the problems.

Using Subsidies to Redistribute Income

Leaders Cling to Subsidies

The Financial Times
September 13, 2012

Popular revolts sweeping the Arab world are throwing up a financial dilemma for struggling governments who want to scrap expensive energy subsidies but fear they will provoke riots if they do. Countries in the Middle East and north Africa spent $212 billion (U.S.) last year on food and energy subsidies, the equivalent of more than 7 percent of the region's gross domestic product, according to the International Monetary Fund estimates.

Fuel subsidies accounted for a striking four-fifths of the total cost. But it is the much less wealthy Arab oil-importing countries that face the biggest subsidy problem. Egypt's budget deficit is 11 percent of gross domestic product.

Officials in Egypt, where 20 percent of the state budget is eaten by keeping fuel prices low, promised the total cancellation of subsidies in energy-intensive industries and the enforcement of a nationwide coupon distribution system to help limit the impact on the poorest people.

So far, there has been scant evidence of this policy taking place.

It is a reminder of the difficulty that Arab world governments face in convincing their populations that removing subsidies will ultimately help them, because energy subsidies are not only a drag on the economy but can also disproportionately benefit wealthy, high consumers of energy. . . .

ESSENCE OF THE STORY

- Subsidies, mainly of food and fuel, account for over 7 percent of the value of the Middle East's production (gross domestic product) and for more than 20 percent of Egypt's state budget.

- Egypt's government fears that cutting subsidies would be extremely unpopular.

- The subsidy system disproportionately benefits the rich because they consume more fuel than the poor.

- To ensure that subsidized fuel reaches only the poor, the Egyptian government has promised to end subsidies to energy-intensive industries and to introduce a nationwide coupon distribution system.

- This new system is not yet operating.

ECONOMIC ANALYSIS

- The governments of developing nations redistribute income with the aim of alleviating poverty in the short run and encouraging choices that have long-term effects.

- Some governments provide cash and some provide specific goods or services—called "in-kind" transfers—to targeted families.

- Cash and in-kind transfers help the poor in the short run but often lock them in poverty.

- To get better long-run outcomes, many governments in developing nations have started using Conditional Cash Transfers (CCT).

- As the term implies, CCTs come with conditions. Their recipients must take steps to enhance their productivity and help pull themselves and their future generations out of poverty.

- Two standard conditions are (1) that recipient households attend an illiteracy eradication program, and (2) that they enroll their children in schools and ensure their regular attendance.

- More than 30 developing countries have active CCT programs and many more are starting them.

- CCT programs are costly to operate. These costs include those of identifying the target families and monitoring them to ensure compliance with the conditions imposed.

- Because of the cost of operating a CCT program, many developing nations redistribute income by subsidizing consumer goods and services.

- If the items subsidized are consumed mainly by the lower income quintiles, subsidies achieve a more equal distribution—they lower the Gini ratio and move the Lorenz curve closer to the line of equality.

- But if the items subsidized are consumed mainly by the higher income quintiles, subsidies result in a *less equal* distribution—they raise the Gini ratio and move the Lorenz curve away from the line of equality.

- In Egypt, one of the countries that uses subsidies, the items subsidized most heavily are food and fuel.

- Families in the high-income quintiles consume much more fuel than do families in the low-income quintiles. So Egypt's fuel subsidies end up making the distribution of income *less equal*.

- Egypt's inequality also has a regional dimension and an urban versus rural dimension.

- Figure 1 shows these two dimensions of inequality using the Gini ratio.

- Income is distributed more unequally in Upper Egypt (higher Gini ratio) than in Lower Egypt.

- And income is distributed more unequally (higher Gini ratio) in urban Egypt than in rural Egypt.

- The large degree of urban inequality might be one of the reasons why the Egyptian political revolution was more an urban rather than a rural phenomenon.

- If the Egyptian government were to use information on the regional degree of poverty, it might target programs more accurately at the urban poor, especially those in Upper Egypt.

- If the Egyptian government is to succeed in achieving less inequality (lowering the Gini ratio) in urban regions, it must replace its current general fuel subsidies with CCTs that target the poor, especially those in urban regions.

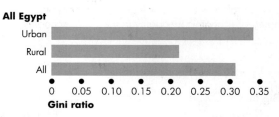

Figure 1 Gini Ratios for Egypt in 2010

Source of data: United Nations Development Program Database, International Human Development Indicators, 2010.

SUMMARY

Key Points

Economic Inequality in the United States (pp. 444–450)

- In 2011, the mode money income was $22,000 a year, the median money income was $50,054, and the mean money income was $69,677.
- The income distribution is positively skewed.
- In 2011, the poorest 20 percent of households received 3.2 percent of total income and the wealthiest 20 percent received 51.1 percent of total income.
- Wealth is distributed more unequally than income because the wealth data exclude the value of human capital.
- Since 1971, the distribution of income has become more unequal.
- Education, type of household, age of householder, and race all influence household income.

Working Problems 1 to 7 will give you a better understanding of economic inequality in the United States.

Inequality in the World Economy (pp. 451–452)

- Incomes are distributed most unequally in Brazil and South Africa and least unequally in Finland, Sweden, and some other European economies.
- The U.S. income distribution lies between the extremes.
- The distribution of income across individuals in the global economy is much more unequal than in the United States.
- The global income distribution has been getting less unequal as rapid income growth in China and India has lifted millions from poverty.

Working Problems 8 to 11 will give you a better understanding of economic inequality in the world economy.

The Sources of Economic Inequality (pp. 453–456)

- Inequality arises from differences in human capital and from contests among superstars.
- Trends in the distribution of human capital and in the rewards to superstars that arise from technological change and globalization can explain some of the trend in increased inequality.
- Inequality might arise from discrimination.
- Inequality between men and women might arise from differences in the degree of specialization.
- Intergenerational transfers of wealth lead to increased inequality because people can't inherit debts and assortative mating tends to concentrate wealth.

Working Problems 12 to 15 will give you a better understanding of the sources of economic inequality.

Income Redistribution (pp. 457–459)

- Governments redistribute income through progressive income taxes, income maintenance programs, and subsidized services.
- Redistribution increases the share of total income received by the lowest 60 percent of households and decreases the share of total income received by the highest quintile. The share of the fourth quintile barely changes.
- Because the redistribution of income weakens incentives, it creates a tradeoff between equity and efficiency.
- Effective redistribution seeks to support the long-term solution to low income, which is education and job training—acquiring human capital.

Working Problems 16 and 17 will give you a better understanding of income redistribution.

Key Terms

Big tradeoff, 458

Gini ratio, 447

Lorenz curve, 445

Market income, 444

Money income, 444

Poverty, 449

Progressive income tax, 457

Proportional income tax, 457

Regressive income tax, 457

Wealth, 446

STUDY PLAN PROBLEMS AND APPLICATIONS

MyEconLab   You can work Problems 1 to 17 in MyEconLab Chapter 19 Study Plan and get instant feedback.

Economic Inequality in the United States

(Study Plan 19.1)

1. What is money income? Describe the distribution of money income in the United States in 2011.

2. The table shows money income shares in the United States in 1991.

Households (percentage)	Money income (percentage of total)
Lowest 20	3.8
Second 20	9.6
Middle 20	15.9
Next highest 20	24.2
Highest 20	46.5

   a. Draw a Lorenz curve for the United States in 1991 and compare it with the Lorenz curve in 2011 shown in Fig. 19.3 on p. 445.

   b. Was U.S. money income distributed more equally 1991?

Use the following news clip to work Problems 3 to 6.

Household Incomes Rise but ...

As household income crept higher last year, more people in each household had to work because median earnings for those working full-time year-round actually fell. As the poverty rate edged lower, the percent of Americans living below the poverty line slipped to 12.3 percent in 2006.

The poverty threshold is based on personal data and not on the local cost of living, so the poverty threshold is the same in rural towns and large cities. Also it does not reflect the value of household subsidies such as food stamps, tax credits, and Medicaid, which are intended to alleviate the effects of poverty. Over the years, the gap between high-income and low-income households has grown, but income inequality remained unchanged between 2005 and 2006.

Source: CNN, August 28, 2007

3. Why is the recent increase in median household income a misleading statistic when attempting to measure the change in economic inequality?

4. How does using set poverty thresholds that apply to the entire United States complicate the attempt to measure poverty?

5. Why does excluding household subsidies lead to a misleading measurement of the percentage of people actually living in poverty?

6. Why has the gap between high-income and low-income households grown in recent decades?

7. **Census: Income Fell Sharply Last Year**

   The U.S. Census Bureau reported that in 2008 the median household income fell 3.6%. The share of people living in poverty rose to 13.2% in 2008 from 12.5% in 2007. Only households led by people aged 65 or older enjoyed income gains—a 1.2% increase.

   Source: *USA Today,* September 11, 2009

   a. What does the information in this news report tell you about changes in the distribution of income in 2008?

   b. What additional information would you need to know how the changes described changed the U.S. Lorenz curve?

Inequality in the World Economy (Study Plan 19.2)

8. Incomes in China and India are a small fraction of incomes in the United States. But incomes in China and India are growing at more than twice the rate of those in the United States.

   a. Explain how economic inequality in China and India is changing relative to that in the United States.

   b. How is the world Lorenz curve and world Gini ratio changing?

Use the following table to work Problems 9 to 11. The table shows the income shares in the United States, Canada, and the United Kingdom in 2009.

Households (percentage)	United States	Canada	United Kingdom
	(percentage of total income)		
Lowest 20	3	7	3
Second 20	8	13	5
Middle 20	15	18	14
Next highest 20	23	25	25
Highest 20	50	37	53

9. Create a table that shows the cumulative distribution of Canadian and U.K. incomes. Is the distribution of income more unequal in Canada or in the United Kingdom?

10. Draw the Lorenz curves for the United States and Canada. In which country was money income less equally distributed in 2009?

11. Draw the Lorenz curves for the United States and the United Kingdom. In which country was income less equally distributed in 2009?

The Sources of Economic Inequality (Study Plan 19.3)

12. The following figure shows the market for low-skilled labor.

The value of marginal product of high-skilled workers is $16 an hour greater than that of low-skilled workers at each quantity of labor. The cost of acquiring human capital adds $12 an hour to the wage that must be offered to attract high-skilled labor.

Compare the equilibrium wage rates of low-skilled labor and high-skilled labor. Explain why the difference between these wage rates equals the cost of acquiring human capital.

Use the following information to work Problems 13 and 14.

In 2010, 828,000 Americans had full-time management jobs that paid an average of $96,450 a year while 4.3 million Americans had full-time retail sales jobs that paid an average of $20,670 a year. Managers require a high school certificate while retail sales people don't but they undergo training.

Source: Bureau of Labor Statistics

13. Explain why managers are paid more than retail salespeople.

14. If the online shopping trend continues, how do you think the market for salespeople will change in coming years?

15. The figure shows the market for a group of workers who are discriminated against. Suppose that other workers in the same industry are not discriminated against and their value of marginal product is perceived to be twice that of the workers who are discriminated against. Suppose also that the supply of these other workers is 2,000 hours per day less at each wage rate.

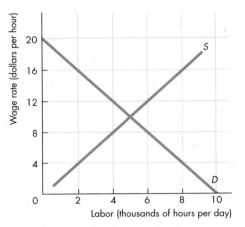

a. What is the wage rate of the workers who are discriminated against?

b. What is the quantity of workers employed who are discriminated against?

c. What is the wage rate of the workers who do not face discrimination?

d. What is the quantity of workers employed who do not face discrimination?

Income Redistribution (Study Plan 19.4)

Use the following table to work Problems 16 and 17. The table shows three redistribution schemes.

Before-tax income (dollars)	Plan A tax (dollars)	Plan B tax (dollars)	Plan C tax (dollars)
10,000	1,000	1,000	2,000
20,000	2,000	4,000	2,000
30,000	3,000	9,000	2,000

16. Which scheme has a proportional tax? Which scheme has a regressive tax? Which scheme has a progressive tax?

17. Which scheme will increase economic inequality? Which scheme will reduce economic inequality? Which scheme will have no effect on economic inequality?

ADDITIONAL PROBLEMS AND APPLICATIONS

MyEconLab   You can work these problems in MyEconLab if assigned by your instructor.

Economic Inequality in the United States

Use the following table to work Problems 18 and 19. The table shows the distribution of market income in the United States in 2007.

Households (percentage)	Market income (percentage of total)
Lowest 20	1.1
Second 20	7.1
Middle 20	13.9
Next highest 20	22.8
Highest 20	55.1

18. a. What is the definition of market income?
    b. Draw the Lorenz curve for the distribution of market income.

19. Compare the distribution of market income with the distribution of money income shown in Fig. 19.3 on p. 445. Which distribution is more unequal and why?

Inequality in the World Economy

Use the following table to work Problems 20 to 22. The table shows shares of income in Australia.

Households (percentage)	Income share (percentage of total)
Lowest 20	7
Second 20	13
Middle 20	18
Next highest 20	24
Highest 20	38

20. Draw the Lorenz curve for the income distribution in Australia and in Brazil and South Africa (use the data in Fig. 19.6 on p. 451). Is income distributed more equally or less equally in Brazil and South Africa than in Australia?

21. Is the Gini ratio for Australia larger or smaller than that for Brazil and South Africa? Explain your answer.

22. What are some reasons for the differences in the distribution of income in Australia and in Brazil and South Africa?

The Sources of Economic Inequality

Use the following news clip to work Problems 23 to 26.

Bernanke Links Education and Equality

Ben Bernanke, the chairman of the Federal Reserve, said that increased education opportunities would help reduce the increased economic inequality that has occurred over the last 30 years. He also said that globalization and the advent of new technologies, the two main causes of income inequality, will lead to economic growth, but inhibiting them will do far more harm than good in the long run.

It is time to recognize that education should be lifelong and can come in many forms: early childhood education, community colleges, vocational schools, on-the-job training, online courses, adult education. With increased skills, lifetime earning power will increase.

Source: *International Herald Tribune,* June 5, 2008

23. Explain how the two main causes of increased income inequality in the United States identified by Mr. Bernanke work.

24. Draw a graph to illustrate how the two main causes of increased income inequality generate this outcome.

25. What are the short-term costs and long-term benefits associated with these two causes of inequality?

26. Explain Bernanke's solutions to help address growing income inequality.

27. **Where Women's Pay Trumps Men's**

Men work more than women on the job, at least in terms of overall hours. That's just one reason why in most fields, men's earnings exceed women's earnings. But Warren Farrell found 39 occupations in which women's median earnings exceeded men's earnings by at least 5 percent and in some cases by as much as 43 percent. In fields like engineering, a company may get one woman and seven men applying for a job. If the company wants to hire the woman, it might have to pay a premium to get her. Also, where women can combine technical expertise with people skills—such as those required in sales and where customers prefer dealing with a woman—that's likely to contribute to a premium in pay.

Source: CNN, March 2, 2006

a. Draw a graph to illustrate why discrimination could result in female workers getting paid more than male workers for some jobs.

b. Explain how market competition could potentially eliminate this wage differential.

c. If customers "prefer dealing with a woman" in some markets, how might that lead to a persistent wage differential between men and women?

Income Redistribution

28. Use the information provided in Problem 18 and in Fig. 19.3 on p. 445.
    a. What is the percentage of total income that is redistributed from the highest income group?
    b. What percentages of total income are redistributed to the lower income groups?

29. Describe the effects of increasing the amount of income redistribution in the United States to the point at which the lowest income group receives 15 percent of total income and the highest income group receives 30 percent of total income.

Use the following news clip to work Problems 30 and 31.

The Tax Debate We Should be Having

A shrinking number of Americans are bearing an even bigger share of the nation's income tax burden. In 2005, the bottom 40 percent of Americans by income had, in the aggregate, an effective tax rate that's negative: Their households received more money through the income tax system, largely from the earned income tax credit, than they paid. The top 50% of taxpayers pay 97% of total income tax and the top 10% of taxpayers pay 70%. The top 1% paid almost 40% of all income tax, a proportion that has jumped dramatically since 1986.

Given the U.S. tax system, any tax cut must benefit the rich, but in terms of the change in effective tax rates: The bottom 50% got a much bigger tax cut under the Bush tax cut than the top 1%. Did the dollar value of Bush's tax cuts go mostly to the wealthy? Absolutely.

Source: *Fortune*, April 14, 2008

30. Explain why tax cuts in a progressive income tax system are consistently criticized for favoring the wealthy.

31. How might the benefits of tax cuts "trickle down" to others whose taxes are not cut?

Economics in the News

32. After you have studied *Reading Between the Lines* on pp. 460–461, answer the following questions.
    a. Why have some Arab governments ended energy subsidies?
    b. What is the difference between a conditional cash transfer and a commodity subsidy?
    c. Looking at Fig. 1 on p. 461, how would you explain the fact that the Gini ratios for the whole of Egypt are larger than those for both Upper Egypt and Lower Egypt?
    d. How might the Egyptian government lessen the degree of income inequality in urban Upper Egypt?

33. **The Best and Worst College Degrees by Salary**
    Business administration is always a strong contender for honors as the most popular college major. This is no surprise since students think business is the way to make big bucks. But is business administration really as lucrative as students and their parents believe? Nope.

    In a new survey by PayScale, Inc. of salaries by college degree, business administration didn't even break into the list of the top 10 or 20 most lucrative college degrees. A variety of engineering majors claim eight of the top 10 salary spots with chemical engineering ($65,700) winning best for starting salaries. Out of 75 undergrad college majors, business administration ($42,900) came in 35th, behind such degrees as occupational therapy ($61,300), information technology ($49,400), and economics ($48,800).

    Source: moneywatch.com, July 21, 2009

    a. Why do college graduates with different majors have drastically different starting salaries?
    b. Draw a graph of the labor markets for economics majors and business administration majors to illustrate your explanation of the differences in the starting salaries of these two groups.

20

UNCERTAINTY AND INFORMATION

After studying this chapter, you will be able to:

- Explain how people make decisions when they are uncertain about the consequences

- Explain how markets enable people to buy and sell risk

- Explain how markets cope when buyers and sellers have private information

- Explain how uncertainty and incomplete information influence the efficiency of markets

When you buy a car, you could get stuck with a lemon. How do you make a decision when you don't know what its consequences will be?

Although markets do a good job of allocating resources efficiently, they face some obstacles. Can markets lead to an efficient outcome when there is uncertainty and incomplete information? This chapter answers these questions. And in *Reading Between the Lines*, you will see why grade inflation really doesn't help you.

Decisions in the Face of Uncertainty

Tania, a student, is trying to decide which of two summer jobs to take. She can work as a house painter and earn enough to save $2,000 by the end of the summer. There is no uncertainty about the income from this job. If Tania takes it, she will definitely have $2,000 in her bank account at the end of the summer. The other job, working as a telemarketer selling subscriptions to a magazine, is risky. If Tania takes this job, her bank balance at the end of the summer will depend on her success at selling. She will earn enough to save $5,000 if she is successful but only $1,000 if she turns out to be a poor salesperson. Tania has never tried selling, so she doesn't know how successful she'll be. But some of her friends have done this job, and 50 percent of them do well and 50 percent do poorly. Basing her expectations on this experience, Tania thinks there is a 50 percent chance that she will earn $5,000 and a 50 percent chance that she will earn $1,000.

Tania is equally as happy to paint as she is to make phone calls. She cares only about the money. Which job does she prefer: the one that provides her with $2,000 for sure or the one that offers her a 50 percent chance of making $5,000 but a 50 percent risk of making only $1,000?

To answer this question, we need a way of comparing the two outcomes. One comparison is the expected wealth that each job creates.

Expected Wealth

Expected wealth is the money value of what a person expects to own at a given point in time. An expectation is an average calculated by using a formula that weights each possible outcome with the probability (chance) that it will occur.

For Tania, the probability that she will have $5,000 is 0.5 (a 50 percent chance). The probability that she will have $1,000 is also 0.5. Notice that the probabilities sum to 1. Using these numbers, we can calculate Tania's expected wealth, EW, which is

$$EW = (\$5,000 \times 0.5) + (\$1,000 \times 0.5) = \$3,000.$$

Notice that expected wealth decreases if the risk of a poor outcome increases. For example, if Tania has a 20 percent chance of success (and 80 percent chance of failure), her expected wealth falls to $1,800—

$$(\$5,000 \times 0.2) + (\$1,000 \times 0.8) = \$1,800.$$

Tania can now compare the expected wealth from each job—$3,000 for the risky job and $2,000 for the non-risky job.

So does Tania prefer the risky job because it gives her a greater expected wealth? The answer is we don't know because we don't know how much Tania dislikes risk.

Risk Aversion

Risk aversion is the dislike of risk. Almost everyone is risk averse but some more than others. In football, running is less risky than passing. Coach John Harbaugh of the Baltimore Ravens, who favors a cautious running game, is risk averse. Indianapolis quarterback Peyton Manning, who favors a risky passing game, is less risk averse. But almost everyone is risk averse to some degree.

We can measure the degree of risk aversion by the compensation needed to make a given amount of risk acceptable. Returning to Tania: If she needs to be paid more than $1,000 to take on the risk arising from the telemarketing job, she will choose the safe painting job and take the $2,000 non-risky income. But if she thinks that the extra $1,000 of expected income is enough to compensate her for the risk, she will take the risky job.

To make this idea concrete, we need a way of thinking about how a person values different levels of wealth. The concept that we use is *utility*. We apply the same idea that explains how people make expenditure decisions (see Chapter 8) to explain risk aversion and decisions in the face of risk.

Utility of Wealth

Wealth (money in the bank and other assets of value) is like all good things. It yields utility. The more wealth a person has, the greater is that person's total utility. But each additional dollar of wealth brings a diminishing increment in total utility—the marginal utility of wealth diminishes as wealth increases.

Diminishing marginal utility of wealth means that the gain in utility from an increase in wealth is smaller than the loss in utility from an equal decrease in wealth. Stated differently, *the pain from a loss is greater than the pleasure from a gain of equal size.*

Figure 20.1 illustrates Tania's utility of wealth. Each point *A* through *F* on Tania's utility of wealth curve corresponds to the value identified by the same letter in the table. For example, at point *C*, Tania's wealth is $2,000, and her total utility is 70 units. As Tania's wealth increases, her total utility increases and her marginal utility decreases. Her marginal utility is 25 units when wealth increases from $1,000 to $2,000, but only 13 units when wealth increases from $2,000 to $3,000.

We can use a person's utility of wealth curve to calculate expected utility and the cost of risk.

Expected Utility

Expected utility is the utility value of what a person expects to own at a given point in time. Like expected wealth, it is calculated by using a formula that weights each possible outcome with the probability that it will occur. But it is the utility outcome, not the money outcome, that is used to calculate expected utility.

Figure 20.2 illustrates the calculation for Tania. Wealth of $5,000 gives 95 units of utility and wealth of $1,000 gives 45 units of utility. Each outcome has a probability of 0.5 (a 50 percent chance). Using these numbers, we can calculate Tania's expected utility, *EU*, which is

$$EU = (95 \times 0.5) + (45 \times 0.5) = 70.$$

FIGURE 20.1   The Utility of Wealth

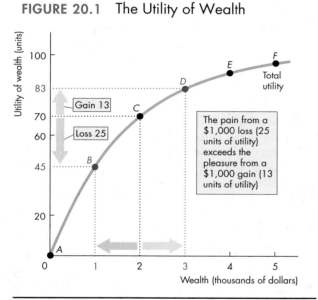

	Wealth (dollars)	Total utility (units)	Marginal utility (units)
A	0	0	
			45
B	1,000	45	
			25
C	**2,000**	**70**	
			13
D	3,000	83	
			8
E	4,000	91	
			4
F	5,000	95	

The table shows Tania's utility of wealth schedule, and the figure shows her utility of wealth curve. Utility increases as wealth increases, but the marginal utility of wealth diminishes.

MyEconLab animation

FIGURE 20.2   Expected Utility

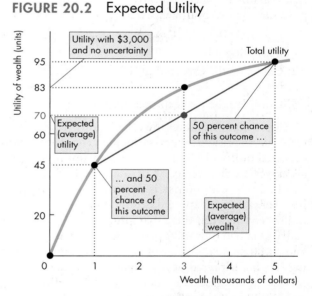

Tania has a 50 percent chance of having $5,000 of wealth and a total utility of 95 units. She also has a 50 percent chance of having $1,000 of wealth and a total utility of 45 units. Tania's expected wealth is $3,000 (the average of $5,000 and $1,000) and her expected utility is 70 units (the average of 95 and 45). With a wealth of $3,000 and no uncertainty, Tania's total utility is 83 units. For a given expected wealth, the greater the range of uncertainty, the smaller is expected utility.

MyEconLab animation

Expected utility decreases if the risk of a poor outcome increases. For example, if Tania has a 20 percent chance of success (and an 80 percent chance of failure), her expected utility is 55 units—

$$(95 \times 0.2) + (45 \times 0.8) = 55.$$

Notice how the range of uncertainty affects expected utility. Figure 20.2 shows that with $3,000 of wealth and no uncertainty, total utility is 83 units. But with the same expected wealth and Tania's uncertainty—a 50 percent chance of having $5,000 and a 50 percent chance of having $1,000—expected utility is only 70 units. Tania's uncertainty lowers her expected utility by 13 units.

Expected utility combines expected wealth and risk into a single index.

Making a Choice with Uncertainty

Faced with uncertainty, a person chooses the action that maximizes expected utility. To select the job that gives her the maximum expected utility, Tania must:

1. Calculate the expected utility from the risky telemarketing job
2. Calculate the expected utility from the safe painting job
3. Compare the two expected utilities

Figure 20.3 illustrates the calculations. You've just seen that the risky telemarketing job gives Tania an expected utility of 70 units. The safe painting job also gives Tania a utility of 70 units. That is, the total utility of $2,000 with no risk is 70 units. So with either job, Tania has an expected utility of 70 units. She is indifferent between these two jobs.

If Tania had only a 20 percent chance of success and an 80 percent chance of failure in the telemarketing job, her expected utility would be 55 (calculated above). In this case, she would take the painting job and get 70 units of utility. But if the probabilities were reversed and she had an 80 percent chance of success and only a 20 percent chance of failure in the telemarketing job, her expected utility would be 85 units—$(95 \times 0.8) + (45 \times 0.2) = 85$. In this case, she would take the risky telemarketing job.

We can calculate the cost of risk by comparing the expected wealth in a given risky situation with the wealth that gives the same total utility but no risk. Using this principle, we can find Tania's cost of bearing the risk that arises from the telemarketing job. That cost, highlighted in Figure 20.3, is $1,000.

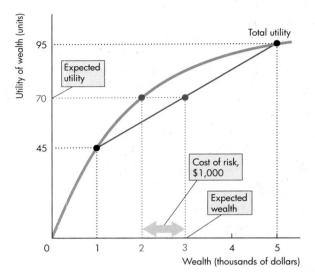

FIGURE 20.3   Choice Under Uncertainty

With a 50 percent chance of having $5,000 of wealth and a 50 percent chance of having $1,000 of wealth, Tania's expected wealth is $3,000 and her expected utility is 70 units. Tania would have the same 70 units of total utility with wealth of $2,000 and no risk, so Tania's cost of bearing this risk is $1,000. Tania is indifferent between the job that pays $2,000 with no risk and the job that offers an equal chance of $5,000 and $1,000.

MyEconLab animation

REVIEW QUIZ

1 What is the distinction between expected wealth and expected utility?
2 How does the concept of utility of wealth capture the idea that pain of loss exceeds the pleasure of gain?
3 What do people try to achieve when they make a decision under uncertainty?
4 How is the cost of the risk calculated when making a decision with an uncertain outcome?

You can work these questions in Study Plan 20.1 and get instant feedback.   *MyEconLab*

You've now seen how a person makes a risky decision. In the next section, we'll see how markets enable people to reduce the risks they face.

Buying and Selling Risk

You've seen at many points in your study of markets how both buyers and sellers gain from trade. Buyers gain because they value what they buy more highly than the price they must pay—they receive a *consumer surplus*. And sellers gain because they face costs that are less than the price at which they can sell—they receive a *producer surplus*.

Just as buyers and sellers gain from trading goods and services, so they can also gain by trading risk. But risk is a bad, not a good. The good that is traded is risk avoidance. A buyer of risk avoidance can gain because the value of avoiding risk is greater than the price that must be paid to someone else to get them to bear the risk. The seller of risk avoidance faces a lower cost of risk than the price that people are willing to pay to avoid the risk.

We're going to put some flesh on the bare bones of this brief account of how people can gain from trading risk by looking at insurance markets.

Insurance Markets

Insurance plays a huge role in our economic lives. We'll explain

- How insurance reduces risk
- Why people buy insurance
- How insurance companies earn a profit

How Insurance Reduces Risk Insurance reduces the risk that people face by sharing or pooling the risks. When people buy insurance against the risk of an unwanted event, they pay an insurance company a *premium*. If the unwanted event occurs, the insurance company pays out the amount of the insured loss.

Think about auto collision insurance. The probability that any one person will have a serious auto accident is small. But a person who does have an auto accident incurs a large loss. For a large population, the probability of one person having an accident is the proportion of the population that has an accident. But this proportion is known, so the probability of an accident occurring and the total cost of accidents can be predicted. An insurance company can pool the risks of a large population and enable everyone to share the costs. It does so by collecting premiums from everyone and paying out benefits to those who suffer a loss. An insurance company that remains in business collects at least as much in premiums as it pays out in benefits.

Why People Buy Insurance People buy insurance and insurance companies earn a profit by selling insurance because people are risk averse. To see why people buy insurance and why it is profitable, let's consider an example. Dan owns a car worth $10,000, and that is his only wealth. There is a 10 percent chance that Dan will have a serious accident that makes his car worth nothing. So there is a 90 percent chance that Dan's wealth will remain at $10,000 and a 10 percent chance that his wealth will be zero. Dan's expected wealth is $9,000—($10,000 × 0.9) + ($0 × 0.1).

Dan is risk averse (just like Tania in the previous example). Because Dan is risk averse, he will be better off by buying insurance to avoid the risk that he faces, if the insurance premium isn't too high.

Without knowing some details about just how risk averse Dan is, we don't know the most that he would be willing to pay to avoid this risk. But we do know that he would pay more than $1,000. If Dan did pay $1,000 to avoid the risk, he would have $9,000 of wealth and face no uncertainty about his wealth. If he does not have an accident, his wealth is the $10,000 value of his car minus the $1,000 he pays the insurance company. If he does lose his car, the insurance company pays him $10,000, so he still has $9,000. Being risk averse, Dan's expected utility from $9,000 with no risk is greater than his expected utility from an expected $9,000 with risk. So Dan would be willing to pay more than $1,000 to avoid this risk.

How Insurance Companies Earn a Profit For the insurance company, $1,000 is the minimum amount at which it would be willing to insure Dan and other people like him. With say 50,000 customers all like Dan, 5,000 customers (50,000 × 0.1) lose their cars and 45,000 don't. Premiums of $1,000 give the insurance company a total revenue of $50,000,000. With 5,000 claims of $10,000, the insurance company pays out $50,000,000. So a premium of $1,000 enables the insurance company to break even (make zero economic profit) on this business.

But Dan (and everyone else) is willing to pay more than $1,000, so insurance is a profitable business and there is a gain from trading risk.

The gain from trading risk is shared by Dan (and the other people who buy insurance) and the insurance company. The exact share of the gain depends on the state of competition in the market for insurance.

If the insurance market is a monopoly, the insurance company can take all the gains from trading risk. But if the insurance market is competitive, economic profit will induce entry and profits will be competed away. In this case, Dan (and the other buyers of insurance) gets the gain.

A Graphical Analysis of Insurance

We can illustrate the gains from insurance by using a graph of Dan's utility of wealth curve. We begin, in Figure 20.4, with the situation if Dan doesn't buy insurance and decides to bear the risk he faces.

Risk-Taking Without Insurance With no accident, Dan's wealth is $10,000 and his total utility is 100 units. If Dan has an accident, his car is worthless: he has no wealth and no utility. Because the chance of an accident is 10 percent (or 0.1), the chance of not having an accident is 90 percent (or 0.9). Dan's expected wealth is $9,000—($10,000 × 0.9) + ($0 × 0.1)—and his expected utility is 90 units—(100 × 0.9) + (0 × 0.1).

You've just seen that without insurance, Dan gets 90 units of utility. But Dan also gets 90 units of utility if he faces no uncertainty with a smaller amount of wealth.

We're now going to see how much Dan will pay to avoid uncertainty.

The Value and Cost of Insurance Figure 20.5 shows the situation when Dan buys insurance. You can see that for Dan, having $7,000 with no risk is just as good as facing a 90 percent chance of having $10,000 and a 10 percent chance of having no wealth. So if Dan pays $3,000 for insurance, he has $7,000 of wealth, faces no uncertainty, and gets 90 units of utility. The amount of $3,000 is the maximum that Dan is willing to pay for insurance. It is the value of insurance to Dan.

Figure 20.5 also shows the cost of insurance. With a large number of customers each of whom has a 10 percent chance of making a $10,000 claim for the loss of a vehicle, the insurance company can provide insurance at a cost of $1,000 (10 percent of $10,000). If Dan pays only $1,000 for insurance, his

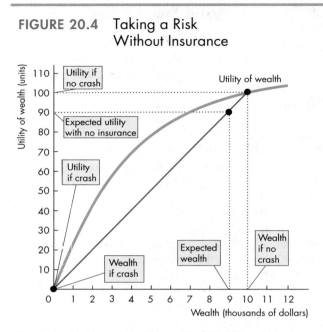

FIGURE 20.4   Taking a Risk Without Insurance

Dan's wealth (the value of his car) is $10,000, which gives him 100 units of utility.

With no insurance, if Dan has a crash, he has no wealth and no utility.

With a 10 percent chance of a crash, Dan's expected wealth is $9,000 and his expected utility is 90 units.

——— MyEconLab animation ———

wealth is $9,000 (the $10,000 value of his car minus the $1,000 he pays for insurance), and his utility from $9,000 of wealth with no uncertainty is about 98 units.

Gains from Trade Because Dan is willing to pay up to $3,000 for insurance that costs the insurance company $1,000, there is a gain from trading risk of $2,000 per insured person. How the gains are shared depends on the nature of the market. If the insurance market is competitive, entry will increase supply and lower the price to $1,000 (plus normal profit and operating costs). Dan (and the other buyers of insurance) enjoys a consumer surplus. If the insurance market is a monopoly, the insurance company takes the $2,000 per insured person as economic profit.

FIGURE 20.5   The Gains from Insurance

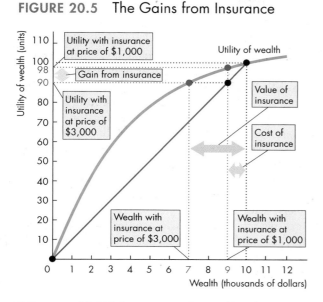

If Dan pays $3,000 for insurance, his wealth is $7,000 and his utility is 90 units—the same utility as with no insurance—so $3,000 is the value of insurance for Dan.

If Dan pays $1,000 for insurance, which is the insurance company's cost of providing insurance, his wealth is $9,000 and his utility is about 98 units.

Dan and the insurance company share the gain from insurance.

MyEconLab animation

Risk That Can't Be Insured

The gains from auto collision insurance that we've studied here apply to all types of insurance. Examples are property and casualty insurance, life insurance, and health-care insurance. One person's risks associated with driving, life, and health are independent of other persons'. That's why insurance is possible. The risks are spread across a population.

But not all risks can be insured. To be insurable, risks must be independent. If an event causes everyone to be a loser, it isn't possible to spread and pool the risks. For example, flood insurance is often not available for people who live on a floodplain because if one person incurs a loss, most likely all do.

Also, to be insurable, a risky event must be observable to both the buyer and seller of insurance. But much of the uncertainty that we face arises

Economics in Action
Insurance in the United States

We spend 7 percent of our income on private insurance. That's more than we spend on cars or food. In addition, we buy Social Security and unemployment insurance through our taxes. The figure shows the relative sizes of the four main types of private insurance. More than 80 percent of Americans have life insurance, and after 2010 most have health insurance. The United States only recently made health insurance compulsory.

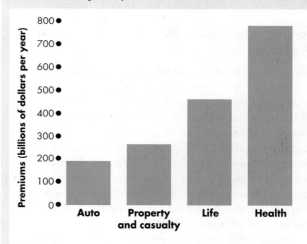

The U.S. Insurance Industry

Source of data: U.S. Bureau of the Census, *Statistical Abstract of the United States 2010*, Tables 128, 1184, and 1185.

REVIEW QUIZ

1 How does insurance reduce risk?
2 How do we determine the value (willingness to pay) for insurance?
3 How can an insurance company offer people a deal worth taking? Why do both the buyers and the sellers of insurance gain?
4 What kinds of risks can't be insured?

You can work these questions in Study Plan 20.2 and get instant feedback.   *MyEconLab*

because we know less (or more) than others with whom we do business. In the next section, we look at the way markets cope when buyers and sellers have different information.

◆ Private Information

In all the markets that you've studied so far, the buyers and the sellers are well informed about the good, service, or factor of production being traded. But in some markets, either the buyers or the sellers—usually the sellers—are better informed about the value of the item being traded than the person on the other side of the market. Information about the value of the item being traded that is possessed by only buyers or sellers is called **private information**. And a market in which the buyers or sellers have private information has **asymmetric information**.

Asymmetric Information: Examples and Problems

Asymmetric information affects many of your own economic transactions. One example is your knowledge about your driving skills and temperament. You know much more than your auto insurance company does about how carefully and defensively you drive—about your personal risk of having an accident that would cause the insurance company to pay a claim. Another example is your knowledge about your work effort. You know more than your employer about how hard you are willing to work. Yet another example is your knowledge about the quality of your car. You know whether it's a lemon, but the person to whom you are about to sell it does not know and can't find out until after he or she has bought it.

Asymmetric information creates two problems:

- Adverse selection
- Moral hazard

Adverse Selection **Adverse selection** is the tendency for people to *enter into agreements* in which they can use their private information to their own advantage and to the disadvantage of the uninformed party.

For example, if Jackie offers her salespeople a fixed wage, she will attract lazy salespeople. Hardworking salespeople will prefer not to work for Jackie because they can earn more by working for someone who pays by results. The fixed-wage contract adversely selects those with private information (knowledge about their work habits) who can use that knowledge to their own advantage and to the disadvantage of the other party.

Moral Hazard **Moral hazard** is the tendency for people with private information, *after entering into an agreement*, to use that information for their own benefit and at the cost of the less-informed party. For example, Jackie hires Mitch as a salesperson and pays him a fixed wage regardless of how much he sells. Mitch faces a moral hazard. He has an incentive to put in the least possible effort, benefiting himself and lowering Jackie's profits. For this reason, salespeople are usually paid by a formula that makes their income higher, the greater is the volume (or value) of their sales.

A variety of devices have evolved that enable markets to function in the face of moral hazard and adverse selection. We've just seen one, the use of incentive payments for salespeople. We're going to look at how three markets cope with adverse selection and moral hazard. They are

- The market for used cars
- The market for loans
- The market for insurance

The Market for Used Cars

When a person buys a car, it might turn out to be a lemon. If the car is a lemon, it is worth less to the buyer than if it has no defects. Does the used car market have two prices reflecting these two values—a low price for lemons and a higher price for cars without defects? It turns out that it does. But it needs some help to do so and to overcome what is called the **lemons problem**—the problem that in a market in which it is not possible to distinguish reliable products from lemons, there are too many lemons and too few reliable products traded.

To see how the used car market overcomes the lemons problem, we'll first look at a used car market that has a lemons problem.

The Lemons Problem in a Used Car Market

To explain the lemons problem as clearly as possible, we'll assume that there are only two kinds of cars: defective cars—lemons—and cars without defects that we'll call good cars. Whether or not a car is a lemon is private information that is available only to the current owner. The buyer of a used car can't tell whether he is buying a lemon until after he has bought the car and learned as much about it as its current owner knows.

Some people with low incomes and the time and ability to fix cars are willing to buy lemons as long as they know what they're buying and pay an appropriately low price. Suppose that a lemon is worth $5,000 to a buyer. More people want to buy a good car and we'll assume that a good car is worth $25,000 to a buyer.

But the buyer can't tell the difference between a lemon and a good car. Only the seller has this information. And telling the buyer that a car is not a lemon does not help. The seller has no incentive to tell the truth.

So the most that the buyer knows is the probability of buying a lemon. If half of the used cars sold turn out to be lemons, the buyer knows that he has a 50 percent chance of getting a good car and a 50 percent chance of getting a lemon.

The price that a buyer is willing to pay for a car of unknown quality is more than the value of a lemon because the car might be a good one. But the price is less than the value of a good car because it might turn out to be a lemon.

Now think about the sellers of used cars, who know the quality of their cars. Someone who owns a good car is going to be offered a price that is less than the value of that car to the buyer. Many owners will

be reluctant to sell for such a low price. So the quantity of good used cars supplied will not be as large as it would be if people paid the price they are worth.

In contrast, someone who owns a lemon is going to be offered a price that is greater than the value of that car to the buyer. So owners of lemons will be eager to sell and the quantity of lemons supplied will be greater than it would be if people paid the price that a lemon is worth.

Figure 20.6 illustrates the used car market that we've just described. Part (a) shows the demand for used cars, D, and the supply of used cars, S. The market equilibrium occurs at a price of $10,000 per car with 400 cars traded each month.

Some cars are good ones and some are lemons, but buyers can't tell the difference until it is too late to influence their decision to buy. But buyers do know what a good car and a lemon are worth to them, and sellers know the quality of the cars they are offering for sale. Figure 20.6(b) shows the demand curve for good cars, D_G, and the supply curve of good cars, S_G. Figure 20.6(c) shows the demand curve for lemons, D_L, and the supply curve of lemons, S_L.

At the market price of $10,000 per car, owners of good cars supply 200 cars a month for sale. Owners

FIGURE 20.6   The Lemons Problem

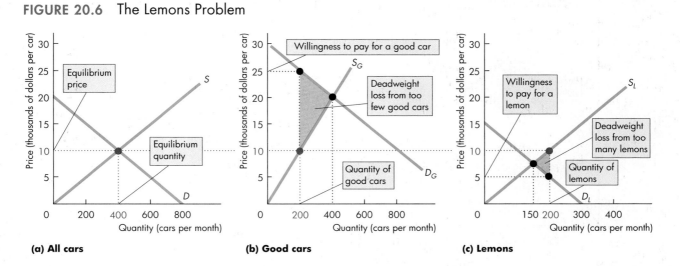

(a) All cars

(b) Good cars

(c) Lemons

Buyers can't tell a good used car from a lemon. Demand and supply determine the price and quantity of used cars traded in part (a). In part (b), D_G is the demand curve for good used cars and S_G is the supply curve. At the market price, too few

good cars are available, which brings a deadweight loss. In part (c), D_L is the demand curve for lemons and S_L is the supply curve. At the market price, too many lemons are available, which brings a deadweight loss.

MyEconLab animation

of lemons also supply 200 cars a month for sale. The used car market is inefficient because there are too many lemons and not enough good cars. Figure 20.6 makes this inefficiency clear by using the concept of deadweight loss (see Chapter 5, pp. 113–114).

At the quantity of good cars supplied, buyers are willing to pay $25,000 for a good car. They are willing to pay more than a good car is worth to its current owner for all good cars up to 400 cars a month. The gray triangle shows the deadweight loss that results from there being too few good used cars.

At the quantity of lemons supplied, buyers are willing to pay $5,000 for a lemon. They are willing to pay less than a lemon is worth to its current owner for all lemons above 150 cars a month. The gray triangle shows the deadweight loss that results from there being too many lemons.

You can see *adverse selection* in this used car market because there is a greater incentive to offer a lemon for sale. You can see *moral hazard* because the owner of a lemon has little incentive to take good care of it. The market for used cars is not working well. Too many lemons and too few good cars are traded.

A Used Car Market with Dealers' Warranties

How can used car dealers convince buyers that a car isn't a lemon? The answer is by giving a guarantee in the form of a warranty. By providing warranties only on good cars, dealers signal which cars are good ones and which are lemons.

Signaling occurs when an informed person takes actions that send information to uninformed persons. The grades and degrees that a university awards students are signals. They inform potential (uninformed) employers about the ability of the people they are considering hiring.

In the market for used cars, dealers send signals by giving warranties on the used cars they offer for sale. The message in the signal is that the dealer agrees to pay the costs of repairing the car if it turns out to have a defect.

Buyers believe the signal because the cost of sending a false signal is high. A dealer who gives a warranty on a lemon ends up bearing a high cost of repairs—and gains a bad reputation. A dealer who gives a warranty only on good cars has no repair costs and a reputation that gets better and better. It pays

---

FIGURE 20.7   Warranties Make the Used Car Market Efficient

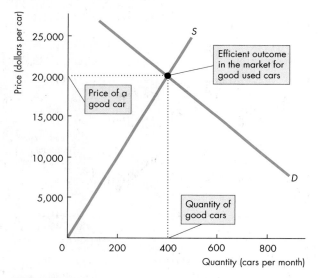

(a) Good cars

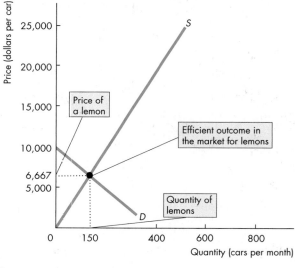

(b) Lemons

With dealers' warranties as signals, the equilibrium price of a good used car is $20,000 and 400 cars are traded. The market for good used cars is efficient. Because the signal

enables buyers to spot a lemon, the price of a lemon is $6,667 and 150 lemons are traded. The market for lemons is efficient.

dealers to send an accurate signal, and it is rational for buyers to believe the signal.

So a car with a warranty is a good car; a car without a warranty is a lemon. Warranties solve the lemons problem and enable the used car market to function efficiently with two prices: one for lemons and one for good cars.

Figure 20.7 illustrates this outcome. In part (a) the demand for and supply of good cars determine the price of a good car. In part (b), the demand for and supply of lemons determine the price of a lemon. Both markets are efficient.

Pooling Equilibrium and Separating Equilibrium

You've seen two outcomes in the market for used cars. Without warranties, there is only one message visible to the buyer: All cars look the same. So there is one price regardless of whether the car is a good car or a lemon. We call the equilibrium in a market when only one message is available and an uninformed person cannot determine quality a **pooling equilibrium**.

But in a used car market with warranties, there are two messages: Good cars have warranties and lemons don't. So there are two car prices for the two types of cars. We call the equilibrium in a market when signaling provides full information to a previously uninformed person a **separating equilibrium**.

The Market for Loans

When you buy a tank of gasoline and swipe your credit card, you are taking a loan from the bank that issued your card. You demand and your bank supplies a loan. Have you noticed the interest rate on an unpaid credit card balance? In 2007, it ranged between 7 percent a year and 36 percent a year. Why are these interest rates so high? And why is there such a huge range?

The answer is that when banks make loans, they face the risk that the loan will not be repaid. The risk that a borrower, also known as a creditor, might not repay a loan is called **credit risk** or **default risk**. For credit card borrowing, the credit risk is high and it varies among borrowers. The highest-risk borrowers pay the highest interest rate.

Interest rates and the price of credit risk are determined in the market for loans. The lower the interest rate, the greater is the quantity of loans demanded and for a given level of credit risk, the higher the interest rate, the greater is the quantity of loans supplied. Demand and supply determine the interest rate and the price of credit risk.

If lenders were unable to charge different interest rates to reflect different degrees of credit risk, there would be a pooling equilibrium and an inefficient loans market.

Inefficient Pooling Equilibrium To see why a pooling equilibrium would be inefficient, suppose that banks can't identify the individual credit risk of their borrowers: they have no way of knowing how likely it is that a given loan will be repaid. In this situation, every borrower pays the same interest rate and the market is in a pooling equilibrium.

If all borrowers pay the same interest rate, the market for loans has the same problem as the used car market. Low-risk customers borrow less than they would if they were offered the low interest rate appropriate for their low credit risk. High-risk customers borrow more than they would if they faced the high interest rate appropriate for their high credit risk. So banks face an *adverse selection* problem. Too many borrowers are high risk and too few are low risk.

Signaling and Screening in the Market for Loans Lenders don't know how likely it is that a given loan will be repaid, but the borrower does know. Low-risk borrowers have an incentive to signal their risk by providing lenders with relevant information. Signals might include information about the length of time a person has been in the current job or has lived at the current address, home ownership, marital status, age, and business record.

High-risk borrowers might be identified simply as those who have failed to signal low risk. These borrowers have an incentive to mislead lenders; and lenders have an incentive to induce high-risk borrowers to reveal their risk level. Inducing an informed party to reveal relevant private information is called **screening**.

By not lending to people who refuse to reveal relevant information, banks are able to screen as well as receive signals that help them to separate their borrowers into a number of credit-risk categories. If lenders succeed, the market for loans comes to a separating equilibrium with a high interest rate for high-risk borrowers and a low interest rate for low-risk borrowers. Signaling and screening in the market for loans act like warranties in the used car market and work to avoid the deadweight loss of a pooling equilibrium.

Economics in Action
The Sub-Prime Credit Crisis

A sub-prime mortgage is a loan to a homebuyer who has a high risk of default. Figure 1 shows that between 2001 and 2005, the price of risk was low. Figure 2 shows why: The supply of credit, S_0, was large and so was the amount of risk taking. In 2007, the supply of credit decreased to S_1. The price of risk jumped and, faced with a higher interest rate, many sub-prime borrowers defaulted. Defaults in the sub-prime mortgage market spread to other markets that supplied the funds that financed mortgages.

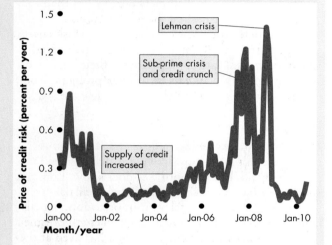

Figure 1 The Price of Commercial Credit Risk

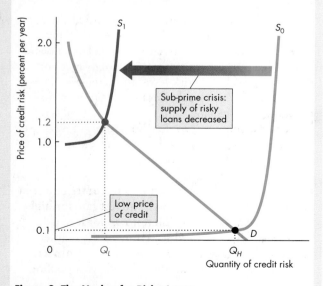

Figure 2 The Market for Risky Loans

The Market for Insurance

People who buy insurance face moral hazard, and insurance companies face adverse selection. *Moral hazard* arises because a person with insurance against a loss has less incentive than an uninsured person to avoid the loss. For example, a business with fire insurance has less incentive to install a fire alarm or sprinkler system than a business with no fire insurance does. *Adverse selection* arises because people who create greater risks are more likely to buy insurance. For example, a person with a family history of serious illness is more likely to buy health insurance than is a person with a family history of good health.

Insurance companies have an incentive to find ways around the moral hazard and adverse selection problems. By doing so, they can lower premiums for low-risk people and raise premiums for high-risk people. One way in which auto insurance companies separate high-risk and low-risk customers is with a *no-claim bonus*. A driver accumulates a no-claim bonus by driving safely and avoiding accidents. The greater the bonus, the greater is the incentive to drive carefully. Insurance companies also use a *deductible*. A deductible is the amount of a loss that the insured person agrees to bear. The premium is smaller, the larger is the deductible, and the decrease in the premium is more than proportionate to the increase in the deductible. By offering insurance with full coverage—no deductible—on terms that are attractive only to the high-risk people and by offering coverage with a deductible on more favorable terms that are attractive to low-risk people, insurance companies can do profitable business with everyone. High-risk people choose policies with a low deductible and a high premium; low-risk people choose policies with a high deductible and a low premium.

◆ REVIEW QUIZ

1 How does private information create adverse selection and moral hazard?
2 How do markets for cars use warranties to cope with private information?
3 How do markets for loans use signaling and screening to cope with private information?
4 How do markets for insurance use no-claim bonuses to cope with private information?

You can work these questions in Study Plan 20.3 and get instant feedback.   MyEconLab

⬛▶ Uncertainty, Information, and the Invisible Hand

A recurring theme throughout microeconomics is the big question: When do choices made in the pursuit of *self-interest* also promote the *social interest?* When does the invisible hand work well and when does it fail us? You've learned about the concept of efficiency, a major component of what we mean by the social interest. And you've seen that while competitive markets generally do a good job in helping to achieve efficiency, impediments such as monopoly and the absence of well-defined property rights can prevent the attainment of an efficient use of resources.

How do uncertainty and incomplete information affect the ability of self-interested choices to lead to a social interest outcome? Are these features of economic life another reason why markets fail and why some type of government intervention is required to achieve efficiency?

These are hard questions, and there are no definitive answers. But there are some useful things that we can say about the effects of uncertainty and a lack of complete information on the efficiency of resource use. We'll begin our brief review of this issue by thinking about information as just another good.

Information as a Good

More information is generally useful, and less uncertainty about the future is generally useful. Think about information as one of the goods that we want more of.

The most basic lesson about efficiency that you learned in Chapter 2 can be applied to information. Along our production possibilities frontier, we face a tradeoff between information and all other goods and services. Information, like everything else, can be produced at an increasing opportunity cost—an increasing marginal cost. For example, we could get more accurate weather forecasts, but only at increasing marginal cost, as we increased the amount of information that we gather from the atmosphere and the amount of money that we spend on supercomputers to process the data.

The principle of decreasing marginal benefit also applies to information. More information is valuable, but the more you know, the less you value another increment of information. For example, knowing that it will rain tomorrow is valuable information.

Knowing the amount of rain to within an inch is even more useful. But knowing the amount of rain to within a millimeter probably isn't worth much more.

Because the marginal cost of information is increasing and the marginal benefit is decreasing, there is an efficient amount of information. It would be inefficient to be overinformed.

In principle, competitive markets in information might deliver this efficient quantity. Whether they actually do so is hard to determine.

Monopoly in Markets that Cope with Uncertainty

There are probably large economies of scale in providing services that cope with uncertainty and incomplete information. The insurance industry, for example, is highly concentrated. Where monopoly elements exist, exactly the same inefficiency issues arise as occur in markets where uncertainty and incomplete information are not big issues. So it is likely that in some information markets, including insurance markets, there is underproduction arising from the attempt to maximize monopoly profit.

▶ REVIEW QUIZ

1 Thinking about information as a good, what determines the information that people are willing to pay for?
2 Why is it inefficient to be overinformed?
3 Why are some of the markets that provide information likely to be dominated by monopolies?

You can work these questions in Study Plan 20.4 and get instant feedback.   MyEconLab

◆ You've seen how people make decisions when faced with uncertainty and how markets work when there is asymmetric information. *Reading Between the Lines* on pp. 480–481 looks at the way markets in human capital and labor use grades as signals that sort students by ability so that employers can hire the type of labor they seek. You'll see why grade deflation can be efficient and grade inflation is inefficient. Discriminating grades are in the social interest and in the self-interest of universities and students.

Grades as Signals

Baruch College Has Initiated A Draconian Policy To Fight Grade Inflation

http://www.businessinsider.com
April 12, 2012

Teachers in the accounting department of Baruch College who give too many A's "automatically and permanently become disqualified to be rehired by the department," reports Gizelle Lugo. . . .

Professor Jimmy Ye, chair of the Stan Ross Department of Accountancy, said in an email that the school was at risk of losing its accreditation for having too many students and too few professors. He blamed this situation on grade inflation, stating that it helps keep the weak students in the accounting program, stretches the department's resources, and lowers the department's CPA passing rate. . . .

Stuart Rojstaczer and Christopher Healy, authors of "Where A Is Ordinary," say that grade inflation can make students complacent and not study as hard. "When college students perceive that the average grade in a class will be an A, they do not try to excel," they write. . . .

[And it] . . . makes it harder for employers to determine who is an excellent, good, and mediocre student.

The reaction among Baruch students seems to be mixed, with some agreeing that the policy will help weed out weak students not suited for accounting early on, while others are concerned that their efforts might be unfairly evaluated. "If I get a 96, I want the A I deserve, instead of settling for the B because 20% of the students got a 97," Shamima Akter, a Baruch student, told Lugo. . . .

From businessinsider.com. Reprinted with permission.

ESSENCE OF THE STORY

- In the accountancy department at Baruch College, teachers who give too many A's will not be rehired.

- Grade inflation keeps weak students in the accounting program.

- When grades are inflated, students don't try to excel and employers can't separate excellent, good, and mediocre students.

ECONOMIC ANALYSIS

- Accurate grades provide valuable information to students and potential employers about a student's ability.

- Baruch College accountants want to provide accurate information and avoid grade inflation—awarding a high grade to most students.

- The labor market for new college graduates works badly with grade inflation and works well with accurate grading.

- Figure 1 shows a labor market for new college graduates when there is grade inflation.

- Students with high ability are not distinguished from other students, and the supply curve represents the supply of students of all ability levels.

- The demand curve shows the employers' willingness to hire new workers without knowledge of their true ability.

- Students get hired for a low wage rate. Eventually, they get sorted by ability as employers discover the true ability of their workers from on-the-job performance.

- Figures 2 and 3 show the outcome with accurate grading.

- In Fig. 2, students with high grades get high-wage jobs and in Fig. 3, students with low grades get low-wage jobs.

- The outcomes in Figs. 2 and 3 that arise immediately with accurate grading occur eventually with grade inflation as employers accumulate information about the abilities of the workers.

- But the cost to the student and the employer of discovering true ability is greater with grade inflation than with accurate grading.

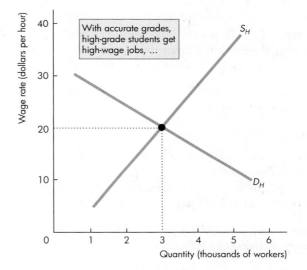

Figure 2 The Market for A Students

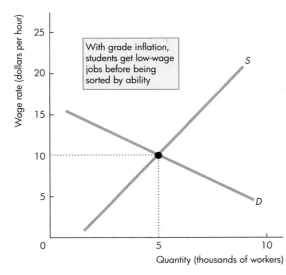

Figure 1 Market with Grade Inflation

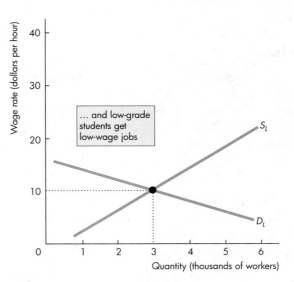

Figure 3 The Market for D Students

SUMMARY

Key Points

Decisions in the Face of Uncertainty (pp. 468–470)

- To make a rational choice under uncertainty, people choose the action that maximizes the expected utility of wealth.
- A decreasing marginal utility of wealth makes people risk averse. A sure outcome with a given expected wealth is preferred to a risky outcome with the same expected wealth—risk is costly.
- The cost of risk is found by comparing the expected wealth in a given risky situation with the wealth that gives the same utility but with no risk.

Working Problems 1 to 3 will give you a better understanding of decisions in the face of uncertainty.

Buying and Selling Risk (pp. 471–473)

- People trade risk in markets for insurance.
- By pooling risks, insurance companies can reduce the risks people face (from insured activities) at a lower cost than the value placed on the lower risk.

Working Problems 4 to 6 will give you a better understanding of buying and selling risk.

Private Information (pp. 474–478)

- Asymmetric information creates adverse selection and moral hazard problems.

- When it is not possible to distinguish good-quality products from lemons, too many lemons and too few good-quality products are traded in a pooling equilibrium.
- Signaling can overcome the lemons problem.
- In the market for used cars, warranties signal good cars and an efficient separating equilibrium occurs.
- Private information about credit risk is overcome by using signals and screening based on personal characteristics.
- Private information about risk in insurance markets is overcome by using the no-claim bonus and deductibles.

Working Problems 7 to 11 will give you a better understanding of private information.

Uncertainty, Information, and the Invisible Hand (p. 479)

- Less uncertainty and more information can be viewed as a good that has increasing marginal cost and decreasing marginal benefit.
- Competitive information markets might be efficient, but economies of scale might bring inefficient underproduction of information and insurance.

Working Problems 12 and 13 will give you a better understanding of uncertainty, information, and the invisible hand.

Key Terms

Adverse selection, 474
Asymmetric information, 474
Credit risk or default risk, 477
Expected utility, 469
Expected wealth, 468

Lemons problem, 474
Moral hazard, 474
Pooling equilibrium, 477
Private information, 474
Risk aversion, 468

Screening, 477
Separating equilibrium, 477
Signaling, 476

STUDY PLAN PROBLEMS AND APPLICATIONS

MyEconLab   You can work Problems 1 to 14 in MyEconLab Chapter 20 Study Plan and get instant feedback.

Decisions in the Face of Uncertainty (Study Plan 20.1)

1. The figure shows Lee's utility of wealth curve.

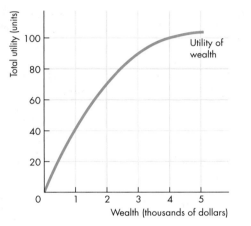

Lee is offered a job as a salesperson in which there is a 50 percent chance that she will make $4,000 a month and a 50 percent chance that she will make nothing.

a. What is Lee's expected income from taking this job?

b. What is Lee's expected utility from taking this job?

c. How much would another firm have to offer Lee with certainty to persuade her not to take the risky sales job?

d. What is Lee's cost of risk?

Use the following news clip to work Problems 2 and 3.

Larry Page on How to Change the World

As president of Google, Larry Page said that the risks that Google has taken have led to hot new applications like Gmail and Google Maps. In 2004, Page set out Google's risk strategy: Google would do some things that would have only a 10 percent chance of making $1 billion over the long term, but not many people will work on those things; 90 percent work on everything else. So that's not a big risk. Many of Google's new features come from the riskier investments. Before we began, we thought that Google might fail and we almost didn't do it. The reason we started Google was probably Stanford's decision that

we could go back and finish our Ph.D.s if we didn't succeed.

Source: *Fortune*, May 12, 2008

2. If much of Google's success has come from "riskier investments," then why doesn't Google dedicate all of their resources toward these riskier innovations?

3. In spite of the many risks that Larry Page has taken with Google, what evidence does this news clip provide that he is risk averse?

Buying and Selling Risk (Study Plan 20.2)

4. Lee in Problem 1 has built a small weekend shack on a steep, unstable hillside. She spent all her wealth, which is $5,000, on this project. There is a 75 percent chance that the house will be washed down the hill and be worthless. How much is Lee willing to pay for an insurance policy that pays her $5,000 if the house is washed away?

Use the following information to work Problems 5 and 6.

Larry lives in a neighborhood in which 20 percent of the cars are stolen every year. Larry's car, which he parks on the street overnight, is worth $20,000. (This is Larry's only wealth). The table shows Larry's utility of wealth schedule.

Wealth (dollars)	Utility (units)
20,000	400
16,000	350
12,000	280
8,000	200
4,000	110
0	0

5. If Larry cannot buy auto theft insurance, what is his expected wealth and his expected utility?

6. High-Crime Auto Theft, an insurance company, offers to sell Larry insurance at $8,000 a year and promises to provide Larry with a replacement car worth $20,000 if his car is stolen. Is Larry willing to buy this insurance? If not, is he willing to pay $4,000 a year for such insurance?

Private Information (Study Plan 20.3)

Use the following information to work Problems 7 and 8.

Zaneb is a high-school teacher and is well known in her community for her honesty and integrity. She is shopping for a used car and plans to borrow the money from her local bank to pay for the car.

7. a. Does Zaneb create any moral hazard or adverse selection problems for either the bank or the car dealer? Explain your answer.

    b. Does either the bank or the car dealer create any moral hazard or adverse selection problems for Zaneb? Explain your answer.

8. What arrangements is Zaneb likely to encounter that are designed to help her cope with the moral hazard and adverse selection problems she encounters in her car buying and bank loan transactions?

9. Suppose that there are three national football leagues: Time League, Goal Difference League, and Bonus for Win League. The leagues are of equal quality, but the players are paid differently. In the Time League, they are paid by the hour for time spent practicing and time spent playing. In the Goal Difference league, they are paid an amount that depends on the points that the team scores minus the points scored against it. In the Bonus for Win League, the players are paid one wage for a loss, a higher wage for a tie, and the highest wage of all for a win.

    a. Briefly describe the predicted differences in the quality of the games played by each of the leagues.

    b. Which league is the most attractive to players?

    c. Which league will generate the largest profits?

10. **We All Pay for the Uninsured**

    When buying health care, most of us don't behave like regular consumers: Seven out of the eight dollars we spend is somebody else's money, and we don't have very good information about doctors or hospitals. You can go online and find out your physician's fee before you make an appointment. That's helpful for a routine service, but when you have a serious condition, you really want to know about the physician's quality. Now, with physicians collaborating to agree on quality standards and all health plans willing to pool their data, consumers can look at a set of performance indicators that physicians think are appropriate, and be able to judge the quality of their physicians.

    Source: *Fortune*, May 12, 2008

    a. Explain how the adverse selection problem applies to health care.

    b. How does the moral hazard problem apply to health insurance?

11. You can't buy insurance against the risk of being sold a lemon. Why isn't there a market in insurance against being sold a lemon? How does the market provide a buyer with some protection against being sold a lemon? What are the main ways in which markets overcome the lemons problem?

Uncertainty, Information, and the Invisible Hand (Study Plan 20.4)

12. In Problem 10, what role can better information play in the health care market? Is it possible for there to be too much information in this market?

13. **Show Us Our Money**

    I have no clue what my colleagues make and I consider my salary my own business. It turns out that could be a huge mistake. What if employers made all employee salaries known? If you think about it, who is served by all the secrecy? Knowing what other workers make might be more ammunition to gun for a raise.

    Source: *Time*, May 12, 2008

    Explain why a worker might be willing to pay for the salary information of other workers.

Economics in the News (Study Plan 20.N)

14. **Making the Grade**

    Grade inflation is unfair to students who truly deserve exceptional marks. It also is unfair to graduate applicants who come from schools that don't inflate grades.

    Source: NJ.com, September 25, 2007

    What economic role do accurate grades play? Who benefits from grade inflation: students, professors, universities, or future employers? Who bears the cost of grade inflation? How do you think grade inflation might be controlled? Is grade inflation efficient?

ADDITIONAL PROBLEMS AND APPLICATIONS

MyEconLab   You can work these problems in MyEconLab if assigned by your instructor.

Decisions in the Face of Uncertainty

Use the following table, which shows Jimmy's and Zenda's utility of wealth schedules, to work Problems 15 to 17.

Wealth	Jimmy's utility	Zenda's utility
0	0	0
100	200	512
200	300	640
300	350	672
400	375	678
500	387	681
600	393	683
700	396	684

15. What are Jimmy's and Zenda's expected utilities from a bet that gives them a 50 percent chance of having a wealth of $600 and a 50 percent chance of having nothing?

16. a. Calculate Jimmy's and Zenda's marginal utility of wealth schedules.

    b. Who is more risk averse, Jimmy or Zenda? How do you know?

17. Suppose that Jimmy and Zenda each have $400 and are offered a business investment opportunity that involves committing the entire $400 to the project. The project could return $600 (a profit of $200) with a probability of 0.85 or $200 (a loss of $200) with a probability of 0.15. Who goes for the project and who hangs on to the initial $400?

Use the following information to work Problems 18 to 20.

Two students, Jim and Kim, are offered summer jobs managing a student house-painting business. There is a 50 percent chance that either of them will be successful and end up with $21,000 of wealth to get them through the next school year. But there is also a 50 percent chance that either will end up with only $3,000 of wealth. Each could take a completely safe but back-breaking job picking fruit that would leave them with a guaranteed $9,000 at the end of the summer. The table in the next column shows Jim's and Kim's utility of wealth schedules.

Wealth	Jim's utility	Kim's utility
0	0	0
3,000	100	200
6,000	200	350
9,000	298	475
12,000	391	560
15,000	491	620
18,000	586	660
21,000	680	680

18. Does anyone take the painting job? If so, who takes it and why? Does anyone take the job picking fruit? If so, who takes it and why?

19. In Problem 18, what is each student's maximized expected utility? Who has the larger expected wealth? Who ends up with the larger wealth at the end of the summer?

20. In Problem 18, if one of the students takes the risky job, how much more would the fruit-picking job have needed to pay to attract that student?

Buying and Selling Risk

Use the following table, which shows Chris's utility of wealth schedule, to work Problems 21 and 22.

Chris's wealth is $5,000 and it consists entirely of her share in a risky ice cream business. If the summer is cold, the business will fail, and she will have no wealth. Where Chris lives there is a 50 percent chance each year that the summer will be cold.

Wealth (dollars)	Utility (units)
5,000	150
4,000	140
3,000	120
2,000	90
1,000	50
0	0

21. If Chris cannot buy cold-summer insurance, what is her expected wealth and what is her expected utility?

22. Business Loss Recovery, an insurance company, is willing to sell Chris cold-summer insurance at a price of $3,000 a year and promises to pay her

$5,000 if the summer is cold and the business fails. Is Chris willing to buy this loss insurance? If she is, is she willing to pay $4,000 a year for it?

Private Information

Use the following information to work Problems 23 to 25.

Larry has a good car that he wants to sell; Harry has a lemon that he wants to sell. Each knows what type of car he is selling. You are looking at used cars and plan to buy one.

23. If both Larry and Harry are offering their cars for sale at the same price, from whom would you most want to buy, Larry or Harry, and why?

24. If you made an offer of the same price to Larry and Harry, who would sell to you and why? Describe the adverse selection problem that arises if you offer the same price to Larry and Harry.

25. How can Larry signal that he is selling a good car so that you are willing to pay Larry the price that he knows his car is worth, and a higher price than what you are willing to offer Harry?

26. Pam is a safe driver and Fran is a reckless driver. Each knows what type of driver she is, but no one else knows. What might an automobile insurance company do to get Pam to signal that she is a safe driver so that it can offer her insurance at a lower premium than it offers to Fran?

27. Why do you think it is not possible to buy insurance against having to put up with a low-paying, miserable job? Explain why a market in insurance of this type would be valuable to workers but unprofitable for an insurance provider and so would not work.

Uncertainty, Information, and the Invisible Hand

Use the following news clip to work Problems 28 and 29.

Why We Worry About the Things We Shouldn't ... and Ignore the Things We Should

We pride ourselves on being the only species that understands the concept of risk, yet we have a confounding habit of worrying about mere possibilities while ignoring probabilities, building barricades against perceived dangers while leaving ourselves exposed to real ones: 20% of all adults still smoke; nearly 20% of drivers and more than 30% of back-seat passengers don't use seat belts; two thirds of us

are overweight or obese. We dash across the street against the light and build our homes in hurricane-prone areas—and when they're demolished by a storm, we rebuild in the same spot.

Source: *Time*, December 4, 2006

28. Explain how "worrying about mere possibilities while ignoring probabilities" can result in people making decisions that not only fail to satisfy social interest, but also fail to satisfy self-interest.

29. How can information be used to improve people's decision making?

Economics in the News

30. After you have studied *Reading Between the Lines* on pp. 480–481, answer the following questions.
   a. What information do accurate grades provide that grade inflation hides?
   b. If grade inflation became widespread in high schools, colleges, and universities, what new arrangements do you predict would emerge to provide better information about student ability?
   c. Do you think grade inflation is in anyone's self-interest? Explain who benefits and how they benefit from grade inflation.
   d. How do you think grade inflation might be controlled?

31. **Are You Paid What You're Worth?**
   How do you know if your pay adequately reflects your contributions to your employer's profits? In many instances, you don't. Your employer has more and better information than you do about how your salary and bonus compare to others in your field, to others in your office, and relative to the company's profits in any given year. You can narrow the information gap a bit if you're willing to buy salary reports from compensation sources. For example, at $200, a quick-call salary report from Economic Research Institute will offer you compensation data for your position based on your years of experience, your industry and the place where your company is located.

Source: CNN, April 3, 2006

   a. Explain the role that asymmetric information can play in worker wages.
   b. What adverse selection problem exists if a firm offers lower wages to existing workers?
   c. What will determine how much a worker should actually pay for a detailed salary report?

For Whom?

During the past 35 years, the gap between the richest and the poorest in America has widened. But millions in Asia have been lifted from poverty and are now enjoying a high and rapidly rising standard of living. What are the forces that generate these trends? The answer to this question is the forces of demand and supply in factor markets. These forces determine wages, interest rates, rents, and the prices of natural resources. These forces also determine people's incomes.

In America, human capital and entrepreneurship are the most prized resources, and their incomes have grown most rapidly. In Asia, labor has seen its wage rates transformed. And in all regions rich in oil, incomes have risen on the back of high and fast-rising energy prices.

Many outstanding economists have advanced our understanding of factor markets and the role they play in helping to resolve the conflict between the demands of humans and the resources available. One of them is Thomas Robert Malthus.

Another is Harold Hotelling, whose prediction of an ever-rising price of nonrenewable natural resources implies an ever-falling rate of their use and an intensifying search for substitutes.

Yet another is Julian Simon, who challenged both the Malthusian gloom and the Hotelling Principle. He believed that people are the "ultimate resource" and predicted that a rising population lessens the pressure on natural resources. A bigger population provides a larger number of resourceful people who can discover more efficient ways of using scarce resources.

Thomas Robert Malthus *(1766–1834), an English clergyman and economist, was an extremely influential social scientist. In his best-selling* Essay on the Principle of Population, *published in 1798, he predicted that population growth would outstrip food production and said that wars, famine, and disease were inevitable unless population growth was held in check by marrying at a late age and living a celibate life. (He married at 38 a wife of 27, marriage ages that he recommended for others.)*

Malthus had a profound influence on Charles Darwin, who got the key idea that led him to the theory of natural selection from the Essay on the Principle of Population. *But it was also Malthus's gloomy predictions that made economics the "dismal science."*

"The passion between the sexes has appeared in every age to be so nearly the same, that it may always be considered, in algebraic language, as a given quantity."

THOMAS ROBERT MALTHUS
An Essay on the Principle of Population

DAVID CARD is Class of 1950 Professor of Economics and Director of the Center for Labor Economics at the University of California, Berkeley, and Faculty Research Associate at the National Bureau of Economic Research.

Born in Canada, Professor Card obtained his B.A. at Queen's University, Kingston, Ontario, and his Ph.D. at Princeton University. He has received many honors, the most notable of which is the American Economic Association's John Bates Clark Prize, awarded to the best economist under 40.

Professor Card's research on labor markets and the effects of public policies on earnings, jobs, and the distribution of income is published in more than 100 articles and several books. His most recent books include two volumes of the *Handbook of Labor Economics* (co-edited with Orley Ashenfelter). An earlier book (co-authored with Alan B. Krueger), *Myth and Measurement: The New Economics of the Minimum Wage* (Princeton, NJ: Princeton University Press, 1995), made a big splash and upset one of the most fundamental beliefs about the effects of minimum wages.

Michael Parkin talked with David Card about his work and the progress that economists have made in understanding how public policies can influence the distribution of income and economic well-being.

> The most difficult thing that empirical economists try to do is infer a causal relationship.

Almost all your work is grounded in data. You are an empirical economist. How do you go about your work, where do your data come from, and how do you use data?

The data I use come from many different sources. I have collected my own data from surveys; transcribed data from historical sources and government publications; and used computerized data files based on records from Censuses and surveys in the United States, Canada, Britain, and other countries.

An economist can do three things with data. The first is to develop simple statistics on basic questions such as "What fraction of families live in poverty?" For this, one needs to understand how the data were collected and processed and how the questions were asked. For example, the poverty rate depends on how you define a "family." If a single mother and her child live with the mother's parents, the income of the mother and the grandparents is counted as "family income."

The second thing economists do with data is develop descriptive comparisons. For example, I have compared the wage differences between male and female workers. Again, the details are important. For example, the male-female wage differential is much bigger if you look at annual earnings than at earnings per hour, because women work fewer hours per year.

Once you've established some simple facts, you start to get ideas for possible explanations. You can also rule out a lot of other ideas.

The third and most difficult thing that empirical economists try to do is infer a causal relationship. In rare instances, we have a true experiment in which a random subgroup of volunteers is enrolled in a "treatment group" and the remainder become the "control group." . . .

If we can't find a compelling comparison group, we have to be cautious.

*Read the full interview with David Card in **MyEconLab**.

Abatement technology A production technology that reduces or prevents pollution. (p. 397)

Absolute advantage A person has an absolute advantage if that person is more productive than another person. (p. 40)

Adverse selection The tendency for people to *enter into agreements* in which they can use their private information to their own advantage and to the disadvantage of the uninformed party. (p. 474)

Allocative efficiency A situation in which goods and services are produced at the lowest possible cost and in the quantities that provide the greatest possible benefit. We cannot produce more of any good without giving up some of another good that we *value more highly*. (p. 35)

Antitrust law A law that regulates oligopolies and prevents them from becoming monopolies or behaving like monopolies. (p. 356)

Asymmetric information A market in which buyers or sellers have private information. (p. 474)

Average cost pricing rule A rule that sets price to cover cost including normal profit, which means setting the price equal to average total cost. (p. 314)

Average fixed cost Total fixed cost per unit of output. (p. 254)

Average product The average product of a factor of production. It equals total product divided by the quantity of the factor employed. (p. 249)

Average total cost Total cost per unit of output. (p. 254)

Average variable cost Total variable cost per unit of output. (p. 254)

Barrier to entry A natural or legal constraint that protects a firm from potential competitors. (p. 298)

Behavioral economics A study of the ways in which limits on the human brain's ability to compute and implement rational decisions influences economic behavior—both the decisions that people make and the consequences of those decisions for the way markets work. (p. 192)

Benefit The benefit of something is the gain or pleasure that it brings and is determined by preferences. (p. 10)

Big tradeoff The tradeoff between efficiency and fairness. (pp. 117, 458)

Bilateral monopoly A situation in which a monopoly seller faces a monopsony buyer. (p. 427)

Black market An illegal market in which the equilibrium price exceeds the legally imposed price ceiling. (p. 128)

Budget line The limit to a household's consumption choices. It marks the boundary between those combinations of goods and services that a household can afford to buy and those that it cannot afford. (pp. 178, 202)

Capital The tools, equipment, buildings, and other constructions that businesses use to produce goods and services. (p. 4)

Capital accumulation The growth of capital resources, including *human capital*. (p. 38)

Capture theory A theory that regulation serves the self-interest of the producer, who captures the regulator and maximizes economic profit. (p. 313)

Cartel A group of firms acting together—colluding— to limit output, raise the price, and increase economic profit. (p. 343)

Ceteris paribus Other things being equal—all other relevant things remaining the same. (p. 24)

Change in demand A change in buyers' plans that occurs when some influence on those plans other than the price of the good changes. It is illustrated by a shift of the demand curve. (p. 58)

Change in supply A change in seller's plans that occurs when some influence on those plans other than the price of the good changes. It is illustrated by a shift of the supply curve. (p. 63)

Change in the quantity demanded A change in buyers' plans that occurs when the price of a good changes but all other influences on buyers' plans remain unchanged. It is illustrated by a movement along the demand curve. (p. 61)

Change in the quantity supplied A change in sellers' plans that occurs when the price of a good changes but all other influences on sellers' plans remain unchanged. It is illustrated by a movement along the supply curve. (p. 64)

Coase theorem The proposition that if property rights exist, if only a small number of parties are involved, and transactions costs are low, then private transactions are efficient, and it doesn't matter who has the property rights. (p. 398)

Collusive agreement An agreement between two (or more) producers to form a cartel to restrict output, raise the price, and increase profits. (p. 346)

Command system A method of allocating resources by the order (command) of someone in authority. In a firm a managerial hierarchy organizes production. (pp. 106, 229)

Common resource A resource that is rival and nonexcludable. (p. 372)

Comparative advantage A person or country has a comparative advantage in an activity if that person or country can perform the activity at a lower opportunity cost than anyone else or any other country. (p. 40)

Competitive market A market that has many buyers and many sellers, so no single buyer or seller can influence the price. (p. 56)

Complement A good that is used in conjunction with another good. (p. 59)

Compound interest The interest on an initial investment plus the interest on the interest that the investment has previously earned. (p. 436)

Constant returns to scale Features of a firm's technology that lead to constant long-run average cost as output increases. When constant returns to scale are present, the *LRAC* curve is horizontal. (p. 262)

Consumer equilibrium A situation in which a consumer has allocated all his or her available income in the way that, given the prices of goods and services, maximizes his or her total utility. (p. 181)

Consumer surplus The excess of the benefit received from a good over the amount paid for it. It is calculated as the marginal benefit (or value) of a good minus its price, summed over the quantity bought. (p. 109)

Contestable market A market in which firms can enter and leave so easily that firms in the market face competition from *potential* entrants. (p. 354)

Cooperative equilibrium The outcome of a game in which the players make and share the monopoly profit. (p. 352)

Credit risk The risk that a borrower, also known as a creditor, might not repay a loan. (p. 477)

Cross elasticity of demand The responsiveness of the demand for a good to a change in the price of a substitute or complement, other things remaining the same. It is calculated as the percentage change in the quantity demanded of the good divided by the percentage change in the price of the substitute or complement. (p. 92)

Deadweight loss A measure of inefficiency. It is equal to the decrease in total surplus that results from an inefficient level of production. (p. 113)

Default risk The risk that a borrower, also known as a creditor, might not repay a loan. (p. 477)

Demand The entire relationship between the price of the good and the quantity demanded of it when all other influences on buyers' plans remain the same. It is illustrated by a demand curve and described by a demand schedule. (p. 57)

Demand curve A curve that shows the relationship between the quantity demanded of a good and its price when all other influences on consumers' planned purchases remain the same. (p. 58)

Deregulation The process of removing regulation of prices, quantities, entry, and other aspects of economic activity in a firm or industry. (p. 313)

Derived demand Demand for a factor of production—it is derived from the demand for the goods and services produced by that factor. (p. 419)

Diminishing marginal rate of substitution The general tendency for a person to be willing to give up less of good *y* to get one more unit of good *x*, while at the same time remaining indifferent as the quantity of good *x* increases. (p. 206)

Diminishing marginal returns The tendency for the marginal product of an additional unit of a factor of production to be less than the marginal product of the previous unit of the factor. (p. 251)

Diminishing marginal utility The tendency for marginal utility to decrease as the quantity consumed of a good increases. (p. 180)

Direct relationship A relationship between two variables that move in the same direction. (p. 18)

Discounting The calculation we use to convert a future amount of money to its present value. (p. 436)

Diseconomies of scale Features of a firm's technology that make average total cost rise as output increases—the *LRAC* curve slopes upward. (p. 262)

Doha Development Agenda (Doha Round) Negotiations held in Doha, Qatar, to lower tariff barriers and quotas that restrict international trade in farm products and services. (p. 163)

Dominant strategy equilibrium An equilibrium in which the best strategy for each player is to cheat *regardless of the strategy of the other player*. (p. 345)

Dumping The sale by a foreign firm of exports at a lower price than the cost of production. (p. 164)

Duopoly A market structure in which two producers of a good or service compete. (p. 342)

Economic depreciation The *fall* in the market value of a firm's capital over a given period. (p. 225)

Economic efficiency A situation that occurs when the firm produces a given output at the least cost. (p. 227)

Economic growth The expansion of production possibilities. (p. 38)

Economic model A description of some aspect of the economic world that includes only those features of the world that are needed for the purpose at hand. (p. 12)

Economic profit A firm's total revenue minus its total cost, with total cost measured as the opportunity cost of production. (p. 224)

Economic rent Any surplus—consumer surplus, producer surplus or economic profit. (p. 306)

Economics The social science that studies the *choices* that individuals, businesses, governments, and entire societies make as they cope with *scarcity* and the *incentives* that influence and reconcile those choices. (p. 2)

Economies of scale Features of a firm's technology that make average total cost fall as output increases—the *LRAC* curve slopes downward. (pp. 238, 262)

Economies of scope Decreases in average total cost that occur when a firm uses specialized resources to produce a range of goods and services. (p. 239)

Efficient Resource use is efficient if it is not possible to make someone better off without making someone else worse off. (p. 5)

Efficient scale The quantity at which average total cost is a minimum—the quantity at the bottom of the U-shaped *ATC* curve. (p. 328)

Elastic demand Demand with a price elasticity greater than 1; other things remaining the same, the percentage change in the quantity demanded exceeds the percentage change in price. (p. 86)

Elasticity of supply The responsiveness of the quantity supplied of a good to a change in its price, other things remaining the same. (p. 94)

Entrepreneurship The human resource that organizes the other three factors of production: labor, land, and capital. (p. 4)

Equilibrium price The price at which the quantity demanded equals the quantity supplied. (p. 66)

Equilibrium quantity The quantity bought and sold at the equilibrium price. (p. 66)

Excess capacity A firm has excess capacity if it produces below its efficient scale. (p. 328)

Excludable A good or service or a resource is excludable if it is possible to prevent someone from enjoying the benefit of it. (p. 372)

Expected utility The utility value of what a person expects to own at a given point in time. (p. 469)

Expected wealth The money value of what a person expects to own at a given point in time. (p. 468)

Exports The goods and services that we sell to people in other countries. (p. 152)

Externality A cost (external cost) or a benefit (external benefit) that arises from production or consumption of a private good and that falls on someone other than its producer or consumer. (p. 372)

Factors of production The productive resources used to produce goods and services. (p. 3)

Firm An economic unit that hires factors of production and organizes those factors to produce and sell goods and services. (pp. 44, 224)

Four-firm concentration ratio A measure of market power that is calculated as the percentage of the value of sales accounted for by the four largest firms in an industry. (p. 234)

Free-rider problem The problem that the market would provide an inefficiently small quantity of a public good. (p. 375)

Game theory A set of tools for studying strategic behavior—behavior that takes into account the expected behavior of others and the recognition of mutual interdependence. (p. 344)

General Agreement on Tariffs and Trade (GATT) An international agreement signed in 1947 to reduce tariffs on international trade. (p. 158)

Gini ratio The ratio of the area between the line of equality and the Lorenz curve to the entire area beneath the line of equality. (p. 447)

Goods and services The objects that people value and produce to satisfy human wants. (p. 3)

Government failure A situation in which government actions lead to inefficiency—to either underprovision or overprovision. (p. 370)

Herfindahl–Hirschman Index A measure of market power that is calculated as the square of the market share of each firm (as a percentage) summed over the largest 50 firms (or over all firms if there are fewer than 50) in a market. (p. 234)

Hotelling Principle The idea that traders expect the price of a nonrenewable natural resource to rise at a rate equal to the interest rate. (p. 432)

Human capital The knowledge and skill that people obtain from education, on-the-job training, and work experience. (p. 3)

Implicit rental rate The firm's opportunity cost of using its own capital. (p. 224)

Import quota A restriction that limits the maximum quantity of a good that may be imported in a given period. (p. 160)

Imports The goods and services that we buy from people in other countries. (p. 152)

Incentive A reward that encourages an action or a penalty that discourages one. (p. 2)

Incentive system A method of organizing production that uses a market-like mechanism inside the firm. (p. 229)

Income effect The effect of a change in income on buying plans, other things remaining the same. (p. 211)

Income elasticity of demand The responsiveness of demand to a change in income, other things remaining the same. It is calculated as the percentage change in the quantity demanded divided by the percentage change in income. (p. 91)

Indifference curve A line that shows combinations of goods among which a consumer is *indifferent*. (p. 205)

Individual transferable quota (ITQ) A production limit that is assigned to an individual who is free to transfer (sell) the quota to someone else. (p. 406)

Inelastic demand A demand with a price elasticity between 0 and 1; the percentage change in the quantity demanded is less than the percentage change in price. (p. 85)

Inferior good A good for which demand decreases as income increases. (p. 60)

Interest The income that capital earns. (p. 4)

Inverse relationship A relationship between variables that move in opposite directions. (p. 19)

Labor The work time and work effort that people devote to producing goods and services. (p. 3)

Labor union An organized group of workers that aims to increase the wage rate and influence other job conditions. (p. 426)

Land The "gifts of nature" that we use to produce goods and services. (p. 3)

Law of demand Other things remaining the same, the higher the price of a good, the smaller is the quantity demanded of it; the lower the price of a good, the larger is the quantity demanded of it. (p. 57)

Law of diminishing returns As a firm uses more of a variable factor of production with a given quantity of the fixed factor of production, the marginal product of the variable factor of production eventually diminishes. (p. 251)

Law of supply Other things remaining the same, the higher the price of a good, the greater is the quantity supplied of it; the lower the price of a good, the smaller is the quantity supplied. (p. 62)

Legal monopoly A market in which competition and entry are restricted by the granting of a public franchise, government license, patent, or copyright. (p. 298)

Lemons problem The problem that in a market in which it is not possible to distinguish reliable products from lemons, there are too many lemons and too few reliable products traded. (p. 474)

Limit pricing The practice of setting the price at the highest level that inflicts a loss on an entrant. (p. 355)

Linear relationship A relationship between two variables that is illustrated by a straight line. (p. 18)

Long run The time frame in which the quantities of *all* factors of production can be varied. (p. 248)

Long-run average cost curve The relationship between the lowest attainable average total cost and output when the firm can change both the plant it uses and the quantity of labor it employs. (p. 261)

Lorenz curve A curve that graphs the cumulative percentage of income or wealth against the cumulative percentage of households. (p. 445)

Macroeconomics The study of the performance of the national economy and the global economy. (p. 2)

Margin When a choice is made by comparing a little more of something with its cost, the choice is made at the margin. (p. 11)

Marginal benefit The benefit that a person receives from consuming one more unit of a good or service. It is measured as the maximum amount that a person is willing to pay for one more unit of the good or service. (pp. 11, 36)

Marginal benefit curve A curve that shows the relationship between the marginal benefit of a good and the quantity of that good consumed. (p. 36)

Marginal cost The *opportunity cost* of producing *one* more unit of a good or service. It is the best alternative forgone. It is calculated as the increase in total cost divided by the increase in output. (pp. 11, 35, 254)

Marginal cost pricing rule A rule that sets the price of a good or service equal to the marginal cost of producing it. (p. 313)

Marginal external benefit The benefit from an additional unit of a good or service that people other than the consumer enjoy. (p. 379)

Marginal external cost The cost of producing an additional unit of a good or service that falls on people other than the producer. (p. 394)

Marginal private benefit The benefit from an additional unit of a good or service that the consumer of that good or service receives. (p. 379)

Marginal private cost The cost of producing an additional unit of a good or service that is borne by the producer of that good or service. (p. 394)

Marginal product The increase in total product that results from a one-unit increase in the variable input, with all other inputs remaining the same. It is calculated as the increase in total product divided by the increase in the variable input employed, when the quantities of all other inputs remain the same. (p. 249)

Marginal rate of substitution The rate at which a person will give up good *y* (the good measured on the *y*-axis) to get an additional unit of good *x* (the good measured on the *x*-axis) while at the same time remaining indifferent (remaining on the same indifference curve) as the quantity of *x* increases. (p. 206)

Marginal revenue The change in total revenue that results from a one-unit increase in the quantity sold. It is calculated as the change in total revenue divided by the change in quantity sold. (p. 272)

Marginal social benefit The marginal benefit enjoyed by society—by the consumer of a good or service (marginal private benefit) plus the marginal benefit enjoyed by others (marginal external benefit). (p. 379)

Marginal social cost The marginal cost incurred by the producer and by everyone else on whom the cost falls—by society. It is the sum of marginal private cost and marginal external cost. (p. 394)

Marginal utility The *change* in total utility resulting from a one-unit increase in the quantity of a good consumed. (p. 179)

Marginal utility per dollar The marginal utility from a good that results from spending one more dollar on it. It is calculated as the marginal utility from the good divided by its price. (p. 182)

Market Any arrangement that enables buyers and sellers to get information and to do business with each other. (p. 44)

Market failure A situation in which a market delivers an inefficient outcome. (p. 113)

Market income The wages, interest, rent, and profit earned in factor markets and before paying income taxes. (p. 444)

Markup The amount by which the firm's price exceeds its marginal cost. (p. 329)

Microeconomics The study of the choices that individuals and businesses make, the way these choices interact in markets, and the influence of governments. (p. 2)

Minimum efficient scale The *smallest* quantity of output at which the long-run average cost reaches its lowest level. (p. 263)

Minimum wage A regulation that makes the hiring of labor below a specified wage rate illegal. The lowest wage at which a firm may legally hire labor. (p. 131)

Mixed good A private good the production or consumption of which creates an externality. (p. 372)

Money Any commodity or token that is generally acceptable as the means of payment. (p. 44)

Money income Market income plus cash payments to households by the government. (p. 444)

Money price The number of dollars that must be given up in exchange for a good or service. (p. 56)

Monopolistic competition A market structure in which a large number of firms make similar but slightly different products and compete on product quality, price, and marketing, and firms are free to enter or exit the market. (pp. 233, 324)

Monopoly A market structure in which there is one firm, which produces a good or service that has no close substitutes and in which the firm is protected from competition by a barrier preventing the entry of new firms. (pp. 233, 298)

Monopsony A market in which there is a single buyer. (p. 427)

Moral hazard A tendency for people with private information, *after entering into an agreement*, to use that information for their own benefit and at the cost of the less-informed party. (p. 474)

Nash equilibrium The outcome of a game that occurs when player A takes the best possible action given the action of player B and player B takes the best possible action given the action of player A. (p. 345)

Natural monopoly A market in which economies of scale enable one firm to supply the entire market at the lowest possible cost. (p. 298)

Natural monopoly good A good that is nonrival and excludable. When buyers can be excluded if they don't pay but the good is nonrival, marginal cost is zero. (p. 372)

Negative externality An externality that arises from either production or consumption and that imposes an external cost. (p. 372)

Negative relationship A relationship between variables that move in opposite directions. (p. 19)

Neuroeconomics The study of the activity of the human brain when a person makes an economic decision. (p. 193)

Nonexcludable A good or service or a resource is nonexcludable if it is impossible (or extremely costly) to prevent someone from enjoying its benefits. (p. 372)

Nonrenewable natural resources Natural resources that can be used only once. (p. 418)

Nonrival A good or service or a resource is nonrival if its use by one person does not decrease the quantity available for someone else. (p. 372)

Normal good A good for which demand increases as income increases. (p. 60)

Normal profit The return to entrepreneurship is normal profit and it is the profit that an entrepreneur earns *on average*. (p. 225)

Offshore outsourcing A U.S. firm buys finished goods, components, or services from firms in other countries. (p. 165)

Oligopoly A market structure in which a small number of firms compete. (pp. 233, 342)

Opportunity cost The highest-valued alternative that we must give up to get something. (pp. 10, 33)

Payoff matrix A table that shows the payoffs for every possible action by each player for every possible action by each other player. (p. 344)

Perfect competition A market in which there are many firms each selling an identical product; there are many buyers; there are no restrictions on entry into the industry; firms in the industry have no advantage over potential new entrants; and firms and buyers are well informed about the price of each firm's product. (pp. 233, 272)

Perfectly elastic demand Demand with an infinite price elasticity; the quantity demanded changes by an infinitely large percentage in response to a tiny price change. (p. 85)

Perfectly inelastic demand Demand with a price elasticity of zero; the quantity demanded remains constant when the price changes. (p. 85)

Perfect price discrimination Price discrimination that occurs when a firm sells each unit of output for the highest price that anyone is willing to pay for it. The firm extracts the entire consumer surplus. (p. 310)

Pigovian taxes Taxes that are used as an incentive for producers to cut back on an activity that creates an external cost. (p. 398)

Political equilibrium The situation in which the choices of voters, firms, politicans, and bureaucrats are all compatible and no group can see a way of improving its position by making a different choice. (p. 371)

Pooling equilibrium The equilibrium in a market when only one message is available and an uninformed person cannot determine quality. (p. 477)

Positive externality An externality that arises from either production or consumption and that creates an external benefit. (p. 372)

Positive relationship A relationship between two variables that move in the same direction. (p. 18)

Poverty A state in which a household's income is too low to be able to buy the quantities of food, shelter, and clothing that are deemed necessary. (p. 448)

Predatory pricing Setting a low price to drive competitors out of business with the intention of setting a monopoly price when the competition has gone. (p. 358)

Preferences A description of a person's likes and dislikes and the intensity of those feelings. (pp. 10, 36, 179)

Present value The amount of money that, if invested today, will grow to be as large as a given future amount when the interest that it will earn is taken into account. (p. 436)

Price cap A regulation that makes it illegal to charge a price higher than a specified level. (p. 128)

Price cap regulation A rule that specifies the highest price that the firm is permitted to set—a price ceiling. (p. 315)

Price ceiling A regulation that makes it illegal to charge a price higher than a specified level. (p. 128)

Price discrimination The practice of selling different units of a good or service for different prices. (p. 299)

Price effect The effect of a change in the price of a good on the quantity of the good consumed, other things remaining the same. (p. 209)

Price elasticity of demand A units-free measure of the responsiveness of the quantity demanded of a good to a change in its price, when all other influences on buyers' plans remain the same. (p. 84)

Price floor A regulation that makes it illegal to trade at a price lower than a specified level. (p. 131)

Price taker A firm that cannot influence the price of the good or service it produces. (p. 272)

Principal–agent problem The problem of devising compensation rules that induce an *agent* to act in the best interest of a *principal*. (p. 229)

Principle of minimum differentiation The tendency for competitors to make themselves similar to appeal to the maximum number of clients or voters. (p. 377)

Private good A good or service that is both rival and excludable. (p. 372)

Private information Information about the value of an item being traded that is possessed by only buyers or sellers. (p. 474)

Producer surplus The excess of the amount received from the sale of a good or service over the cost of producing it. It is calculated as the price of a good minus the marginal cost (or minimum supply-price), summed over the quantity sold. (p. 111)

Product differentiation Making a product slightly different from the product of a competing firm. (pp. 233, 324)

Production efficiency A situation in which goods and services are produced at the lowest possible cost. (p. 33)

Production possibilities frontier The boundary between the combinations of goods and services that can be produced and the combinations that cannot. (p. 32)

Production quota An upper limit to the quantity of a good that may be produced in a specified period. (p. 139)

Profit The income earned by entrepreneurship. (p. 4)

Progressive income tax A tax on income at an average rate that increases with the level of income. (p. 457)

Property rights The social arrangements that govern the ownership, use, and disposal of anything that people value. Property rights are enforceable in the courts. (pp. 44, 397)

Proportional income tax A tax on income at a constant average rate, regardless of the level of income. (p. 457)

Public choice A decision that has consequences for many people and perhaps for the entire society. (p. 370)

Public good A good or service that is both nonrival and nonexcludable. It can be consumed simultaneously by everyone, and no one can be excluded from enjoying its benefits. (p. 372)

Public production The production of a good or service by a public authority that receives its revenue from the government. (p. 381)

Quantity demanded The amount of a good or service that consumers plan to buy during a given time period at a particular price. (p. 57)

Quantity supplied The amount of a good or service that producers plan to sell during a given time period at a particular price. (p. 62)

Rate of return regulation A regulation that requires the firm to justify its price by showing that its return on capital doesn't exceed a specified target rate. (p. 314)

Rational choice A choice that compares costs and benefits and achieves the greatest benefit over cost for the person making the choice. (p. 10)

Real income A household's income expressed as a quantity of goods that the household can afford to buy. (p. 203)

Regressive income tax A tax on income at an average rate that decreases with the level of income. (p. 457)

Regulation Rules administered by a government agency to influence prices, quantities, entry, and other aspects of economic activity in a firm or industry. (p. 313)

Relative price The ratio of the price of one good or service to the price of another good or service. A relative price is an opportunity cost. (pp. 56, 203)

Rent The income that land earns. (p. 4)

Rent ceiling A regulation that makes it illegal to charge a rent higher than a specified level. (p. 128)

Rent seeking The lobbying for special treatment by the government to create economic profit or to divert consumer surplus or producer surplus away from others. The pursuit of wealth by capturing economic rent. (pp. 167, 306)

Resale price maintenance An agreement between a distributor and a manufacturer to resell a product *at or above a specified minimum price*. (p. 357)

Risk aversion The dislike of risk. (p. 468)

Rival A good, service, or a resource is rival if its use by one person decreases the quantity available for someone else. (p. 372)

Scarcity Our inability to satisfy all our wants. (p. 2)

Scatter diagram A graph that plots the value of one variable against the value of another variable for a number of different values of each variable. (p. 16)

Screening Inducing an informed party to reveal relevant private information. (p. 477)

Search activity The time spent looking for someone with whom to do business. (p. 128)

Self-interest The choices that you think are the best ones available for you are choices made in your self-interest. (p. 5)

Separating equilibrium The equilibrium in a market when signaling provides full information to a previously uninformed person. (p. 477)

Short run The time frame in which the quantity of at least one factor of production is fixed and the quantities of the other factors can be varied. The fixed factor is usually capital—that is, the firm uses a given plant. (p. 248)

Short-run market supply curve A curve that shows the quantity supplied in a market at each price when each firm's plant and the number of firms remain the same. (p. 278)

Shutdown point The price and quantity at which the firm is indifferent between producing the profit-maximizing output and shutting down temporarily. The shutdown point occurs at the price and the quantity at which average variable cost is a minimum. (p. 276)

Signal An action taken by an informed person (or firm) to send a message to uninformed people. (p. 332)

Signaling A situation in which an informed person takes actions that send information to uninformed persons. (p. 476)

Single-price monopoly A monopoly that must sell each unit of its output for the same price to all its customers. (p. 299)

Slope The change in the value of the variable measured on the y-axis divided by the change in the value of the variable measured on the x-axis. (p. 22)

Social interest Choices that are the best ones for society as a whole. (p. 5)

Social interest theory A theory that the political and regulatory process relentlessly seeks out inefficiency and introduces regulation that eliminates deadweight loss and allocates resources efficiently. (p. 313)

Strategies All the possible actions of each player in a game. (p. 344)

Subsidy A payment made by the government to a producer. (pp. 140, 381)

Substitute A good that can be used in place of another good. (p. 59)

Substitution effect The effect of a change in price of a good or service on the quantity bought when the consumer (hypothetically) remains indifferent between the original and the new consumption situations—that is, the consumer remains on the same indifference curve. (p. 212)

Sunk cost The past expenditure on a plant that has no resale value. (p. 248)

Supply The entire relationship between the price of a good and the quantity supplied of it when all other influences on producers' planned sales remain the same. It is described by a supply schedule and illustrated by a supply curve. (p. 62)

Supply curve A curve that shows the relationship between the quantity supplied of a good and its price when all other influences on producers' planned sales remain the same. (p. 62)

Symmetry principle A requirement that people in similar situations be treated similarly. (p. 118)

Tariff A tax that is imposed by the importing country when an imported good crosses its international boundary. (p. 157)

Tax incidence The division of the burden of the tax between the buyer and the seller. (p. 133)

Technological change The development of new goods and of better ways of producing goods and services. (p. 38)

Technological efficiency A situation that occurs when the firm produces a given output by using the least amount of inputs. (p. 227)

Technology Any method of producing a good or service. (p. 226)

Total cost The cost of all the productive resources that a firm uses. (p. 253)

Total fixed cost The cost of the firm's fixed inputs. (p. 253)

Total product The maximum output that a given quantity of labor can produce. (p. 249)

Total revenue The value of a firm's sales. It is calculated as the price of the good multiplied by the quantity sold. (pp. 88, 272)

Total revenue test A method of estimating the price elasticity of demand by observing the change in total revenue that results from a change in the price, when all other influences on the quantity sold remain the same. (p. 88)

Total surplus The sum of consumer surplus and producer surplus. (p. 112)

Total utility The total benefit that a person gets from the consumption of all the different goods and services. (p. 179)

Total variable cost The cost of all the firm's variable inputs. (p. 253)

Tradeoff A constraint that involves giving up one thing to get something else. (p. 10)

Tragedy of the commons The absence of incentives to prevent the overuse and depletion of a commonly owned resource. (p. 402)

Transactions costs The opportunity costs of making trades in a market. The costs that arise from finding someone with whom to do business, of reaching an agreement about the price and other aspects of the exchange, and of ensuring that the terms of the agreement are fulfilled. (pp. 115, 238, 398)

Tying arrangement An agreement to sell one product only if the buyer agrees to buy another, different product. (p. 357)

Unit elastic demand Demand with a price elasticity of 1; the percentage change in the quantity demanded equals the percentage change in price. (p. 85)

Utilitarianism A principle that states that we should strive to achieve "the greatest happiness for the greatest number of people." (p. 116)

Utility The benefit or satisfaction that a person gets from the consumption of goods and services. (p. 179)

Value of marginal product The value to the firm of hiring one more unit of a factor of prodeuction. It is calculated as the price of a unit of output multiplied by the marginal product of the factor of production. (p. 419)

Voucher A token that the government provides to households, which they can use to buy specified goods and services. (p. 381)

Wages The income that labor earns. (p. 4)

Wealth The value of all the things that people own—the market value of their assets—at a point in time. (p. 446)

World Trade Organization (WTO) An international organization that places greater obligations on its member countries to observe the GATT rules. (p. 163)

Lottery, 107
Lugo, Gizelle, 480
Luxuries, 86

Macroeconomics, 2
Mad cow disease (BSE), 163
Majority rule, 106, 115
Malthus, Thomas Robert, 487
Mankiw, N. Gregory, 166
Manning, Peyton, 468
Margin, 11
Marginal analysis, 184, 275
Marginal benefit, 11, 379
  decreasing, 36
  demand and, 58
  preferences and, 36
Marginal benefit curve, 36
Marginal cost, 11, 254
  decrease in, 140
  increasing, 62, 140, 403
  marginal revenue and, 302
  PPF and, 35
  principle of, 403
  supply and, 109–110
Marginal cost curve, 254
Marginal cost pricing rule, 313
Marginal external benefit, 379
Marginal external cost, 394, 403
Marginal private benefit, 379
Marginal private cost, 394, 403
Marginal product, 249
  of capital, 260
  value of, 419, 430, 453
Marginal product curve, 250–251
Marginal rate of substitution, 206
Marginal returns
  diminishing, 251, 403
  increasing, 250–251
Marginal revenue, 272
  elasticity and, 301
  marginal cost and, 302
  price and, 300
Marginal social benefit, 109, 379
  common resources and, 403
  of housing, 129
  of innovation, 330
  of public good, 375
Marginal social cost, 110, 394
  common resources and, 403
  of housing, 129
  of public good, 376
Marginal utility, 179–180
  theory, 185–191
Marginal utility per dollar, 182
Markets, 44. See also Factor markets;
    Global markets; Labor markets
  alternatives to, 115
  black, 128–129
  circular flows through, 44–45
  commodity, 418
  competitive, 56, 112–118
  competitive environments and, 233–237
  constraints, 226
  contestable, 354–355
  coordination, 238
  for drugs, 142
  efficiency of competitive, 112–115
  equilibrium, 66–67, 77, 128, 397
  with exports, 154

  fairness of competitive, 116–118
  geographical scope of, 236
  government action in, 380–381
  housing, 128–130
  illegal goods, 142–143
  with imports, 153
  industry correspondence and, 236–237
  insurance, 471–473, 478
  for loans, 477
  for oil, 433
  political, 370–371
  power, 367
  prices, 56, 106
  rental, 418, 430–431
  structure, 236
  understanding, 175, 487
  for used cars, 474–477
  value, 225
Market capitalism, 8
Market demand, 56, 108–109
  for labor, 422
Market failure, 113–115, 415
Market income, 444, 458
Marketing, in monopolistic competition,
    324–325, 330–333
Market supply, 110
  of labor, 422–423
Market supply curve, 110, 423
  short-run, 278
Markup, 329
  advertising and, 332
Marriage, wealth concentration and, 456
Marshall, Alfred, 175
Marshall, Bob, 176
Marshall, Mary Paley, 175
Marx, Karl, 8
Maximum points, 20–21
Maximum profit, 8, 347
Mazumdar-Shaw, Kiran, 6
McDonald's (Reading Between the Lines), 264
McKenzie, Richard B., 428
Mean income, 444
Measures of concentration, 234–236
  limits of, 236–237
Median income, 444
Medicaid, 385, 457, 458
Medicare, 385, 458
Medicare Part C for All (Kotlikoff), 384
Mergers and acquisitions, 359
Mexico, 164–165. See also North
    American Free Trade Agreement
MGM, 429
Microeconomics, 2
Microsoft, 7, 233, 297, 299, 312, 357,
  358, 367
Military, 229
Mill, John Stuart, 116
Minimum differentiation, 377
Minimum efficient cost, 381
Minimum efficient scale, 263, 272
Minimum points, 20–21
Minimum wage, 131–132, 144
  employment increased by, 131
  fairness of, 131–132
  in Hong Kong and Singapore (Reading
    Between the Lines), 144–145
  inefficiency of, 132–133
  monopsony and, 429
  unemployment brought by, 131
Minus sign and elasticity, 85

Mixed economy, 8
Mixed goods, 372
  education as, 373
  with external benefits, 373, 380–381
  with external costs, 373–374
  government and, 380–381
  health care as, 373
Mode income, 444
Model economy, 32
Momentary supply, 96
Money, 44
Money income, 444, 458
Money price, 56
Monopoly, 115, 233–234, 297–317.
    See also Cartel; Oligopoly;
    Single-price monopoly
  antitrust law and, 356–358
  bilateral, 427, 429
  buying, 306
  creating, 306
  deadweight loss and, 306
  elasticity of demand in, 301
  information-age, 7, 299
  legal, 298
  natural, 298, 313–315, 342, 372, 374
  price discrimination, 307–311
  price-setting strategies, 299–300
  regulation, 313–315
  single-price, 299–306
  uncertainty and, 479
Monopolistic competition, 233, 323–335
  advertising in, 330–332
  efficiency of, 305, 329
  entry and exit in, 325
  examples of, 325
  firms in, 367
  HHI and, 325
  innovation in, 330
  marketing in, 324–325, 330–333
  output in, 326–329
  perfect competition compared with,
    328–329
  price in, 326–329
  product development, 330–333
  product differentiation, 334
Monopsony, 427, 429
Moore, Gordon, 7
Moral hazard, 474
Morgan, J. P., 356
Morgenstern, Oskar, 344
Motorola, 237
Movies and DVDs, 210–211
MSN, 326
Multifiber Arrangement, 164
Murdoch, Rupert, 359
Murphy, Kevin, 132
MySpace, 359

NAFTA. See North American Free Trade
    Agreement
Nash, John, 345
Nash equilibrium, 345, 349, 350
National Collegiate Athletic Association
    (NCAA), 428
National comparative advantage, 152
National market, 236
Natural barrier to entry, 298
Natural disaster generator shortage
    study, 118

The Pearson Series in Economics

Abel/Bernanke/Croushore
*Macroeconomics**

Bade/Parkin
*Foundations of Economics**

Berck/Helfand
The Economics of the Environment

Bierman/Fernandez
Game Theory with Economic Applications

Blanchard
*Macroeconomics**

Blau/Ferber/Winkler
The Economics of Women, Men and Work

Boardman/Greenberg/ Vining/ Weimer
Cost-Benefit Analysis

Boyer
Principles of Transportation Economics

Branson
Macroeconomic Theory and Policy

Brock/Adams
The Structure of American Industry

Bruce
Public Finance and the American Economy

Carlton/Perloff
Modern Industrial Organization

Case/Fair/Oster
*Principles of Economics**

Caves/Frankel/Jones
World Trade and Payments: An Introduction

Chapman
Environmental Economics: Theory, Application, and Policy

Cooter/Ulen
Law & Economics

Downs
An Economic Theory of Democracy

Ehrenberg/Smith
Modern Labor Economics

Farnham
Economics for Managers

Folland/Goodman/Stano
The Economics of Health and Health Care

Fort
Sports Economics

Froyen
Macroeconomics

Fusfeld
The Age of the Economist

Gerber
*International Economics**

González-Rivera
Forecasting for Economics and Business

Gordon
*Macroeconomics**

Greene
Econometric Analysis

Gregory
Essentials of Economics

Gregory/Stuart
Russian and Soviet Economic Performance and Structure

Hartwick/Olewiler
The Economics of Natural Resource Use

Heilbroner/Milberg
The Making of the Economic Society

Heyne/Boettke/Prychitko
The Economic Way of Thinking

Hoffman/Averett
Women and the Economy: Family, Work, and Pay

Holt
Markets, Games and Strategic Behavior

Hubbard/O'Brien
*Economics**

*Money and Banking and the Financial System**

Hubbard/O'Brien/Rafferty
*Macroeconomics**

Hughes/Cain
American Economic History

Husted/Melvin
International Economics

Jehle/Reny
Advanced Microeconomic Theory

Johnson-Lans
A Health Economics Primer

Keat/Young
Managerial Economics

Klein
Mathematical Methods for Economics

Krugman/Obstfeld/Melitz
*International Economics: Theory & Policy**

Laidler
The Demand for Money

Leeds/von Allmen
The Economics of Sports

Leeds/von Allmen/Schiming
*Economics**

Lipsey/Ragan/Storer
*Economics**

Lynn
Economic Development: Theory and Practice for a Divided World

Miller
*Economics Today**

Understanding Modern Economics

Miller/Benjamin
The Economics of Macro Issues

Miller/Benjamin/North
The Economics of Public Issues

Mills/Hamilton
Urban Economics

Mishkin
*The Economics of Money, Banking, and Financial Markets**

*The Economics of Money, Banking, and Financial Markets, Business School Edition**

*Macroeconomics: Policy and Practice**

Murray
Econometrics: A ModernIntroduction

Nafziger
The Economics of Developing Countries

O'Sullivan/Sheffrin/Perez
*Economics: Principles, Applications and Tools**

Parkin
*Economics**

Perloff
*Microeconomics**

*Microeconomics: Theory and Applications with Calculus**

Phelps
Health Economics

Pindyck/Rubinfeld
*Microeconomics**

Riddell/Shackelford/Stamos/ Schneider
Economics: A Tool for Critically Understanding Society

Ritter/Silber/Udell
*Principles of Money, Banking & Financial Markets**

Roberts
The Choice: A Fable of Free Trade and Protection

Rohlf
Introduction to Economic Reasoning

Ruffin/Gregory
Principles of Economics

Sargent
Rational Expectations and Inflation

Sawyer/Sprinkle
International Economics

Scherer
Industry Structure, Strategy, and Public Policy

Schiller
The Economics of Poverty and Discrimination

Sherman
Market Regulation

Silberberg
Principles of Microeconomics

Stock/Watson
Introduction to Econometrics

Studenmund
Using Econometrics: A Practical Guide

Tietenberg/Lewis
Environmental and Natural Resource Economics Environmental Economics and Policy

Todaro/Smith
Economic Development

Waldman
Microeconomics

Waldman/Jensen
Industrial Organization: Theory and Practice

Walters/Walters/Appel/ Callahan/Centanni/ Maex/O'Neill
Econversations: Today's Students Discuss Today's Issues

Weil
Economic Growth

Williamson
Macroeconomics

* denotes MyEconLab titles   Log onto www.myeconlab.com to learn more

Reading Between the Lines

Reading Between the Lines, which appears at the end of each chapter, helps students think like economists by connecting chapter tools and concepts to the world around them.

Economics in Action

Economics in Action boxes apply economic theory to current events to illustrate the importance of economic forces in the world around us.

Economics in the News

Economics in the News boxes shows students how to use the economic toolkit to understand the events and issues they are confronted with in the media.

At Issue

At Issue boxes shows two sides of a controversial issue and helps students to apply the economic way of thinking to clarify and debate the issues.

1973	1974	1975	1976	1977	1978	1979	1980	1981	1982	1983	1984	1985	1986
3.2	2.8	2.7	2.3	2.0	2.1	2.2	1.8	2.0	1.8	1.3	1.6	1.5	1.4
1.0	1.4	1.5	1.4	1.6	1.5	1.7	2.4	2.9	2.5	1.9	1.8	1.5	1.0
4.8	4.7	4.3	4.4	4.4	4.6	4.7	4.4	3.9	3.7	3.7	3.9	4.1	4.4
13.0	12.3	11.5	12.1	12.5	12.7	12.3	11.3	11.0	10.0	9.8	10.3	9.8	9.5
8.7	8.8	8.8	8.9	8.8	8.6	8.6	8.5	8.5	8.2	7.8	7.4	7.2	6.6
3.9	3.8	4.1	4.1	4.1	4.1	3.8	4.0	4.1	4.5	4.4	4.3	4.2	4.1
6.6	6.9	6.9	6.6	6.5	6.6	6.6	6.5	6.4	6.3	6.1	6.3	6.2	6.1
9.0	8.7	8.9	9.0	9.0	8.9	8.6	8.3	8.2	8.3	8.5	8.6	8.7	8.7
3.3	3.3	3.0	3.2	3.2	3.2	3.2	3.1	2.9	2.7	2.7	2.8	2.7	2.7
11.7	11.8	12.0	11.7	11.8	11.9	11.8	12.3	12.5	13.1	13.4	13.4	13.6	14.0
—	—	—	—	—	—	—	—	—	—	—	—	—	—
—	—	—	—	—	—	—	—	—	—	—	—	—	—
—	—	—	—	—	—	—	—	—	—	—	—	—	—
—	—	—	—	—	—	—	—	—	—	—	—	—	—
—	—	—	—	—	—	—	—	—	—	—	—	—	—
40.7	40.0	39.4	40.1	40.3	40.4	40.2	39.7	39.8	39.0	40.1	40.6	40.5	40.7
4.9	4.8	4.7	4.5	4.2	4.1	3.8	3.8	3.7	3.6	3.5	3.2	2.8	2.6
0.9	0.9	1.0	1.0	1.0	1.0	1.1	1.1	1.2	1.3	1.1	1.0	1.0	0.8
5.2	5.0	4.5	4.4	4.6	4.8	4.9	4.7	4.5	4.3	4.3	4.6	4.8	4.8
23.0	22.5	20.9	21.1	21.1	20.9	20.8	19.9	19.7	18.7	18.2	18.4	17.8	17.2
66.1	66.9	68.9	69.0	69.1	69.2	69.5	70.5	71.0	72.2	73.0	72.9	73.8	74.6
4.51	4.93	5.40	5.72	6.12	6.62	7.25	8.04	8.76	9.51	9.68	10.13	10.69	11.03
16.0	16.1	16.1	16.1	16.2	16.4	16.6	16.8	16.8	17.2	16.8	16.9	17.3	17.5
924.1	759.1	802.9	975.2	894.3	821.1	844.4	891.1	932.9	884.5	1,190.8	1,178.6	1,328.0	1793.1
3,284.6	2,473.1	2,390.8	2,745.8	2,367.5	2,031.6	1,928.1	1,864.5	1,784.7	1,594.9	2,065.9	1,970.5	2,155.0	2,846.7
7.4	8.6	8.8	8.4	8.0	8.7	9.6	11.9	14.2	13.8	12.0	12.7	11.4	9.0
1.2	−2.5	−0.3	2.7	1.5	1.1	−1.7	−1.6	3.9	7.6	8.8	8.4	7.8	7.2
397.0	438.1	448.5	513.2	576.6	653.3	736.5	807.4	926.9	949.4	1,008.6	1,121.8	1,223.6	1,300.1
400.7	453.8	535.2	575.6	622.6	685.2	763.1	883.1	1,000.5	1,110.7	1,210.4	1,312.2	1,439.1	1,538.6
−3.8	−15.7	−86.7	−62.5	−46.0	−31.9	−26.7	−75.7	−73.5	−161.3	−201.8	−190.4	−215.5	−238.5
265.7	263.1	309.7	382.7	444.1	491.6	524.7	591.1	664.9	790.1	981.7	1,151.9	1,337.5	1,549.8

Microeconomic Data

These microeconomic data series show some of the trends in what, how, and for whom goods and services are produced — the central questions of microeconomics. You will find these data in a spreadsheet that you can download from your MyEconLab Web site.

		1987	1988	1989	1990	1991	1992	1993	1994	1995	1996	1997
WHAT WE PRODUCE												
Percentage of gross domestic product												
1	Agriculture, forestry, fishing, and hunting	1.7	1.6	1.7	1.7	1.5	1.6	1.4	1.5	1.3	1.5	1.3
2	Mining	1.5	1.4	1.4	1.5	1.3	1.1	1.1	1.0	1.0	1.1	1.1
3	Construction	4.6	4.6	4.5	4.3	3.8	3.7	3.7	3.9	3.9	4.0	4.1
4	Durable goods	10.2	10.2	9.9	9.4	9.0	8.9	8.9	9.2	9.2	9.0	9.1
5	Nondurable goods	6.9	7.0	7.0	7.0	6.9	6.8	6.7	6.7	6.8	6.4	6.3
6	Utilities	2.6	2.4	2.5	2.5	2.5	2.5	2.5	2.5	2.5	2.3	2.2
7	Wholesale trade	6.0	6.2	6.2	6.0	6.0	6.0	6.0	6.3	6.2	6.3	6.3
8	Retail trade	7.4	7.2	7.1	6.9	6.8	6.8	6.9	7.0	7.0	7.0	6.9
9	Transportation and warehousing	3.2	3.2	3.0	2.9	3.0	2.9	3.0	3.1	3.1	3.0	3.1
10	Finance, insurance, real estate, rental, and leasing	17.7	17.8	17.8	18.0	18.4	18.6	18.6	18.4	18.7	18.8	19.2
11	Professional and business services	8.7	9.1	9.4	9.8	9.7	9.9	9.9	9.9	10.0	10.4	10.8
12	Information	3.9	3.8	3.8	3.9	3.9	4.0	4.1	4.2	4.2	4.3	4.2
13	Educational services, health care, and social assistance	6.0	6.1	6.3	6.7	7.1	7.3	7.3	7.2	7.2	7.1	6.9
14	Arts, entertainment, recreation, accommodation, and food services	3.2	3.3	3.3	3.4	3.4	3.4	3.4	3.3	3.4	3.4	3.5
15	Other services, except government	2.4	2.4	2.4	2.5	2.4	2.4	2.5	2.4	2.4	2.4	2.4
HOW WE PRODUCE												
16	Average weekly hours	41.0	41.0	40.9	40.5	40.4	40.8	41.2	41.7	41.3	41.3	41.7
	Employment (percentage of total)											
17	Agriculture	2.6	2.5	2.4	2.3	2.3	2.3	2.1	2.2	2.2	2.0	1.9
18	Mining	0.7	0.7	0.7	0.7	0.7	0.6	0.6	0.6	0.5	0.5	0.5
19	Construction	4.9	4.8	4.8	4.7	4.3	4.1	4.2	4.4	4.4	4.5	4.6
20	Manufacturing	16.8	16.6	16.3	15.8	15.4	15.1	14.8	14.6	14.4	14.1	13.9
21	Services	75.0	75.4	75.9	76.6	77.3	77.9	78.3	78.3	78.5	78.8	79.0
	FOR WHOM WE PRODUCE											
22	Wage rate (dollars per hour)	11.42	12.06	12.55	13.30	13.91	14.46	14.75	15.00	15.66	16.15	16.62
23	Real wage rate (2005 dollars per hour)	17.6	18.0	18.0	18.4	18.6	18.9	18.8	18.8	19.2	19.4	19.6
24	Stock price index (Dow Jones)	2,277.5	2,061.5	2,510.3	2,679.5	2,929.0	3,284.1	3,524.9	3,794.6	4,499.4	5,743.9	7,443.2
25	Real stock price index (2005 dollars)	3,514.1	3,075.1	3,608.2	3,707.9	3,914.8	4,287.8	4,502.6	4,747.1	5,513.8	6,907.5	8,795.6
26	Interest rate Aaa (percent per year)	9.4	9.7	9.3	9.3	8.8	8.1	7.2	8.0	7.6	7.4	7.3
27	Real interest rate (percent per year)	5.7	5.6	4.4	3.9	4.6	5.1	4.2	5.4	4.8	4.4	5.0
GOVERNMENT IN THE ECONOMY												
28	Government receipts (billions of dollars)	1,413.8	1,513.6	1,639.6	1,725.0	1,775.3	1,860.9	1,965.9	2,112.1	2,235.5	2,403.5	2,584.2
29	Government expenditures (billions of dollars)	1,622.1	1,700.2	1,821.3	1,976.9	2,076.7	2,234.0	2,304.1	2,374.4	2,480.1	2,583.2	2,658.0
30	Government surplus(+)/deficit(−) (billions of dollars)	−208.4	−186.7	−181.7	−251.8	−301.3	−373.1	−338.3	−262.3	−244.5	−179.7	−73.8
31	Government debt (billions of dollars)	1,677.7	1,822.4	1,970.6	2,177.1	2,430.4	2,703.3	2,922.7	3,077.9	3,230.3	3,343.1	3,347.8

1998	1999	2000	2001	2002	2003	2004	2005	2006	2007	2008	2009	2010	2011
1.2	1.0	1.0	1.0	0.9	1.0	1.2	1	0.9	1	1.1	1	1.1	1.2
0.9	0.9	1.2	1.2	1.0	1.3	1.3	1.5	1.7	1.8	2.2	1.5	1.6	1.9
4.3	4.4	4.4	4.6	4.6	4.5	4.7	4.9	4.9	4.7	4.3	3.9	3.5	3.4
9.2	8.9	8.8	7.7	7.4	7.0	6.9	7	6.9	6.7	6.3	5.7	6.3	6.6
6.1	6.0	5.7	5.6	5.5	5.4	5.6	5.5	5.4	5.4	5.1	5.3	5.4	5.6
2.1	2.0	1.9	2.0	2.0	2.0	1.8	1.6	1.8	1.8	1.8	1.9	1.8	1.7
6.2	6.2	6.0	6.0	5.9	5.8	5.8	5.7	5.8	5.8	5.8	5.5	5.5	5.6
6.8	6.9	6.7	6.8	6.9	6.9	6.7	6.6	6.5	6.3	5.9	6	6.1	6.1
3.1	3.1	3.1	2.9	2.9	2.9	2.9	2.9	2.9	2.9	2.9	2.8	2.8	2.8
19.3	19.4	19.7	20.3	20.5	20.5	20.3	20.6	20.7	20.4	20.4	21.3	20.7	19.9
11.2	11.5	11.6	11.5	11.4	11.4	11.4	11.6	11.7	12.1	12.5	12	12.3	12.6
4.4	4.7	4.7	4.7	4.6	4.5	4.7	4.6	4.4	4.5	4.5	4.4	4.3	4.4
6.9	6.8	6.9	7.3	7.6	7.8	7.6	7.6	7.6	7.7	8.1	8.7	8.8	8.7
3.5	3.5	3.6	3.6	3.6	3.6	3.9	3.8	3.8	3.9	3.8	3.7	3.8	3.9
2.4	2.3	2.3	2.4	2.4	2.4	2.5	2.5	2.5	2.5	2.4	2.4	2.5	2.4
41.5	41.4	41.2	40.4	40.5	40.4	40.8	40.6	41.1	41.2	40.8	39.8	41.1	41.4
1.8	1.7	1.6	1.6	1.6	1.6	1.5	1.5	1.4	1.3	1.3	1.3	1.3	1.3
0.5	0.5	0.4	0.5	0.4	0.4	0.4	0.5	0.5	0.5	0.6	0.5	0.5	0.6
4.8	5.0	5.1	5.1	5.1	5.1	5.2	5.4	5.6	5.5	5.2	4.5	4.2	4.2
13.7	13.2	12.9	12.3	11.5	11.0	10.7	10.5	10.3	10.0	9.7	8.9	8.8	8.8
79.2	79.6	80.0	80.6	81.4	81.9	82.1	82.2	82.3	82.7	83.3	84.6	85.2	85.1
17.72	18.65	19.75	20.80	21.28	22.08	22.68	23.63	24.24	25.13	26.20	26.97	26.84	27.58
20.7	21.5	22.3	22.9	23.1	23.5	23.4	23.6	23.5	23.7	24.1	24.6	24.2	24.3
8,631.9	10,482.6	10,723.8	10,205.8	9,214.9	9,006.6	10,315.5	10,546.7	11,409.8	13,178.0	11,244.1	8,885.7	10,668.6	11,957.6
10,086.5	12,071.6	12,087.5	11,249.0	9,995.1	9,568.5	10,658.8	10,547.4	11,053.0	12,406.1	10,354.7	8,112.6	9,612.3	10,548.8
6.5	7.0	7.6	7.1	6.5	5.7	5.6	5.2	5.6	5.6	5.6	5.3	4.9	4.6
5.0	4.8	4.3	4.2	4.9	3.4	3.0	1.9	2.4	2.7	1.8	5.7	3.6	1.5
2,762.2	2,939.2	3,168.1	3,155.6	3,000.5	3,071.4	3,296.0	3,691.6	4,028.3	4,228.8	4,085.6	3,730.4	3,926.7	4,100.6
2,735.2	2,874.8	3,021.5	3,220.8	3,422.9	3,624.6	3,827.0	4,109.9	4,319.8	4,636.9	5,022.9	5,398.7	5,577.8	5,642.9
27.0	64.4	146.6	−65.1	−422.4	−553.3	−531.1	−418.3	−291.6	−408.1	−937.3	−1,668.3	−1,651.0	−1,542.3
3,262.9	3,135.7	2,898.4	2,785.5	2,936.2	3,257.3	3,595.2	3,855.9	4,060.0	4,255.5	5,311.9	6,775.5	8,207.2	8,463.5

Microeconomic Data

These microeconomic data series show some of the trends in what, how, and for whom goods and services are produced — the central questions of microeconomics. You will find these data in a spreadsheet that you can download from your MyEconLab Web site.

		1962	1963	1964	1965	1966	1967	1968	1969	1970	1971	1972
WHAT WE PRODUCE												
Percentage of gross domestic product												
1	Agriculture, forestry, fishing, and hunting	3.0	2.8	2.5	2.6	2.5	2.3	2.1	2.2	2.1	2.1	2.3
2	Mining	1.2	1.2	1.1	1.1	1.0	1.0	1.0	0.9	1.0	1.0	1.0
3	Construction	4.3	4.4	4.5	4.5	4.5	4.5	4.5	4.6	4.6	4.7	4.7
4	Durable goods	14.5	14.7	14.7	15.3	15.4	14.8	14.8	14.4	12.7	12.4	12.7
5	Nondurable goods	10.6	10.5	10.4	10.3	10.3	10.0	10.0	9.7	9.4	9.1	8.9
6	Utilities	4.1	4.1	4.1	4.0	3.9	3.9	3.9	3.9	4.0	4.0	4.0
7	Wholesale trade	6.6	6.6	6.6	6.5	6.5	6.5	6.5	6.5	6.6	6.5	6.6
8	Retail trade	8.9	8.9	9.1	9.0	8.8	8.9	9.1	9.1	9.2	9.2	9.1
9	Transportation and warehousing	3.6	3.5	3.5	3.5	3.4	3.3	3.2	3.2	3.2	3.2	3.3
10	Finance, insurance, real estate, rental, and leasing	11.9	11.9	11.8	11.7	11.4	11.6	11.6	11.7	11.9	12.1	12.0
11	Professional and business services	—	—	—	—	—	—	—	—	—	—	—
12	Information	—	—	—	—	—	—	—	—	—	—	—
13	Educational services, health care, and social assistance	—	—	—	—	—	—	—	—	—	—	—
14	Arts, entertainment, recreation, accommodation, and food services	—	—	—	—	—	—	—	—	—	—	—
15	Other services, except government	—	—	—	—	—	—	—	—	—	—	—
HOW WE PRODUCE												
16	Average weekly hours	40.4	40.6	40.8	41.2	41.4	40.6	40.8	40.7	39.8	39.9	40.5
	Employment (percentage of total)											
17	Agriculture	9.5	8.8	8.2	7.5	6.7	6.1	5.8	5.4	5.3	5.1	5.0
18	Mining	1.2	1.1	1.1	1.1	1.0	1.0	0.9	0.9	0.9	0.9	0.9
19	Construction	4.9	4.9	4.9	5.0	4.9	4.7	4.7	4.9	4.9	5.0	5.1
20	Manufacturing	25.2	25.1	25.0	25.2	25.8	25.5	25.2	24.9	23.8	22.8	22.7
21	Services	59.3	60.0	60.8	61.2	61.6	62.7	63.3	63.9	65.1	66.1	66.3
FOR WHOM WE PRODUCE												
22	Wage rate (dollars per hour)	2.33	2.41	2.52	2.62	2.82	3.03	3.26	3.50	3.79	4.00	4.19
23	Real wage rate (2005 dollars per hour)	12.2	12.5	12.9	13.2	13.8	14.3	14.8	15.2	15.6	15.7	15.7
24	Stock price index (Dow Jones)	639.1	714.7	834.1	910.7	872.8	879.5	904.0	875.7	753.1	884.9	950.1
25	Real stock price index (2005 dollars)	3,350.1	3,706.9	4,260.1	4,568.6	4,257.5	4,162.0	4,103.7	3,788.0	3,094.4	3,462.9	3,564.9
26	Interest rate Aaa (percent per year)	4.3	4.3	4.4	4.5	5.1	5.5	6.2	7.0	8.0	7.4	7.2
27	Real interest rate (percent per year)	3.3	2.9	3.1	2.9	2.3	2.4	2.0	1.6	2.3	3.0	4.0
GOVERNMENT IN THE ECONOMY												
28	Government receipts (billions of dollars)	153.2	165.1	169.9	183.9	206.7	221.7	256.2	288.2	291.6	309.4	353.8
29	Government expenditures (billions of dollars)	161.5	169.1	177.8	189.1	214.7	242.9	268.3	286.7	313.2	340.7	370.7
30	Government surplus(+)/deficit(−) (billions of dollars)	−8.3	−4.1	−7.9	−5.2	−8.0	−21.2	−12.1	1.4	−21.5	−31.3	−16.8
31	Government debt (billions of dollars)	218.3	222.0	222.1	221.7	221.5	219.9	237.3	224.0	225.5	237.5	251.0